INTERNATIONAL
BANK SECRECY

AUSTRALIA
The Law Book Company
Brisbane * Sydney * Melbourne * Perth

CANADA
Carswell
Ottowa * Toronto * Calgary * Montreal * Vancouver

Agents
Steinmatzky's Agency Ltd., Tel Aviv
N. M. Tripathi (Private) Ltd., Bombay
Eastern Law House (Private) Ltd., Calcutta
M. P. P. House, Bangalore
Universal Book Traders, Delhi
Aditya Books, Delhi
MacMillan Shuppan KK, Tokyo
Pakistan Law House, Karachi, Lahore

INTERNATIONAL
BANK SECRECY

General Editor

DENNIS CAMPBELL, B.A., J.D., LL.M.
Member of the New York and Iowa State Bars
Director, Center for International Legal Studies
Salzburg, Austria

LONDON
SWEET & MAXWELL
1992

Published in 1992 by
Sweet & Maxwell Limited
South Quay Plaza, 183 Marsh Wall
London E14 9FT, England

Typeset in Optima and Palatino by
the Center for International Legal Studies
Salzburg, Austria

Printed in England
by Clays Ltd., St. Ives plc

Published under the auspices
of the Center for International Legal Studies

*A CIP catalogue record for this book is available
from the British Library*

ISBN 0 421 47250 2

DEDICATION

This book is dedicated to the memory

of Nicholas N. Campbell.

PREFACE

Tangential references in the Code of Hamourabi imply that confidentiality in banking existed more than 4,000 years ago in Babylon. Ancient Romans may have practiced banking secrecy, and it was then probably recognized as well by barbarian tribes in other parts of Europe.

Customary Austrian law of the sixteenth century acknowledged rules of financial confidentiality, and later associations of Italian and German bankers are known have sanctioned its breach. Financial privacy even acquired the status of an accepted constitutional right in nineteenth century Germany. Today, some concept of financial confidentiality between a client and his banker exists in nearly every country.

The savings and loan association collapses in the United States, the Bank of Commerce and Credit International scandal, the evasion of United States taxes through the use of Swiss accounts, the use of secret accounts by dictators to plunder and stash away the patrimonies of their countries, and the exploitation of banking secrecy in laundering drug-money and clandestine espionage operations are among the activities that have caused lawyers, bankers, and governments to re-examine the concept and scope of banking confidentiality.

Undeniably, banking secrecy may have been an element of greater or lesser importance in many of the scams perpetrated in recent years in the international financial system. However, part of the problem in assessing banking secrecy is that, while the concept has been almost universally acknowledged, its expression, application, role, and legal regime are far from uniform.

The rules providing for banking secrecy may be no more than vague custom. They may be contractually set out in varying degrees of detail by account agreements, or they may be stipulated by law. By the same token, no rights of action may accrue to protect confidentiality, or they may accrue variously to professional associations, public administrators, prosecutors or the betrayed client.

In some jurisdictions, the breaching bank may be faced with nothing more than bad publicity; in others, it may obliged to compensate the client for direct or even hypothetical losses.

Through their employment contracts, some indiscreet bankers might be obliged to indemnify their employers, and they also could still be directly liable to the client on a tort basis. Fines and possible incarceration are deemed appropriate in some jurisdictions to protect the public interest in financial privacy.

Obviously, that public interest is appreciated very differently. Some of banking secrecy's supporters argue that, while some activities exploiting confidentiality may be immoral, banking secrecy itself is not, and thus this concept should not be tarred with the same brush as the criminals who abuse it. On the other hand, many contend that merely "looking the other way", when done so resolutely and profitably, is in itself worthy of condemnation.

There are, of course, numerous justifications offered for banking secrecy, and each seems to provoke its own counter argument. These rationales include hindering unlawful (or simply unpleasant) confiscation, fostering professional confidence, and promoting fundamental rights.

The first argument encompasses situations in which a public authority wrongly attempts to appropriate private assets. In this respect, one might imagine a foreign investor, a national in a politically volatile state, or a dissident author who wishes to secure his illegal royalties.

How "unlawful" and "illegal" are understood is not always consistent. Beyond this rather philosophical issue, it is sometimes argued that interests like these could be protected equally well by other devices without so much potential for abuse. In the case of the foreign investor, this could be through international conventions.

Tax evaders maintain that secrecy is a legitimate defense against unfair tax systems. They maintain that oppressive or merely progressive taxation is unjustified confiscation and such systematic and plundering regimes should be prevented. Accepting taxes and their legitimacy as an undebatable certainty, opponents dismiss this charge, questioning the principles behind such convictions.

While traditionally few states recognize foreign revenue claims, even fewer would tolerate their tax authorities to be blocked by their own banking secrecy laws. The proliferation of tax treaties and cooperation among sovereign states indicates growing international consensus on the legitimate objectives of revenue collection and perhaps the role that banking secrecy should be allowed to play.

The second argument views confidentiality between financial adviser and account holder as a form of professional secrecy comparable to that between lawyer and client, doctor and patient, or priest and penitent. It is said that such confidence fosters full disclosure and thus more competent and complete service.

However, professional secrecy must be appreciated in a balance. The resulting social utility must outweigh the likelihood and severity of social detriment. The lawyer-client privilege is a corollary to the rights of access to legal counsel and against self-incrimination, as required by the competitive and antagonistic nature of litigation and business. Medical privacy is justified by how an embarrassed silence might exacerbate the consequences of disease, if doctors were not bound to guard information on their patients' health. Finally, many societies offer their reverence to religion to justify confessional privilege.

Banking secrecy's detractors do not recognize such social utility in restricting access to financial information, and they point out that, where these other privileges are accepted, they remain subject to limitations and exceptions.

Many advocates of the third argument regard financial privacy as a fundamental right. This may be attractive in light of trends toward privacy rights. It is asserted that in as much as individuals' homes, images, or actions should be protected from public scrutiny, so too should their financial matters. Financial privacy should be an individual liberty, essential to and protected by democratic systems.

However, according to its opponents, banking secrecy is just as wrongly equated with financial privacy as it is with criminality. It may involve matters which should not be characterized as private, but which the individual merely wishes to conceal.

Nowhere is there found unfettered access to the information that a bank holds on its clients. Neither is there anywhere hermetic silence on these matters. The very debate on banking secrecy demonstrates the limits that are imposed and the exceptions that apply.

Helping to rein in insider dealing, Switzerland has supplied United States law enforcement authorities with information under the 1982 and 1987 Memoranda of Understanding. Indeed, enough information leaks out of more obscure and more strict jurisdictions to whet official appetites. Many jurisdictions, such as the Cayman Islands, contemplate exceptions for criminal matters and where the client has waived his right to secrecy.

Such waivers have created their own little controversies. Some judicial authorities, notably those in the United States, have attempted to circumvent foreign banking secrecy rules by ordering those at least theoretically falling within their personal jurisdiction to authorize disclosure.

These less-than-completely voluntary waivers can create multiple dilemmas for banks. On the one hand, the bank may not wish to disclose prejudicial information that its client would really rather keep secret. On the other, neither does the bank want to risk placing its client in contempt by complying with those true preferences and refusing to disclose confidential information.

Such disregard for a compelled waiver could expose the banks to liability in the United States, and disclosure might have the same consequence in their own jurisdictions. Even if the banks could freely avail themselves of an "in bank's interest to disclose" exception, that interest is not always easy to identify.

These issues also touch upon the unsettled conflict of laws problems in banking secrecy. Generally, the law of the place where the account is kept applies. Nevertheless, banks with foreign branches may be constrained by the requirements of their home jurisdictions. The emergence of banking groups and the transfer of information within them, cross-border banking, and a decline in comity have increased the need for collaboration.

After years of an aggressive unilateral approach, the United States appears to be willing to compromise and cooperate. While the European Community has recognized the need for at least coordination, many of its efforts have yet to bear fruits. At least on paper, some international actions to crack down on the abusers of banking secrecy, rather than the practice itself, look more promising. If they succeed, the debate on banking secrecy may become less heated and more considered.

A thoughtful relationship between the protected interests and the sanctions for breach might ameliorate the more repugnant aspects of banking secrecy. Where legitimate financial interests are prejudiced by disclosure, the bank should be liable, but not where the information is necessary for investigating extraditable offenses. Authorities requesting information might guarantee this and offer indemnities but, for the time being, such solutions are perhaps too simplistic and the hope for a utopia of uniformity naive.

While the patchwork of laws persists, and the demands of more liberal financial systems and more aggressive regulatory bodies pull at its seams, banking secrecy will continue to intrigue and perplex not only lawyers, government officials, and businesspersons, but also the public. It is the former group that will have to concern itself with the ever-changing intricacies of this institution.

In their contributions which follow, lawyers from Australia, Austria, the Bahamas, Belgium, the British Virgin Islands, Canada, Denmark, England, Finland, France, Germany, Gibraltar, Grenada, Greece, Hong Kong, India, Ireland, the Isle of Man, Japan, Liechtenstein, Korea, Luxembourg, Macao, Mexico, The Netherlands, New Zealand, Norway, Pakistan, Portugal, Scotland, Singapore, Spain, Sweden, Switzerland, the United States, and the European Community have surveyed the rules and practice prevailing in their respective jurisdictions under the laws in effect at September 1992.

The result offers an opportunity to assess and compare not only the laws of particular countries but also the social and business practices in which their banking systems operate.

DENNIS CAMPBELL
Salzburg, Austria
October 30, 1992

THE AUTHORS

PETER ANTHONI, Bützow & Co., Helsinki, Finland.

FINN ARNESEN, Advokatene Haavind & Haga, Oslo, Norway.

ANDREAS BATLINER, Dr.Dr. Batliner & Partner, Vaduz, Liechtenstein.

PAUL R. BECKETT, Deutsche Bank (Switzerland) Limited, Geneva, Switzerland

RAFFAELLA BETTI BERUTTO, Gianni, Origoni, Tonucci, Rome, Italy.

MARC BILLIAU, Berlioz & Co., Paris, France.

JANE BOGATY, Osler Renault Ladner, Montreal, Quebec, Toronto, Ontario, and Vancouver, British Columbia, Canada.

HANS BOLLMANN, Pestalozzi Gmuer & Patry, Zürich, Switzerland.

RON L. BOZZER, Osler Renault Ladner, Montreal, Quebec, Toronto, Ontario, and Vancouver, British Columbia, Canada.

JON BROADLEY, Minter Ellison Morris Fletcher, Brisbane, Australia.

JAMES E. CARROLL, Altheimer & Gray, Chicago, Illinois.

MELANIE ROVNER COHEN, Altheimer & Gray, Chicago, Illinois.

G. V. DAVIS, Marrache & Co., Gibraltar.

DANIEL DEL RÍO, Basham, Ringe & Correa, Mexico City, Mexico.

STELIOS N. DEVERAKIS, Deverakis Law Office, Piraeus, Greece.

JAMES DUDLEY, Gerrard, Scallan & O'Brien, Dublin, Ireland.

JAMES E. FORDYCE, Osler Renault Ladner, Montreal, Quebec, Toronto, Ontario, and Vancouver, British Columbia, Canada.

WENDY FOWLER, Richards Butler, London, England.

SIMON FRASER, Rudd Watts & Stone, Auckland, New Zealand.

GILL GOODWIN, Rudd Watts & Stone, Auckland, New Zealand.

M. LINDA GRANT, Grant & Grant, St. George's, Grenada, West Indies.

GUY HARLES, Arendt & Medernach, Luxembourg.

RITA L. JOSEPH, Grant & Grant, St. George's, Grenada, West Indies.

HARALD JUNG, Peltzer & Riesenkampff, Frankfurt am Main, Germany.

TERRY ROBIN HORWITZ KASS, Altheimer & Gray, Chicago, Illinois.

YOUNG MOO KIM, Kim & Chang, Seoul, South Korea.

KATARINA KIVENHEIMO, Bützow & Co., Helsinki, Finland.

MICHAEL KUTSCHERA, Binder Grösswang & Partner, Vienna, Austria.

ODILE LAJOIX, Berlioz & Co., Paris, France.

FELIX LÓPEZ ANTÓN, Abogado, Madrid, Spain.

DAVID LYONS, Lyons & Caplan, St. Helier, Jersey, Channel Islands.

MARCUS MANDEL, Marcus Mandel, Shakenovsky, Kretzmer & Hershkowitz, Tel Aviv, Israel.

B. J. S. MARRACHE, Marrache & Co., Gibraltar.

RUTSEL S. J. MARTHA, Robeco Antillen N.V., Willemstad, Curacao, Netherlands Antilles.

FINN MARTENSEN, Advokaterne Vingardshus, Aalborg, Sweden.

BARRIE MEERKIN, Robert W. H. Wang & Co., Hong Kong.

IAIN MEIKLEJOHN, Shepherd & Wedderburn, Edinburgh, Scotland.

MICHAEL L. PATON, Lennox Paton, Nassau, Bahamas.

SOO MAN PARK, Kim & Chang, Seoul, South Korea.

DANCIA PENN, Dancia Penn & Co., Road Town, Tortola, Virgin Islands.

MONICA PETERSSON, Advokatfirman Vinge, Stockholm, Sweden.

FERGUS RANDOLPH, Brick Court Chambers, Brussels, Belgium.

JOSÉ F. SALEM, Basham, Ringe & Correa, Mexico City, Mexico.

FRANCISCO SANTANA GUAPO, Advogado, Lisbon, Portugal.

CHRIS SUNT, DeBandt, Van Hecke & Lagae, Brussels, Belgium.

ANDERS TOLBORG, Advokaterne Vingardshus, Aalborg, Sweden.

ANGELINE YAP, Allen & Gledhill, Singapore.

ALIYA YUSUF, Orr, Dignam & Co., Karachi, Pakistan.

JOE VARLEY, Gerrard, Scallan & O'Brien, Dublin, Ireland.

CESARE VENTO, Gianni, Origoni, Tonucci, Rome, Italy.

OLOF WAERN, Advokatfirman Vinge, Stockholm, Sweden.

W. S. WALKER, W. S. Walker & Company, George Town, Grand Cayman.

CONTENTS

Chapter 12

Chapter 13

Chapter 14

Chapter 15

Chapter 16

Chapter 17

Chapter 18

Chapter 19

Chapter 20

Chapter 21

Chapter 22

Chapter 23

Chapter 28

Chapter 29

Chapter 30

Chapter 31

Singapore

Chapter 32

South Korea

Chapter 33

Spain

Chapter 34

Chapter 35

Chapter 36

Chapter 37

TABLE OF CASES

TABLE OF LEGISLATION

CHAPTER 1

AUSTRALIA

Jon Broadley
Minter Ellison Morris Fletcher
Brisbane, Australia

Chapter 1

AUSTRALIA

INTRODUCTION

Under the Australian Constitution, the federal government has **1-001** power to legislate throughout Australia with respect to banking except "state banking", which covers the business of banking carried on by a State itself as banker.

The federal government also has the power to legislate with respect to incorporation of banks and the issue of currency. The Federation of Australia is comprised of six states and two territories, as well as the federal or commonwealth government. The power given to the federal government is not exclusive, and each of its states and territories also can introduce legislation with respect to banking where there is a proper territorial nexus.

Although there is power in all of these legislatures to define the banker's duty to maintain secrecy, that duty also is described in the cases and elsewhere as a duty of confidence or an obligation of confidentiality. There is no distinct legislation that defines or codifies the duty, but there are many statutes on a Federal and State level which touch various aspects of the banker's duty to maintain confidentiality.

Such statutes mostly require disclosure under specified circumstances and are, therefore, exceptions to the general duty, but there is some legislation that prohibits disclosure for privacy and other reasons. The state, territorial, and federal governments operate as separate jurisdictions but one must turn to the Common Law and equity to determine the scope of the banker's duty of confidentiality.

3

CONFIDENTIAL NATURE OF BANKER/CUSTOMER RELATIONSHIP

At Common Law

1-002   The essence of the obligation of confidentiality is that the law implies a term into the contract regulating the banker/customer relationship that the banker is to keep the affairs of the customer secret and is not to disclose them to anyone without just cause.

The classic statement of the obligation of secrecy that is imposed upon a banker, and the exceptions to that obligation are the statements of Bankes L.J. of the English Court of Appeal in *Tournier* v. *National Provincial and Union Bank of England*:

> "At the present day I think it may be asserted with confidence that the duty is a legal one arising out of contract, and that the duty is not absolute but qualified. It is not possible to frame an exhaustive definition of the duty. The most that can be done is to classify the qualification, and to indicate its limits."[1]

Bankes L.J. pointed to four qualifications to the obligation of secrecy: [2]

(1) Where disclosure is under compulsion by law;

(2) Where there is a duty to the public to disclose;

(3) Where the interests of the bank require disclosure, and

(4) Where the disclosure is made with the express or implied consent of the customer.

Nature of information protected

1-003   The information protected must be acquired by the banker in his character as a banker. In that case, the protected information was acquired by the bank's manager in ascertaining the identity of the person in favor of whom the customer had endorsed or drawn checks.

In the same case, Bankes L.J. said:

> "The case of the banker and his customer appears to me to be one in which the confidential relationship between the parties

---

[1] *Tournier* v. *National Provincial and Union Bank of England* [1924] 1 K.B. 461, at pp. 471-472.

[2] *Id.,* at p. 473.

is very marked. The credit of the customer depends very largely upon the strict observance of that confidence. I cannot think the duty of non-disclosure is confined to information derived from the customer himself or from his account."[3]

The only limitation mentioned by Bankes L.J. is that the information must be acquired by the banker in his character as a banker. In the *Tournier* case, the protected information was acquired by the bank's manager in ascertaining the identity of the person in favor of whom the customer had endorsed or drawn checks.

Scrutton L.J., in the same case, expressed the view that the bankers duty of secrecy owed to its customer did not extend to knowledge acquired by the bank before the relationship of the banker and customer was in contemplation, or after it had ceased, or to knowledge derived from other sources during the continuance of the relationship.

However, it would seem that the courts require a banker to maintain confidentiality in respect of all information required about the customer in the course of the banker/customer relationship.

Usually, the existence of a banker/customer relationship will be clear. The courts have held that the appropriate test of the existence of such a relationship is that "the customer" maintain an account with the bank, through which transactions are passed. This may be as expected, but there are instances where the existence or otherwise of an account can prove to be important.

For example, in *Great Western Railway Co. v. London & County Banking Co. Ltd.*,[4] a man had, for some years, been exchanging his crossed checks for cash at a bank where he had no account. The bank charged him nothing for this service. The court held that he was not a customer of the bank.

The extent of the duty of non-disclosure is not clear, but the kinds of information that will be protected is indicated by Atkin L.J. in *Tournier*:

"It clearly goes beyond the state of the account, that is, whether there is a debit or a credit balance, and the amount of the balance. It must extend to at least all the transactions that go through the account, and to the securities, if any, given in respect of the account; and in respect of such matters it must, I think, extend beyond the period when the account is closed, or ceases to be an active account."[5]

[3] *Id.*, at p. 474.
[4] *Great Western Railway Co. v. London & County Banking Co. Ltd* [1901] A.C. 414.
[5] *Tournier v. National Provincial and Union Bank of England, supra* n.1, at p. 485.

Extent of duty

1-004   The texts on banking law usually describe the exceptions to the rule regarding confidentiality rather than the scope of the duty itself. Although uncertainties exist, it is better that, unless protected by one of the exceptions, a bank should not disclose any information about the customer's affairs acquired by the bank in the course of the banker/customer relationship.

One could suggest that, if a customer has a current account, he will be revealing the details of his bankers and the number of his bank account every time he draws a check. However, this may not necessarily indicate that the customer does not consider that he or she confidentially keeps an account with that particular bank. Further, a bank may not disclose the state of a company's account to that company's parent or subsidiary.[6]

A difficult question is whether the banks are the only financial institutions to which a duty of confidentiality applies. Building societies, for example, originally were established primarily to finance the purchase of housing by owner/occupiers. Their operations in Australia have increased significantly since the mid-1960s. The services offered by building societies are continually expanding with interstate groupings of building societies being formed to develop the joint provision of electronic and other banking services.

It is suggested that, with respect to the provision of such services, the general principles of confidentiality in banking law should extend to other sorts of financial institutions such as building societies.

Conflict of duties

1-005   The decision of the Federal Court of Australia in *Kabwand Pty Ltd. v. National Australia Bank Limited*[7] is an interesting illustration of the operation of the duty of confidentiality conflicting with a statutory duty not to mislead or deceive.

In that case, the customer alleged that the bank officer represented that a strawberry farming business that the customer was intending to purchase was "a sound and prosperous" one, had failed to advise that the business was unprofitable and that the vendor (who was a customer of the bank) was heavily indebted to the bank.

6 *Bank of Tokyo Ltd.* v. *Karoon* [1986] 3 All E.R. 468.
7 *Kabwand Pty Ltd.* v. *National Australia Bank Limited* [1989] A.T.P.R. 40-950.

The trial judge (whose decision was upheld on appeal) disbelieved the customer's allegation of a positive misstatement. That left the question of whether the bank's conduct by silence was misleading or deceptive prohibited by section 52 of the Trade Practices Act (Commonwealth) 1974. On appeal, the Full Court of the Federal Court found that the bank officer knew that the business was unprofitable but said:

> "In the present circumstances, however, it could not be said that there was any duty on the part (of the bank officer) to impart to the 'purchasing customer' any information at all concerning the business or financial affairs of (the vendor customer). Quite the contrary. (The) Bank Manager had an implied contractual duty to keep confidential the business and financial affairs of (the vendor customer) . . . . The Bank's duty of confidence is not absolute. It may . . . be overridden by statute or by the express or implied consent of the customer. It may be overridden where the bank has some duty to the public generally to disclose . . . . In our view the present circumstance did not fall within any of the . . . qualifications to the duty (of confidentiality) and, for (the bank officer) to have said anything at all about the business or affairs of his (vendor) customer, would have been in clear breach of (the bank officer's) obligations to him."[8]

The decision of the English Court of Appeal in *Tournier* has also been approved by the High Court of Australia in a number of cases involving the Federal Commissioner of Taxation, the ANZ Banking Group Limited, and Smorgon Family.[9]

Fiduciary relationships

In some circumstances, the relationship between a bank and its customer can become a fiduciary relationship. Another case of conflicting duties arose recently in *Smith* v. *Commonwealth Bank of Australia*[10] where a banker was banker to both parties to a commercial transaction. **1-006**

The fiduciary relationship that was held to exist prevented the banker from continuing to act for both parties. This was because the

---

[8] *Id.*, at p. 50-377.

[9] (1976) 6 A.T.R. 690, (1977) 8 A.T.R. 140, and (1979) 9 A.T.R. 483, together called "the *Smorgon* cases".

[10] Unreported decision of Von Doussa J., Federal Court, March 11, 1991.

banker's duty of confidentiality to each customer conflicted with his fiduciary duty to disclose to one customer all that he knew about the transaction. In this case, the bank manager was banker to both the vendor and purchasers of a leasehold hotel business.

The manager was found to have approached the purchasers and informed them that he knew of a hotel for sale, privately. He was found to have then assumed the role of advisor to the purchasers in the merits of the transaction. The business was proved to have been purchased at an over-value. The court found that the bank had become a fiduciary because the bank's manager assumed a role that was not simply that of banker. The judge found that the bank had breached its fiduciary obligation to the purchasers of full disclosure.

He said that, even if the bank's manager had disclosed to the purchasers that he was acting for the vendor, he would "... still have been placed in an impossible position and the purchasers sought his advice on the merits of the transaction, and inquired whether they should offer less than the vendor's asking price. He could give no answer on these matters without running into a conflict with his duty to at least one side in the negotiations". The bank manager could not properly discharge his duty to maintain confidentiality.

In equity

1-007   A duty of confidentiality also may arise in equity, quite apart from duty arising out of the contract between the customer and banker. Such a duty may arise in equity where disclosures are made to a bank by a prospective customer in the course of discussing the question whether he or she will become a customer.

In such a case, a contract may never arise between the banker and customer, but equity may intervene to prevent the banker disclosing that confidential information.

There is no doubt that equitable obligations as to confidentiality can exist without there being any contract between the parties. However, where contract is the basis of the relationship between the parties, the contract is sufficient to define, by express words or necessary implication, what the obligations of the parties are. The discussion by Stephen J., in the first of the *Smorgon* cases, of the banker's duty of secrecy is limited to this contractual basis[11] that an

---

[11] See this discussion at (1976) 6 A.T.R. 697-699; further, it has been suggested in the work by P.D. Finn, *Fiduciary Obligations*, at p. 134.

imposed equitable duty of confidence would never differ in extent from an implied contractual duty arising out of the same circumstances.

Each of the exceptions to the contractual duty of non-disclosure will be discussed.

DISCLOSURE UNDER COMPULSION BY LAW

Growth of exception

The extent of this exception has grown in importance. Many governmental and regulatory bodies have legislatively conferred powers to call for the disclosure of banking records and documents.

1-008

For example, the production of documents by a bank may be compelled under legislation relating to stamp duties, or in accordance with provisions of the Corporations Law 1990, Bankruptcy Act 1969, Income Tax Assessment Act 1936, the Cash Transactions Reports Act 1988, the Fair Trading Acts of various states, the Commonwealth Trade Practices Act 1974, Proceeds of Crime Act 1987,[12] and the National Crime Authority Act 1984. The scope of this exception has widened in an uncoordinated fashion. Many, but not all, of these exceptions are discussed below.

A similar situation exists in the United Kingdom, which prompted the Jack Committee, in its report, *Banking Services: Law and Practice*,[13] to comment that "customers may already be forgiven for wondering at times, if the duty of confidentiality has not been replaced by a duty to disclose."

The Committee recommended the statutory codification of the rule in the *Tournier* case. In particular, it suggested that all of the existing circumstances where disclosure is justified under compulsion by law should be consolidated. This recommendation of codi-

---

12 With the Mutual Assistance in Criminal Matters Act 1987, this legislation enables Australian orders for freezing and confiscation of assets to be enforced overseas and orders made in overseas countries to be enforced against assets located in Australia. Protection is granted to financial institutions that disclosed suspected criminal conduct to law enforcement agencies and requires financial institutions to preserve the money trail by retaining certain documents, including documents necessary to reconstruct transactions, for seven years. See article by W.S. Weerasooria, "Money Laundering, Cash Transactions Legislation and the Banker-Customer Relationship", *Journal of Banking and Finance Law and Practice*, Law Book Co., June 1991, at p. 84.

13 Published in 1989.

fication was rejected by the government of the United Kingdom in its White Paper on Banking Services: Law and Practice.[14]

Instead, it proposed that the duty of confidentiality and its exceptions should be set out in a Code of Banking Practice. A similar recommendation has been made in Australia and will be discussed later in this chapter.

To whom the right accrues

1-009 The right of confidentiality belongs to the customer and not the banker. Accordingly, if the court considers that the customer should be compelled to disclose information, then the bank also will be compelled.

Australian courts are empowered to subpoena confidential information in litigation involving a customer of the bank, where it is appropriate.

Diplock L.J., in *Parry-Jones* v. *Law Society*, indicated the basis of this exception:

"A duty of confidence is subject to, and overridden by the duty of any party to that contract to comply with the law of the land. If it is the duty of such a party to a contract, whether at Common Law or under statute to disclose in defined circumstances confidential information then he must do so and any express contract to the contrary will be illegal and void. For example, in the case of banker and customer the duty of confidence is subject to the overriding duty of the banker at Common Law to disclose and answer questions as to his customer's affairs when he is asked to give evidence on them in the witness box in a court of law."[15]

Applying the exception

1-010 In applying this exception, the courts have recognized that the duty of confidentiality adds to the integrity and standing of banking institutions. This is illustrated by statements of Lord Denning in *Bankers Trust Company* v. *Shapira*:

14 Published in 1990.
15 *Parry-Jones* v. *Law Society* [1969] 1 ch 1, at p. 9.

"It is a strong thing to order a bank to disclose the state of its customers accounts and the documents and correspondence relating to it."[16]

In that case, two rogues obtained money by presenting to the plaintiff bank in New York a check purportedly drawn on it by a bank in Saudi Arabia and made payable to one of the men. The bank paid more than US $1-million and, on instruction from the two men, credited US $600,000 and later US $108,203 to accounts of the two men at the local branch of the Discount Bank (Overseas) Limited ("Discount"). Discount was a Swiss bank having a London branch.

On discovering that the checks were forgeries, the plaintiff bank in New York reimbursed the amount debited to the account of the Saudi Arabian bank and sought to recover its losses from the two rogues. During its attempts to locate the two men, the plaintiff bank applied for an order instructing Discount to permit the plaintiff bank to inspect and take copies of all correspondence between the rogues and Discount.

This order was granted by the English Court of Appeal, but it was expressed to be subject to an implied undertaking by the plaintiff bank that the information disclosed would be utilized solely for the purpose of the action to trace the funds.

Income Tax Assessment Act (Commonwealth) 1936

Powers to compel documents

The provisions of sections 263 and 264 of the Income Tax Assess- **1-011**
ment Act give the Commissioner for Taxation wide powers in respect of obtaining copies of relevant documents and information pursuant to requests in writing to the bank concerned.

These provisions have operated since the statute's enactment in 1936, but it is only in recent years that the Commissioner has put it to extensive use when investigating tax evasion.

Section 263 provides that a Commissioner of Taxation or any authorized officer "shall at all times have full and free access to all buildings, places, books, documents and other papers for any of the purposes of the Tax Act, and for that purpose may make extracts from or copies of any such books, documents or papers".

---

[16] *Bankers Trust Company* v. *Shapira* [1980] 1 W.L.R. 1274, at p. 1282.

Not only is the bank's privacy invaded, but the bank also must provide the Commissioner or his officer with all reasonable facilities and assistance for the effective exercise of powers under that Section.

Section 264 allows the Commissioner to give a notice in writing requesting any person to furnish such information as the Commissioner may require. The Commissioner also may ask that person to attend and give evidence before him on oath concerning his or any other person's income or tax assessment, and may require that person to produce all books, documents, and other papers whatsoever that he may have in his custody or under his control.

Limits to the powers

1-012   These provisions in the Tax Act are very wide. However, recent cases have indicated two limits upon the power to the Commissioner.

Because of the banker's duty of confidentiality, the banker is under a duty to claim legal professional privilege for those of a customer's documents that may be privileged. The properly advised banker should, therefore, request a delay of access by the tax officer to enable him to obtain instructions from the customer about which documents are subject to a claim of legal professional privilege.

It would be prudent to advise a client banker that, if time allows, the bank should obtain written confirmation from the customer stating that either none of the customer's documents are privileged or specifying the documents that are the subject of legal professional privilege. The problem usually is, however, that the tax officer arrives unannounced and there is little time to obtain such confirmation.

Authority for this proposition can be found in the case of *Allen Allen & Hemsley* v. *Deputy Federal Commission of Taxation*.[17] In that case, a taxation officer sought access to the trust account records of a firm of solicitors. The firm objected on the grounds that the accounts were privileged documents. Pincus J. stated the basic proposition that documents relating to the giving of legal advice could not be requisitioned by the tax officers under section 263 because they were privileged communications.

However, he concluded that only in the most unusual case would a solicitor's trust account records be privileged. Before they

---

[17] *Allen Allen & Hemsley* v. *Deputy Federal Commission of Taxation* (1988) 88 A.T.C. 4734.

could be classified as privileged, the records would need to have written on them some memorandum of legal advice. This decision was applied in the case of *Clarke* v. *Deputy Federal Commission of Taxation*.[18]

Thus, money laundering through trust accounts or records of particular payments under a tax evasion scheme are unlikely to be protected.

If a customer does not wish to claim legal professional privilege for any document that has been identified as privileged, the banker should obtain written confirmation of this from the customer.

The banker should himself also consider whether any of the bank's own documents are subject to a claim for legal professional privilege.

Protection against unnecessary disclosure

The Australian courts recognize that the right of a customer should be protected from unnecessary disclosure of information. In *Citibank Limited* v. *Commissioner of Taxation (Commonwealth)*,[19] section 263 of the Tax Act was considered after 37 Tax Department officers arrived unannounced at the Citibank premises in Sydney. The purpose of the visit was to search for and remove copies of documents relating to an investigation by the Commissioner of Taxation into certain corporate customers of Citibank and, in particular, an offshore redeemable preference share arrangement. **1-013**

Lockhart J. granted an interim injunction preventing tax officers from coming into Citibank premises and exercising their power pursuant to section 263. As a matter of principle, he considered that section 263 should be construed so that the encroachment that it may make upon the liberty, rights, and privacies of individuals is no greater than the statute allows, either expressly or by necessary implication. As such, a section 263 search cannot be used for a general fishing expedition of a person's documents. There must be a reasonable basis for the review of the documents.

For example, in this case, the tax officers needed to have formed the sound view that the bankheld documents relevant to the preference share arrangements. This decision was upheld by the Full Court of the Federal Court.

---

18 *Clarke* v. *Deputy Federal Commission of Taxation* (1989) 20 A.T.C. 701.
19 *Citibank Limited* v. *Commissioner of Taxation (Commonwealth)* (1988) 88 A.T.C. 4714.

Tax file number legislation

1-014 Federal tax file number legislation[20] requires all taxpayers and potential taxpayers to be given a tax file number. This requirement is designed to assist the taxation authorities in reducing tax evasion.

The Taxation Commissioner is able to match up information supplied by taxpayers in their income tax returns with information which banks and other financial institutions are required to give about customer's accounts.

Although banks must disclose the required information to the Taxation Commissioner, the Commissioner cannot disclose that information to other persons or to government bodies. It can use it only in checking the accuracy of tax returns and then taking action against taxpayers for discrepancies. The Privacy Act 1988 allows the Privacy Commissioner to investigate complaints about interferences with privacy arising out of the tax file number system.

Cash Transactions Reports Act 1988

Duty to report

1-015 This legislation poses many problems for banks. First, it imposes a duty upon banks to prepare a report and communicate the information contained therein to the Director of the Cash Transactions Reports Agency whenever a bank has reasonable grounds to suspect that information in its possession concerning a transaction to which it is a party may be relevant to the investigation of an evasion or attempted evasion of a taxation law or relevant to the investigation of, or the prosecution for, an offense against a law of the commonwealth or a territory or may be of assistance in the enforcement of the Proceeds of Crime Act 1987.

In providing information under this section, the bank is placed in a position of jeopardy because the Act provides protection only in relation to an action taken "pursuant to the relevant section".

This may mean that, should it be held ultimately that, in relation to a particular disclosure, there were no reasonable grounds for a suspicion of the required character, then the disclosure would not have been effected pursuant to the section and the bank will receive no statutory protection.

[20] Income Tax Assessment Act 1936, section 202, .

Significant cash transactions

Further, section 7 of the Cash Transactions Reports Act requires a   **1-016**
cash dealer who is a party to a significant cash transaction to
prepare a report of the transaction and communicate the information contained in that report to a Director of the Agency.

A "significant cash transaction" is defined by the Act as meaning
a cash transaction involving the transfer of currency of not less than
Aus. $10,000 in value. The meaning of the term "transaction" has a
wider scope than at first appears because, in Guideline Number 1
issued by the Cash Transactions Reports Agency, it is stated that the
expression includes negotiations or discussions that may not result
in an actual dealing.

Accordingly, if the following situation occurs the bank would be
required to compile a report:

"X" enters the bank with a suitcase containing Aus. $60,000 in
cash and requests Swiss franc travellers checks totalling this sum.
The bank's officer advises "X" that the bank requires a tax clearance
certificate or a completed declaration before the request can be
processed. "X" asks if there is any way to avoid obtaining such a
document. When "X" is advised that a certificate or declaration is
essential, "X" says he will have to consult his solicitor and leaves the
office with his money.

The difficulties are multiplied because most of these kinds of
transactions are dealt with, in the first instance, by the less experienced people at the front counter of the bank. It is in circumstances
in which the person seeking the dealing is not a current account
holder that the bank is required to be more alert.

Thus, the Common Law duty of confidentiality that a banker has
to preserve in relation to his customer's account has been modified
by a statutory protection and immunity for disclosure of information under this statute (which was modelled on United States legislation).

Cash Transactions Reports Act

Further, other significant changes to well established account and   **1-017**
banking practice involving bank secrecy were affected by the Cash
Transactions Reports Act.

With effect from July 1988, it was made an offense to open or
operate an account in a false name and, from February 1, 1991, a
statutory regime of account verification has to be followed for the
identification of a person opening a new account or for a new
signatory to an existing account.

Thus, it can be seen that there is no scope in Australia for anonymous accounts that may exist in other jurisdictions.

The initial response of the banking industry to this legislation was negative. It was considered that the provisions of this legislation were effectively making banks and other financial institutions additional arms of the law enforcement agencies. In addition, the implementation of the legislation has come at substantial cost to the banking industry.

Subpoenas and search warrants

1-018 A subpoena issued out of a court is one instance of lawful compulsion in accordance with the general law, under statute or under the rules of court.

In such case, the documents are produced to the court, and the production does not allow the party issuing the subpoena access to the documents or witnesses until the court expressly grants such access.

There are limits on this procedure and, in *Commissioner for Railways* v. *Small*,[21] the issue of a subpoena *duces tecum* requiring the production of an excessively wide range of documents was held to be a serious abuse of the process of the court.

Another method of compulsion is the use of search warrants in criminal matters. Banks which are presented with a warrant should ensure that the warrant is properly issued, that is, with evidence having been adduced before a magistrate as to the necessity for its issue.

Australian Securities Commission

Supervision of corporate transactions

1-019 Very wide powers have been given to the Australian Securities Commission, which is the corporate watchdog overseeing the enforcement of the new Corporations Law that came into force on January 1, 1991.

Under section 33 of the Australian Securities Commission Act 1989, the Commission may give to a bank a written notice requiring the production of specified books in the bank's possession and which may "relate to affairs of a body corporate".

---

[21] *Commissioner for Railways* v. *Small* (1938) 38 S.R. (N.S.W.) 564.

In a judgment by Spender J. of the Federal Court in *Australian Securities Commission* v. *Pasqual Zarro and Others*,[22] the court held that the above wording required Westpac Bank to comply with the notice to produce documents relating to Zarro's personal account (Zarro being a former director of the company being investigated) although there was no apparent connection between the documents sought and the corporation being investigated by the Commission.

The court adopted a broad interpretation of documents "related" to the affairs of a body corporate. The bank was ordered to provide the documents and Spender J. said that "it would be an impossible imposition upon the Australian Securities Commission if inquiries were to be predicated on an obligation in every case, [to ascertain] the detailed basis of the asserted connection between the documents sought and the bodies corporate, the subject of investigation".[23]

No duty to avoid disclosure

It is important to note that there is no duty imposed upon a bank to seek to avoid disclosure under compulsion of law. Thus, if a bank receives notice from the police, for example, that an order will be sought authorizing the police to inspect the current account and the bank complies with that order, the bank is not obliged to contest the application or to probe the evidence in support of it unless it is aware of relevant information that is not apparent on the face of the application or notice and which may not be known to the police.[24] **1-020**

However, in *Zarro* above, Westpac Banking Corporation seemed to take the view that the relevance of an individual's account was not apparent from the face of the notice to produce books. Accordingly, the bank objected to the issue of the section 33 notice (albeit unsuccessfully).

A bank usually will consider notifying its customer if the bank receives notice that a customer's records are to be inspected, seized, or produced in court. However, the ability of a bank to disclose to customers that documents are being inspected under compulsion of law can be limited. For example, section 74(1) of the Proceeds of Crime Act 1987 declares that a financial institution subject to a monitoring order under section 73 of the Act shall not disclose the existence or the operation of the order to any persons, except those

---

[22] *Australian Securities Commission* v. *Pasqual Zarro and Others* (1992) 10 A.C.L.C. 11.

[23] *Id.*

[24] *Barclays Bank PLC* v. *Taylor* [1989] 3 All E.R. 563.

mentioned in a specified list which does not include the customer or customer whose accounts are or have been subject to monitoring.

Trade Practices Act

1-021   Section 155 of the Trade Practices Act (Cth) 1974 gives the Trade Practices Commission wide powers to call for production of documents and information that relate to any matter that could constitute a contravention of the legislation.

A bank could be required to produce evidence that may be used, for example, in prosecuting a customer in relation to price discrimination or a similar practice.

Bankruptcy provisions

1-022   Under section 125(1) of the Bankruptcy Act (Cth) 1966, a banker is obliged to inform the trustee in bankruptcy in writing of the existence of any account of an undischarged bankrupt, unless the banker is satisfied that the account is held on behalf of another person.

Naturally, a bankruptcy trustee also has power to seize any assets or documents of the bankrupt that may be held by a banker. The provisions of the Bankruptcy Act vest the bankrupt's property in the trustee.

There are also additional powers under section 77A of the Bankruptcy Act for the trustee to have access to the books of any entity associated with a bankrupt and which books may be in the possession of the bank.

Bankers books

1-023   Legislation in each state of Australia[25] facilitates the proof of bankers' books in evidence to court by the production of verified copies of entries in such books in place of the books themselves. This legislation usually provides that access to the original books is only to be made with the leave of a court or a judge.

The purpose of this legislation is to relieve banks of the necessity of bringing their actual books to court under a subpoena. Nevertheless, this kind of legislation commonly includes provisions that empower the courts to make orders permitting the inspection of

[25] For example, see Evidence Act (Queensland) 1977, sections 83-91.

bank records and the taking of copies. This legislation was relied upon in *Bankers Trust Company* v. *Shapira*.[26]

In *A* v. *C*,[27] the point was made that one of the benefits of making an order permitting bank records to be inspected is that a knowledge of the amounts standing to the credit of the defendant's bank account can avoid a situation where, as the consequence of a Mareva injunction, an excessive amount of money is frozen.

There is also some concern about subpoenas issued out of foreign courts, particularly those situated in the United States, where the scope of the documents that are accessible is wider than under Australian law.

The question to be addressed is whether an Australian bank that complied with such a subpoena would be able to use the plea of lawful compulsion, if the customer queried the bank's right to rely on that exception. This is a difficult question and is referred to later in this chapter in a reference to international aspects.

DISCLOSURE PURSUANT TO DUTY TO PUBLIC

Definition of the exception

This exception is ill-defined. In relation to this exception, Bankes   **1-024** L.J., in the *Tournier* case[28] said, ". . . there would be many instances in which it would be necessary to consider the duty to the public" and ". . . danger to the state or public duty may supersede the duty of the agent to his principal."[29]

What the courts will consider to be the public interest can only be decided on the basis of the facts of each case. However, it should be noted that the term "interested" here does not mean that which is interesting from gratifying curiosity or a love of information or amusement, but that in which a class of the community has a pecuniary interest, in which their legal rights and liabilities are affected.[30]

It is possible to gain guidance from cases relating to commercial information in the context of industry when trying to define this particular duty in relation to the banking sector. In *Attorney-General*

---

26 *Bankers Trust Company* v. *Shapira, supra* n. 16.

27 *A* v. *C* 1980 2 All E.R. 347.

28 *Tournier* v. *National Provisional and Union Bank of England, supra* n. 1.

29 Bankes L.J. quoted Viscount Finlay's dictum in *Weld Blundall* v. *Stephens* [1920] A.C 956, at p. 965.

30 Campbell C.J. in *R* v. *Bedfordshire* (1855) 24 L.J.Q.B. 81, at p. 84.

v. *Guardian Newspapers Ltd. (No. 2)*,[31] the House of Lords considered whether to restrain two newspapers from publishing material obtained from former members of the security service. Lord Goff of Chieveley suggested:

> "Although the basis of the law's protection of confidence is that there is a public interest that confidences should be preserved and protected by the law, nevertheless the public interest may be outweighed by some other countervailing public interest which favours disclosure".[32]

In *Lion Laboratories Ltd. v. Evans*,[33] the plaintiff sought to restrain the publication of some confidential internal memoranda that cast doubt on the accuracy of the functioning of an instrument authorized by the Home Office in the United Kingdom for use by police for measuring intoxication by alcohol. Stephenson L.J. suggested:

> "The Courts will restrain breaches of confidence, and breaches of copyright, unless there is just cause or excuse for breaking confidence or infringing copyright. The just cause or excuse with which this case is concerned is the public interest in admittedly confidential information. There is confidential information that the public may have a right to receive and others, in particular the press, now extended to the media, may have a right and even a duty to publish, even if the information has been unlawfully obtained in flagrant breach of confidence and irrespective of the motive of the informer."[34]

Balancing competing interests

1-025   The balancing process with respect to competing public interests of confidence and disclosure will not be easy and bankers should be extremely cautious in considering whether to disclose confidential information under this exception to *Tournier*.

Learned Commentators Messrs Walter and Erlich[35] propose several strict tests that a court may consider in banking confidentiality cases:

---

[31] *Attorney-General* v. *Guardian Newspapers Ltd* (No. 2) [1988] 3 W.L.R. 776.

[32] *Id.*, at p. 807.

[33] *Lion Laboratories Ltd.* v. *Evans* [1985] 1 Q.B. 526.

[34] *Id.*, at p. 536.

[35] J..M. Walter and N. Erlich, "Confidences - Bankers & Customers: Power of Banks to Maintain Secrecy and Confidentiality", 63 A.L.J. 404, at p. 415.

(1) Whether the facts before the court display a situation that a reasonable banker would understand to be one that would be in the public's interest to disclose;

(2) Whether a clear, real, and extensive danger to the public exists;

(3) Whether the sole intent of making public the confidential information is in society's best interest (constructive interest); the bank must be purely motivated at the time of the announcement; there should be no collateral purpose such as a personal reason between the customer and the bank;

(4) Whether the bank has carefully considered if its action will be constructive (constructive effect);

(5) Whether the bank has considered if there is an alternate course of action against the potential harm that will be caused if the information is not made public (lack of alternative), and

(6) Whether, in considering the possibility of harm, the bank has weighed and balanced the harm that might flow from consequential disclosure of other information and not merely the harm flowing from the disclosure of the particular information (consequential harm).

DISCLOSURE IN INTEREST OF BANK

Disclosure by necessity

By necessity, a bank may disclose in its pleading in court action **1-026** against a customer what otherwise may amount to confidential information. This would be the case when detailing the state of its customer's indebtedness when it is taking legal proceedings to recover the amount of an overdraft or other loan facility.

Similarly, the necessary disclosures can be made in proceedings relating to the enforcement of protection of the security that the bank may hold. With this exception, there has been little argued before the courts.

However, in *Sunderland* v. *Barclays Bank Ltd.*,[36] the bank dishonored the plaintiff's checks, there being insufficient funds in her account to meet them. The real reason for the refusal to pay was the knowledge that the plaintiff was betting. She complained to her husband, and on his advice telephoned the bank. During the wife's

---

[36] *Sunderland* v. *Barclays Bank Ltd.* (1938) 5 Legal Decisions Affecting Bankers 163.

telephone conversation with the bank, the husband interrupted the conversation to take up his wife's case and was told that most checks passing through his wife's account were in favor of book-makers.

The wife sued for breach of duty to maintain secrecy. Du Parcq L.J. thought that, in the circumstances, the interests of the bank required disclosure and that it had, moreover, the customer's im-plied consent. He went on to say that, if this judgment had been for the plaintiff, he would have ordered only nominal damages since the plaintiff had suffered little damage, if any.[37]

Where disclosures are made under this exception, it must be limited strictly to information necessary to protect the bank's inter-est. Disclosure also will be necessary if the bank brings an action against a guarantor.

Release within banking group

1-027 The growing practice of banks in releasing confidential information about a customer within a banking group (and sometimes its non-banking subsidiaries) was considered in the case of *Bank of Tokyo Ltd v. Karoon*.[38] That case involved a parent bank and subsidiary bank.

It was alleged that an American subsidiary of the Bank of Tokyo Ltd. had committed a breach of confidentiality with respect to Karoon, a customer of both banks, because the American bank had passed on information relating to the customer's account in that branch to its parent company. The court refused to accept the view that the information passed by a subsidiary to its parent company was not disclosure. The fact that the subsidiary was in practice the same organization was found to be immaterial as, at law, the two companies were regarded as separate entities.

DISCLOSURE WITH EXPRESS OR IMPLIED CONSENT

1-028 The issue of express or implied consent is likely to arise in the case of guarantees and bankers' opinions or references.

---

37 *Id.*
38 *Bank of Tokyo Ltd. v. Karoon* [1987] 1 A.C. 45.

Guarantees

Conflicts of disclosure and confidentiality often arise in the consideration of guarantee situations.[39] It is likely that the guarantor will wish to know the extent of his obligations under the guarantee, and it is crucial that the bank correctly represents the relevant facts to a proposed guarantor.

1-029

Commentators in this area of law do not agree whether a bank has an implied authority of its customer to disclose customer information to a guarantor.[40]

Information subject to disclosure

The case authorities are also unclear whether a customer gives an implied authority to disclose information when he introduces a guarantor or intending guarantor to a bank.

1-030

For example, Harvey C.J., in *Ross v. Bank of New South Wales*,[41] indicated that the guarantor of a customer's account is not entitled to demand from the bank a copy of the account but is entitled to demand information as to the balance owing, the rate of interest charged, and the amount (if any) realized by the bank in respect of collateral securities.

However, Barwick C.J., in *Goodwin v. National Bank of Australasia*,[42] said the bank is only bound to disclose to the intending surety anything that has taken place between the bank and the principal debtor "which was not naturally to be expected".

Recent commentators have suggested the safest and the usual course is to arrange for a joint meeting between the guarantor, the customer, and the banker at which the guarantor may, in the presence of a customer, ask for information on any the matters concerning the customer's affairs.[43]

Certainly, a bank can be liable if it provides details of the financial stability of a company whose obligations are to be guaranteed and this information is incorrect. If a bank merely stated a set of facts and remained silent in dealing with questions as to the financial ability of a subject company, then liability may not attach. A contract of guarantee is not a contract of the "utmost good faith", and

---

39 *Kabwand Pty Ltd. v. National Australia Bank Limited, supra* n. 7.

40 See, for example, Lord Chorley, *Law of Banking*, (6th ed., 1974), at p. 335, and compare Paget's *Law of Banking*, (9th ed., 1982), at p. 502.

41 *Ross v. Bank of New South Wales* (1928) S.R. (N.S.W.) 539.

42 *Goodwin v. National Bank of Australasia* (1968) 42 A.L.J.R 110, at p. 111.

43 Walter and Erlich, *supra* n. 34, at p. 418.

the obligation of the bank in these circumstances to provide information to guarantors is "limited".[44] There is clear authority that the bank may not have to provide information unless specifically asked.[45]

Implied consent to release information

1-031   In certain circumstances, a court will find an implied consent to release information.

In *Lee Gleeson Pty Ltd.* v. *Sterling Estates Pty Ltd.*,[46] the New South Wales Supreme Court held that, where a bank customer has authorized the bank to reveal to a third party information that would otherwise have been confidential to the customer and the customer then changes the instructions to the bank relating to that information, the customer impliedly authorized the officers of the bank to advise the third party of those changed instructions.

In this instance, a builder, before promising to complete certain works within a set time, sought an assurance from a bank that he would be paid. The bank gave that assurance upon which the builder gave the promise and completed the works within the set time, enabling the bank to improve its position against the owner of the works. The bank should have told the builder that, meanwhile, payment instructions had been countermanded by the owner.

Banker's opinions or references

1-032   There is a well-established banking practice that banks supply to other banks opinions concerning their customers' credit worthiness and the reliability and standing of those who bank with them, without the express authority of their customers. Banks rely on the customer's implied assent to this banking custom and practice that has developed over the years.

It is at least arguable that, if banks do not take the initial step of obtaining a standard of authority from customers at the time an account is opened, to be able to furnish references to other institutions and information to credit reference agencies, they should not be allowed to rely on banking custom and practice. It would now appear to accord with the usual banking practice to have written conditions incorporated into the banker/customer contract. This

[44] *Henjo Investments Pty Ltd.* v. *Collins Marrickville Pty Ltd* (1988) A.T.P.R. 40-850.
[45] Professor Baxt, "Commercial Law Note" (1989) 63 A.L.J. 429, at p. 430.
[46] *Lee Gleeson Pty Ltd* v. *Sterling Estates Pty Ltd.* (1991) 23 N.S.W.L.R. 571.

could easily include an express consent to supply such opinions or references. In the United Kingdom, the practice seems to have developed (and been accepted) that the opinions are expressed in conventional and general terms and are given only to a carefully controlled list of organizations.

Some deviation from that practice appears to have occurred and was apparent from evidence given to the Jack Committee[47] that information was being released by banks to non-banking subsidiaries, with a justification that this was for the protection of the group as a whole.

Certainly, the banks did not seriously dispute the fact that information was carefully released, not just for such protection but for marketing purposes.

The Australian Law Reform Commission, in its report entitled "Privacy", concluded that in Australia institutions other than banks solicit and are given bankers' opinions, and there is no carefully controlled list of organizations. In addition, the Commission considered that this practice was not widely accepted by customers.

Privacy Act and Code of Conduct

As a result, the Privacy Act 1988 was passed by Federal Parliament in December 1988 and came into force on January 1, 1989. Originally, the Act was concerned with laying down detailed information on privacy standards to be observed by Commonwealth Government departments and statutory bodies. 1-033

It also is concerned with the handling of tax file numbers that are reference numbers given to all assessable individuals, trusts, or corporations by the Tax Department in an effort to monitor assessable income and therefore increase tax revenue receipts. At that time, the Act did not provide any guidelines concerning credit reporting and credit reporting agencies.

Credit reporting came under the purview of the Act after an amendment was passed in December 1990. In September 1991, a Code of Conduct for credit reporting agencies and credit providers was issued by the Privacy Commissioner. That Code of Conduct must be complied with on and from February 25, 1992.

The Privacy Act and Code have a significant impact on bankers. Information may be obtained only by a lender from an individual's credit file only for certain purposes set out in section 18K. These

---

[47] "Banking Services: Law and Practice", Report by the Review Committee (Chairman: Professor R.B. Jack), February 1989, Cmnd.622.

include assessing applications of credit, assessing guarantors and collecting overdue payments.

Information obtained by a lender from the credit file can be disclosed only for the reasons set out in section 18N. These include disclosures to debt collection agencies, to guarantors, to other lenders, but only with the consent of the individual concerned, and where otherwise permitted by law.

The apparently time-honored ability to solicit a bank's opinion in relation to its customer due to an implied term in the banker/customer relationship has now been curtailed as a result of the amendments to the Privacy Act.The specific consent of the individual concerned must be obtained. Lenders are bound by the Code of Conduct that is now in force:

(1) To notify a proposed borrower or guarantor if his or her credit file will be consulted;

(2) Not to report a default to a credit reporting agency unless certain conditions have been complied with in respect of that default;

(3) To notify a proposed borrower if the borrower's application for finance has been refused because of information on the borrower's credit file, and

(4) To train staff in the requirements of the Act and Code for handling information obtained from a credit report.

It is important to note, however, that the Privacy Act is largely concerned with consumer credit lending where monies are being borrowed for an individual's domestic or family purposes. However, the provision by a bank of an opinion relating to an individual's "commercial" creditworthiness is unaffected by the provisions of the Code of Conduct or the Privacy Act. Similarly unaffected is the provision by a bank of opinions relating to corporations since the definition of "individual" only refers to a natural person.

REMEDIES

1-034 Because the duty of confidentiality is basically a contractual one within the banking customer relationship (although a duty in equity also has been discussed), the customer has two remedies; he may sue for damages after the disclosure or for an injunction to restrain disclosure or a repetition of previous disclosure.

Damages often will be an inadequate remedy after the disclosure has taken place and the damage done. It is unlikely that punitive or exemplary damages would be awarded except in exceptional circumstances.

The chief protection for the customer is his ability to obtain an injunction restraining the bank from making disclosure. The failure to comply with such an order by the bank could constitute a contempt of court. It is necessary, however, for the court to be satisfied that there is some evidence that disclosure is threatened. It is often difficult for the customer because disclosure can take place before he knows about it.

If a *prima facie* case is shown by the customer such that on the balance of convenience, a court is likely to grant an injunction, it will usually be on condition that the customer gives an undertaking to pay damages to the bank if any loss occurs as a result of the wrongful imposition of the injunction.

Where an action is successful on the basis of a breach of the equitable duty of confidence or is based in tort, for example where a third party is instituting a claim, then equitable remedies such as an account of profits or an order requiring delivery up of documents containing confidential information may be available in certain circumstances.

There is also legislation requiring certain disclosures that, if not complied with, may lead to criminal penalties.

Where a bank does not comply with the statutory obligation to produce documents or disclose information, and even when a fine is prescribed in the legislation it has been held that if the default continues, an injunction can lie to compel obedience with legislation.[48]

REFORM IN AUSTRALIA

In November 1991, the Commonwealth House of Representatives **1-035** Standing Committee on Finance and Public Administration ("Martin Committee") handed down its conclusions and recommendations after a lengthy inquiry into banking and the effects of deregulation.

There were more than 100 recommendations made by the Committee in respect of the banking industry. Included was a recommendation that the Australian Law Reform Commission be

---

[48] See *Attorney General v. Thomas* (1983) 13 A.T.R. 859, with respect to section 264 of the Income Tax Assessment Act.

requested to conduct a review of the law of banker and customer and draft recommendations for appropriate legislation.

Proposed Code of Banking Practice

1-036   Importantly, it was recommended that a Code of Banking Practice, contractually enforceable by bank customers and subject to ongoing monitoring by the Trade Practices Commission, be developed as a result of a consultation process among the banking industry, consumer organizations, Commonwealth Government agencies, and relevant state government authorities. This Code would include stated general conditions upon which the banker/customer relationship could operate.

The Martin Committee acknowledged that, in the area of confidentiality, there was a need for modernization and clarification of the law; "although banks now possess major data bases, they are not fully subject to the regulation relating to them".[49]

Specifically, the Martin Committee recommended that:

> "84. the obligation of banks to maintain customer confidences should be expressly recognized by law and should be subject to express exceptions. The exceptions to the duty of confidentiality should include the following circumstances:
>
>> disclosure of information where subpoenaed for the purposes of litigation;
>>
>> disclosure under due process of law;
>>
>> disclosure pursuant to express consent in writing obtained by the customer and for a particular purpose; and
>>
>> disclosure to other credit providers and agencies subject to the restrictions imposed by the Privacy Act 1988 (as amended) and the Credit Reporting Code of Conduct;

---

[49] "A Pocket Full of Change: Banking and Deregulation - Conclusions and Recommendations", House of Representatives Standing Committee on Finance and Public Administration (Chairman: Stephen Martin, MP), 1991, Australian Government Publishing Service, at p. 6.

85. the duty of confidentiality should extend to all information obtained by the bank in relation to its customer, other than information readily available to the public;

86. customers should have access to all personal information concerning them contained in the records of the bank;

87. customers should be advised upon opening an account or commencing a relationship with a bank and at intervals thereafter of their right of access to personal information about them held by the bank; and

88. the obligation imposed upon credit reporting agencies by the Privacy Act 1988, to take reasonable steps to ensure that accurate files are maintained, should apply to personal information held by banks in relation to customers."

With respect to guarantors, the Martin Committee regarded as justifiable an intrusion on the borrowers privacy, where a borrower wants a guarantor to undertake a significant financial responsibility. The Martin Committee suggested that the banks be required to disclose to intending guarantors relevant information. If guarantors do not proceed with the transaction and loans are not made, that was regarded as better than guarantors entering improvident transactions unaware of the possible risks involved.

Accordingly, the Martin Committee recommended that the Code of Banking Practice require a bank to disclose to prospective guarantors all material facts known to it relating to the borrower and those transactions. It suggested that failure to so disclose should render a guarantee voidable unless the bank can show that the failure was inadvertent and the guarantor knew of or was in a position to know of the relevant fact or would have entered the transaction if the fact had been disclosed.[50]

Privacy Act revision

The recommendation by the Martin Committee that the Privacy Act **1-037** be amended to permit banks, with the consent of borrowers, to disclose information about the borrower or prospective borrower to a prospective guarantor has already been included in the legislation.

[50] *Id.*, at p. 47.

As to a detailed government response to the remainder of the recommendations of the Martin Committee, it is expected that some time may be required for that to occur.[51]

CROSSBORDER ASPECTS

1-038   Because of the development of a more global economy, it is appropriate to comment upon these aspects here.

The Rules of Court for various tribunals in Australia have the usual powers for taking evidence in civil proceedings on behalf of the courts in other countries. Some of these procedures include the production of documents and examination of witnesses. Evidence relating to bank accounts and other banking transactions are dealt with the same way as any other evidence.

Comity of law and sovereignty

1-039   The process of obtaining information by "letter of request" (or letters rogatory) involves a request for the provision of evidence made by a court in the inquiring country, to a court in the location where the records are maintained.

This process does not infringe the sovereignty of the other country where the records are maintained. If, however, a subpoena is issued, this can raise complex matters of international comity of law and sovereignty. A difficult position is presented to the bank as to whether it should not comply with the subpoena and be at risk of being held in contempt of court in the foreign jurisdiction. If the subpoena is obeyed, the bank runs the risk of breaching its duty of confidence that applies in Australia.

By section 5 of the Foreign Proceedings (Prohibition of Certain Evidence) Act 1976, the Federal Attorney-General can prohibit the production of documents, or evidence concerning them, except with his written consent. It is also possible for Australian citizens or residents to be prohibited from giving evidence before a foreign

---

[51] The Federal Treasurer, by Press Release Number 101 on June 25, 1992, stated the federal government's response to the Martin Committee's recommendation. Particularly, the government has endorsed the development of a comprehensive Code of Banking Practice to establish requirements and specific standards in key areas such as the obligations of guarantors. However, the specific recommendation of more complete disclosure is to be further considered before its inclusion in the Code of Banking Practice. The Treasurer expected to have the Code in place by the end of 1992.

tribunal about documents in Australia. The definition of a "tribunal" is very wide and includes a court or grand jury and any authority, officer, examiner, or person having authority to take or receive evidence.

The Federal Attorney-General may only use these powers when he is satisfied that a foreign tribunal may be acting inconsistently with international law of comity or where restrictions are desirable to protect the national interest. In any event, he can only act in matters involving the laws or the executive powers of the Commonwealth.

Under the Foreign Proceedings (Excess of Jurisdiction) Act 1984, the Federal Attorney-General can make an order prohibiting the right of a foreign court to request documents to be produced from Australia or persons within Australia to be called in proceedings involving a foreign court.

The legislation may be wide enough to cover matters within the constitutional power of the Commonwealth. Although it could apply to any federal laws concerning banking, the duty of confidentiality is a matter of Common Law, not one of federal statute law. The situation may change should recommendations of the 1991 Martin Committee on banking be implemented with respect to the establishment of a Federal Code of Banking Practice (including bankers' confidentiality).

Australian court assistance to foreign tribunal

Problems can arise in two ways. The assistance of an Australian **1-040** court may be sought, to conclude that the information or documents requested by a foreign tribunal need not be produced.

These cases are more usual. Alternatively, the Australian court may be asked to consider the validity of a request or requirement to produce documents or information imposed locally from the bank where that order would require production of documents or information in a foreign jurisdiction. There would appear to have been no real authorities on these points in Australia. Therefore, reference can be made to English cases, which are discussed below.

The United States approach

Many of the authorities seem to involve the United States, and it is **1-041** perhaps relevant and instructive to consider the position involving orders from the American courts.

Extra-territorial reach of subpoena

1-042 The regular and robust view of the courts in the United States has been that, when a subpoena is served on the office of a foreign bank in the United States, that subpoena can properly require the production of information concerning a bank customer from anywhere in the world.

With the development of a global economy and particularly with the continued emphasis by United States law enforcement agencies on discovering insider trading conducted from foreign accounts, the United States Department of Justice, the United States Securities Exchange Commission, and private litigants in the United States have increasingly sought to compel financial institutions to disclose customer account records located in jurisdictions that have civil or penal provisions prohibiting such disclosure.

The real problem for the non-party bank caught in the middle of conflicting demands can have serious ramifications. United States courts have imposed daily fines of US $25,000 and US $50,000 to enforce compliance with their discovery orders or subpoenas on financial institutions whose customer account records located abroad were pertinent to claims being litigated in a United States court.[52]

Several factors were traditionally taken into account by United States courts in balancing whether to issue and compel compliance with a subpoena or a discovery order in the face of conflicting obligations arising from other nations' laws. Not surprisingly, this balancing very frequently causes the United States courts to uphold the discovery demand at issue and compel compliance.

However, there has been a change in the United States position in this area. The 1965 *Restatement* has been revised by section 442 of the *Restatement of the Law* 3d, Foreign Relations of the United States (1987).

Most importantly, it is provided that a penalty should not be imposed on the party that has failed to comply "unless the party or witness has engaged in deliberate concealment or removal of information" or has not acted in "good faith" to attempt to obtain permission from foreign authorities to comply with the order.

Good faith defense

1-043 Section 442 of the Restatement provides a presumption that a party or witness that has made an effort in good faith to comply with the

---

[52] *United States* v. *Bank of Nova Scotia*, 740 F2d. 817 (11th Cir., 1984).

court's discovery order, short of violating foreign law, should not be penalized.

This good faith defense has its roots in the decision of the United States Supreme Court in *Sociètè Internationale Pour Participations Industrielles et Commerciales* v. *Rogers*.[53] There, the Supreme Court reversed the imposition of the harsh sanction against the plaintiff - dismissal of its complaint - for its failure to comply with a discovery order compelling it to produce information in violation of Swiss law.

The Supreme Court held that such a sanction was too severe in light of the good faith efforts made by the plaintiff to comply; nonetheless, the court remanded the matter to the lower court to determine whether a lesser penalty was appropriate.

In the decision of *Ings* v. *Ferguson*,[54] the United States court refused to order New York officers of two Canadian banks to produce records from Canadian branches.

The judge doubted whether the New York manager could direct Canadian officers to send branch records out of Canada in violation of a statutory provision in Quebec; but the judge emphasized more "fundamental principles of international comity", saying that courts

". . . should not take such action as may cause a violation of laws of a friendly neighbor or, at the least, an unnecessary circumvention of its procedures".[55]

Other means were available for securing evidence, namely, by letters of request (letters rogatory). It is arguable that this principle should apply to Australia although the duty of confidence does not itself involve a breach of statute. A question of whether the Attorney-General also may make an order under the Foreign Proceedings (Prohibition of Certain Evidence) Act 1976 should be considered.

Absolute prohibition of disclosure

Prior to the revised *Restatement* referred to above, United States **1-044** courts tended to suggest that the prohibition of disclosure under a foreign law must be absolute before this justifies the United States court in refusing to make the order against the bank.

[53] *Sociètè Internationale Pour Participations Industrielles et Commerciales* v. *Rogers*, 357 U.S. 197 (1958).
[54] *Ings* v. *Ferguson* 282 F2d. 149 (1960).
[55] *Id.*, at p. 152.

Consequently, in the face of a conflict between a duty of confidentiality and an obligation to comply with an overseas court order, it appears unlikely that an Australian bank could successfully plead compulsion of law as its defense.

However, if the Australian bank were restrained by an injunction in Australia from releasing the information to the United States court, then a breach of it would make a bank subject to Common Law penalties. United States courts would not usually make orders that will result in a breach of criminal or contempt laws in a foreign country.

It appears that a more sensible approach is to utilize the usual procedures involving an approach to the Australian courts by letter of request (letters rogatory).[56]

Likely attitude of Australian courts

1-045   In *Mackinnon* v. *Donaldson Lufkin & Jenrette Securities Corp.*,[57] the plaintiff sued the defendant for international fraud and had obtained in the United Kingdom:

(1) An order against the defendant bank (a United States bank with branches throughout the world, including London), under section 7 of the United Kingdom Bankers Books Evidence Act 1879, requiring the bank to allow the plaintiff to take copies of the bank's books relating to the defendant's accounts, and

(2) A subpoena requiring the bank to attend by its proper officer to give evidence of the trial and produce documents.

The London branch of the bank was served with the order and subpoena and the relevant books and papers relating to the defendants account were located in the United States where the account was maintained.

The bank applied to have the order and subpoena set aside on the grounds that in principle they exceeded the international jurisdiction of the court and infringed the sovereignty of the United States. The court allowed the bank's request and discharged the subpoena and order.

It was apparent from MacKinnon's case that a registered presence within the jurisdiction is not sufficient; British courts are reluc-

---

56 See generally E.W. Wallace, Chapter One, *Bank Confidentiality* (Neate and McCormick, eds., IBA and Butterworths, 1990).

57 *Mackinnon* v. *Donaldson Lufkin & Jenrette Securities Corp.* [1986] ch. 482

tant to impose obligations on foreigners to disclose documents outside its jurisdiction, and British courts are reluctant to infringe sovereignty.

In the case of *XAG* v. *A Bank*,[58] an injunction was granted restraining the bank from disclosing its records kept in England pursuant to a subpoena served on the United States bank's head office for the production in the United States of the London records. It involved investigations by the United States Department of Justice into the crude oil industry, where the investigators wished to produce before a Federal grand jury documents belonging to the customer.

These records related to a customer who did not carry on business in the United States and who had accounts with the London branch of the defendant, a United States bank. The court held the proper law of the contract was English law so that banker/customer confidentiality applied to the relationship of the members of the group within the bank.

In the *XAG* case, the court held that the duty of confidence in an international conflict can be a matter of "public interest" and not just a private matter between banker and customer. Further, the question of sovereignty also was a matter to which particular attention should be given when considering the balance of convenience as to whether to continue the injunction.

In *Libyan Arab Foreign Bank* v. *Bankers Trust Co.*,[59] the United States bank was held to have come within the public interest exception recognized in Tournier's case when it disclosed information to the Federal Reserve Board of New York that had power to obtain information from banks. A comparison was made with the power in the United Kingdom of the Bank of England to obtain similar information from banks.

In Australia, section 62 of the Banking Act 1959 allows the Reserve Bank, Australia's central bank, to direct banks (other than state banks) to furnish information, but any such direction shall not require the giving of information that identifies any individual customer. The use of such a power may eliminate problems facing a bank when caught in a conflict between its duty to maintain confidentiality and an obligation to comply with the order of a foreign court.

A foreign court is unlikely to resort to contempt proceedings if the bank involved is prohibited from disclosing information by its own courts. In the *XAG* case, the court, in considering whether, on a balance of convenience, the injunction ought to be vacated or continued, found it important that the American order would lead

---

58 *XAG* v. *A Bank* [1983] 2 All E.R. 464.
59 *Libyan Arab Foreign Bank* v. *Bankers Trust Co.* [1988] 1 Lloyds Rep. 259.

to a breach of secrecy, and the fact that the United States court would be unlikely to resort to contempt proceedings if the bank was prohibited from making disclosure by a court in the place where the records were kept.

Reference was made in *XAG* to the case of *United States* v. *First National City Bank*.[60] In that case, it was held it that a defense based on German bank secrecy laws was speculative, based on exposure to civil liability or loss of standing in the financial community and, on appeal, the distinction was made between Swiss bank secrecy law that is a mandatory law backed by criminal sanction and German law for breach of which there was at most a civil liability.

In the *XAG* case, it was said that:

> ". . . the Bank, having properly pursued its good faith efforts to relieve itself from the consequences of an injunction in this country, ought not to be held liable for contempt in any proceedings brought to that end in New York."[61]

The above cases give some guidelines to the likely approach that Australian courts will adopt in response to attempts by United States courts to obtain information within Australia.

The orders originating from the United States often may be seen as an invasion on local sovereignty, and the economic or other interests of the United States that are being enforced are seen as different from those of Australia.

---

[60] *United States* v. *First National City Bank*, 396 F2d. 897 (1968), was cited.
[61] *XAG* v. *A Bank, supra* n. 56, at p. 474.

CHAPTER 2

AUSTRIA

Michael Kutschera
Binder, Grösswang & Partner
Vienna, Austria

Chapter 2

AUSTRIA

INTRODUCTION[1]

Credit System Act

Sections 23, 23a, 34, and 35a of the Credit System Act (KWG) contain **2-001** the most important provisions on Austrian bank secrecy. These provisions are supplemented by several provisions which are of a procedural nature, in particular by the Revenues Penal Code (FinStrG).

Duties of confidentiality of a more general nature, such as those established by the Data Protection Act, are not dealt with in this contribution.

Sections 23 and 34 of the KWG came into force in early 1979, and section 23a was added and section 23, KWG, amended as of January 1, 1987. In July of 1988, section 35a was enacted as a provision of constitutional law which has afforded special protection to the provisions of section 23, KWG.

Since the codification of bank secrecy in the KWG, many treatises have been published, but only a few cases have been decided by the courts. Thus, there is no firmly settled Austrian law on bank secrecy.

The Austrian provisions on bank secrecy receive a special touch, as Austrian law and banking practice have, at least so far, permitted the establishment of anonymous bank accounts in certain cases.

---

[1] Kutschera, Austrian Contribution in *Bank Confidentiality*, Ed. Francis Neate, Roger McCormick, Butterworths, 1990, on which this contribution is based (hereinafter, "Kutschera").

Uniform declaration

2-002   In order to avoid abuses, in particular the laundering of money in connection with criminal offenses (primarily income from illegal drug dealing and organized crime), the Austrian banks have agreed on the wording of a uniform declaration, dated January 13, 1992, by which banks voluntarily undertake a number of duties to prevent such abuse.

In addition to the general undertaking of the banks to turn away clients or discontinue the business relationship in case of suspicion that funds originate from criminal activity, or that business partners have made misrepresentations as to their identity, the declaration contains the following main provisions:

(1) Banks will request disclosure of the identity of owners of bank vaults and continue to request such disclosure for the owners of accounts which serve for money transfer and payment transactions;

(2) Banks will request disclosure and documentary proof of the identity of any client who wishes to engage in over-the-counter transactions involving foreign currency equivalents in excess of ATS 200,000 (originally, the delivery to the bank of United States currency in amounts exceeding US $50,000);

(3) Banks will request disclosure of the identity of any foreign beneficiary in accordance with foreign exchange regulations in case a physical or legal person acting as trustee deposits funds with an Austrian bank, and

(4) Special care will be exercised if the nature of a transaction or the involvement of certain countries gives rise to suspicion that there may be a connection with money-laundering activities.

Further, the Austrian National Bank has issued a ruling that foreigners may not have anonymous securities accounts with a value in excess of ATS 10-million.

STATUTORY FOUNDATION

2-003   Section 23(1), KWG, reads:

"The banks, their shareholders, organ members, employees, as well as persons otherwise becoming active for the banks are prohibited from disclosing or exploiting secrets which were entrusted to or, to which access was made available for them on the basis of the business relationship with clients or on the basis of section 16(2)[2] hereof exclusively (bank secrecy). If, in the conduct of their official activities, organs of public authorities or of the Austrian National Bank receive information which is subject to bank secrecy, they shall maintain bank secrecy as an official secret from which they may be released only in one of the cases set forth in section 23(2). The duty to confidentiality applies without limit as to time."

Private and public administrative law

The provisions contained in section 23, KWG, embody elements of private and public administrative law.[3]   **2-004**

The confidentiality obligations of public authorities which gain access to information subject to bank secrecy; and the supervision of the banks' compliance with the bank secrecy rules by the bank regulatory authorities; involve public administrative law.

On the other hand, section 23, KWG, also defines a duty of private law which forms part of every contractual relationship between a bank and its customers. The latter raises the issue of whether or not bank secrecy duties can be contracted away in whole or in part.[4] Finally, section 34, KWG, subjects certain breaches of the duty of confidentiality pursuant to section 23, KWG, to criminal punishment.

---

[2] Section 16, KWG, provides that banks must give certain data on large borrowings to the Austrian National Bank which collects them and must pass them to other banks and to contract insurance businesses upon request. Section 23, KWG, also applies to contract insurance businesses in respect of section 16(2), KWG.

[3] Arnold, "Das Bankgeheimnis", ZGV Service 1/1981, at p. 20 (hereinafter "Arnold, Bankgehimenis"); Avancini-Iro-Koziol, *Österreichisches Bankvertragsrecht* I (1987), at pp. 103 *et seq.* (hereinafter "Avancini-Iro-Koziol"); Frotz, "Die Bankauskunft nach österreichischem Recht", Hadding-Schneider (Hrsg), *Bankgeheimnis und Bankauskunft in der Bundesrepublik Deutschland und in ausländischen Rechtsordnungen* (1986), at p. 257) (hereinafter "Frotz"); Jabornegg-Strasser-Floretta, *Das Bankgeheimnis*, at pp. 31 *et seq.* (Hereinafter "Jabornegg-Strasser-Floretta"); Laurer, "Das Bankgeheimnis in der Entwicklung von Lehre und Rechtsprechung", ÖJZ 1986, at p. 385 (Hereinafter "Laurer, Bankgeheimnis"),.

[4] Arnold, Bankgeheimnis, *supra* n. 3, at p. 20; Arnold, "Zum Bankgeheimnis, Anmerkungen zu einer kontroversiell diskutierten Rechtsthematik - zugleich eine Buchesprechung", ÖBA 1986, at p. 359, p. 360 (Hereinafter "Arnold, Zum Bankgeheimnis"); Avancini-Iro-Koziol, *supra* n. 3, at p. 104; for a mandatory nature, see Jabornegg-Strasser-Floretta, *supra* n. 3, at pp. 34 *et seq.*

Following is a brief summary of the main elements contained in section 23(1), KWG.

Bank defined

2-005   Section 1(1), KWG, defines a bank as one authorized to conduct banking transactions on the basis of the KWG or any other provision of federal law. The Austrian National Bank is not subject to the bank secrecy provisions of the KWG but to its own regulations. Building and loan associations are also not subject to the KWG provisions on bank secrecy with respect to those banking transactions which are typical for them, according to section 2(2)1, KWG.

It is the prevailing view that the term "shareholders", as used in section 23, KWG, means all shareholders of a bank, including shareholders of banks which are publicly traded.[5] Organ members are the holders of offices which are provided for by applicable corporate law. A trustee in bankruptcy is deemed an organ member of the bank.

Persons otherwise active for the banks are natural and other persons not integrated into the banks internal organization, including their outside counsel and other banks employed for the accomplishment of banking transactions.[6]

Physical persons may simultaneously be shareholders, organ members, employees of, or persons otherwise active for the same bank.

Secrets are facts which are known only to a limited group of persons and to which other persons cannot gain access at all or can gain access only with difficulties. An objective interest to keep the facts in question secret is required but presumed on the part of the clients.[7]

Clients are persons who deal with banks in the context of banking transactions. If a bank gains access to a secret relating to a client in a manner other than through the business relationship, there is no duty of confidentiality upon the bank pursuant to bank secrecy; an exception is provided by section 16(2), KWG.

[5] Arnold, Bankgeheimnis , supra n. 3, at p. 5; Avancini-Iro-Koziol, supra n. 3, at p. 108; Jabornegg-Strasser-Floretta, supra n. 3, at pp. 56 et seq.; Kastner, "Kreditwesen- gesetz und Gesellschaftsrecht", JBl 1980, p. 62, at p. 70.

[6] Avancini-Iro-Koziol, supra n. 3, at pp. 110 et seq.; Jabornegg-Strasser-Floretta, supra n. 3, at pp. 65 et seq.

[7] Arnold, Bankgeheimnis, supra n. 3, at p. 7; Burgstaller, "Der strafrechtliche Schutz wirtschaftlicher Geheimnisse", Ruppe (Hrsg.), Geheimnisschutz im Wirtschaftsleben (1980), at p. 5, p. 13; Frotz, supra n. 3, at p. 237; Jabornegg-Strasser-Floretta, supra n. 3, at p. 37.

Not clients - and therefore not directly entitled to bank secrecy - are third parties with respect to which the banks receive confidential information by clients. The banks are nevertheless obliged towards their clients not to disclose secrets relating to third parties and which they have learned from clients.[8]

Disclosure of bank secret

Disclosing a bank secret means generally its being made known (or **2-006** allowing it to become known because of refraining from taking reasonable action to prevent disclosure).[9] There is a dispute as to the scope of those persons to whom bank secrets may be disclosed on the grounds that such persons also would be subject to bank secrecy with respect to the relevant information (e.g., other bank employees), i.e., whether bank secrets shall be disclosed only to those others within the same organization (bank) who reasonably need to learn about the secret in question[10] or whether bank secrets may be freely passed on within the same organization (bank).[11]

Exploiting a bank secret is generally interpreted as an economic exploitation of a bank secret to the detriment of the bank's client.[12] One view holds that a bank is entitled to use client secrets for its own disposition, provided such use does not adversely affect the client in question, for its own disposition towards the client even if that would affect them adversely, and for its usual counselling of other clients, provided that the secret is thereby not indirectly disclosed or that the client in question is not otherwise adversely affected.[13]

---

[8] Arnold, Bankgeheimnis, *supra* n. 3, at p. 8; Avancini-Iro-Koziol, *supra* n. 3, at pp. 114 *et seq.*; Haushofer-Schinnerer-Ulrich, *Die österreichischen Kreditwesengesetze* 23/16 (hereinafter "Haushofer-Schinnerer-Ulrich"); Jabornegg-Strasser-Floretta, *supra* n. 3, at pp. 40 *et seq.*

[9] Erlaß Zl FS-130/1-III/9/79; Arnold, Bankgeheimnis, *supra* n. 3, at p. 8; Frotz, *supra* n. 3, at p. 239; Jabornegg-Strasser-Floretta, *supra* n. 3, at p. 46.

[10] Avancini-Iro-Koziol, *supra* n. 3, at p. 125; Jabornegg-Strasser-Floretta, *supra* n. 3, at pp. 137 *et seq.*

[11] Laurer, Bankgeheimnis, *supra* n. 3, at p. 389.

[12] Avancini-Iro-Koziol, *supra* n. 3, at pp. 125 *et seq.*; Haushofer-Schinnerer-Ulrich, 23/7, *supra* n. 8; Jabornegg-Strasser-Floretta, *supra* n. 3, at p. 86; Schinnerer, "Zur Problematik einer gesetzlichen Regelung des börslichen Insider-Geschäftes in Österreich", ÖBA 1985, at p. 271.

[13] Avancini-Iro-Koziol, *supra* n. 3, at p. 126.

Bank secrets disclosed to courts or other public authorities become official secrets and generally must not be disclosed to other courts or public authorities or exploited by the latter as a basis for the initiation of proceedings of any kind. To this extent, bank secrecy prevails over the general duty of public authorities to provide mutual assistance.[14] However, the provisions governing criminal proceedings do not address the problem explicitly, and official secrecy is lifted once a trial has begun.[15] The provisions on penal administrative law are more specific in that regard (see text below).

UNLAWFUL DISCLOSURE

Injunction

2-007   If a breach of bank secrecy is threatening, whether for the first time or continuing, the affected client will be entitled to injunctive relief, which relief does not require the demonstration of fault (negligence or intent) on the part of the party against whom such remedy is asked.[16]

Damages

2-008   A client who suffers damages through a violation of bank secrecy is entitled to reimbursement in accordance with the general principles of tort law. In accordance with these principles, a client generally will be entitled to reimbursement of the property damages which have been caused by such violation through a tortfeasor at fault.

It is the prevailing view that the right to damages may be contracted away in respect of a tortfeasor's lower levels of fault (at least for slight negligence) and that provisions to that effect contained in a bank's general conditions are valid if such conditions have become a part of the contractual relationship between the bank and the client in question.[17]

14 Avancini-Iro-Koziol, *supra* n. 3, at p. 127; Jabornegg-Strasser-Floretta, *supra* n. 3. at pp. 69 *et seq.*, pp. 124 *et seq.*

15 Avancini-Iro-Koziol, *supra* n. 3, at p. 127; Liebscher, "Das Bankgeheimnis im In- und Ausland", ÖJZ 1984, at p. 253 (Hereinafter "Liebscher").

16 Avancini-Iro-Koziol, *supra* n. 3, at pp. 163 *et seq.*; Jabornegg-Strasser-Floretta, *supra* n. 3, at pp. 160 *et seq.*

17 Avancini-Iro-Koziol, *supra* n. 3, at pp. 165 *et seq.*; Frotz, *supra* n. 3, at pp 267 *et seq.*; against, Jabornegg-Strasser-Koziol, *supra* n. 3, at p. 163.

A bank will be liable for all its agents and other personnel, whether employed or not, which cause damages to clients through faulty breach of bank secrecy as if the bank itself had committed such breach. On the other hand, such agents and other personnel will be protected by the above disclaimer as to lower degrees of negligence, as well.[18]

Criminal punishment

Under section 23, KWG, a natural person who discloses or exploits **2-009** facts subject to bank secrecy, with malicious intent to enrich himself or a third party or to adversely affect another, is subject to criminal punishment (imprisonment of up to one year or fines), but a person who has committed such crime shall be prosecuted only upon application of the party whose interest in confidentiality was infringed, as provided by section 34(1) and (3), KWG.

Public officials in breach of bank secrecy may be subject to more severe criminal punishment for breach of official secrecy.

Action by bank regulatory authorities

The bank regulatory authority (the Federal Minister of Finance) **2-010** must intervene if breaches of bank secrecy attributable to a bank have led or threaten to lead to a grievance (*Mißstand*).

The most severe consequence in such event could be the withdrawal of the bank's concession.[19]

EXCEPTIONS TO BANK SECRECY

Section 23(2), KWG, provides for six exceptions to bank secrecy. **2-011** This listing is not conclusive as to the duties stipulated in section 23, KWG.[20] Following is a description of those exceptions set forth in section 23(2), KWG, and those which are based on other provisions or principles of law.

18 Avancini-Iro-Koziol, *supra* n. 3, at pp. 165 *et seq.*
19 Avancini-Iro-Koziol, *supra* n. 3, at pp. 170 *et seq.*; Jabornegg-Strasser-Floretta, *supra* n. 3, at pp. 165 *et seq.*
20 Arnold, Bankgeheimnis, *supra* n. 3, at p. 12, 18 *et seq.*; Avancini-Iro-Koziol, *supra* n. 3, at p. 129; Jabornegg-Strasser-Floretta, *supra* n. 3, at p. 93.

Customer's consent

2-012   There is no bank secrecy if the client expressly consents in writing to the disclosure or exploitation of a secret, under section 23(2)3, KWG. A valid consent requires a clearly formulated writing signed by the client which, within certain limits, also may be given in advance.[21] If a secret relates to persons who are not clients, the waiver nevertheless has to be issued by the client who passed the secret to the bank.

    Apparently, no Austrian court has ruled on the relevance of a consent obtained as a consequence of a foreign court order under the threat of fines or imprisonment (*e.g.*, a subpoena issued by a United States court and served in the United States upon the client of an Austrian bank). Even if the consent were deemed to have been obtained by undue force (which is doubtful in case the foreign court acts in accordance with applicable law), it would nevertheless be deemed to have been validly given until declared invalid by a court in the course of civil litigation. In any event, the issuer of the consent declaration could revoke it at any time.

Litigation between bank and client

2-013   That there is no bank secrecy in the disclosure is indispensably necessary for the resolution of legal issues arising out of the relationship between banks and clients, as provided by section 23(2)5, KWG.

    This exception relates to litigation and permits the bank to disclose secrets relating to and learned from the client in a litigation with such client.

Information on customer's financial situation

2-014   There is no bank secrecy for generally phrased information on the fiinancial situation of a business, as usually given by banks, unless the client expressly objects thereto, according to section 23(2)4, KWG.

---

[21] Arnold, Bankgeheimnis, *supra* n. 3, at pp. 17 *et seq.*; Avancini-Iro-Koziol, *supra* n. 3, at pp. 131 *et seq.*, Frotz, *supra* n. 3, at pp. 244 *et seq.*; Jabornegg-Strasser-Floretta, *supra* n. 3, at pp. 99 *et seq.*

This exception permits the banks to generally inform the public as to their clients' financial situations (unless a client objects in advance). In these cases, the bank will have to carefully balance the frequently conflicting interests of the clients and those of the recipients of the bank's information. The limitation as to "general information" prevents the banks from passing on specific and detailed data.

Banks only may give a general picture of their clients' states of affairs without directly or indirectly disclosing exact data. In order to comply with the above duties of care, the banks normally issue such information by using standard formulations, and the banks may rely on the assumption that the information recipient understands the meaning of such terminology.[22]

Balancing of interest

There is probably no bank secrecy if, upon a balancing of the client's   **2-015** interest in confidentiality with conflicting interests of the bank or third parties, the bank's or such third parties' interests appear to be significantly overriding,[23] although this exception is not set forth in a special statutory provision. Therefore, careful scrutiny must be applied upon determining whether those interests which conflict with bank secrecy prevail.

Typical cases are those in which the bank is asked by persons who actually have posted, or are contemplating posting, security for an obligation by a bank's client towards such bank for information on the debtor's financial state.[24]

In one case, the Austrian Supreme Court (OGH) has held that section 23, KWG, did not prevent the issuer of credit cards from disclosing the address of a credit card holder to a business from

---

22 Arnold, Bankgeheimnis, *supra* n. 3, at pp. 17 *et seq.*; Avancini-Iro-Koziol, *supra* n. 3, at pp. 153 *et seq.*; Frotz, *supra* n. 3, at pp. 242 *et seq.*; Jabornegg-Strasser-Floretta, *supra* n. 3, at pp. 105 *et seq.*

23 Arnold, Bankgeheimnis, *supra* n. 3, at p. 19; Avancini, "Der Auskunftsanspruch des Bürgen gegenüber dem Gläubiger - Zugleich ein Beitrag zum Bankgeheimnis", JBl 1985, at p. 193, pp. 204 *et seq.* (Hereinafter "Avancini, Auskunftsanspruch"); Avancini-Iro-Koziol, *supra* n. 3, at pp. 161 *et seq.*; Frotz, *supra* n. 3, at pp. 254 *et seq.*; Jabornegg-Strasser-Floretta, *supra* n. 3, at pp. 142 *et seq.*; Steiner, "Zur Aufklärungspflicht der Kreditunternehmung bei Wechseldiskontgeschäften", JBl 1983, at p. 189 (Hereinafter "Steiner").

24 Avancini, Auskunftsanspruch, *supra* n. 23, at pp. 193 *et seq.*; Steiner, *supra* n. 23, at pp. 189 *et seq.*

which the credit card owner had purchased goods but who subsequently requested the issuer of the card not to pay the invoice.[25]

Payment of another's debt

2-016   There is a further exception to bank secrecy towards third parties who have paid a client's debt to the bank and for which debt such third parties were personally liable or had posted other security. Such third parties are assignees of the (bank) creditor's rights by operation of law.

Such third parties are entitled to delivery of all other security posted for the debt in question and of such other documents or information necessary to pursue their right to recourse against the debtor and against others who have posted security, as per section 1358, Civil Code, ABGB.

The OGH has held twice that section 1358, ABGB, prevails over section 23, KWG.[26]

In the older case, the OGH held that a surety who had paid the secured debt was entitled to receive the underlying credit agreements, other suretyship agreements, drafts, and the correspondence executed by the other sureties or the debtor and relating to the debtor's credit account (but not internal memoranda and correspondence signed by the bank).

In the more recent case, the OGH held that a mortgagor's rights under section 1358, ABGB, prevailed over section 23, KWG, as well.[27]

Inventory of estates by probate court

2-017   There is no bank secrecy towards the probate court in connection with the inventory or other determination of the assets and obligations of the estate of a deceased person under section 23(2)2, KWG.

The exception pursuant to section 23(2)2, KWG, applies only to requests for information by Austrian probate courts in Austrian probate proceedings. There is no exception to bank secrecy for

[25] OGH, March 8, 1988. ÖJZ 1989/1 = ÖBA 1988, 1021; Jabornegg, "Neues zum Bankgeheimnis", WBl 1990, 29 et seq. (Hereinafter "Jabornegg").

[26] OGH, February 2, 1984, SZ 57/29; OGH 29 April 1986, JBl 1986, 511.

[27] OGH in SZ 57/29 and JBl 1986, 511; Avancini-Iro-Koziol, supra n. 3, at p. 157; Frotz, supra n. 1.3, at pp. 252 et seq.; Jabornegg-Strasser-Floretta, supra n. 3, at pp. 151 et seq.

requests by foreign probate courts, whether made directly or through letters rogatory.[28]

Criminal proceedings

There is no bank secrecy towards Austrian penal courts in connection with initiated judicial criminal proceedings and towards Austrian fiscal penal authorities (*Finanzstrafbehörden*) in connection with initiated penal proceedings because of international fiscal offenses (*vorsätzliche Finanzvergehen*), except for fiscal irregularities (*Finanzordnungswidrigkeiten*).

2-018

Criminal proceedings are those with respect to such crimes or offenses (including certain crimes and offenses provided for in the Revenues Penal Act, *e.g.*, tax fraud and smuggling) and other fiscal offenses defined as such in other (federal) statutes.

Fiscal offenses may be subject to judicial criminal punishment or to administrative (fiscal) penal punishment. Fiscal irregularities are fiscal offenses of a lesser degree. Fiscal penal authorities are administrative agencies. Decisions of the final-instance fiscal penal authorities generally may be appealed to the Administrative Court or the Constitutional Court.

Whether or not courts or fiscal penal authorities may request the disclosure of bank secrets depends on two main issues, namely, whether a relevant proceeding is deemed "initiated" and whether there is sufficient "connection" between the proceeding and the requested disclosure.

A resolution of these issues must take into consideration that the exception to bank secrecy in connection with criminal and certain administrative penal proceedings does not enable the prosecution to gather indicia for potential crimes or offenses (fishing expeditions) but only to corroborate (or dispel) well founded and reasonably defined suspicions of such crimes or offenses.[29]

---

[28] Arnold, Bankgeheimnis, *supra* n. 3, at pp. 15 *et seq.*; Avancini, "Auskünfte über Sparbücher im Verlassenschaftsverfahren", NZ 1985, at p. 21; Avancini-Iro-Koziol, *supra* n. 3, at pp. 150 *et seq.*; Frotz, *supra* n. 3, at pp. 251 *et seq.*; Jabornegg-Strasser-Floretta, *supra* n. 3, at pp. 126 *et seq.*

[29] Arnold, "Entscheidungsanmerkung", AnwBl 1986, at p. 417; Avancini-Iro-Koziol, *supra* n. 8, at p. 141; see also, Jabornegg-Strasser-Floretta, *supra* n. 3, at pp. 110 *et seq.*; Bertel, "Das Bankgeheimnis im Strafverfahren", ÖBA 1992, at p. 711 (Hereinafter "Bertel"), and Fuchs, "Gewinnabschöpfung und Geldwäscherei", ÖJZ 1990, at p. 544 (Hereinafter "Fuchs").

"Initiated" criminal proceedings

2-019   Under Austrian law, a criminal proceeding normally is conducted
in three stages (exceptions are not dealt with herein). The initial
stage is the preliminary inquiry (*Vorerhebung*), which is conducted
under the guidance of the public prosecution which, in turn, employs police or courts for the actual inquiry actions.

The next phase is the preliminary investigation (*Vorunter-
suchung*) in which a judge is in charge and which is followed by the
trial as the last stage. A preliminary investigation can be directed
against one or more identified persons only, whereas a preliminary
inquiry also may be directed against unknown perpetrators.

The issue of whether a criminal proceeding should be deemed
initiated upon the commencement of preliminary inquiries, or only
upon the opening of a formal preliminary investigation, has probably been resolved by a decision of the OGH,[30] which held that the
taking of any measures against known or unknown perpetrators in
the course of criminal proceedings, including the stage of preliminary inquiries, constituted the initiation of criminal proceedings.

There remains a dispute as to whether a court in charge of
investigations or entrusted with inquiries may employ the police
for the opening of bank secrets.[31] Although the above question has
not been the subject of a court decision, it is the prevailing practice[32]
that the courts may have the actual investigation conducted by the
police.

"Initiated" fiscal penal proceedings

2-020   Fiscal penal proceedings are formally initiated by an appealable
decree pursuant to sections 82 and 83, FinStrG. The suspect must
receive notice of such initiation.

A fiscal penal proceeding is to be initiated if there is suspicion of
a fiscal offense unless the offense probably cannot be proven, the
suspected facts do not constitute a fiscal offense, or the suspect has
not committed the offense or cannot be prosecuted or punished for it.

---

30 OGH, January 18, 1989, JBl 1989, 454 = ÖJZ 1989/99 = ÖBA 1989, 526, see also,
Weber, "Das Bankgeheimnis bei eingeleiteten gerichtlichen Strafverfahren -
Banken im Zwiespalt", RdW 1990, at p. 435 (Hereinafter "Weber") and
(advocating the contrary view) Jabornegg, *supra* n. 25, at pp. 33, 34.

31 Avancini-Iro-Koziol, *supra* n. 3, at p. 142; against, Jabornegg-Strasser-Floretta,
supra n. 3, at p 118.

32 Bertel, *supra* n. 29, at pp. 711 *et seq.*

Sufficient "connection"

There is a sufficient connection between proceeding and bank secret   2-021
if there is an objectively ascertainable relevance of the requested
information to the proceeding in question.

It is the prevailing view that such relevance also may exist for the
bank secrets of one party in relation to a crime or fiscal offense of a
third party in which the former did not participate.[33]

Search and seizure

Scope of power

The scope of the court and fiscal penal authorities' right to obtain   2-022
bank secrets, by way of search and seizure and to use bank secrets
obtained in such manner, is of particular significance because an
obligation to disclose is only relevant to the extent it actually can be
enforced.

It should be mentioned that there is a theoretical possibility to
indirectly enforce disclosure by fining a bank (or its shareholders)
which refuses to disclose a bank secret upon a request issued by a
fiscal penal authority.

After the KWG's coming into force in March 1979, the fiscal penal
authorities continued their former practice to conduct searches and
seizures with banks because of particular fiscal offenses but to seize
as well any evidence which indicated the commission of intentional
fiscal offenses (including offenses totally unrelated to those in respect of which the actual searches had been ordered) by other bank
clients which had nothing to do with the subject matter of the
original search order.[34]

Ruling of the Constitutional Court

In 1986, the Constitutional Court (in another context) struck down   2-023
several provisions of the Revenues Penal Code, holding that a

---

[33] Avancini-Iro-Koziol, *supra* n. 3, at pp. 141, 144; Jabornegg-Strasser-Floretta,
supra n. 3, at pp. 108 *et seq.*; Liebscher, *supra* n. 15, at p. 254; against a lifting of
bank secrecy, Arnold, Bankgeheimnis, *supra* n. 3, at p. 13; LG f. *Strafsachen Graz*,
March 21, 1990, ÖBA 1990, at p. 849.

[34] Doralt, "Das Bankgeheimnis im Abgabeverfahren", ÖJZ 1981, at p. 652; Doralt,
"Entscheidungsanmerkung", RdW 1984, at p. 128.

legally acknowledged right to refuse testimony because of the privilege of self-incrimination could not be thwarted by obtaining the denied evidence through search and seizure or other undue means (*e.g.*, indirect pressure, such as assessments based on estimates).[35] Based on this ruling, the provisions on the right to search and seizure, as contained in the Revenue Penal Code were amended. Although the provisions on search and seizure pursuant to the Criminal Procedure Code (StPO), were not changed, particularly their interpretation will have to consider principles underlying the amendment of the Revenues Penal Code, the latter in view of a statement made by the Constitutional Court which indicates that its holding on the provisions of the Revenues Penal Code should apply to the comparable provisions of the Criminal Procedure Code, as well.[36]

The new section 89(4), FinStrG, provides that evidence for breaches of the law other than those which form the basis of the initial (lawful) search order, which are accidentally found by the searching authorities in the custody of banks, and which concern secrets in the meaning of section 23(1), KWG, may be seized only if directly connected with the intentional fiscal offense(s) (not just fiscal irregularities) for which bank secrecy was lifted pursuant to section 23(1)1, KWG.

That means that such means of evidence can be seized to the extent they relate to a fiscal offense (not to a crime, another fiscal offense, or other contraventions of the law) which is not just a fiscal irregularity and which is directly connected with the financial offense(s) for which the search was originally conducted.

This limitation applies for the benefit of the party suspected of the fiscal offense and in particular for the benefit of third parties.[37]

If the bank formally alleges that information was seized in violation of bank secrecy (*i.e.*, the requirements of section 23(2)1, KWG, or those of section 89(4), FinStrG, were not fulfilled), such information must be sealed and a formal decision on the legality of the seizure must be issued. Such decision can be appealed.

[35] VfGH, December 3, 1984, AnwBl 1985, at p. 43; see Arnold, "Die Finanzstrafgesetznovelle 1985", ZGV 1986, at p. 5 (Hereinafter "Arnold, Finanzstrafgesetznovelle"); Arnold, "Aktuelles zum Bankgeheimnis", ÖBA 1985, at p. 19; Beiser, "Entscheidungsanmerkung", OStZ 1985, at p. 24; Avancini, Bankgeheimnis, *supra* n. 23, at pp. 298 *et seq.*; Avancini-Iro-Koziol, *supra* n. 3, at p. 145.

[36] Arnold, Finanzstrafgesetznovelle, *supra* n. 35, at p. 9; Avancini, Bankgeheimnis, *supra* n. 23, at pp. 298 *et seq.*; Avancini-Iro-Koziol, *supra* n. 3, at pp. 145, 147.

[37] Arnold, Finanzstrafgesetznovelle, *supra* n. 35, at p. 7; Avancini-Iro-Koziol, *supra* n. 3, at p. 146.

Finally, section 98(4), FinStrG, provides that evidence seized in violation of the above must not be used for the rendering of the decision (punishment order) to the detriment of the accused or of an accessory. This provision is interpreted to mean that the fiscal authorities must not use such evidence in an initiated proceeding, and no court or other public authority may use it to commence proceedings against those involved.[38]

The corollary to section 89(4), FinStrG, is section 144, StPO, which, as indicated above, does not contain a comparable limitation but rather provides broadly that objects may be seized if they are found during a search and indicate the commission of other crimes which shall be prosecuted *ex officio*.

Impact of the Constitutional Court's ruling

It is the prevailing view[39] that a limitation as contained in section **2-024**
89(4), FinStrG, has to be read into section 144, StPO, in view of the Constitutional Court's ruling. If that is the case, a seizure of objects beyond such limitation will be illegal and a (criminal) judgment rendered on the basis of such evidence could be appealed as void.

It is difficult to predict whether and, if so, to what extent the courts will follow the above line of reasoning. According to information informally received by the author, the courts do not apply the principles of section 89(4), FinStrG, to section 144, StPO, at present.

Consequently, there is, at present, no limit to the use of crime-related information accidentally gathered in the course of an official and legal search conducted in relation to criminal proceedings.

Bank secrecy and foreign legal proceedings

There is no exception to bank secrecy if foreign courts or other **2-025**
public authorities approach a bank directly, irrespective of whether in a civil or criminal matter, themselves. But there may be exceptions to bank secrecy if foreign courts (and other public authorities)

---

[38] Arnold, Finanzstrafgesetznovelle, *supra* n. 36, at p. 9; Avancini, Bankgeheimnis, *supra* n. 23, at p. 299; Avancini-Iro-Koziol, *supra* n. 3, at p. 146.
[39] Arnold, Finanzstrafgesetznovelle, *supra* n. 36, p. 9; Avancini, Bankgeheimnis, *supra* n. 23, at p. 299; Avancini-Iro-Koziol, *supra* n. 3, at p. 147.

request the assistance of Austrian courts or other Austrian public authorities in criminal proceedings by way of letters rogatory.[40]

Letters rogatory

2-026 In the absence of applicable treaties, the Act on Extradition and Legal Assistance in Matters of Criminal Law (ARHG) of December 1979 governs the grant of legal assistance to foreign authorities. Pursuant to section 50, ARHG, legal assistance may be granted by or through Austrian courts to foreign courts, foreign public prosecutors, and foreign prison authorities, provided there is reciprocity.

Legal assistance shall not be granted if (among other factors) the offense on which the request for legal assistance is based is not subject to judicial criminal punishment under Austrian law or is not a violation of revenues, monopolies, or customs, exchange control, rationing, import, or export control laws.

Further, the legal assistance must not lead to a breach of Austrian law providing for duties to confidentiality which shall be maintained in regard to penal courts as well; and the compliance with the request of legal assistance must not be contrary to the public policy or other essential interests of the Republic of Austria.

The majority view[41] holds that legal assistance shall be granted on the basis of the ARHG if its conditions are met and special requirements and limits under which bank secrecy may be lifted in purely domestic proceedings are fulfilled (*i.e.*, initiated criminal proceedings, sufficient connection, and safeguard against the use of accidentally gathered evidence which is not directly related to the offense which formed the basis for the request for legal assistance; according to information informally received by the author, the Austrian authorities do not request safeguard against undue use of accidentally gathered evidence by foreign courts at present.).

---

[40] Avancini-Iro-Koziol, *supra* n. 3, at p. 149; Jobornegg-Strasser-Floretta, *supra* n. 3, at p. 156; Laurer, Bankgeheimnis, *supra* n. 3, at p. 393; doubtful, Arnold, Bankgeheimnis, *supra* n. 3, at p. 15; Binder, "Österreichs Bankgeheimnis im internationalen Steuerrecht", SWK 1985/13, at p. 9.

[41] Avancini-Iro-Koziol, *supra* n. 3, at p. 149; Jabornegg-Strasser-Floretti, *supra* n. 3, at p. 156; Laurer, Bankgeheimnis, *supra* n. 3, p. 393; Weber, *supra* n. 30, at pp. 439, 440.

European Convention on Mutual Assistance

Austria is signatory to the European Convention on Mutual Assis-   2-027
tance in Criminal Matters of April 20, 1959. The most relevant
requirements for and exceptions to Austria's duty to render legal
assistance under the treaty (in its original version) are that legal
assistance will only be granted for offenses subject to judicial criminal punishment in the requesting country and in Austria (article
1(1) and Austrian Reservation thereto) but will not be granted in
respect of fiscal offenses (Austrian Reservation to article 2a).

In addition, legal assistance will not be granted if it impairs
Austria's essential interests (article 2b; Austria has made a reservation to article 2b, declaring that it understands as "other essential
interests" in particular the respecting of the duties of confidentiality
provided by Austrian law).

In 1983, Austria ratified the Additional Protocol to the European
Convention on Mutual Assistance in Criminal Matters (BGBl
296/1983) in which it waived the exception as to fiscal offenses.

Later, Austria withdrew the exception as to fiscal offenses also
with respect to those countries signatory to the Convention but
which had not subscribed to the Additional Protocol, and it issued
another declaration in which it referred to the protection of confidentiality by domestic law. Thus, it remains unclear whether and
within which limits Austria will grant legal assistance under the
above Convention with respect to criminal proceedings of a fiscal
nature.[42]

Austria has entered into a number of bilateral treaties, some of
which supplement the above Convention.

Nature of assistance

Austrian authorities will not render legal assistance to foreign   2-028
authorities in civil matters if such assistance is contrary to bank
secrecy.

Austria will render legal assistance in criminal matters in accordance with applicable treaties or the ARHG, even if that requires a
lifting of bank secrecy, provided the requirements for and the limits
to a lifting of bank secrecy in a purely domestic situation are

---

[42] Beiser, "Das österreichische Bankgeheimnis (23, KWG) im Verhältnis zum
Ausland, insbesonders zur Bundesrepublik Deutschland", ÖJZ 1985, at p. 178
(Hereinafter "Beiser, Bankgeheimnis"), and Kutschera, *supra* n. 1, at pp. 45, 46.

fulfilled and respected. If provided in applicable treaties, such (foreign) criminal matters may include fiscal offenses.

Tax liabilities of deceased persons

2-029   There is no bank secrecy in respect of the banks' duty to give notice to the fiscal authorities of assets belonging to or deposited with them for the disposition of a deceased person (section 25, Estate Tax Act).

Enforcement proceedings

2-030   There is no bank secrecy with respect to requests for information on a person's claims against banks which were attached in enforcement proceedings.[43]

Assessment of bank taxes

2-031   There is no bank secrecy to the extent a disclosure of bank secrets is necessary for the assessment of taxes to be paid by the banks themselves, according to section 23(3), KWG.

Certainly, bank secrets obtained by the (fiscal) authorities in such manner are subject to official secrecy, must not be passed on to other public authorities, and must not be used in regard to third parties to which such bank secrets relate.

OTHER ASPECTS

2-032   There is no bank secrecy with respect to the Austrian National Bank's right to certain information in matters of exchange control, with respect to certain notice requirements under the Income Tax Act or other revenue laws, in regard to the right to information of the bank regulatory authority and the Audit Office (*Rechnungshof*), and towards the trustee in bankruptcy or reorganization proceedings.

[43] Arnold, Bankgeheimnis, *supra* n. 3, at p. 22; Avancini-Iro-Koziol, *supra* n. 3, at p. 158; Jabornegg-Strasser-Floretta, *supra* n. 3, at pp. 153 *et seq.*

Naturally, bank secrets disclosed to the Austrian National Bank, the bank regulatory authorities, or the Audit Office are subject to official secrecy and must not be passed to other authorities.[44]

Foreign bank regulatory authorities

Pursuant to section 23a, KWG, the Federal Minister of Finance may   2-033
give official information to foreign bank regulatory authorities provided:

(1) The *ordre public*, other essential interests of the Republic of Austria, and bank secrecy are not violated thereby;
(2) There is reciprocity, and
(3) A similar request for information made by the Federal Minister of Finance would be in accordance with the purposes of the KWG.

The above does not apply if applicable treaties provide to the contrary. At present, however, there is no such treaty.

CONCLUSION

Austrian bank secrecy has come under closer international observa-   2-034
tion, and some pressure, as the ability to investigate the flow of money from unclear origins becomes indispensable in the battle against drug trafficking and organized crime.

The statutory protection of Austrian bank secrecy was granted with the primary intent to avoid the flow of untaxed funds out of Austria. Rather than forcing Austrian tax evaders to waste their grey money in manners which do not leave traces, hide it in cash at home, or deposit it in foreign countries, it was intended that it be attractive to deposit it within the Austrian economy.

In addition, the Austrian legislature thought that at least a part of money from comparable sources abroad would be attracted by Austrian banks rather than (as had been the case before) nearly

---

[44] Avancini-Iro-Koziol, *supra* n. 3, at pp. 159, 160; Jabornegg-Strasser-Floretta, *supra* n. 3, at pp. 129 *et seq.*

exclusively by competitors in certain Caribbean and European countries. No one thought about the danger that Austrian banks might become a haven for money originating in drug trafficking or organized crime.

With the increased concern regarding drug trafficking and organized crime, the primary reaction was to encourage the banks to employ self-policing measures and to continue close supervision of the banking industry by the bank regulatory authorities, the latter including a very restrictive policy on issuing bank licenses.

It is the author's impression that the Austrian banking industry has no interest to become involved with crime-related money and that they are quite skillful and effective in their efforts to distinguish between such funds (which would be rejected) and those connected to fiscal offenses of a lesser degree.[45] It may be that this handling of the problem is not well understood and evaluated by experts from countries which take a more formal approach to such problems.

The ongoing developments which make a more efficient countering of money-laundering necessary and Austria's move towards European Community (EC) membership will not leave the Austrian statutory situation unaffected.

It appears more likely that the Austrian legislature will define certain money-laundering practices as new crimes and further limit, if not abolish altogether, the possibility to have anonymous accounts rather than to change the bank secrecy laws (in view of the public perception of Austrian bank secrecy as a principle close to a fundamental right).

Thus, any changes of this rather romantic legal concept, the origins of which can be related to the consequences of the currency reform of 1948,[46] will have to be sold to the public with care and feeling, even if the above-described pragmatic reality in Austrian banking practice is certainly supported by the public without reservation.

---

[45] Fuchs, *supra* n. 29, at p. 553.

[46] For other views on the future of Austrian bank secrecy, see Luther, "Österreichisches Bankgeheimnis - das unbekannte Wesen oder Was Sie schon immer über das österreichische Bankgeheimnis wissen wollten", NZ 1990, at p. 8; Weber, "Die 'Geldwäsche' Richtlinie (Vorschlag der Kommission der EG) und mögliche Anpassungserfordernisse im österreichischen Recht", WBl 1990, at p. 294; Jabornegg, *supra* n. 25, at pp. 60, 61.

CHAPTER 3

THE BAHAMAS

Michael L. Paton
Lennox Paton
Nassau, Bahamas

Chapter 3

THE BAHAMAS

INTRODUCTION

The concept of bank secrecy is shrouded in mystery and has been **3-001** subject to much publicity. The resultant misconceived notion of secrecy has been effectively used as a marketing tool by the offshore banking industry in its effort to attract deposits. This chapter will endeavor to dispel the various myths associated with bank secrecy and outline the realities of the subject relative to The Bahamas.

For the purposes of this chapter, it is assumed that banks (including trust companies where the context so allows) in The Bahamas fall into three principal categories. Firstly, there are banks that are incorporated in a jurisdiction other than The Bahamas and which do business through a branch in The Bahamas. Secondly, there are banks that are incorporated in The Bahamas and are wholly-owned subsidiaries of foreign banks. Finally, there are banks that are incorporated in The Bahamas and are owned by a group of investors.

Further, it is assumed for this article that the account opening forms signed by a customer stipulate that the administration of the bank account is intended to be governed by the laws of The Commonwealth of The Bahamas.

Bank secrecy in The Bahamas is governed by the provisions of section 10 of The Banks and Trust Companies Regulation Act, 1965 (as amended),[1] and by the Common Law, which is best expressed in the judgment of Bankes J. in *Tournier* v. *National Provincial and Union Bank of England*.[2]

---

[1] The Banks and Trust Companies Regulation Act, 1965 [Ch. 287 1987 Revised Edition].

[2] *Tournier* v. *National Provincial and Union Bank of England* [1924] 1 K.B. 461.

THE BANKS AND TRUST COMPANIES REGULATION ACT

3-002   The principal provisions of this Act are summarized below.[3]

Section 3

3-003   A license is required in order to carry on banking business or trust business from or within The Bahamas.

Section 4

3-004   Application for license is to be in a required format. As a condition precedent to the granting of a license, any bank or trust company with its head office or its registered office outside The Bahamas must designate, by notice to the Minister of Finance, its principal office in The Bahamas and the name of its authorized agent and deputy authorized agent in the Bahamas. "Authorized agent" in this context should not be confused with an authorized agent under exchange control regulations. Subsequent changes in this information also must be notified to, and these appointments must be approved by, the Central Bank.

Authority is given for a license to be revoked if the licensee has ceased to carry on banking business or trust business or if the licensee becomes bankrupt, goes into liquidation, is wound up, or is otherwise dissolved, or in the circumstances set out in section 9 (see text below).

Section 5

3-005   Unless otherwise exempted, no shares in a company or certificates of deposit or any other securities of such company which is a licensee under the Act shall be issued, and no issued shares shall be transferred or disposed of in any manner without prior approval.

In appropriate circumstances, the Bank Supervision Department of the Central Bank can be expected to give sympathetic consideration to proposals designed to minimize any practical inconvenience which may be experienced as a result of the requirement to obtain prior approval to such transactions, or to an application for exemption from the provisions of this section.

---

[3] The summary of statutory regulation is provided by John M. Cates, Pettit & Martin, Nassau, The Bahamas.

Section 7

If it appears likely that a licensee is or may become unable to meet   **3-006**
its obligations or is carrying on business in a manner detrimental to
the public interest or to the interest of its creditors or depositors, its
manager or authorized agent may be required to submit an audited
financial statement of the licensee as at a date within the previous
15 months, together with any other required information.

Section 8

An inspector may be appointed to examine the business of any   **3-007**
licensee in order to satisfy himself that the provisions of the Act are
being complied with and that the licensee is in a sound financial
position. An inspector so appointed shall be entitled at all reasonable times to have access to any books, records, or documents of the
licensee and may call for such information and explanations as he
may reasonably require for the purpose of enabling him to perform
his functions under the Act.

The inspector may only have access to the account of a depositor
of a licensee or to any information relating to or concerning the
affairs of any customer of a licensee pursuant to a court order.

Section 9

If a licensee is carrying on its business in a manner detrimental to   **3-008**
the public interest or to the interests of its depositors or other
creditors or is contravening the provisions of any relevant legislation or any term or condition subject to which the license was
issued, the licensee may be required to take such steps as may be
considered necessary to rectify the matter, or the license may be
revoked with the requirement that the licensee's business be wound
up.

Section 10

Preservation of secrecy, as provided by the 1980 amendment to   **3-009**
section 10, is, as explained above, of fundamental importance to the
continued development of The Bahamas as an offshore financial
center; this section is, therefore, quoted below in full:

"(1) No person who has acquired information in his capacity as:

(a) director, officer, employee or agent of any licensee or former licensee;

(b) counsel and attorney, consultant or auditor of the Central Bank of The Bahamas, established under section 3 of the Central Bank of The Bahamas Act, 1974, or as an employee or agent of such counsel and attorney, consultant or auditor;

(c) counsel and attorney, consultant, auditor, accountant, receiver or liquidator of any licensee or former licensee or as an employee or agent of such counsel and attorney, consultant, auditor, accountant, receiver or liquidator;

(d) auditor of any customer of any licensee or former licensee or as an employee or agent of such auditor;

(e) the Inspector under the provisions of this Act, shall, without the express or implied consent of the customer concerned, disclose to any person any such information relating to the identity, assets, liabilities, transactions, accounts of a customer of a licensee or relating to any application by any person under the provisions of this Act, as the case may be, except:

(i) for the purpose of the performance of his duties or the exercise of his functions under this Act, if any; or

(ii) for the purpose of the performance of his duties within the scope of his employment; or

(iii) when a licensee is lawfully required to make disclosure by any court of competent jurisdiction within The Bahamas, or under the provisions of any law of The Bahamas.

(2) Nothing contained in this section shall:

(a) prejudice or derogate from the rights and duties subsisting at common law between a licensee and its customer; or

(b) prevent a licensee from providing upon a legitimate business request in the normal course of business a general credit rating with respect to a customer.

(3) Every person who contravenes the provisions of subsection (1) of this section shall be guilty of an offense against this Act and shall be liable on summary conviction to a fine not exceeding fifteen thousand dollars or to a term of imprisonment not exceeding two years or to both such fine and imprisonment."

Section 11

Under certain circumstances, a license may be suspended for a period not exceeding ninety days. 3-010

OTHER BANKING REGULATIONS

The Central Bank of The Bahamas Act 1974[4] gives the Central Bank the power to require any financial institution or trust company to supply to the Central Bank such information as the Central Bank considers necessary to enable it to carry out its functions. 3-011

The Central Bank requires each licensee, whether engaged in banking or trust business, to file with it on an annual basis within four months of the end of the licensee's financial year; a complete set of audited financial statements (including a statement of operations).

In the case of a Bahamian incorporated company, the filed financial statements are those of that company, whilst, in the case of a bank operating as a branch of a foreign company, it is the combined statements of the bank as a whole that must be filed. The power to request information additional to that disclosed in a licensee's financial statements is being increasingly used by the Central Bank, particularly in the areas of loan portfolios, deposit maturity profiles, and investments.

[4] The Central Bank of The Bahamas Act, 1974 [Ch. 321 1987 Revised Edition].

. Directors, officers, and employees of the Central Bank are required by statute to preserve and aid in preserving secrecy with regard to any matter relating to the affairs of any financial institution, or of any customer thereof, coming to his knowledge in the course of the performance of his duties.

In 1980, legislation[5] was enacted to exempt banks and trust companies from the provision of the Rate of Interest Act,[6] which prohibits interest in excess of 20 per cent per annum. The 20 per cent ceiling continues to apply to non-licensed entities and individuals dealing in Bahamian currency.

Regulation at Common Law

3-012   At Common Law, the duty is a legal one, arising out of contract. It is not an absolute duty, but qualified, and subject to certain exceptions as set out in the judgment of Banks J. in *Tournier*,[7] as follows:

(1) Where disclosure is under compulsion of law;
(2) Where there is a duty to the public to disclose;
(3) Where the interest of the bank requires disclosure, and
(4) Where the disclosure is made by the express or implied consent of the customer.

Situation laws

Statutory exceptions

3-013   The statute laws of The Bahamas do not require absolute confidentiality or secrecy and are subject, *inter alia*, to the following exceptions.

A director, officer, or employee of a bank may, not without the express or implied consent of the customer, disclose information relating to the identity, assets, liabilities, transactions, and account of the customer except:

---

5 Rate of Interest Act, 1980.
6 Rate of Interest Act, 1948 [Ch. 314 1987 Revised Edition].
7 *Tournier* v. *National Provincial and Union Bank of England* [1924] 1 K.B. 461.

(1) For the purpose of the performance of his duties or in the exercise of his functions under the Banks and Trust Companies Regulations Act;

(2) For the purpose of the performance of his duties within the scope of his employment, or

(3) When the bank is lawfully required to make disclosure by any court of competent jurisdiction within The Bahamas or under any provisions of any laws of The Bahamas.

The penalties for breach of customer account secrecy are severe, including fines and/or imprisonment.

Impact of foreign law

If a customer's account should be opened in any country other than **3-014** The Bahamas (which may be even if the account should be booked to a Nassau bank or Nassau branch), the contract will be governed by the proper law of the contract (which may be expressed) or by the law of the country where the contract is made, and the existence and extent of the requirement of confidentiality will be determined by the governing law.

Whatever law governs, there must be an implied term that the bank shall be bound to comply with the requirements of the authorities (including the judicial system) by reason of which the bank exists and operates. If such compliance requires disclosure of information relating to a customer's account, the implied term would encompass the right of the bank to make such disclosure and would obviously extend also to the right of the bank to make such disclosure under an order of a court of competent jurisdiction both within and without The Bahamas.

Even if the customer were to open the account at a Nassau branch of a foreign bank, or if the proper law of the contract were otherwise expressed to be the laws of The Bahamas, there is a further implied term that the relevant secrecy laws of The Bahamas shall apply only insofar as they are not inconsistent with the requirements of the authorities referred to above (which includes the judicial system) by which the bank exists and operates. Any contrary conclusion would be unreasonable.

If an officer of a branch of a foreign bank doing business in The Bahamas, or of a Bahamian bank incorporated and doing business both within and without The Bahamas and registered pursuant to the laws of a foreign state, is required to make available records of his branch or his bank for the purpose of compliance with the requirements of a supervisory or controlling authority (which includes the judicial system), then he is performing his duties within the scope of his employment if he makes disclosure at the request of a bank officer who acts pursuant to the compulsion of a foreign court.

He is bound to comply with such requirements, and nothing in the legislation of The Bahamas or in the Common Law prevents him from doing so or imposes any criminal or civil liability upon him for doing so.

DUTY OF CONFIDENTIALITY

Nature of duty

3-015 At Common Law, the duty of confidentiality does not apply where the interest of the bank requires disclosure. However, where disclosure is justified under this head, it must be limited to such disclosure as may be strictly necessary to protect the bank's interests.

Where the attempt to obtain information pertaining to a Bahamian bank account derives from a foreign litigation or investigation, the correct procedure is for the foreign court to make an application to the Bahamian court by letters rogatory under the Foreign Tribunals Evidence Act, 1856.

The Bahamian court will, in a "proper" case, direct the bank in question to turn over the sought after account information. The key issue then is defining what is a "proper" case. This requires a close examination of the current body of case law on the subject.

The Bahamas is a Common Law jurisdiction and a member of the British Commonwealth, with the ultimate court of appeal being the Judicial Council of the Privy Council, in London, England.

Consequently, Commonwealth decisions are persuasive authority and are instructive.

English authority

3-016 In an English High Court decision in 1983, in which the bank was not named, Legatt J. ordered a London branch of a leading United States bank not to obey a subpoena issued by a New York grand jury, requiring disclosure of a customer's affairs, on the grounds that it would be a breach of the bank's duty of confidentiality to its customer because the evidence showed that "in practice there is no secrecy in regard to matters entrusted to grand jurors".[8]

At issue was the sanctity of the professional relationship between bank and customer. The judge recognized that the bank was bound by United States law to comply and looked to the New York court for relief: "It is for the New York court to relieve the bank of the dilemma in which it has placed its own national, by refraining from holding it in contempt if contempt proceedings are issued." It is worth noting that the issue in this case was alleged tax evasion.

Bank of Nova Scotia Judgment

This is not what happened in the celebrated Bank of Nova Scotia 3-017 case[9] where, in 1983, the United States District Court for the Southern District of Florida ordered the enforcement of a subpoena which was served on the Miami branch of the bank for the disclosure of account information of one Mr. Twist, a customer of The Bahamas branch of the bank.

The United States court's decision is extraordinary, especially considering the bank is incorporated in Canada, and it bears close examination as it clearly sets forth the United States judiciary's view on the subject of banking secrecy. The court, cognizant of the risk of criminal charges being levied against the bank, considered the following factors in reaching its decision:

(1) The vital interests of each of the states;
(2) The extent and the nature of the hardship that inconsistent enforcement actions would impose upon the person;
(3) The extent to which the required conduct is to take place in the territory of the other state;
(4) The nationality of the person, and
(5) The extent to which enforcement by action of either State can reasonably be expected to achieve compliance with the rule prescribed by that state.

The court held that, on balance, the subpoena should be enforced. The court ruled that the interest of the United States in enforcing the subpoena in order to further the investigatory function of the grand jury was greater than the Bahamian interest in secrecy. In addition, the court declared that it was anomalous to give the target of the

---

[8] *Re A Bank, Financial Times,* January 28, 1983.
[9] *In re Grand Jury Proceedings, U.S. v. Bank of Nova Scotia,* 722. F.2d.657 (11th Cir. 1983).

investigation, an American citizen, greater protection of concealed Bahamian banking records than he could expect in his United States bank accounts.

Further, the court held that, while the records must be gathered in the Bahamian branch and sent to the Florida branch of the Bank of Nova Scotia, the actual disclosure would be made in the United States rather than in The Bahamas. As to the last factor, the court held that enforcement of the subpoena would help to ensure compliance with the grand jury's goals of investigating criminal matters.

The court recognized that, while enforcement in some respects ameliorated the privacy interests which the Bahamian statute attempted to protect, it felt that the stated exceptions to the non-disclosure provisions of the statute indicated that enforcement was not an unreasonable diversion from these concerns.

Facing significant sanctions if it did not, the bank capitulated and disclosed the information. No action was taken against the bank in The Bahamas. The decision of the United States court was staggering. It was an affront to the comity of nations and showed a disregard for the sovereignty of an independent nation and the established rules of procedure. Had the proper procedure been followed, it is likely the same result would have been achieved.

Caymans authority

3-018   In 1983, the Cayman Court of Appeal ordered the disclosure of account information pertaining to one Mr. LeMire.[10] The Court of Appeal held that disclosure is mandatory if the request is for specific documents relevant to a prosecution in which charges have been filed, and if the offense would be a crime in the Cayman Islands.

It was held that these elements were present in Mr. LeMire's case. The court went further and emphasized that the Cayman's business confidentiality law was not intended to shield criminals, as to do so would be contrary to public policy.

Bahamas authority

3-019   Indeed, the Supreme Court of The Bahamas held that, although the policy of the secrecy of banks in The Bahamas should be scrup-

10 *U.S.* v. *LeMire, The Wall Street Journal*, January 11, 1983.

ulously observed, it was equally as important that such a policy of secrecy should not become a screen for facilitating fraud.[11]

The court will not, however, entertain an application for the disclosure of information where the court is of the opinion that such request is a general "fishing expedition" for information.[12] It is clear, therefore, that the litigant must have a *bona fide* and *prima facie* case and that the request for disclosure must be specific and directly relate to the case in question.

The Bahamas Legislature has passed The Mutual Legal Assistance (Criminal Matters) Act, 1988,[13] which enables the government to enter into treaties with foreign governments for mutual legal assistance in criminal matters. This would not extend to assistance by the Bahamas Government in matters relating to tax or exchange control laws or regulations of a foreign state.

It is intended primarily to counter drug trafficking and the laundering of drug money. To date, the Bahamas Government has entered into treaties with the governments of the United Kingdom, the United States, and Canada pursuant to the provisions of this Act. An application by a court of one of these countries for bank account information in a criminal matter would, therefore, be under this Act rather than The Foreign Tribunals Evidence Act, 1856.[14]

CONCLUSION

In conclusion, The Bahamas can be said to provide a large degree of bank secrecy for depositors seeking a safe-haven for flight capital from the provisions of exchange control or fiscal laws of a foreign country or for an investor seeking anonymity and confidentiality for any variety of legitimate reasons. The Bahamas is not, however a sanctuary for illicit proceeds.   **3-020**

If satisfied with the cogency of a plaintiff's case, the court will readily compel the disclosure of account information. While marginal operators are present in every jurisdiction, the Bahamian offshore banking industry is determined in its efforts to eliminate the problem.

[11] *Royal Bank of Canada* v. *Apollo Development Ltd.* (1985), unreported.

[12] *Re Nissan Motor Corporation* (1990), unreported.

[13] The Mutual Legal Assistance (Criminal Matters) Act, 1988, (No.2 of 1988)

[14] The Foreign Tribunals Evidence Act, 1856; United Kingdom Statute extended to the Commonwealth of The Bahamas.

The Bahamas is a leading offshore financial center and is well positioned to take advantage of the opportunities that will assuredly arise in the global financial marketplace.

APPENDIX

Code of Conduct for Members of the Association of International **3-021**
Banks and Trust Companies in The Bahamas

Preamble

This Code of Conduct has been adopted by the Association of **3-022**
International Banks and Trust Companies in The Bahamas (the
"Association") to provide for its member institutions resident in The
Bahamas ("members") standards of conduct and professional ethics
governing certain basic relationships between members and their
customers. The board of directors of the association may reject the
new or continued membership of any institution that refuses to
adhere to this code or being a member knowingly commits infractions of the code.

The objectives of the Code are to:

1. Maintain and enhance the reputation of The Bahamas as an
   international financial center.
2. Prevent the use of banks and trust companies in The Bahamas for criminal purposes.
3. Adhere to the principles of banking confidentiality/secrecy
   as embodied in Bahamian legislation.

To attain these objectives, this Code sets forth guidelines for members under the following headings:

Part I - Cooperation with the Central Bank of The Bahamas

Part II - Know your Customer

Part III - Rejection of Customers Involved in Criminal Activity

Part IV - Avoidance of Acts Violating Fiscal or Foreign Exchange
Laws

Part V - Maintenance of Confidentiality

Part VI - Disclosure of Members' Ownership

This Code of Conduct in no way supersedes the banking laws and
regulations in effect in The Bahamas nor alters the legal relationships between a member bank or trust company and its customers.

Part I - Cooperation with the Central Bank of The Bahamas

3-023   It shall be the responsibility of every member to accord the fullest cooperation to the Central Bank in following all guidelines and regulations which may be prescribed to implement the operation of this code and in all cases of doubt or difficulty to confer with and seek the advice of the Central Bank. In particular, members shall conform to the requirements of the Central Bank with regard to the acceptance of large case deposits.

Part II - Know Your Customer

3-024   Members shall take all reasonable measures to determine the identity of the beneficial owners of all accounts and will not open or maintain accounts unless they are satisfied as to the relationship and have obtained proper references.

Part III - Rejection of Customers Involved in Criminal Activity

3-025   Members shall take all reasonable measures to ensure that accounts are not used for the purpose of holding assets obtained as the result of, or for facilitating the commission of, criminal activity or for any objects that infringe Bahamian law, and shall take appropriate steps to close any accounts so used at the earliest possible opportunity. 'Criminal activity' shall include drug trafficking, embezzlement, larceny, extortion, misappropriation of funds, bribery and similar crimes fundamentally offensive to the public or private welfare.

Part IV - Avoidance of Acts Violating Fiscal or Foreign Exchange Laws

3-026   Members shall not knowingly commit any acts in any foreign country that would be an offense under the fiscal or exchange control laws of that country, and in particular shall not accept cash deposits in any foreign country that might constitute such an act. Members shall not provide customers with false attestations or documentation for the purpose of evading the fiscal or exchange control laws of any country.

Part V - Maintenance of Confidentiality

3-027   Confidentiality, as well as by applicable provisions of Bahamian banking legislation, shall be respected.

Part VI - Disclosure of Members' Ownership

Members shall fully observe the requirements of the Central Bank 3-028
now or hereafter in effect with regard to disclosure of the identity
of members' beneficial shareholders.

Provisions

A. This code of conduct has been approved by a resolution adopted 3-029
at a general meeting of the association held on January 17, 1985,
with the written approval by the Central Bank of The Bahamas.

B. The board of directors of the association is authorized to withhold or withdraw membership from any bank or trust company
which refuses to adhere to this code of conduct. Any such action by
the board of directors shall be a public document and the board of
directors shall be reported to the Central Bank.

C. This code of conduct shall be a public document and the board
of directors of the association may circulate it and arrange such
publicity as the board deems appropriate for it to become generally
known in The Bahamas and abroad.

D. The board of directors of the association or any member is
authorized to propose any modifications to this code, in furtherance
of the objectives stated in the preamble, which may prove necessary
or desirable in the light of experience, which modifications shall
only be approved by the same procedure as in paragraph A above.
However, minor modifications to correct any technical deficiencies
in the wording of the code not amounting to changes of substance,
may be authorized by the board of directors alone.

CHAPTER 4

BELGIUM

Chris Sunt and Jacques Richelle
De Bandt, Van Hecke & Lagae
Brussels, Belgium

Chapter 4

BELGIUM

INTRODUCTION

The aspects of Belgian banking secrecy law which distinguish it **4-001** from its European counterparts are contained more in the exceptions to the rule than in the rule itself. The duty of confidentiality in principle is similar to that in other European countries. Most of the exceptions, however, are derived from specific procedural rules in various areas of the law and from recent financial legislation providing for specific disclosure rules.

Banking secrecy in Belgium is based largely on tradition. Unlike in other European countries, it was never embodied in any statutory provision. Furthermore, courts have rarely had the opportunity to apply the concept and, therefore, have not been of much help in determining the nature and the scope of the duty, the remedies available to the customer in case of breach of the banker's obligation or the exceptions to the rule of confidentiality. Instead, this area of the law has been developed primarily by legal doctrine.

As far as terminology is concerned, it seems more correct to use the expressions "duty of confidentiality" or "duty of discretion" (as used by the *Cour de Cassation*; see text below) than "banking secrecy" (*secret bancaire* or *bankgeheim*), as it is usually referred to in Belgium. In that respect, it must be noted that article 458 of the Criminal Code (see text below), which uses the term "professional secrecy", applies to physicians, lawyers, and others, but not to bankers. In addition, a duty with so many exceptions of disclosure can hardly be called one of "secrecy".

NATURE OF DUTY OF CONFIDENTIALITY

Breach of duty of confidentiality not a criminal offense

4-002   In its decision of October 25, 1978, the Belgian *Cour de Cassation* (Supreme Court) clearly determined that the breach of the bankers' duty of confidentiality was not a criminal offense.[1] The issue before the court was whether bankers should fall under article 458 of the Criminal Code, which provides that physicians, surgeons, health officers, pharmacists, and all other persons who, because of their status or profession, are confided secrets will be, subject to certain exceptions, fined and/or imprisoned if they reveal these secrets.

The court held that this article does not apply to bankers because they are merely held to a duty of "discretion". The court added that neither the nature of their duties nor any statutory provision makes them subject to article 458 of the Criminal Code.

The judgment of 1978 is very short. Hints as to the court's reasoning can be found in previous decisions and in the comments of various legal authors:

(1) Bankers do not have any legal monopoly as is the case with the professions mentioned in article 458;

(2) Entering into a relationship with a banker does not necessarily involve confiding secrets in him; at least, it is not the banker's primary function, and

(3) It is not deemed as socially important for a banker to keep the secrets he is told as it is for a lawyer or a physician; the latter have a much more intimate relationship with their clients, whose trust is essential to their respective functions.

These arguments have been the subject of controversy among legal authors. However, whatever the underlying reasoning, the rule of law is clear: bankers are not criminally liable for revealing secrets confided to them by their clients.

Duty of confidentiality as a Civil Law concept

4-003   The banker may be liable for damages incurred by his clients due to the breach of his duty of confidentiality. The nature of the duty and its resulting liability depend on the circumstances.

[1] Supreme Court, October 15, 1978, Pasicrisie 1979, I., at p. 237.

When the banker and his client reach an agreement, the duty arises out of the contract itself. Whether expressly provided for in the agreement or, as in most cases, merely implied, the duty is undoubtedly contractual.

The nature of the duty is not so clear, however, in the absence of a contract, *e.g.*, during the negotiation process or when a person cashes a bank check as a one-time operation. Authors have put forward many legal grounds on which to enforce the banker's duty in such circumstances:

(1) In torts, under article 1382 of the Civil Code;
(2) On an implied pre-contractual agreement;
(3) On a *sui generis* contract, or
(4) On the *culpa in contrahendo* doctrine.

It seems that, in most cases, liability could be based on an implied agreement of confidentiality, independent from any later formal contract.

If evidence of such an agreement cannot be shown, however, article 1382 of the Civil Code is always applicable.

CLIENT'S REMEDIES

If the duty of confidentiality is contractual, the client may claim **4-004** damages for breach of contract under articles 1142 and 1145 of the Civil Code.

As far as tortious liability is concerned, pursuant to article 1382 of the Civil Code, the client may be awarded damages if he can establish that there has been a breach of the duty of confidentiality, an injury and a causal link between the two.

SCOPE OF DUTY OF CONFIDENTIALITY

As in other countries, the scope of the bankers' duty of confidenti- **4-005** ality in Belgium is very broad. It may be approached from three different perspectives:

Type of operations

4-006   The duty applies to banking operations in the broad sense: deposit taking, credit, transfer of funds, foreign exchange, financial advice, safe rental, and letter of credit. It would not apply to activities unrelated to banking, such as operating a travel agency.

Origin of information

4-007   The duty extends to all facts the banker comes across in the course of his business relationship with his client. This includes information released directly by the client himself, as well as that known by the banker from any other source (*e.g.*, banker's own investigation or "black lists" of clients; see text below). Mere hints or facts suspected by the banker are also included.

Some authors have suggested that facts known by the banker in another capacity (*e.g.*, as a friend) and facts discovered by the banker by a mere coincidence are not included in the scope of the duty because they do not come to the banker's attention "in the course of his business relationship with the client". Such fine line drawing must be handled very cautiously.

Type of information

4-008   The duty of confidentiality applies to various types of information, including:

(1) Facts regarding the customer himself, *e.g.*, financial situation, commercial practices or strategy;
(2) Types of banking operations, *e.g.*, opening of an account, of a line of credit, transfer of funds, reception of funds, and
(3) Amounts involved and account balances.

It must be added that the mere disclosure of the existence of a business relationship does not seem to constitute a breach of the banker's duty of confidentiality under Belgian law.

EXCEPTIONS TO DUTY OF CONFIDENTIALITY

In general

"Higher social interests" may sometimes override the need for 4-009
bankers' discretion, thus creating numerous exceptions to the bankers' duty of confidentiality. In all of these situations, however, it
must be kept in mind that confidentiality remains the rule and
disclosure the exception. Therefore, the bankers' duty of disclosure
is strictly limited to the protection of these higher interests. This
limit has to be carefully appraised by the banker, as any unnecessary disclosure may expose him to liability.

Client's consent

The client can relieve the banker of his duty of confidentiality, either 4-010
expressly or implicitly. The underlying reasoning for this rule is that
the banker's duty only protects his client's private material interests, not any larger public interest.

Interest of the bank

A banker is allowed to release information about his client when his 4-011
own material interest is at stake. Whether or not such disclosure is
limited to judicial proceedings to which the banker is a party is the
subject of controversy among authors.

Information to persons in sphere of confidentiality

Certain persons may require information from the banker because 4-012
of their special relationship to the client. Such persons may be those
associated with, or those that have taken over, the management of
the client's assets and are, therefore, included in the sphere of
confidentiality. These situations should not be considered as real
exceptions but rather as flexible applications of the rule of confidentiality.
   The following categories can be distinguished:

   (1) Persons representing the client, including representatives
       of persons lacking legal capacity, the client's agents (*e.g.*, the
       directors of a corporation), the administrator of a bankrupt
       company, the company's liquidator;

(2) Persons continuing the client's legal status after his death, *e.g.*, the legal heir or the heir by will having accepted the estate as a whole (*légataire universel*);

(3) Persons having the same right as the client to assets in the banker's possession, *e.g.*, the spouse under certain circumstances. The banker must advise the client's spouse of the opening of any account or renting of a safe.[2] The spouse may request information from the banker as to the client's assets, provided he or she shows evidence that such money or property is jointly owned by the couple.

Criminal proceedings

In general

4-013 A banker can be compelled to disclose information regarding his client's operations at various stages of a criminal proceeding, *i.e.*, during the investigation process and by the court at the trial hearings. In these cases, his duty of confidentiality is irrelevant; the banker must testify or accept a search, just like any other person.

The same rules apply if the banker is himself under investigation or on trial. In that case, however, his fundamental right to remain silent supersedes any duty of disclosure. Therefore, he cannot be forced to testify.

Investigation stage

4-014 The judge leading the investigation (*Juge d'instruction*) has the power:

(1) To compel the banker to disclose confidential information regarding his client,[3] based on the Code of Criminal Procedure (*Code d'Instruction Criminelle*; hereinafter CIC). The judge may delegate this power to the Public Prosecutor (*Procureur du Roi* and his *Subsituts*) or to the Judicial Police (*Police Judiciaire*). If the banker refuses to testify, he can be fined and forced to appear.[4] At this stage, false testimony is not a criminal offense. The witness can modify his testimony up until the close of the trial. This traditional rule,

---

2 Article 218 of the Civil Code.
3 Articles 71 *et seq.* of the Code of Criminal Procedure.
4 *Id.*, Article 80.

however, has been called into question by some authors and courts.

(2) To order a search (*perquisition*) at the bank.[5] This is the judge's most effective alternative since the banker may not oppose the search. The banker may, however, write down comments on the official minutes of the search. He will do so when:

(a) a procedural rule has been violated, *e.g.*, if the judge lacks territorial jurisdiction, or

(b) the search is unrelated to the charges brought against the person under investigation.

This may lead the trial court to eventually reject as evidence material found during the search.

It is important for the banker to distinguish the official, formal investigation just described from an unofficial one (*enquête officieuse* or *information*) led by the Public Prosecutor. In the latter case, as there is no legal obligation for the banker to answer any questions, his duty of confidentiality should keep him from disclosing any confidential information.

Trial stage

At the trial hearings, the trial court may order a banker, as any other person, to testify.[6] A refusal to testify then leads to the same consequences as at the investigation stage.[7]   **4-015**

Spontaneous disclosure

The CIC provides that anybody who witnesses an attempt to commit a crime against the "public safety" or the life or property of an individual must advise the Public Prosecutor.[8] Faced with such situation, the banker would not be liable to the client for disclosing information evidencing the attempted crime.   **4-016**

---

[5] *Id.*, Article 87.
[6] *Id.*, Articles 153, 190, and 315.
[7] *Id.*, Articles 157, 189, and 355.
[8] *Id.*, Article 30.

Subpoenas from foreign jurisdictions

4-017 Belgium is a party to the European Convention on Judicial Assistance in Criminal Matters[9] and to various other bilateral and multilateral treaties. Under the European Convention, a subpoena from a signatory state must be executed by the judicial authorities of the receiving state in accordance with the latter's own procedural rules.

Therefore, once the subpoena is accepted by the Belgian authorities, the banker finds himself in the same situation as when faced with a subpoena from a Belgian judge.

In the absence of an international treaty, the foreign subpoena must be authorized by the Belgian Minister of Justice.[10] A specific procedure for foreign subpoenas ordering searches or the production of documents is set forth in article 11 of the 1874 Law on Extradition.

Banker's conduct

4-018 A banker faced with criminal proceedings has very little room within which to maneuver. In most cases, he will have no other option but to disclose information regarding his client or suffer a search in order to avoid criminal sanctions. In these circumstances, the banker will not be liable to his client for breach of the duty of confidentiality, provided that he stays within the general limits of disclosure (see text above).

This would require him, for instance, to limit his answers to the precise questions asked during the testimony and to mention any procedural illegalities related to the search that he is aware of. The banker will never be liable to his customer if the latter is eventually convicted of the charges pending at the time of the investigation or trial.

Civil proceedings

Bankers' testimony and production of documents

4-019 **Principles** The rules relating to evidence in Belgian civil procedure are based on two principles:

---

[9] Signed in Strasbourg, France, on April 4, 1959.
[10] Article 873 of the Judicial Code.

(1) Litigants and third parties must cooperate in the search for the truth, and

(2) The court may force them to do so.

Under the Judicial Code (*Code Judiciaire*; hereinafter CJ), the court may compel litigants[11] and third parties[12] to disclose documents. If they fail to comply with the court's order, they may have to pay damages to the party to which their conduct causes injury.[13] Similar rules apply to testimony.[14] Besides possible damages, a refusal to testify also may lead to criminal penalties, including imprisonment.[15]

This broad duty of disclosure is, however, qualified by two rules:

(1) The court's subpoena must be valid, and

(2) The subpoena may be opposed for a "legitimate reason".

As in criminal proceedings, the banker, despite his duty of confidentiality, is subject to the same rules of disclosure as any other person.

The subpoena must be valid The tests for the validity of a subpoena   **4-020**
are laid down in the CJ.[16] They can be summarized as follows, the first test applying to both testimony and presentation of documents and the other two to the latter only:

(1) It must present the evidence of a relevant and precise fact; requests which are too broad (*e.g.*, "all documents in your possession") or too vague (*e.g.*, "any relevant document available") do not meet this test;

(2) There must be precise and serious presumptions that the document is in the hands of the person requested to produce it; a mere suspicion of the possession of the document is, therefore, not enough, and

(3) The document must exist at the time of the request; a demand to draft a new document will be rejected.

---

11 *Id.*, Articles 871 and 877.
12 *Id.*, Articles 877 and 878.
13 *Id.*, Article 882.
14 *Id.*, Articles 915 and 916.
15 Articles 495 bis of the Criminal Code.
16 Articles 877 (production of documents), 915 (testimony at the request of the litigant), and 916 (testimony at the request of the court) of the Judicial Code.

4-021   **Opposition to the subpoena for a legitimate reason** Article 929 of the CJ provides that:

(1) Witnesses may ask the court to be relieved of their duty to testify because of a legitimate reason (*motif légitime*);
(2) Professional secrecy, among others, is to be deemed a legitimate reason, and
(3) The court must hear the witness and the (other) parties before reaching a decision as to this request.

By its terms, this provision only applies to testimony. It is, however, widely accepted that the same rules apply to the production of documents.[17] The bankers' duty of confidentiality is not generally deemed a duty of professional secrecy within the meaning of article 929. In specific circumstances, however, it can constitute a legitimate reason for not testifying or producing documents.

Therefore, the judge would have to take the banker's request into consideration and balance his duty of confidentiality with the requirements of the search for the truth. Authors agree that such request by the banker is not likely to succeed, as courts would construe the "legitimate reason" concept narrowly.

4-022   **Subpoenas from foreign jurisdictions** As was the case with criminal matters, Belgium is a party to many bilateral or multilateral treaties, including the International Convention on Civil Procedure.[18] The same general principle of execution of the subpoena following the requested party's own procedural rules applies (see text above). Article 873 of the CJ is applicable in the absence of an international treaty (see text above).

4-023   **Banker's conduct** As with criminal proceedings, the banker does not have many options when requested to testify or produce documents about his clients. He will not be liable to his client for breach of his duty of confidentiality, provided he has verified the validity of the subpoena, has raised any available legitimate reason to oppose disclosure and has stayed within the general limits of his duty of disclosure (see text above).

---

[17] See articles 878 and 882 of the Judicial Code and the Van Reepinghen Report, on which the 1967 enactment of the Judicial Code was based.
[18] Signed in The Hague, The Netherlands, on March 1, 1954.

Garnishee orders (Saisies-arrêts)

Premise A creditor of the banker's client may have the banker **4-024**
garnished as a third party owing money or property to the client-
debtor. The garnishment order may be either a mere sequestration
pending the outcome of litigation (*saisie-arrêt conservatoire*), or a step
in the execution of a judgment (*saisie-arrêt exécution*). The procedures are strictly regulated in the CJ.[19] Garnishment obviously entails disclosure of information by the garnishee, *i.e.*, by the bank.

The banker must be the client's debtor There are specific problems **4-025**
in this regard. In order for the garnishment procedure to be valid,
the banker must be the client's debtor for a particular amount of
money or property, which corresponds to the garnishee order.
Questions which arise concern the definition of a debt in the banker-
client relationship:

Safe If the client leaves property to be kept by the banker in the **4-026**
bank's safe, the banker owes him a duty of delivering it back to him,
at his request. The banker is thus the client's debtor. If the client
rents a private safe at the bank, however, the banker is a mere lessor
and is not a debtor as to any of the property contained therein.

Line of credit The issue is not yet settled in Belgian law. The Van **4-027**
Reepinghen Report and a recent decision by the Attachment Judge
(*Juge des Saisies*) of Brussels have declared valid the application of
the garnishment procedure to a line of credit, but some authors
disagree. The practical significance of such order in this case, however, is limited as the banker can revoke the line of credit for loss of
confidence vis-à-vis his client at the time he receives the notice.

Pending operations The debt is equal to the credit balance of an **4-028**
account at the time notice of the order is given to the banker. Some
operations prior to that date, but affecting the balance at a later
stage also must be taken into account. Such is the case for checks
signed by the account holder but not yet presented for payment at
the bank. Such is not the case, however, for transfers of funds
ordered prior to the garnishee order but not yet executed by the
bank. Operations taking place after the notice is given do not affect
the amount of the debt subject to the order.

[19] Articles 1386 *et seq.* of the Judicial Code.

4-029 **Banker's duty to disclose** Upon receipt of notice of a garnishee order related to one of his clients, the banker must disclose to the creditor (with a copy for the client), within a 15-day period, the following information:[20]

(1) In the case where he is currently the client's debtor:
   (a) origin of the debt, *i.e.*, type of account or other banking operation the debt derives from;
   (b) amount of the debt;
   (c) terms of payment, if any, and
   (d) particular conditions of the debt, if any;
(2) In the case where he has never been the client's debtor, the banker may simply declare so, or
(3) In the case where he is no longer a debtor, he must state when and how the debt was paid off and produce any relevant document evidencing such fact.

The banker also must disclose prior orders of which he received notice. It is not clear whether he must inform the creditor about accounts with a credit balance. The banker may always turn to the Attachment Judge for information regarding the extent of the required disclosure.

Failure to issue such statement within the 15-day period or any misrepresentation of facts may result in the banker being held liable for part or all of his client's debts.

The Van Reepinghen Report mentions fraud, bad faith, or negligence as possible grounds for such measure, but it is left entirely up to the Attachment Judge whether and to what extent such a penalty will be imposed. For instance, a short delay due to technical reasons or which causes the client's creditor no harm will normally not be sanctioned by the Attachment Judge.

4-030 **Banker's conduct** Given the penalty at stake, the banker must be careful to strictly adhere to the requirements of the garnishee order. His role is not to protect his client, who has at his disposal various means of opposing wrongful or abusive garnishments by his creditors. The banker is not expected, for instance, to oppose an order relating to amounts much greater than the client's debt.

Many bankers seem, however, to have the habit of disclosing and blocking any increase in the account's credit balance after notice of the garnishee order is given, until the credit equals the client's debt to his creditor. Such a practice is overly cautious and lacking in any legal grounds.

[20] Articles 1452-1456 of the Judicial Code.

Information to tax authorities

Registration tax

Various types of operations, such as the sale of real estate, are 4-031
subject to registration and payment of a tax to the Registration
Administration (*Administration de l'Enregistrement et des Domaines*).
Bankers may be compelled by the Registration Administration to
disclose any information and documents deemed relevant to the
determination of the exact tax to be paid, when the bank or one of
its clients is subject to such taxation.[21]

Inheritance tax

The following rules of disclosure only apply when the deceased is 4-032
a Belgian resident. Non-residents are not subject to Belgian inheritance taxes, except in case of real estate, but which is irrelevant in a
banker-client relationship.

Bankers' passive duty of disclosure Bankers have a similar passive 4-033
duty of disclosure as the one related to registration taxes; the Registration Administration (which is also in charge of the collection of
the inheritance taxes) may ask bankers to provide information
related to any operation of the deceased, his or her spouse, heir, or
any third party, that took place before or after the death and that
may affect the taxation of the inheritance.[22]

Bankers' active duty of disclosure Bankers must keep record of all 4-034
clients depositing sealed envelopes or boxes or renting safes, along
with the identity of their spouses. They must also keep a list of
signatures of all of the client's mandatees or co-lessees who ask to
have access to the envelope, box, or safe. These records are transmitted to the Registration Administration.[23] The following disclosures occur in the event of death of a client or his or her spouse:

   (1) The banker must transmit to the Registration Administra-
      tion a list of all of the client's funds, securities, or other
      properties in the bank's possession, before paying or deliv-
      ering it back to the estate;[24]

[21] Article 183 of the Registration Tax Code.
[22] Article 100 of the Inheritance Tax Code.
[23] Article 102-1 of the Inheritance Tax Code.
[24] *Id.*, Article 97.

    (2) If the banker is in possession of sealed envelopes or boxes or if the client has rented a safe, the banker must:

    (a) notify the Administration of the upcoming opening of the envelope, box, or safe, at least five days in advance, and

    (b) transmit a list of the contents of the envelope, box or safe at the time it is opened; the Registration Administration may send one of its agents to witness the opening.[25]

Value added tax

4-035   Bankers, like any other person subject to value added tax (VAT), must list all operations with clients which are themselves subject to VAT. Bankers also owe a passive duty of disclosure; they must, if requested, transmit any relevant information and document enabling the VAT Administration to establish correct tax liability.[26]

Revenue tax

4-036   **Taxation stage** The Revenue Tax Administration (*Administration des Contributes Directes*) may request from any individual, corporation, or other entity information and relevant material necessary to determine the tax liability of that party or of any third party.[27]

As far as bankers are concerned, this broad duty of disclosure is qualified by the Revenue Tax Code,[28] which provides that the Revenue Tax Administration may not check banks' books or records in order to determine their client's tax liability. Some case law has complemented this rule by rendering it illegal for the Revenue Tax Administration to request bankers to disclose information about clients that the Administration is not itself allowed to look for in the bank's records.

However, if in the course of an inquiry related to the banker's own tax situation the Administration discovers relevant information leading to the suspicion that an arrangement exists in which the banker and his customer are trying to illegally avoid the taxation of the latter's revenues, then the Administration is allowed to investi-

---

[25] *Id.*, Articles 98 and 101.
[26] Article 61, paragraph 2 of the Value Added Tax Code.
[27] Articles 221, 222, 223, 228 *et seq.* of the Revenue Tax Code.
[28] *Id.*, Article 224.

gate into the banker's records in order to determine the client's tax liability.[29]

If the Banking and Finance Commission, whose mission includes the control of banks, discovers such a mechanism, it must advise the Revenue Tax Administration, thus broadening the latter's power of investigation to the same extent.[30]

The Code provides that information discovered by one tax administration may be used by another to determine another category of tax.[31] It seems, however, that the Revenue Tax Administration may not use this provision as a basis for requesting other tax administrations to obtain from a bank the information it needs about one of its clients.

Such a construction of the statute would render meaningless the limits to the Revenue Tax Administration's power of investigation. Article 224 of the Code was enacted in 1980, more than 40 years after articles 242 and 243, and it should be understood as limiting the rule of cooperation among the various tax administrations.

Complaint stage When the taxpayer contests the taxation of his revenue, the Revenue Tax Administration may require information from his banker, to investigate the validity of the complaint.[32] It is accepted, however, that the taxpayer may forbid his banker from disclosing any information, even though such attitude will obviously greatly undermine his chances of a successful complaint. Bankers often spontaneously refuse to release information that could reveal the identity of other clients.   4-037

Information to regulatory authorities

Banking and Finance Commission

The Banking and Finance Commission supervises bankers through the use of auditors. Neither auditors nor members of the Banking and Finance Commission may reveal any information they come across in the course of their supervisory activities, subject to certain exceptions such as judicial proceedings. A breach of this rule leads to the criminal sanctions provided for in article 458 of the Criminal Code (see text above).[33]   4-038

29 *Id.*, Article 224, paragraph 2.
30 *Id.*, Article 235, paragraph 5.
31 *Id.*, Articles 242-243.
32 *Id.*, Article 275.
33 Articles 40 and 45 of Royal Decree Number 185 of July 9, 1935.

Bankers also have a duty of disclosure to the Banking and Finance Commission, and the National Bank, as to credits and loans of more than BEF 1-million.

Foreign exchange control

4-039 Various types of operations must be disclosed by banks to the *Institut Belgo-Luxembourgeois du Change.*[34]

Communication of information among bankers

The Credit Risks Central Office (Centrale des Risques de Crédit)

4-040 Bankers are compelled to notify the National Bank and the Banking and Finance Commission of any grant of a credit or a loan of an amount above BEF 1-million. Both institutions may ask the bank for further details, such as the level of withdrawals.

The Credit Risks Center is operated by the National Bank and is accessible to banks which have granted, or are negotiating, a credit or a loan of more than BEF 1-million. The information disclosed includes the total amount of the client's credits from all banks in Belgium and the amount actually drawn, without any reference to specific banks or operations. The Credit Risks Center is "positive", *i.e.*, it discloses all credit information, whether or not the client defaulted.

Consumer credit and databases

4-041 The Law of June 12, 1991, on Consumer Credit (the "Law") allows, under specific conditions, the setting-up of private databases on consumers and their credit standing and entrusts the National Bank with the task of gathering information on all defaults under consumer credits in the Central Database.

4-042 **Private databases** The Law determines the type of information that may be included in the databases, as well as the categories of persons to whom and the purpose for which the information may be disclosed. Such private databases may be positive.

---

[34] Decree Law of October 6, 1944, and related statutes and regulations.

A consumer must be informed of his first inclusion in such a database. Consumers involved may have access to the information at all times and request false or irrelevant data to be amended or omitted.

The Central Database Prior to the Law, the National Bank already 4-043 had operated the Central Consumer Credit Office in accordance with the Law of July 9, 1957, on Sales with Installment Plans and their Financing (repealed by the Law of June 12, 1991). The Central Database operates under similar conditions. Consultation of the Central Database is mandatory for bankers prior to any offer of credit to a consumer, as defined in the Law. The Central Database is negative, as it is limited to the recording of consumers' defaults.

Private "black lists"

Prior to the Law of June 12, 1991, private organizations already had 4-044 established databases to gather information for their members about their clients, especially in case of defaults or frauds. Such private black lists are not necessarily limited to information on consumers. They include:

(1) The *Secrétariat Eurochèque;*
(2) The *Union Professionnelle du Crédit* and its *Mutuelle d'Information sur le Risque,* and
(3) The Belgian Association of Bankers and its *Mutuelle d'Information pour favoriser la sécurité des opérations bancaires.*

Some authors seem to agree that such private black lists are legal, whether they are positive or merely negative. This exception to the banker's duty of confidentiality is accepted on the following grounds:

(1) Disclosure is made to other bankers; their duty of discretion prevents information from being revealed to the general public;
(2) Such disclosure is justified by a higher social and economic interest, *i.e.,* safer and healthier credit for the public as a whole, and
(3) The system only affects "bad" clients, *i.e.,* the ones who do not faithfully disclose the existence of other credits to their bankers and the ones who have defaulted on previous credits.

The Civil Court of Liège has held a Belgian bank and the *Union Professionnelle du Crédit* liable for damages to a client for keeping outdated information on the black list.[35] The client's default was partly due to technical problems and had been cleared soon after. The default, however, was still mentioned on the black list.

Notwithstanding the absence of evidence that the client had been refused other credits because of the wrong data, the court nevertheless held that the burden of the investigation undertaken by the client to discover the existence of the black list constituted recoverable damages.

The court held that the plaintiff's right to privacy had been violated because the black list was secret and did not allow amendments to the data in case of later change in the debtor's situation, *e.g.*, the reimbursment of his debt or a judicial decision declaring the debt to be null and void.

The court seemed to agree that black lists are lawful provided they meet certain tests regarding disclosure and up-dating. These tests are similar to those laid down in the Law of June 12, 1991 (see text above).

Money laundering

4-045   The Law of July 17, 1990, on money laundering has extended the scope of the crime of receiving and concealing goods or funds deriving directly from criminal activities by amending articles 42 and 505 of the Criminal Code in the following ways:

(1) Such a crime is no longer limited to movable goods and funds directly derived from criminal activity but also covers all "financial advantages", whether derived directly or indirectly from a criminal activity, as well as the revenues derived from the investment of those financial advantages, and

(2) Not only receiving and concealing, but also managing those financial advantages, is now prohibited.

In accordance with previous case law, it is now provided that the activities mentioned hereabove constitute a crime where the perpetrator knew or should have known that the financial advantage has a criminal origin.

---

[35] President of the Civil Court of Liège, June 6, 1986, *Journal de Droit Fiscal*, 1986, at p. 359.

These new provisions are clearly aimed at bankers who must now shoulder the heavy burden of checking the origin of the funds and financial advantages they receive from and/or manage on behalf of their clients. The new wording of articles 42 and 505 raises the following issues in the case where a bank, which is currently holding or managing funds, learns of their criminal origin:

(1) Is the bank committing a crime? Despite the ambiguity of article 505, Parliamentary reports clearly exclude such possibility; for the crime to be established, the banker must know or should have known at the time he receives the funds that they were of criminal origin;

(2) Is the banker compelled to disclose the fact that he holds such funds to the authorities? The Law is not clear in that respect. It must be noted that the Belgian Association of Banks is currently examining a common position to be taken on this issue.

Brokerage in transferable securities

The Law of December 4, 1990, on financial operations and markets **4-046** includes provisions on the brokerage of transferable securities (*valeurs mobilières* or *effecten*). Such brokerage is reserved to certain categories of individuals and companies, including banks.

In case indications lead to the belief that a crime related to the trading of securities has been committed, including insider trading, or that certain formalities with regard to the disclosure of important holdings in companies listed on a stock exchange have not been fulfilled, the Banking and Finance Commission may request banks to disclose information about their clients and the transactions carried out for them.

The Law requires the bankers to inform their clients of such a potential disclosure obligation prior to carrying out any transaction on their behalf.

CONCLUSION

This description of the bankers' duty of confidentiality has put **4-047** much more emphasis on the exceptions to the rule, which are more specific to Belgian law, than on the duty itself. In many circumstances, the banker will not be allowed to use his duty of discretion to oppose requests for disclosure.

It must be remembered, however, that the rule of confidentiality, in its principle and scope, and the potential liability in case of breach are clearly established in Belgium. Therefore, the banker, if required to disclose information about his client's operations to public authorities or private persons, must not depart from his traditional cautious conduct; he must ensure that procedural rules have not been violated and limit the release of information or documents to the required minimum.

CHAPTER 5

BRITISH VIRGIN ISLANDS

Dancia Penn
Dancia Penn & Co.
Road Town, Tortola, Virgin Islands

Chapter 5

BRITISH VIRGIN ISLANDS

INTRODUCTION

This chapter examines the law on banking secrecy in the British **5-001**
Virgin Islands. The Virgin Islands (now commonly called the British
Virgin Islands) is a group of islands located in the Caribbean approximately 40 miles east of the island of Puerto Rico and is referred
to in this chapter as "BVI". The group consists of some 56 islands,
most of which are uninhabited. The capital and main center of
business is in Road Town on the island of Tortola.

The BVI is a colony of the United Kingdom and has a Constitu-
tion that provides for a Governor as the Queen's Representative, a
Legislative Council, and an Executive Council. The Legislative
Council is comprised of nine members who are elected every four
years. The Executive Council consists of four of the nine elected
members, including the Chief Minister who is the Head of the
Government, the Attorney General, and the Governor, who is its
Chairman.

By virtue of the Common Law (Declaration of Application) Act,[1]
the Common Law of England is in force in the BVI. Accordingly,
any discussion of the law in the BVI involves, to some extent, a
consideration of the law of England, save as it is abrogated by
statute.

There is a hierarchical system of courts, consisting of a Magistrate's Court, a High Court, and a Court of Appeal. There is a final
right of appeal to Her Majesty in Council.

There are four commercial banks licensed to carry on the full
spectrum of commercial and business services in the BVI, and seven
banks have been granted restricted banking licenses.

---

[1] Common Law (Declaration of Application) Act [Act 31/1705], Cap. 14, Laws of
the Virgin Islands, passed on June 20, 1705.

LAW ON BANKING SECRECY

5-002   It is settled law that a banker is under a duty not to make disclosure
of his customer's accounts except under certain conditions. It is a
legal rather than a moral duty and arises out of the contract between
a banker and his customer. As a duty arising out of contract, it is a
duty the breach of which gives a successful plaintiff a remedy in
damages.

The duty on the banker not to disclose is one that is not absolute
but is qualified and is subject to certain exceptions. The case of
Tournier v. *National Provincial and Union Bank of England* [2] settled the
law on this point. In his oft-quoted judgment, Bankes L.J. said:

> "In my opinion is it necessary in a case like the present to direct
> the jury what are the limits and what are the qualifications of
> the contractual duty of secrecy implied in the relation of
> banker and customer. There appears to be no authority on the
> point. On principle I think that the qualifications can be clas-
> sified under four heads: (a) where disclosure is under compul-
> sion by law; (b) where there is a duty to the public to disclose;
> (c) where the interests of the bank require disclosure; (d)
> where the disclosure is made by the express or implied con-
> sent of the customer."[3]

The duty of secrecy on the part of the banker begins at the time of
the establishment of the relationship between the banker and the
customer, and it continues except when the information is released
in accordance with one of the four exceptions identified by the court
in the *Tournier* case. An examination of the question of banking
secrecy, therefore, requires an examination of the exceptions laid
down in the *Tournier* case, and substantially of the first exception.

Where disclosure is by compulsion of law

5-003   The usual and best illustration of this is the duty of a bank to obey
an order made under the Banker's Books (Evidence) Act.[4] The
Banker's Books was enacted in the Virgin Islands on November 21,
1881. The Act, which remains on the books in most of the English-
speaking jurisdictions of the Caribbean, was passed to give relief to

2 *Tournier* v. *National Provincial and Union Bank of England* [1924] 1 K.B. 461.
3 *Id.*
4 The Banker's Books (Evidence) Act, 1881, Cap. 8, Laws of the Virgin Islands.

bankers and to abrogate the rigors of the Common Law, which required them, when necessary, to attend court with their books when proof of their contents was required.

Section 7 of the Act provides:

"7. On the application of any party to a legal proceeding, a Court or Judge may order that such party be at liberty to inspect and take copies of any entries in a banker's book for any of the purposes of such proceeding. An order under this section may be made either with, or without, summoning the bank or any other party, and shall be served on the bank three clear days before the same is to be obeyed, unless the Court or Judge otherwise directs."

"Bank" or "banker" is defined in section 2 of the Act to mean:

". . . any person, persons, partnership or company carrying on the business of bankers".

No definition is given for the expression "the business of bankers". It is perhaps important to note, however, that section 2 of the Banks and Trust Companies Act[5] defines "bank" to mean "a person carrying on banking business", and "banking business" as:

". . . the business of receiving (other than from a bank or trust company) and holding on current, savings, deposit or similar account money that is repayable by cheque or order and is capable of being invested by way of advances to customers or otherwise but does not include the receiving on savings, deposit, or similar account money that is paid by one company to another at a time when -

(a) one is the subsidiary of the other; or
(b) both are subsidiaries of another company."

The Banks and Trust Companies Act 1990 repealed the Banking Ordinance Cap. 9 of 1972 and is an Act to provide for the licensing and control of banking business and trust business and related matters.

---

[5] Banks and Trust Companies Act 1990, Cap. 9, Laws of the Virgin Islands.

THE CASES

5-004   The question of banking secrecy has not much attracted the attention of the courts in the BVI, or indeed, the Caribbean. However,
there is a recent relevant decision of the Eastern Caribbean Court of
Appeal on the subject. The case is *Robertson v. The Caribbean Imperial
Bank of Commerce (CIBC).*[6] The case, which is still unreported, is a
decision that is of binding precedent in the BVI courts, because the
BVI is a member of the Eastern Caribbean Court of Appeal.

In this case, Dr. Robertson, a medical doctor practicing in the
island of St. Vincent, and CIBC, a commercial bank doing business
in the island of St. Vincent, appealed against the findings of a High
Court judge. The judge had ruled, *inter alia:*

(1) That the Respondent bank was in breach of the implied
term of confidentiality in the contract of banking between
the Bank and Dr. Robertson when the bank disclosed Dr.
Robertson's accounts to the High Court in response to a
subpoena duces tecum.[7] The accounts disclosed were, in fact,
more than were needed to prove the case against Dr.
Robertson.

(2) That the breach occurred as a result of the negligence of the
bank in not obtaining the consent of Dr. Robertson before
disclosing the accounts and in not claiming the privilege
afforded by the banker/customer relationship.

(3) That the bank was protected by an absolute privilege because the disclosure was made in the witness box in the
course of legal proceedings.

It was on the latter ground that the judge gave judgment for the
bank.

Byron J.A. delivered the judgment of the Court of Appeal and the
other two members, then Chief Justice Sir Lascelles Robotham and
Moe J.A. concurred. The court seemed to find favor with the view
that the duty of confidentiality did not impose any duty on a bank
to abstain from answering questions in a Court of Justice as to a
customer's account.

The question of whether it was for the bank to enforce the duty
of confidentiality before there had been disclosure and whether the

---

6 *Robertson v. The Caribbean Imperial Bank of Commerce,* Civil Appeal No. 4 of 1990
(Unreported).

7 A Common Law writ to compel a person to attend court at a specified date and
time to produce material documents.

bank's duty to maintain confidentiality was all embracing was eloquently answered by Byron J.A. in the following manner:

> "Counsel's argument that the banks did owe such a duty was based on a contention that the bank's duty to maintain confidentiality was all-embracing, subject to the four exceptions set out in *Tournier v. National Provincial Union Bank of England* [1924] 1 K.B. 461 at 473, [1923] All E.R. 550 at 554. From this it followed, so he submitted, that there was an implied obligation to do everything possible to prevent the application of the exceptions. I do not agree. The duty to maintain confidentiality is not all-embracing, subject to exceptions. It does not exist in the four exceptional circumstances and it is no part of the duty of confidentiality to seek to avoid disclosure under compulsion by law.
>
> "The real question is whether in order to give business efficacy to the relationship of banker and customer, there must be an implied obligation to contest a s.9 [section 7 in the BVI law] application or to probe it or inform its customers. Since the responsibility for deciding is firmly placed on the Circuit Judge, and such an order cannot be made by consent of the parties, I can see no reason for implying an obligation to contest the application unless the bank knew something relevant to it or might not be known to the police. The primary purpose of the notice being given to the bank is to enable it to safeguard its own interests by, for example, pointing out that it did not hold the accounts to which the application related."[8]

The case *Saunders v. The Bank of Nova Scotia,*[9] a decision of the Court of Appeal of the Bahamas also deals, *inter alia,* with the question of banking secrecy. It shows how a court, the decisions of which would be of persuasive precedent in the BVI, dealt with the question of what constitutes "banker's books".

In this case, the appellant Saunders opened a special account with the respondent bank. The account was subject to the bank's standard terms. The appellant on at least two occasions endorsed checks that were credited by the bank to his account. It was later found that the endorsements by the payee on the checks were forgeries but, in any event, the respondent bank honored the requests of the paying banks to be reimbursed the sums represented by the two checks which bore the forged signatures. At the trial in

---

8 *Robertson v. The Caribbean Imperial Bank of Commerce, supra,* n. 6.
9 *Saunders v. The Bank of Nova Scotia* 35 W.I.R. 1.

which the bank sought to recover from the appellant the sums represented by the two checks, the puisne judge, in addition to admitting the direct evidence of the forgeries, admitted under the Bankers Books Evidence Act 1968 affidavits with reference to the authenticity of the signatures on the checks and other documents supporting the claims of the paying banks to reimbursement on the grounds of forgery.

The appeal was upheld, and the court held, *inter alia*, that:

> ". . . neither the affidavits to the effect that the signatures on the cheques were false nor the other documents supporting the claims of the paying banks for the return of the monies paid out on the cheques fell within the term 'banker's books' in the Bankers Books Evidence Act 1968, section 2(2), since section 4 of the Act made it clear that the term referred only to documents in the permanent record of a bank that related to its ordinary business; the affidavits and other documents did not relate to the ordinary business of the bank but to a particular situation and were not admissible . . . ."

"Banker's books" are defined in section 2(2) of the Bahamas Act to:

> "(a) include any records used in the ordinary business of a bank, or used in the transfer department of a bank acting as registrar of securities, whether comprised in bound volumes, looseleaf binders or other looseleaf filing systems, looseleaf ledger sheets, pages, folios or cards, and
>
> (b) cover documents in manuscript, documents which are typed, printed, stenciled or created by any other mechanical or partly mechanical process in use from time to time and documents which are produced by any photographic or photostatic process."

Section 2 of the BVI Act defines "banker's books" to include:

> ". . . ledgers, daybooks, cashbooks, account books and all other books used in the ordinary business of the bank . . . ."

Section 4 in the BVI Act and the Bahamas Act is identical and provides as follows:

> "A copy of an entry in a banker's book shall not be received in evidence under this Act unless it be first proved that the book was at the time of the making of the entry one of the ordinary books of the bank, and that the entry was made in the usual

and ordinary course of business, and that the book is in the custody or control of the bank. Such proof may be given by a partner or officer of the bank, and may be given orally or by an affidavit sworn before any notary public or justice of the peace or person authorised to take affidavits."

THE STATUTES

The Evidence Act

Section 12 of the Evidence Act[10] of the Laws of the Virgin Islands **5-005** provides that:

"12. Every document, which, by any law now in force, or hereinafter to be in force, is or shall be admissible in evidence in any Court of Justice in England, shall be admissible in evidence in the like manner, to the same extent, and for the same purpose, in any Court in the Colony, or before any person having by law, or by consent of the parties, authority to hear, receive and examine evidence."

Accordingly, copies of entries in banker's books used in the ordinary business of a bank, whether those records are on microfilm, magnetic tape or any other form of mechanical or electronic data retrieval mechanism would be admissible in a BVI court.

This is, of course, provided that the book was at the time of the entry one of the ordinary books of the bank, that it was kept in the custody and control of the bank (or its successors), and that the entry was made in the ordinary course of business.[11]

The Evidence (Proceedings in Foreign Jurisdictions) Act[12]

On October 1, 1988, the Evidence (Proceedings in Foreign Jurisdic- **5-006** tions) Act that had been passed by the Legislature of the Virgin Islands in 1984, came into effect. Similar statutes exist in several other British Dependent Territories in the Caribbean, either by

---

[10] Evidence Act 1984, Cap. 24, Laws of the Virgin Islands.

[11] *Phipson on Evidence*, (14th ed.), at p. 751.

[12] Evidence (Proceedings in Foreign Jurisdictions) Act 1984, Cap. 1, Laws of the Virgin Islands.

extension to the individual Territory by Order in Council of the United Kingdom Parliament or by enactment by the local Legislative Council.

The statute provides for the obtaining of evidence in the BVI on the application of, and for the use of, civil proceedings in a foreign jurisdiction. The High Court in the BVI may, *inter alia*, make provision for the production of documents and the inspection, photographing, preservation, custody, or detention of any property.

The statute is expressed in section 9(3) to be "enabling and shall in its application be given such construction as would as nearly as possible afford it conformity with the Convention contained in the Schedule."

That Convention is the Hague Convention on the Taking of Evidence Abroad in Civil or Commercial Matters 1970.

The Convention seeks to facilitate the taking of evidence in a country at the request of a foreign court or tribunal where the evidence is for use in civil proceedings, is relevant, and is taken before a court in the country to which the request is addressed. Based on adherence to the principle of international comity, the municipal court will usually grant the request of the foreign court. To the writer's knowledge, no application has to date been made to the BVI Court under this statute.

However, in any such proceeding, there would have to be respect for territorial sovereignty. The request would have to be for "particular documents", and the court will not allow "a fishing expedition". Reliance would quite likely be on relevant United Kingdom decisions, such as *Rio Tinto Zinc Corp* v. *Westinghouse* [13] and the cases following thereon.

The case *U.S.* v. *Carver et. al.*,[14] a decision of the Cayman Islands Court of Appeal, would likely provide good guidance to a BVI court. In the Carver case, the court held that an order to a banker to produce "all correspondence, ledgers, day books, and account books used in its ordinary course of business" in which the bank recorded the receipt of a particular sum, on a particular day, which funds it credited to a particular account, would satisfy the statutory requirement of particular documents. The court severed the words "all other books, documents and papers" as being too wide and likely to lead to a fishing expedition.[15]

[13] *Rio Tinto Zinc Corp.* v. *Westinghouse* [1978] 1 All E.R. 434.
[14] *U.S.* v *Carver et. al.*, Cayman Islands Civil Appeal No. 5 of 1982.
[15] *Id.*

Mutual Legal Assistance (United States of America) Act

The Mutual Legal Assistance (United States of America) Act[16] was **5-007** passed by the Legislature of the Virgin Islands on September 17, 1990. It is an Act "to make provision for giving effect to the terms of a treaty made between the Government of the United States of America, the Government of the United Kingdom of Great Britain and Northern Ireland, concerning the Cayman Islands dated 3 July 1986, for improving the effectiveness of the law enforcement authorities of the United States of America and the British Virgin Islands in the prosecution and suppression of crime, through cooperation and mutual legal assistance in criminal matters and for purposes connected therewith."[17]

This Act is far reaching in its scope and specifically provides that it applies for the purpose of giving effect to the Treaty above-mentioned, which has legal effect in the BVI for the provision of mutual assistance between the authorities in the United States and the BVI for the suppression of the types of criminal offenses specified in the Treaty and "including any such ancillary civil or administrative proceedings by the parties" to the Treaty as are mentioned in the Treaty. The criminal activities covered include racketeering, drug trafficking, insider trading and fraudulent securities practices.

The Act, in section 4, constitutes the Attorney General as "the British Virgin Islands Mutual Legal Assistance Authority", and it requires any person (which, of course, includes banks) when a request is made to testify or produce in BVI documentary information in his possession or under his control.

Section 9 of the Act has important implications for banking secrecy in the BVI. It provides that:

> "9. A person who divulges any confidential information or gives any testimony in conformity with a request shall be deemed not to commit any offence under any law for the time being in force in the British Virgin Islands, by reason only of such disclosure or the giving of such testimony; and shall be deemed not to commit any offence under any law by reason only of such disclosure of the giving of such testimony; and such disclosure or testimony shall be deemed not to be a breach of any confidential relationship between that person and any other person, and no civil claim or action whatsoever

[16] Mutual Legal Assistance (United States of America) Act 1990 (Cap. 5 of 1990).
[17] *Id.*

shall lie against the person making such disclosure or giving such testimony or against such person's principal or employer by reason of such disclosure or testimony."

However, article 7(1) of the Treaty places a limitation on the use of information obtained under the Act. It states that:

"1. The Requesting Party shall not use any information or evidence obtained under this Treaty for any purposes other than for the investigation, prosecution or suppression in the territory of the Requesting Party of those criminal offences stated in the request without the prior consent of the Requested Party."

The Drug Trafficking Offences Act 1992

5-008   The Drug Trafficking Offences Act 1992[18] was passed by the Legislature of the Virgin Islands on May 15, 1992, and the Proclamation bringing it into effect has not, as of the time of writing, been published in the Gazette. This no doubt will be done in the near future. The Act is in several material aspects similar to the Drug Trafficking Act 1986 of the United Kingdom, and there are similar statutes in force in most of the British Dependent Territories.

Section 23(1) makes it an offense to assist a person to retain the benefit of drug trafficking. Most significantly in terms of banking secrecy, section 23(4) of the Act gives immunity from suit for breach of contract to any person who "discloses to a police officer a suspicion or belief that any funds or investments are derived from or used in connection with drug trafficking or any matter on which such a suspicion or belief is based. . .".

Section 23(4) provides a defense to a person charged with the offense under the section if he can prove that he did not know or suspect that the arrangement related to drug trafficking. This can clearly present difficulty for banks, especially if there is a prior awareness of the suspicions of the police.

The Act further provides for the enforcement of external confiscation orders that are defined as orders "made by a court in the designated country for the purpose of recovering payments or other rewards received in connection with drug trafficking or their value".

18 Drug Trafficking Offences Act 1992, Laws of the Virgin Islands.

EXTRA-TERRITORIAL ORDERS

It is important to note that all the four commercial banks in the BVI **5-009**
are branches of major commercial banks with headquarters elsewhere. The law is that any order under section 7 of the Banker's
Books Evidence Act, or by subpoena requiring the production of
documents held outside the jurisdiction concerning business transacted outside its jurisdiction, should not be imposed on a foreigner
and, in particular, a foreign bank.

This is based on the principle that a state should refrain from
demanding obedience to a sovereign authority by foreigners in
respect of their conduct outside the jurisdiction.[19]

Once more, the matter has not been tested in the BVI courts, but
a BVI court is likely to follow a case such as *R. v. Grossman* [20] and
decisions following thereon. In the *Grossman* case, an inspection
order was made *ex parte* requiring Barclays Bank Ltd., at its head
office in London, to allow the Inland Revenue to inspect and take
copies of certain documents of a company that maintained an
account with Barclays Bank in the Isle of Man. The Court of Appeal
set aside the inspection order. Lord Denning M.R. stated:

> "The branch of Barclays Bank in Douglas, Isle of Man, should
> be considered as a different entity separate from the head office
> in London. It is subject to the laws and regulations of the Isle
> of Man. It is licensed by the Isle of Man government. It has its
> customers there who are subject to the Manx laws. It seems to
> me that the court here ought not in its discretion to make an
> order against the head office here in respect of the books of the
> branch in the Isle of Man in regard to the customers of that
> branch .... Any order in respect of the production of the books
> ought to be made by the courts in the Isle of Man - if they will
> make such an order. It ought not to be made by these courts.
> Otherwise there would be danger of a conflict of jurisdictions
> between the High Court here and the courts of the Isle of Man.
> That is a conflict which we must always avoid. ... It seems to
> me that, although this court has jurisdiction to order the head
> office here to produce the books, in our discretion it should not
> be done."[21]

---

[19] See Grace A. Smith, "Bank Secrecy in the Cayman Islands" 1986, vol. 10, *West Indian Law Journal*, particularly at p. 117.
[20] *R. v. Grossman* [1981] 73 Cr. App. Rep. 302.
[21] *Id.*

OTHER EXCEPTIONS AS SET OUT IN *TOURNIER*

5-010 The other exceptions to the banker's duty of secrecy are as follows:[22]

(1) Where disclosure is required in the public interest - Such instances are rare and are likely to be in circumstances where considerations of national security are involved.

(2) Where disclosure is required in the interests of the bank - Such instances are also rare and are likely to arise in cases where there is litigation between a bank and its customer.

(3) Where disclosure is made with the customer's authority - These cases are fairly obvious and usually occur where a customer authorizes the bank to provide a credit reference.

Conclusion

5-011 In sum, therefore, while the question of banking secrecy remains essentially untested in the BVI courts, it is obvious that recent statutory provisions have made some significant incursions into the confidentiality that classically existed between the banker and his client.

It is likely that the banks doing business in the BVI would comply with the provisions of the law.

---

[22] *Paget's Law of Banking*, (10th ed.), Mark Hapgood, ch. 20, at p. 353.

CHAPTER 6

CANADA

Jane Bogaty, Ron L. Bozzer and James E. Fordyce
Osler Renault Ladner
Montreal, Quebec, Toronto, Ontario, and
Vancouver, British Columbia, Canada

Chapter 6

CANADA

INTRODUCTION

This chapter concerns the obligations of banks and other financial 6-001
institutions operating in Canada to maintain the affairs of their
customer secret - an obligation also commonly referred to as a "duty
of confidentiality". This chapter deals with the federal laws of
Canada and the laws applicable in the provinces of British Columbia, Ontario, and Quebec, which are the principal Canadian provinces.

The analysis of the duty of secrecy under Canadian law is complicated because of the constitutional separation of powers between
the federal and provincial governments. In addition, Canada has
made a sweeping reform of the laws governing federally regulated
financial institutions. For example, Canadian banks are able, to
venture into new areas of financial services, such as securities
dealing, investment banking, and providing trust services.

Until recently, the financial sector in Canada was separated by
function into "four pillars". These pillars represented banking, insurance, trust operations, and the securities industry. The reform
legislation was expected to have the effect of breaking down the
pillars.

Other reforms made effective on June 1, 1992, provide increased
powers to some federally regulated financial institutions.[1] For ex-

---

[1] The Bank Act, the Trust Companies Act, the Loan Companies Act, the Canadian
and British Insurance Companies Act, the Foreign Insurance Companies Act,
and the Cooperative Credit Associations Act have been replaced by new
financial institutions legislation, which was passed by the Canadian
Parliament and received Royal Assent on December 13, 1991, and proclamed
in force on June 1, 1992. The new legislation broadens the lending and
investment powers of federally regulated financial institutions and updates the
regulatory regime under which they operate.

ample, insurance companies will be permitted to issue credit or charge cards and now have full consumer lending powers. The government's intention is to benefit consumers by increasing competition with a movement to "one-stop shopping".

All federally regulated financial institutions are permitted to network financial services by selling or offering for sale products of affiliated and non-affiliated entities. The new legislation contains restrictions on the ability to use confidential information in targeting customers.

The new powers also brings concerns in areas such as disclosure of information about customers' identity and needs. Financial services regulatory reform poses new secrecy concerns for financial institutions as they attempt to provide a broader range of financial services to their customers.

Canadian constitutional context

6-002   Canada is a federation of 10 provinces. The constitution of Canada is based on an 1867 English Act of Parliament which has been repatriated to Canada and updated by the Constitution Act, 1982.[2]

The Constitution Act divides legislative authority between the central federal parliament and the 10 provincial legislatures. The Constitution Act provides that the federal parliament has exclusive legislative jurisdiction over banking and the incorporation of banks.[3] However, the provinces have exclusive legislative jurisdiction over property and civil rights within their territory.[4]

This separation of powers is not water tight. As a result, banks face overlapping regulation by the federal and provincial governments. Although banking is a federal matter governed by the Bank Act, other financial transactions in which banks or their subsidiaries are involved, such as securities matters, are primarily under provin-

---

[2] Canada is currently debating further constitutional amendments. This process began with a proposal issued by the Federal Cabinet on September 24, 1991, entitled "Shaping Canada's Future Together". It has culminated in a "Consensus Report on the Constitution", issued in Charlottetown, P.E.I., on August 28, 1992. Neither of these documents contain any specific proposal for constitutional amendments which would impact on the matters described in this chapter. There is a suggestion that there be a rationalization of the involvement of both levels of government — federal and provincial — in some aspects of financial sector regulation and bankruptcy law. This particular suggestion is simply a call for early discussion with the provinces of Canada and no imminent rationalization is expected.

[3] Constitution Act, section 91(15).

[4] *Id.*, section 92(13).

cial jurisdiction. Moreover, to the extent not specifically dealt with by federal banking legislation, matters such as contract law and agency are governed by the Common Law and statutory law of each province.

There is variation among the laws of Canada's nine Common Law provinces, mainly as a result of statutory provisions. Generally, the laws applicable to commercial operations are similar in each of the Common Law provinces. The laws of the Province of Quebec are based on the French Civil Law system. Although this legal system often provides similar results to those found in the Canadian Common Law provinces, this factor nevertheless further complicates the regulatory system.

Application of duty of secrecy

Who are the "banks" to which the obligation of secrecy applies? **6-003** This chapter is concerned not only with financial institutions which are designated as "banks" and which operate in Canada but also to other financial institutions which are subject to the Common Law duty of secrecy. The Bank Act[5] differentiates between Schedule I banks, which are banks which must be widely held, and in respect of which no single shareholder may own more than 10 percent of the outstanding shares and Schedule II banks.

The Schedule I banks comprise seven operating Canadian banks. The Bank Act permits foreign banks to operate in Canada through Schedule II banks which are wholly-owned subsidiaries of foreign banks. There are 57 such subsidiaries licensed to operate in Canada.[6] References in this chapter to banks include both Schedule I and Schedule II banks.

The duty of confidentiality is arguably also applicable to investment and securities firms, trust companies, credit unions, and insurance companies, some of which are licensed to accept deposits from the public. These institutions often are referred to as "near-banks" because of their powers to undertake business similar to banks themselves. References in this chapter to "banks" should also be taken to include such "near banks".

[5] S.C. 1991, chap. 46.
[6] Annual Report of Superintendent of Financial Institutions, October 1991.

SECRECY FOUNDED ON CONTRACTUAL PRINCIPLES

Nature of banker-customer relationship

6-004   The nature of the relationship between a bank and its customer is multi-faceted. The relation is primarily contractual, as between a debtor and creditor or a principal and agent, but on occasion may extend into a fiduciary relationship. "The basic meaning of a bank deposit is that it is a loan of money by the depositor to the bank."[7] Under this contract, the customer has no right to the money he has deposited, nor to the profit the bank has made through the use of his money.[8] The money, in fact, becomes the property of the bank.

A customer simply has a claim to return of a certain amount of money from the bank, pursuant to contract. Insofar as an agency relation is concerned, as an incident to the depositing of funds with a banker, there is an implied term (unless specifically negated, as is the case with some types of savings accounts) that the customer may direct the banker, by means of a check or other bill of exchange, to pay such funds to third parties.[9]

In certain circumstances, the relationship between a customer and the bank is fiduciary rather than simply contractual. The existence of a fiduciary relationship must be proven by the customer, since it is an "exception" to the general rule that the relation between a bank and its customer is simply one of debtor and creditor.[10]

The requirements for the courts to find a fiduciary relationship are that the bank has stepped beyond its traditional role and given advice to a customer, upon which the customer relied (to the bank's knowledge) and from which the bank stood to receive a benefit.[11]

There is no basis in Canadian federal statutes for the relationship between a bank and its customer, even though banking is a federal regulatory concern. Rather, the nature of the relationship has been determined under the Common Law and, in the case of Quebec, crystallized in the Civil Code, based upon centuries of banking. It is open to the Federal Parliament to enact legislation defining the banking relationship.

---

[7] Baxter, *The Law of Banking*, 3rd ed., at p. 2.

[8] *Foley* v. *Hill* (1848), 2 H.L. Cas. 28, 35-36; 9 E.R. 1002.

[9] *London Joint Stock Bank* v. *Macmillan* [1918] A.C. 777, 789.

[10] *First Calgary Financial Savings and Credit Union Ltd.* v. *Meadow and Meadows* [1989] 66 Alta. L.R. (2nd) 7, 14, affirmed on appeal [1991] 73 D.L.R. (4th) 705. Alberta Court of Appeal, October 4, 1990.

[11] The leading Canadian case is *Standard Investments Ltd. et. al.* v. *Canadian Imperial Bank of Commerce*, [1985] 52 O.R. (2d) 472 (C.A.), leave to appeal refused [1986] 53 O.R. (2d) 663 (S.C.C.).

Indeed, as will be noted later in this chapter, there is a substantial body of federal legislation which affects the nature of the relationship. However, in general, Canadian legislators have not seen fit to disturb the traditions of the Common Law and the English law merchant as the foundation for the nature of the relationship.

In order to discuss the question of confidentiality or secrecy as it relates to the banker-customer relationship, we must first determine how the duty of confidentiality arises.

Nature of the relationship giving rise to the duty of secrecy

For purposes of determining the question of bank secrecy, the 6-005 banker-customer relationship is a contractual one. This is the analysis used in the seminal case of *Tournier* v. *National Provincial and Union Bank of England*.[12] In that case, a customer sued the bank where he kept an account, because the bank had told the customer's employer that the customer owed money to the bank, and that the customer made payments to a bookmaker. The employer subsequently fired the customer. The customer claimed that he had been slandered by the bank and that the bank had breached a duty of confidentiality owed to him.

Each member of the Court of Appeal agreed that a duty of secrecy existed in law and not just in morality, and the duty was founded upon the contractual relationship of the parties.[13] It is an implied term of every contract between a bank and its customer that the bank will maintain in confidence the dealings of the customer with the bank.

Each member of the court then went on to say that the duty was not absolute. The judgments are chiefly occupied with the limits of the duty. How much information about a customer must the bank keep secret? Are there circumstances in which a bank is subject to a duty to disclose that overrides its duty of secrecy to the customer?

There is still little authority other than *Tournier* itself concerning the first question. As Scrutton L.J. remarked in *Tournier*, the fact that there is so little authority on the duty of secrecy "appears to be greatly to the credit of English" - and, one may add, Canadian - bankers, "who have given so little excuse for its discussion."[14]

---

12 *Tournier* v. *National Provincial and Union Bank of England* [1924] 1 K.B. 461.
13 *Id.*, at pp. 471-472, 480, and 483-484.
14 *Id.*, at p. 479.

Nature of information subject to disclosure limitations

6-006   One of the implied terms of the banker-customer contract is that the banker shall not divulge information relating to the customer. The question arises, what information is subject to the banker's duty of secrecy? In *Tournier*, Bankes L.J. said that while the existence of a duty of secrecy was clear, it was "more difficult to state . . . the limits of the duty[and] as to the nature of the disclosure."[15]

But he did say that the state of the customer's account is definitely within the scope of the duty of secrecy, "the confidence is not confined to the actual state of the customer's account," but "extends to information derived from the account," and the confidence may extend "to information in reference to the customer and his affairs derived not from the customer's account but from other sources, as, for instance, from the account of another customer of the customer's bank."[16]

The information which is subject to the rule must have been obtained by the banker in his "character of banker"[17] either from his customer or from other sources.

The reasoning of Bankes L.J. in *Tournier* is that the confidential relationship between a banker and his client "is very marked" - perhaps even more marked than that existing between a lawyer or a doctor and his client, it is suggested - because "the credit of the customer depends very largely upon the strict observance of that confidence."[18]

This passage is useful because it suggests a test for deciding upon the scope of the duty of secrecy. When deciding whether a certain kind of information is caught by the implied term of confidentiality, one may look at what would have motivated a customer to have insisted upon such a broad term at the time the contract was made. Bankes L.J. suggests, for instance, that the customer cannot be said to have impliedly consented to a term that would allow the banker to divulge information that would hurt the credit of the customer.

The trouble with this analysis is that it goes too far. To be safe, the customer would want the banker never to divulge anything concerning the customer - even personal information acquired on social occasions unrelated to the banker's work. However, such a term would be onerous to the banker as a private person, and could scarcely be implied as a term "necessarily" part of the banker-customer contract.

[15] *Id.*, at p. 473.
[16] *Id.*
[17] *Id.*, at p. 474.
[18] *Id.*, at p. 475.

Bankes L.J. also outlined a second, more practical test for determining what information is subject to the duty of secrecy. To be subject to the duty, the information must have been gained by the banker "in the character of banker."[19] This analysis makes the limits of the duty of secrecy both more and less broad than it might otherwise be. Information about a customer acquired while playing golf with a third party on a purely social basis would not be subject to the legal duty of confidentiality, even though release of this information could hurt a customer's credit. On the other hand, information about a customer that is acquired from another customer who is independent of the first customer may nevertheless be information acquired in the character of a banker, and would therefore be subject to the duty of secrecy existing between the banker and the first customer.

Applying these principles to the facts in *Tournier*, Bankes L.J. was of the view that information that a customer was making payments to a bookmaker, which was discovered after inquiry at the bookmaker's bank, was information gained in the banker's character as a banker.[20] Only if the information fell into one of the four classes of exception to the duty of secrecy would disclosure not be a breach of the duty.

Scrutton L.J. dissented on the issue of the extent of the duty. He felt that the duty *vis-à-vis* one customer would apply only to information the bank had derived from its dealings with that customer. Information about a customer that was received from an independent source such as another customer, even if the information was received in one's character as a banker, would not be subject to the duty of secrecy. Disclosure of such information to a third party would thus not give rise to a right of action for the first customer.

This narrow view of the scope of the duty of secrecy has not been followed in subsequent cases.[21] It also runs contrary to the implied term doctrine of secrecy, since it cannot be presumed that a customer would have agreed to have its financial affairs, whether derived from an independent source or not, made subject to disclosure.

However, the limitation on the scope of the duty placed by the requirement of Bankes L.J. that the information have been acquired "in the character of a banker" is also arguably not a restriction to which an experienced business customer would have lightly con-

---

[19] *Id.*, at pp. 474-475.

[20] *Id.*, at p. 475.

[21] The issue does not appear to have been litigated. Baxter, *The Law of Banking*, 3rd ed., pp. 11-12, simply refers to the view of Scrutton L.J. as the dissenting view in *Tournier*.

sented. It is possible, of course, that what Bankes L.J. was alluding to is the possibility that there might be more than one type of relationship between the parties at the same time.

In such case information clearly arising from the other relationship would not be acquired in the character of a banker. If however, the only relationship between the parties is that of banker and customer it could very well be argued that any information concerning the customer received by the banker, whether on the golf course or in the office, is information acquired by him in his character as a banker.

The better view is that the scope of the information that is subject to the duty of secrecy is very wide. A wide duty would greatly benefit the customer without imposing an undue burden on the banker. Thus, a wide duty is the duty most likely to have been agreed upon by the parties to the contract. The duty of secrecy, therefore, encompasses not only account balances or loan balances but also general or personal information about the customer - at least, if acquired by the banker in his capacity as banker.

Legislative basis for secrecy

6-007   As noted above, the basis for the banker's duty of secrecy in Canada outside of Quebec is founded in the Common Law.[22] In these jurisdictions, there are many legislative provisions requiring disclosure, as an exception to the duty of secrecy. These provisions are discussed below.

In Quebec, it may be argued that the basis for secrecy is founded in the Civil Code. The point is moot because it is not clear whether, under the Constitution, provinces have the power to regulate any aspect of banking, including banking secrecy. The banks have always taken the position that the provinces are without jurisdiction.

Sections 1017 and 1024 of the Civil Code of Lower Canada, which are applicable only in the province of Quebec, provide respectively that "customary clauses must be supplied in contracts, although they may not be expressed" and that "the obligation of a contract extends not only to what is expressed in it, but also to all the consequences which, by equity, usage, or law, are incident to the contract, according to its nature".

---

[22] Certain acts do legislate secrecy. For example, section 8 of the Consumer Reporting Act (Ontario), R.S.O. 1980, c. 89, as amended, provides that no consumer reporting agency shall knowingly furnish information except in certain defined circumstances. This legislation is not applicable to banks.

These statutory provisions may provide the legal basis in Quebec for the banker's duty of confidentiality, to the extent that the express terms of the contract setting forth the relation between the banker and his customer have not specifically provided for this duty. Such a result would coincide with the holding in the *Tournier* decision.[23]

As well, the Quebec Charter of Rights and Freedoms provides that "every person has a right to respect for his private life".[24] In addition, section 9 thereof states that "every person has a right to non-disclosure of confidential information" and that "no person bound to professional secrecy by law. . .may, even in judicial proceedings, disclose confidential information revealed to him by reason of his position or profession, unless he is authorized to do so by the person who confided such information to him or by an express provision of law. . .". These rules arguably also may apply to a banker-customer relationship.

Industry policy to protect policy

The Canadian Bankers' Association (CBA) is an industry associa-   **6-008** tion which represents all the banks operating in Canada. In December 1990, the CBA issued a "Model Privacy Code for Individual Customers", a non-binding policy statement by the CBA which sets out the industry's objectives and practices in the protection of privacy.

The policy statement shows support for the Canadian government's adherence to the Organization for Economic Co-operation and Development (OECD) "Guidelines on the Protection of Privacy and Transborder Flows of Personal Data". While the policy statement is not binding on individual banks, it serves as a basic model for the implementation of a code by individual members of the CBA.

The policy statement is limited in its coverage to "personal information", which includes the identity and relevant personal credit and financial information of an individual. It recites that "banks preserve carefully the confidentiality of the banker-customer relationship". It further enumerates the circumstances in which disclosure of personal information may be made to third parties. The exceptions are drawn from the *Tournier* decision which is discussed in the following section of this chapter.

---

[23] L'Heureux, L., *Le Droit Bancaire*, Les Editions Revue du Droit. Université de Sherbrooke, Sherbrooke, 1988, at pp. 30-31 and 60-61.
[24] R.S.Q., chap. C-12. section 5.

Is prospective customer or borrower also protected by secrecy?

6-009   There are two features to this question. First, does a one-time borrower enjoy the same benefits of banker secrecy as does a continuing client of the bank such as the client in *Tournier*? Second, does a prospective customer, who may never in fact consummate a transaction with the bank, enjoy the right of secrecy? The answer to both questions is yes.

First, there is no doubt that the standard of confidentiality applied in relation to bank customers as creditors of the bank also applies to borrowers from a bank. *Tournier* itself concerned information about a customer's indebtedness to the bank, in addition to extrinsic information about the plaintiff's payment to a bookmaker.

Second, the reasoning of *Tournier*, which relies on the presumed intentions of the contracting parties, applies equally to all those who reveal information to a bank in contemplation of the creation of some financial contractual relationship. The fact that the relationship may not materialize does not affect the existence of the obligation, since the state of mind of the bank and the customer is the same whether or not a transaction is ultimately consummated. One could say that the bank impliedly agrees to keep secret the prospective customer's information in consideration for the chance of gaining the custom of the prospective customer.

A prospective borrower from a bank also will be owed fiduciary duties by the bank, if the circumstances are such as to create a fiduciary relation between a bank and the prospective borrower. Thus, in *Woods* v. *Martins Banks Ltd.*,[25] a bank gave investment advice to a person who later opened an account at the bank. The court was of the view that the person was a customer of the bank when the advice was given, but went on to say that even if it was wrong in this view, the bank nevertheless owed to potential customers the same duty to exercise ordinary skill and care that it owed to actual customers.[26]

By the same reasoning, disclosure of confidential information relating to a prospective customer in such a situation would amount to a breach of the banker's fiduciary duty.

Where a customer gives the bank certain confidential information (beyond simply opening an account, for example), the bank may find itself no longer simply owing the customer a duty of

[25] *Woods* v. *Martins Banks Ltd.* [1959] 1 Q.B. 55, at p. 63, [1958] 3 All E.R. 166, at p. 173, approved, *Warren Metals Ltd.* v. *Colonial Catering Co. Ltd.* [1975] N.Z.L.R. 273.

[26] *Woods* v. *Martins Banks Ltd.* [1959] 1 Q.B. 55, at p. 63, [1958] 3 All E.R. 166, at p. 172.

non-disclosure but also a fiduciary duty to disclose any conflicts of interest it may have or decline the customer's business and, in any event, not to misuse the information.

Thus, in the leading Canadian case of *Standard Investments Ltd. et. al.* v. *Canadian Imperial Bank of Commerce,*[27] the plaintiffs "bared their souls" to the bank by revealing their plans to take over a trust company. This company was, unbeknownst to the plaintiffs, also a customer of the bank. The bank had recently purchased for its own account a 10 percent stake in the trust company to help prevent a takeover attempt which it was rumored might be made by the plaintiffs.

The plaintiffs, in revealing this information to the bank, had subsequently relied upon the bank for advice. The bank was aware of that reliance. The Ontario Court of Appeal therefore found that a fiduciary relationship existed between the bank and the plaintiffs. The existence of a fiduciary relationship triggered an obligation on the bank either to disclose its conflict of interest to the plaintiffs, or to refuse to advise them. The failure of the bank to do either of these things made it liable for damages.

This additional fiduciary duty will not arise unless there is an element of special confidence or reliance placed by the customer on advice given by the bank, that changes the character of the relationship between the bank and the customer to something more than just a debtor-creditor relationship. There must be "special circumstances".[28]

These circumstances include reliance by the customer on advice given by the bank, awareness by the bank of the reliance placed on it, the possibility of the bank benefiting from the transaction or relationship, and "confidentiality," which refers to an "extra quality", "beyond . . . the confidence that can well exist between trustworthy persons" who deal at arm's length.[29]

Where a fiduciary relationship exists, the fact that the confidential information has entered the public realm makes no difference to the continuing fiduciary duties of the bank toward the customer.[30] In contrast, the implied contractual duty of secrecy disappears once the information has entered the public realm since, after this point, the customer would suffer no injury from the bank's disclosure.

---

27 *Standard Investments Ltd. et. al.* v. *Canadian Imperial Bank of Commerce* [1985] 52 O.R. (2d) 473 (C.A.), leave to appeal refused, [1986] O.R. (2d) 663 n. (S.C.C.).

28 *Standard Investments Ltd. et. al.* v. *Canadian Imperial Bank of Commerce* [1985] 52 O.R. (2d) 473 (C.A.), n. 10 at p. 495, quoting the trial judge, with whom the court concurred on this point.

29 *Id.*, at p. 496, citing *Lloyds Bank Ltd.* v. *Bundy*, [1975] Q.B. 326.

30 *Id.*, at p. 503.

Where no fiduciary relationship exists, a bank would not be liable to a customer on Common Law principles for using confidential information relating to a customer on its own account. Such use, in contrast to disclosure of the information, would breach no implied term of the debtor-creditor relationship between the parties.

However, other laws may be broken. For example, a bank which trades in shares of the customer based on non-public material facts derived from that customer would be in breach of Canadian insider trading laws.

When does duty of secrecy terminate?

6-010   In *Tournier*, Bankes L.J. held as follows:

> "I certainly think that the duty does not cease the moment a customer closes his account. Information gained during the currency of the account remains confidential unless released under circumstances bringing the case within one of the classes of qualification I have already referred to."[31]

The bank, in other words, has no right to release information about a customer until the customer expressly or impliedly consents to the release, or until some rule of law, either under the exceptions set out in *Tournier* or under statutory provisions, compels disclosure.

WHEN IS DISCLOSURE PERMITTED?

6-011   The *Tournier* decision, as previously stated, is the leading case in Canada with respect to the issue of the duty of banks to keep information about their customers' business confidential. The English Court of Appeal was unanimous in holding that the source of such a duty is an implied incident or term of the contract giving rise to the relationship between a bank and its customer.

Clearly, it was the desire of the English Court of Appeal to enunciate a rule of general application to the banking relationship since, on the facts of the case, the court might have held that such a duty arises only where the contract between a bank and its customer contains an express term to such effect.

---

[31] *Tournier v. National Provincial and Union Bank of England, supra* n. 13, at p. 473.

Having concluded that, unless excluded by the parties, every contract between a bank and its customer contains either as an express or as an implied term the duty of confidentiality or secrecy on the part of the bank, each member of the court stressed that such a duty was not absolute but qualified and that it was not possible to frame any exhaustive definition of the duty.[32]

The *Tournier* case also remains as authority for the four general situations which the English Court of Appeal identified within which the banker is no longer bound to his contractual or legal duty of confidentiality and may disclose to third parties information regarding his customer's affairs. These four situations are summarized concisely by Bankes L.J. as follows:

(1) Where there is a duty to the public to disclose;
(2) Where the interest of the bank requires disclosure;
(3) Where the disclosure is made with the express or implied consent of the customer, and
(4) Where disclosure is under compulsion by law.[33]

Canadian law recognizes these four situations as the exceptions to the rule calling for the duty of banks to hold secret the affairs of their customers. As well, Canadian courts, when confronted with the issue of disclosure by a bank of its customer's affairs, have considered the facts in question to see whether such disclosure falls under one of the qualifications raised in the *Tournier* decision. Let us examine each of these qualifications in turn as they have been considered in Canada.

Public duty to disclose

In Canada, where a banker has direct knowledge of criminal activ- **6-012** ity such as fraud, such banker is free and probably obliged to disclose it to the appropriate authority. However, unfounded suspicion of wrongdoing, communicated to persons other than the police, will constitute a breach of the duty of secrecy. Moreover, if disclosure is made and either no charges are laid or charges are dismissed, a bank could, subject to a recent amendment to the Criminal Code[34]

---

[32] *Id., per* Bankes L.J., at p. 472; *per* Scrutton L.J., at pp. 480–481; *per* Atkin L.J., at p. 484.
[33] *Id.,* at p. 473.
[34] R.S.C. 1985, chap. C-46, section 462.47.

referred to below, find itself liable for damages for breach of the duty of secrecy or even liable for slander.[35]

The exception in *Tournier* encompassed within the public duty to disclose has been considered primarily in Canada in the context of the disclosure of information in the hands of a liquidator of a failed financial institution.

One of the instances in Canada where the duty to the public exception has been raised is in *Canada Deposit Insurance Corp.* v. *Canadian Commercial Bank.*[36] The case involved an application by the Canada Deposit Insurance Corporation (CDIC) and the Government of Canada, as petitioners, for an order directing the Canadian Commercial Bank (CCB) to provide them with access to and production of certain documents. The CCB had been the object of a liquidation order subsequent to which the petitioners had paid in excess of one billion dollars to creditors of the CCB.

In this context, the petitioners took legal action against former officers and directors of the CCB. To pursue their litigation, they needed documents then in the possession of the liquidator of the CCB. The petitioners alleged that it was in the public interest to allow complete access to documents relating to the CCB in order that they might seek recovery of the money paid by them to the CCB's depositors.

This contention was in part grounded on the "public duty" qualification raised in *Tournier*. The court granted the order sought, stating that there was "an overriding public interest" requiring disclosure "on a broader basis than would be obtainable by way of discovery of documents in the possession of a third party".[37]

While the precise basis for the court's decision is not clear, the decision was based upon the *Tournier* decision, certain federal legislative provisions and the Alberta rules of court.

The *CDIC* v. *CCB* case was considered and applied in a recent decision of the British Columbia Court of Appeal in *Surrey Credit Union* v. *Willson.*[38] This decision involved a similar application to

---

35 J.T. Burnett, "The Banker's Duty of Confidentiality", *Insight Banking Law and Practice* (1984), pp. 17-18, reports the American case in which a young banker in the State of Maryland, certain that he had uncovered criminal activity by observing various transactions in an account, advised the police who then proceeded to harass the customer. Ultimately, it was discovered that the transactions in question were legitimate. The customer sued the bank and was awarded US $50,000 in damages. (*Suburban Trust* v. *Haller* 408 A. 2d 758 (Maryland C.A., 1979)).

36 *Canadian Deposit Insurance Corp.* v. *Canadian Commercial Bank* [1989] A.J. No. 44, No. 8503-23319, (Alta Q.B.); (1989) 64 Alta L.R. (2d) 329; 71 C.B.R. (N.S.) 239; 95 A.R. 24.

37 *Id.*, 71 C.B.R. 239, at p. 244.

38 *Surrey Credit Union* v. *Willson* [1990] 79 C.B.R. 24.

have information in the hands of a liquidator of a failed bank disclosed in a civil proceeding against the bank's directors and others. The Appeal Court upheld the decision of the trial judge allowing the production of the documents based upon provincial subpoena legislation and the rules of court.

In *Glover v. Glover (No. 2)*,[39] a telephone company (Bell Canada) sought to quash a court order compelling it to produce telephone records which would establish the whereabouts of an absconding spouse. The court considered whether there "would be any real prejudice to the public interest" if such records were produced. It held that it could not order a third party to provide information concerning a party to an action by delivering to the court documents which might turn out not to contain any relevant information, particularly when such information was commonly regarded as confidential.

The dissenting judge, relying on the *Tournier* decision, felt however that the duty of confidentiality "owed by Bell Canada . . . must give way in this case to the paramount public interest in the enforcement of custody orders affecting the well-being of children"[40] and would have ordered the release by Bell Canada of its records. In drawing an analogy with the situation of a banker, it is apparent that there is a great deal of subjectivity involved in the determination of when a public duty may supersede a private duty of confidentiality.

The issue of the public duty to disclose has been simplified by the introduction of money-laundering legislation and legislation relating to evidence which relieves the banker from having to decide whether he must disclose information in relation to a customer in circumstances where "danger to the State or public duty"[41] is involved. Such legislation, as it exists in Canada, is described in the context of the fourth exception, namely, where disclosure is under compulsion by law.

Bank's own interest

As recognized in the *Tournier* decision, a bank is not bound by its **6-013** duty of confidentiality when it is in its interest to disclose its customer's affairs. This is clearly the situation when a bank is suing to

---

[39] *Glover v. Glover* (1981) 29 O.R. (2d) 401 (Ont. C.A.).

[40] *Id., per* Wilson J.A., at pp. 410-411.

[41] First *Calgary Financial Savings and Credit Union Ltd.* v. *Meadow and Meadows, supra* n. 11, *per* Bankes L.J., at p. 473, quoting Lord Finlay in *Weld-Blundell* v. *Stephens* [1920] A.C. 956, at p. 965.

recover monies owing to it by its customer or to enforce its security, or when a bank is sued by its customer.

Furthermore, a bank may be justified in disclosing information about a customer's affairs when the customer in question has made public statements concerning its transactions with the bank. In such circumstances, a bank is entitled to set the record straight in order to protect its public reputation.[42]

A recent example of disclosure, when recovering a debt owed by a customer, is the case of the British Columbia Supreme Court in *Canadian Imperial Bank of Commerce* v. *Sayani*.[43] The court relied upon this particular exception in *Tournier* to allow a solicitor acting for the bank to reveal the existence of a dispute involving the bank's customer to a third party in order to protect the interests of his client bank in collecting on its debt. The disclosure was made before the matter had become public by way of court litigation.

While the *Sayani* decision would appear to expand this exception by permitting disclosure at an earlier time than commencement of the litigation process, the disclosure which was made was limited in that no details were provided to the third party of the amount or circumstances of the account or even of the identity of the bank involved in the dispute.

Where a bank is a third party to a proceeding, this exception would not necessarily apply unless disclosure could fall under another classification, such as the public duty or compulsion by law exceptions.

Customer's consent

6-014   The third exception raised in *Tournier* allows for disclosure where the customer has authorized the release of information in respect of

---

[42] *See* Crawford and Falconbridge, *Banking and Bills of Exchange*, 8th ed. (Toronto, Canada, Law Book Inc., 1986), Volume 1, p. 813. An example arose of newspaper coverage in a Canadian national newspaper (*The Globe and Mail*, December 15, 1981, p. CL-1) of a customer of a Toronto bank, with personal loans of about one million dollars, who drew public attention to his allegation of unfair dealings by his bank by dumping on the steps of the bank the carcasses of several cows that he alleged had died of starvation. The bank, in response to heavy public criticism for its apparently insensitive treatment of the customer, released information which resulted in deflecting much criticism. It is said that such a situation is one in which the interest of the bank becomes a consideration. The case law canvassing the scope of the defense of fair comment on a matter of public interest, which may be raised in actions of defamation, provides a sensible analogy.

[43] Unreported. Vancouver Registry, Case No. C886400, November 19, 1991.

its affairs. There is little Canadian authority on this exception. The obvious example is when a customer has given, to establish its credit-worthiness or character, its banker as a reference.

It may be argued that, when a banker has been called upon to give credit information about its customer without having been asked specifically by its customer to do so, the banker may disclose such information on the basis of the customer's implicit consent to do so.[44]

That being said, a banker should, in all circumstances, be cautious in releasing any information about its customer's affairs without the customer's explicit consent.[45] In particular, a court might refuse to hold that a customer gave its implied consent to have information in respect of its financial situation disclosed if such information were found to be negative and its release jeopardized the customer's credibility or otherwise caused damage to its affairs. In such a situation, a bank, clearly, would be best to obtain the express authorization of its customer prior to releasing any such information.

Several provinces in Canada have consumer credit reporting laws which require the written consent of the customer in a credit application to the obtaining of a consumer report from a credit bureau by a lender for use in connection with the credit application. Although it is not clear whether such laws may apply to banks, bankers are prudent in respecting such provincial legislation. Accordingly, a form of consent to the release of information is generally incorporated in certain bank standard forms, such as applications for credit.

---

[44] *First Calgary Financial Savings and Credit Union Ltd.* v. *Meadow and Meadows, supra* n. 11, *per* Atkin L.J., at p. 486.

[45] In *Hull* v. *Childs and the Huron and Erie Mortgage Corporation* (1951) O.W.N. 116 (H.C.J.), the plaintiff, about to undergo a serious operation from which he believed he would not recover, had signed a number of checks in blank to the order of three of his relatives so that they would be able to cover his funeral expenses and their own expenses in attending the funeral. The plaintiff recovered from his illness and learned that his account had been closed, his bank manager having revealed the full amount left in his account to the three relatives in question who emptied the account. The plaintiff took action against one of the relatives and the bank. The court held that the bank had breached its duty of confidentiality on the basis that the mere signing of a check in blank could not impute to the signer the desire that the amount in his account be made known to whoever presented the instrument. However, on the facts of the case, the Court felt that the breach was not the cause of the loss sustained by the plaintiff. The action against the bank was therefore dismissed without costs but maintained against the other defendant. Clearly, the customer's implied consent to having certain information revealed about his account does not extend to all information related thereto.

Disclosure by legal compulsion

6-015 The fourth category of authorized disclosure contemplated by the *Tournier* decision is that which is made under compulsion by law. This disclosure entails the banker being directed, generally by way of a court order or other legal directive, to disclose secret information. The legal basis for disclosure is extensive and is detailed below.

STATUTORY DISCLOSURE REQUIREMENTS

6-016 A multitude of federal and provincial laws can impact on the banker's duty of secrecy. While this chapter is not designed to be a complete compendium of such legislation, some of the primary legislation is detailed in this section. Our review of the primary legislation focuses on four disclosure areas. These areas are statutory provisions and court procedural rules relating to the provision of evidence in legal proceedings, laws relating to the enforcement of taxation statutes, laws requiring disclosure in a bankruptcy context, and money laundering and record-keeping requirements.

Laws relating to provision of evidence in legal proceedings

6-017 There are federal and provincial statutes which generally provide that a bank must disclose records in its possession where the records are required as evidence in the course of civil, criminal or arbitral proceedings not involving the bank. However, a court order is usually required before the bank can be compelled either to appear as a witness or to produce a customer's records.

An example is the Evidence Act (Canada).[46] The provisions in the Evidence Act (Canada) ensure that bank records are not seized every time one of its customers is in litigation. These provisions take precedence over the Criminal Code (Canada) which permits seizure of records where there are reasonable grounds to believe the records will afford evidence of the commission of an offense.[47]

There is also provincial legislation such as the Subpoena (Interprovincial) Act[48] which permits parties to a proceeding, under the authority of a court, to compel the appearance of witnesses and the

[46] R.S.C. 1985, chap. C-5, section 29(5).
[47] *R. v. Mowat, ex parte Toronto Dominion Bank* [1967] 1 O.R. 179 (Ont. H.C.J.).
[48] R.S.B.C. 1979, chap. 396, as amended.

production of documents in a legal proceeding. This particular statute was considered in the case of *Surrey Credit Union* v. *Willson*, referred to above.

Enforcement of tax statutes

Canadian federal and provincial taxing statutes generally provide investigatory powers to the taxing authorities to enable them to administer and enforce tax legislation. As a result of the separation of powers in Canada there are taxing statutes at both the federal and provincial level. The provisions vary but generally entail rights to require information from third parties, including financial institutions and various search and seizure powers. **6-018**

The Canadian Income Tax Act[49] permits Revenue Canada, for the purpose of the administration or enforcement of the Income Tax Act, to examine a third party's books and records, including bank accounts and statements if they relate to a taxpayer. Revenue Canada also may require the third party who has custody or ownership of the books and records to provide reasonable assistance and answer any proper questions.

Therefore, a bank may be required to provide to Revenue Canada for inspection a customer's bank records and respond to inquiries on the customer's transactions. These provisions have been interpreted to mean that a bank can be required to disclose records of transactions, even if the result would mean disclosing private information of the bank's customers who are not themselves under investigation.[50]

Revenue Canada recognizes that proceedings taken by its officials in seeking information from financial institutions may have serious effects on a taxpayer's relationship with its financial institution. The information is generally requested by the issue by Revenue Canada of a "Requirement to Provide Information" under the authority of the Income Tax Act.

The information requested must be relevant to the administration or enforcement of the Income Tax Act. As a result of the potentially serious effects on taxpayers, Revenue Canada's policy is to closely control the use of the "Requirement to Provide Information". These are used by Revenue Canada generally for the following cases and proceedings:

[49] R.S.C. 1985, as amended, section 231.1.
[50] *Canadian Bank of Commerce* v. *A-G of Canada* [1962] 35 D.L.R. (2nd) 49 (S.C.C.).

(1) Cases involving fraud;

(2) Tax avoidance cases;

(3) Significant cases where the taxpayer refuses to permit examination of his bank accounts and where the bank information is essential to the case, and

(4) Collection proceedings where the taxpayer is using evasive tactics.

Bankruptcy laws

6-019 The Constitution Act reserves to the federal parliament the exclusive legislative authority over bankruptcy and insolvency.[51] The federal government has, in pursuance of such power, passed the Bankruptcy and Insolvency Act (Canada).[52] The Bankruptcy Act (Canada) vests powers in and exercisable by a trustee in bankruptcy relating to the bankrupt and its affairs including the power to examine under oath "any person reasonably thought to have knowledge of the affairs of a bankrupt". The trustee has the power to compel the production of documents, correspondence or papers.[53] This provision is intended to assist the trustee in carrying out his duty to administer the bankrupt's estate.

Similarly, the court may, on application of any creditor or other interested person, require such examination or disclosure of documents.[54] Such provision was recently used by a bank creditor who was successful in obtaining a court order permitting the questioning of wives of two bankrupts and requiring the production of "banking and investment records" of other financial institutions.[55]

Money laundering and record-keeping requirements

6-020 Canada is a member of the G-7 group of nations. As such and like the other G-7 members, it has enacted laws and taken initiatives which seek to control money laundering in Canada. These laws and initiatives have a direct impact on the banker's duty of secrecy.

[51] Section 91(21).

[52] Originally passed in 1919, the most recent version is R.S.C. 1985, chap. B-3, but amended in 1992. Certain provisions of the 1992 amendment were not yet in force, but none of those provisions affect this chapter.

[53] Bankruptcy and Insolvency Act, sections 163 and 164.

[54] *Id.*, section 163(2).

[55] *Royal Bank v. Oliver*, [1991] 5 W.W.R. 281, Saskatchewan Queen's Bench, Osborn J., June 12, 1991.

Money laundering legislation

Canada's most significant measure to prevent money laundering 6-021
was the enactment on January 1, 1989, of amendments to the Canadian Criminal Code,[56] the Food and Drugs Act,[57] and the Narcotic
Control Act.[58] These amendments made money laundering a criminal offence and provided for confiscation of proceeds of crime,
including intangible property, benefits, and advantages. In addition, the law expanded police search and seizure powers and extended protection to informants from both civil and criminal
liability.

The offense of laundering the proceeds of crime is committed
when a person "uses, transfers the possession of, sends or . . .
otherwise deals with . . . any property or any proceeds of any
property with intent to conceal or convert that property or those
proceeds" and knowing the property to be derived directly or
indirectly from certain illegal activities. The illegal activities are
known as "enterprise crime offenses" or "designated drug offenses".

"Enterprise crime offenses" include a wide array of offenses such
as bribery, fraud, secret commission and illegal gambling. "Designated drug offenses" include trafficking in restricted or controlled
drugs, and importing, cultivating or trafficking in narcotics,
whether inside or outside Canada.

There is a further offense of possession of property or proceeds
knowing they were obtained or derived from drug trafficking.

This proceeds-of crime-legislation impacts directly on the duty
of confidentiality owed by a bank to its customers concerning the
client's identity and disclosure of his financial affairs and the duty
to report suspected criminal activity to the police. The legislation
does not create a positive obligation on a financial institution to
report a suspicious transaction to the authorities.

However, in making a disclosure of facts which give rise to a
suspicion that any property is the proceeds of a crime or that a crime
is or is about to be committed, the financial institution may rely on

---

[56] Criminal Code, R.S.C. 1985, chap. C-46, Part XII.2, "Proceeds of Crime", sections
462.3 to 462.5.

[57] Food and Drugs Act, R.S.C. 1985, chap. F-27, as amended, sections 44.2 and
44.3.

[58] Narcotic Control Act, R.S.C. 1985, chap. N-1, as amended, sections 19.1 and
19.2.

the statutory protection in the Criminal Code (Canada). This provision is a significant statutory exception to the duty of secrecy. It provides as follows:

> "No Civil or Criminal Liability Incurred by Informants.
>
> "462.47 For greater certainty but subject to section 241 of the Income Tax Act,[59] a person is justified in disclosing to a peace officer or the Attorney General any facts on the basis of which that person reasonably suspects that any property is proceeds of crime or that any person has committed or is about to commit an enterprise crime offense or a designated drug offense."

There has not been any reported decision thus far on the application of this section. The section has been carefully worded so as to avoid any infringement on the provincial domain of property and civil rights. As such it does not contain a clear statement that no civil liability will attach. To determine whether a reasonable suspicion is justified, informants would presumably rely on policies of the financial institutions and of the regulatory bodies, such as those detailed in the text below.

The financial institution also would rely on the recognized exception for public duty disclosure referred to above.

Record-keeping legislation

6-022   On October 1, 1991, the Canadian federal government proclaimed in force the Proceeds of Crime (Money Laundering) Act.[60] The statute is record-keeping legislation by which financial institutions operating in Canada will be required to keep and retain adequate records to assist law enforcement authorities in investigating and prosecuting the money-laundering offenses described above.

The effect of the new record-keeping legislation is to require the retention of specified records for specified periods. Certain designated groups of financial institutions including banks, trust and

---

[59] Section 241 of the Income Tax Act (Canada) imposes an obligation on government officials which restricts their communication of information received under that Act. Disclosure is permitted where the officials are required to disclose in a legal proceeding or criminal prosecution under certain conditions detailed in the legislation. A more detailed review of this legislation is found in Edwin G. Kroft, "Disclosure to and by Revenue Canada", Canadian Tax Foundation (B.C. Tax Conference, 1991).

[60] S.C. 1991, c. 26.

insurance companies must keep and retain records relating to financial activities. The Proceeds of Crime Act (Canada) empowers the federal cabinet to make detailed regulations, including regulations requiring measures to ascertain the identity of persons with whom the financial institution is dealing.

The details of the types of records, retention periods, and verification procedures are to be contained in regulations issued by the federal government. Drafts of the regulations have been[61] published under the authority of this new legislation. The draft regulations were to become effective in late 1992.

The Proceeds of Crime Act (Canada) applies to banks, credit unions, *caisses populaires*, and loan, life insurance, and trust companies, whether federally or provincially incorporated. It also applies to other non-bank financial institutions, including securities dealers, portfolio managers, and persons engaged in the business of foreign exchange dealing. The Canadian federal government also can, by regulation, expand the record-keeping requirements to other businesses and activities as well as to professions, such as lawyers and accountants.

When formally promulgated, the regulations will specify in detail the records which the designated institutions must maintain as well as the minimum period of retention. The minimum retention period is expected to be at least five years from closure of accounts in the case of account documentation and from the creation of the documents in all other cases. The records to be kept by the designated institutions will vary according to the type of institution.

Deposit-taking institutions, such as banks, credit unions, and loan and trust companies, will be required to keep signature cards, account operating agreements, account statements, and customer credit files. A customer credit file will include the documents relating to a credit arrangement, such as credit applications, approvals, and lending documents, as well as all documents establishing the identity and financial capacity of the financial institution's client.

Businesses dealing in foreign exchange transactions must also retain transaction records. Securities dealers must keep information concerning trade confirmations and authorizations. Life insurance companies are required to keep all client application forms for annuities and products containing significant investment components.

All institutions which are subject to the Proceeds of Crime Act (Canada) must keep "large cash transaction records". These are defined as records of the receipt of cash of Cdn. $10,000 or more.

[61] Proposed "Regulations to Combat the Laundering of Proceeds of Crime" were published on June 13, 1992, in draft form. *Canada Gazette*, Part I, at p. 1742.

The records must identify the client name, address, occupation, and nature of business and include such additional information as the customer accounts affected and the amount and currency of the cash received. If the recipient has reasonable grounds to believe the customer is acting on behalf of a third party, then the identity of the third party must be disclosed. There also will be provisions which aggregate a number of smaller cash transactions by the same individual on the same business day.

All institutions will be required to obtain verification of the identity of every individual signing a signature card, every individual conducting a foreign currency transaction in excess of Cdn. $1,000 and every individual carrying out a "large cash transaction", except in respect of a corporate account. The regulations will require identification by way of passport or birth certificate, driver's licence or social insurance card or other similar document.

There is no provision in either the Proceeds of Crime Act (Canada) or anticipated in the Regulations to be issued under this legislation which impacts or will impact directly on the duty of secrecy and confidentiality. However, the legislation and the expected regulations define the nature of the records which must be maintained in respect of customers and which a financial institution will be expected to disclose in reporting transactions under the money laundering offense statutes. Such information can also be compelled to be produced by a judge under the provisions of the Criminal Code (Canada) referred to above.

Policy of the Canadian Superintendent of Financial Institutions

6-023   The central regulatory authority in Canada for banks and other federal financial institutions is the Office of the Superintendent of Financial Institutions (OSFI). OSFI has issued a Policy, effective January 1, 1990, known as "Best Practices for Deterring and Detecting Money Laundering".

The Policy enunciates the Canadian federal regulator's expectations concerning implementation by federally regulated financial institutions of the "Statement of Principles" of the Committee on Banking Regulations and Supervisory Practices of the Bank for International Settlements, published in December 1988, concerning the "Prevention of Criminal Use of the Banking System for the Purposes of Money Laundering".

Canada is a signatory to this document, which calls for stricter customer identification, cooperation with the law enforcement authorities, and training within the financial institutions to detect money laundering.

The Policy requires that specific policies be adopted by federally regulated financial institutions, such as designating an officer responsible for anti-money laundering procedures in each unit, implementing control systems for detection and deterrence of money laundering and record retention procedures.

One of the minimum measures in the Policy is the requirement of referral of suspicious transactions, examples of which are set out in the policy, to the designated officer responsible for anti-money laundering procedures. The designated officer is required to complete a "source of funds declaration" which identifies the customer and the source of cash funds. The referral of suspicious transactions entails divulging information which is subject to the duty of confidentiality, such disclosure being permitted by the Criminal Code (Canada) disclosure provision referred to above.

COURT-ORDERED DISCLOSURE

Disclosure in interests of justice

The *Tournier* case and its four exceptions were approved in a recent **6-024** Alberta decision which decided that disclosure of confidential information by an order of a court fell within the compulsion by law exception in *Tournier*.[62] In this case, there is a hint that there may be developing a fifth category of permissible disclosure of privileged information, that is where "the interest of justice require disclosure". The court permitted the disclosure of the affairs of another bank customer to the non-bank defendant claiming breach of fiduciary duty and conflict of interest against the plaintiff bank.

The decision was easy to reach based on the fact that the customer whose affairs were to be disclosed was insolvent and insolvency proceedings had been concluded. That customer could not suffer any prejudice as a result of the disclosure due to its financial situation. This proposed fifth exception, where the interests of justice require disclosure, has apparently not yet gained judicial acceptance elsewhere in Canada.

---

[62] *Royal Bank of Canada* v. *Art's Welding & Machine Shop Ltd.* [1989] 34 Carswell's Practice Cases (2d), p. 190, Alberta Court of Queen's Bench, Master Breitkreuz, May 26, 1989.

Extra-territorial aspects

6-025   The issue has arisen in Canada as to the conditions under which Canadian courts will require the disclosure of information and records from a foreign bank or from the foreign branches of a Canadian bank.

This issue was recently considered in the Ontario case of *Comaplex Resources International* v. *Schaffhauser Kantonalbank.*[63] The motion before Master Sandler of the Ontario High Court of Justice was whether a representative of the defendant bank should be required to produce documents and answer questions concerning the bank's customers in an examination for discovery in a civil action in Ontario.

Invocation of Swiss law

6-026   The issue considered was whether the Swiss banking secrecy laws, which apparently prohibited disclosure by the defendant bank of such documents and information, could form a valid basis for the defendant bank's refusal to answer the questions and produce the documents in Canada.

The Ontario Master considered a number of American cases as well as two previous Canadian cases. Canadian judicial authority has thus far been inconsistent. The primary Canadian cases include the civil case of *Frischke* v. *Royal Bank of Canada*[64] and the criminal case of *Spencer* v. *The Queen.*[65]

In the *Frischke* case, the Ontario Court of Appeal refused to compel the Royal Bank of Canada and two of its employees to inform themselves about information which would have required the Royal Bank of Canada to disclose information contrary to Panamanian laws. On the other hand, in the *Spencer* case, the Supreme Court of Canada required disclosure by a Royal Bank of Canada employee, now living in Canada, of the affairs of the bank's customer in the Bahamas even though that disclosure was a breach of Bahamian law.

---

63 *Compalex Resources International* v. *Schaffhauser Kantonalbank* [1989] 42 C.P.C. (2d) 230.

64 *Frischke* v. *Royal Bank of Canada* [1977], 80 D.L.R. (3rd) 393.

65 *Re Spencer and The Queen* (1983) 145 D.L.R. (3rd) 344 (Ontario Court of Appeal), affirmed [1985], 21 D.L.R. (4th) 756 (Supreme Court of Canada).

The court decided that the giving of evidence in Canada was a right of the courts and the public and the fact that giving the evidence in Canada constituted a crime in the Bahamas did not permit a witness to refuse to testify.

Frischke and Spencer distinguished

In the *Comaplex* case, the Ontario master decided that these two **6-027** Canadian cases were not applicable to the situation he was required to consider. He distinguished the *Frischke* case on the basis that the bank was not really a litigant but was involved in the case to effectuate an injunction application. In the *Comaplex* case, the bank was a party to the litigation.

The master distinguished the *Spencer* case on the basis that the information sought was really only in the memory of the bank witness. However, in the case before him, the information and documents requested were in Switzerland.

The master based his decision on United States cases which have held that, procedurally, a person should not be permitted to invoke foreign law prohibitions against the disclosure of information in an application to compel the disclosure. Rather, the objection should only be raised at the time that the court is considering sanctions for breach of an order to disclose.

He, therefore, ruled that the defendant bank in this case was required to disclose information relating to the identity of certain customers of the bank and details of their dealings with and at the bank, even though this information was confidential information under the laws governing the bank in Switzerland and that such disclosure would expose the bank and its representatives to criminal and civil sanction under the laws of Switzerland.

Further proceeding

An appeal on this issue was dismissed by consent of the parties. On **6-028** a subsequent motion, the master required disclosure of the names of the bank's customers. In a further proceeding, the Ontario Court of Justice[66] had to weigh conflicting evidence as to whether Swiss bank secrecy laws prohibited disclosure of the identity of the bank's customers and, if so, whether such laws relieve the bank of its obligations not to disclose such information.

[66] [1991] Ontario Judgments No. 1643, Action No. 33378/88. Judgment, October 2, 1991.

Justice Southey found as a fact that the Swiss bank secrecy laws did not prohibit disclosing the customers' identity. He could not then excuse the bank in Ontario from divulging information which the bank would be obliged to divulge in Switzerland.

If the decision of the Ontario master is applied by other Canadian courts, the result in Canada could be a trend to bring banks into civil actions more frequently in order to require disclosure of confidential information whether or not such information is protected by secrecy laws of other countries.

CONCLUSION

6-029 In Canada, the need for the protection of confidential information has, in recent years, received heightened awareness and concern both by the courts and by the financial services industry. However, one of the significant examples illustrating this heightened awareness does not come from the financial services industry.

The example is the Supreme Court of Canada's leading pronouncement on fiduciary duty and confidential information in *Lac Minerals* v. *International Corona Resources*,[67] which dealt with the disclosure of information made by a business entity in a mine development context.

Although not a case which deals with financial institutions, it has resulted in much discussion both because of the monetary significance of the case and the extent to which courts will protect confidential information generally. Another example is the model Privacy Code for individual customers, issued by the Canadian Bankers' Association and referred to above.

Balancing this heightened awareness are the legislative encroachments into bank secrecy made by government, particularly in the tax and money laundering areas.

---

[67] *Lac Minerals* v. *International Corona Resources* 61 D.L.R. (4th) 14 (S.C.C.).

These initiatives appear to be accepted in Canada as they represent intrusions into bank secrecy for justifiable public policy reasons. In this context, they should not be seen as a trend to a lessening of the duty of secrecy imposed on financial institutions in Canada.[68]

NOTE: Osler Renault Ladner is an international partnership of three Canadian law firms: Osler, Hoskin & Harcourt of Toronto, Ontario, Ogilvy Renault of Montreal, Quebec, and Ladner Downs of Vancouver, British Columbia.

[68] The International Financial Business (Tax Refund) Act, B.C. 1988, c. 17 (the "B.C. IFB Act") presents another example of statutes imposing duties on administrative officials. Each of the metropolitan areas of Vancouver, B.C., and Montreal, Quebec, have been designated by the Canadian Federal government under the Income Tax Act as International Banking Centres entitling eligible financial institutions to income tax relief for certain international banking center business. The provinces of Quebec and British Columbia in which those cities are located have also enacted complementary legislation providing deductions or refunds for a broader range of eligible international financial activities carried on by registered international financial centre businesses, primarily with non-resident persons. Many Canadian banks, foreign bank subsidiaries operating in those provinces, and other financial institutions are registered for these tax benefits. The B.C. IFB Act is the provincial legislation which creates the tax refund for B.C. income taxes otherwise payable in respect of these international financial activities. Section 17 of the B.C. IFB Act imposes a statutory duty of secrecy on any person who has custody or control over information or records under the B.C. IFB Act. Such a person must not disclose the information or records, except in the course of the administration or enforcement of the B.C. IFB Act or in court proceedings relating thereto. The name of any registered financial institution may also be disclosed. Records are broadly defined to include books, documents, letters, vouchers and anything on which information is recorded or stored by any means. We interpret such provision to extend to the international clients and transactions which are recorded in the books of the IFC business. While it is clear that such secrecy provision extends to government officials who are responsible for the administration or enforcement of the B.C. IFB Act, the provision appears to be sufficiently broad in scope as to also impose a statutory duty of secrecy on employees of the financial institution who have custody or control of the records at the financial institution.

CHAPTER 7

THE CAYMAN ISLANDS

W. S. Walker
W. S. Walker & Company
George Town, Grand Cayman

Chapter 7

THE CAYMAN ISLANDS

INTRODUCTION

The Cayman Islands, which are a British Dependent Territory situated in the North West Caribbean, are a major international financial and banking center.   **7-001**

There are approximately 547 banks licensed by the Cayman Government and operating in the Islands, and all banks licensed in the Cayman Islands (whether or not they operate their own office in the Island and whether a branch or subsidiary) are subject to the secrecy requirements of the Islands. There are three types of banking license.

Category "A" license

A Category "A" banking license allows a bank to carry on local and international business from within the Cayman Islands. There are approximately 31 Category "A" licenses in existence.   **7-002**

Most Category "A" licenses operate their own fully staffed offices in the Islands and are branches, subsidiaries, or affiliates of international banks.

Category "B" license

A Category "B" license (which includes the majority of the banks licensed in the Islands) allows a bank to carry on banking business anywhere in the world from within the Cayman Islands and with non-resident persons and non-resident companies within the Cayman Islands.   **7-003**

A number of these licenses operate their own fully staffed offices in the Islands, but most use the facilities of a Category "A" licensee.

Category "B" restricted license

7-004　A Category "B" restricted license is a restricted form under which the bank may carry on business with a small number of named clients. This is intended for private in-house banks which function as part of an international corporate structure.

　　As in the case of Category "B" unrestricted licenses, most Category "B" restricted licensees operate through a Category "A" licensee.

SECRECY REQUIREMENTS

7-005　Bank secrecy in the Cayman Islands is governed by both statute and decided cases.

Banks and Trusts Companies Law, 1989

7-006　The Banks and Trust Companies Law, 1989,[1] provides for the preservation of secrecy on the part of the Inspector of Banks and Trust Companies and any person authorized to assist him in his functions.

　　It prohibits the disclosure of any information, by the Inspector or his staff, of the affairs of a licensee or any customer of a licensee and provides a penalty of a fine not exceeding CI $10,000, or a term of imprisonment not exceeding one year, or both for contravention of this law.

Confidential Relationships (Preservation) Law, 1976

7-007　The Confidential Relationships (Preservation) Law, 1976,[2] as amended, provides that, if any person in possession of confidential information, however obtained, divulges it or attempts, offers, or threatens to divulge it to any person not entitled to possession, or who willfully obtains or attempts to obtain confidential information

---

[1] The Banks and Trust Companies Law, 1989 (Law 4 of 1989 of the Laws of the Cayman Islands).

[2] The Confidential Relationship (Preservation) Law, 1976 (Law 16 of 1976 of the Laws of the Cayman Islands); The Confidential Relationships (Preservation) (Amendment) Law 1979 (Law 26 of 1979 of the Laws of the Cayman Islands).

is guilty of an offense and is liable on summary conviction to a fine not exceeding CI $5,000, or for imprisonment of a term not exceeding two years, or both.

In addition, where such person solicits such information for himself or another for reward or being a professional person entrusted with such information, the above-mentioned penalties are doubled.

Section 3(2)(b) of the Law provides a number of cases in which the Law has no application. These are as follows:

(1) Any professional person acting in the normal course of business or with the consent, express or implied, of the relevant principal;

(2) A constable of the rank of Inspector or above investigating an offense committed or alleged to have been committed within the jurisdiction;

(3) A constable of the rank of Inspector or above, specifically authorized by the Governor in that regard, investigating an offense committed or alleged to have been committed outside the Islands which offense, if committed in the Islands, would be an offense against its laws; or

(4) The Financial Secretary, the Inspector or, in relation to particular information specified by the Governor, such other person as the Governor may authorize;

(5) A bank in any proceedings, cause, or matter when and to the extent to which it is reasonably necessary for the protection of the bank's interest, either as against its customers or as against third parties in respect of transactions of the bank for, or with, its customer, and

(6) The relevant professional person with the approval of the Financial Secretary when necessary for the protection of himself or any other person against crime.

The Confidential Relationships (Preservation) Law, 1976, as amended, provides in section 3A that, where it applies (that is, in all cases apart from the six detailed above), the following provisions shall apply:

Whenever a person intends or is required to give in evidence in, or in connection with, any proceeding been tried, inquired into, or determined by any court, tribunal, or other authority (whether within or without the Islands), any confidential information within the meaning of the Law, he shall, before so doing, apply for directions, and any adjournment necessary for that purpose may be granted.

Application for directions under subsection (1) shall be made to, and be heard and determined by, a judge of the Grand Court sitting alone and in camera. At least seven days notice of any such application shall be given to the Attorney General and, if the judge so orders, to any person in the Islands who is a party to the proceedings in question.

The Attorney General may appear as *amicus curiae* at the hearing of any such application, and any party on whom notice has been served as aforesaid shall be entitled to be heard thereon, either personally or by counsel.

Upon hearing an application under subsection (2), a judge shall direct:

(1) That the evidence be given; or
(2) That the evidence shall not be given, or
(3) That the evidence be given subject to conditions which he may specify whereby the confidentiality of the information is safeguarded,

In order to safeguard the confidentiality of a statement, answer, or testimony ordered to be given under subsection (3)(c), a judge may order:

(1) Divulgence of the statement, answer or testimony to be restricted to certain named persons;
(2) Evidence to be taken in camera, and
(3) Reference to the names, addresses, and descriptions of any particular persons to be by alphabetical letters, numbers, or symbols representing such persons, the key to which shall be restricted to persons named by him.

Every person receiving confidential information by operation of subsection (2) is as fully bound by the provisions of the Law as if such information had been entrusted to him in confidence by a principal.

Normally, where a criminal investigation is involved, the Cayman court will order that the evidence be given, but the order is usually subject to conditions, as the judges are very aware of the necessity for the preservation of general confidentiality.

In most cases, the court orders that accompanying information not necessary for the investigation at hand be blacked out before the evidence is given, in order to ensure that innocent third parties are not implicated.

English Common Law and English cases

Pursuant to the leading English Case of *Tournier* v. *National Provin-* **7-008**
cial and Union Bank of England,[3] which case is declared under The
Confidential Relationships (Preservation) Law, 1976, as amended,
to have application to the Cayman Islands, there is a duty of a
Cayman Bank to preserve the confidentiality of the business of its
customers.

This duty would be the same as would be the duty of a bank in
the United Kingdom and is not derogated from by The Confidential
Relationships (Preservation) Law, 1976, as amended.

Although the decision of *Tournier* v. *National Provincial and Union
Bank of England* dates from 1924, the basic decision is still good law.
Briefly, the case states that there are four cases in which a bank
should disclose information as follows:

(1) Where disclosure is under compulsion by law - Such a case
    would be under the Mutual Legal Assistance Treaty (see
    below) or the Misuse of Drugs Law (of the Cayman Is-
    lands);

(2) Where there is a duty to the public to disclose - Although
    initially the English courts held that the duty to the public
    was somewhat limited, recent cases have expanded this
    duty and, today, the courts support the idea that, in most
    cases, when a serious criminal matter is being investigated
    there is a duty to the public to disclose; this would be the
    case also in the Cayman Islands;

(3) Where the interest of the bank requires disclosure - This
    would normally be when disclosure was necessary in order
    to preserve a bank's legal position, and

(4) Where the disclosure is made by the express or implied
    consent of the customer - The Cayman Islands courts have
    held that the consent of the customer must be voluntary
    and that a consent obtained under duress or obtained un-
    der a threat of further action is not a proper consent and is
    to be disregarded.

---

[3] *Tournier* v. *National Provincial and Union Bank of England* [1924] 1 K.B. 461.

The Mutual Legal Assistance Treaty

7-009   The Mutual Legal Assistance Treaty,[4] signed by the United Kingdom, the United States, and the Cayman Islands, relating to mutual legal assistance in criminal matters (but specifically excluding tax matters and tax enquiries), was signed in 1986 and laid before the British Parliament and subsequently ratified by the United States Senate. It is now in full force and effect.

Pursuant to this Treaty, the Cayman Islands enacted the Mutual Legal Assistance (United States of America) Law, 1986,[5] which is also in effect. This Law provides that the Cayman Mutual Legal Assistance Authority shall be the Chief Justice of the Cayman Islands or another judge designated by the Chief Justice to act on his behalf.

There have been a number of applications to the Chief Justice pursuant to the Treaty (although most relate to matters which took place in the Cayman Islands in past years), and the procedure under the Treaty and Law have been working generally satisfactorily.

The Treaty has been extended to the other British Dependent Territories in the Caribbean (British Virgin Islands, Turks & Caicos Islands, Anguila and Monsterrat), and somewhat similar treaties have been negotiated by the United States with the Bahamas, Panama, and other countries.

CONCLUSION

7-010   The exceptions to the Confidential Relationships (Preservation) Law, 1976, as amended, and to *Tournier v. National Provincial and Union Bank of England* clearly show the determination of the Cayman Islands Government not to allow criminals to hide behind the country's strong secrecy laws.

This effort culminated in the signing of the Mutual Legal Assistance Treaty with the United States. This Treaty reflects the Cayman Governments' continued determination to assist in stamping out international crime and particularly drug dealing and money laundering.

[4] The Treaty between the United States of America and the United Kingdom of Great Britain and Northern Ireland concerning the Cayman Islands relating to Mutual Legal Assistance in Criminal Matters, July 3, 1986.

[5] The Mutual Legal Assistance (United States of America) Law, 1986 (Law 16 of 1986 of the Laws of the Cayman Islands).

The exception in the Treaty to exclude tax matters shows, how-ever, that outside the perimeters of criminal matters, bank secrecy remains effective in the Cayman Islands.

CHAPTER 8

DENMARK

Finn Martensen and Anders Tolborg
Advokaterne Vingardshus
Aalborg, Denmark

Chapter 8

DENMARK

INTRODUCTION

Danish legislation and Danish legal literature have focused little on banking secrecy. This is true even if the topic has, in fact, practical relevance.   **8-001**

The obligation of the bank to not disclose its knowledge regarding its customers traditionally has been an important and leading principle in Denmark. This principle is important due to the fact that it helps to support the relationship of trust between bank and customer. The principle is the main basis for the customer's willingness to give economical and personal information to the bank. The customer must rest assured that such important information is not released to unauthorized persons.

Today, it is indisputable that very important principles in banking secrecy have been weakened. This is partly due to legislative regulation and partly due to the banks' own practices in releasing information regarding creditworthiness of their customers.

In Denmark, four kinds of financial institutions are found, namely banks, saving banks, cooperative banks, and mortgage banks. This chapter will deal only with the first three types of financial institutions, hereafter collaterally referred to as banks. It should be mentioned, however, that mortgage banks, which are rather institutional in nature, never or rarely release information regarding their customers' creditworthiness.

DEFINITION OF BANK SECRECY

Banking secrecy in Denmark has traditionally been defined as follows: "The bank's obligation to keep secure what the customers   **8-002** have entrusted the banks, which should lead to a more specific relationship of trust than what is usual amongst business connections."[1]

This principle of secrecy, which for many years has rested solely on banking usage and practices, was not regulated by any Danish code until 1974 when a rather simplistic regulation was inserted in the Banking Code. The current principle is now found in section 54, subsection 2, of the Code on Banks and Saving Banks (*Bank og Sparekesseloven*),[2] hereafter referred to as the Banking Code of 1991.

The core of section 54, subsection 2, of the Banking Code of 1991 is still that persons who, via their professional position in a bank, obtain knowledge of confidential information regarding bank customers are prohibited from releasing such information. However, a number of exceptions are found.

The fact that banking secrecy in Denmark has survived without being legally regulated until 1974 indicates that the concept has found favor in Denmark, not only seen from the customer's perspective but also from the bank's perspective. Seen from the bank's perspective, maintenance of banking secrecy is requisite for the bank's business. If the customers could not entrust information to the banks, then the customers would tend not to use Danish banks and might instead prefer using foreign banks where banking secrecy would be more strictly upheld.

Such a situation would not be desirable for the Danish banks which, in turn, leads to the result that there has been a mutual interest between customers and banks in upholding the principle of banking secrecy.

The legislative interest in regulating banking secrecy is first due to the point of view that it is advantageous to obtain uniform rules regarding banking secrecy. Second it is in the interest of the general society to assure that banking secrecy will not be used as a cover for illegal transactions in the form of laundering money or as a tax shelter.

The legal regulation of banking secrecy should balance, on one side, the interest in protecting information entrusted to the bank from customers and, on the other side, the society's general interest in preventing banking secrecy from being used as a shelter for criminal dispositions.

This balance is reflected in the wording of section 54, subsection 2, of the Banking Code of 1991. This regulation prohibits banks from releasing information regarding private matters such as race, religion, political views, criminal records, sexual behavior, and informa-

---

[1] T. Wad, *Handelsvidenskabeligt Tidsskrift* (1947), at p. 68.
[2] Banks and Savings Banks Code, Number 22, of January 9, 1991.

tion regarding health or social problems. Regarding information that is purely of an economic nature, the regulation contains many exceptions to the principle of banking secrecy. All these exceptions will be in the text relating to limitations on the banking secrecy.

LIMITATIONS ON BANK SECRECY

The obligation to keep secret remains the main rule to which a **8-003** number of exceptions are attached. The limitation on banking secrecy is, therefore, most practically described by reference to all the exceptions to the main rule stating the principle of secrecy.

Credit reports

An important modification to the principle of banking secrecy is the **8-004** bank's release of credit reports regarding the bank's customers.

Until 1982, credit reports were released according to customers that varied from bank to bank. In 1982, the Danish Banking Society (*Den Danske Bankforening*) and the Danish Savings Banks Association (*Danmarks Sparekasseforening*) published the Rules for the Financial Institutes' Release of Credit Reports.

This publication has been revised twice, and the title is now "Rules and Instructions for the Financial Institutions' Release of Credit Reports, 1988".[3] The instructions now are based on the rules in the Ministry of Justice's Regulation,[4] regarding release of credit reports by financial institutions. This regulation was effective as of April 1, 1988, and issued as the result of certain regulations in the Danish Code on Private Registers.[5]

The instructions regarding credit reports have created a uniform set of rules for issuing credit reports. Credit reports can only be released to "serious" recipients. Such recipients consist of:

(1) Other banks and the banks' own business customers;
(2) Domestic and foreign banks;
(3) Domestic and foreign credit information institutions, and
(4) Embassies and public institutions.

---

[3] *Regler og Vejledning for Pengeinstitutternes afgivlese af soliditetsoplysininger* (Rules and Regulations for Issuance of Credit Reports by Financial Institutions) (1988).
[4] Regulation Number 122 of March 11, 1988.
[5] Code Number 622 of October 2, 1987.

The banks issue the credit reports under secrecy. Therefore, the bank must be convinced that the applicant will treat the information as confidential and that the applicant has a recognizable business interest in having the information issued.

The contents of the credit report must be in compliance with the bank's general obligation to keep information confidential. This means that the credit report must be issued in general terms, not containing specific amounts on deposit accounts, amounts of debts or specific instances of delay in payment. Such specific information can be given only if the customer has given its express consent to the bank.

Furthermore, the bank is not allowed to release information containing specific information regarding matters such as assets, liabilities, and turnover, which cannot be obtained from otherwise publicly accessible accounts or from the Danish Business Register (*Erhvervs- og Selskabsstyrelsen*).

The credit report should contain an assessment of the customer's economic solidity. In accordance with the regulations in the Code on Private Registers, the information cannot contain information regarding matters such as race, or religion, as described above.

It follows furthermore from section 4, subsection 2, of the Code on Private Registers that information regarding circumstances more than five years old cannot be given without consent from the customer unless it is evident that such information is of crucial importance for the circumstances that should be described in the credit report. This regulation gives the banks much discretion in releasing information that is more than five years old.

A customer, however, may give written instructions to his bank that no credit reports can be issued. Such message is binding on the bank.

If credit reports are issued by the bank, the bank has an obligation to inform the customer not later than four weeks after such information is given.

The bank has an obligation to rectify a credit report to the extent that the credit report contains misleading information based on the information that the bank used to issue the credit report. Information that comes to the bank's knowledge after the credit report was issued, for example, that the customer had filed for bankruptcy or suspension of payments, does not obligate the bank to rectify the report.

This is of crucial importance for the recipient of the report because the report is only based on the information available to the bank when the report was issued. In other words, the bank has no obligation to conduct research in the process of issuing the report nor any obligation to follow up if the bank receives crucial information after the report is issued.

If the customer becomes aware that the contents of the report did not correctly reflect the customer's current economic status, the customer can instruct the bank to correct the report. If the bank declines or refuses to make such corrections, the customer is entitled to bring the issue to the Board of Supervision of Registers (*Registertilsynet*), which will rule on the matter.

A credit report should contain the following information:

(1) Name and address of the customer;
(2) Kind of business that the customer carries out;
(3) Year of establishment of the business;
(4) Ownership and leadership;
(5) Capital structure;
(6) Turnover and income, and
(7) Liquidity.

Credit reports concerning private customers can be given only in the following instances:

(1) In connection with the establishment of suretyship in favor of a bank;
(2) On the basis of the customer's specific consent, or
(3) On the basis of the customer's specific request.

The practice regarding issuing of credit reports contains an important exception to the general principle of banking secrecy. The issuing of credit reports has been an integrated part of the banks' business functions, and it is viewed as a necessary tool for participating in the business environment.

The customers of the bank have a general interest in the issuance of credit reports since such reports will often be a prerequisite for establishment of financial agreements between the customer and the parties with whom he carries out business.

Public supervision

Banks in Denmark are closely controlled by public institutions. This **8-005** control is carried out by the Financial Supervisory Board (*Finanstilsynet*). The main function of the Financial Supervisory Board is to see that all regulations in the Banking Code of 1991 are observed.

As part of this control function, the Financial Supervisory Board controls the banks functions. In this connection, the banks are obliged to release to the Financial Supervisory Board all necessary information. Such information will, to a large degree, contain information relating to the banks customers; thus, this release is an important exception to the general principle of banking secrecy.

In order to avoid misuse of the information given to the Financial Supervisory Board, it is stated in section 50a, subsection 1, of the Banking Law of 1991 that all employees in the Financial Supervisory Board who receive such information are responsible according to sections 152-152E, of the Danish Criminal Code.[6]

According to these provisions, the employees in the Financial Supervisory Board become obligated to keep secret the information they receive in the course of carrying out their tasks. Breach of this secrecy requirement is a criminal act.

There is an important exception to the rule just mentioned. The Financial Supervisory Board is entitled to transfer the confidential information to other public authorities such as the police, certain courts, the Danish National Bank, and foreign central Banks. Generally, employees in all public institutions in Denmark to which the information can be transferred have the same obligation to maintain confidentiality, as described above, regarding employees of the Financial Supervisory Board.

These regulations should assure that no information given to the Financial Supervisory Board or transferred to other public authorities will be released to private parties.

Witnesses in court

8-006   According to section 168 of the Danish Administration of Justice Code (*Retsplejeloven*),[7] the principle rule is that anyone demanded must appear as a witness in court. This rule also embraces employees in banks.

An exception to the main rule is found in section 170, subsection 3, of the Danish Administration of Justice Code. According to this exception, the court can determine that the witness shall be excluded regarding facts that the witness should treat as confidential according to legal regulations and if confidentiality is of importance.

The first of the two conditions is clearly fulfilled because the general principle of banking secrecy is expressed in section 54, subsection 2, of the Banking Code of 1991. It is ambiguous, how-

---

[6] Danish Criminal Code, Number 607, of September 6, 1986, as amended by Code Number 385 of May 20, 1992.

[7] Danish Administration of Justice Code Number 748 of December 1, 1987, as amended by Code Number 3 of January 6, 1992.

ever, whether banking secrecy generally is of importance. The courts have ruled on that question in only a very few instances.

In the only published judgment relevant to the issue, the superior court (*Vestre Landsret*) ruled that section 170, subsection 3, of the Danish Administration of Justice Code should not bar a creditor from obtaining information from employees in a bank regarding a debtors' assets (accounts) in the bank.[8] The court's ruling is very specific, and the decision cannot be taken as a precedent for a general principle allowing employees of banks to disclose otherwise confidential information when the employees act as witnesses in a court case.

Section 170, subsection 3, of the Danish Administration of Justice Code should be used only in situations where the party who seeks to obtain otherwise confidential information through questioning employees of banks as witnesses can demonstrate a compelling interest in obtaining this information. To prevail, such interest should greatly outweigh the opposite party's interest in keeping the information confidential.

Seizure and search

The general objective of clearing criminal acts has led to regulations **8-007** allowing seizure and search of otherwise confidential documents that are believed to be of importance as evidence in criminal cases.

The authority for this rule is found in sections 824 to 830 of the Danish Administration of Justice Code. According to these rules, the court can compel any person who has control of such documents or information to release such documents or information to the court, unless the information released would contain information that the person would not be obliged to release as a witness according to sections 169-172 of the Danish Administration of Justice Code.

The exceptions referred to in sections 169-172 have a very limited scope because they refer only to situations where release of the information would severely affect the witness. This will rarely be the situation where the bank releases information regarding its customers. The rule is, therefore, from a practical perspective, that the banks in general have an obligation to release otherwise confidential information on the request of the court if the information is to be used as evidence in a criminal proceeding.

---

[8] See *Ugeskrift For Retsvaesen* (1979), at p. 216.

In order to avoid bank employees at lower levels obtaining knowledge of pending criminal procedures, the normal practice is that the court decision regarding release of material is sent to the board of directors of the bank who will deal with the matter as discreetly as possible.

The Tax Control Code

8-008   The most dramatic exception to the general principle of banking secrecy is found in the Tax Control Code (*Skattekontrolloven*).[9] The Code contains two sets of regulations. One set gives the tax authorities the ability to request information from the banks, and the second set provides that the banks have an obligation to release information to the tax authorities regarding all the bank's customers.

The release of information is grossly in conflict with the general principle of secrecy, and there is a strong trend toward the release of more and more information in order to provide the basis for the tax authorities to assure that all taxable income and all taxable assets are reported. In other words, the legislature in Denmark has found that tax assessment outweighs the general principle of banking secrecy.

The banks have a general obligation to furnish the tax authorities with all the following types of information regarding all of the bank's customers:

(1) Information regarding interest on all kinds of deposit accounts - The information shall specifically describe the amount of interest, dates the interest accrued and the total sum deposited in the bank at the end of each calendar year.

(2) Information regarding interest paid to the bank on loans that in any fiscal year have been established in the bank - Information also must be given regarding loans that have been established but paid out before the end of the calendar year.

(3) Information regarding interest and outstanding debt on loans secured by a mortgage in real property to the extent that such securities are administered by the bank.

(4) Information regarding interest and value of bonds belonging to the bank's customers and administered by the bank - It should be noted here that all Danish bonds are now administered via electronic media. This means that no Dan-

9 Tax Control Code, Number 551, of July 9, 1991.

ish bond can be purchased or sold without establishment of a certain account in a bank. This, in turn, means that no bond can be purchased, owned, or sold without giving information to the tax authorities.

(5) Information regarding forwarding contracts and option contracts if one of the parties to the contract is a natural person.

All the above-mentioned information is given to the tax authorities on a regular basis at the end of each calendar year.

In addition to this annual reporting, the banks are obliged to provide the tax authorities with the types of information mentioned plus almost any other type of financial information at any time where a specific request is issued from the tax authorities.

If the tax authorities find that it is uncertain to whom an account in a bank belongs, the tax authorities are entitled to freeze the account for six months while investigations regarding the ownership of the account are conducted. The freezing of the account can be extended if investigations have not proven who owns the account at the end of the initial period.

Thus, the tax authorities virtually and without any court order have access to any economic information held by the bank regarding the customers of the bank.

Information between companies and subsidiaries

In section 54, subsection 2, of the Banking Code of 1991, it is **8-009** expressly stated that general information regarding the relationship between customer and bank can be given to the customer's concern-related company if the following three conditions are all fulfilled:

(1) The information given must be usual information regarding the customer;
(2) The person who receives the information must keep the information confidential, and
(3) The release of the information must be for a reasonable business purpose.

The information that can be given covers general matters such as name and address, and specific information regarding deposits and loans.

The definition of concern-related companies is found in section 1, subsection 2, number 8, of the Code on Annual Accounts (*Aas-regnskabsloven*).[10] The provision basically covers the relationship between parent companies and subsidiaries.

Internal information among branches of a bank

8-010 It is a well established, but not legally regulated principle that release of otherwise confidential information from one section of a bank to another is not protected by the general principle of banking secrecy. This statement is general as far as the information released is released to the board of managers in the bank or only released to a specific numbers of high ranking personnel in the bank.

If, however, release is given broadly to employees of the bank, such release would probably (there are no court decisions) violate the general principle of banking secrecy.

Consent from bank's customer

8-011 The last and obvious exception to the principle of banking secrecy is found in the situation where the customer consents to release of otherwise confidential material. Such consent is valid to the extent that it relates to release of information in one or more specific situations.

A general agreement between the bank and the customer allowing the bank to release otherwise confidential material would probably violate section 54, subsection 2, of the Banking Code of 1991 because this subsection imposes a general obligation upon the banks to not break the general principle of banking secrecy.

CONCLUSION

8-012 The most important legislation regarding banking secrecy is found in Code Number 22 of January 9, 1991, on Banks and Saving Banks (*Bank og Sparekasseloven*). Section 54, subsection 2, of the Code sets standards and exceptions for banking secrecy. Regulations related

10 Code on Annual Accounts, Number 661, of September 25, 1991.

specifically to credit reports are found in Regulation number 122 of March 11, 1988, regarding release of credit reports by financial institutions.

The traditional and well-established principle of banking secrecy in Denmark has been derived from a number of specific areas. The two most important deviations are found in the bank's routinely released credit reports and in the legally regulated obligations for the banks to release basically all information regarding accounts to the tax authorities.

The first derivation is commonly accepted since it is advantageous and understandable from a business point of view. It is generally in the interest of the business participants to be able to obtain credit information regarding current or prospective business partners. The second deviation, release of information to the tax authorities, has been criticized as being overly broad.

The legislature has not paid much attention to such criticism since, in Denmark, it is a well established principle that the tax authorities should have ready access to information that is crucial in controlling tax returns and the tax assessments.

The two deviations mentioned, combined with the other possible release of information of otherwise confidential material, results in the final conclusion that banking secrecy in Denmark is considerably watered down compared to that in many other countries of Europe.

There are only a very few court cases or accessible administrative decisions that have dealt with banking secrecy. This leads to the impression that Danish banks have had no great difficulty in administering banking secrecy in a way that generally satisfies both the banks' customers and the public authorities.

CHAPTER 9

FINLAND

Peter Anthoni and Katariina Kivenheimo
Bützow & Co.
Helsinki, Finland

Chapter 9

FINLAND

INTRODUCTION

A new law on deposit banks and several new laws concerning different forms of banking activity entered into force on January 1, 1991, in Finland. The purpose of the law reforms was to harmonize the regulations concerning Finnish banks so that these regulations would be in conformity with the provisions of the relevant European Community directives. Another objective of the reforms was to restrict the right of the banks to own shares of other companies.

The amendments to the provisions concerning banking secrecy were not substantive, and the present regulation on banking secrecy is very much the same as before the law reform.

9-001

BANKING TRADITION IN FINLAND

The first Finnish banks were established in early 1800s. These banks were either savings banks or cooperative banks. The country did not have any law on commercial banks until 1862, and the establishment of the first commercial bank immediately succeeded the law in the same year.

The Finnish banking tradition has a phenomenon of its own, *Postipankki Oy*, which is a state-owned company limited by shares with a part of its offices located in local post offices throughout the country. After the law reform in 1991, *Postipankki Oy* is now considered one of the commercial banks.

9-002

The legal structure of the different types of banks is surveyed below since the banking secrecy obligation binds the organs as well as the functionaries of the banks.

Savings banks

9-003   A savings bank was the first bank to be established in Finland in 1822. The savings banks have a legal structure of their own, resembling a trust but without the supporting legislation as have the other forms of banks.[1]

A savings bank is a consortium of persons who own proportions of the original fund of the bank. An original fund of FiM 25-million is a minimum requirement for the establishment of a savings bank.[2]

The savings banks are administered by a board of managers which represents the portions of the original fund and the depositors. The board of managers selects the board of directors and the board of directors selects the managing director. A savings bank also can have a board of governors which is chosen by the board of directors.

The savings banks have a saving banks inspectorate of their own which is supervised by the Banking Supervision Authority.

Cooperative banks

9-004   A cooperative bank is legally a cooperative society. A cooperative bank is owned by owners of portions of investments. The minimum capital of investments is also FiM 25-million.

A meeting of a cooperative bank selects an administrative board of directors and a managing director and, depending on the by-laws of the bank, an assembly of representatives of the members of the cooperative also can be chosen.

The cooperative banks also have an inspectorate of cooperative banks of their own which is obliged to function under the supervision of the Banking Supervision Authority.

---

[1] For example, commercial banks are subject to the Companies Act and cooperative banks are subject to the Cooperative Societies Act.

[2] At writing, FiM 25-million was equal to approximately ECU 5-million.

Commercial banks

The legal form of a Finnish commercial bank is that of a company   **9-005**
limited by shares. The minimum capital stock is FiM 25-million. The
commercial banks are administered by a board of directors which is
selected according to the articles of association of the bank. A board
of directors selects a board of governors and a managing director
and is responsible for the internal inspection of the bank.

The Act on Commercial Banks also is applied to the state-owned
Postipankki Oy.

Banking Supervision Authority

The Banking Supervision Authority controls all banking activity in   **9-006**
Finland, including the activities of subsidiaries of foreign banks.
The Banking Supervision Authority issues general instructions to
banks concerning the principles of banking activity, controls savings bank and cooperative bank inspectorates, and supervises the
conditions of banking activity in general. It has a right to extensive
inspection measures.

The Banking Supervision Authority nominates a special inspector for a bank if a lack of skill, carelessness, or abuses are detected
in the activity of the bank.

PROVISIONS ON BANKING SECRECY

The business and professional secrets of a bank, as well as informa-   **9-007**
tion concerning its financial standing, must be separated from that
of a client. A bank has discretionary power where its own business
and commercial secrets are concerned and can disclose or publish
such information at its own discretion, but this does not apply to
similar information regarding its clients.

The individual employees of a bank cannot dispose of this discretionary power. The employees are not entitled to communicate
any information regarding their employer, and this includes plans
of the employer concerning marketing and development.

Deposit Banks Act

9-008 The general provision on banking secrecy is codified in the Deposit Banks Act,[3] which was entered into on January 1, 1991. The Act imposes an obligation to keep secret all facts concerning the financial situation, any private matter, or a business or a professional secret of bank clients on all the members or substitute members of the organs of banks, as well as on bank employees. This obligation is not binding if:

(1) Law or other regulation obligates the disclosure of such information;

(2) A client or clients in question give their permission to communicate such information, or

(3) A bank considers the disclosure of the confidential information essential for the risk management of an entity belonging to the same group of companies as the deposit bank itself. This rule can be applied only if the employees and the members of the organs of the entity are bound to a similar secrecy obligation as the organs and the employees of the bank in question.

Confidential matters, as mentioned above, may not be communicated to the board of managers of a savings bank, the shareholders' meeting of a commercial bank, the assembly of the representatives of the members of a cooperative bank, to the individual owners of a share, portion of an original fund or investment, or to an individual depositor.

The deposit banks are allowed to collect credit information if the collection of information is limited to normal banking activity.

Savings Banks Act and Cooperative Banks Act

9-009 Both the Savings Banks Act and the Cooperative Banks Act contain similar provisions on banking secrecy. The banking secrecy provision in both Acts prescribes a secrecy obligation to the employees of the savings bank inspectorate and the cooperative bank inspectorate concerning the financial standing and the business and professional secrets of the banks and their subsidiaries, as well as that of the clients.

---

[3] The Deposit Banks Act, section 58.

Exceptions

This obligation is not binding if: 9-010

   (1) The information is needed by the police or the prosecution authorities for the investigation of a crime;

   (2) Other authorities, prescribed by law, are in need of the information, or

   (3) A debtor has considerable debts and commitments in different savings or cooperative banks or in their subsidiaries or if it otherwise can be suspected that the activities of a client can damage savings or cooperative banks or their subsidiaries.

Mutual organizations

Business secrets of individual banks, as well as of their subsidiaries, 9-011
can be communicated to guarantee funds, insurance companies, and central organizations of the banks in question, according to the Savings Banks Act and the Cooperative Banks Act.

Banking Supervision Authority

The officials of the Banking Supervision Authority are bound to the 9-012
secrecy obligation concerning any information obtained regarding an inspected bank, its clients, or other persons. This information includes, at minimum, information regarding financial standing and business or professional secrets. In case an official reveals such facts, such offense can lead to dismissal from office, as well as fines or imprisonment.

SCOPE OF SECRECY OBLIGATION

The Finnish Association of Banks has, in cooperation with the 9-013
Association of Savings Banks and the Association of Cooperative Banks, prepared a directive on banking secrecy in Finland. The following analysis is based on the requirements in the law and the directive.

Persons bound to secrecy obligation

9-014   The following persons are bound by the secrecy obligation:

(1) Functionaries and fiduciaries of a deposit bank, including the members of the organs of the deposit banks and their mutual organizations;

(2) Bank personnel not directly connected with the banking activity, *i.e.*, messengers, caretakers, cleaners, kitchen staff, chauffeurs, and porters;

(3) Auditors of a bank or of a combination of banks;

(4) Personnel of a service business, such as for posting, cleaning, or other services provided by an outside company, and

(5) Other persons outside the banking activity but located in the premises of a bank, for example, sale of insurances arranged in the premises of a bank.

Information under secrecy obligation

9-015   All information obtained in the course of bank activity or employment is under the secrecy obligation whether it concerns the financial position or a private matter of a client or the business or professional secrets of a client. On this ground, for example, profitability calculations, business agreements, information about new products, and other business arrangements cannot be revealed to an outsider without violating the secrecy obligation.

Client relationship

9-016   The secrecy obligation is not dependent on whether the client relationship is temporary or permanent. The secrecy obligation also is binding in regard to the previous clients of a bank.

In addition, information which is obtained outside the banking relationship between a bank and a client cannot be disclosed if the information has been acquired on account of the banking relationship. The way in which the information is obtained does not affect this obligation; for example, some information can be received from another bank in relation to the transfer of payments between banks.

Expertise services

Information, which is obtained in the so-called "expertise services" offered by a bank, is also under the secrecy obligation. Expertise services can, for example, include various registers kept on behalf of the client. **9-017**

Common knowledge

The secrecy obligation does not extend to persons or entities beyond those involved in a bank-client relationship and where the information can be considered a matter of common knowledge. **9-018**

Temporal scope of secrecy obligation

The secrecy obligation of the functionary or of the fiduciary of a bank begins as the information is obtained and continues until the employment or the fiduciary relationship is ended. **9-019**

Information regarding a client, whether it is obtained before or after a banking relationship, also falls under the secrecy obligation.

Confidential matters should not be discussed by bank functionaries among themselves more than is required in the work assignment, *i.e.*, matters under the secrecy obligation should not be revealed to other functionaries unnecessarily.

EXCEPTIONS TO SECRECY OBLIGATION

Permission

The permission of a client releases a bank from the secrecy obligation. A client can limit this right as to the scope or the group of recipients of the information. An oral permission is considered to be sufficient, although normally this permission would be asked to be given in writing for the sake of good order. **9-020**

Authorities

Certain authorities are entitled to obligate a bank to disclose information which normally is under the secrecy obligation, regardless of the permission of a client. **9-021**

Banking Supervision Authority

9-022   The Banking Supervision Authority has the right to inspect all documents concerning the bank under inspection, as well as information acquired by it in relation to its clients.

The Banking Supervision Authority also has the right to inspect a branch office of a bank located abroad and take possession of documents there in case this is permitted according to the legislation of the country in question. This right also includes the right to obtain necessary information and documents concerning other entities owned or controlled[4] by the group of companies to which the bank under inspection itself belongs.

The Finnish Banking Supervision Authority has a right to communicate information concerning a Finnish bank and its foreign subsidiary to a corresponding foreign authority responsible for the same or similar duties on basis of law in its own country and where reciprocity is accorded to the Finnish Banking Supervision Authority.

Tax authorities

9-023   The tax authorities have a right to claim information from a bank according to various tax laws. Nevertheless, this right is not so extensive as the right of the Banking Supervision Authority and, therefore, the request for information must be specified.

There can be no doubt as to the identity of the client in question, and the nature of the requested information must be sufficiently specific.

Disclosure of information to the tax authorities must be limited to only that which is necessary to satisfy the request. Therefore, for example, the names of possible sureties cannot be disclosed, although the amount of the debt must be revealed to tax authorities.

In case the tax inspection applies to the bank itself, the tax authorities have no right to inspect any material which is directly connected with the clients of the bank or their deposits.

9-024   **National and municipal taxes** A bank is obliged to give information regarding the interest income of a client, the amount of money deposited on an account, and credits granted to a client if requested by the national and municipal tax authorities.

---

[4] The rule applies where 50 per cent or more ownership is held.

This list is exhaustive, *i.e.*, the bank in question is not obliged to give any other information about the client to the tax authorities. Therefore, for example, the tax authorities are not entitled to receive information regarding a right of a taxpayer to control another person's account.

All companies limited by shares are obliged to give information to the tax authorities regarding the possible distributed dividend and also to disclose the names of the shareholders in question. This regulation also includes the commercial banks which, as stated above, are companies limited by shares.

The revenue law also includes a general provision stating that everyone possessing any information liable to affect another's taxation is obliged to disclose this information to the tax authorities. This regulation is limited only if the person was entitled to refuse to testify in the matter. This right is constituted only for the persons themselves, their close relatives, or other certain persons.

Inheritance and gift tax A bank is not obliged to disclose any information in connection with inheritance and gift tax matters. 9-025

Tax at source concerning distributed interest Information concerning distributed interest must be disclosed only when requested. This obligation is limited to the information already in the possession of the bank in question. 9-026

Other tax laws A bank also is obliged to provide information regarding factors influencing a client's credit, stamp duty, turnover, and customs and excise taxation if requested by the tax authorities. 9-027

Nordic cooperation The Nordic countries[5] have entered into a treaty concerning administrative aid in taxation and, therefore, Finnish banks are obligated to disclose information to the tax authorities of other Nordic countries in the same way as to the Finnish tax authorities. 9-028

Bank of Finland

The central bank, the Bank of Finland, exercises control over the exchange of foreign currency in Finland and is entitled to have information which is relevant for its duties as defined by Finnish foreign exchange legislation. 9-029

[5] Finland, Sweden, Denmark, Norway, and Iceland.

The policy concerning the movement of capital and foreign exchange in general has been liberalized in the last years. Permission must be applied for only as to foreign credits to private persons living in Finland and for foreign loans. In October 1991, the restriction on foreign credits was lifted.

Police and prosecuting authority

9-030   The police are entitled, in connection with the investigation of a crime, to conduct a search of the premises of a bank and to confiscate documents, records of payment, and other objects.

A search of the premises of a party other than the suspect can be conducted only if the most severe punishment for the suspected crime is more than imprisonment of six months or if the suspect has been taken into custody.

Courts

9-031   If a functionary of a bank is called as a witness in a court of law, the functionary is not entitled to communicate any facts concerning the business and professional secrets of the bank in question or its clients, unless permitted to do so by the bank or by the client, respectively.

Nevertheless, the functionary can be obligated to make disclosure, for example, if necessary for the solving of a serious crime or for the freeing of an obviously innocent person. The court has the right, at its discretion, to obligate the witness to testify for especially important reasons.

Execution authorities

9-032   Generally, a debtor has an obligation to disclose all relevant facts concerning his financial standing, and execution can be levied upon such individualized deposits as disclosed by the debtor.

The execution authorities cannot obligate a bank to reveal possible further deposits or possessions of a debtor, in the event the debtor does not disclose all of his possessions. The execution authorities also must individualize all property in the custody of a bank before execution can be levied on it.

Other authorities

Privacy protection and consumer protection authorities have rights   **9-033**
to obtain information from a bank. This information must be necessary for the duties of these authorities. Privacy protection authorities supervise the keeping of the registers of persons, and the
consumer protection authorities have a particular concern with
consumer credit.

In addition, government authorities for social affairs[6] have limited rights to acquire information, which is normally under the
secrecy obligation if this information is connected with their duties.

Private persons

Joint-ownership or joint-responsibility

Private persons are sometimes authorized to obtain confidential   **9-034**
information on account of their own responsibility or joint-ownership. The parties to a joint credit are entitled to the same information
separately in the same way as the sole debtor of a credit. This
applies as well to the situation in which two or more parties own
something together and the possession is in the custody of a bank,
for example, a shared account or safe.

A person owing a right to use another's account has a right to the
information about this account in the same way as the owner of the
account. This also applies to the party to whom an account has been
transferred.

Authorization

The owner of an account also can authorize someone to dispose of   **9-035**
his account or to obtain information in general or connected with
some particular aspect of the account. The scope of this right is
determined by the authorization, which must be explicit.

Supporters and guardians

The supporter of a person under age or a guardian has an extensive   **9-036**
right to obtain all information concerning the bank accounts of the

---

[6] These include the Social Insurance Institution, the Committee and Appellate
Board for Social Insurance, and the Insurance Court.

minor or the ward despite the exclusive right of the latter to dispose of the account.

Spouse

9-037   A spouse or a party to cohabitation without marriage has no right to receive information concerning the matters of the other spouse from the bank without permission.

Death estate

9-038   A distributee of a death estate is entitled to receive information only about the banking affairs of the deceased regarding the day of death and the time after the death. The distributees can dispose of this right separately.

A trustee of an estate is only entitled to receive information regarding banking affairs of a deceased if the trustee has been nominated by a court of law. If he is elected entirely by the distributees of the death estate, he must present to the bank a proxy signed by one of the distributees.

An administrator of an estate and an executor or the distributor of an estate, when appointed by a court of law, have the right to receive information about the banking matters of the deceased which took place before the date of death.

Bankruptcy and liquidation

9-039   An administrator of a bankrupt's estate, a liquidator of a company limited by shares, limited partnership company, and other entities have the right to acquire information regarding the banking matters of the entity in question.

Pledge and other guarantees

9-040   An owner of any property pledged as collateral for creditors is entitled to receive information concerning those credits for which the pledge in question stands.

Any holder of a lien (*i.e.*, a holder of a second mortgage) is entitled to receive information only regarding the assets or property in question.

A surety or guarantor is entitled to receive information regarding the credit for which he has pledged himself.

Checks and bank cards

A holder of a check is entitled to know whether the amount of money deposited on the account in question is sufficient for the redemption of the check. The same applies to a holder of a receipt of a bank card purchase.

9-041

Persons acting for company

Members of the board of directors, the managing director, a holder of procuration, or a partner of a partnership company have a right to receive information regarding the bank account of the company in question.

9-042

Banks and insurance companies

Banks have a right to disclose information to companies belonging to the same group of companies if functionaries and fiduciaries of the company are bound to a similar secrecy obligation.

Savings and cooperative banks cannot disclose information to another savings or cooperative bank without the permission of the client.

9-043

CREDIT INFORMATION ACTIVITY

The banks have a right to collect credit information concerning their own clients to an extent which is normal in the banking business. This right is limited by the law on the registration of private persons. Credit information about private persons can be collected only in connection with the banking relationship unless a private person has a substantial influence on a business entity on account of ownership or position.

According to the privacy protection law, a bank can collect information regarding persons who actively engage in business life by practising a profession or by owning a company, although these persons would not be the clients of the bank.

9-044

SANCTIONS

9-045   The sanctions for violating the secrecy obligation can range from fines to a maximum sentence of imprisonment of six months; for disclosing a business secret of a bank, sanctions may range from fines to imprisonment for two years, if the person in question is still employed in the bank.

In case the employment relationship has been terminated, a disclosure of a business secret of a bank can be punished only when the disclosure is made in order to gain financial benefit.

In case a person has acted as a counsel in the counseling and expertise services which are provided by a bank and discloses a private or a family matter which has come into his knowledge in this activity, the person can be fined or sentenced to imprisonment of a maximum duration of six months. This also applies to the disclosure of a business secret which is acquired as a counsel.

In case the secrecy obligation is violated, the bank is liable for compensating the resulting damage. The person who has violated the obligation can be held responsible for reimbursing all or part of the indemnity to the bank. If the person has communicated a business secret of a bank, he can be obliged to compensate for any resulting damage.

CONCLUSION

9-046   Court proceedings concerning banking secrecy have been very few in Finland. Nevertheless, in 1990, the Supreme Administrative Court ordered a bank to reveal the identity of parties to a security purchase to the Banking Supervision Authority. In this case, the bank itself had acted as an intermediary in the security purchase.

In general, it can be stated that very few amendments to the prevailing provisions on banking secrecy can be expected because the Deposit Bank Act, as well as the other laws on banking activity, are relatively new. Finland will, in all likelihood, follow the general development in Europe and especially in the European Community, as the recent reform has indicated.

FRANCE

Odile Lajoix and Marc Billiau
Berlioz & Co.
Paris, France

Chapter 10

FRANCE

INTRODUCTION

Until recently, the scope and penalties of banking secrecy were the   **10-001**
subject of debate and discussion in France. However, the Banking
Law of January, 24, 1984, cut short any discussion of principle by
stating in article 57(1) that "any member of the board of directors,
and as the case may be any person who, in whatever capacity, takes
part in the management or administration of a credit establishment
or who is employed by a credit establishment, is bound by professional secrecy under conditions and penalties prescribed by article
378 of the Penal Code".

Article 57(1) affirms unambiguously the existence of banking
secrecy, the disregard of which is sanctioned by a prison sentence of
one to six months and a fine ranging from FF 500 to FF 15,000.

The persons embraced by the article are numerous since, in
reality, it concerns any person working in a credit establishment and
who has knowledge of confidential information through his office.[1]

It is clearly stated that bankers are liable for the violation of the
duty of secrecy. Such liability is not linked with the intent to carry
out the violation as it would be under the principles of penal law.
Such liability relates, instead, to a contractual action, or to tort,
depending on whether the claimant has been a client of the bank,
although a distinction can be made in the first case where gross
negligence (*faute lourde* or *faute grave*) has been committed.

---

[1] It was decided that an internal rule which restricts itself to reminding bank
employees of the existence of the secrecy obligation does not interfere with the
employees' right of expression; CE June 1, 1990, JCP ed. E1990 I 20060 - CE June
3, 1988, JCP ed. EI 1988 I. 17567.

Banking secrecy nevertheless reveals a distinctive feature in comparison with other secrecies, of which medical secrecy is one. Indeed, unlike medical secrecy,[2] banking secrecy is not absolute because it is enacted in the private interest of clients. Therefore, it can be lifted in certain circumstances. It also is possible that the client can release the bank from its duty.

Some persons view professional secrecy as "a not inconsiderable asset in international financial relations"[3] because it has the power of attracting foreign capital. The comment is not inaccurate, and the reputation of certain foreign banks is built on this assumption. However, the source of the money deposited has sometimes appeared questionable as shown by the large number of scandals in the 1980s, resulting particularly in the Law of July 12, 1990, regarding money laundering.

It appears that banking secrecy is, first of all, "the expression of a right to confidentiality". However, since it is relative, it can be lifted by the legislator in certain cases. Though it exists and in no event can the bank on its own initiative exempt itself from its secrecy obligation, it cannot be invoked against certain authorities; it is the expression of public order (*ordre public*).

INVOCABILITY OF BANKING SECRECY: RIGHT TO CONFIDENTIALITY

10-002   Banking secrecy is expressed as a right to confidentiality. Following the example of numerous subjective rights, banking secrecy is framed within certain limits, hence the necessity to determine its scope. Once this is determined, it will be possible to view the sanctions which ensure its effectiveness.

Scope of right to confidentiality

10-003   The right to confidentiality, as we have seen, is provided by article 57 of the Banking Law, but this article lacks precision. It is, therefore, necessary to refer to case law and to legal commentators in order to resolve a certain number of practical questions indispensable for its implementation. It is thus important to specify the persons against

[2] See, on the absolute nature of medical secrecy, *Cass. Crim.* June 5, 1985.
[3] See Gavalda and Stoufflet, *Le droit de la banque* 1974, n. 311.

whom the banker can invoke secrecy and the nature of information covered by the secrecy.

Persons against whom secrecy can be invoked

Obligation to all third parties. As a rule, the obligation of the credit **10-004** establishment concerns all third parties, that is to say all those who have not entrusted it with confidential information.[4]

For example, the Court of First Instance of Paris issued a decision in a case in which the drawer of a check requested his bank to transmit to him a photocopy of both sides of the check and the name of payee's bank. The bank refused this request. It restricted itself to sending to its client the photocopy of the first side of the check. The client then instituted proceedings against the bank, which invoked professional secrecy to support its refusal. In its judgment of March 21, 1991, the court allowed this argument on the ground:

> ". . .that article 57 of the law of January 24, 1984, defines as professional secrecy; besides the cases provided for by law, professional secrecy cannot be invoked either against the Bank Committee (*Commission bancaire*) or against the Bank of France or against the judicial authorities acting in the context of criminal proceedings; that in this particular case, the request is neither necessary in the context of criminal proceedings nor within a case provided by law; that the bank is therefore entitled to refuse the delivery of the banking information sought by L whose request must be rejected".[5]

Nevertheless, in the absence of express contrary legislative provisions, the answer to the question of whether banking secrecy can be invoked against third parties does not appear as simple as at first sight.

It is accepted that the bank cannot invoke secrecy against the authorized representative of the bank's client with regard to the performance of his task.[6] In fact, one must consider that the client has tacitly released the banker from his secrecy obligation to the

---

[4] Even if it is obvious that the beneficiary of the secrecy is not a third party, the Supreme Court has, in a decision of June 19, 1990 (*Bull. civ.* IV, n 179, at p. 123), stated that the bank could not invoke banking secrecy in litigation since it was summoned not "as third party's confidant but as a party to a proceedings brought against it by the beneficiaries of the banking secrecy".

[5] *Banque* 1991, at p. 985.

[6] The representative nevertheless must justify his capacity. The banker who delivers information covered by secrecy without taking elementary precautions is liable to his client.

authorized representative.[7] This explanation complies with the nature of the banker's duty.[8]

To this basic assumption we must add the cases where one of the spouses is authorized by a court to represent the other in the exercise of powers arising from marital status.[9] The nature of the authorization (*mandat*) - contractual, judicial, or legal - is indeed immaterial in the determination of the persons authorized to share the banking secrecy.

In the course of marital life, save in the case mentioned above, banking secrecy may be invoked by the bank against its client's spouse by virtue of the principle of the banker's autonomy enacted by article 221, paragraph 1 of the Civil Code. According to this text, "Each of the spouses can without the consent of the other open any deposit account or any portfolio account in his/her name".

However, at the time of dissolution of the marital status, one must recognize that the surviving spouse can, for the purpose of liquidation of this status, obtain information from the banker, without the latter being able to invoke banking secrecy. In fact, in community estates (*régimes de communauté de biens*), the surviving spouse has a right to one half of the communal estate. This right can be exercised only if the surviving spouse is in a position to obtain the information on the accounts opened personally by his or her spouse during the marriage in which communal assets (*valeurs de communauté*) have been deposited.

Furthermore, banking secrecy cannot be invoked against the client's heirs and legatees because they are the successors of the deceased person.[10]

10-005 **Joint accounts and minor's accounts** All these assumptions do not create specific difficulties. On the other hand, one can ask questions about the scope of the banker's obligation when several persons have competing rights on the same account, *i.e.*, joint accounts, or when the account is opened in a minor's name.[11]

As regards accounts on which several holders have rights, the question arises whether only one of the holders can release the banker from his secrecy obligation against third parties. It seems

---

[7] See Rives-Lange and Contamine-Reynaud, *Droit bancaire*, 5th edition, Dalloz n 175.

[8] CE June 1, 1990, JCP ed. E1990 I 20060 - CE June 3, 1988, JCP ed. EI 1988 I. 17567.

[9] Article 219, Civil Code.

[10] Rives-Lange and Contamine-Reynaud, *supra* n. 7, which however limits access to secrecy to "information strictly patrimonial"; see also Gavalda and Stoufflet, *supra* n. 3, n 317.

[11] One knows that a minor 16 years old, even non-emancipated, can freely deposit and withdraw savings bank funds; see Decree of June 27, 1952.

that a qualified answer is necessary. Indeed, certain information is indivisible from the general running of the account; other information can, on the contrary, have no effect on the rights of other holders of the account. In the latter case, there is no legal impediment to the client concerned releasing the banker from his obligation.

On the other hand, in the first case, only one holder of the account cannot interfere with the right to confidentiality, of which the other holders can take advantage. Unanimous agreement is, therefore, required.

Concerning accounts opened by minors, when this is possible,[12] the question arises in other ways. Can the minor's representative, generally his parents, have access to information known to the banker? The reply is likely to be found in the regulations pertaining to the powers granted to the holders of parental authority.

By virtue of article 371-2, paragraph 2, of the Civil Code, parents have with regard to the child "right and duty of custody, supervision, and education". The reference to supervision may, by inference, confer a right to the parents to be communicated the child's financial situation from the banking establishment. In addition, the parents can be held liable by third parties on the basis of lack of supervision, pursuant to article 1384, paragraph 4, of the Civil Code.[13]

Furthermore, the minor is legally represented by his administrators. These administrators, in their capacity as representatives, then find themselves in a similar position to that of an authorized representative.[14] Thus, one can come to the conclusion that, in this particular case, banking secrecy cannot be invoked against the parents.

Accounts of a corporate body In addition, the courts have been   10-006
faced with some difficulties when the account has been opened in the name of a corporate body. If it is a fact that banking secrecy cannot be invoked against legal or statutory representatives of

---

[12]See Huet, *Détournement bancaire de mineurs (rappel des règles de capacité dans les contrats)*, D. 1987, chron. XXXIX, pp. 215 *et seq.*

[13]See Ghestin, "*Traité de droit civil*", t. IV. *La responsabilité: conditions* by G. Viney, ns 881 and *et seq.* It is necessary to add that the contracts put forward by the bankers generally provide for joint and several liability of the parents; see Huet, *supra* n. 12, at p. 216, 2nd column, in fine, at p. 217, 1st column in limine.

[14]See *supra* n. 6; Huet, *supra* n. 12, at p. 220, 1st column, paragraph 2, even suggests creating a special obligation to supervise the account opened in the name of a minor and to compel the banker to inform the parents when the operations carried out are not sound.

the corporate body, including the supervisory bodies[15] because they are the beneficiaries of the secrecy, the question whether the secrecy can be invoked by the banker against the shareholders must be discussed.

On March 20, 1990, the Appeal Court of Paris[16] decided that the qualification of shareholder alone was insufficient to lift the banking secrecy. It held that the shareholder must make his request to the company since the law specially sets out the information to be given to the shareholders. This solution, also adopted by the Court of First Instance of Paris,[17] is unanimously approved by the doctrine.[18]

Writers, however, distinguish this from the case of shareholders of a *société en nom collectif* (a type of a private company) because they are personally and indefinitely liable to third parties.[19]

The position of the shareholder can be compared to that of the guarantor. The guarantor has a clear interest in wanting to know the banking situation of the principal debtor since he can be brought in to substitute the debtor. This interest, nevertheless, does not appear sufficient to exempt the banker from his secrecy obligation.

It is for the guarantor to contact the debtor at the time of issuance of the guarantee, even if it means drawing the necessary inferences from a refusal to inform, and during the guarantee period, subject to the provisions of article 48 of the Law of March, 1, 1984, relating to companies in administration and receivership which compel the credit establishments having granted a financial assistance to an undertaking to deliver on March 31 of each year certain information to the guarantor.

10-007 **Refusal to create exceptions** In reality, the extenuating circumstances set out above with respect to persons against whom banking secrecy can be invoked are more apparent than real. In fact, far from constituting exceptions, they justify themselves either by the presumed intention of the holder of the right to confidentiality or by rules of representation.

---

[15] On statutory auditors' right to disclosure, see article 229, paragraph 5, of the Law of July 24, 1966: "Statutory auditors also can collect all useful information in the exercise of their tasks to third parties who have carried out operations for the account of the company. However, this right to disclosure cannot extend to disclosure of papers contracts and documents of whatever nature held by third parties unless they are authorized by a court order. Professional secrecy cannot be invoked against statutory auditors except by court representatives".

[16] Credot and Gerard-Adde, Order of the President of the Court of First Instance, Arras of April 9, 1989, *Rev. dr. bancaire*, 1989, at p. 91.

[17] November 20, 1990, JCP E. 1991, pan p. 147, n 401.

[18] Rives-Lange and Contamine-Reynaud, *supra* n. 7.

[19] Gavalda and Stoufflet, *supra* n. 3.

This explains why courts refuse to create real exceptions, notably by rejecting the claims of a shareholder which would conflict with the right to secrecy. The right to confidentiality, therefore, appears real. However, the nature of the information covered by secrecy needs to be specified.

Nature of information covered by secrecy

In theory, one can argue that secrecy covers all information given by **10-008** the client. However, such a position would not be realistic. As Dean Roblot emphasized:

> "The duty of professional secrecy is likely to put the banker in a tricky position when he is requested by a client to provide information on another client."[20]

One of the bank's clients, indeed even a third party when it grants a loan, can have a legitimate interest in seeking certain information. In other words, it is necessary to find a balance between the requirement of commercial information and the respect of banking secrecy. To achieve this balance, substantive law adopts a distinction depending on the nature of the information entrusted to the banker.[21]

Some information is thus excluded from the domain of banking secrecy while other information is subject to it. The criterion to be considered is that of confidentiality.

Confidentiality must be specified. For Dean Roblot, "Confidential information is that which shows a precise nature, notably by figures which accompany them: contents of balance sheet, movement of accounts."[22] Conversely, the disclosure of general information, notably on the solvency of a person, does not conflict with secrecy.[23]

Court decisions on this issue are scarce, but one can cite a few decisions which provide useful information. To determine whether

---

[20] Ripert and Roblot, *Traité de droit commercial* t. II 11th edition n 2282.

[21] Virassamy, "Les limites à l'information sur les affaires d'une entreprise", *Rev. trim. dr. com.*, 1988, nos. 11 *et seq.*, at pp. 188 *et seq.*

[22] *Id.*

[23] See Gavalda and Stoufflet, *supra* n. 3, at n. 318, citing Colmar, March 24, 1961, Gaz. Pal., II, at p. 56.

information is confidential or not is not an easy task, and case law is not very clear on this question as the matter has been mainly decided on a case-by-case basis.

10-009   **All information held confidential** In its Judgment of February 6, 1975,[24] the Third Division of the Appeal Court of Paris laid down the principle that all information given by a client to his bank was covered by professional secrecy. It nevertheless emphasized that there was a practice by virtue of which the bank could transmit to third parties certain information, but it stated that the practice "can only constitute a dispensation from the rule of secrecy which remains essential both in the field of the banking profession in that of contractual relationship."

The court concluded that:

> "Consequently, the onus is on the banker whose liability is being sought to justify the grounds which have prompted him to communicate to third parties information on the financial and commercial position of its client and to establish that this communication was made with the necessary reserve and objectivity and under conditions and in accordance with the customary rules prevailing in the profession".

This decision is significant on more than one count.

First, it establishes that the existence of a customary rule justifies dispensation from the principle of secrecy. Recourse to the customary rule can be criticized since the enactment of criminal sanctions in 1984. Indeed, the above-mentioned article 57 does not make a distinction, and a customary rule cannot be *contra legem*. In reality, the ground for limiting the confidentiality obligation is based only on the nature of the information; certain information is confidential while other information is not. Consequently, it is not necessary to have recourse to a customary rule to justify the position taken.[25]

Second, the judgment draws attention to the fact that the burden of proof is placed on the banker to establish that the information delivered to third parties is not covered by banking secrecy. It appears that this situation remains unchanged because the Banking Law of 1984 has established a right to confidentiality essentially similar to that which existed previously. Further, the attribution of the burden of proof to the banker is in the client's advantage and ensures, at least partially, the effectiveness of the right to confidentiality.

[24] D. 1975, at p. 318, note J. Vezian.
[25] See Virassamy, *supra* n. 21, article, n 12.

Limiting the scope of secrecy A second judgment, rendered by the **10-010** Commercial Division of the Supreme Court (*Chambre Commerciale de la Cour de Cassation*) on June 19, 1990, also is worth citing.[26] In this case, the liability of the bank was alleged for having allowed its client to carry on business which was incurring losses.

In summary proceedings, the court made an order for an audit to be carried out and required the bank to hand over to the auditor various documents. The bank appealed against this order by invoking banking secrecy and issued a writ against the auditor in order to have the order rescinded. This contention was rejected by the judges deciding on the merits of the case, and the Supreme Court upheld the judgment on the same ground as that given by the Court of Appeal:

> ". . . after having stated that the bank was basically appealing against the order on the basis both that it was bound by professional secrecy and by the lack of interest of the documents requested which were only for the purposes of internal use and having noted the contradictory nature of the bank's contention. . .has not modified the object of the dispute, it being given that, the bank was not seriously claiming that the delivery of the information requested would constitute a disclosure of secrets entrusted to it".

This decision established unambiguously that not all the information held by a banker is covered by banking secrecy. On the other hand, it implies that it is for the banker to assess the confidential nature of the information held by him. In fact, the dismissal of the ground was justified by the fact that the bank did not assert seriously that the delivery of the information requested would constitute a disclosure of secrets entrusted to it.

This part of the decision is open to criticism. Issue is not taken with the fact that the banker must carry out an assessment. However, it is difficult to accept that the judges can entrench themselves behind such an assessment to order the delivery of documents whose scope is in dispute. In fact, it is for the judge to settle the conflict and thus to make an assessment himself.

Some writers are of the opinion that the more the information relating to the client is precise or specific, the more it must be covered by the duty of secrecy. This would be the case for the contents of the balance sheet or a balance of the bank account.

---

[26] *Bull. civ.*, IV. n 179, at p. 123.

Any information of which the banker would have been aware, although he had no relationship with the person concerned, should not be considered as confidential. This would be the case for information well-known in the world of finance, or that resulting, for instance, from bankruptcy proceedings or default of payment of negotiable investments since they are the object of publicity.

10-011   *Requirement of accuracy* Lastly, it is necessary to stress that, if banking secrecy cannot be invoked against the delivery of certain information, the information which is in fact delivered must be accurate.

The Commercial Division of the Supreme Court decided, in its Judgment of January 9, 1978 that:

> ". . .if it is for a bank, which considers itself bound by banking secrecy, to refuse to provide information on a client, this secrecy obligation does not authorize it to give inaccurate information".[27]

Generally, the delivery of inaccurate information entails liability for the banker. However, when the bank confines itself to transmitting information which has been conveyed to it by other sources, it is only liable to its client if it has undertaken to guarantee its accuracy.[28] Having raised the question of the banker's liability, we shall now consider the sanctions applicable when the banker has disregarded his secrecy obligation.

Sanctions

10-012   Sanctions can be civil or criminal.

Civil sanctions

10-013   It is indisputable that the banker who disregards professional secrecy to which he is bound commits a wrongful act (*faute*). This wrongful act can be a source of liability.[29] For example, a banker

---

[27] *Bull. civ.*, IV. n 12, at p. 9.

[28] Supreme Court (Commercial Division), December 12, 1964, Gaz. Pal., June 16-18, 1984, at p. 115; see also, Orléans, Aud. sol., March 24, 1988, JCP. E. I. 17572. See, however, Paris, 25e Ch., section A, June 19, 1987, JCP. ed. E.I. 16910: for the Court of Paris, the banker is liable if he does not state that the information transmitted comes from third parties and that he was not in a position to verify them.

[29] Virassamy, *supra* n. 21, at p. 191, n 14.

who reports on the cash flow problems of the corporate client to its suppliers, supported by figures, is providing information of a nature to destroy the confidence between the commercial partners and break the business relationship, leading the corporation into liquidation.

In such case, the bank's corporate client will seek the liability of the banker. Third party suppliers also can suffer damage and can implicate the banker.

The nature of the banker's liability will depend on the existence or absence of a contract. Thus, the banker's liability to his client will be on the basis of contractual liability,[30] while to third parties the liability will be based on tort. Liability based on tort is seldom to be found in practice. Generally, the third party will negotiate with the banker, and it is only if the negotiation fails that proceedings will follow.

Damages will be awarded to cover the damage suffered, being moral and commercial. Generally, when the liability derives from a tortious act, not only the damage which could be foreseeable will be covered by virtue of article 1150 of the Civil Code as in contractual matters but also any damage suffered arising directly from the negligence of the bank, as provided by article 1151 of the Civil Code.

Criminal sanctions

The disclosure of a secret is a criminal offense since the reform of **10-014** the Banking Law.[31] Its commission requires the existence of two factors, one material and the other intentional (*élément matériel and élément intentionnel*).

The Commercial Division of the Supreme Court has clarified the nature of these two factors in a recent decision of March 7, 1989.[32] Strictly speaking, this decision is not on banking secrecy, but the position adopted, concerning professional secrecy to which the avocat is bound is *mutatis mutandis* applicable, to the extent that the charges are identical, as provided under article 378, Penal Code.

In setting forth the principle, the Supreme Court held that:

[30] See Gavalda and J. Stoufflet, *supra* n. 3, at n. 318. It is in this sense it was pronounced by the Court of Appeal of Paris in its decision of February 6, 1975, above-mentioned.

[31] Previously, the question was discussed by doctrine; see the comments of Vezian, under C. A. Paris, February 6, 1975, *supra* n. 30, at p. 320, 2e col., paragraph 4, references cited.

[32] *Bull. crim.*, n. 101, at p. 291.

". . .on the one hand the principle laid down by article 378 of the Penal Code is general and absolute even if this is an event known in its entirety when the intervention of the holder of the secret brings about the disclosure of information which the holder alone knew; that on the other hand the fraudulent intention consists of the accused's awareness that he is revealing the secret in his possession, whatever may be the motive which compelled him to do so".

This decision is significant for two reasons. First, it confirms that not all information is covered by banking secrecy. That information which is well known in a particular place is excluded from it.

Next, the intentional factor of the tort is objectivized. It is sufficient that the accused is aware of the nature of the information which he is revealing to others. The accused cannot invoke a moral duty to justify his conduct and avoid sanction.

However, the law can release the banker from his duty of professional secrecy. This arises in cases of the non-invocability of banking secrecy.

NON-INVOCABILITY OF BANKING SECRECY: PUBLIC POLICY

10-015 The exceptions to the banking secrecy principle are provided by the laws and regulations in force. However, on a consensual basis, there is the possibility that the information concerned is authorized or requested by the person concerned. The authorization can be express or tacit within the frame of a mandate resulting for instance from a provision of the law (such as the agent of a minor).

Such exception applies also when delivery of such information is requested by a person, sharing with the person concerned the interest in the disclosure. This relates to heirs, spouses, or guarantors (see text above).

In addition, the banker might be willing to disclose information in the event a suit is instituted by him against the person concerned.

Owing to the general nature of article 57 of the Banking Law of 1984, professional secrecy can only be lifted by specific provisions which are considered as exceptions. A few are only justified by social considerations. This entails:

(1) The obligation to deliver information to French authorities - Tax, Customs, Bank Committee, Banque de France, Securities Exchange Commission (*Commission des Opérations de Bourse*), *Cour des Comptes* (body controlling accounts of public-owned companies or related companies), *Commission nationale de l'informatique et des libertés* (body controlling the compliance with the laws regarding the disclosure of computerized data);

(2) The lifting of banking secrecy in case of penal procedure and in some instances before the civil and commercial judge, such as divorce matters or a rehabilitation procedure;

(3) The obligation to deliver some type of documents in specific cases:
  (a) Attachment;
  (b) Collection of alimony or penalties;
  (c) Regarding the auditor (*Commissaire aux comptes*) of a company by virtue of the Law of January 24, 1966, on commercial companies.

In practice, it is for the banker to determine whether the information to be disclosed falls within the scope and the limits of the exception.

Exceptions which the substantive law makes to the principle of banking secrecy are justified by public policy (*ordre public*). It seems possible to classify them on the basis of the nature of the public policy in question; some of them are connected to the political public policy (*ordre public politique*) and others to economic and social policy (*ordre public économique et social*).

Political public policy

The legislator has defined four cases in which banking secrecy may **10-016** not be invoked and which are linked to political public policy. Secrecy cannot be invoked against judicial authorities acting within the context of criminal proceedings, against tax and customs authorities, in cases of money laundering, and in the case of international cooperation.

Judicial authorities acting in criminal r civil proceedings

10-017 This exception is found in article 57 of the Banking Law. The position was discussed above.[33] It is justified by the relative nature of the secrecy and by the nature of criminal proceedings which bring into play the public interest.

The practice before the courts has involved particularly the following scenarios.

The banker might be called to testify before a court, an examining magistrate (*juge d'instruction*), before a special police officer (*officier de police judiciaire*) or an expert appointed by a penal judge, investigating a penal case.

In such case, the banker may not inform the client of such pending investigation or testimony.

It is generally accepted that the preliminary investigation falls within the context of criminal proceedings (article 75 of the Criminal Procedure Code).[34]

As regards civil procedure itself, the exception to the secrecy could result from the enforcement of an order demanding that a bank forward a document under article 11, paragraphs 138 to 141, of the New Code of Civil Procedure, but it is generally admitted that the principle of banking secrecy set out by article 57 of the Law of January 24, 1984, would prevent such disclosure once the information is deemed "confidential".

Tax authorities

10-018 Article L 83 of Tax Procedure Code[35] provides:

> "The authorities of the State, the departments and communes, the undertakings licensed or controlled by the State, departments or communes, as well as establishments or organizations of any nature subject to the control of administrative authorities, must deliver to the Central Authority, upon its request, the service documents which they hold without the power to invoke professional secrecy".

---

[33] Ripert and Roblot, *supra* n. 20, n 2281.
[34] See Lamy, *Droit du financement*, n 2129.
[35] Formerly article 1987 of the General Tax Code.

On the basis of this provision, the Administrative Supreme Court (*Conseil d'Etat*) decided in its Judgment of December 22, 1982,[36] that banking secrecy could not be invoked against tax authorities. The court founded its decision by accepting that

"... all banks are placed under the control of the State by virtue of the provisions of the Law of June 13, 1941, and by the ordinance of December 2, 1945, notably those which set up the controlling commission of the banks (*Commission de contrôle des banques*) and the National Council of Credit (*Conseil National du crédit*)".

It concluded therefrom that "the tax authorities were entitled to obtain the transmission by the operations recorded in the accounts of the person concerned".

The reform carried out by the Banking Law does not call into question this approach because the banks, through the Banking Committee, remain under the control of the State as provided by articles 27 to 49, Law of January, 24, 1984.

In a directive of March 18, 1988,[37] the authorities clarified to their staff the mode of exercising the right of control. As a rule, control must be carried out only in the event of default of the taxpayer who is first asked to provide the statement of account or other banking documents.

Furthermore, the authorities retain a principle of selection of requests under which they prohibit requests for all credit or debit documents. In this way, the tax authorities take into consideration the difficulty of investigators. As a rule, the right to delivery is exercised on the spot, but the cost of photocopies is reimbursed to the banks. In any case, the directive states that the implementation of article L 83 of the Tax Procedure Code is subject to prior authorization of the General Tax Division.

Customs authorities

The tax authorities' right to disclosure, which bypasses banking **10-019** secrecy must be linked to the provisions of the Customs Code which invests the customs authorities with similar powers.[38]

---

[36] *Dr. fiscal*, 1983, 1888, at p. 1244, conc. Schricke; D. 1983, *Inf. rap.*, at p. 407, comments M. Vasseur.

[37] *Bull. off. impôts* 13 K-2-88.

[38] Pannier, "Le droit de communication de l'administration des douanes", *Rev. dr. bancaire*, 1989, at pp. 101 *et seq.*

According to article 455 of the Customs Code:

> "The various rights to disclosure provided for the benefit of the tax authorities can be exercised to control the application of the law and regulation of the financial relationships with foreign countries."

This article, therefore, refers back to article L 83 of the Tax Procedure Code.[39]

A second article enables the customs authorities to bypass banking secrecy. Article 65 sets out a right to disclosure as regards papers and documents of any nature which may interest the customs authorities.

The Criminal Division of the Supreme Court tends to restrict the exercise of this power within narrow limits. In a decision of January 25, 1977,[40] the Criminal Division of the Supreme Court decided that:

> ". . . if article 65-1(c) of the Customs Code allows the customs authorities to exercise their right to disclosure of documents of any nature held by a bank, it is on the condition that the documents requested are related to lawful or unlawful operations falling within the jurisdiction of the customs authorities; that such is not the case judging by the statement of the Court of Appeal; on the bank's request, one of its agents had made a study on the financial situation of one of its clients, the accused bank, invoking professional secrecy, refused to disclose this report".

This decision overturns a previous decision of January 30, 1975.[41]

In this last case, the customs authorities requested a bank to deliver documents permitting the identification of all the holders of safes rented to clients. The bank refused by invoking banking secrecy. The Court of Appeal condemned this attitude, and this was approved by the Criminal Division of the Supreme Court which accepted that the bank could not oppose the request since the documents asked for were likely to facilitate the performance of the customs authorities's task.

Consequently, the right to disclosure could be exercised in an impersonal manner. Such is no longer the case following the deci-

---

[39] Article 64 A of the Customs Code reproduces almost word for word article L.83 of the Tax Procedure Code.

[40] D. 1977, at p. 666, note Vasseur; JCP. 1977. II. 18651, comments Gavalda.

[41] *Bull. crim.*, at p. 95, n 36; D. 1975, Inf. rap., at p. 51; Banque 1975, at p. 542, comments Martin; JCP. 1975 II. 18137, note Gavalda; *Rev. trim. dr. com.*, 1975, at p. 346, comments Cabrillac and Rives-Lange.

sion of 1977. This having been said, any document can be requested by virtue of the Customs Code. That is how it was decided that an internal note drawn up by bank on a group of companies fell within the provisions of the Code and that the bank could not refuse its disclosure to the customs authorities.[42]

The Customs Code provides criminal penalties for all unjustified refusals to disclose, with a prison sentence ranging from ten days to one month and a fine from FF 600 to FF 3,000.[43]

Money laundering

The problem of money laundering arises notably from drug traf- **10-020**
ficking. Certainly as we have seen,[44] with regard to the substantive law (*droit positif*) in France, banking secrecy cannot be invoked against judicial authorities acting within the context of criminal proceedings.

However, it has become obvious that this exception to banking secrecy is clearly insufficient in the battle against money laundering by many States.[45] France has taken a drastic measure in this area. Although allowing the general exception to the bank's duty of confidentiality to remain, it removed the concept of banking secrecy by imposing particularly[46] on the organizations governed by the provisions of the Law of January 24, 1984, a positive obligation to denounce.

This is the object of Law Number 90-614 of July 12, 1990, on the involvement of the financial institutions in the battle against the laundering of money coming from drug trafficking.[47]

---

[42] *Crim.*, n. 199, at p. 546.

[43] Articles 413 bis, Customs Code.

[44] See Virasammy, *supra* n. 21.

[45] Mr. Beregovoy, Minister of the Economy, Finance and Budget, stressed, in a speech at the Commercial Court of Paris on November 12, 1990 (*Notes bleues*, 517): "It is the first time that banking secrecy can be lifted on the bank's intiative. This departure from a fundamental rule of banking law is justified by the seriousness of the crimes in question. It is a necessity. Most of the suspicious operations can only be detected by banks. To confine oneself to silence would be to protect money laundering".

[46] The area of application of the law as regards persons referred to is very wide since article 3 of the law states that any person who (in the exercise of his profession), exercises control over or gives advice on operations involving movements of funds is subject to an obligation to denounce.

[47] Completed by Decree Number 91-160 of February 13, 1991, a circular from the Minister of Justice of September 28, 1990 (n Crim. 90, n 10 F3), and a decision of February 28, 1991, on approval of the regulation 91-07 of February 15, 1991, from the committee on bank regulation (*Comité de la règlementation bancaire*).

Article 3 of the law states that financial institutions are obliged to notify a department placed under the authority of the Ministry of Economy and Finance of:

"(1) the sums recorded in their books if they appear to them as coming from one of the offences set out by article L. 627 of the Public Health Code (*Code de la Santé Publique*),[48] or by article 415 of the Customs Code (*Code des douanes*);[49] (2) the operations relating to sums which appear to them to come from one the offences mentioned in (1) above".

Article 8 of the law provides that no civil liability action can be instituted and that no professional sanction can be pronounced against a credit establishment which has complied with the provisions of article 3, provided it has acted in good faith. This restriction is, of course, of a nature to give rise to litigation.[50]

At present, the only certain point is that the good faith of the person making the declaration must be presumed, in accordance with general legal rules.

Banking secrecy cannot, therefore, be invoked in such cases. However, it appears in reality that the scope of the text is wider. Indeed, the creation of an obligation to denounce indicates that it is the existence of banking secrecy itself which is called into question. In other words, banking secrecy does not exist from the moment one is within the ambit of the Law of July 12, 1990. It also is significant that article 7 of the law sanctions financial institutions which omit to make the declaration following a failure of control or a default in the organization of their services.

The battle against money laundering is also led by the European Community (EC) whose Council issued Directive 91/308/EEC on June 10, 1991, on the prevention of the use of the financial system for money laundering.[51] This Directive adopts a view identical to that of the French law with respect to the role that credit establishments must take on in the fight against laundering. Its scope of application is, however, wider since it concerns proceeds of other criminal activities.[52] In theory, therefore, France, was required to amend its law on this point before January 1, 1993.

---

[48] Offense of money laundering.

[49] Offense of international transfer of funds from drug trafficking.

[50] See for comments on the law, Credot and Gerard, "Législation et règlementation bancaire", *Rev. banking law* 1990, at pp. 199 *et seq*. For comments on the Decree, see Credot and Gerard, "Législation et règlementation bancaire", *Rev. Législation et Règlementation* 1991, at pp. 95 *et seq*.

[51] ECOJ, June 28, 1991.

[52] See preamble and 1st article, which refers to "criminal activity".

Banking secrecy and international cooperation

This question will be raised once a decision is issued by a foreign **10-021** court or tribunal rules on the disclosure of documents or information held by a bank.

France has ratified treaties by virtue of which French authorities are empowered to provide assistance to a foreign authority. Briefly, this involves the Law of March 10, 1927, regarding enforcement of written interrogatories (*commissions rogatoires*) issued by foreign authorities; the Treaty of April 20, 1979, regarding cooperation in penal matters, and the Hague Convention of March 18, 1970, for obtaining of proof in a foreign jurisdiction. In each case, the request must be conveyed through the French authorities.

On the other hand, the Law of July 25, 1968, amended by the Law of July 16, 1980, provides:

> "Subject to any international treaty and the laws and regulations in force, it is prohibited to anyone to request, to search, or to disclose, in writing or verbally or under any other form, documents or information of economic commercial, industrial, financial or technical nature aiming towards the gathering of evidence with a view to a foreign judicial or administrative procedure or within the frame thereof".

A violation will be punished by a prison sentence of from two to six months, or fine of FF 15,000, or both.

The question is debatable whether a bank's client can force the bank to disclose, to foreign authorities, documents covered in France by banking secrecy.

Economic and social public order

Economic and social public order first of all justifies that banking **10-022** secrecy cannot be invoked against certain organizations responsible for the control of banking institutions. Article 57, paragraph 2, of the Law of January 24, 1984, states that professional secrecy cannot be invoked either against the Bank Committee or the Bank of France.

It is clear that, if secrecy could be invoked against them, these organizations would not be able to carry out their tasks.

In the same way, secrecy cannot be invoked against the Securities Exchange Commission. Article 5 B of the Law of September 28, 1967, modified by Law Number 89-531 of August 2, 1989, provides that:

". . . the investigators can, for the requirements of the investigation, have all documents of whatever nature handed over to
them and to obtain copies thereof. They can summon and hear
any person who are likely to provide them with information.
They can enter the premises for professional use".

Article 5 states that "professional secrecy cannot be invoked against
the commission's staff except by the representatives of the law". The
compliance with these provisions is ensured by criminal sanctions.[53]

Specific provisions governing civil and commercial matters

10-023 In, for example, divorce matters, the banker cannot raise his secrecy
obligation when maintenance and capital payments are being fixed.
According to article 259-3, paragraph 2, of the Civil Code, "The
judge can carry out all necessary inquiries into the debtors or those
who hold money for the account of the spouses without their being
able to invoke secrecy".

In the same way, to allow the creditor to recover his debt, banking secrecy could not be raised against him in matters of attachment
under article 559 of the old Civil Procedure Code.[54] This text was
repealed by Law Number 91-650 of July 9, 1991, on the reform of
civil execution proceedings.[55]

This law includes a section on "the search for information".
Under article 39, the information referred to is:

". . .the address of organizations where an account is opened
in the name of the debtor as well as the address of the debtor
and the address of his employer to the exclusion of any other
information."

[53] Article 10, ordannace of September 28, 1967: "Any person who obstructs the
task of the investigators carried out under the conditions provided by article 5
B shall be punished by a prison sentence ranging from 15 days to two years
and/or a fine from FF 15,000 to FF 2,000,000".

[54] Supreme Court (Commercial Division), May 6, 1981, JCP. 1982 II. n 19708,
comments M. Vasseur; Rev. trim. dr. civ., 1982, at p. 216, comments R. Perrot;
Rev. trim. dr. com., 1981, at p. 806, comments Cabrillac and Teyssie. See also
Paris 15e Ch. A., February 12, 1991, D. 1991, Inf. rap., at p. 89.

[55] D. 1991, L., at pp. 317 *et seq.*

The request for information is a matter for the court bailiff responsible for enforcement. The court bailiff nevertheless can meet with the refusal of the banker. Article 24, paragraph 1, of the law specifies that "third parties cannot obstruct proceedings instituted with a view to enforcing or preserving claims. They must give their assistance to these proceedings when they are legally required".

However, paragraph 2 adds that "one who, without legitimate ground, avoids his obligations can be compelled to perform them, if necessary by a daily fine for delay in performance of the obligations, without prejudice to compensation".

Professional secrecy appears as a legitimate ground in view of article 57 of the Banking Law. It then remains for the court bailiff the possibility of referring it to the public prosecutor. The public prosecutor can then, by virtue of article 40, paragraph 2,

> ". . . ask the establishments authorized by law to hold deposit accounts whether one or more accounts, joint or merged accounts are opened in the name of the debtor as well as the place or places where the account or accounts are held exclusive of any other information".

It does not seem that the banker can hide behind professional secrecy. In fact, it would be useless to grant the public prosecutor the power to make a request for information if the banker could raise secrecy to refuse to reply to the request.

In addition, paragraph 1 of article 24 states that, when the inquiry is made against an organization "subject to the control of the administrative authority", the organization cannot invoke banking secrecy. Banks are subject to such a control.

Further, it is necessary to take into account article 47, paragraph 1, of the Law of July 9, 1991, on attachment (*saisie-attribution*),[56] which provides:

> ". . .when the attachment is carried out in an establishment authorized by law to hold deposit accounts, the establishment is obliged to declare the balance of the debtor's account (s) as at the date of attachment".

On the basis of this article, the banker cannot invoke professional secrecy against the enforcing creditor. The Law of July 9, 1991, thus constitutes an exception to article 57 of the Banking Law, which is justified by the need to protect the legitimate rights of the creditors.

[56] Applicable equally to attachment, article 75, paragraph 3.

Administration and receivership

10-024 Lastly, it is essential to cite the provisions governing administration and receivership proceedings. These enact a waiver of banking secrecy justified on the basis of safeguarding the common interest.

Article 36 of the Law of March 1, 1984, on the administration and receivership of companies gives the President of the Court the power to obtain from banking institutions information necessary to assess the debtor's situation.

There is an equivalent power for the official receiver (*Juge-Commissaire*) when drawing up the economic and social report (*bilan économique et social*), and rehabilitation plan of the undertaking in the judicial rehabilitation proceedings governed by the Law of January 25, 1985.

By virtue of the Law of January 25, 1985, banking secrecy cannot be invoked against the receiver or the liquidator since they act as legal representatives of the bank's client.

In addition, under articles 13 and 67, the judicial receiver may obtain all information from various authorities including credit establishments, that is "information of such nature as to give accurate information on the economic and financial standing of the company" and in the event of continuation or sale of the undertaking the judge in charge of the plan can request "any document or information useful for his task".

Equally, when sanctions are imposed against the director in fact or law (*dirigeant de fait ou de droit*) of a corporate body subject to rehabilitation proceedings or judicial liquidation proceedings, the court can by virtue of article 184, lift banking secrecy to assess the totality of the director's wealth.

Finally, it is necessary to cite article 4 of the Law Number 89-1010 of December 31, 1989, on the prevention and settlement of disputes linked to the over-indebtedness of individuals and families. According to this text, the board of examiners of situations of over-indebtedness of individuals can obtain from credit establishments.

> ". . . any information of a nature to give it accurate information on the debtor's situation, of the possible evolution of the debtor's situation, and of the amicable arrangement proceedings in progress".

All these exceptions are manifestly justified by considerations of economic and social public policy. Only a clear knowledge of content of the economic assets and liabilities permits the rehabilitation of the undertakings and thus the maintenance of the overall economic activity. Concerning civil rehabilitation, it is the social aspect which prevails.

Finally, one notes that, if the exceptions to banking secrecy are relatively important, they are all justified by public order considerations which necessarily prevail over private interest which itself justifies the relative nature of the banker's confidentiality obligation.

CONCLUSION

Despite a number of exceptions, it is possible to affirm that banking **10-025** secrecy is an essential principle of French law. In fact, as we have seen, the Supreme Court does not admit exceptions in the relationship between individuals.

It is only in the face of interests considered superior, because they concern the community, that the right to confidentiality gives way to the right to disclosure. However, it remains that the information so disclosed is limited to certain persons defined by law and provided they keep the information confidential.

The scope of banking secrecy is thus merely diluted since there is only a widening of the circle of persons entitled to share information which remains confidential.

CHAPTER 11

GERMANY

Harald Jung
Peltzer & Riesenkampff
Frankfurt am Main, Germany

Chapter 11

GERMANY

INTRODUCTION

A generally valid, express regulation on banking secrecy does not **11-001** exist in the German legal system. Nor, as under Swiss and Austrian law, is banking secrecy offered any protection under German criminal law.[1]

Only paragraph 6, Post Law, provides that information on post office giro accounts and post office savings accounts must not be released unless required by law. Nevertheless, it is generally accepted that banking secrecy exists in general and does warrant protection.

Opinions differ as to the legal source for banking secrecy. Though not a majority viewpoint, some commentators believe that banking secrecy is a customary right. Others have argued that banking secrecy stems from constitutional rights. Article 2(1) of the Basic Law (*Grundgesetz*) grants every individual the right to freely develop his personality.

The general law on personality is derived from this general freedom of action and from the dignity of man, which is, according to article 1(1), Basic Law, inviolable and to be respected and protected by the state.

The general law on personality comprises, among other things, the right to secrecy. This right includes the individual's right to hold secret that information which he seeks to keep confidential.[2] Other authorities have also taken the view that the right to free development of the individual, pursuant to article 2(1), Basic Law, ensures constitutional protection for banking secrecy.

---

[1] Article 47, Swiss Banking Law; paragraphs 34(1) and 23, Austrian Banking Law.
[2] Hubmann, *Juristenzeitung* 1957, at p. 524; Sichtermann, *Monatszeitschrift für Deutsches Recht* 1965, at p. 679.

This constitutional right also guarantees, according to this view, freedom of business and freedom of contract. The latter is violated when the contractual parties are barred from comprehensively securing banking secrecy in their legal transactions.

The overwhelming majority view assumes correctly that banking secrecy is based on the contractual relations between customer and bank. These two parties develop a relationship of mutual trust.[3] The duty of confidentiality is, therefore, a secondary duty resulting from the bank contract. If no effective bank contract is actually concluded, the duty of confidentiality results from the particular relationship of trust established at the inception of the business relationship.

According to this view, a bank is bound to secrecy on information it has come to know during preliminary contract negotiations. Since the duty of confidentiality in banking forms an inherent part of the business relationship between customer and bank, no express agreement is required.

SUBJECT MATTER AND EXCEPTIONS TO BANKING SECRECY

Facts pertaining to banking secrecy

11-002   Normally, a bank is bound to maintain confidentiality unless it is entitled to disclosure. In this respect, all information which the bank comes to know through its relationship with its customer, and which the customer does not wish to have revealed, must remain confidential.

In the German language, not all banking organizations are called banks (*Banken*), *e.g.*, savings banks (*Sparkassen*) and public law credit institutions (*öffentlich - rechtliche Kreditinstitute*). Nevertheless, the German expression for banking secrecy (*Bankgeheimnis*) applies to all "banks", not only to private banks.

Negative facts also are subject to the duty of confidentiality, *e.g.*, the fact that there has been no transaction, that a customer does not have an account, or that a credit line has not been exhausted. Information under banking secrecy consists not only of facts in the actual sense of the word, but also impressions and assessments

---

3 Canaris, *Bankvertragsrecht*, 4th ed., ann., at pp. 36 *et seq.*; Sichtermann, *Bankgeheimnis und Bankauskunft*, at pp. 40 - 65; Musielak in Hadding/Schneider, *Bankgeheimnis und Bankauskunft*, at p. 13.

which the bank could not have made without processing the information to which it became privy.

The duty of confidentiality does not apply to evident facts, *i.e.*, information that is available to the public or that could be learned without any expertise.[4]

Banking secrecy applies to all information the customer wishes to keep confidential.[5] The customer's subjective intent is decisive in determining what information shall remain confidential. It is irrelevant whether the customer's intent is reasonable and in furtherance of his interests. If the actual intent cannot be ascertained, the customer's presumed intent plays a role.

Only when the presumed intent cannot be determined does the criteria of objective interest become the deciding factor. In case of doubt, all information to which the bank becomes privy in connection with its business relations with the customer is subject to confidentiality.

The bank must obtain the information in connection with its business relations with the customer. A bank is subject to a heightened degree of confidentiality because the customer has put a great degree of trust in the bank and because the bank is privy to information which, if released to an unintended party, could have serious ramifications for the customer's affairs.

Therefore, the connection between banking secrecy and business relations is to be interpreted broadly; there is no prerequisite that a concrete transaction has taken place or that actual business relations have been established. The duty of confidentiality begins with the initiation of business, for example, when an application for credit has been submitted and the credit negotiations are discontinued without result.

Further, it is not important whether the bank has gathered the information from the customer or from a third party. This applies in particular to information the customer revealed regarding his financial position such as balance sheets, by-laws, land register excerpts, tax returns, tax value assessments, lists of stocks, inheritance, divorce, and payment of alimony, as well as state of accounts and deposits, both at the initiation of his business relations with the bank and subsequently.

Since it often happens that a customer's creditor contacts the bank to inquire whether a customer has an account with the intention of attaching the assets, the fact that a person is a customer and has an account with a particular bank also is confidential. Of course,

---

[4] Musielak, *supra* n. 3.

[5] *Entscheidungen des Bundesgerichtshofes in Zivilsachen*, volume 27, at p. 246.

the discontinuance of business relations does not affect the duty of confidentiality with regard to information obtained prior to that period.

Since the scope of the duty of confidentiality depends on the customer's intent, he can, in principle, exclude certain facts from the duty of confidentiality. Beyond that, a bank does not need to withhold information from persons with the assistance of whom it does business. Since the customer realizes that this information will be shared, the bank can assume his consent. This also is not considered to be contradictory to the customer's interests because the bank's assistants are, likewise, bound to secrecy.

The duty of confidentiality is further limited insofar as there may be a requirement to release information by force of law (see text below). Finally, a bank also is not bound to secrecy if it is generally entitled, according to an arrangement, to give information (see text below).

Indirect protection of banking secrecy

11-003   Although there are no definitions or general statutory regulations on banking secrecy, there are quite a number of statutory rules which indirectly relate to banking secrecy. They include the right to refuse to testify in court proceedings.

The regulations do not state that a bank's representative or employee is required, in order to keep banking secrets, to refuse to testify. However, if such person did not make use of his right to refuse to testify he would violate his duty of confidentiality on banking secrets.

There are, however, rare cases when, in order to protect the higher interests of the general public or legally protected rights of higher rank, it is necessary for the bank's representative or employee to testify. For instance, a bank is acknowledged to have the right to reveal information subject to banking secrecy in it's own interest if it cannot otherwise defend itself against defamatory allegations in court proceedings.[6]

The most important rights to refuse to testify under German law are the following.

According to paragraph 383(1), number 6, and paragraph 384, number 3, Code of Civil Procedure (*Zivilprozeßordnung*), in civil proceedings a witness has the right to refuse to testify regard-

---

[6] Canaris, *supra* n. 3, ann. 65; *Bundesgerichtshof in Neue Juristische Wochenschrift* 1952, at p. 151; Lenkner in Schönke/Schroeder, *Strafgesetzbuch*, paragraph 203, ann. 33.

ing information he was entrusted with by virtue of his office and that is confidential by its nature. As early as 1914, courts acknowledged that banking secrecy is included in the secrets protected hereby.[7]

Owners and legal representatives of banks, as well as employees and assistants, all have the right to refuse to testify. Legal representatives and legal successors of bankers, *e.g.*, receivers, administrators, executors, also may subscribe to this right.

Since employees at several public law banks, such as savings banks or the German Federal Bank (*Deutsche Bundesbank*), are bound to secrecy according to the duty of official secrecy.[8] Such persons, when revealing facts protected by the right to refuse to testify, may be guilty of a crime pursuant to paragraph 203(2), Penal Code (*Strafgesetzbuch*). This regulation renders the unauthorized revelation of someone else's secrets a punishable offense.

Similar to civil proceedings, it is expressly stated, in both bankruptcy proceedings and composition proceedings, that banks have the right to refuse to testify.[9]

The regulations on the right to refuse to testify in civil proceedings are also applicable to labor court proceedings.[10] Thus, banks also can refuse to testify in labor courts.

There are similar regulations in social court proceedings,[11] according to which the right to refuse to testify also applies to the petition for information (*Auskunftsersuchen*) preceding the actual court proceedings.[12] According to this regulation, the president of the chamber of a social court must take all measures necessary to settle the litigation in a meeting prior to the hearing.

The regulations found in the Administrative Court Act (*Verwaltungsgerichtsordnung*) also refer to the right to refuse to testify in civil proceedings.[13] Banks, therefore, also are entitled to refuse to testify in administrative court proceedings.

---

[7] *Bundesgerichtshof in Juristische Wochenschrift* 1914, at p. 830.

[8] Paragraphs 21 and 23, Law on Savings Banks of North Rhine-Westphalia; paragraph 21, Law on Savings Banks of Schleswig-Holstein; paragraph 32, German Federal Bank Law.

[9] Paragraph 72, Bankruptcy Law; paragraph 115, Law on Composition Procedure.

[10] Paragraphs 46(2) and 80(2), Labor Court Law.

[11] Paragraphs 118 and 202, Social Court Law.

[12] Paragraph 106, Social Court Law.

[13] Paragraph 98, Administrative Court Law.

Legal duties to give information and testify

11-004   The scope and limits of banking secrecy are conclusively determined by regulations expressly stating the duty to give information despite banking secrecy.

Seizure of debts under paragraph 840, Code of Civil Procedure

11-005   Paragraph 840, Code of Civil Procedure , grants a creditor who is seeking to execute a judgment or comparable title the right to demand information from a third party debtor of the judgment debtor (garnishee). According to this regulation, the garnisee must provide information to the judgment creditor as to the extent, if any, to which he acknowledges the debt owed to the judgment debtor and is willing to pay, and what claims, if any, other persons may have raised against this debt.

Finally, the garnishee must provide information on whether the debt has already been seized by other creditors, and if so, for what claims.

In principle, the duty to give such information applies to anyone, including banks who cannot, in this connection, base a refusal to provide such information on an appeal to banking secrecy.

Criminal and administrative offense proceedings

11-006   In criminal proceedings, owners and employees of banks are bound to appear as witnesses before the prosecutor to testify.[14] The same applies to hearings before the criminal court during the main hearing.[15] Witnesses do not have the right to refuse to testify unless they do so pursuant to paragraphs 53 to 55, Code of Criminal Procedure (*Strafprozeßordnung*).

Since banking secrecy is not mentioned in the list of trade secrets to which the right to refuse to testify applies, bank owners and bank employees also must testify as to information that, though banking secrets, comes under the duty of confidentiality.

However, according to paragraph 54, Code of Criminal Procedure, employees of public law banks must be authorized by the appropriate superior to give information.

---

[14] Paragraph 161a, Code of Criminal Procedure.
[15] Paragraph 162, Code of Criminal Procedure.

There is no duty to give information to a foreign authority or court so long as the duty is not recognized by a German authority or by a German court.[16]

Regardless of whether a question relates to a banking secret, a bank employee, of course, can refuse to answer if he would otherwise incriminate himself or one of his relatives.

The witness testifying before the court or the prosecutor must do so truthfully and fully, *i.e.*, he has the duty to familiarize himself with the facts so as not to carelessly make incorrect statements. Therefore, a witness who has neglected to take this action prior to his testimony must declare that his recollection might not coincide with the evidentiary documents.

Banking secrecy is further restricted by the prosecutor's right to confiscate evidentiary business documents without prior written court approval; however, such right exists only in urgent situations.[17] To carry out the confiscation, a search of the bank's offices may be ordered. Both the search and the confiscation must be restricted to evidence essential for the investigation.

The documents must be described specifically and accurately to limit the search to its stated purpose. A search is not permitted without supporting information indicating that the evidence is in the area to be searched.

Although the evidence must be described as accurately as possible as to its form or possible content, evidence found during the search that was not included in the search warrant may be confiscated. In addition, evidence found during the search but which has no relation to the search may be confiscated temporarily if it indicates another criminal offense.

However, the Code of Criminal Procedure prohibits a search for evidence which does not relate to the offense being investigated. To use the search as a pretext for a systematic search for incriminating evidence which does not relate to the criminal offense being investigated is unlawful. Both the use and confiscation of such evidence is prohibited.[18]

With respect to banking secrecy, the Code of Criminal Procedure also is applicable to the prosecution of administrative offenses, *i.e.*, proceedings for violation of mere administrative regulations which are not penal laws in the strict sense.[19]

In those proceedings, the investigating authority also has the right to summon and question bank employees as witnesses, ask

[16] Landgericht Kiel in *Recht der Internationalen Wirtschaft* 1983, at p. 206.
[17] Paragraphs 94 *et seq.*, Code of Criminal Procedure.
[18] Landgericht Bonn in *Wertpapiermitteilungen* 1980, at p. 1211.
[19] Paragraph 41, Law on Administrative Offenses.

banks for information and, in case of danger of delay, give orders to search and confiscate, or to carry out such actions pursuant to court order.

Tax law

11-007   **General** The bank's duty to reveal information to the tax authorities pursuant to a petition for information is treated differently in taxation proceedings, criminal tax proceedings, administrative offense tax proceedings, and tax investigation proceedings.

In criminal tax proceedings and administrative offense tax proceedings, the general principles, as described above, are applicable.

In tax investigation proceedings, the scope of the duty to give information and submit evidence depends on whether the tax authority has instituted taxation proceedings or criminal tax proceedings. When a criminal tax offense or infringement of tax law is being investigated, it is a criminal tax proceeding. The examination of taxation bases and exposure of unknown tax cases constitutes a taxation proceeding.

In taxation proceedings against one of its customers, a bank is required to give the tax authority information necessary to ascertain a fact pertinent to taxation. Although paragraph 102, Tax Code (*Abgabenordnung*), gives the right to refuse to testify to protect certain trade secrets, banks may claim this right in order to refuse information to tax authorities, since banking secrets are not considered trade secrets. The same applies to the submission of documents.[20]

Therefore, paragraph 93, Tax Code, is applicable and provides that parties, as well as other persons, including banks, must reveal information necessary to ascertain a fact pertinent to taxation.

Official secrecy, which applies to employees of banks organized under public law, such as the German Federal Bank and savings public law banks, does not apply to tax authorities' petitions for information and requests for submission.[21]

11-008   **Paragraph 30a, Tax Code** However, the wording of paragraph 30a, Tax Code, considerably limits the tax authorities' right to investigate banks in general taxation proceedings, without establishing a general right to refuse to give information. This provision is similar

[20] Paragraph 104(1), Tax Code.
[21] Paragraphs 21 and 23, Law on Savings Banks of North Rhine-Westphalia; paragraph 21, Law on Savings Banks of Schleswig-Holstein; paragraph 32, German Federal Bank Law.

to regulations, known as "banking enactments" (*Bankenerlaß*), that had been in force for decades within the Federal Ministry of Finance. It did not become a statutory regulation, and thus, part of the Tax Code, until August 3, 1988. It provides as follows:

"Paragraph 30a, Protection of Bank Customers

(1) When examining the facts of a case (paragraph 88), tax authorities must show particular consideration for the relationship of trust between the bank and its customers.

(2) Tax authorities must not demand from credit institutions for the purpose of general control, once or periodically, information about accounts of specific kinds or exceeding a specific amount.

(3) Deposit accounts or securities accounts, at the opening of which an identity check of the holder was conducted pursuant to paragraph 154(2) must not be reviewed during a tax audit of a credit institution in order to control the correctness of taxation. No control statements shall be made on such accounts.

(4) The account number of deposit or securities accounts which a taxpayer holds at a bank shall not be requested on tax declaration forms unless tax deductible costs are claimed in connection therewith or because of payments to the tax authority.

(5) Paragraph 93 is applicable to petitions for information submitted to banks. If the taxpayer is of known identity and no criminal tax proceedings or administrative offense tax proceedings have been instituted against him in a proceeding pursuant to paragraph 208(1), sentence 1, a credit institution may be asked for information and submission of documents only if a petition for information submitted to the taxpayer has been unsuccessful or is unlikely to be successful."

Questions have been raised repeatedly[22] regarding the constitutionality of this regulation. The Federal Constitution Court (*Bundesverfassungsgericht*) also has questioned the constitutionality of the

---

[22] Hellwig in Hellermann/Hepp/Spitaler, *Kommentar zur Abgabenordnung*, paragraph 30a, ann. 7; Tipke/Kruse, *Kommentar zur Abgabenordnung*, paragraph 30a, ann. 10; Tipke/Lang, *Steuerrecht*, 12th ed., paragraph 21, 3.44.

regulation in a decision of June 27, 1991.[23] Commentators consider part of paragraph 30a, Tax Code, a violation of the principle of equality guaranteed by article 3, Basic Law.

According to their view, the principle of equality requires that the state's substantive tax claim, once established, must be enforced equally towards all citizens who meet the statutory preconditions for taxation. It is argued that the principle of equality is violated by the statutory regulation of paragraph 30a, Tax Code, since it prevents tax authorities from considering an important part of taxable income for taxation, *i.e.*, interest and the underlying bank accounts.

It is further argued that there are no objective plausible reasons justifying a different treatment of interest income from other income. Experience has shown that a withholding tax on interest, which had been provided for in German law for only a short time, resulted in a substantial and unacceptable exodus of capital. A similar effect, unwelcomed by economic policy makers, is to be expected when the duty to reveal information to the authorities takes precedence over banking secrecy.

Such effects, however, do not justify violating the principle of equality since they cannot be accepted as objective grounds, pursuant to German constitutional law, for permitting unequal treatment.

Since, according to this view, the risk of disturbance in the capital market results from substantive tax law, only amendments to this law can reduce this risk.

Hence, paragraph 30a, Tax Code is, in certain parts, unconstitutional. In its judgment of June 27, 1991, the Federal Constitutional Court gave the German legislature until December 31, 1992, to amend the regulation of paragraph 30a, Tax Code, in such a way that the principle of equal treatment is no longer violated. However, the judgment did not specifically provide as to how this was to be implemented.

This regulation restricts a number of general examination and investigation rights tax authorities have available in instances where capital and capital income is concerned, *i.e.*, interest in particular. If this regulation is applied to the letter, tax authorities will not have any information on interest income unless it has been properly declared.

Paragraph 30a(1), Tax Code, provides that tax authorities examining information relevant for taxation must show particular discretion regarding the relationship of trust between banks and their

---

23 *Finanz-Rundschau* 1991, at p. 375.

customers. This regulation favors the customer to some degree, as it limits the scope of the investigation.[24] Most commentators hold such an interpretation to be unconstitutional.[25]

According to paragraph 30a(2), Tax Code, banks are not, at any time, required to give tax authorities information on accounts of a particular kind or state for general supervision. There is no doubt as to the constitutionality of this rule because the Federal Constitutional Court decided in 1987[26] that a body investigating suspected tax evasion may not make general examinations unless there is sufficient and concrete evidence of tax evasion.

Subsection 2 could further be interpreted to mean that tax authorities do not have the right to information on transactions even if there is concrete indication that the interest for a particular account has not been taxed. This interpretation is refuted partly for constitutional reasons.[27]

However, if there are indications in a particular case, that a taxpayer received interest and failed to declare it, subsection 2 does not prohibit the tax authorities from submitting a petition for information to the bank.

Subsection 3 is the most important part of paragraph 30a, Tax Code. According to this regulation, tax authorities must not use statements made during a tax audit of a bank which relate to a particular customer (control statements) if the bank has followed the proper procedure in confirming the background of the customer when opening the account. This regulation restricts the general rights tax auditors have pursuant to paragraph 194(3), Tax Code. This restriction also is considered to be unconstitutional because it deviates greatly from the principle of equality in taxation proceedings.[28]

Subsection 4 of the regulation is considered constitutional. It states that tax declaration forms may not request information on numbers of accounts and securities accounts at banks, unless tax-deductible costs or other reductions are claimed in this connection, or the information is necessary for payment transactions. However, this regulation does not limit the tax authorities' right to information on a particular account.

Such demands for information on a particular account are permissible, with the customer's knowledge, pursuant to paragraph 30a(5), Tax Code.

[24] Tipke/Kruse, *supra* n. 22, paragraph 30a, ann. 4.
[25] Hellwig, *supra* n. 22, ann. 13.
[26] *Bundessteuerblatt II* 1987, at p. 484.
[27] Hellwig, *supra* n. 22, ann. 16.
[28] *Id.*

Until the regulation is changed, or declared unconstitutional, both the bank and the customer can lodge an appeal against orders by tax authorities to reveal information that is not covered by paragraph 30a, Tax Code. However, if the period to appeal passes, the order becomes incontestable and must be satisfied.

When a bank is asked for information or submission of documents by a tax authority, it is within its discretion to inform the customer. Neither tax law regulations nor criminal law regulations prohibit such information from being passed to the customer. However, banks do not have a duty to inform the customer when such information is requested.

Whether a petition from the tax authorities for information is permissible also depends on its precision as to the content. For instance, a general petition for information on a customer's business relations is not sufficiently precise. The investigative character of such a petition runs counter to the principles of necessityand specificity.

11-009 **Paragraph 33, Inheritance Tax Law** The bank's obligation to report in case of a customer's death pursuant to paragraph 33, Inheritance Tax Law, is an especially serious limitation of banking secrecy. Banks are required to give the tax authority in charge of inheritance tax information on the accounts and other assets which are in the safekeeping of the bank and over which the deceased had the power to dispose.

This limitation of banking secrecy is exacerbated by the Additional Order of the Highest Tax Authorities (*Zusatzerlaß der Obersten Finanzbehörden*) of February 17, 1986,[29] which provides that inheritance tax authorities must submit a report to the authorities responsible for income and net-worth tax if an estate exceeds a fixed amount (a total value of more than DM 250,000 or capital assets of more than DM 50,000).

Banking supervision

11-010 The Banking Act (*Kreditwesengesetz*) imposes on banks the obligation to give the Federal Banking Supervisory Authority (*Bundesaufsichtsamt für das Kreditwesen*) and the German Federal Bank certain information, thereby restricting banking secrecy.

According to paragraph 14, Banking Act, the banks must notify the German Federal Bank four times a year regarding borrowers who had a debt of DM 1-million or more at any time within the three

29 *Bundessteuerblatt* 1986 I., at p. 82.

months preceding the day of notification. If a borrower has been granted several such loans, the German Federal Bank must inform the banks concerned regarding the borrower's total debt and the number of banks concerned.

In addition, large loans, *i.e.*, loans exceeding 15 per cent of the bank's liable capital, generally must be made known to the German Federal Bank (paragraphs 13 and 13a, Banking Act).

Loans of a certain amount to a bank's managers, members of the supervisory board, officials, and employees. must be made known to the Federal Supervisory Authority and to the German Federal Bank (paragraphs 15 and 16, Banking Act).

Paragraph 44, Banking Act, is the most drastic restriction of banking secrecy in this Act. According to this provision, the Federal Banking Supervisory Authority has the right to demand information on any business matter, to request the submission of books and documents, and to carry out investigations without giving specific reasons. In order to do so, employees at the Federal Banking Supervisory Authority may enter the bank's offices.

No reason must be given to justify the petition for information, but it is limited to the discretion of the administrative authority in such a way that the Federal Banking Supervisory Authority may not demand information except that which is necessary to fulfil the tasks provided in the Banking Act.

In practice, the limitations on banking secrecy favoring the Federal Banking Supervisory Authority and the German Federal Bank have not had a negative impact because these rights have been exercised with great discretion. Employees at the Federal Banking Supervisory Authority and at the German Federal Bank also are bound to observe confidentiality under the provisions of paragraph 19, Banking Act.

Foreign trade law

According to paragraph 44, Foreign Trade Law (*Außenwirtschaftsge-* **11-011** *setz*), the German Federal Bank, and all other authorities mentioned in that paragraph, may demand information insofar as it is necessary to meet the requirements of this Act and the regulations promulgated pursuant thereto.

All parties involved in foreign trade, whether directly or indirectly, are required to give information (paragraph 44(2), Foreign Trade Law). Banks also are bound by this requirement insofar as they are involved in foreign trade. Involvement in payment transactions of a foreign trade business suffices to trigger the requirement.

Authorities which have the right to information can demand that business documents be submitted. They also may question the parties bound to give the information and, in order to carry out the investigation, enter their offices. The party bound to give information need not necessarily be suspected of having violated the regulations of Foreign Trade Law.

Depending on the business purpose, the authorities will decide what supervisory measures, if any, shall be taken to obtain the information, observing however, the principles of necessity, appropriateness, suitability, and reasonableness.

The employees of authorities which have the right to information are bound by an obligation to official secrecy, the violation of which constitutes a criminal offense (paragraph 203, Penal Code).

Banking secrecy and rights to information

Bank information

11-012 "Bank information" is general information a bank gives to a third party regarding the financial position, business practices, and business principles of one of its customers.

Thus, bank information reveals the financial position of a customer which he would normally wish to remain confidential. Hence, there is tension between banking secrecy and bank information.

All German banks - large banks , small private banks, and banks organized under public mandate - traditionally open business relations with their customers only on the basis of "General Terms of Business of Private Banks" or "General Terms of Business of Savings Banks", respectively.[30] They define the term "bank information" as follows:

> "Bank Information is general statements and remarks on the financial position of a customer, his creditworthiness and solvency; information on the state of accounts, savings accounts, securities accounts and other assets the bank has been entrusted with, as well as on borrowings, is not included."

To what extent, if any, banks have the right to give bank information concerning customers was in dispute until the general terms of

[30] Number 10, paragraph 2, General Terms of Business of Private Banks, or number 7, paragraph 1, General Terms of Business of Savings Banks, respectively.

business of banks was amended in 1984. It is now clearly provided as to what information may be released.[31]

The bank has the right to give information on legal entities and merchants registered in the commercial register if the customer has not given a contrary order. The bank should not give information on any other entity or association unless it has been given express approval in general or in a particular case.

According to this regulation, banks are entitled to give information on the following commercial customers without express consent: stock corporations, limited share partnerships, limited liability companies, registered cooperatives, mutual insurance societies, general commercial partnerships, limited partnerships, and registered merchants, including general partners of commercial partnerships.

There is no general right to give bank information on registered merchants who are natural persons. The crucial point here is whether the customer has the account for personal or business purposes. Therefore, bank information may be revealed only if the merchant is registered in the commercial register and has come to the bank as a commercial customer.

Even though a bank can give negative information on such commercial customers, it nevertheless may be bound to refuse to give information in a particular case because all banks and savings banks, pursuant to the preliminary remarks to their general terms of business, have obliged themselves to protect the interests of their customers.

For this reason, they cannot refer to the general consent of commercial customers that information may be given if it is evident to the bank concerned that giving the information is against the customer's interest in a particular case.

However, when weighing the interests, the bank should consider that, in practice, a refusal to give information is often regarded as unfavorable information. Therefore, it may happen that negative information is more favorable to the customer than a refusal to give information that could give rise to unfounded speculation.

Except with their express consent, banks may not give out information on customers who are neither legal entities nor merchants registered in the commercial register. If confronted with such a request, the bank will generally ask for a written declaration. If no prior express consent has been given, banks normally will refuse to

---

[31] Number 10, paragraph 1, General Terms Business of Private Banks, or number 7, paragraph 2, General Terms of Business of Savings Banks, respectively.

give information since they are not bound to obtain the consent for themselves. Banks generally avoid consulting the customer because he may limit his consent to that information which was specifically discussed with him.

Bank information can be given to other banks and to the bank's customers. It may not be given to non-customers.

However, the non-customer has the opportunity to submit the name and the account number of the customer in question to his bank and have that bank forward the petition for information to the appropriate bank. Therefore, a bank asking for information must make it clear whether it is acting in its own interest or on behalf of a customer.

Information also can be given to foreign banks, but the principle of reciprocity is carefully observed.

Bank information must be limited to the following data; otherwise, it is not covered by the general consent of a commercial customer or the express consent of a private customer:

    (1) Commercial customer -
        (a) Name, firm, and domicile of customer in question;
        (b) Foundation;
        (c) Legal form;
        (d) Business purpose;
        (e) Partners and capital;
        (f) Management, and
        (g) Creditworthiness.
    (2) Private customer -
        (a) Surname, first name, and domicile of customer in question;
        (b) Age;
        (c) Marital status;
        (d) Occupation/profession, and
        (e) Creditworthiness.

If information on the financial situation of a firm is asked for, no information on the financial situation of the managers is given.

Upon request by the customer in question, the bank is bound to tell him what information it has revealed.

"Schufa" proceedings

11-013   *"Schufa"* is the abbreviation for "Protection Association for the General Securing of Credits" (*Schutzgemeinschaft für allgemeine Kreditsicherung*). This is an association of which almost all German banks and savings banks are contractual members. The task of *Schufa* is to give its members formal information in order to protect them from losses in consumer credit transactions.

Besides mail order firms and department stores, only firms granting cash credits or retail financing to customers by trade can become members of *Schufa*.

Whereas the bank information procedure is limited to commercial customers, *Schufa* procedures apply exclusively to private customers.

Schufa acts in accordance with the principle of reciprocity, *i.e.*, only those providing *Schufa* with information are able to obtain information. The information given to a contractual partner is based on information *Schufa* has received from other members or has drawn from public registers.

A member may not ask *Schufa* for information except on such persons who seek cash credits, retail financing, or wish to enter into an obligation of suretyship. Beyond that, banks can obtain *Schufa* information before opening a current account.

In addition to the information given on petition, *Schufa* provides members with information it has learned subsequently. For instance, the member receives information concerning irregularities during the performance of a loan transaction a customer undertakes with another *Schufa* member. Permission for transmitting relevant data to *Schufa* is the express and written consent of the customer concerned.

At present, banks that have the customer's appropriate consent transmit to *Schufa* the following data: characteristics of the application for credit, the assumption of a guaranty including the bank's conclusion as stipulated in the contract, information about a customer's failure to perform pursuant to a contract, and the introduction of judicial measures. This includes, among other things, the closing of a current account, the cancellation of credit, and an application for a court order for repayment (*Mahnbescheid*) in case of an outstanding debt or enforcement measures.

Beyond that, *Schufa* uses data from public registers such as a declaration in lieu of an oath by which the debtor declares that he has no assets against which the creditor can enforce his claim, the opening of bankruptcy proceedings, and the refusal to open bankruptcy proceedings for lack of assets.

Information on checks and bills of exchange

In cases concerning checks not honored, the holder can ask the **11-014** relevant bank for information on the drawer. The bank is entitled to give all data necessary to process the check claims. This may include the name and address of the drawer being revealed.

By drawing the check, the drawer has conclusively empowered the bank to reveal this information. The bank is not allowed to give additional information on the drawer's financial situation.

Although the bank is entitled to give information, it is not required to do so in any way.

Furthermore, the bank has the right to inform the check holder, upon request, whether the check will be paid. The drawer also has conclusively given consent to such affirmation of payment, but the bank must make sure that the petition for affirmation is not fraudulent.

Beyond that, the bank has the right to inform the drawer about the payee and the circumstances of payment.

LEGAL CONSEQUENCES OF VIOLATIONS OF BANKING SECRECY

11-015 If a bank willfully or negligently violates banking secrecy, the customer can seek damages for the resultant loss. The violation is willful if the bank knows, when giving the information, that it is revealing a secret of the customer or if it recklessly discloses information.

The bank is negligent if, though not knowing that it is revealing a secret of the customer, it could and should have realized by applying the care a reasonable bank must observe[32] that its actions would result in revealing a secret of the customer.

If a bank violates banking secrecy, the customer also has the right to terminate the business relationship with immediate effect.

If a bank fails to observe its obligation of secrecy, the customer is entitled to seek a court order directing that the bank refrain from disclosing the information. Such an enforceable claim exists if there is concern that the bank might reveal a secret, especially in cases where the bank disputes its obligation to maintain secrecy. Such claims also can be made in interim injunction proceedings.

Note: The author would like to thank Jörg Rehder, Attorney at Law, Washington, DC, for assistance in editing this article.

[32] Hellwig, *supra* n. 22.

GIBRALTAR

B.J.S. Marrache and G.V. Davis
Marrache & Co.
Gibraltar

Chapter 12

GIBRALTAR

INTRODUCTION

Even before the full opening of the frontier with the mainland of   **12-001**
Spain in 1985, great interest in Gibraltar as a banking and financial
center was shown by major banking institutions and by investors
alike. Ever since 1967, with the arrival of the Companies (Taxation
and Concessions) Ordinance,[1] which developed the concept of Gibraltar exempt companies, Gibraltar has encouraged both investing
and banking activity and accordingly has been recognized as a
financial center.

Gibraltar entered the European Community (EC) as a dependent
territory under article 227(4) of the Treaty of Rome in 1973, following the accession to the Community of the United Kingdom and, for
the purposes of banking and other commercial businesses, Gibraltar is essentially established as the thirteenth Member State of the
Community.

Gibraltar's membership in the EC is, however, conditioned by
the specific non-application of Community law in three following
areas: the Common Agricultural Policy, harmonization of value
added norms and other turnover taxes, and the Common Customs
Tariff.

Well aware of its unique position within the EC and of its increasingly sophisticated financial services and banking legislation, the
Gibraltar Government has consciously and deliberately created an
hospitable environment for achieving the growth of its financial
center. With the globalization of banking and the financial services
market, Gibraltar's continually updated banking legislation reflects
a commitment to financial vitality and banking stability.

[1] Companies (Taxation and Concessions) Ordinance 1967.

FINANCIAL CENTER

12-002 Gibraltar's official currency is the British pound or pound sterling, although Government of Gibraltar notes denominated in sterling also are legal tender. There is no capital gains tax in Gibraltar and, for non-residents of Gibraltar, there is no investment income surcharge, no value added tax, no sales tax, no capital transfer tax, no income tax, and no estate duty.

No exchange control regulations exist in Gibraltar on the investment of capital and, therefore, Gibraltar companies and individuals may hold and operate bank accounts in any foreign currency and may, for example, purchase real and personal property anywhere in the world without restriction. Gibraltar exempt companies created under the Companies (Taxation and Concessions) Ordinance are liable only for a flat annual tax of £225 to the Government of Gibraltar.

Banking in Gibraltar is currently governed by the Banking Ordinance,[2] which specifically provides for implementation of various Community directives in Gibraltar and which regulates banking operations in the territory and introduces a minimum capital requirement for such operations.

Gibraltar's new Banking Ordinance of 1992 has been implemented, and it is this new piece of legislation which offers a particularly interesting framework for the parameters of banking confidentiality.

NEW AND OLD LEGISLATION: GENERAL COMPARISON

12-003 Under the 1992 Ordinance, Part IV, as under the 1982 Ordinance, a minimum capital requirement for banking operations is maintained. Licensing is strictly regulated, and the criteria for the issue of a banking license includes the need to protect the interests of depositors and potential depositors, the need to protect the reputation of Gibraltar in relation to financial matters, the reputation of the institution and its ability to provide a full range of services, and the minimum paid-up capital and reserves of ECU 5-million (or an amount of equivalent value denominated wholly or partly in another unit of account) or such greater amount as may be prescribed by an instrument of the European Community.

2 Banking Ordinance of 1982.

Of course, the institution also must carry on its business with integrity and prudence and must maintain adequate liquidity, as well as make provision for bad and doubtful debts and for obligations of a contingent nature, and the whole of the business must effectively be directed by not fewer than two individuals. Thus, the new Ordinance makes no substantial alterations to the 1982 restrictions on licensing.

As the regulatory framework supporting the banking and financial sector continues to be improved, however, certain distinctions and changes are reflected in the new Banking Ordinance. Any once-recognized distinction, for example, between class "A" (*i.e.*, on-shore) and class "B" (*i.e.*, off-shore) banking licences will be abolished, meaning that all banks licensed in Gibraltar now are able to carry on both on-shore and off-shore business under the same license.

Under the new Ordinance, the Gibraltar Banking Supervisor is able to grant licences to Gibraltar banks wishing to open branches in the European Community. Those distinctions between branches and subsidiaries of European banks conducting business in Gibraltar are maintained under the 1992 Ordinance.

BANKING CONFIDENTIALITY

The concept of confidentiality with respect to tax planning and **12-004** other financial matters has long been an integral part of Gibraltar's legislation. For example, in the case of trusts settled in Gibraltar according to certain conditions, the identity of both the settlors and the beneficiaries is kept confidential, and there is no record of the trust instrument filed in any official registry.

Further, although the Companies (Taxation and Concessions) Ordinance provides, in certain circumstances, for disclosure of those persons ultimately entitled to the shares in an exempt company under sections 5(3) and 14(3), these provisions do not apply where those shares are held under the terms of a discretionary trust.

Thus, the trustees of a discretionary trust can incorporate an exempt company whose shares are held by the trust and, upon application for an exemption certificate in respect of the company, they need only disclose the existence of the discretionary trust and the identity of the trustees because since the trust is discretionary, the beneficiaries may not yet be ascertainable.

In the banking and financial sectors, however, specific legislation concerning banking secrecy or confidentiality is only now further elevating the already high level previously maintained, due, in large part, to Gibraltar's independent taxing structure. Until this recent legislation, Gibraltar was guided by the principles of Common Law alone where banking secrecy or confidentiality was concerned.

Now, with the enactment of the Banking Ordinance 1992, Gibraltar will join those Common Law jurisdictions, such as the Bahamas and the Cayman Islands, which insure banking confidentiality under both Common Law and statute.

The Common Law duty of secrecy, to which the sanction of damages attaches, characterizes a breach of this duty as a civil wrong. This Common Law duty is derived from the leading English case of *Tournier* v. *National Provincial and Union Bank of England* [3] where it was held that, subject to certain exceptions, a bank has a contractual duty to maintain secrecy on behalf of its customers with respect to the customer's accounts and with respect to any other information which the bank possesses about the customer relating to or concerning the customer's accounts.

This contractual duty of secrecy naturally continues throughout the duration of the contract and has, in some cases, even been found to continue after a customer's accounts are closed. The protection against disclosure is generally thought to belong to the customer and not to the bank, and even a statement which discloses that a person is not a customer of a bank could be construed to be a breach of the bank's duty of secrecy.

There are four established Common Law exceptions to this duty of secrecy, and they are as follows:

(1) Disclosure of information by compulsion of law (in this case, disclosure may be made only to persons authorized and acting in pursuance of an actual legal power, and the information obtained may be used only for those specific and limited purposes required);

(2) Disclosure where there is a duty to the public to do so;

(3) Disclosure where the interests of the bank require it, and

(4) Disclosure where there is express or implied consent of the customer (*e.g.*, where a customer gives a bank as a reference).

The Common Law duty of banking secrecy, however, is by no means comprehensive, and the Banking Ordinance 1992 therefore provides legislation which introduces banking confidentiality in

---

[3] *Tournier* v. *National Provincial and Union Bank of England* [1924] 1 K.B. 461.

the context of a criminal offense with penalties in order to fill in certain gaps which persist in relying solely on the Common Law approach.

Disclosure, confidentiality, and privilege

Part XI, sections 82(9), 82(10), 83, 84, 85, 86, and 89, of the Banking Ordinance 1992 all deal with disclosure of information, confidentiality, and privilege under the Banking Ordinance.   **12-005**

Section 82 of the Ordinance itemizes that conduct which constitutes an offense under the banking laws and, when section 86 of the Ordinance is read in conjunction with subsections 82(9) and 82(10), it is clear that confidentiality is carefully regulated. These sections provide the following:

"Offences

82(9) A person who discloses otherwise than for any purpose specified in sub-section (10), any information obtained by him under the Ordinance, is guilty of an offense and is liable on conviction on imprisonment for two years and to a fine of four times the amount at level 5 on the standard scale.

(10) sub-section (9) shall not apply to the disclosure -

(a) of any information that is permitted or required under the Ordinance; or

(b) of any information to or by any person concerned with the administration of the Ordinance, for the purposes of carrying the Ordinance into effect; or

(c) of any information by the Commissioner or Banking Supervisor, or by any officer on the staff of the Commissioner, to any person qualified in law, accountancy or valuation or any other matter requiring the exercise of professional skill, in order to take advice from that qualified person for the purposes of the Ordinance; or

(d) of any information with the consent of the person to whom it relates; or

(e) of any information that is a matter of public record or knowledge; or

(f) of any information with a view to the institution of, or otherwise for the purposes of, any criminal proceedings whether under the Ordinance or otherwise;

(g) of any information in relation to any proceedings arising out of the Ordinance;

(h) of any information in connection with any winding-up or administration proceedings under the Companies Ordinance in respect of an authorised institution or former authorised institution except for information relating to a person (not being a controller of the institution concerned) who to the knowledge of the person making the disclosure is participating in an attempt to secure the survival of the institution as a going concern;

(i) by the Commissioner or Banking Supervisor of any information, being information relating to the nature or conduct of the business of an authorised institution or the business of any other relevant person as defined in section 59, to any authority responsible for the control or supervision of institutions carrying on the business of banking, financial services or insurance in any other country where it appears to the Commissioner or Banking Supervisor -

(i) that the person to whom the information relates carries on or proposes to carry on or has or proposes to acquire an interest in any deposit-taking business in that country; and that the disclosure of the information would assist that authority in its prudential control or supervision of deposit- taking instructions in that country; or

(ii) that the disclosure of the information is necessary for supervision of a deposit-taking institution to be effected on a consolidated basis in accordance with Council Directive 83/350/EEC or any successor thereto;

(j) of any information in the form of a summary or collection of information, in such manner as not to enable information relating to any particular person to be ascertained from it.

Disclosure of Confidential Information obtained under this Ordinance

86(1) All persons who are entitled to obtain confidential information under the Ordinance may not subsequently divulge any information obtained in the course of their duties to any other person or authority not entitled under the Ordinance to obtain such information is divulged in a summary or collective form such that individual institutions cannot be identified.

(2) Subsection (1) above shall not apply to information divulged by the Commissioner or Banking Supervisor and to which paragraphs (d), (e), (f), (g) or (h) of section 82(10) applies."

Section 83 of the Ordinance provides for joint and several liability of officers, and it states that, where a person other than an individual commits an offense under any subsection of section 82, including, of course, subsection (9), then every director, controller or manager of that person is guilty of the same offense and liable in the same manner unless he can demonstrate that the offense was committed without his knowledge or that where the offense was committed with his knowledge, it was nevertheless committed without his consent and that he took all reasonable steps both to prevent its commission and to report its commission as soon as practicable to the Commissioner.

The protection of legal privilege is insured in section 84, which provides that neither a barrister nor a solicitor be required to disclose any privileged information or document to anyone. Finally, in order to incorporate EC Council Directive 83/350/EEC which insures the efficient supervision of banking institutions, section 85 of the Ordinance permits authorised institutions, and their controllers and subsidiaries, to exchange information with institutions of which the authorised institutions are controlled, if that information is necessary to facilitate supervision of institutions on a consolidated basis in accordance with the Community directive.

Effect of new legislation

While it is possible that Gibraltar's new banking legislation may not **12-006** be found to be completely watertight upon implementation, it is nevertheless clear that significant improvements have been made to create an environment in Gibraltar in which bank customers will find privacy and trust.

Questions are bound to remain, even in the early stages of the new Bill's enactment, and obvious concerns about a confidentiality policy which acts to screen or facilitate fraud will, it must be assumed, be carefully monitored once the new legislation is securely in place.

Grey areas, such as, for example, the negligent breach of a duty of secrecy, will still exist, and it remains to be seen what the interplay will be between the Common Law and statute once the new legislation is enacted. In the meantime, Gibraltar can count itself among the most regulated of off-shore centers.

CONCLUSION

12-007   In 1970, the total deposits found in commercial banks in Gibraltar amounted to £14.4-million. Twenty-two years later, in 1992, Gibraltar is a significant financial center with 30 resident banks and total deposits which reached £1.75-billion, with £4.4-billion in bank assets and £1.75-billion in loans and other advances.

A special emphasis is being made in promoting Gibraltar in non-Community countries as a significant European banking and financial Center. Of course, the significance of direct access to the Single European Market is a major feature for Gibraltar's position in the banking world. To this end, Gibraltar has attempted to ensure that its legislation conforms to European Community standards so that its regulations are automatically consistent with those of the Community.

One immediate result is that any non-Community bank opening in Gibraltar will have gained the right, subject of course to certain conditions, to open a branch elsewhere in the Community.

CHAPTER 13

GREAT BRITAIN

Wendy Fowler
Richards Butler
London, England

Chapter 13

GREAT BRITAIN

INTRODUCTION

The English courts have recognized for more than 65 years that 13-001
there is implied into the relationship between banks and their
customers a duty of secrecy or confidentiality, owed by banks to
their customers.[1]

In *Tournier v. National Provincial and Union Bank of England*,[2]
which is the leading authority on this subject, the Court of Appeal
unanimously held that, subject to certain qualifications, banks owe
their customers a duty not to disclose to third parties information
concerning their affairs.

Until the *Tournier* decision, there was no clear authority on
whether a duty of secrecy exists between banks and their customers
and, if it does, whether it is a legal duty or merely a moral duty. The
uncertainty surrounding the law relating to banking secrecy in the
period prior to *Tournier* is illustrated by three nineteenth century
cases which are considered below.

Some 60 years prior to *Tournier*, in *Foster v. The Bank of London*,[3]
Erle C.J. referred to the jury the question of whether there was a
duty on the plaintiff's bankers not to disclose to another of its
customers the state of the plaintiff's account.

The jury was of the opinion that such a duty existed, and Erle
C.J., in response, said that "he was not aware of any law against
that".[4] This case was not, however, a positive affirmation of the duty
and gave no consideration to its scope or application.

---

[1] There is little Scottish case law relating to banking secrecy. It is likely that the
Scottish courts would regard the English authorities as persuasive and that the
English decisions from *Tournier* onwards would be followed in Scotland.

[2] *Tournier v. National Provincial and Union Bank of England* [1924] 1 K.B. 461.

[3] *Foster v. Bank of London* (1862) 3 F.& F. 213.

[4] *Id.*, at p. 218.

The decision in *Foster* v. *The Bank of London* was considered in the 1868 case of *Hardy* v. *Veasey and Others*.[5] In that case, the court was not required to determine whether the banker's duty of secrecy exists. However, Kelly C.B., in considering *Foster* v. *The Bank of London*, remarked that it was impossible to reconcile the opinion of Erle C.J. in that case with a total absence of any such duty.

Another judge, Martin B, conceded that "there may be such a duty but I confess I should like to see some authority in its support".[6] His apparent reluctance to treat the decision in *Foster* v. *The Bank of London* as authority for the existence of the duty may be due to the facts of that case, which indicated a clear conspiracy between the bank and one of its customers against the plaintiff.

It may be that he considered that the court had decided in the favor of the plaintiff in *Foster* because there had clearly been a breach of the moral duty of the bank to its customer, even if there had been no breach of a legal duty.

In his judgment in *Hardy* v. *Veasey and Others*, Martin B. also referred to the case of *Tassell* v. *Cooper*.[7] In *Tassell* v. *Cooper*, the judges, in particular Williams J., found that the count in the plaintiff's action based on there being a duty on a bank not to disclose information concerning a customer's account to a third party, disclosed no cause of action.

However, the case is not necessarily strong authority for the non-existence of the duty because, in that case, counsel for the plaintiff abandoned the count of breach of duty before the judges delivered their judgments.

THE DECISION IN *TOURNIER*

13-002 The starting point of any discussion of English law relating to banking secrecy is the *Tournier* case, which has been referred to above. The *Tournier* case concerned a customer of the defendant bank called Tournier whose account with the bank was overdrawn.

Tournier and the bank had agreed that Tournier should reduce his overdraft by weekly installments. He had no fixed address and gave his bank branch manager the name and address of his new employer. Shortly afterwards, Tournier defaulted in the payment of the agreed weekly installments.

---

[5] *Hardy* v. *Veasey and Others* (1868) L.R. 3 Ex. 107.
[6] *Id.*, at p. 112.
[7] *Tassell* v. *Cooper* (1850) 9 C.B. 509.

Subsequently, another customer of the defendant bank drew a check in Tournier's favor, but Tournier did not pay it into his account at the bank. The check was eventually returned to the bank by the London City and Midland Bank. The branch manager of the defendant bank inquired of the London City and Midland Bank as to the identity of their customer and was told that he was a book-maker.

The branch manager then telephoned Tournier's employer to find out his address and spoke to two of its directors. While doing so, he disclosed the existence of the overdraft and Tournier's default. He also expressed the opinion that Tournier was betting heavily. As a result, Tournier's employer refused to renew his employment at the end of his probationary period.

Tournier sued the bank for slander and for breach of an implied term of the contract between him and the bank that the bank would not disclose to third parties the state of his account or any transaction relating to it. He won his case on appeal, and a new trial was ordered.

At first instance in the *Tournier* case, Avory J. directed the jury that Tournier's claim for breach of contract turned on whether the communication of the state of Tournier's account was made on a reasonable and proper occasion. This direction was described by the Court of Appeal as an insufficient explanation of the law relating to banking secrecy. The Court of Appeal went on to consider the law on this subject in some detail.

Implied duty of confidentiality

The Court of Appeal judges in the *Tournier* case were in no doubt **13-003** that a duty of confidentiality is implied into the relationship of banker and customer, notwithstanding the absence of clear authority on the point. However, the views of Scrutton L.J. on the nature of the duty differed from those of Atkin L.J. and Bankes L.J.

The majority view of the extent of the duty was described by Atkin L.J. as follows:

> "It [the obligation of secrecy] clearly goes beyond the state of the account, that is, whether there is a debit or a credit balance, and the amount of the balance. It must extend at least to all the transactions that go through the account, and to the securities, if any, given in respect of the account; and in respect of such matters it must, I think, extend beyond the period when the account is closed or ceases to be an active account. It seems to me inconceivable that either party would contemplate that once the customer had closed his account the bank was to be

at liberty to divulge as it pleased the particular transactions which it had conducted for the customer when he was such. I further think that the obligation extends to information obtained from other sources than the customer's actual account, if the occasion upon which the information was obtained arose out of the banking relations of the bank and its customers - for example, with a view to assisting the bank in conducting the customer's business or in coming to decisions as to its treatment of its customers . . . . In this case, however, I should not extend the obligation to information as to the customer obtained after he had ceased to be a customer."[8]

Bankes L.J. agreed that the duty of secrecy does not cease the moment a customer closes his account. He was more cautious on the question of whether the duty extends to information derived from sources other than the customer's account but was satisfied that, on the particular facts of the case, the information obtained by the branch manager of the defendant bank as a result of his inquiry of the London City and Midland Bank was covered by the duty.

The minority view expressed by Scrutton L.J. was that the duty of secrecy does not extend to knowledge that the bank acquires before the relationship of banker and customer was contemplated or after it ceases to exist. Scrutton L.J. was also of the opinion that the duty does not apply to knowledge derived from sources other than the customer's account.

Thus, he held that if, as in the circumstances of the *Tournier* case, the bank acquires information about one of its customers ("customer A") through the account of another customer ("customer B"), his duty not to disclose that information is owed to customer B, not customer A. However, he considered that, on the facts of the *Tournier* case, this argument could not be applied to avoid a new trial.

Duty not absolute

13-004   The Court of Appeal was unanimously of the opinion that the duty of secrecy owed by banks to their customers is not absolute but qualified.

In considering the qualifications to the duty, Bankes L.J. described the duty of secrecy as a difficult and only partially investigated branch of law and held that "It is not possible to frame any

---

[8] *Tournier, supra* n. 2, at p. 485.

exhaustive definition of the duty. The most that can be done is to classify the qualification, and to indicate its limits".[9]

Bankes L.J. classified the qualifications under four heads:

(1) Where disclosure is under compulsion by law;
(2) Where there is a duty to the public to disclose;
(3) Where the interests of the bank require disclosure, and
(4) Where the disclosure is made with the express or implied consent of the customer.

These qualifications were not disputed by the other Court of Appeal judges and are considered below. They were recently examined in detail by the Review Committee on Banking Services, chaired by Professor R. B. Jack, when it considered the subject of banking secrecy in the context of a review of the provision of banking services as a whole.

The recommendations of that Committee[10] were published in February 1989. The Report (which is referred to here as the "Jack Report") suggested a number of significant changes to the law relating to banking secrecy. The recommendations of the Jack Report are considered, where appropriate, throughout this chapter.

QUALIFICATIONS TO DUTY

Where disclosure is under compulsion by law

The duty of secrecy owed by a bank to its customers is subject to the **13-005** bank's duty to comply with the general law.

Under English law,[11] a bank must disclose information that would otherwise be subject to the duty of confidentiality if required to do so by order of court or by statute notwithstanding that it is a contractual term of the banker/customer relationship to keep such information secret.

---

[9] *Id.,* at p. 472.
[10] Banking Services: Law and Practice Report by the Review Committee, Cmnd 622.
[11] Applicable in Scotland.

Compulsion by order of court

13-006   **Bankers' Books Evidence Act 1879** The main purpose of the Bankers' Books Evidence Act 1879[12] ("the 1879 Act") was to relieve bank officials from the obligation to appear personally in court.

Section 3 of the 1879 Act provides that "a copy of any entry in a banker's book shall in all legal proceedings be received as *prima facie* evidence of such entry, and of the matters, transactions, and accounts therein recorded".

Section 7 of the 1879 Act provides that:

> "On the application of any party to a legal proceeding a court or judge may order that such party be at liberty to inspect and take copies of any entries in a banker's book for any of the purposes of such proceedings. An order under this section may be made either with or without summoning the bank or any other party, and shall be served on the bank three clear days before the same is to be obeyed, unless the court or judge otherwise directs".

13-007   *Scope of 'legal proceeding'* The expression "legal proceeding" includes any civil or criminal proceeding or inquiry in which evidence is or may be given and covers arbitrations.[13]

"Banker's books" are defined to include ledgers, day books, cash books, account books, and all other books used in the ordinary business of the bank, whether those records are in written form or are kept on microfilm, magnetic tape or any other form of mechanical or electronic data retrieval mechanism.[14]

The case of *Barker* v. *Wilson*[15] also establishes that, when written records are reduced to microfilm, the microfilm records are the "banker's books" for the purpose of the definition. Correspondence does not fall within the definition;[16] nor do checks and paying-in slips retained by a bank after conclusion of a banking transaction to which they relate.[17]

The expression "bank" is defined as institutions authorized under the Banking Act 1987 or a municipal bank within the meaning of that Act, a building society,[18] the National Savings Bank, and the

---

[12] Applicable in Scotland.

[13] Section 10, Bankers' Books Evidence Act 1879.

[14] Section 9(2), Bankers' Books Evidence Act 1879, which was substituted by the Banking Act 1979, and which also is applicable in Scotland.

[15] *Barker* v. *Wilson* [1980] 2 All E.R. 81.

[16] R.V. Dadson (1983) 77 Cr. App. Rep. 91.

[17] *Williams* v. *Williams* [1987] 3 All E.R. 257.

[18] See Schedule 18 of the Building Societies Act 1986.

Post Office in the exercise of its powers to provide banking services. Thus, the definition extends to branches of foreign banks established in England and Wales[19] that are authorized institutions under the Banking Act 1987.

The 1879 Act provides for verification of the relevant banker's book by a partner or officer of the bank, either orally or by affidavit, confirming that the book was at the time of the making of the entry one of the ordinary books of the bank, that the entry was made in the usual and ordinary course of business and that the book is in the custody or control of the bank. Evidence must also be provided that the copy has been examined with the original and is correct.

Distinction of proceedings The application of the 1879 Act distinguishes between criminal and civil proceedings. In *Williams* v. *Summerfield*, Lord Widgery L.J. described the way in which section 7 should be applied in criminal proceedings: **13-008**

> ". . . in criminal proceedings, justices should warn themselves of the importance of the step which they are taking in making an order under section 7; should always recognise the care with which the jurisdiction should be exercised, should take into account among other things whether there is other evidence in the possession of the prosecution to support the charge; or whether the application under section 7 is a fishing expedition in the hope of finding some material upon which the charge can be hung. If justices approach these applications with a due sense of responsibility and a recognition of the importance of that which they are being asked to do, if they are always alive to the requirement of not making the order extend beyond the true purposes of the charge before them, and if in consequence they limit the period of the disclosure of the bank account to a period which is strictly relevant to the charge before them; and if finally they recognise the importance of considering whether there is other evidence in the possession of the prosecution before they provide the bank account as perhaps the only evidence . . . if they observe those precautions and pay heed to those warnings, they will in fact produce a situation in which the section is used properly, wisely and in support of the interests of justice, and will not allow it to be used as an instrument of oppression which on its face it might very well be."[20]

---

[19] And in Scotland.
[20] *Williams* v. *Summerfield* [1972] 2 Q.B. 512, at p. 518.

In civil proceedings, the usual approach to section 7 is that the statutory power to order disclosure should not overreach the general law of discovery.[21] Such orders are usually made only against the account of a party who is involved in the litigation.

The court will occasionally make orders against a third party who is not a party to the litigation, for instance, if the court is satisfied that the account is, in fact, the account of a party to the litigation, although maintained in the name of a third party or if the party to the action is so closely concerned with the account that it can be properly used as evidence against him.[22]

In *Williams* v. *Summerfield,* [23] an order was made in respect of the account of a near relative of the accused on that basis. In *Ironmonger & Co.* v. *Dyne,*[24] inspection of the account of the husband of the accused was ordered on the grounds that the wife had been using the account to mask her own activities. A similar order was made in *R* v. *Andover Justices ex p Rhodes,*[25] where the wife admitted depositing stolen money in her husband's account.

In *Bankers Trust Co.* v. *Shapira,*[26] the Court of Appeal held that where fraud is alleged, a customer who is prima facie guilty of fraud cannot rely on the confidential relationship between him and his bank to prevent an order for discovery of information that would otherwise be subject to the banker's obligation of confidentiality. However, it appears from the case that strong evidence of fraud is needed before such an order may be made.

13-009   **R.S.C. Order 38, rule 13 / *subpoena duces tecum*** [27]Order 38, rule 13, of the Rules of the Supreme Court enables the court to order any person to attend any proceeding in the action other than the trial and to provide any document that the court considers necessary for that proceeding.

This rule does not enable an order to be made for the inspection of documents in the hands of persons who are not parties to the action (*Straker* v. *Reynolds*[28]) and is, of course, subject to the provi-

---

[21] *R* v. *Bono* (1913) 29 T.L.R. 635; *Williams* v. *Summerfield, supra* n. 20.

[22] *South Staffordshire Tramways Co.* v. *Ebbsmith* [1895] 2 Q.B. 669.

[23] *Williams* v. *Summerfield, supra* n. 20.

[24] *Ironmonger & Co.* v. *Dyne* (1928) 44 T.L.R. 579.

[25] *R.* v. *Andover Justices ex* p Rhodes [1980] Crim. L.R. 644.

[26] *Bankers Trust Co.* v. *Shapira* [1980] 3 All E.R. 353.

[27] Not applicable in Scotland.

[28] *Straker* v. *Reynolds* (1889) 22 Q.B.D. 262.

sions of the Bankers' Books Evidence Act 1879 permitting the production of copies of entries in the relevant bankers' books.[29]

The court also may issue a *subpoena duces tecum* requiring a bank to produce documents at the trial of an action.[30]

Extra-territorial orders The attitude of the English courts to applications for orders for disclosure of documents against foreign banks having branches in England and Wales is of considerable interest.

    13-010

A court will not usually make an order against the head office of a bank in England in respect of documents held by a foreign branch relating to a customer of that branch.

This is particularly the case if the laws of the country where the documents are located prohibit disclosure and where the customer is not a party to the proceedings.

Inspection order set aside In *R* v. *Grossmann*,[31] the Court of Appeal set aside an inspection order made on the head office of Barclays Bank Ltd. in London. The order required it to permit the Inland Revenue to inspect and take copies of an account maintained by an Isle of Man company with the Isle of Man branch of Barclays Bank Ltd. An application for a similar order had previously been made to the court in the Isle of Man and refused.

    13-011

Lord Denning M.R. held that any order in respect of production of the particular books should be made by the courts of the Isle of Man and that, if the English courts were to make the order sought, it might lead to a conflict of jurisdictions. Oliver L.J. described the order which was subject to the appeal as "very unusual". His response to the application was as follows:

> "The English court is asked to order, because of the fortuitous fact that the head office of Barclays Bank is situated in this country, the disclosure of a foreign banker's account maintained at a foreign branch of Barclays Bank. That is sought in the face of a subsisting injunction of a court of competent jurisdiction in the Isle of Man . . . . I do not say that an order in

---

[29] In Scotland, the Court of Session can grant, under Rule of Court 95, a commission and diligence for recovery of documents. The Sheriff Court can, under section 80 of the Sheriff Courts (Scotland) Act 1907, also order the production of documents.

[30] Not applicable in Scotland.

[31] *R.* v. *Grossmann* (1981) 73 Cr. App. Rep. 302.

such unusual circumstances can never be made, but it would, I think, be one that ought to be made only on a case very much stronger than that which the Inland Revenue have been able to deploy in the instant case."[32]

R v. *Grossman* was applied in *Mackinnon* v. *Donaldson, Lufkin and Jenrette Securities Corporation and Others.*[33] This case concerned an order obtained *ex parte* under section 7 of the Bankers' Books Evidence Act 1879 against the London branch of Citibank requiring it to produce books and papers held at its head office in New York that related to transactions on a New York account maintained by a Bahamian company.

Citibank was not a party to the litigation. Citibank sought the discharge of the order on the grounds that, in principle, it exceeded the international jurisdiction of the English courts and infringed the sovereignty of the United States.

In discharging the order, Hoffmann J. held that the court should not, save in exceptional circumstances, require the production by a foreigner, who is not a party to the litigation, of documents outside the jurisdiction concerning business that was transacted outside the jurisdiction. He considered that this was particularly the case when the foreigner is a bank.

He made the point that "the principle . . . that a state should refrain from demanding obedience to its sovereign authority by foreigners in respect of their conduct outside the jurisdiction" has been frequently insisted upon by the United Kingdom government in response to the application by the United States courts of United States antitrust laws to British companies in respect of conduct outside the United States.[34] He gave as an example of that insistence the case of *XAG* v. *A Bank*,[35] which is considered below.

Hoffmann J. also made the point that, although it is a general principle of international law that a state may regulate the conduct of its own nationals even outside its jurisdiction, provided that this does not conflict with the national's obligations under local law, banks are in a special position.[36] He described the special position of banks as follows:

---

[32] *Id.*, at p. 309.
[33] *Mackinnon* v. *Donaldson, Lufkin and Jenrette Securities Corporation and Others* [1986] Ch. 482.
[34] *Id.*, at p. 493.
[35] *XAG* v. *A Bank* [1983] 2 All E.R. 464.
[36] *Id.*, at p. 496.

"The nature of banking business is such that if an English court invokes its jurisdiction even over an English bank in respect of an account at a branch abroad, there is a strong likelihood of conflict with the bank's duties to its customer under the local law. It is therefore not surprising that any bank, whether English or foreign, should as a general rule be entitled to the protection of an order of the foreign court before it is required to disclose documents kept at a branch or head office abroad".

Exceptional circumstances required Hoffmann J. interpreted the **13-012** *Grossman* decision as establishing that an order in respect of documents held at a bank's foreign branch or head office should not be made save in exceptional circumstances. He applied that principle to the circumstances in the *Mackinnon* case and discharged the order.

In doing so, he noted that alternative legitimate procedures were available to the plaintiff to obtain the relevant documents and that there appeared to have been delay on the plaintiff's part in taking advantage of those procedures.

This raises the question of when the court will consider the circumstances to be exceptional so as to order disclosure of documents held at a foreign branch or head office. Perhaps one such example is the unreported 1978 case of *London and County Securities Ltd (In Liquidation)* v. *Caplan*. In that case, Templeman J. ordered an English bank to obtain from its foreign banking subsidiaries documents relating to accounts connected to the defendant in order to trace assets that he was accused of embezzling.

Templeman J. described the relief that he was granting as "to be granted only in the most exceptional circumstances". He was prepared to grant the order because otherwise "justice may well become impossible because the evidence and the fruits of crime and fraud may disappear."

Balance of convenience As noted above, the case of *XAG* v. *A Bank* **13-013** was cited by Hoffmann J. in the *Mackinnon* case as an example of a case where the English courts objected to the application of United States law to a bank operating in the United Kingdom. In that case, three corporate customers of the London branch of a United States bank applied for the continuation of injunctions restraining the bank from disclosing documents relating to their accounts pursuant to a subpoena of a New York court.

In considering whether to grant the order, Leggatt J. sought to determine the balance of convenience between the plaintiffs and the defendant. Counsel for the bank contended that an English court will respect the order of a foreign court and, if it finds the order to be in conflict with the private law of confidentiality, will proceed with caution to uphold the order of the foreign court unless there is a compelling reason not to do so.

In considering that contention, Leggatt J. remarked that, if it were correct, "It would be necessary for this court in particular to consider the nature, scope, quality and effect of the foreign order and to analyze it with some care, because the fact is that to allow that order to take effect on a bank conducting its business in the City of London would be, as it would appear, to allow a fairly large cuckoo in the domestic nest".[37] He summarized the balance of convenience between the plaintiffs and the defendant as follows:

> "On the one hand, there is involved in the continuation of the injunction impeding the exercise by the United States court in London of powers that, by English standards, would be regarded as excessive, without in so doing causing detriment to the bank; on the other hand, the refusal of the injunctions, or the non-continuation of them, would cause potentially very considerable commercial harm to the plaintiffs, which cannot be disputed, by suffering the bank to act for its own purposes in breach of the duty of confidentiality admittedly owed to its customers".[38]

Leggatt J. ordered that the injunctions should continue.

Compulsion by statute

13-014   The Jack Report makes the point that, whereas at the time of the *Tournier* case, there was little legislation compelling banks to release confidential information, ". . . the last two decades have seen a torrent of new legislation, which has become a spate in the past few years requiring or permitting bankers, in a wide range of specified situations, to disclose confidential information." [39]

The Jack Report listed, in Appendix Q, nineteen such statutory requirements. The more significant examples of the legislation referred to in the Jack Report are considered below, as are examples of more recent legislation that are relevant to the issue of banking secrecy. It will be seen that some legislation not only requires banks

37 *Id.*, n. 35, at p. 478.
38 *Id.*, n. 35, at p. 480.
39 The Jack Report, paragraph 5.07.

to produce information when requested but also places a duty on banks to report to the authorities confidential information relating to their customers on their own initiative.

Insolvency Act 1986 Section 234[40] of the Insolvency Act 1986 provides that, where an administration order or winding-up order has been made in relation to a company or an administrative receiver or
provisional liquidator is appointed or the company goes into liquidation, the court may require any person having in his possession or control property, books, papers, or records to which the company appears to be entitled to transfer it to the person holding the office of administrator, administrative receiver, liquidator, provisional liquidator, or official receiver.

13-015

Section 236[41] of the Insolvency Act 1986 applies in the same circumstances as section 234 and empowers the court to summon any person "known or suspected to have in its possession any property of the company or supposed to be indebted to the company" or "any person whom the court thinks capable of giving information concerning the affairs of the company". Such a person can be required to submit an affidavit to the court or to produce any books, papers or other records in his possession or under his control relating to the company's affairs.

Building Societies Act 1986 Section 52 of the Building Societies Act 1986[42] enables the Building Societies Commission to require a building society's agents, including its bankers, to produce information or documents or to provide an explanation relating to the business of the building society or its plans for future development.

13-016

Financial Services Act 1986 Under section 105 of the Financial Services Act 1986,[43] the banker of a person carrying on investment business whose affairs are being investigated may be required to attend before the Secretary of State to answer questions or to produce documents if the Secretary of State considers it necessary for the investigation.

13-017

Section 106(2A)[44] provides that the requirement to disclose information and to produce documents does not apply to persons who owe an obligation of confidence by virtue of carrying on the busi-

---

[40] Applicable in Scotland.
[41] Applicable in Scotland.
[42] Applicable in Scotland.
[43] Applicable in Scotland.
[44] Inserted by section 73(5), Companies Act 1989, and applicable in Scotland.

ness of banking. The exceptions to this are where they are themselves under investigation or are related to the person under investigation or the person to whom the obligation is owed is itself under investigation or consents to disclosure by the banker or in circumstances where the Secretary of State authorizes disclosure.

Section 177 of the Financial Services Act 1986[45] confers on inspectors appointed to investigate insider dealing the power to require any person whom they consider is or may be able to give information concerning the alleged insider dealing to produce documents in his possession or control, to attend before the inspectors or otherwise to give the inspectors all assistance that such person is reasonably able to give.

Failure to comply with the inspectors' requirements without reasonable excuse may be punished as if the person were guilty of contempt of court.

13-018   **Companies Act 1985** Section 434[46] of the Companies Act 1985 provides that, when inspectors are appointed to investigate a company's affairs, it is the duty of all officers and agents of the company and of any subsidiary or holding company of the company under investigation whose affairs the inspectors consider relevant to produce books and documents, attend before the inspectors and to otherwise give the inspectors all assistance that they are reasonably able to give.

For these purposes, "agents" include the bankers of the company, subsidiary or holding company. If the person concerned refuses, he may be punished as if he had been guilty of contempt of court.

Section 443[47] of the Companies Act 1985 confers on inspectors appointed by the Secretary of State to investigate the ownership of a company the same power to require production of documents and evidence, as is set out in section 434.

Under section 447 of the Companies Act 1985,[48] any bank that is a company may be directed by the Secretary of State at any time to produce specified documents, if the Secretary of State thinks there is a good reason for the direction. The Secretary of State may delegate this power to an officer of his or any other competent person.[49]

Section 449 restricts the publication or disclosure of information obtained under section 447 other than to a competent authority or

---

[45] Applicable in Scotland.
[46] Applicable in Scotland.
[47] Applicable in Scotland.
[48] Amended by section 63 of the Companies Act 1989, and applicable in Scotland.
[49] Section 447(3), Companies Act 1985.

for one of the purposes set out in that section. The definition of "competent authority" includes the Secretary of State or an inspector appointed by him, the Treasury, the Bank of England and the Director of Public Prosecutions.[50]

The purposes for which information may be disclosed include the institution of criminal proceedings and to enable the Bank of England to discharge its functions under the Banking Act 1987.

Section 452(1A)[51] excludes from the disclosure requirements contained in sections 434 and 443 persons who owe an obligation of confidence by virtue of carrying on the business of banking unless the person to whom the obligation is owed is under investigation or consents to disclosure or the requirement to disclose is specifically authorized by the Secretary of State.

Banking Act 1987 Section 39 of the Banking Act 1987[52] empowers   13-019
the Bank of England to require an authorized institution to provide such information and documents as the Bank of England reasonably requires for the performance of its functions under that Act.

These powers also may be exercised in relation to a holding company or subsidiary of the authorized institution, other members in the same group and the directors, controllers, and managers of the authorized institution.

Under section 41 of the Banking Act 1987, every person who is or was a director, controller, manager, employee, agent, banker, auditor, or solicitor of an unauthorized institution that is under investigation by the Bank of England under that section is under a duty to produce to the investigators appointed by the Bank of England all documents that the investigators require, to attend before them, and to give them all assistance that they are reasonably able to give. Failure to do so is an offense.

Section 84 of the Banking Act 1987 permits disclosure by the Bank of England of information obtained for the purposes of the Act to a number of persons, including the Secretary of State or one of his inspectors, the Building Societies Commission, Self Regulating Organizations and the Official Receiver, if the Bank of England considers that disclosure would enable or assist that person to discharge the functions specified in the section, *e.g.*, functions under the Companies Act 1985, the protection of the shareholders and depositors of building societies and the investigation of an authorized institution in respect of which a winding-up order has been made.

---

[50] The Lord Advocate in Scotland.
[51] Inserted by section 69(3) of the Companies Act 1989.
[52] Applicable in Scotland.

13-020 **Taxes Management Act 1970** Under section 13 of the Taxes Management Act 1970,[53] banks which are in receipt of money, value, profits, or gains of any other person which is chargeable to income tax, may be required to deliver a return to the tax inspectors setting out a statement of the amount held and the name and address of the person to whom it belongs.

Section 20 confers upon tax inspectors the power to require banks to deliver or make available for inspection documents in their possession or power which contain information relevant to the inspectors' enquiries into any person's tax liability.

Section 24 of the Taxes Management Act 1970 provides that the Commissioners of the Inland Revenue may require a bank to give them information as to the receipt of income from United Kingdom securities by persons other than the holders or from United Kingdom bearer securities.

Similar powers are conferred on tax inspectors by section 17 of the Act in respect of interest paid to customers without deduction of tax.

13-021 **Income and Corporation Taxes Act 1988** Under section 745(1) of the Income and Corporation Taxes Act 1988,[54] the Commissioners of the Inland Revenue may require any person to furnish such particulars as the Commissioners think necessary relating to the provisions of the Act relating to the transfer of assets abroad.

Section 745(5) provides that a bank is under no obligation to furnish particulars of any ordinary banking transactions between it and a customer carried out in the ordinary course of banking business unless the bank acted for the customer in connection with the formation or management of any body corporate resident or incorporated outside the United Kingdom or, if resident in the United Kingdom, a close company that is not a trading company or the creation or execution of trusts in consequence of which income becomes payable to a person resident or domiciled outside the United Kingdom.

In *Royal Bank of Canada* v. *IRC*,[55] Megarry J. considered the meaning of "ordinary banking transactions". He concluded that not every transaction lawfully carried out by a bank is a "banking transaction" and even if it is a banking transaction, the transaction is not necessarily "ordinary". The burden is on counsel for the bank to establish that the transaction in question is "ordinary".

---

53 Applicable in Scotland.
54 Applicable in Scotland.
55 *Royal Bank of Canada* v. *IRC* [1972] 1 All E.R. 225.

Drug Trafficking Offences Act 1986 Section 24(1) of the Drug Traf- **13-022**
ficking Offences Act 1986[56] makes it an offense for a person, knowing or suspecting that another person is a drug trafficker, either:

(1) To retain or control the proceeds of drug trafficking;
(2) To place funds so obtained at the person's disposal, or
(3) To assist in the investment of the proceeds of the drug
    trafficking.

It is a defense under section 24(4) to prove lack of knowledge or
suspicion that the person was a drug trafficker or to have disclosed
that knowledge or suspicion to the authorities. The section specifically provides in section 24(3)(a) that disclosure to the police of a
suspicion or belief that funds are derived from drug trafficking will
not be treated as a breach of any contractual confidentiality restriction.

Section 27(1) provides that the police may apply to a Circuit
Judge[57] for an order for the production of or access to particular
material or material of a particular description. Section 27(9) provides that such an order takes effect notwithstanding any obligation
as to secrecy.

Prevention of Terrorism (Temporary Provisions) Act 1989 Section **13-023**
11(1) of the Prevention of Terrorism (Temporary Provisions) Act[58]
makes it an offense to facilitate the retention or control of funds that
may be applied or used for the commission of, in the furtherance of
or in connection with, acts of terrorism, the proceeds of such acts or
the resources of a proscribed organization.

Acts of terrorism for these purposes are acts connected with the
affairs of Northern Ireland and certain acts of international terrorism. Under section 11(2), it is a defense to prove that the person did
not know and had no reasonable cause to suspect that the arrangements that he facilitated related to terrorist funds.

Section 12(1) specifically provides that a person may disclose to
the police his suspicion or belief that money or other property is or
is derived from terrorist funds or any matter on which such a
suspicion or belief is based notwithstanding any restriction on the
disclosure of confidential information.

---

[56] Section 24(1) does not apply in Scotland but see section 43 of the Criminal
Justice (Scotland) Act 1987. Sections 24(3)(a) and 27 apply in Scotland.
[57] In Scotland, the application is made by the procurator fiscal to the Sheriff
Court.
[58] Applicable in Scotland.

Under section 12(2), it is a defense to the offense created by section 11(1) if the person concerned discloses his suspicion or belief to a constable on his own initiative and as soon as it is reasonable for him to do so.

13-024 **Criminal Justice Act 1988** Section 98(1) of the Criminal Justice Act 1988[59] provides that where a person discloses to the police a suspicion or belief that any property has been obtained in connection with an indictable offense, that disclosure shall not be treated as a breach of any restriction on the disclosure of information.

13-025 **Police and Criminal Evidence Act 1984** Where there are reasonable grounds for believing that a serious arrestable offense has been committed, a constable may obtain access to special procedure material for the purposes of a criminal investigation under section 9(1) of the Police and Criminal Evidence Act[60] by making an application under Schedule 1 of the Act. The definition of "special procedure material" includes material in the possession of a person who holds it subject to an express or implied undertaking to hold it in confidence.

13-026 **Criminal Justice (International Co-operation) Act 1990** Section 7 of the Criminal Justice (International Co-operation) Act 1990 extends the power to obtain access to special procedure material contained in section 9(1) of the Police and Criminal Evidence Act 1984 to conduct that is an offense under the law of a country or territory outside the United Kingdom and which would constitute a serious arrestable offense if it had occurred in the United Kingdom.

Section 14 of the Criminal Justice (International Co-operation) Act 1990[61] makes it an offense for a person who knows or has reasonable grounds to suspect that property is derived wholly or in part from the proceeds of drug trafficking to conceal, disguise, convert, transfer or remove that property from the jurisdiction of the English courts[62] for the purpose of assisting any person to avoid prosecution for a drug trafficking offense.

Other examples where statute provides for the disclosure of confidential information are very wide ranging and cover a broad spec-

---

[59] Section 98(1) does not apply in Scotland.
[60] Section 9(1) does not apply in Scotland. Section 38 of the Criminal Justice (Scotland) Act 1987 empowers the Sheriff Court, on the application of the procurator fiscal, to order the production of material in connection with investigations into drug trafficking.
[61] Applicable in Scotland.
[62] And the Scottish courts.

trum of subject matter from investigation of charities and consumer protection through to mental incapacity.

Inter-relationship of compulsion by statute with duty of secrecy The **13-027** case of *Barclays Bank plc v. Taylor, Trustee Savings Bank of Wales and Border Counties and Another v. Taylor and Another,*[63] is interesting in that it illuminates the inter-relationship of the "compulsion by statute" qualification with the duty of secrecy.

In that case, the Court of Appeal was asked to consider whether there is implied in the contract between banker and customer a term that the banker must notify its customer of any application made under section 9 of the Police and Criminal Evidence Act 1984 for disclosure of the customer's account and also must resist such an application.

The implied term, the existence of which the Court of Appeal had to consider, was described by Croom-Johnson L.J. as an undertaking by the bank "to use its best endeavors to prevent the confidentiality [in the banker/customer relationship] from being destroyed by legal orders made under a number of statutes on different subjects."[64]

He pointed out that such a term, if it exists, would be applicable not only to the Police and Criminal Evidence Act 1984, in respect of which the case was brought, but also to statutes such as the Bankers' Books Evidence Act 1879, the Drug Trafficking Offences Act 1986, the Taxes Management Act 1970, and the Companies Act 1985.

The term also would have to apply in circumstances where there is a duty to the public to disclose.

The Court of Appeal unanimously held that a term of the sort suggested is not to be implied into the banker/customer relationship. In considering whether the bank should have informed Mr. Taylor, their customer, of the application, Lord Donaldson M.R. remarked that he should have been "surprised and disappointed if they (*i.e.,* the bank) had done so in the context of a criminal investigation unless they were under a legal duty to do so".[65]

The reason for this is that, in certain circumstances, by notifying the customer, the bank might frustrate the investigation. He was clear on the point that no such duty exists in relation to the notification of applications under the Police and Criminal Evidence Act 1984 and went on to say:

---

[63] *Barclays Bank PLC v. Taylor, Trustee Savings Bank of Wales and Border Counties and Another v. Taylor and Another* [1989] 3 All E.R. 563.
[64] *Id.,* at p. 570.
[65] *Id.,* at p. 569.

> "There is a public interest in assisting the police in the investigation of crime and I can think of no basis for an implied obligation to act in a way which, in some circumstances, would without doubt hinder such inquiries."[66]

The Jack Report recommended that all existing statutory exemptions from the duty of secrecy should be consolidated in new legislation that makes it clear that the duty applies to all providers of banking services and covers all information that the bank acquires about the customer while providing banking services to him.

It further recommended that any new statutory exemptions from the duty of secrecy should be made by reference to the new legislation; failure to do so would mean that the exemption would not override the duty.

The Review Committee on Banking Services also recognized that the burden placed on banks by statutory provisions that require them to report suspicious transactions on their own initiative is a heavy one. This was further highlighted by the Guidance Notes to Banks and Building Societies relating to Money Laundering, which were issued by the Bank of England in December 1990, and the Guidance Notes for Investment Business on Money Laundering dated September 1991.

The Guidance Notes recognized that a suspicious transaction will often be one that is recognizable only because it is inconsistent with a customer's known, legitimate business or personal activities or with the normal business for that type of account and that, to identify such transactions, banks must be sufficiently familiar with their customers' normal activities so as to recognize transactions which are in any way unusual.

The Guidance Notes recommended that banks institute comprehensive internal measures to ensure that their staff are made aware of banks' responsibility in respect of suspicious transaction and are able to identify such transactions so as to report them.

On June 10, 1991, the EC Council issued a Directive on money laundering.[67] The Directive was issued against a background of greatly increased free movement of capital within the European Community and a recognition of the enhanced opportunities for money laundering which that liberalization brought. Its aim was to coordinate national measures to combat money laundering.

The Directive requires member states to implement its provisions by January 1, 1993. It obliges member states to ensure,

---

66 *Id.*

67 Council Directive on prevention of the use of the financial system for the purpose of money laundering (91/308/EEC).

amongst other things, that banks and financial institutions (including branches of such institutions with head offices both within and outside the European Community) cooperate fully with the authorities responsible for combating money laudering by giving them information on their own intiative.

Article 9 of the Directive specifically provides that such disclosure, when done in good faith, will not render the bank or financial institution concerned liable for breach of any contractual restriction on disclosure. Member states are able, if they wish, to adopt or retain stricter provisions in the field covered by the Directive.

Where there is duty to public to disclose

In *Tournier* v. *National Provincial and Union Bank of England*, Atkin L.J. **13-028** said that a bank may disclose its customer's affairs "to the extent to which it is reasonably necessary. . .to protect the bank, or persons interested, or the public, against fraud or crime".[68]

This position was reinforced in the judgments of Scrutton L.J. and Bankes L.J.[69]

The Jack Report made the point that the volume of legislation passed since the *Tournier* decision compelling banks to release information relating to their customers has considerably eroded the significance of the "duty to the public" qualification and that:

> "If banks are already under so many specific obligations to disclose in the public interest, disclosure on the generalised basis of exception (b) ['the duty to the public' qualification] will require a very special justification."[70]

The Jack Report recommended that the generalized ground of public interest should be specifically abolished by legislation. Its reasons for that conclusion were set out as follows:

> "Statutory specification of this type of disclosure . . . has now been carried so far that it is hard to see in what circumstances the generalised provision, with its uncertainty of application, could any longer be needed, given that emergency legislation could always be enacted in time of war. Some light might be shed on what, in modern conditions, are the public interest

---

[68] *Tournier, supra* n. 1, p. 486.
[69] See also *Libyan Arab Foreign Bank* v. *Bankers Trust Co.* [1989] 3 All E.R. 252, at p. 285.
[70] The Jack Report, paragraph 5.09.

considerations likely to justify a bank in departing from the obligations of confidentiality by reference to the circumstances in which a journalist can be required to disclose his 'sources' under the Contempt of Court Act 1981. These circumstances are that the disclosure is 'necessary in the interests of justice or national security or the prevention of crime'. These are however still vague concepts, and do not provide the measure of certainty which we consider essential if banks, without the authority of an order of the court, are to be released from the obligation of confidentiality they owe to their customers".[71]

Where interests of bank require disclosure

13-029   In the *Tournier* case, Bankes L.J. gave as an example of this exception circumstances where the bank issues a writ for repayment of an overdraft, with the amount of the overdraft stated on the writ.

Other examples are the use of the bank's books to defend itself in circumstances where a customer sues it for repayment of his credit balance or where the bank discloses the debt due from its customer to the guarantor in order to sue the guarantor.

In the case of *XAG* v. *A Bank*,[72] the defendant bank argued that their interests justified disclosure of confidential documents and information to comply with a subpoena of a United States court on the grounds that failure to do so would put them in contempt of court in the United States.

In this case, Leggatt J. balanced the interests of the bank against those of the customers concerned. He said that he was not convinced that the bank would suffer any significant detriment if it failed to comply with the subpoena in that it appeared from evidence produced to the court that an action for contempt would be unlikely to be brought. However, he was satisfied that the customers would be significantly damaged if the duty of confidentiality was breached and he gave judgment in their favor.

The Jack Report considered the "interests of the bank" qualification to the duty of confidentiality in some detail. It identified two areas of concern relating to the qualification.

---

71 *Id.*, paragraph 5.30.
72 *XAG, supra* n. 35.

Disclosure within bank's group

The first area concerns the release by banks of confidential informa- **13-030**
tion about customers to other companies in the bank's group without the express consent of the customer. In some cases, disclosure is
made to non-banking companies within the group such as travel
and estate agencies or brokers.

The argument advanced by the banks to justify disclosure to
other group members is that it is necessary to protect themselves
and the group from the increasingly serious problem of customer
default; they also contend that, in any event, their customers have
given implied consent to such disclosure under the general principles governing the banker/customer relationship.

The Jack Report noted that suggestions that confidential information is used not simply for the protection of the group but for
marketing purposes as well do not "appear to be seriously disputed" by the banks and that there is widespread concern about this
practice among both private customers and corporate treasurers.

Disclosure to credit reference agencies

The second area of concern that the Jack Report considered relates **13-031**
to the disclosure of confidential information to credit reference
agencies. Such agencies exist for the purpose of providing information about the credit worthiness of individuals with whom lenders
propose to do business.

Information is collected from public sources and from providers
of credit who are prepared to contribute. The information is then
sold to potential lenders who subscribe to the agency.

Extent of disclosure

The Jack Report recommended that the extent of permissible disclo- **13-032**
sure "in the interests of the bank" should be confined to particular
situations by statute. The Jack Report accepted that the transfer of
information between banking subsidiaries is necessary for banks to
be able to fulfil their reporting obligations under the Banking Act
1987.

It recommended that the passing of confidential information
without customer consent within a banking group to such members
of the group as are banks should be sanctioned by statute on the
basis that the purposes for which the information is passed are
strictly defined and do not include the marketing of services.

The Jack Report stated that the Review Committee could "see no justification in any event for the transmission of such information, without customer consent, to non-banking subsidiaries within the Group".[73]

The Jack Report also conceded that disclosure should be permitted by statute in circumstances where there is to be a transfer of ownership of a bank that requires the bank to disclose the state of its customers' accounts. It also recommended that statutory recognition should be given to the release to agencies of information concerning customers who are in default. It proposed that this be dealt with by way of a new qualification based on there having been a breakdown of the banker-customer relationship arising through customer default.

The Jack Report suggested that default should be defined as a case where no security has been given and no satisfactory response has been received from the customer within 28 days of demand for repayment. Disclosure should, according to the Review Committee, be limited to the release of information to approved credit reference agencies.

Where disclosure is made with consent of customer

13-033   The most obvious example of disclosure on the basis of express or implied consent of the customer is where a customer authorizes its bank to issue a reference or, as the Jack Report referred to it, a "banker's opinion".

The Jack Report suggested that the new statutory definition of the duty of secrecy should amend the fourth qualification so that it is confined to disclosure with the express consent of the customer, given in writing where the consent states the purpose for which it is given.

The Report stated,

> ". . . while . . . we in general see no difficulty in banks, if they so choose, continuing to conduct relations with their customers on the basis of implied contract, in the particular matter of confidentiality it is insufficiently clear what, in present-day conditions, the contract should be taken to imply."[74]

Therefore, the Jack Report considered that disclosure by implied consent should no longer be permitted. However, it suggested that

---

[73] The Jack Report, paragraph 5.31.
[74] Id., paragraph 5.33.

if new legislation is introduced it should include a limited exception in the case of bankers' opinions where consent is often given in tacit form.

In order to rely on such consent, the Jack Report stated that a bank should be able to demonstrate that the customer had been made aware of the purpose for which the consent was required and that he was free to give or withhold his consent but could be assumed to have given it if he did not notify his bank to the contrary within a reasonable time.

The Review Committee was firmly of the view that confidential information concerning customers who are not in default should not be made available to credit reference agencies without the customers' express consent.

CONCLUSION

It will be readily apparent from the above that the banker's duty of **13-034** secrecy has been considerably eroded since the time of the *Tournier* decision. The extent of the erosion prompted the Review Committee to remark in the Jack Report:

> ". . . customers may already be forgiven for wondering, at times, if the duty of confidentiality has not been replaced by a duty to disclose".[75]

As well as highlighting the growth in the practice of releasing confidential information to other members of a bank's group and the development of credit reference agencies, the Jack Report also identified a further potential threat to the duty of secrecy in the spread of automated banking. The Review Committee did not regard the growth of electronic fund transfer systems as a direct threat to the principle of banking secrecy but pointed out that it "has brought new threats of its own to the privacy a customer expects".[76] The subject of automated banking is, of course, outside the scope of this chapter.

However, the most significant inroads into the duty to date have undoubtedly been statutory and this was recognized by the Review Committee when it called upon the Government not to extend the

---

[75] *Id.*, paragraph 5.26.
[76] *Id.*, paragraph 5.25.

statutory exceptions further, without taking full account of the consequences for the banker-customer relationship.

Although the implications of further statutory exceptions for banking secrecy as a whole are of primary concern, due consideration also should be given to the burden placed on banks by measures that require them to report suspicious transactions on their own initiative. Such a burden is undoubtedly onerous and should be taken into account by the legislators when formulating such measures.

To date, the only change which has been made in the area of banking secrecy in response to the Jack Report is the publication of a voluntary code of practice by the British Bankers' Association, The Building Societies Association and the Association for Payment Clearing Services in December 1991.[77]

The code became effective in March 1992 and requires banks and building societies to observe a strict duty of confidentiality about their customers', and former customers', financial affairs. It prohibits them from disclosing details of customers' accounts or their names and addresses to any third party, including other companies in the same group, other than in the four exceptional cases set out in the *Tournier* case.

The code specifically provides that the "interests of the bank" qualification should not be used to justify disclosure for marketing purposes to any third party, including other companies within the same group. Such information may only be passed on with express consent of the customer.

Although the code has gone some way to dealing with the Jack Report recommendations relating to disclosure based on the "interests of the bank" qualification, it has not addressed the other areas of concern relating to banking secrecy which the Jack Report highlighted. It now seems unlikely that the code will be followed by legislation on banking secrecy in the foreseeable future so the problems which the Jack Report identified are likely to remain.

If the United Kingdom decides to adopt legislation in the area of banking secrecy in the future, there may be some inter-relationship between that legislation and the Second Banking Directive.[78] The United Kingdom was required to implement the Directive by January 1, 1993. As well as providing for increased cooperation between member states for the exchange of confidential information acquired by their supervisory authorities, it will, when implemented,

---

[77] Good Banking - Code of practice to be observed by banks, building societies and card issuers when dealing with personal customers.

[78] Second Council Directive on the co-ordination of laws, regulations and administrative provisions relating to the taking up and pursuit of the business of credit institutions and amending Direcive 780/EEC (89/646/EEC).

transfer the burden of supervision of branches of foreign banks set up in the United Kingdom to the supervisory authorities of the member states where the branches' head offices are situated.

However, one area of supervision where the United Kingdom will retain responsibility is for activities of foreign branches which are contrary to legislation adopted in the United Kingdom in the interests of the general good. While it is unclear which areas of legislation will fall within that category, banking secrecy legislation which the United Kingdom may choose to implement in the future may be one such area.

The Review Committee on Banking Services described the principle of confidentiality as:

> ". . . a tradition which should be respected and, when under threat, emphasized the more strongly, because its roots go deeper than the business of banking: it has to do with the kind of society in which we want to live."[79]

It warned of serious consequences for customer confidence if nothing is done to strengthen the law on this subject. It remains to be seen whether its warning will be heeded and statutory measures taken to institute some or all of the Review Committee's recommendations or whether the banker's duty of secrecy will continue to be eroded piecemeal, as has been the case over the last two decades.

Note - Commentary regarding Scots Law and banking secrecy is provided by Iain Meiklejohn of Shepherd & Wedderburn, Edinburgh, Scotland.

[79] The Jack Report, paragraph 5.26.

CHAPTER 14

GREECE

Stelios N. Deverakis
Deverakis Law Office
Piraeus, Greece

Chapter 14

GREECE

INTRODUCTION

The following definition of banking secrecy would seem to be **14-001** generally accepted:

> "By the term banking secrecy we mean a right and an obligation, which was primarily created through commercial practice of the Banks, that various facts or statements which were disclosed to them by a third party or otherwise came to their knowledge during the exercise of their professional activity, be kept secret for an indefinite time, in accordance with the presumed will or interest of above third party." [1]

Customary development

It is also generally held that banking secrecy became a rule of law **14-002** in Greece through custom, that is, following long established practice by the banks and the ensuing conviction that it represented law.[2]

The first written law which expressly provided for a banking secrecy obligation of the employees of a bank was enacted in 1909 and constituted the Post Office Savings Bank.

---

[1] A. D. Loukopoulos, *Banking Secrecy, A Theoretical and Comparative Study* (1950), at pp. 10-11.
[2] A. Constantinides, *Duty of Witnessing and Professional Secrecy in the Criminal Trial* (1991), volume 2, at pp. 136-138.

In 1929, by Law 4316, banking companies were allowed to refuse the disclosure of information relating to (money) deposits of their customers or debentures delivered to them for safe keeping, and each and every of their customers' accounts, to the extent that above information was requested by the tax authorities for the determination of the taxable income of their customers.

Secrecy towards the tax authorities was severely limited in 1942, 1947, and 1949, but eventually secrecy was largely preserved with regard to money deposits as this was reflected in Law 3323 of 1955 regarding income tax.

Article 50 of Law 3323 provided that banks were entitled to refuse the disclosure of information to tax authorities with regard to deposits made by their customers.

In 1951, the Code of Criminal Law, Law 1492 of 1950, article 371, currently in force, provided for the crime of breach of professional confidence. Though the banking profession was not expressly listed, it was generally interpreted that above provision included bankers and banking employees in its general expression of "any others to whom, due to their profession or capacity, personal matters of a confidential nature are entrusted".

Law Decree 1059

14-003　Banking secrecy was elevated to a distinctive feature of Greek banking upon introduction of Law Decree 1059 of 1971. A strict duty and obligation was placed upon the banks, their officers and employees to observe an almost absolute secrecy with regard to deposits placed with banks in Greece.[3]

Law Decree 1059 was amended in 1988 and 1989 but, even following these amendments, the secrecy introduced by it essentially still constitutes the backbone of Greek legislation on this matter.

BANKING SECRECY AND PENAL LAW

Code of Criminal Law

14-004　Article 371 of the Code of Criminal Law introduces a criminal sanction for breach of professional secrecy and makes such breach

3 *Id.*, at p. 138.

a crime for lawyers, physicians, nurses, pharmacists and their assistants, as well as any others (*e.g.* bankers) to whom, due to their profession or capacity, personal matters of a confidential nature are entrusted.

In addition, any person who, following the death of any of the above professional persons, comes into possession of client records, is also under an obligation of confidence.

Breach of the above duty of confidentiality is prosecuted only upon a complaint by the one(s) prejudiced, not *ex officio* by the public prosecutor or upon complaint by a member of the public at large.

By way of exception to the above duty (of bankers), article 371 expressly provides that disclosure of confidential information would be excusable if done in discharge of another duty (*e.g.*, witness evidence in judicial proceedings) or in the interest of a custody of a lawful or other justifiable interest which could in no other manner be protected or performed (*e.g.*, disclosure of personal information of a customer given by him to the bank in the past in defending interests of the bank in court).

It would appear that the above obligation limits its scope of protection to the customer(s) of the bank and would not extend to the protection of the bank itself upon disclosure of confidential information by its employees to the detriment of the bank.[4]

Code of Criminal Procedure

Further article 260 of the Code of Criminal Procedure, Law 1493 of **14-005** 1950, makes provision for a power of an investigating judge or other officer to investigate correspondence and premises of a bank and if appropriate proceed to attachment of funds held in accounts or safes at the bank.

Items subject to attachment need not belong to the accused provided that they relate to the investigated crime. However, in accordance with the prevailing view, Law Decree 1059 of 1971 made article 260 inoperative with regard to bank deposits.[5]

All above provisions of written and customary law on banking secrecy may be distinguished from the secrecy obligation relating to deposits, and this is dealt with below.

[4] G. Grammatikas, *Banking Secrecy* (1991), at p. 52; and especially at p. 135.
[5] N. Androulakis, *Banking Secrecy* (1988), at pp. 48-50.

SECRECY OF DEPOSITS

14-006 Pursuant to article 1 of Law Decree 1059 of 1971, deposits placed with Greek banks are termed secret. Disclosure of any information on banking deposits by the bank's governor, directors, or members of other collective bodies or employees who, in the course of performing their duties take knowledge of such information, is punishable with imprisonment of at least six months.

The consent or approval by the customer does not preclude the criminal character of disclosure to third parties.

Upon breach of secrecy relating to banking deposits, criminal proceedings may be initiated *ex officio* by the public prosecutor, as well as upon complaint by the person prejudiced, as is the case of breach of professional confidence of article 371 of the Criminal Code.

Governors, members of the board of directors or of other collective bodies, or employees of a bank, if called upon as witnesses in any civil or criminal trial may not be examined regarding secret deposits. This restriction is not lifted even if the customer (depositor) concerned were to seek or consent to such an examination.

Originally, Law Decree 1059 of 1971 contained only one express and narrowly worded exception to the duty of absolute secrecy under strict conditions and involving a time-consuming procedure.

Provided and to the extent that disclosure of information relating to the secret banking deposits was absolutely necessary in order to trace and punish criminal actions which took place in Greece and qualified as a crime punishable with imprisonment of at least five years and a domestic court expressly waived the duty of secrecy, then such information could be lawfully disclosed to the competent judicial authority.

A second and insignificant exception to the duty of secrecy for banking deposits was introduced by Law Decree 1325 of 1972 with regard to bad checks. In the instance of non-payment of a check drawn on a bank due to lack of sufficient available funds of the issuer, the bank is under an obligation to confirm in writing the insufficiency of funds and further report the matter to the public prosecutor for an *ex officio* prosecution of the issuer.

Banking Secrecy Practice and Court Precedents

There do not seem to be reported court precedents on matters of general banking secrecy. The contrary is observed with regard to secrecy of bank deposits. **14-007**

Since the enactment of Law Decree 1059 of 1971, a number of issues were raised with regard to defining which persons were entitled to be given access to and information on bank deposits. Should the bankruptcy trustee, the wife of the depositor, the heirs, or the creditors who have obtained an injunction or final debt judgment be considered third parties who should not be supplied with information on the deposits?

Would foreign banks operating in Greece be under the same duty? Furthermore, should the Central Bank, as supervisor of the functions of banking institutions, and the tax authorities, in assessing inheritance and income tax on the depositor, be allowed to obtain information on the deposits of specific customers?

Attachment of money and other deposits held with a bank

The procedure provided by the Code of Civil Procedure for interim or compulsory attachment of funds of a person in debt (*e.g.*, a depositor) held or due to him by a third party (*e.g.*, a bank) in broad terms is the following: **14-008**

The claimant should notify the third party with copy of the court decision or other lawful title (*e.g.*, arbitration award which allows him to effect an attachment). Within eight days of date of notice of attachment, the third party is under a statutory obligation to file a written declaration with his local Justice of the Peace Court whether or not funds or other property of the debtor are in his possession.

Failure to comply with this duty or an untrue disclosure would expose the third party to liability for damages to the prejudiced claimant. With regard to limited companies (*e.g.*, banks), an attachment becomes effective as to the particular branch notified, not as to all branches of the banking company concerned.

Funds held by a customer with a bank are probably a most common example of a debtor-third party relationship of interest to a claimant.

Within the context of this procedure for effecting attachment, the introduction of Law Decree 1059 of 1971 created uncertainty. The courts gave conflicting interpretations as to whether banks, as third parties, were exempted due to secrecy duties from the statutory obligation to file the written declaration with their local Justice of the Peace Court, disclosing deposits of money and other assets which their concerned customers kept with them.

The Supreme Court (Plenary Session), in Decision 1234 of 1975,[6] resolved the matter by holding that Law Decree 1059 of 1971 prohibits Greek banks from making a declaration to the Justice of Peace Court upon notification of an attachment of their customer's deposit. Thus, an omission by a bank to file a declaration may not be challenged by a claimant. Any attachment of deposits in the hands of a branch of a bank as a third party is prohibited and, therefore, void.

In the matter before it, the Supreme Court set aside the decision of the lower courts which had found the attachment, pursuant to an injunction of a deposit of United States Dollars with the appellant bank, as lawful and valid.

A strong minority of the Supreme Court dissented:

> "Banking secrecy does not extend to the point of releasing banks from their statutory obligation, following notice of attachment, to disclose whether funds or other property of a debtor were held by them. The attaching creditor is exercising rights of the depositor himself, and a bank should not be entitled to refuse making the declaration required by the Code of Civil Procedure. The interpretation given by the majority of the court would make bank deposits exempt from attachment which the law would have done in clear and express terms due to the grave consequences of such an exemption. Those who commit pecuniary crimes would easily and safely secure the money produce of their criminal activity by depositing it with a bank whilst debtors of bad faith would escape their creditors by liquidating their assets and placing the money proceeds with a Greek bank."

Despite the minority opinion and criticism of the decision by commentators,[7] the Supreme Court's interpretation of the law has been consistently followed by the courts. The policy of widening the financial resources of the Greek banking system, rather than any considerations of justice, would seem to have prevailed.

The Supreme Court (Plenary Session), in Decision 1225 of 1975,[8] had limited the scope of the exemption of banks from interim and

---

6 Supreme Court (Plenary) Decision 1234 of 1975, reported in *Epitheorisi Emboricou Dikaeou* (1976), volume 27, at pp. 218-220.

7 I. Brinias, *The Law of Enforcement* (1980), 2nd ed., at pp. 1280-1284.

8 Supreme Court (Plenary) Decision 1225 of 1975, reported in *Epitheorisi Emboricou Dikaeou* (1976), volume 27, at pp. 220-221.

compulsory attachment to money deposits only. Attachment was held permissible against shares, debentures, or other negotiable instruments deposited with a bank.

However, the Law 1868 of 1989 would seem to have inadvertently extended secrecy to negotiable instruments, as well.

Attachment of money deposits held with foreign banks in Greece

In October 1975, a creditor notified the branch of an American bank **14-009** operating in Athens of a seizure report against a company allegedly a depositor.

The claimant had previously obtained a court payment order and was attempting to collect the funds due by attaching that amount in the debtor's account. The bank filed a written declaration with the Athens Justice of Peace Court, admitting the existence of an account of the particular company but refusing to provide any further information, invoking the law on banking secrecy.

Nevertheless, it reserved its option to comply with any interpretation of the law in an *ad hoc* case pending before the Plenary Session of the Supreme Court.

The creditor filed an objection writ against such declaration by the bank and sought a payment order against the bank for the amount seized.

The Athens Appeal Court held that:

"The objection writ had to be rejected as inadmissible in law. No seizure of money deposit with a bank operating in Greece was allowed. Relevant provisions of the Civil Procedure Code prescribing the option available to a creditor to place a seizure of a claim of its debtor owed to the latter by a bank operating in Greece in the context of a money deposit relationship were inapplicable. Whilst the letter of Law Decree 1059 of 1971 expressly refers to secrecy for the deposits placed with Greek banks, the true will of the legislator was that deposits maintained with all banks operating in Greece be termed secret.

The above interpretation is supported by following considerations:

"I) The purpose of the legislator was the increase of money deposits with banks so that the accumulation of funds available for the finance of the national economy be increased. Any discrimination against Foreign banks would not promote above purpose of the legislator in that money deposits with foreign banks operating in Greece would decline to the detriment of the national economy.

II) The secrecy was enacted not in favor of the banks but in favor of the depositors as this is expressly stated in articles 2, paragraph 1, and 3 of Law Decree 1059 of 1971. Secrecy encompassing only the depositors of Greek banks and excluding those of non Greek banks would introduce a discrimination against depositors not permitted by the principle of equality of Greek citizens embodied in article 4, paragraph 1, of the Constitution.

III) An interpretation that secrecy of deposits relates to Greek banks only would be contrary to a fundamental principle of Greek Legislation that in principle foreigners enjoy the same civil law rights as Greeks do.

IV) As far as American banks operating through branches in Greece are concerned, any exclusion of the privilege of secrecy for their depositors would be contrary to article 13 of Law 2893 of 1954 which ratified the Treaty of Friendship, Commerce and Shipping between Greece and the United States. The above article provides that companies of both countries shall enjoy the right to establish themselves and shall engage in commercial activities under the same conditions as the companies of the home country."[9]

With reference to branches of foreign banks of European Community (EC) countries, Law Decree 1059 of 1971 was found applicable to them by virtue of article 44, article 48, paragraph 2, article 52, paragraph 2, and article 58 of the Treaty of Rome of March 25, 1957.[10]

---

[9] Athens Appeal Court Decision 7060 of 1976, reported in *Nomico Vima* (1978), volume 26, at pp. 947-948.

[10] Athens One-Member Court Decision 691 of 1983, reported in *Epitheorisi Emborikou Dikaeou* (1983), volume 34 , at pp. 404-405.

Information sought by former spouse

Greek Family Law makes a number of provisions for a right of **14-010** alimony between husband and wife and a right of participation in the wealth accumulated during the currency of marriage by the other spouse.

By way of illustration, article 1445 of the Civil Code expressly provides for

> ". . . an obligation among former spouses to provide each other with accurate information provided that this would be expedient in determining the amount of alimony. Upon application by one of the former spouses submitted through the competent public attorney the employer, the competent office and the competent tax authority officer have to provide every information relating to the financial position of the other spouse and especially his (or her) income".

Upon submission of a request for information relating to deposits placed with a bank by the other spouse, the Supreme Court's deputy public prosecutor issued an opinion against the disclosure.[11] Following are extracts from the deputy public prosecutor's opinion:

> "The Law (Law Decree 1059/1971) places a paramount confidentiality clause in each and every contract whereby a bank accepts a money deposit. A bank has a right and an obligation for an indefinite time to preserve secrecy with regard to facts of existence and operation of the contract and of all events and disclosures of its customer that its employees became aware of during the pre-contractual, contractual, and post-contractual stage of the banking business."

> "By the general provision of article 1445 of the Civil Code, one should not consider that indirectly the special (secrecy) principle established by article 1 of Law Decree 1059 of 1971 was abolished in this field."

> "In particular, one may not enlarge and construe the meaning of the term 'office' (or 'service') used in article 1445 of the Civil

---

[11] Legal Opinion 23 of 1986, Supreme Court Deputy Public Prosecutor, reported in *Elliniki Dikaeosyni* (1987), volume 28, at pp. 1150-1152.

Law in such a broad way as to encompass the banks too, including their line of business which consists in the acceptance of money deposits in consideration for the payment of interest."

"By the abstract term 'competent office' one may really mean the civil service, corporations of the broader public sector, public law legal entities, etc., which provide wages or fees to one of the former spouses or a pension fund providing pension or other similar social security funding in money or other value, the land registrar with regard to property owned by one of the former spouses . . ." but not banks.

Information sought by heirs

14-011   In principle, upon the death of a person, his estate passes pursuant to his will (testament) to the designated heirs, subject to rules on compulsory inheritance.

In the absence of a valid will, the estate passes by virtue of the law to intestate heirs. Descendants and parents of the deceased, as well as his (or her) spouse (compulsory heirs), are by law entitled to a minimum percentage of the estate, irrespective of any different provision in the will.

Heirs are entitled, as substitute beneficiaries of the depositor, to seek and obtain information relating to deposits of the deceased. However, the issue becomes complicated with regard to joint and several banking accounts. Law 5638 of 1932, article 3, provides that a clause may be added to such accounts to the effect that the heirs of a joint and several account depositor (as long as there remains a surviving joint and several depositor) maintain no interest in the deposit which passes as a whole to the surviving account holders.

In this instance, the law expressly excludes the specific assets of the joint and several account from the inheritance estate. Thus, one would conclude that heirs are not entitled to seek and obtain information on such an account from the bank. However, article 117 of the Law Introducing the Civil Code provides that, if by virtue of a deposit into a joint and several account a donation was effected in favor of the other joint and several holders of the account, this is treated as donation and is subject to partial rescission in order to preserve for the compulsory heirs the minimum share to which they are entitled, irrespective of the will of the deceased.

In this context, the compulsory heir, if he were to challenge the donation in order to rescind it, should first establish particulars of the deposits made by the deceased. These particulars may be extracted from the balances of the joint and several account on and before the date of death.

It was proposed[12] that the heir in these circumstances should apply to a court and, in particular pursuant to articles 902-903 of the Civil Code, seek a court order forcing the bank to disclose the information relating to the joint and several account on and prior to the date of death of the deceased.

However, this view, although approved by a few courts, recently was rejected by a first instance court which denied an application by compulsory heirs against a bank for release of information relating to joint and several accounts of a deceased. The court declared:

> "The compulsory heir, even if the deposit by the inherited deceased constituted donation, may apply against the joint account holder who obtained benefit but has no direct and *ipso jure* entitlement on the deposit . . . the secrecy of the deposit is not lifted due to the presence of a lawful interest in the person of applicant."[13]

Information sought by bankruptcy trustee

In 1984, a ship management company, incorporated in Liberia and lawfully operating from Piraeus, Greece, was declared bankrupt by the Court of Piraeus. The court appointed a lawyer as bankruptcy trustee. **14-012**

The trustee applied to the branch of the Dutch bank where the bankrupt company held a U.S. dollar current account and sought copies of the debit notes and other instruments by virtue of which funds had been withdrawn from the account.

The bank refused to offer the required information on grounds of banking secrecy. The First Instance Court of Piraeus (Interim Measures) held that:

> "The representatives and employees of banks operating in Greece pursuant to Law 1059 of 1971, which was intended to

---

[12] V. Douvlis, *Joint and Several Account: Infringement of the Right to Compulsory Inheritance and Lifting of Secrecy of Banking Deposits* (1987), at pp. 46-57.

[13] First Instance Court of Larissa (Interim Measures) Decision 170 of 1990, reported in *Nomico Vima* (1990), volume 38, at pp. 1469-1471.

achieve an increase of banking deposits and through it a service to the national economy, are under a duty to refuse all information relating to the money deposits of their customer whether this was sought through a court process or not.

Such prohibition, however, is not applicable to the bankruptcy trustee (pursuant to Greek Law) of a foreign company lawfully operating from Greece. Indeed, the rights of a bankrupt upon the assets of bankruptcy are exercised by the trustee under the same conditions that the bankrupt would exercise them, whether the trustee be considered as representing the bankrupt or the group of his creditors even under the alternative that the trustee represents neither the bankrupt nor the group of creditors but derives his powers from the law. He is the one who represents the bankrupt and his bankruptcy assets."

The application was admissible in law and on the evidence was granted. The bank involved was ordered to provide the trustee with the information on bank deposits which he was seeking.[14]

Information sought by the Bank of Greece

14-013 Pursuant to Law 1665 of 1951, the Bank of Greece (the Central Bank) exercises supervision and control over all credit institutions operating in Greece.

Pursuant to such function, the Bank of Greece is authorized to investigate all books and records of the examined banks. Law 1665 provides:

"The Central Bank and its officers are entitled to proceed and investigate all books and records of the (examined) bank, to examine as witnesses the governors, directors and employees of the (examined) banks, who are obliged to supply in writing, if so requested, all required information."

Scope of authority

14-014 It was suggested that such authority included the investigation of money deposits of all kinds. However, it was argued that the

---

[14] First Instance Court of Piraeus Decision 3629 of 1984, reported in *Epitheorisi Naftiliakou Dikaeou* (1986), volume 13, at pp. 144-145.

authority of the Bank of Greece had been restricted following the introduction of Law 1059 of 1971 on secrecy of banking deposits.

In July 1988, the Bank of Greece obtained an opinion from its legal counsel that, following introduction of Law Decree 1059 of 1971, it had no power to investigate and collect information on the banking deposits held at the examined banks.

Pursuant to this opinion, the examined banks were entitled to consider the inspectors of the Bank of Greece as third parties who should be denied access and information on banking deposits. Thus, the Bank of Greece sought authority to investigate deposits through enactment of new legislation.

One may note that banking deposits with banks in Greece do not enjoy any insurance cover in the eventuality that a bank becomes insolvent. There is no law providing that the State should salvage banks (and their depositors) from failure.[15]

However, it has been the practice that the State would intervene and directly or indirectly would provide financial support to banks in distress to enable them to pay their depositors.

It was pointed out in 1988 that any view that the Bank of Greece could not investigate the deposits held with banks in Greece could lead to an immunity of the latter to the extent that the depositor, having secured the secrecy of his deposits/accounts, might lose the deposits precisely due to lack of effective banking supervision and control.[16]

Bank of Crete case

A case involving the Bank of Crete raised the issue of the extent of **14-015** authority of the Bank of Greece to supervise and investigate banks operating in Greece.

The governor of the bank, having risen from the rank of employee, embarked on a major business expansion, buying daily newspapers, building a major printing facility, and investing an estimated US $100-million.[17]

The Bank of Greece, following major press publicity, commenced an investigation into the Bank of Crete and discovered that the funds originated from a personal account of the governor of the Bank of Crete.

[15] L. Georgakopoulos, *The Law of Limited Companies* (1991), volume 4, at pp. 481-482, paragraph 64.
[16] P. Floros, "Thoughts on Banking Secrecy", *Nomico Vima* (1988), volume 36, at pp. 1518-1519.
[17] Androulakis, *supra* n. 5, at pp. 11-15.

The governor declared to bank inspectors that most of those drachma funds had been produced by conversion of foreign currency funds from abroad. However, he refused to supply official conversion receipts and maintained that Law 1059 of 1971 entitled him to refuse investigation of his personal accounts.

An application by an Appeal Court's deputy public prosecutor for judicial investigation of the accounts was rejected. The Council of Appeal Court Judges held it could not entertain the application because, prior to commencement of criminal prosecution, it lacked jurisdiction and proceedings in the instance case were still at the investigatory stage.[18]

Shortly thereafter, the Bank of Greece received a written advice from a New York bank which revealed that the governor of the Bank of Crete had been presenting the Bank of Greece with falsified deposit certificates concerning the deposits of the Bank of Crete with the New York bank.

Were it possible for the American banks to plead secrecy of bank deposits, the Bank of Greece might never have uncovered the fraud.

On the motion of the Bank of Greece, the government placed the Bank of Crete under the command of a governor appointed by the Bank of Greece. Criminal proceedings against the former governor were expedited, and the Council of Appeal Court Judges, on the motion of the investigating judge, lifted the secrecy established by Law 1059 of 1971 and ordered the provision of information on the bank deposits:

> "The Council considers it indispensable to allow the provision of absolutely necessary information (by way of witnessing of persons who know, delivery of documents, response in writing to questions, opinions of experts who might be appointed, reports of the inspectors of the bank of Greece, seizure of documents and other evidence, etc.) regarding the deposits which are related or may turn out that they are related with the allegedly committed by the accused (G.K. and accomplices) crime of embezzlement of the monies involved and any other related crime punishable with imprisonment of at least five years."[19]

---

[18] Athens Appeal Court Decree 1465 of 1988, reported in *Nomico Vima* (1988), volume 36, at pp. 1274-1276.

[19] Athens Appeal Court Decree 2432 of 1988, reported in *Elliniki Dikaeosyni* (1990), volume 31, at pp. 918-921.

Information sought by tax authorities

Article 50 of Law Decree 3323 of 1955, regarding taxation of income **14-016**
of natural persons, expressly provided that banks "are entitled to
refuse the supply of information only with regard to deposits of
their customers with them", thus limiting the extent of information
which tax authorities could seek from banks for checking the accuracy of the annual tax returns.

With the exception of joint and several banking accounts, all
other accounts appear to be subject to inheritance tax. The prevailing view holds that the banks may not raise banking secrecy as to
bank deposits against tax authorities on matters relating to inheritance tax.[20] Joint and several accounts, by express provision of
article 2, paragraph 1, of Law 5638 of 1932, may contain (and, in
practice, invariably do contain) a clause to the effect that, upon the
death of any of several beneficiaries of the deposit, the survivors
become sole beneficiaries to the exclusion of the heirs.

The law also provides that the deposit thus acquired by the
remaining beneficiaries is subject to no charge on account of inheritance tax or other tax.

In relation to banking secrecy and the tax authorities, in a case
where the state attempted to seize a deposit to satisfy an income tax
liability, the Athens Appeal Court has held:

"By express provision of article 1 of Law Decree 1059 of 1971,
deposits maintained with banks located in Greece are secret.
Directors, officers or employees of banks who through their
business at the bank become aware of deposits made are to be
punished with imprisonment of at least six months if they
provide any information relating to deposits. The consent or
approval of the depositor does not release the bank officer
concerned from his duty to secrecy nor his accountability for
violating the above provision of criminal law. Thus, a bank is
restricted from making any statement even if a seizure was
effected through it against the beneficiary of the deposit. Its
duty to secrecy relieved it from having to disclose by official
statement the availability or not of funds under seizure. Thus,
the writ issued against the bank is rejected as inadmissible in
law."[21]

---

[20]Grammatikas, *supra* n. 4, at pp. 174-175.
[21] Athens Appeal Court Decision 11194 of 1986 reported in *Epitheorisis Emborikou
Dikaeou* vol 39 (1988) at pp. 42-43.

In another case, the tax authorities in 1986 sought information from a Greek bank on the amounts collected by its shopkeeper customers during the year 1982 through sales under a particular credit card. The bank refused to supply the required information. The Administrative First Instance Court of Athens held that the refusal of the bank was justified on grounds of banking secrecy. Secrecy of deposits included not only the amounts of deposited funds but also all operations of the account (withdrawals, deposits, and interest).[22]

Set off by a bank against its depositor

14-017 Pursuant to article 451 of the Civil Code, no set off is allowed against claims which are excluded from attachment.

Given that Law Decree 1059 of 1971, through the secrecy it establishes as interpreted by the courts, makes bank deposits immune from attachment, one might conclude that even the bank where the deposit is maintained is not allowed to exercise set off for its claims against the depositor.

There appear to be no court judgments dealing with this matter, although among commentators it is held almost unanimously[23] that a bank may effect such a set off.

RECENT AMENDMENTS AND LAWS AFFECTING BANKING SECRECY

Bank of Greece supervision

14-018 Following the Bank of Crete case, Law Decree 1059 of 1971 was amended by Law 1806 of September 20, 1988, which shortly thereafter was largely repealed by Law 1868 of October 10, 1989.

The definition of secrecy as per article 1 of Law Decree 1059 of 1971 was not affected, but the conditions for lifting secrecy were amended to allow disclosure in more instances, although still in strictly defined circumstances:

> "By way of exception, the disclosure of information for secret deposits of money or other values kept with banks operating

---

[22] Athens Administrative First Instance Court Decision 12877 of 1989, unpublished.

[23] Douvlis, *supra* n. 12, at pp. 44-45.

in Greece is permitted; subject to a specifically justified order or application or decision of the official competent to initiate criminal proceedings or preliminary investigation or investigation either through the Council of Judges or the Court before which the relevant proceedings are pending, provided that the provision of such information is absolutely necessary for tracing and punishing a crime punishable with imprisonment of five years at least".

New scope of Law Decree 1059

The new language of article 3 of Law Decree 1059 of 1971 appears to: **14-019**

(1) Expressly place under its scope all banks operating in Greece, without distinction between Greek and non-Greek banks;

(2) Enlarge the scope of banking secrecy by adding deposits other than money, *e.g.*, deposits of negotiable instruments and securities within the object of protection of secrecy;

(3) Allow lifting of secrecy at the preliminary stage of criminal investigation prior to commencement of criminal prosecution, and

(4) Allow lifting of secrecy on account of major crimes committed outside Greece, provided that the Greek Criminal Courts had jurisdiction.

Confirmation of supervisory powers

In particular with regard to supervision and control over all banks operating within Greece, Law 1868 of 1989 confirmed power of the Bank of Greece and other government authorities as follows: **14-020**

"The secrecy, which is enacted by article 1 of Law 1059 of 1971, of deposits in all kinds of credit institutions operating within the country is not operative towards the inspector and the monetary authorities of the bank of Greece, the Judicial Authorities, the Investigating Parliamentary Committees to which the Law delegates the relevant control of the credit institutions, with regard to deposits which are maintained in the respective credit institutions, provided that the aforesaid persons or bodies exercise competence relating to the control of the banking system and the correct application of the credit and monetary legislation or the legislation relating to protection of national currency."

Thus, it appears that pursuant to above new provision:

(1) Not only the Bank of Greece but also the judicial authorities and the Investigating Parliamentary Committees (the latter within the limits prescribed by the Law governing function of Parliament) are afforded a right to seek and obtain information on deposits, and

(2) Grounds for inspection and supply of information on deposits were extended beyond the requirements of control of the banking system also to the matters of correct application of credit and monetary laws and the laws on protection of the national currency.

Additional ground for setting aside secrecy

14-021   The Joint Ministerial Decision of the Ministers of National Economy and Commerce 376 of November 29, 1988, regarding lifting of secrecy of banking deposits, introduced a new ground for setting banking secrecy aside.

Pursuant to the Ministerial Decision, which was ratified by article 38 of Law 1828 of 1989, provided the following cumulative conditions are satisfied, banking secrecy with regard to all deposits effected during a period under investigation may be lifted:

(1) Nomination by the Bank of Greece of a compulsory governor of a bank, and

(2) Commencement of criminal prosecution against management of a bank for a crime relating to the administration and function of a bank and which crime has aroused a public outcry.

Organized crime limitations

14-022   Law 1916 of December 28, 1990, regarding protection of society from organized crime, introduced provisions limiting banking secrecy. Article 1 of Law 1916 defines a number of instances in which banking secrecy might be limited.

These include the actions of a group of two or more persons aiming at habitually or cumulatively committing one or more of following: murder, serious injury, hostage taking, hijacking, arson, attacks against military or police installations, and drug trafficking.

Article 12 of Law 1916 provides for lifting of banking secrecy and attachment of funds with regard to the deposits and accounts of any person accused of the above crimes. Such lifting and attachment of funds may be authorized by an investigating judge or, prior to commencement of criminal prosecution, by an investigation officer subject to the consent of a deputy public prosecutor of the Supreme Court.

Tax law limitations

Article 50 of Law Decree 3323 of 1955, which expressly provided **14-023** that banks "are entitled to refuse the supply of information only with regard to deposits of their customers with them", following its amendment by Law 1828 of 1989 is not repeated.

Instead article 57, paragraph b, of Law 3323 of 1955 provides that the tax authorities are entitled to:

> ". . . seek from public, district and communal authorities, legal entities of public law, banks, private businesses and in general from any professional, commercial, industrial, agricultural concern any information which they consider expedient for facilitating their work".

This very broad wording is not considered by commentators as actually lifting banking secrecy;[24] nor have the tax authorities been reported as having sought from any bank information on bank deposits on the basis of the revised provision.

This view also would seem to align with the recently introduced taxation of deposit interest earned from banks in Greece. With effect as of January 1, 1991, Law 1921 of 1991 introduced a 10 percent withholding taxation on interest of deposits which had been free of tax. The tax is withheld by the bank and relevant tax return makes a reference in bulk to the gross interest payable by the bank without disclosure of particulars of depositors and their individual deposits.

[24]Grammatikas, *supra* n. 4, at pp. 101-103.

Transparency of financial resources of public officials

14-024 Law 1738 of 1987, in articles 6 to 9, makes provision for members of parliament, ministers and leaders of political parties, government appointed officers or members of boards of directors of corporations of the public sector, and members of their families to file annual financial statements with a Parliament or the deputy public prosecutor of the Supreme Court.

The annual financial statements should include the deposits of money or other valuables deposited with banks or other financial institutions. Under article 8, the verification of financial statements is delegated to inspectors appointed by Parliament or the deputy public prosecutor, respectively.

By express provision of the law, banking secrecy (as well as stock exchange and tax secrecy) may not be raised against duly appointed inspectors who are entitled to obtain information on the banking deposits of investigated persons of any of the above classes of persons.

Law 1868 of 1989 introduced an obligation of financial disclosure for:

(1) Publishers, editors, and managers of newspapers, radio, and television stations;
(2) Registered shareholders of five percent of the stock of any Greek bank;
(3) Individuals, groups, or company institutions engaged in editing of newspapers, radio, and television stations;
(4) The representatives of any business concern in which persons mentioned above under (1), (2), or (3) participate at or in excess of 10 percent of their stock, and
(5) Immediate relatives of persons mentioned above under (1), (2), (3), and (4).

Again, banking secrecy may not be raised against the public inspectors.

European Community limitations

14-025 The Treaty of Rome in article 214, recognizes a duty of professional secrecy for its own bodies and employees with regard to information which by its nature is considered professional secret (*e.g.* bank deposits).

At a different level, the EC Directive of June 13, 1983, on the supervision of credit institutions on a consolidated basis requires EC Member States to eliminate legal impediments which prevent a credit institution from supplying to another credit institution to which it is linked information necessary for consolidated supervision. In practice, these provisions result in the abolition of banking secrecy in this context.[25]

Greek Law 1914 of 1990, in articles 19-24, introduces provisions for cooperation of the Greek tax authorities with the tax authorities of other EC Member States and for the exchange of information.

However, no assistance is granted "...if, pursuant to Greek Laws, the collection or the investigations for the collection or the use of the information required for tax purposes is prohibited".

One might suggest that, due to banking secrecy restrictions, the Greek tax authorities would not be allowed to provide assistance and information on banking deposits to tax authorities in other Member States.

Finally, within the EC framework, consideration also should be given to the published intention of the Greek government to introduce new laws to implement EC Directive 91/308/EEC of June 10, 1991, on money laundering.[26] Under the proposed legislation, banks would be placed under a duty to report to the authorities any deposits of suspect origin (drug trafficking or trade in drugs and/or in arms) for investigation. Such a law would have a major impact on banking secrecy in Greece.

CONCLUSION

Throughout the legislation and court decisions noted above, one **14-026** may note an underlying reluctance of the legislator and the courts to lift banking secrecy.

Judicial interpretation of the law and practice have elevated the duty of secrecy to an almost absolute one, and this was exemplified by the complexity of the process and the time required for lifting of secrecy in the Bank of Crete case. In that instance, the abuse of banking secrecy prompted new legislation which allows the Bank of Greece to exercise effective control over all banking institutions operating in Greece.

A lender would find it difficult to seize monies and obtain recovery out of funds which his debtor may have placed with a bank operating in Greece. Even if one possessed a final debt judgment,

---

[25] M. Dassesse, *EEC Banking Law* (1985), at pp. 100-101.
[26] EC Directive 91/308/EEC of June 10, 1991.

one would not be allowed, as a third party, to enforce it against funds deposited in a bank account.

Despite the eloquent arguments of the minority in Supreme Court Decision 1234 of 1975 and the concern expressed by legal commentators, there does not appear any intention to reform the law in this respect.

Over the last few years, the law on banking secrecy has been revised and amended repeatedly. However, despite these changes, banking secrecy has been essentially preserved.

Although the government faces a major challenge in containing its public debt and public expenses and raising its revenue from taxes, it is doubtful it will find the will (or, indeed, the capacity) to limit or abolish banking secrecy towards the tax authorities.[27]

Compared to the practice in other EC Member States, banking secrecy in Greece is quite restrictive as regards the tax authorities, lenders, and victims of minor crimes. Thus, the banking system in Greece, despite inroads into secrecy remains an attractive place for deposit of funds by those concerned with confidentiality.

[27] Law 2065 of June 30, 1992, introduced an express, though limited, lifting of banking secrecy regarding deposits and a right of attachment in cases of tax evasion.

Appendix

Code of Criminal Law (Law 1492 of 1950)

Article 371

Breach of Professional Confidence

1. Clergymen, attorneys, and all defense lawyers, notaries public, medical doctors, midwifes, nurses, pharmacists and their assistants and any others to whom, because of their profession or capacity, personal matters of a confidential nature, are entrusted, shall be punished by pecuniary penalty or imprisonment not exceeding one year if they disclose such matters entrusted to them.

2. One who, following the death of any professional under paragraph 1, comes into possession of such person's documents or papers related to such person's profession or capacity and disclosed personal matters of a confidential nature contained therein shall be subject to the same punishment.

3. Criminal prosecution shall be initiated only upon complaint.

4. An act (of disclosure) shall be justified and shall not be punished if the perpetrator acted in accordance with a duty or in the interest of the custody of a lawful or otherwise justifiable legal interest, public or private, whether his own or of another which could in no other manner be protected or preserved.

Code of Criminal Procedure (Law 1493 of 1950)

Attachment at Banks and Other Institutions

Article 260

1. At banks or other institutions, public or private, the investigating judge and all investigating officers may personally proceed to the attachment of securities, amounts placed in a current account, and every other deposited thing or document even if they are contained in safe boxes and even if these do not belong to the accused or are not registered in his name, provided that they are related to the crime.

2. The judge and the officers mentioned hereinabove are entitled to examine the correspondence and all actions of the Bank or institution, in order to sort out the items subject to attachment or in order to determine other circumstances expedient to the finding of truth and in the instance of refusal, to proceed with search and attachment of items and documents of use.

14-029   **Law Decree 1059 of 1971 Regarding Banking Secrecy**

Article 1. Deposits made with Greek Banks are termed secret.

Article 2. (1) Governors, members of the Board of Directors or of other collective organs or employees of Banks who in the course of performing their duties take knowledge of banking deposits if they were to anyhow provide any information shall be punished with imprisonment of a term of at least six months. The consent or approval by the depositor in whose favor the secrecy is enacted would by no means preclude the criminal character of such an action.

(2) Upon finding the accused guilty of the action defined in the previous paragraph, the Court may not order the suspension of execution of imprisonment nor its conversion into monetary punishment (abolished by article 6 of Law 1419/1984).

(3) The persons which are mentioned in paragraph 1 if called upon as witnesses in any civil or criminal trial shall never be examined about secret deposits, even if the depositor in whose favor the secrecy is enacted were to consent to such examination.

Article 3. By way of exception the provision of information about the secret bank deposits is allowed only following a domestic court decision containing specific reasons provided and to the extent that relevant information is absolutely necessary in order trace and punish criminal actions which took place in Greece and qualify as major crime.

(The above article 3 was replaced by article 27 of Law 1868 of 1989 which is set out below)

Article 27

By way of exception the provision of information for the secret deposits of money or other value kept with banks operating in Greece is permitted following a specifically justified order or application or decision of the (official) competent to initiate criminal proceedings or preliminary investigation or investigation through the council of judges or the court before which the relevant proceedings are pending, provided that the provision of such information is absolutely necessary for tracing and punishing a major crime.

Law Decree 1325 of 1972 Regarding Bad Checks

14-030

By way of exception to the provisions of Law Decree 1059 of 1971 in the instance of non-payment of a check drawn on a bank due to lack of sufficient available funds of the issuer, the bank is under an obligation to confirm this either on the instrument of the check itself or in a separate document along with a note on the date of presentation of the check.

Law 1806 of 1988, As Amended By Law 1868 of 1989, Article 40 (In Part)

14-031

Paragraph 2

The secrecy, which is enacted by article 1 of Law 1059/ 1971, of the deposits in all kinds of credit institutions operating within the country is not operative towards the inspector and the monetary authorities of the Bank of Greece, the Judicial Authorities, the Investigating Parliamentary Committees to which the Law delegates the relevant control of the credit institutions, with regard to the deposits which are maintained in the respective credit institution, provided that the aforesaid persons or bodies exercise competence relating to the control of the banking system and the correct application of credit and monetary legislation or the legislation relating to protection of national currency.

Law 1914 of 1990

14-032

Articles 19-24 on mutual assistance within the Community

Cooperation with Tax Authorities of Other Member States and Exchange of Information

Article 21, Instance C

. . . if, pursuant to Greek Laws, the collection or the investigations for the collection or the use of information required for tax purposes is prohibited" no assistance is granted.

14-033 Law 1916 of 1990 Regarding Protection of Society from Organized Crime

Article 12

During a judicial investigation relating to crimes prescribed by this Law, the secrecy of bank deposits and accounts of the accused is lifted pursuant to a decree of the competent investigating judge and the funds therein are attached. During a preliminary investigation, it is possible for the secrecy of bank deposits and accounts of the accused to be lifted and the funds therein to be attached subject to a concurring opinion of the competent deputy public prosecutor of the Supreme Court.

14-034 Draft Commercial Code (1987)

Article 171

Secrecy

1. With regard to every deposit a bank has to observe secrecy towards any third party. The consent of the depositor or beneficiary does not release the bank from the above obligation. Those who violate secrecy are punished with imprisonment not exceeding a term of three years.

2. The secrecy is lifted when the supply of information is ordered by judicial decision or decree in relation with criminal charges for a crime punishable with imprisonment of a term of at least five years.

CHAPTER 15

GRENADA

M. Linda Grant and Rita L. Joseph
Grant & Grant
St. George's, Grenada, West Indies

Chapter 15

GRENADA

INTRODUCTION

Grenada is a three-island nation situated in the West Indies which **15-001**
obtained its independence from the United Kingdom on February
7, 1974.

The legal system of Grenada is based on the Common Law of
England and statute. The benefit of the laws of England was extended to Grenada by virtue of various Royal Proclamations made
in 1763, 1764, and 1784. These proclamations declared that the laws
of Great Britain were in force in Grenada as far as the nature and
circumstances of Grenada would permit and that all other jurisdictions, offices, commissions, and proceedings for the future not
founded on the laws of England were declared to be absolutely
determined, utterly void and totally abolished.

Between the Proclamations of 1763 and 1784, Grenada had been
a French colony. The last-mentioned proclamation recited the
Treaty of Peace with France of September 3, 1783, after which
Grenada returned to British rule.

This position was maintained throughout the period of British
Rule. On independence, Grenada preserved its existing laws.

The civil law of Grenada is administered by the Supreme Court
of Grenada, which forms part of the court system of the Organization of Eastern Caribbean States. A right of appeal lies to the Appeal
Court of the Eastern Caribbean and, as in other parts of the British
Commonwealth, a final appeal lies on a point of law to Her Majesty's Privy Council in England.

BANKING SECRECY

Duty

15-002 The relationship of banker and customer is based on contract and necessarily involves certain duties and obligations. For the purpose of this chapter, we are concerned with the duty of secrecy imposed upon a banker both at Common Law and by statute.

Duty at Common Law

15-003 At Common Law, it is an implied term of the contract between a banker and his customer that the banker will not divulge to third parties, without the consent of the customer, express or implied, either the state of the customer's account, any of his transactions with the bank, or any information relating to the customer acquired through the keeping of his account.

However, the banker may divulge information where he is compelled to do so by order of a Court, or where the circumstances give rise to a public duty of disclosure, or where the protection of the banker's own interests require it. This duty arises only when the relationship of banker and customer exists and does not cease when a customer closes his account.

Express authority

15-004 Where a customer gives express authority to his banker to disclose information to a third party, the banker commits no breach of duty in complying with that request.

Implied authority

15-005 The Common Law implies authority to disclose in certain situations, for example, where a banker receives a query from an intending surety which may have a material bearing as to whether or not he gives a guarantee.

The banker must give the information honestly and to the best of his ability because this situation necessarily implies authority for disclosure when a customer introduces a surety to his banker.

Public duty of disclosure

There are very few reported cases which touch upon a bank's duty   **15-006**
to make disclosure in the public interest and no cases on the subject
have been considered by the Supreme Court of Grenada.

The usual instance where a Bank might be justified in disclosing
information is where, in time of war, a customer's dealings indicate
trading with the enemy. However, it is apparent from the dicta of
Bankes L.J. in *Tournier* v. *National Provincial and Union Bank of England*[1] that disclosure to the police regarding a customer suspected of
criminal activities is unwarranted.

Disclosure in bank's interest

The only reported case on the issue of disclosure in the bank's   **15-007**
interest is that of *Sutherland* v. *Barclays Bank Ltd.*[2] In that case, the
bank dishonored the plaintiff's checks as there were insufficient
funds in the account.

However, the real reason for the refusal to pay was that the bank
was cognizant of the fact that the plaintiff was gambling. The
plaintiff complained to her husband who telephoned the bank and
was advised that most of his wife's checks were made out to
bookmakers.

The plaintiff sued the bank for breach of its duty of secrecy. It was
held that in the circumstances the bank's interest required disclosure. It also was held that the bank had the customer's implied
consent to disclose.

Compulsion by law

The Supreme Court of Grenada is empowered by various legisla-   **15-008**
tive provisions to make orders requiring a bank to disclose information touching or concerning its customers. The statutory provisions
in Grenada are so diverse that it is necessary to comment briefly on
each provision.

For the purposes of the legislation hereinafter referred to, "person" includes any company or association or body of persons,
corporate or unincorporate. Therefore, banks and bankers would be
included within that definition.

[1] *Tournier* v. *National Provincial and Union Bank of England* [1924] 1 K.B. 461.
[2] *Sutherland* v. *Barclays Bank Ltd.* (1938) 5 Legal Decisions Affecting Bankers 163.

Evidence Act

15-009   The Evidence Act[3] provides, *inter alia*, that a bank shall not be compelled to produce its books in any legal proceeding to which the bank is not a party in any case where the contents of its books can be proved by secondary evidence, unless a judge so orders for special cause.

Any party to a suit may apply to a judge for an order to inspect and take copies of any entries in a banker's book, for any of the purposes of the suit. This order may be made *ex parte* and must be served on the bank three days before it is to be obeyed unless the judge directs otherwise.

"Banker's book" includes any ledger, day book, cash book, account book, and any other book used in the ordinary business of a bank.

This position is akin to that which pertained in England under the Banker's Books Evidence Act 1879.[4] Thus, in interpreting the provisions in Grenada, the courts will apply the same principles employed by the English Court in interpreting the English Act.

The power to order inspection of bankers' books is discretionary and will be exercised with great caution and only on sufficient grounds. The order, if made, would be limited to relevant entries which would be admissible in law at the trial.

Bankruptcy Act

15-010   The Bankruptcy Act[5] provides, *inter alia*, that, where a receiving order has been made against a debtor, the court may, on the application of the receiver or a trustee, summon before it any person known or suspected to have in his possession any of the estate or effects of the debtor or supposed to be indebted to the debtor or any person whom the court may deem capable of gaining information respecting the debtor, his dealings or property.

In addition, the court has power to require such person to produce any documents in his custody or power relating to the debtor, his dealings, or property.

The provisions of this Act are similar to those contained in the Bankruptcy Act 1883 of England.[6]

[3] The Evidence Act (Chapter 109, Revised Laws of Grenada, 1958 ed.).
[4] The Banker's Books Evidence Act 1879 (U.K.).
[5] The Bankruptcy Act (Chapter 29, Revised Laws of Grenada, 1958 ed.).
[6] See the Bankruptcy Act 1914 (U.K.).

Business Levy Act 1987

The Business Levy Act[7] imposes a tax on sales and services. Under the provisions of this Act, a comptroller, appointed by the Governor-General for the purposes of administration and enforcement of the Act, has power to require any bank to furnish him with statements of any banking accounts and to inspect the records of the bank with respect to the banking accounts of any person or may require the attendance of any officer of a bank to give evidence before him in respect of any bank account or other asset which may be held by the bank on behalf of any person.

15-011

Collector-General Act 1971

The Collector-General Act 1971[8] was promulgated to confer power on one official, namely the Collector-General, to collect taxes due under all fiscal legislation once a warrant is given to him to so act.

15-012

This Act gives the Collector-General, appointed thereunder, all the powers relating to collection and enforcement of taxes which the appropriate authority would have under the relevant law once a warrant is given to him.

For example, if the Comptroller under the Business Levy Act gives the Collector-General a warrant to collect business levy, then the Collector-General will have all the powers of collection which the Comptroller has under that Act. Where a warrant is given, only the Collector-General can then enforce and collect.

Commissions of Inquiry Act

Under the Commissions of Inquiry Act,[9] a Commissioner has all the powers of the Supreme Court to summon witnesses and to call for the production of books and documents. The powers of the Supreme Court are dealt with later in this chapter.

15-013

---

[7] The Business Levy Act 1987 (Number 5 of 1987), as amended.
[8] The Collector-General Act 1971 (Number 19 of 1971).
[9] The Commissions of Inquiry Act (Chapter 64, Revised Laws of Grenada, 1958 ed.).

Companies Act

15-014   The Companies Act[10] contains similar provisions to those set out in the aforesaid Bankruptcy Act, which powers are in *pari materia* to those contained in the Companies Act 1908[11] of England.

United States-Grenada (Taxes Exchange of Information) Act 1987

15-015   On December 18, 1986, at Washington D.C., Grenada entered into an agreement with the United States with the object to provide mutual assistance to ensure the accurate assessment and collection of taxes, to prevent fiscal fraud and evasion, and to develop improved information sources for tax matters.

The United States-Grenada (Taxes Exchange of Information) Act was promulgated to give effect to the agreement.[12] The taxes covered by the Act are:

(1) In relation to Grenada -
   (a) business levy,
   (b) value added tax,
   (c) alien land-holding tax,
   (d) real property tax,
   (e) excise taxes, and,
(2) In relation to the United States -
   (a) federal income taxes,
   (b) federal taxes on self-employment,
   (c) federal taxes on transfers to avoid income tax,
   (d) federal estate and gift taxes, and
   (e) federal excise taxes.

This Act empowers the Director-General of the Ministry of Finance in Grenada, upon receiving a request from a senior official of the Government of the United States, to compel persons in Grenada, named in the request, to deliver to him information sought by the request.

---

[10] The Companies Act (Chapter 47, Revised Laws of Grenada, 1934 ed.).

[11] The Companies Act 1908 (U.K.).

[12] United States-Grenada (Taxes Exchange of Information) Act 1987 (Number 10 of 1987).

Further powers are given by this Act to the Director-General to apply to a judge for a warrant authorizing entry upon premises where there is reasonable ground for suspecting that an offence against the Act has been, or is being, or is about to be committed on any premises which would result in endangering any information sought by the request.

An officer entering any premises by virtue of such warrant is empowered to seize and remove any things found on the premises which he reasonably believes may contain information relevant to the request.

The Act specifically provides that the Director-General, in performing his functions thereunder, is not restricted by any law relating to confidentiality except that relating to the solicitor-client privilege.

The Act provides that it will come into force upon the day appointed by the Minister of Finance upon notice being given in the *Government Gazette*. However, no such notice has been published in the *Gazette*. By the Statutes (Date of Commencement) Act 1990,[13] the Act was purportedly brought into effect retroactive to May 14, 1987. As this method of effecting the Act has been utilized, rather than by notice as stipulated in the Act, it is doubtful whether the Act has the force of law.

The Act gives the Director-General extremely wide powers of discovery. At the time of writing, no action or proceeding had been instituted in any court in Grenada touching or concerning this Act.

The ramifications of the Act do not appear to have been fully considered. For example, there are few stipulations concerning the content of the request to be made or whether *prima facie* evidence of tax evasion has to be given. It seems, therefore, that a request simpliciter under this Act is all that is needed to trigger the Director-General's powers.

Exchange Control Act

The Exchange Control Act[14] confers powers and imposes duties and restrictions in relation to gold, currency, and securities and the import, export, transfer, and settlement of property.   **15-016**

This Act gives the Minister of Finance wide powers of enforcement, including powers to request information and documents

---

13 The Statutes (Date of Commencement) Act 1990 (Number 14 of 1990).
14 The Exchange Control Act (Chapter 110, Revised Laws of Grenada, 1958 ed.).

from any person which the Minister of Finance may require for the purpose of securing compliance with or detecting evasion of this Act. Information or documents may be requested from any person other than a person who holds privileged information as counsel or solicitor.

LEGISLATION NOT YET IN FORCE

Banking Act 1988

15-017   The Banking Act 1988[15] was passed by Parliament on March 25, 1988, but has not yet been brought into operation. This Act purports to regulate banking business in Grenada.

Grenada and the other Eastern Caribbean States entered into an agreement on July 5, 1983, establishing the Eastern Caribbean Central Bank. The Central Bank has certain powers to regulate banking business in the participating states. This agreement was given legal effect by the Eastern Caribbean Central Bank Act 1983.[16]

Under the Banking Act, the Central Bank or the Minister of Finance may apply to the Supreme Court for an order to ascertain whether a person carrying on banking business is doing so without a valid license under this Act.

The Act is silent on the type of order the Supreme Court may make. It is, therefore, doubtful whether this provision can be properly enforced.

The Banking Act further provides that a person refusing to make its books, accounts, and records available for examination upon request by the Central Bank commits an offence. It is not readily ascertainable from the particular provision whether the person referred to is any person or the person allegedly carrying on banking business without a valid license.

Grenadian International Companies Act 1989

15-018   The Grenadian International Companies Act 1989[17] was passed on August 9, 1989, but it is not yet in force.

15 The Banking Act 1988 (Number 14 of 1988).
16 Eastern Caribbean Central Bank Act 1983 (Number 23 of 1983).
17 The Grenadian International Companies Act 1989 (Number 29 of 1989).

The object of the Act is to provide for the incorporation, operation, and regulation of companies incorporated under the Act. Companies incorporated thereunder are not entitled to carry on business in Grenada, to accept banking deposits, to enter contracts of insurance, or to own real property other than for offices.

The Act specifically provides that no information relating to the assets, liabilities, transactions, members, directors, or any other information relating to any company incorporated thereunder shall be disclosed to any person or governmental authority within or outside Grenada except in the following circumstances:

(1) Where the Attorney-General obtains an order for disclosure from the Supreme Court;
(2) Under the provisions of the United-Grenada (Taxes Exchange of Information) Act 1987;
(3) Company gives written authorization, or
(4) When lawfully compelled by a court of competent jurisdiction in Grenada.

The Attorney General can make an application for a disclosure order only when he considers that the disclosure of information is relevant to the investigation of criminal activities under the laws of Grenada.

It is a criminal offense to make disclosure other than as permitted by the Act, punishable on summary conviction by a fine not exceeding $15,000 and/or to imprisonment for a term not exceeding two years.

COMPULSION BY COURT

Discovery orders

The general rule is that discovery is not available against a person **15-019** who is not a party to an action. However, under the rules of the Supreme Court, the court has power, by virtue of the *subpoena duces tecum*, to order any person, who is not a party to the matter before the court, to attend before it as a witness and to produce any document which he has in his custody which appears to the court to be necessary for the purposes of the matter.

Further, in *Norwich Pharmacal Co. v. Customs and Excise Commissioners*,[18] the House of Lords held that, where a person through no fault of his own and voluntarily or as a matter of duty becomes involved in the tortious acts of others so as to facilitate their wrongdoing, he may incur no personal liability, but he comes under a duty to assist the person who has been wronged by giving him full information and disclosing the identify of the wrongdoers.

The principle in this case has not been elucidated further, but dicta therein indicate it must be limited to a third party who is involved with the wrongdoing, not a mere stranger who is uninvolved but happens to have some information concerning the wrongdoers.

Mareva injunction

15-020 In an application for a Mareva injunction, the Supreme Court has power to make such ancillary discovery orders as are just and convenient to ensure the effective exercise of the Mareva jurisdiction.

This power is exercised in accordance with the principles set out in the English cases. There are no local cases on point, although Mareva injunctions have been granted.

CONCLUSION

15-021 It is apparent, therefore, that the basic duty of secrecy, although subsisting in law, has been consistently whittled away, primarily by the legislature.

As part of regional development, it is envisaged that legislation will be passed for mutual benefit and conformity. We have already seen the introduction of the United States-Grenada (Taxes Exchange of Information) Act 1987, which provides mutual assistance in the collection and enforcement of payment of taxes.

Currently, the Eastern Caribbean states are debating regional integration. A Regional Constituent Assembly was established by the Eastern Caribbean States to consider the implications of such integration.

18 *Norwich Pharmacal Co. v. Customs and Excise Commissioners* [1974] A.C. 133.

With such integration in view, it is likely that mutual legislation will be passed to assist the participating states in areas of crime prevention and detection with specific reference to drug related crimes, money laundering and tax evasion.

Therefore, an era is rapidly emerging where the public interest will be paramount and, of necessity, will supersede the basic Common Law duty of secrecy.

HONG KONG

Barrie Meerkin
Robert W. H. Wang & Co.
Hong Kong

Chapter 16

HONG KONG

INTRODUCTION

Consistent with its status as a financial center, Hong Kong has **16-001** chosen to import, on a continuing basis, the laws of England on many issues of banking law insofar as such English laws are not inconsistent with the laws of Hong Kong.

However, legislation in the form of the Banking Ordinance, Chapter 155, of the Laws of Hong Kong, was introduced to regulate the banking industry. It does not purport to be a code, and many issues in banking remain to be addressed by case law. It should be noted that there is no central bank in Hong Kong, and the banking industry is governed by a Commissioner of Banking, appointed by the Governor of Hong Kong.

The subject of a centralized monetary authority is currently being considered, and such an authority may be introduced in Hong Kong within the next year.

The Banking Ordinance defines "banking business" to mean:

"The business of either or both of the following:

(a) receiving from the general public money on account, deposit, savings or other similar account repayable on demand or within less than three months or at call or notice of less than three months;

(b) paying or collecting cheques drawn by or paid in by customers".

This definition does not cover the many other areas of business which banks transact today as a matter of course. One must then ask whether a person becomes a "customer" of a bank only in relation to services provided by the bank that constitute "banking business", or whether a person could become a customer of the bank in relation to any service provided by a bank to such person that involves maintaining an account of any sort with it.

The type of activities carried on by banks in Hong Kong that do not fall within the statutory definition of "banking business" are many. They include the performance of nominee and custodian functions in relation to securities, corporate finance activities involving the provision of advice in relation to mergers, acquisitions, public listings, and compliance with stock exchange requirements, treasury activities involving swaps and foreign exchange trading, correspondent banking activities ranging from negotiating or advising trade credits to forfeiting, private banking for high net worth individuals, and managing trusts.

Case law discussing the relationship between banker and customer sheds little light on the issue of the existence of the distinct relationship between the bank and its client in non-traditional banking areas. As a consequence, there is no distinct code of conduct being developed through case law to guide banks in these transactions.

It is unclear to what extent statutory or Common Law duties, such as the duty to maintain secrecy, apply to clients of a bank in relation to non-traditional bank dealings.

The law has not developed a comprehensive perspective of the banker-client relationship, nor of the repercussions of various aspects of their relationship. It will, therefore, be necessary to scrutinize each transaction to determine whether one should imply terms of contract or duties of care that apply to securities dealers, investment advisers, futures brokers, or bankers in the traditional sense.

BANK'S DUTY OF SECRECY

16-002 Hong Kong law recognizes a duty of secrecy (or duty of confidence) owed by a bank to its customer. The right of secrecy belongs to the customer, not to the bank.

As will be discussed later, there are considerable inroads being made into the bank-customer relationship as a result of the introduction of both civil and criminal statutory provisions permitting or compelling disclosure of confidential information by banks.

It is a general rule of Hong Kong law (and of English law) that the contract between a bank and its customer is governed by the laws of the place where the account is kept, in the absence of agreement to the contrary. The duty of the bank to keep its customer's information secret or confidential is an implied term of the contract between bank and customer.

The duty is subject to certain, fairly obvious, exceptions discussed below, but it is otherwise a very strict one and extends to all information that the bank has about its customer.

The implied and statutory duty of secrecy causes problems with bank mergers since it has meant that the banks to be merged cannot exchange information on a particular customer's account or effectively integrate their operations for such an account unless express written consent is obtained from the customer.

Conflict can arise when a foreign bank that is obliged to disclose information under the laws of its head office territory is unable to do so because the information resides with a branch office in another territory. For an example, see the case of *FDC Company Limited and Others* v. *The Chase Manhattan Bank N.A.*[1]

This case arose out of an investigation by the United States Inland Revenue Department into the tax liability of Mr. Aldo Gucci and Gucci Shops Inc. The case is discussed below.

The leading case on the duty of secrecy in Hong Kong is that of *Tournier* v. *The National Provincial and Union Bank of England*[2] and, as stated above, the more recent *FDC* case. Atkin L.J., in Tournier's case, described the extent of the duty thus:

> "It (the obligation of secrecy) clearly goes beyond that state of the account, that is, whether there is a debit or a credit balance, and the amount of the balance. It must extend at least to all the transactions that go through the account, and to the securities, if any, given in respect of the account; and in respect of such matters it must, I think, extend beyond the period when the account is closed, or ceases to be an active account.... I further think that the obligation extends to information obtained from other sources than the customer's actual account, if the occasion upon which the information was obtained arose out of the banking relations of the bank and its customers - for example,

[1] FDC Company Limited and Others v. *The Chase Manhattan Bank N.A.* [1990] 1 H.K.L.R. 277.
[2] *Tournier* v. *The National Provincial and Union bank of England* [1924] 1 K.B. 461.

with a view to assisting the bank in coming to decisions as to its treatment of its customers. . . . In this case, however, I should not extend the obligation to information as to the customer obtained after he had ceased to be a customer."[3]

As implied in this passage, the only information not covered by the obligation of secrecy might be information obtained by the bank in some manner that is clearly independent of the bank-customer relationship, for example, information obtained about the customer supplied by a third party, other than in the course of banking relations between the bank and its customer.

However, a bank should be very careful before relying on this exception, for several reasons.

First, it is derived by reasoning from general principles and there is no conclusive authority in its support.

Second, there is the difficulty of distinguishing between information obtained in consequence of the bank-customer relationship and other information, and the likelihood that the other information is obtained in circumstances which, if not giving rise to a duty of confidence to the customer, nevertheless give rise to a duty of confidence to a third party.

Third, there is the risk of an action for defamation.

In Hong Kong, there is a duty of secrecy implied in a contract between a bank and a customer at Common Law as stated in the recent *FDC* case referred to above. This case develops principles enunciated in the *Tournier* case. Some developments are that:

(1) The exception to the duty of secrecy where disclosure is under compulsion of law, is limited to allude to compulsion of Hong Kong law;
(2) The bank's obligations of secrecy are not subject to territorial limits, although, as a practical matter, the courts cannot restrain disclosure of information in New York;
(3) The bank cannot avoid its duty of secrecy by sending details of the account to its head office in New York by arguing that there is no disclosure to a third party.

As the bank's duty of secrecy is merely an implied contractual obligation, the Legislative Council in Hong Kong can override the duty by statute and impose an obligation to disclose. Thus, it can be

[3] *Id.*

said that Hong Kong law, both statutory law and the Common Law, recognizes the principle that the right of secrecy is the customer's, not the bank's.

CUSTOMER'S REMEDIES FOR BREACH OF CONFIDENCE

The customer has two remedies for breach of confidence; he may sue for damages after disclosure, or he may seek an injunction to restrain disclosure or a repetition of the previous disclosure. **16-003**

Damages

Damages will, in many cases, be an inadequate remedy; once disclosure has taken place, the damage is done and, indeed, it is difficult to see how, in many cases, the customer's loss can be measured in monetary terms. **16-004**

Exemplary or punitive damages would not, except possibly in extreme circumstances, be awarded.

Injunction

Therefore, the main protection for the customer is his ability to obtain an injunction. This is an order of the court restraining the bank from making disclosure; failure to comply with such an order would, in most circumstances, constitute a contempt of court. **16-005**

However, the court will not grant an injunction without some evidence that a disclosure is threatened.

Prima facie, therefore, the customer has a dilemma because disclosure can very easily take place before he knows about it. An injunction can be obtained speedily by means of *ex parte* proceedings. Otherwise, if time allows, the application can be made when both the customer and the bank will be represented.

In both cases, the application is supported by affidavit evidence, and the court must be satisfied that an unauthorized disclosure is threatened. If the injunction is granted, the applicant is required to give an undertaking as to costs and damages in the event that the injunction is subsequently discharged either before or at trial and the bank has suffered damages as a result of the imposition of the injunction.

BANK'S DUTY OF SECRECY - THE RATIONALE

16-006   As previously stated, the bank's duty of secrecy is an implied term of the contract between the bank and its customer. Let us consider the leading *Tournier* case mentioned above in more detail.

Tournier was a customer of the defendant bank. A check was drawn by another customer of the defendant in favor of Tournier who, instead of paying it into his own account, endorsed it to a third person who had an account at another bank. On the return of the check to the defendant, the deposit bank's manager inquired of the other bank to whom it had been endorsed and was told that he was a bookmaker.

The defendant disclosed that information to third persons. Tournier brought an action for slander and for breach of an implied contract that the defendant would not disclose to third persons the state of his account or any transactions relating thereto. The action for slander does not need to be considered for the purposes of this paper. The judge's question to the jury was:

> "Was the communication with regard to the Plaintiff's account at the Bank made on a reasonable and proper occasion?"

This was held in favor of the defendant bank at first instance, and Tournier appealed on the ground that the jury should have been given directions as to the circumstances in which the occasion would be reasonable or proper. On this matter, Bankes L.J. said:

> "A direction to the jury in a case such as the present, must inform the jury of the nature and limits and qualifications of the duty of the bank as a matter of law, leaving to them only questions for the purpose of ascertaining their view whether the communication complained of was, or was not, made, and whether it did, or did not, come within any of the protected occasions to which I have called attention."

Bankes L.J. concluded as follows:

> "The duty is a legal one arising out of contract. . . . It is not absolute but qualified. It is not possible to frame any exhaustive definition of the duty. The most that can be done is to classify the qualifications and to indicate its limits."

The exceptions are expressed as follows:

(1) Where disclosure is made with the express or implied consent of a customer;
(2) Where the interests of the bank require disclosure;
(3) Where disclosure is under compulsion by law, and
(4) Where there is a duty to the public to disclose.

EXCEPTIONS TO DUTY OF NON-DISCLOSURE
IN *TOURNIER*

Disclosure with express or implied consent of customer

If a bank were to notify its customer and state clearly what it **16-007** proposed to do and why, and actually receive consent "preferably in writing" from the customer, there would be no breach of duty if that customer's documents and/or information were disclosed pursuant to that consent.

If, however, the notice were given to a customer by the bank and the customer did not reply, the bank would not be entitled to assume that the customer had impliedly consented. In addition, if the customer were to withdraw his consent prior to the bank making disclosure, the bank probably would be breaching its duty of secrecy if it were to disclose.

When interests of bank require disclosure

This exception was illustrated in Tournier's case and was discussed **16-008** further in the case of *Sunderland* v. *Barclays Bank Ltd.*[4] In this case, the bank dishonored the plaintiff's check because there were insufficient funds in her account.

The real reason, however, was the bank's knowledge that she was gambling. The plaintiff complained to her husband, and on his advice, telephoned the bank. The husband interrupted the conversation to take up his wife's case and was informed that most checks passing through the wife's account were in favor of bookmakers.

[4] *Sunderland* v. *Barclays Bank Ltd.* (1938) *The Times,* November 25, 1938.

The court held that, in the circumstances, the interest of the bank required disclosure since it was being forced to give a reason for the policy it adopted. However, it also was noted by the court that, since the husband joined the conversation, the bank had the customer's implied consent to disclose the information to him.

In the more recent *FDC* decision by the Hong Kong Court of Appeal,[5] the customer of the bank obtained an interlocutory injunction to restrain the bank from disclosing documents/information in order to comply with subpoenas of courts in the United States.

The bank argued that it was in its interest to disclose because otherwise it would be in contempt of court in the United States. These arguments were rejected on the ground that the bank's interest in disclosure was of a different character from that contemplated in *Tournier*.

It should be noted that, where disclosure is made under this exception, it must be limited strictly to information necessary to protect the bank's interests. It is foreseen that generally disclosure will be necessary and permissible under this exception if there is litigation between the bank and its customer and likewise if the bank brings an action against a guarantor.

On the subject of disclosure within a specific banking group, the general view is that each corporate entity within the banking group must be viewed as a separate entity. However, there is the more practical view that, in order to allow a banking group to be run in a cost-effective manner, the law should allow confidential information to be passed between the holding company, being a bank, and such of its subsidiaries as are banks without the need for a customer's consent, provided it is for a strictly defined purpose.

This has not been tested in the courts of Hong Kong. It is felt in any event that a customer's consent should still be required for transmission of such information to non-banking subsidiaries.

Where disclosure is by compulsion of law

16-009   This exception can be dealt with in two categories, being:

(1) Compulsion by order of the court, and
(2) Compulsion by statute.

---

5 *FDC Company Limited and Others* v. *The Chase Manhattan Bank N.A., supra* n. 1.

Compulsion by order of court

An order of the court usually will require a bank official to attend   **16-010**
court and to bring with him specified books, documents, or letters
relating to a customer's affairs. It is important, however, to distinguish between civil and criminal proceedings.

In criminal proceedings, courts generally take the cautious view
and recognize the care with which the jurisdiction should be exercised and take into account, among other things, whether there is
other evidence in the possession of the prosecution to support the
charge.

The courts generally limit the period of the disclosure of the bank
account to a period that is strictly relevant to the charge before
them. In respect of civil proceedings, the rule that has been laid
down is that the statutory power to order inspection should not be
inconsistent with, and not out of reach of, the general law of discovery.

Bankers' books relating to an account of the party to a litigation
will be ordered to be disclosed if they are relevant to the issues in a
litigation and not privileged from production.

In the case of *Bankers Trust Company* v. *Shapira*,[6] the Court of
Appeal extended the circumstances in which an order for discovery
could be used to coerce a bank to reveal details of its customer's
accounts. The court's power to order discovery of information at the
earlier stages of an action may be used to order a bank to disclose
documents and correspondence relating to the account of the customer who is *prima facie* guilty of fraud, although such material
would normally be subject to the bank-customer obligation of confidentiality.

The evidence of fraud against the customer has to be very strong
but, where it is, the customer is not entitled to rely on the confidential relationship between him and his bank to prevent the discovery.

Compulsion by statute

There are several statutory provisions in Hong Kong that either   **16-011**
require or permit disclosure of confidential information by bankers
without the consent of the customer.

The list includes the Companies Ordinance, the Banking Ordinance, the Securities Ordinance, and the Drug Trafficking (Recovery of Proceeds) Ordinance. Only some of these will be considered

---

[6] *Bankers Trust Company* v. *Shapira* [1980] 3 All E.R. 353.

here. Most of these provisions entitle the relevant statutory authority or body to compel a bank to produce information relevant to any matter that it is authorized to investigate.

The general view of the interpretation of "bank records" is that such provisions would include computer data. It should be noted that, at present, there is no specific computer data protection legislation in Hong Kong.

Companies Ordinance, chapter 32, section 221(1)

16-012   Section 221(1) of the Companies Ordinance, chapter 32,[7] of the Laws of Hong Kong, applies in a case where an appointment of a provisional liquidator or the making of a winding-up order is made in relation to a company, the court having the power to summon before it ". . . any person whom the court deems capable of giving information concerning the promotion, formation, trade, dealings, affairs, or property of the company."

The court is further empowered under section 221(4) to apprehend any such person so summoned if such person refuses to come before the court at the time appointed.

Banking Ordinance, chapter 155, section 55(1)

16-013   Section 55(1) of the Banking Ordinance, chapter 155,[8] of the Laws of Hong Kong deals with the examination and investigation of authorized institutions (which, by definition, includes banks) by the Commissioner of banking and states that:

> "The Commissioner may at any time, with or without prior notice of the authorized institution, examine the books, accounts and transactions of any authorized institution and, in the case of an authorized institution incorporated in Hong Kong, any local branch, overseas branch, overseas representative office or subsidiary, whether local or overseas, of such institution."

Section 68 of the Banking Ordinance deals with the examination by authorities outside Hong Kong. This section states that:

---

7 Companies Ordinance, chapter 32, of the Laws of Hong Kong, section 221(1).
8 Banking Ordinance, chapter 155, of the Laws of Hong Kong, section 55(1).

"The appropriate recognized banking supervisory authority of the place outside Hong Kong may, with the approval of the Commissioner, examine the books, accounts and transactions of the principal place of business in Hong Kong or any local branch, or the documents of any local representative office -

(a) of an authorized institution which is incorporated in that place; or

(b) of an authorized institution which is incorporated in or outside Hong Kong and is a subsidiary of the bank or other body corporate which is incorporated in that place."

Securities Ordinance, chapter 333, section 127(1)

Section 127(1) of the Securities Ordinance, chapter 333,[9] of the Laws of Hong Kong empowers the Securities and Futures Commission to appoint an inspector to investigate "any alleged breach of trust, defalcation, fraud or misfeasance; or any matter concerning dealing in securities or the giving of investment advice".   **16-014**

The inspector is further empowered under section 127(3) to require a bank to produce to the inspector such documents relating to a matter under his investigation and that are in the custody of the bank.

Drug Trafficking (Recovery of Proceeds) Ordinance, chapter 405, sections 20 and 23

Sections 20 and 23 of the Drug Trafficking (Recovery of Proceeds) Ordinance, chapter 405,[10] of the Laws of Hong Kong empower an authorized officer for the purpose of an investigation into drug trafficking to obtain an order from the court in relation to particular material where there are reasonable grounds for suspecting that a specified person has carried on drug trafficking, or that there are reasonable grounds to believe that the material to which the application relates is likely to be of substantial value in connection with such a matter.   **16-015**

[9] Securities Ordinance, chapter 333, of the Laws of Hong Kong, section 127(1).
[10] Drug Trafficking (Recovery of Proceeds) Ordinance, chapter 405, of the Laws of Hong Kong, sections 20 and 23.

The sections create potentially wide-ranging instances where the obligation of secrecy in a banking relationship may be overridden.

GUIDELINES FOR PREVENTION OF MONEY LAUNDERING

16-016 The Commissioner of Banking has issued a statement of principles on the prevention of criminal use of the banking system. This is in line with a worldwide practice followed by banks to minimize the risk of their becoming involved in money laundering.

In Hong Kong, the guideline is issued under section 7(3) of the Banking Ordinance, which enables the Commissioner to issue guidelines indicating the manner in which the functions of the Commissioner may be exercised. This worldwide practice was established by the Basle Committee on Banking Regulations and Supervisory Practices that encouraged banks:

(1) To put in place effective procedures to ensure persons conducting banking business are properly identified;
(2) To proceed with transactions only if they appeared legitimate, and
(3) To cooperate, where the law permits, with law enforcement authorities.

It is the latter point that relates to bank-customer secrecy. The guideline in Hong Kong states that banks "should co-operate fully with law enforcement authorities to the extent permitted by contractual obligations relating to customers confidentiality".

Where there is duty to public to disclose

16-017 While not indicating what these instances were, Bankes L.J., in *Tournier's* case, said that many instances might be given where a bank is justified in disclosing its customers' affairs on the grounds that there is a duty to the public to do so.

In the same case, Scrutton L.J. and Atkin L.J. said that a bank may disclose its customers' accounts and affairs to protect the bank, or persons interested, or the public, against fraud or crime.

INSIDER TRADING

Although not falling within the strict parameters of the matters to **16-018** be discussed in this paper, insider trading is of great concern to banks, particularly in the context of securities dealing and mergers and acquisitions. In Hong Kong, insider dealing is covered by statute and dealt with in the Securities Ordinance.[11]

Insider dealing in corporate securities involves the utilization of unpublished price-sensitive information obtained through a privileged relationship to make a profit or avoid a loss by dealing in securities, the price of which could be materially affected by public disclosure of that information.

It only applies to securities of a corporation if they are listed on the Stock Exchange of Hong Kong or have been listed on the Stock Exchange of Hong Kong or an approved stock exchange at any time within five years immediately preceding any insider dealing.

An Insider Dealing Tribunal is established under the Ordinance to inquire whether any insider dealing in relation to the securities of the corporation has taken place. It has wide-ranging powers. Section 141K(2)(a) of the Securities Ordinance allows the Tribunal:

> ". . . to inspect the books and documents of any person where the Tribunal has reasonable grounds to believe or suspect that those books or documents may contain information relevant to the enquiry. . .".

If requested to do so by the Tribunal, banks clearly have a duty to disclose under compulsion by law (being an exception in the *Tournier* case). This again is a situation where a duty to the public to disclose has been recognized and imposed by statute.

CONCLUSION

The rule and exceptions established the *Tournier* case are still the **16-019** basis for the law in Hong Kong relating to the duty of secrecy in the bank-customer relationship.

However, the legislature has subsequently introduced several statutory provisions in Hong Kong that either require or permit disclosure of confidential information by bankers without the con-

---

[11] Securities Ordinance, chapter 333, of the Laws of Hong Kong, Part XIIA.

sent of the customer. These statutory provisions now largely cover matters which might otherwise have fallen under exceptions in the *Tournier* case.

In addition, case law has continued to play its part in dealing with particular circumstances and, indeed, in attempting to reconcile the requirements of different jurisdictions.

IRELAND

Joe Varley and James Dudley
Gerrard, Scallan & O'Brien
Dublin, Ireland

Chapter 17

IRELAND

INTRODUCTION

The duty of secrecy that a banker owes to his client has long been   17-001
recognized as a hallmark of the banker-customer relationship. This
chapter will attempt to explore the extent of this relationship in Irish
law (being the law of the 26 counties of the Republic of Ireland) and
the instances in which the duty may be abrogated by the bank with
impunity.

Ireland was subject to English rule for several hundred years,
culminating with the treaty that was signed on December 6, 1921.

It is understandable, therefore, that the fledgling Irish State that
emerged subsequent to the treaty should inherit the English Common Law system, with the notable exception that Ireland has a
written constitution.

Accordingly, where there is a dearth of Irish authority on a
particular point, the relevant English decision is of high persuasive
value in Ireland. As the law in England in relation to the duty of
secrecy is dealt with in another chapter in this publication, it is not
proposed to examine English authority with the exception of
Tournier's case.

THE TOURNIER CASE

In *Tournier* v. *National Provincial and Union Bank of England*,[1] the   17-002
plaintiff, whose account with the defendant bank had become over-

[1] *Tournier* v. *National Provincial and Union Bank of England* [1924] I K.B. 461.

drawn, came to an arrangement with the bank to repay £1 per week until the overdraft had been cleared.

He subsequently took up employment under a three-month contract as a salesman with a company called Kenyon & Company and, after paying three installments, failed to pay the balance due to the bank.

A check from another customer of the bank, payable to the plaintiff, was endorsed by the plaintiff in favor of a third party who had an account at another bank. On the return of the check to the defendant bank, the manager asked of the last named bank who the person was to whom it had been paid and he was informed that it was a bookmaker.

The manager subsequently telephoned Kenyon & Company, seeking the plaintiff's present address and, in the course of the conversation, revealed to a director of the company that the plaintiff was indebted to the bank, behind in his repayments and appeared to be involved with bookmakers.

As a result, the company refused to renew the plaintiff's employment when the three-month agreement expired. The plaintiff brought an action claiming damages for, *inter alia*, breach of an implied contract that the defendant would not disclose to third parties the state of his account or any transactions relating thereto. The court of first instance found in favor of the defendant, and the plaintiff appealed on the grounds of a misdirection to the jury by the trial judge.

The Court of Appeal held that there had been a misdirection to the jury and that there should be a new trial. It was held that a bank owes a duty of secrecy to its customer, but there are implied four qualifications that allow a bank to disclose what would otherwise be confidential information. A bank is justified in disclosing confidential information where:

(1) There is a public duty to disclose;
(2) The interests of the bank require disclosure;
(3) The disclosure is made with the express or implied consent of the customer, and
(4) Disclosure is required by law.

The court then attempted to define the extent or limits of the duty, either as to time or as to the nature of the disclosure. Bankes L.J. felt that it was:

"... difficult to state what the limits of the duty are either as to time or as to the nature of the disclosure. I certainly think that the duty does not cease the moment a customer closes his account. Information gained during the currency of the account remains confidential unless released under circumstances bringing the case within one of the classes of qualification I have already referred to. Again the confidence is not confined to the actual state of the customer's account. It extends to information derived from the account itself. A more doubtful question but one vital to this case, is whether the confidence extends to information in reference to the customer and his affairs derived not from the customer's account but from other sources, as, for instance, from the account of another customer of the customer's bank".[2]

Bankes, L.J. noted that the identity of the third party in whose favor the check was endorsed was obtained from a source other than the plaintiff's account. He stated that he felt that the relationship between a banker and customer was one in which the confidentiality of the relationship was very marked and that in his opinion the duty of non-disclosure extended to information other than that obtained from the customer or his account.

Therefore, the disclosure made by the defendant's manager was a breach of the duty of secrecy owed to the customer unless the disclosure could be brought within one of the qualifications set out above.

Atkin L.J. agreed with Bankes L.J. and stated that information to which the duty of secrecy extends:

> ". . .clearly goes beyond the state of the account, that is, whether there is a debit or a credit balance, and the amount of the balance. It must extend at least to all the transactions that go through the account, and to the securities, if any, given in respect of the account; and in respect of such matters it must, I think, extend beyond the period when the account is closed, or ceases to be an active account. It seems to me inconceivable that either party would contemplate that once the customer had closed his account the bank was to be at liberty to divulge as it pleased the particular transactions which it had conducted for the customer while he was such. I further think that the obligation extends to information obtained from other sources than the customer's actual account, if the occasion upon which the information was obtained arose out of the banking relations of the bank and its customers. . . ."[3]

[2] *Id.*, at p. 473.
[3] *Id.*, at p. 485.

Atkin L.J., however, felt that the duty of secrecy should not extend to information in relation to the customer obtained after he had ceased to be a customer.

Scrutton L.J., while concurring with Bankes and Atkin L.JJ. on other issues, disagreed on the scope of the duty of secrecy that he felt did not extend to information derived from sources other than the relationship of banker and customer and was limited to information acquired during the continuance of the relationship. As Bankes and Atkin L.JJ. were in the majority, their view must be taken to be a correct statement of the law.

QUALIFICATIONS TO DUTY OF SECRECY

Public duty

17-003 While Bankes L.J. believed that there are many instances where this qualification might apply, he refrained from giving any specific examples and contented himself with quoting Lord Finlay in *Weld-Blundell* v. *Stevens*[4] where he spoke of a higher duty than the private duty as where "danger to the State or public duty may supersede the duty of the agent to its principal".

It would appear that Bankes L.J. would restrict the public duty qualification to something more serious than, for example, fraud as he states that confidential information could not be given to a police officer investigating fraud. One wonders if disclosure is justified where, for example, a crime of murder is being investigated, and one is inclined toward the view that Bankes L.J. intended to restrict this qualification to crimes akin to treason or matters pertaining to the security of the State.

Scrutton L.J., however, goes further and states that the prevention of frauds or crimes would be a sufficient ground for disclosure, and Atkin L.J. agreed that disclosure was warranted ". . . to the extent to which it is reasonably necessary for the protection of. . .the bank or persons interested, or the public, against fraud or crime".[5]

As Scrutton and Atkin L.JJ. are in the majority on this point, their view must be taken as authoritative.

---

[4] *Weld-Blundell* v. *Stevens* [1920] A.C. 956, at p. 965.
[5] *Tournier* v. *National Provincial and Union Bank of England, supra* n. 1, at p. 486.

Where disclosure is in bank's interest

Bankes and Scrutton L.JJ. both cite the example of a writ for the **17-004** recovery of money due to the bank wherein it is necessary to state the amount due to the bank as being examples of this qualification, while Atkin L.J. believed that disclosure under this qualification was justified in circumstances where it was ". . . reasonably necessary for the protection of the bank's interests, either as against their customer or as against third parties in respect of transactions of the bank for or with their customer. . . ." [6]

A case in point is the English judgment in *Sunderland* v. *Barclays Bank Limited*[7] where the plaintiff's check drawn in favor of her dressmaker, was dishonored by the defendant bank. Although there were not sufficient funds in the account to meet the check the real reason for the dishonor was that the plaintiff had indulged in betting operations and, presumably, the manager felt that it would be unwise to grant her an overdraft for the purpose of meeting the check.

The plaintiff complained to her husband about the return of the check and, in the course of a telephone conversation between the husband and the manager, the husband was informed that most of the checks that had passed through his wife's account were drawn to bookmakers.

The plaintiff sued for breach of the duty of secrecy, and it was held that the interests of the bank required disclosure and the disclosure also could be justified on the basis that it was with the implied consent of the customer.

Where disclosure is with consent of customer

There is obviously no breach of confidentiality where a customer **17-005** expressly authorizes his banker to divulge confidential information provided the terms of the authorization are not exceeded. Where, however, the bank seeks to rely on the implied consent of the customer it is on less firm ground.

Bankes and Atkin L.JJ. felt that an example of this third qualification would be the practice of bankers giving references, however, the latter was at pains to convey that he did:

---

[6] *Id.*

[7] *Sunderland* v. *Barclays Bank Limited* (1938) Legal Decisions Affecting Bankers 163.

". . . not desire to express any final opinion on the practice of bankers to give one another information as to the affairs of their respective customers, except to say it appears to me that if it is justified it must be upon the basis of an implied consent of the customer".[8]

Another argument for disclosure in the case of a banker's reference is that it is in the interests of the customer that a reference should issue. Where the reference is unfavorable, however, it can hardly be said to be in the interests of the customer that the disclosure be made.

Scrutton L.J. doubted that disclosure in the interests of the customer would be a sufficient justification if the customer could be consulted in a reasonable time and his consent or dissent obtained.

Where required by Law

Bankers Books Evidence Act 1879

17-006 Section 7 of the Act provides that, on the application of any party to a legal proceeding, a court or judge may order that such party be at liberty to inspect and take copies of any entries in a banker's book for any of the purposes of such proceedings.

An order under section 7 may be made either with or without summoning the bank in question or any other party and must be served on the bank three clear days before it is to be obeyed unless the court or judge otherwise directs. Section 10 goes on to provide that "legal proceeding" is defined as "any civil or criminal proceeding or inquiry in which evidence is or may be given, and includes an arbitration"; "the court" is defined as "the court, judge, arbitrator, persons or person before whom a legal proceeding is held or taken", and "a judge" is defined as a judge of the High Court.

17-007 **Staunton v. Counihan** In *Staunton* v. *Counihan*,[9] the plaintiff sought an order under section 7. The defendant had executed a deed of charge on her freehold premises whereunder she guaranteed the sum of £12,000 that the plaintiff claimed was due to him by her son's company.

8 *Tournier* v. *National Provincial and Union Bank of England, supra* n. 1, at p. 486.
9 *Staunton* v. *Counihan* (1958) 92 I.L.T.R. 33.

The plaintiff claimed that several checks he had received from the defendant's son and presented for payment had been returned marked refer to drawer.

The plaintiff then instituted an action for a declaration that the sum of £12,000 was well charged on the defendant's premises. The defendant admitted executing the deed of charge but alleged that there was, at the time of the execution of the deed, no debt due to the plaintiff by the company, that no real consideration existed for the execution of the charge and that her execution of the charge was procured by a misrepresentation in this respect.

The plaintiff applied, unsuccessfully, for liberty to take copies of all entries in the account of the company at the time of the execution of the charge. Dixon J., refusing the plaintiff's application, stated that, in his opinion:

"The jurisdiction to order inspection of entries in a banking account conferred by section 7 of the Bankers Books Evidence Act 1879 must be exercised with extreme caution even where it is the account of a party to the action. In a case like the present, where it was the account of a person who was not a party to the proceedings, even more caution must be used. It was stated, in *Pollock* v. *Garle* (1898) 1 Ch. 1, that the jurisdiction was intended really to extend only to accounts that were in form and substance those of a party to the action. The account in the present case was not in any sense in form and substance the defendant's account, nor was it so closely connected with her that it could be regarded really as her account in some other name.

Furthermore, the entries must be material to some issue in the action and if they are so must be admissible in evidence on behalf of the applicant".[10]

Dixon J. believed that the real issue in this application was whether the company was indebted to the plaintiff at the time of the execution of the charge and concluded, without indicating what other proof was available to the plaintiff, that the plaintiff's proof of the then existing debt did not essentially depend on the entries in the bank account of the company and, therefore, such entries at that stage were not clearly and necessarily admissible in evidence.

The entries in the account may be admissible at the hearing of the action as being material to some issue, but he felt admissibility had not been established in the instant application. He stated:

[10] *Id.*, at pp. 33-34.

"It may be helpful or useful to see the entries but this is not sufficient. The applicant has to establish on his application that the entries are essential to some issue in the action and would be admissible in evidence to prove his case".[11]

Accordingly, as neither condition above was fulfilled the application was refused. Dixon J. concluded by stating that service of notice of an application under section 7 on an account holder is sufficient and service on the bank is not required.

17-008 **Chemical Bank v. Peter McCormack** Section 7 does not, however, apply to accounts that are located outside the jurisdiction in a branch of a bank registered within the jurisdiction.

In *Chemical Bank v. Peter McCormack*,[12] the plaintiff had sued the defendant in respect of a fraud involving approximately US $800,000 and alleged that the money was paid into the account of Consumark Incorporated, in the United States, and that portion of the money was transferred by the defendant into his personal account with Allied Irish Banks, New York branch. Subsequently, US $600,000 was transferred by the defendant by check presented to Allied Irish Banks in Dublin drawn upon his New York account.

Allied Irish Banks then brought an application to vary an order previously made by Carroll J. to discharge so much of that order as gave the plaintiff liberty to inspect and take copies of entries in the books of Allied Irish Banks at its branch at Park Avenue in New York City and in relation to the accounts of Consumark Incorporated and Consumark (Ireland) Limited (a company wholly owned by the defendant) at its branches at Dame Street and O'Connell Street in Dublin.

Carroll J. cited *R. v. Grossman*[13] where the facts were similar to the facts in the instant case. In that case, an Isle of Man bank maintained an account with a branch of Barclays Bank in the Isle of Man, and an application was made to the court in the Isle of Man for inspection of this account in connection with a prosecution pending in Wales as the accused had used the Isle of Man bank for the purpose of paying in checks made out to a company called J.B.K. Limited and taking monies out in circumstances that led to his being charged with a criminal offense.

---

[11] *Id.*, at p. 34.
[12] *Chemical Bank v. Peter McCormack* [1983] I.L.R.M. 350.
[13] *R. v. Grossman* [1981] Cr. App. Rep. 302.

The Isle of Man court refused the order and an application was made in England directed to Barclays Bank head office, not Barclays Bank Isle of Man, to disclose the account insofar as it related to J.B.K. Limited.

The Court of Appeal refused the order. Lord Denning stated that section 7 covered the proceedings in Wales but that the statute should not be extended to the Isle of Man and continued:

> "It is quite plain, that in the ordinary way, in civil litigation an order of this kind is only made against the account of the party who is involved in a litigation; or if it is in the name of some other person, the account that is really the account of the party. In exceptional circumstances, such an order can be made against another person altogether - who is not a party - but caution must always be used before so doing.
>
> In criminal cases the cases are fewer in number. It is clear that an order under S.7 can be made for the inspection of the account of an accused person. There are also cases in which the account of a near relative - such as a wife's account - has been the subject of an order".[14]

Lord Denning felt that the court should not make an order against Barclays Bank in England in respect of the books of the branch in the Isle of Man and that any order ought to be made by the courts of the Isle of Man, if they would make it; otherwise, there would be a danger of a conflict of jurisdiction which he said must be avoided.

However, it is noteworthy, that he felt that the Court of Appeal had jurisdiction to make an order against Barclays Bank head office but that this jurisdiction should not be exercised in the interests of the comity of courts.

Carroll J. noted that Allied Irish Banks is a named bank in the definition section by virtue of section 2 of the Bankers Books Evidence (Amendment) Act 1959 but felt that:

> ". . . having considered the matter, I am of opinion that the order I made should be amended. There are no clear words in the 1879 Act or the amended 1959 Act that would support the interpretation of an intention to have extraterritorial effect. I do not have power to order inspection in a foreign country and therefore the order which authorises inspection 'at' the branch in New York is in excess of jurisdiction.

[14] *Id.*, at p. 307.

R. v. *Grossman* appears to be authority for the making of an order addressed to AIB as a company incorporated within the jurisdiction to make available for inspection in this country the account of the defendant and that of Consumark Incorporated in the Park Avenue branch of the bank in New York.

However even if it is, I do not propose to make such an order in case there would be a conflict of jurisdiction, which should be avoided in the interests of the comity of courts".[15]

Carroll J. refused to amend her order by deleting reference to Consumark Incorporated and Consumark (Ireland) Limited on the grounds that formal notice had not been given to these two companies because the application for the order had been made in the presence of the defendant's solicitor and counsel and accordingly the defendant was aware of the order.

As the defendant was a 100 percent owner of Consumark (Ireland) Limited, this company was really the defendant under another name and Carroll J. was satisfied that the same applied to the American company. The learned judge concluded that "notice is notice whether it is formal or not".[16]

Citing the case of *Staunton* v. *Counihan* with approval, she said that she was satisfied that the accounts of the two companies in this case were really the defendant's accounts under another name and that, accordingly, the defendant was aware of the order and that through him the companies had actual knowledge.

In conclusion, Carroll J. expressed the view that the disclosure of the American accounts was necessary and relevant as evidence in the instant case and, therefore, it would seem to be a suitable case in which to issue a request to the appropriate American court to assist the courts here in obtaining the required information and she gave liberty to the plaintiff to apply to such American court if necessary.

17-009 **Section 2, Solicitors Act 1954** Section 2 of the Solicitors Act 1954 provides that an inquiry of the Disciplinary Committee of the Law Society shall be a legal proceeding within the meaning of the Bankers Books Evidence Act 1879.

Accordingly, where such an inquiry is ongoing, any party thereto may, subject to the provisions set out above, apply to the High Court or the persons or person before whom the inquiry is being held (the

---

[15] *Id.*, at pp. 353-354.
[16] *Id.*, at p. 354.

Disciplinary Committee) for an order that such party be at liberty to inspect and take copies of any entries in a banker's books for any of the purposes of such inquiry.

Finance Act 1974

Section 57 of the Act provides that, where an individual who is ordinarily resident in the state transfers assets abroad and the income therefrom is payable to persons either resident or domiciled abroad (but where the individual retains the power to enjoy such income), that individual shall be taxed as if it were income received by him in the state. 17-010

For the purpose of detecting such schemes referred to above, section 59 provides that the Revenue Commissioners, or such officer as they may appoint by notice in writing, may require any person to furnish them with such particulars as they think necessary.

Sub-section 4, however, goes on to provide that there shall be no obligation on any bank to furnish any particulars of "any ordinary banking transactions" between the bank and the customer carried out in the ordinary course of banking business unless the bank has acted or is acting on behalf of the customer in connection with the formation or management of any body corporate resident or incorporated outside the State within the meaning of section 530(6) of the Income Tax Act 1967[17] or in connection with the creation or with the execution of the trusts of any settlement in consequence whereof income becomes payable to a person resident or domiciled outside the state.

What constitutes banking operations The question of what constitutes banking operations "in the ordinary course of banking business" was considered in the case of *The Royal Trust Company (Ireland) Limited* and *John Leslie Whelan* v. *The Revenue Commissioners*.[18] 17-011

The defendants, by notice dated January 26, 1976, required the plaintiffs to furnish particulars giving, *inter alia*, the names and addresses of customers and the names of persons to whom the

[17] A private company with less than 50 members and under the control of not more than five persons.

[18] The Royal Trust Company (Ireland) Limited and *John Leslie Whelan* v. *The Revenue Commissioners* [1982] I.L.R.M. 459.

plaintiffs had introduced the customers for the purpose of completing certain specific transactions since 1969.

The plaintiffs replied that, during the period in question, they had introduced persons on several occasions to four companies located abroad with a view to forming a company or operating a settlement out of the State and possibly transferring assets to such a company or settlement. However, the plaintiffs stated that there was no record of the names or addresses of such persons or of the particulars required in the notice with the exception of fourteen instances of which particulars were furnished.

The plaintiffs then asserted that all other transactions were banking operations in the ordinary course of banking business and that section 59(4) applied. The defendants refused to accept the plaintiffs' reply and the plaintiffs sought a declaration that they had complied with the defendants' notice for particulars.

During the period in question, the plaintiffs took part broadly in two forms of transactions.

In the first, a client would approach a bank in Dublin and request a loan to be advanced to him personally. The client would offer as security for the loan a letter of hypothecation of funds on deposit with an acceptable bank within the Sterling area.

In the second, a client would approach a bank in Dublin with a check or other negotiable instrument and request that these funds be transferred to a deposit account with an acceptable bank within the Sterling area. He would request the Dublin bank to grant a loan to him on the security of a letter of hypothecation over the funds in question. The transfer of the funds abroad would not be conditional on the granting of the loan.

McWilliam J. found that the plaintiffs had been involved in 17 of the first type of transactions between 1972 and 1979 and six of the second type, all of which took place in 1972. He referred to and approved the following extract from the judgment of Megarry J. in the case of *Royal Bank of Canada* v. *Inland Revenue Commissioners*,[19] part of which decision referred to section 414(5) of the English Income Tax Act 1952, which is in identical terms with section 59(4) of the Irish 1974 Act:

> "The issue has been that of the ambit of the words which prevent the section from imposing on the bank the obligation 'to furnish any particulars of any ordinary banking transaction between the bank and a customer carried out in the ordinary course of banking business . . .'. Before I turn to the

19 *Royal Bank of Canada* v. *Inland Revenue Commissioners* [1972] 1 Ch. 665.

contentions put before me, let me say at the outset that this seems to me to be a strictly limited provision. The limitations may be ranged under four heads. First, the protection is given not to particulars at large but only to particulars of certain transactions; if the particulars sought are particulars not of any transaction but of the name and address of some person, unrelated to anything that could fairly be called a transaction, then they are outside the protection. Second, there is a limit as to the type of transaction: no transaction will suffice unless it falls within the expression 'ordinary banking transactions'. Third, there is a limit by reference to the parties: only transactions 'between the bank and a customer' qualify. Fourth, there is a limitation as to the circumstances in which the transaction is carried out, namely, that it was 'carried out in the ordinary course of banking business'. This language seems to me to be carefully guarded having regard to the use of the words 'ordinary' and 'banking' twice over, and the cumulative limiting effect of all the phrases used".[20]

Burden of proof McWilliam J. agreed with Megarry J. that it is for   17-012
the bank (in this case *The Royal Trust Company (Ireland) Limited*) to show that the transactions in question are ordinary banking transactions carried out in the ordinary course of banking business.

He noted that there were many different types of bank and felt that he should not be restricted to the type of ordinary banking transactions being carried on by the older banks operating checking accounts.

On the evidence, he found that a senior representative of the City of Dublin Bank, with a distinguished career in banking circles, could only say that with regard to second type of transactions that he knew they are transacted whereas he was familiar with transactions of the first type.

Likewise, a senior representative of the Bank of Ireland appeared to be much more definite with regard to the first type of transactions than to the second. Finally, The Royal Trust Company (Ireland) Limited only engaged in six of the second type of transactions during the year 1972.

Accordingly, the judge declared that the first type of transactions came within the provisions of section 59 (4) of the 1974 Act and that the second type did not.

[20] *Id.*, at p. 678.

Therefore, as is apparent from the foregoing, whether a particular transaction is or is not an ordinary banking transaction, is largely a matter of evidence.

Finance Act 1983

17-013 Section 18(2) of the Act provides as follows:

"Where -

(a) a person who, for the purposes of tax, has been duly required by an inspector to deliver a statement of the profits or gains arising to him from any trade or profession or to deliver to the inspector a return of income, fails to deliver that statement or that return to the inspector, or

(b) the inspector is not satisfied with such a statement or return so delivered,

an authorised officer may, if he is of opinion that that person maintains or maintained an account or accounts, the existence of which has not been disclosed to the Revenue Commissioners, with a financial institution or that there is likely to be information in the books of that institution indicating that the said statement of profits or gains or the said return of income is false to a material extent, apply to a judge for an order requiring that financial institution to furnish the authorised officer -

(i) with full particulars of all accounts maintained by that person, either solely or jointly with any other person or persons, in that institution during a period not exceeding ten years immediately preceding the date of the application, and

(ii) with such information as may be specified in the order relating to the financial transactions of that person, being information recorded in the books of that institution which would be material in determining the correctness of the statement of profits or gains or the return of income delivered by that person or, in the event of failure to deliver such statement or return, would be material in determining the liability of that person to tax".

"Financial institution" is defined as a person who holds or has held a license under section 9 of the Central Bank Act 1971 and a person referred to in section 7(4) of that Act, and "authorised officer" is defined as an inspector or other duly authorised officer of the Revenue Commissioners.

Subsections (3) and (4) Subsection (3) provides that, where a High Court judge is satisfied that there are reasonable grounds for the application, he may make an order requiring the financial institution to furnish such particulars and information as may be specified in the order, and sub-section (4) further provides that on the application of the authorised officer the High Court judge may prohibit any transfer of or any dealing with any assets or moneys of the person to whom the order relates that are in the custody of the financial institution. **17-014**

O'C. v. D. and Another Section 18 of the Finance Act 1983 was considered by both the High Court and the Supreme Court in *O'C. v. D. and Another.* [21] **17-015**

The applicant, an inspector of taxes, applied for an order directing the bank, one of the respondents, to furnish full particulars of all accounts maintained by a certain person (the taxpayer), another of the respondents, with the bank as well as other information relating to the taxpayer's financial transactions.

Murphy J., in the High Court, noted that there were certain preconditions to an application under section 18 and that a judge of the High Court must be satisfied that there are reasonable grounds therefor. He also noted that the use of the word "may" in section 18(3) clearly confers a discretion upon the court in each particular case to grant or refuse the order sought and, where granted, the order is subject to such terms and conditions as the court may decree.

Finally, Murphy J. found that the onus of proof that lies upon an applicant in satisfying the court that the conditions precedent to the exercise of its discretion have been fulfilled is that which exists in any civil case.

The taxpayer contended that he was not a person to whom the section applied, *i.e.*, "an individual who is ordinarily resident in the State", as defined by section 18(1) and that he had not been "duly required by an inspector to deliver a statement of the profits or gains arising to him from any trade or profession or to deliver to the inspector a return of income" as required by section 18(2)(a).

[21] *O'C. v. D. and Another* [1985] I.L.R.M. 123.

As to the first contention Murphy J. noted that, in the special endorsement of claim, the occupation and place of employment of the taxpayer had been deleted and Mr. O'C. in his affidavit stated that the taxpayer carried on a practice but omitted to fill in the blank spaces giving the address and description of the practice. Nevertheless, Murphy J. decided, in the absence of any denial by the taxpayer, that the applicant had discharged the onus of proving as a probability that the taxpayer resided in the state.

In relation to the second contention, counsel for the applicant submitted that the taxpayer had been "duly required" because, as stated in the applicant's affidavit, the taxpayer had been requested under the provisions of section 174 of the Income Tax Act 1967 to submit accounts for the five years ended April 5, 1976, which accounts were not forthcoming. It was then contended that, although the word used in the statement in the affidavit was the word "accounts" rather than "profits or gains", it should properly be interpreted as comprising the latter having regard to the provisions of section 174 of the 1967 Act.

Murphy J., however, rejected this contention and noted that, under section 172 of the 1967 Act, an inspector is given power to require individuals to make returns of income, while an earlier section 169 of the same Act imposes a similar obligation to deliver a statement containing the amount of the "profits or gains" arising during the period specified in such notice.

He felt, therefore, that the reference in the applicant's affidavit to a request for accounts means and was intended to mean accounts as described in section 174 and could not be interpreted as referring to a statement of profits or gains specified in section 169 or returns of income referred to in section 172 and continued:

". . . it is true that the operation of S. 174 presupposes the requirement to deliver a statement of profits or gains but it does not seem to me that there is any other evidence to suggest that the taxpayer was ever requested to deliver a statement of profits or gains and that being so the condition precedent to the right of the applicant to apply for relief under S. 18 of the Finance Act 1983 has not been fulfilled and the application must be refused".[22]

17-016   **Extent of information required** The learned judge then embarked on an examination (*obiter*) of the extent of the information that a financial institution may be requested to furnish under section 18.

[22] *Id.*, at p. 127.

He stated that there are two categories of information that a financial institution may be directed to furnish:

"The first category comprises 'full particulars of all accounts maintained' by the taxpayer in question and the second category comprises 'such information as may be specified in the order relating to the financial transactions' of the person concerned but restricted first to information recorded in the books of the financial institution concerned and then only to such information as would be material in determining the correctness of a statement of profits or gains or in determining liability to tax".[23]

The view which Murphy J. took as to what constitutes "particulars of accounts" was quite restricted. He stated that only the name of the account holder, the nature of the account, and perhaps the date the account was opened and closed constituted particulars of accounts. As to the information that may be required under the second category above, he reiterated that such information is limited to those transactions that are recorded in the "books of that institution" and that would be material to the correctness of returns made.

Section 18 defines "books" as bankers' books within the meaning of the Bankers Books Evidence Acts 1879 and 1959 and the records and documents of persons referred to in section 7(4) of the Central Bank Act 1971.

Therefore, the meaning of books differs depending on whether a particular financial institution is a bank as defined in section 9 of the Bankers Books Evidence Act 1879 as amended by the Bankers Books Evidence (Amendment) Act 1959 or whether the particular financial institution is an institution referred to in section 7(4) of the Central Bank Act 1971, *e.g.*, the Agricultural Credit Corporation Limited and the Post Office Savings Bank.

In the case of a bank, books mean "bankers' books", which is defined in the 1959 Act so as to:

"(a) include any records used in the ordinary business of a bank, or used in the transfer department of a bank acting as registrar of securities, whether comprised in bound volumes, loose-leaf binders or other loose-leaf filing systems, loose-leaf ledger sheets, pages, folios or cards and

---

[23] *Id.*, at pp. 127-128.

(b) cover documents in manuscript, documents which are typed, printed, stencilled or created by any other mechanical or partly mechanical process in use from time to time and documents which are produced by any photographic or photostatic process".

However, in the case of a financial institution that is not a "bank" as defined above, "books" merely means "the records and documents of that institution". In this regard, Murphy J. agreed with Geoffrey Lane L.J. in *Regina* v. *Jones*,[24] when he stated that a file of various letters from various people could not be described as a record.

Accordingly, the word "books" in section 18:

". . . does not extend to files of correspondence or indeed to any documents in the possession of a banker which would not in essence constitute a book within the extended meaning of that word as comprising objects which for convenience are not bound together or fastened permanently and do not necessarily consist of writing or type of any description".[25]

17-017 **Orders of limited scope** Murphy J. concluded by expressing the view that, because an order in broad terms could involve a bank in costly time consuming research, any order given by the court should limit the information sought as closely as possible in the first instance with liberty to the party to apply for further relief in the event of extended disclosure becoming necessary.

The applicant appealed to the Supreme Court, and Finlay C.J. delivered the unanimous decision of the court. He stated that he was satisfied that section 18(2) must be construed as containing a preliminary precondition that the person concerned has been "duly required" to deliver a statement or return and that he was further satisfied that this requirement is applicable to both the situations envisaged by subsection (2), namely a failure to deliver or the delivery of an unsatisfactory statement or return.

The Chief Justice agreed with Murphy J. that the onus of proof on the applicant is that appropriate in a civil case, namely proving the necessary matters as a matter of probability, and he continued:

"I take the view however that the wide and drastic nature of the section is a factor in considering the method by which the evidence of probability is sought to be established. Where the

24 *Regina* v. *Jones* [1978] 1 W.L.R. 195.
25 *Id.*, at p. 130.

plaintiff and deponent in this case has probably got direct knowledge as to whether the taxpayer was duly required to make returns and where the Revenue Commissioners of which he is an officer certainly have easily within their procurement proper proof of that fact, if fact it be, it would, in my view, on an application under this section be wrong to infer from the statement that the taxpayer was served with a notice under S. 174 requiring accounts that the prerequisite for such notice, namely, that he was duly requested to make a return is also proved".[26]

Counsel for the applicant contended that the reference in the applicant's affidavit to the fact that a notice under section 174 of the 1967 Act had been served on the taxpayer, that the taxpayer's accountants had in fact made returns (although it was not stated that they had been duly required to do so) and that there was general evidence of correspondence and communication between the taxpayer and accountants employed on his behalf, was consistent with the attitude of a person who had been duly required to make the return.

The Chief Justice, however, rejected this submission but noted that it did appeal "to one's common sense".[27] He pointed out that section 172 (4) of the 1967 Act provides that:

" . . . if a person delivers to any inspector a return in a prescribed form, he shall be deemed to have been required by a notice under this section to prepare and deliver that return".

If the general law applicable for the making of returns in any form raised an inference of the due requirement for a return, that sub-section would be quite unnecessary.

Finally, the Chief Justice concluded that the *obiter* part of Murphy J.'s judgment had not been argued before the Supreme Court and, therefore, it was not appropriate that he should express any view in relation thereto.

Offences against the State (Amendment) Act 1985

Section 18 of the Offences against the State Act 1939 gives a broad definition of an unlawful organization as, *inter alia*, any organization that is involved with treason, the altering or attempted altering

17-018

---

[26] *Id.*, at p. 132.
[27] *Id.*

of the Constitution by force or violence or the raising of a military or armed force in contravention of the Constitution.

It also is provided that any organization involved in any criminal offense or the non-payment of monies payable to the Central Fund shall be an unlawful organization.

17-019 **Suppression order** Section 19 provides that the Government may make a suppression order in relation to any particular organization that it believes to be an unlawful organization, and section 20 provides that any member of such organization may apply to the High Court for a declaration of legality.

Section 22(a) provides that, immediately upon the making of a suppression order, all the property of such organization shall become and be forfeited to and vested in the Minister for Justice.

Section 2(1)(a) of the 1985 Act provides that any bank shall comply with the direction of the Minister for Justice on production of a document signed by him stating that:

"(i) the moneys described in the document held by the bank stand forfeited to and vested in the Minister for Justice by virtue of section 22 of the 1939 Act;

(ii) the Minister for Justice requires the bank to pay those moneys into the High Court and in the meantime to refrain from doing any act or making any omission inconsistent with that requirement and to notify as soon as may be thereafter the person or persons in whose name or names the moneys are held by the bank of their payment into the High Court".

Section 2(1)(c) provides that section 2(1)(a) shall remain in operation for three months. However, the Government may at any time by order continue its operation for a further period not exceeding three months.

Under section 3, a person claiming to be the owner of the monies so transferred must apply to the High Court within six months for an order directing that the moneys, together with any interest that the court considers reasonable, be paid to him and if that court is satisfied that section 22 of the 1939 Act does not apply, it shall make the order sought.

Section 4 provides that, if the court is of the opinion that there are reasonable grounds for the failure of the person to make an application to the court within the six months provided in section 3 and if the application made under section 4 is made within six years, the court may award compensation to such person.

Section 8 provides that any property of an unlawful organization acquired by it while a suppression order was in effect and all moneys held by any person for the use or benefit of an unlawful organization in respect of which a suppression order under section 19 of the 1939 Act is in force shall be deemed to be the property of such unlawful organization.

As is evident from the foregoing, the provisions of the 1985 Act are quite far reaching and do not merely allow for inspection but allow the Minister for Justice to transfer into the High Court moneys held by a bank on behalf of its customer where he holds the opinion that such moneys are the property of an unlawful organization that is the subject of a suppression order.

Property rights and the Constitution Not surprisingly, the section came under attack as being contrary to the property rights guaranteed by the Constitution in *Alan Clancy and David McCartney v. Ireland and The Attorney General*.[28]   17-020

The Minister for Justice directed the Bank of Ireland, Navan, Co. Meath to pay the sum of £1,750,816.27 into the High Court pursuant to the provisions of the 1985 Act. The plaintiffs instituted proceedings for the return of these moneys and claimed that the Act was unconstitutional as being contrary to article 43 and article 40.3.2 of the Constitution, which guarantee the right of ownership of private property subject to the common good and protect from unjust attack the property rights of every citizen, respectively.

After reviewing the provisions of the 1985 Act, Barrington J. concluded that, contrary to the plaintiff's submission, the Act did not allow for the expropriation of the moneys in question but rather provided that they be frozen pending proof by the owner thereof that the moneys in question were not the property of an unlawful organization or held for the use or benefit of an unlawful organization.

Barrington, J. cited United States authority supporting the view that the seizure of assets without the prior notice of the owner was not contrary to the guarantee of due process in the United States Constitution because notice of an intended seizure of an asset could be frustrated by its destruction, concealment, or removal from the jurisdiction. He noted that there was a provision for the payment of compensation under section 4 of the 1985 Act and quoted a passage from the judgment of Walsh J. in *Dreher v. Irish Land Commission*[29] where he stated:

[28] Barrington J., unreported, High Court, May 4, 1988.
[29] *Dreher v. Irish Land Commission* [1974] I.L.R.M. 94.

"The State in exercising its powers under Article 43 must act in accordance with the requirements of social justice but clearly what is social justice in any particular case must depend on the circumstances of the case. In Article 40.3.2 'The State undertakes by its laws to protect as best it may from unjust attack, and in the case of injustice done vindicate . . . (the) property rights of every citizen'. I think it is clear that any State action that is authorised by Article 43 of the Constitution and conforms to that Article cannot by definition be unjust for the purpose of Article 40.3.2. It may well be that in some particular cases, social justice may not require the payment of any compensation upon a compulsory acquisition that can be justified by the State as being required by the exigencies of the common good. It is not suggested that the present case is one such. . .".[30]

Barrington J. concluded that, in the circumstances of the present case, the provisions of the 1985 Act amounted to a permissible delimitation of property rights in the interests of the common good and, therefore, were not unconstitutional.

Companies Act 1990

17-021   Section 7 of the Act provides that, on the application of a director or creditor or the requisite number of members of a company, or the company itself, the court may appoint one or more inspectors to investigate the affairs of the company.

Under section 8, the Minister for Industry and Commerce may petition the court to have one or more inspectors appointed where there are circumstances suggesting, *inter alia*, that the affairs of the company have been conducted with intent to defraud its creditors or otherwise for a fraudulent or unlawful purpose.

Section 14 further provides that the Minister may appoint one or more inspectors to investigate and report on the membership of any company for the purpose of determining the true persons who are or have been financially interested in the success or failure of the company or able to control, or influence the policy of, the company.

The Minister must hold the opinion, however, that there are circumstances suggesting that it is necessary for the effective administration of company law, the effective discharge of his functions or in the public interest that an inspector be appointed.

30 *Id.*

Section 10(1) provides that it shall be the duty of all officers and agents of the company:

". . . to produce to the inspectors all books and documents of or relating to the company. . .which are in their custody or power, to attend before the inspectors when required so to do and otherwise to give to the inspectors all assistance in connection with the investigation which they are reasonably able to give".

Section 10(2) provides that the inspectors may require any other party other than an officer or agent of the company to produce any books or documents in his custody relating to the company. Section 10(4) provides that an inspector may examine on oath the officers and agents of the company, and section 10(5) contains potentially quite punitive powers in that any officer or agent of the company who refuses to produce to the inspectors any book or document or refuses to attend before the inspectors may on enquiry by the court be punished as if he had been guilty of contempt of court. Section 10(7) provides that:

". . . any reference to officers or to agents shall include past, as well as present, officers or agents, as the case may be and 'agents', in relation to a company. . .shall include the bankers and solicitors of the company. . .".

As the definition in section 3 defines books and documents as including "accounts, deeds, writings, and records made in any other manner", the powers of an inspector extend to accounts of a company under investigation that would otherwise be confidential. It is evident from the foregoing that the powers of an inspector under sections 7 to 10 are quite wide ranging, and a bank official who refuses to comply with an inspector's request for information may have to answer a charge of contempt of court.

The foregoing provisions came under attack in *Chestvale Properties Limited and Hoddle Investments Limited v. John A. Glackin and Ansbacher Bankers Limited, Noel Smyth & Partners and the Attorney General.*[31]

The Court concluded that, while an Inspector appointed under Part 11 of the Companies Act 1990 has extensive powers, he must adhere to the rules of natural and constitutional justice when, and if, he begins to exercise functions of a judicial nature and not merely of an investigative nature, *i.e.,* when he has to "enter a verdict".

[31] (1992) I.L.R.M. 221.

Not least among the principles of natural justice are the rules against bias and *audi alteram partem*, *i.e.*, the right of each party to be heard. Furthermore, it is always open to a bank's client to claim that Part 11 of the Act is unconstitutional; however, it is unlikely that a court would so hold.[32]

Building Societies Act 1989

17-022 Section 41 of the Act provides that the Governor of the Central Bank may authorize in writing a person (an "authorised person") to inspect or investigate the state and conduct of the business of any building society or its subsidiary or associated company or any particular aspect of such business and report to the Central Bank thereon.

Subsection 2 provides that the Central Bank or an authorised person may require a building society to furnish:

> "(a) such information, documents or other material or explanation of matters, which relate to the business or the plans for the future development of the society and its subsidiary or other associated bodies . . .

> "(b) a report . . . on . . . information or documents, or other materials so furnished".

Subsection (3) provides that an authorised person may enter upon the premises of a building society and take copies of or extracts from any documents or material thereon and sub-section 4 extends the ambit of the section to information, documents or other material in the possession or control of a subsidiary or associated body of a building society outside the state.

Although the powers of the Central Bank are quite wide, it is to be noted that, under section 16 of the Central Bank Act 1989, there are significant restrictions on disclosure of such information to third parties.

---

[32] Article 43 of the Constitution provides that the state acknowledges the right to own private property; however, this right ought to be regulated by the principles of social justice. Accordingly, article 43.2.2. provides that the state may limit the exercise of the right to own private property with a view to reconciling its exercise with the exigencies of the common good.

Trustee Savings Banks Act 1989

Section 24 of this Act provides that an officer of the Central Bank   **17-023**
("an authorised officer") may, for the purpose of the performance by
the Central Bank of its functions under the Act:

> "(i) investigate the affairs of a trustee savings bank and report
> to the Central Bank thereon;

> "(ii) at all reasonable times enter any office of the bank and
> examine and take copies of any books, accounts or other re-
> cords related to the business of the bank".

Section 25 further obliges the trustees of a trustee savings bank to
furnish the Central Bank with such information and returns concerning its business as the Central Bank may specify from time to
time, being information and returns that the Central Bank considers
it necessary to have for the due performance of its functions under
the Act. The comments above in relation to section 16 of the Central
Bank Act 1989 also apply here.

Central Bank Act 1989

Section 36 of the Act inserted a new section 17 in the Central Bank   **17-024**
Act 1971. The new section 17 provides that a holder of a
banking
license shall keep at an office within the state such books and
records (including accounts) as may be specified from time to time
by the Central Bank and a duly authorised person ("an authorised
person") may, from time to time and at all reasonable times, inspect
and take copies of and make enquiries as he may consider necessary
in relation to such books and records, any books of account of the
license holder, or any other documents relating to the business of
the said license holder.
Section 16 defines the parameters of the duty of secrecy of the
Central Bank in relation to such information. This section provides
that employees and former employees of the Central Bank shall not
disclose, at any time, any information concerning anyone's business
that came to their knowledge by virtue of their employment or
concerning the Central Bank's activities in respect of the protection
of the integrity of the currency or control of credit unless such
disclosure is to enable the Central Bank to carry out its functions
under the Central Bank Acts 1942 to 1989 or any subsequent legislation. The restriction on disclosure however does not apply to any
disclosure:

"(a) required by a court in connection with any criminal proceedings;

(b) made with the consent of the person to whom the information relates or from whom the information was obtained;

(c) made by the Central Bank acting as agent for the person to whom it relates;

(d) where the Central Bank considers it necessary for the common good, made to any person charged with the supervision of financial institutions who, in the opinion of the Central Bank, has obligations concerning that person duly imposed in respect of non-disclosure of information corresponding to the obligations under section 16;

(e) made to a duly authorised equivalent foreign authority;

(f) made to any European Community's institution for the purpose of the State's membership of any of the Communities;

(g) made to comply with the statutory requirement that a document be laid before a House of the *Oireachtas*".

Moreover, the non-disclosure rule does not apply, so far as an individual's business is concerned, where the disclosure in question is in the Central Bank's opinion necessary for the protection of depositors or with regard to the Central Bank's activities in protecting the integrity of the currency or the control of credit.

The non-disclosure rule does not apply either where disclosure is made with the Central Bank's consent and is not prejudicial to the operation of the Central Bank in any financial market, the issue by the Central Bank of legal currencies or the integrity of the currency. Any contravention of section 16 is an offense and attracts a fine of up to £1000 or six months in prison on summary conviction and £25,000 or five years on conviction on indictment.

Injunctions

17-025   The High Court retains jurisdiction to refuse or grant an injunction in whatever terms it deems necessary where it decides, in its discretion, that the balance of convenience lies in favor of granting or refusing the injunction sought.

In the case of *Larkins, Padmore, Barrells, Hoult and Arnold* v. *National Union of Mineworkers and Bank of Ireland Finance Limited*,[33] Barrington J., on the application of the first four plaintiffs (the sequestrators), made an interim order:

(1) Restraining the National Union of Mineworkers and Bank of Ireland Finance from disposing of or otherwise dealing with any moneys held to the account of the National Union of Mineworkers, and

(2) Requiring Bank of Ireland Finance or any financial institution or bank within the jurisdiction served with notice of the order to produce for inspection to the sequestrators or their solicitors the bankers books including correspondence or computer printouts from electronic recordings relating to any account of the National Union of Mineworkers held by Bank of Ireland Finance or any other financial institution.

The sequestrators had been appointed by an English court to enforce a fine of £200,000 against the union for contempt of court. The fifth named plaintiff, Mr. Arnold, was the receiver appointed on the application of several members of the National Union of Mineworkers claiming that the trustees of the union (the president, vice-president, and secretary) had by their defiance of the English court subjected the union to a fine of £200,000 and placed its funds in jeopardy.

Barrington J. held that it was not immediately obvious who owned the funds in question, *i.e.*, the sequestrators, the receiver, or the trustees, and he continued the injunction until permanent trustees of the union's property were identified or appointed in accordance with the provisions of English law.

Bank of Ireland Finance, which had been dismissed from the action on its undertaking to abide by the terms of the order of the court, applied and was reinstated as a defendant so as to make submissions on the implications of the making of an interim order, as therein, without notice to the bank. Barrington J. emphasized that, as the order in question was then spent, the issue of whether it should or should not have been made was then a moot point and, therefore, he should not be taken as deciding any point of law but rather wished to provide an explanation in deference to the submission advanced by counsel for the bank.

[33] Barrington J., unreported, High Court, June 18, 1985.

The learned judge noted that there was no allegation of fraud in the present case and stated that the applicant for a mareva injunction must prove his case on its merits and also must show that the defendant intends to take his assets out of the jurisdiction or otherwise dispose of them in such a way as to ensure that any judgment obtained by the plaintiff against him will be useless.

The sequestrators in this case claimed that the union had transferred its funds out of the jurisdiction of the English courts in anticipation of being in contempt of court. There was no doubt that the union was the person entitled to ownership of the funds but if the sequestrators' case was valid they were entitled to possession of the funds as against the union and the bank. In the opinion of Barrington J:

> "It appeared to me that they had raised a fair *prima facie* case on this subject and that the balance of convenience lay in favor of granting the injunction".[34]

He continued:

> "Needless to say, this was a very far reaching order and was not lightly made. In the normal course a freezing order would have been sufficient to maintain the status quo and there would have been no justification for making an inspection order such as this *ex parte*. The necessity for the ex parte order arose from the fear that portion of the funds had already been transferred to other financial institutions in Ireland, the identity of which was unknown to the sequestrators".[35]

Finally, Barrington J. rejected a submission on behalf of the bank that bankers books should have the restricted definition given by Murphy J. in *O'C. v. D. and Another*[36] as that decision referred to section 18 of the Finance Act 1983, and he concluded that there was nothing in Murphy J.'s decision or the Bankers' Books Evidence Acts (1879 and 1959) to restrict the power of the High Court to order the production of or inspection of any of a banker's books, documents or computer printouts.

---

34 *Id.*
35 *Id.*
36 *O'C. v. D. and Another, supra* n. 21.

Compulsion of witnesses

The court may compel witnesses to appear before it in any legal   **17-026**
proceeding that is ongoing, and this is achieved by the issue of a
subpoena, being either a subpoena *ad test*, which requires the presence of the person named therein only, or a subpoena *duces tecum*,
which requires that the person named bring with him the documents specified therein.

In *Charles Cully v. Northern Bank Finance Corporation Limited*,[37] a
subpoena *duces tecum* was issued requiring Michael Cleere, an
assistant general manager of the Central Bank, to attend the hearing
of the above legal proceedings and to give evidence on behalf of the
plaintiff and to bring with him all documents relating to the sale or
purchase of certain shares in the Commercial Banking Company
Limited and all documents relating to certain meetings between the
Central Bank and representatives of the Commercial Banking Company Limited.

Michael Cleere applied to the court by way of notice of motion
seeking an order that the subpoena be set aside. His main contention was that, if he complied with the subpoena, he would be in
breach of his oath of secrecy taken pursuant to section 31 of the
Central Bank Act 1942.

Northern Bank Finance Corporation Limited had acted for the
plaintiff in a transaction involving the sale of his entire sharehold-
ing in the Commercial Banking Company Limited some years previous thereto, and the plaintiff in the present proceedings was
claiming damages against the defendant for breach of contract,
negligence and fraud.

It was accepted by both parties that the defendant had been in
communication with the Central Bank in relation to the said transaction and the correspondence passing between the said parties had
been disclosed in the defendant's affidavit of discovery and, therefore, it was possible to procure the said correspondence without
requiring the attendance of Mr. Cleere.

O'Hanlon J. believed that it was difficult to envisage what other
documentation the Central Bank would be likely to have in their
possession that would be relevant to the proceedings. It was noted
that the plaintiff was unable to specify any particular document of

---

[37] O'Hanlon J., unreported, High Court, January 16, 1984.

which he required production and which had not already been included in the defendant's affidavit of discovery but it was suggested that two officers of the defendant who were active in the share transaction may have had communications with the Central Bank after they left the employment of the defendant.

O'Hanlon J., however, felt that the existence or non-existence of any such documents was purely a matter of speculation, and he was unable to hold as a matter of probability that the Central Bank or its officer Michael Cleere had in their possession or procurement any documentation or other evidence relevant to the matters in issue in the instant proceedings over and above the documents that had already been discovered.

Furthermore, he held that the provisions of section 31 of the Central Bank Acts 1942 to 1989 gave rise to a claim of privilege on grounds of public policy against disclosure of any information of the type referred to in the oath of secrecy. O'Hanlon J. then quoted Scarman L.J. in *Senior* v. *Holdsworth*:[38]

> "The law, at it now stands, does not enable the court to refuse to issue a witness summons (or subpoena) for the production of documents on due application. The remedy available to the person served is to move to set the summons aside. On such an application the court will set it aside if what is sought is irrelevant, oppressive, an abuse of the process of the court, or recognised by the law as being privileged from production. Further, even if the document sought be relevant and not otherwise privileged from production, the court has a residual discretion in certain circumstances to protect the document and set the summons aside".

The learned judge adopted this statement of principle and held that section 31 conferred a statutory privilege on the Central Bank on which it is entitled to rely unless and until the validity of that section is sufficiently challenged on constitutional grounds. Section 31 was subsequently repealed by the Central Bank Act 1989; however, the principles adopted above are still relevant where a subpoena *duces tecum* is issued to an employee of a bank or other financial institution.

---

[38] *Senior* v. *Holdsworth* [1975] 2 All E.R. 1009, at p. 1022.

Garnishee orders

Order 45 of the Rules of the Superior Courts provides that the court 17-027
may, upon *ex parte* application of a person who has obtained a
judgment or order for recovery or payment of money (the judgment
creditor) and upon affidavit by such judgment creditor or his solicitors stating that judgment has been recovered, or the order made,
and that it is still unsatisfied, and to what amount, and that another
person is indebted to such judgment debtor and is within the
jurisdiction, the court may order that all debts owing or accruing
from such third person (the garnishee) to such judgment debtor
shall be attached to answer the judgment or order.

The court also may order that the garnishee shall appear before
the court to show cause why he should not pay to the judgment
creditor the debt due from him to such judgment debtor.

The order must be served on the garnishee at least seven days
before the date of the hearing and, unless otherwise ordered, on the
judgment debtor or his solicitor. Service of an order of the court
under the Rules operates to freeze the debt due from the garnishee
to the judgment debtor.

The garnishee may pay the sum due by him to the judgment
debtor into court or dispute that such sum is due and in default. The
court may order the execution of the order against the garnishee.
Payment made by, or execution levied upon, the garnishee shall be
a valid discharge to him as against the judgment debtor to the
amount paid or levied, even though such proceedings may be set
aside or the judgment or order reversed.

CONCLUSION

The duty of secrecy that a bank owes to its client is necessary and of 17-028
paramount importance in a normal commercial environment.
However, there are certain instances in which this duty can and
should be set aside, in particular, to detect tax evasion or hinder the
growth and development of subversive organizations.

While there are numerous statutory instances in which the duty
may be set aside, it is submitted that the Irish courts have strictly
interpreted such statutory infringements of the duty of secrecy,
particularly in the case of taxation legislation as is evident in the
case of *O'C.* v. *D. and Another.* The duty of secrecy is alive and well
in Ireland. It is not an absolute duty, however, but rather a duty that
allows for disclosure in certain necessary circumstances as required
by the common good.

CHAPTER 18

ISLE OF MAN

Paul R. Beckett
Deutsche Bank (Switzerland) Limited
Geneva, Switzerland

Chapter 18

ISLE OF MAN

INTRODUCTION

When considering banking secrecy in the Isle of Man, it is first **18-001** necessary to place the Isle of Man in its correct constitutional and political context, in order to examine more closely the forces working within and from without the Isle of Man which help to shape the policies of its government and guide the application of its principles.

The Isle of Man's unique status is that, while part of the British Isles and acknowledging the Queen of England as its Head of State, it is politically and constitutionally not a part of the United Kingdom. It is a Crown Dependency. As such, it is independent in all matters except foreign affairs and defense, which are the responsibility of the United Kingdom Government.

The Isle of Man legislature, the Tynwald, dates from the Viking Councils of the 9th Century. Scandinavian rule over the Island ended in 1333 with defeat by the Scots, and the Island later passed under the general suzerainty of the English Crown.

The Isle of Man remained, however, outside the English (and later British) political system, and the English monarch continued to fulfil only the role originally played by the ancient Scandinavian kings. Later, the Lordship of Man was granted to a succession of ruling families by the English Kings, until the British Crown itself acquired the Lordship from the Earls of Derby in 1765. The present Lord of Man is the British Queen Elizabeth II, and is represented in the Island by her Lieutenant Governor.

The Lieutenant Governor, who is appointed for a five-year term, now has only a limited role in executive government, the political head of which is the Chief Minister (formally appointed by the Lieutenant Governor after being elected by the Tynwald).

The Tynwald has two branches, a directly elected House of Keys with twenty-four members and the Legislative Council with ten members, eight elected by the House of Keys together with the Island's Bishop and Attorney General. The Tynwald is not a subordinate legislature and does not derive its authority from the United Kingdom Parliament.

It is unlikely that there would be a conflict between an Act of Parliament and an Act of Tynwald, each legislature being closely aware of the other's activities and sensitive to the needs of its neighbor but, were such a conflict to occur (assuming each to have received the Royal Assent), then in the Isle of Man the Act of Tynwald would prevail.

With the passage of the Isle of Man Customs, Harbours and Public Purposes Act in 1866,[1] the Isle of Man gained the separation of its finances from those of the United Kingdom. This enabled the Tynwald to develop the Island's complete financial independence.

The Isle of Man has a special relationship with the European Community (EC). The Treaty of Rome provides for its application to all European territories for whom a Member State is responsible.

However, in the case of the United Kingdom, which is responsible for the Isle of Man's external relations, the Third Protocol was added. This provides that the Treaty shall not apply to the Isle of Man except in certain limited areas concerned with free trade in industrial and agricultural products.

The Isle of Man is not affected by the EC's 1992 "Single Market" program. Being outside the EC for the purpose of trade in financial services and financial products, it is therefore not bound by any legislation emanating from the institutions of the EC.

The Isle of Man has a Customs and Excise Agreement with the United Kingdom dating from 1979,[2] and the two countries therefore constitute a common customs area.

The Isle of Man is a member of the Organization for Economic Cooperation and Development (OECD), the United Kingdom Government having made a declaration that the OECD Convention applied to the Isle of Man in 1990. Isle of Man financial products and financial services, therefore, have access to markets where membership of the OECD is a requirement.

[1] Customs, Harbours and Public Purposes Act 1866 (repealed).
[2] Agreement between the Governments of the United Kingdom and the Isle of Man on Customs and Excise and Associated Matters 1979, Cmnd 7747.

THE MANX LEGAL SYSTEM

The Isle of Man has its own legal system. The High Court of Justice   **18-002**
in the Island is presided over by two "Deemsters". These are the
Island's senior judges, and the office derives from the time of the
Scandinavian Kings when a Deemster was the guardian of the
Island's traditional, unwritten law (still known today, as "Breast
Law").

The senior government law officer is the Attorney General. Appeals are heard by the Staff of Government Division of the High
Court. A further appeal lies, with leave, to the Judicial Committee
of the Privy Council in England.

The sources of law in the Isle of Man are therefore various, and a
minefield for the unwary who would assume its similarity with its
Common Law neighbors in the British Islands and its fellow members of the British Commonwealth. They comprise "Breast Law";
Acts of Tynwald, and (where extended to the Isle of Man or adopted
by Order in Council) of the United Kingdom Parliament; secondary
legislation in the form of Government Circulars, Orders, and Regulations and Extra-Statutory Concessions, together with Practice
Notes issued by the Manx revenue authority, the Assessor of Income Tax; the rules of English and Commonwealth Common Law
and equity (insofar as there is no local rule or custom to the contrary); and international treaty obligations extended to the Isle of
Man by the United Kingdom Parliament.

CONFIDENTIALITY AND REGULATION

There is a climate of confidentiality in the Isle of Man. This is   **18-003**
balanced by the need for the Isle of Man to maintain its record of
excellence as a premier offshore financial center, and it is therefore
one of the most closely regulated of all the offshore jurisdictions.

The Financial Supervision Commission of the Isle of Man was
established in 1983 and is the regulatory and supervisory body for
all financial and banking activities in the Island. Insurance activity
is the domain of the Insurance Supervisor.

The Financial Supervision Commission is an independent statutory body which operates under the general direction of the Manx
Treasury. It is directed by five commissioners, of whom three are
non-executive. Its chairman is the Minister for the Treasury.

The brief given to the Financial Supervision Commission by the
Tynwald is to "take such steps as appear to it to be necessary or

expedient for the effective supervision of the private financial and commercial sector in the Island".

The Financial Supervision Commission has stated its interpretation of that brief to be as follows:[3]

"(a) The purpose of having a banking and financial centre is to provide measurable economic benefits to the Island.

(b) The Isle of Man has nothing to gain from permitting activities or institutions which provide shelter for or facilitate the activities of criminals.

(c) Institutions established on the Isle of Man and their customers will benefit from standards of licensing and supervision which reflect best practice and are acceptable to supervisory bodies in other jurisdictions."

The main functions of the Financial Supervision Commission include:

(1) The licensing and supervision of banking institutions under the Banking Acts 1975 to 1986;[4]
(2) The authorization, recognition and regulation of collective investment schemes under the Financial Supervision Act 1988;[5]
(3) The regulation of all investment businesses (including the managers and trustees of collective investment schemes, as well as third party administrators) under the Investment Business Act 1991;[6]
(4) The authorization and supervision of building societies under the Building Societies Act 1986;[7]
(5) Various miscellaneous functions under the Moneylenders Act 1991[8] and the Companies Acts 1931 to 1992.[9]

---

[3] Financial Supervision Commission, Guide to the Establishment of Banks in the Isle of Man (June 1991), pp. 6-7.

[4] Banking Acts 1975 to 1986 (Banking Act 1975, c. 09; Banking Act 1977, c. 02; Banking (Amendment) Act 1986, c. 02).

[5] Financial Supervision Act 1988, c.16.

[6] Investment Business Act 1991, c.18.

[7] Building Societies Act 1986, c.07.

[8] Moneylenders Act 1991, c.06.

[9] The Companies Acts 1931 to 1992 (Companies Act 1931 XIII, p. 235; Companies Act 1961 XIX, p. 340; Companies Act 1968 XX, p. 413; Companies Act 1974, c. 30; Companies Act 1982, c. 02; Companies Act 1986, c. 45; Companies Act 1992, c. 04).

WHAT CONSTITUTES BANKING?

The Isle of Man is a subscriber to the International Concordat on **18-004**
banking supervision, drawn up by the Basle Supervisors Committee, and adheres to the principle that banking supervision should
aim to be "a seamless robe".

It is necessary to consider what constitutes banking activity in
the Isle of Man in order to assess the level of banking control and
the extent to which the principles of banking secrecy are upheld.

The emphasis is not simply on the taking of deposits. In the Isle
of Man, banking business is defined in section 1(1) of the Banking
Act 1975 as being

> ". . . a business which includes the carrying on of any one or
> more of the following activities, namely:
>
> i) the receipt of money upon any form of running account;
>
> ii) the advance by way of loans of the whole or part of deposits
> received;
>
> iii) the payment and collection of cheques . . .".

The Financial Supervision Commission recognizes that such a
broad definition could encompass activities which ought not properly to be regarded as banking activities; therefore, under the provisions of the Investment Business Act 1991, it has the power to
exempt any person or class of persons from any or all the provisions
of the Banking Acts.

This power was previously exercised by the Manx Treasury itself
under the Banking Acts and, to date, the only exceptions are the
Government of the Isle of Man, the Governments and central banks
of Member States of the EC, the European Investment Bank, the Isle
of Man Post Office Authority, the United Kingdom Post Office, the
National Savings Bank, and Isle of Man registered building societies.

The effect of the supervisory regime is to a certain extent extra-
territorial. Under section 1(1A) of the Banking Act 1975, all Manx
companies, whether resident or non-resident, and all foreign companies having a place of business in the Isle of Man and which carry

on banking business in or from the Isle of Man or abroad are treated as carrying on a banking business in the Isle of Man.

Finally, under section 1(2) of the Banking Act 1975,

". . . where a person carries on a business which in any respect is or in the opinion of the Financial Supervision Commission appears to be of a similar character to banking business, that person upon a declaration made by the Financial Supervision Commission in writing shall be subject to the provisions of [the Banking Acts]".

It should be noted, however, that the Financial Supervision Commission has stated that, in practice, it would not grant a license to a company which was non-resident on the grounds that its activity could not be effectively supervised and controlled.

SECRECY

18-005 In the Isle of Man, banking secrecy can be looked at in three ways: the extent to which an account holder may preserve his anonymity and be confident that all account details will remain confidential to the banking institution with which he is dealing; the obligation placed upon a bank to "know your customer", and the extent to which the bank itself may safeguard the confidentiality of its ownership and control.

The account holder

18-006 The law of the Isle of Man recognizes the contractual duty of a banker to keep the affairs of his customers confidential.

The Bankers' Books Evidence Act 1935[10] provides, in sections 6 and 7, that a banker is not compelled, in any proceedings to which his bank is not a party, to produce banking books or to appear as a witness, unless so ordered by the court. The court may permit a party to inspect and take copies of entries in a banker's books, on giving the banker three days notice.

---

10 Bankers' Books Evidence Act 1935 XIV, p. 300.

The directions which the Financial Supervision Commission is empowered to give to banks do not, under the terms of section 4(2), Banking Act 1975, extend to requests or recommendations with respect to the affairs of any particular customer of a banking institution.

Further, section 5(8), Banking Act 1975, provides that nothing in section 5 of that Act (which deals with inspection and investigation by the Financial Supervision Commission) applies "in respect of the affairs of any particular customer of a banking institution except and in so far as it may be necessary for the purpose of an inspection and investigation . . ." under that section.

Inevitably, in seeking information on a bank's assets, as it is entitled to do, the Financial Supervision Commission will encroach upon customer confidentiality. Nevertheless, sections 22 to 24 of the Financial Supervision Act 1988 restrict the use which the Financial Supervision Commission can make of that information.

With certain important exceptions, such information cannot be disclosed to anyone without the consent of the bank and its customer unless it has already legitimately entered the public domain.

The exceptions are contained in section 23 and cover such matters as civil and criminal proceedings, the workings of the Depositors Compensation Scheme (under section 21 of the Banking Act 1975 and the Regulations made under it), the Treasury and its members, the Financial Supervision Commission and its members, and inspectors appointed under the Companies Acts 1931 to 1992.

Importantly, section 23(5) does not preclude the disclosure of such information

> ". . . for the purpose of enabling or assisting any authority in a country or territory outside the Island to exercise functions corresponding to those of the [Financial Supervision] Commission, the Insurance Supervisor, or the Insurance Authority. . .or any other functions in connection with rules of law corresponding to the provisions of the Company Securities (Insider Dealing) Act 1987".

However, by virtue of section 23(6), section 23(5) is inoperative as regards "the disclosure of any information relating to the affairs of a customer unless the Chief Minister (or in his absence the Minister of Home Affairs) is satisfied:

> "(a) that the disclosure is in the public interest, having regard to the confidential nature of the information and the purpose for which it is required; and

(b) that the disclosure is likely to be of substantial value to the authority to which it is made;

and has given his written concurrence to the disclosure."

It should be noted that there are no powers in statute or in law to disclose information to any foreign revenue authority or under the Banking Acts to the Assessor of Income Tax in the Isle of Man.

"Know your customer"

18-007   In August 1986 the Financial Supervision Commission introduced its "Know Your Customer" policy. In a circular letter to all banking institutions in the Isle of Man, the Banking Supervisor stated:

"The Financial Supervision Commission is concerned at what it understands to be the practice of some if not all banks in opening accounts and undertaking transactions with those they do not know. This applies particularly, though not exclusively, to corporate accounts introduced by local agents where the identity of the ultimate beneficial owner is not disclosed. In the Commission's view, it is not sufficient to rely on the bona fides and assurances of the local agent or the fact that he or his colleagues may be acting in an executive capacity and have signing powers over the bank account.

Failure to identify the beneficial owner and to be satisfied as to the nature of business for which the account will be used increases the risk that the bank concerned may find itself involved in facilitating fraud or the laundering of criminal money. . . .

It is therefore clearly in the commercial interests of all banks that they should establish 'Know Your Customer' principles to which management and staff are requested to adhere. . . ."

The letter went on to warn of the inherent dangers in back-to-back transactions. The Financial Supervision Commission states in its current Guidance Note:

"Arrangements to conceal things from others are not only morally dubious but potentially criminal and those who make such arrangements must be absolutely certain that they are not a party to fraud or money laundering . . . . Much is sometimes made of the need for secrecy as opposed to confidentiality. While there may be a small number of instances where lack of secrecy can be harmful, secrecy is a high risk approach. Anyone who offers secrecy to another takes the risk that he will be involved in criminal activity.

Confidentiality and privacy in one's financial and personal affairs is a long-established right which the Courts are loath to invade or disturb, but that approach is predicated on the assumption that people are open and frank with their bankers and advisers . . . .

Knowing one's customer involves actual verifiable knowledge, but it also involves forswearing the 'hear no evil, see no evil, speak no evil' principle on which some people conduct their business and which critics of offshore centres argue provide the foundation of offshore activity. . . .

The decision as to what kind of business one does and with whom is and always has been a commercial judgement for which the responsibility rests, as it always has done, with the management. But it is also an ethical judgment and ethics lies at the heart of any profession - law, accountancy, banking and so on. Without ethics professional men and women are merely technical functionaries, no more and no less deserving of respect than any technician."

The banking institution

The current banking licensing policy of the Financial Supervision **18-008** Commission requires the disclosure to it of the beneficial ownership of the bank, and once a bank is licensed changes of ownership require the prior consent of the Commission.

"The Commission treats a change of ownership control, though not a change in the structure of ownership, as equivalent to a new licence application. The Commission must be aware at all times of the identity of the owners of an institution licensed under the Banking Act. Related parties are considered to be one shareholder in considering questions of control."[11]

---

[11] Financial Supervision Commission, *supra* n. 3, at p. 20.

CONCLUSION

18-009   The weighing of secrecy with confidentiality and the balancing of these two against public interest is being deftly undertaken.

The Isle of Man has come to terms with its responsibilities as a premier offshore centre, and is facing up to the pressures placed upon its regulatory authorities firmly but with a keen appreciation of commercial reality.

Independent, outside the European Community, able to call upon centuries of legal experience and writings, ably served by a strong judiciary and a thriving professional community, the Isle of Man is taking its place as one of the major financial centers of the world.

Note: The author is a solicitor of the Supreme Court of England and Wales and advocate solicitor and attorney in the Isle of Man.

ISRAEL

Marcus Mandel
Marcus Mandel, Shakenovsky,
Kretzmer & Hershkowitz
Tel Aviv, Israel

Chapter 19

ISRAEL

INTRODUCTION

This survey sets out the law in Israel relating, directly or indirectly, **19-001** to banking secrecy, the practice in Israel relating to this topic, and general conclusions on the subject.

Needless to say, the laws quoted below are Hebrew, and their translations into English are the authorized translations issued by the Ministry of Justice in Israel. While it is Hebrew that is binding on a court of law, these translations are, nevertheless, sufficiently accurate for the purposes of this survey.

THE LAW

In 1969 and in 1981, the Knesset (Israel's sovereign legislative body) **19-002** enacted amendments to the Banking Ordinance of 1941.[1] (It is to be noted that, although the State of Israel became independent only in 1948, a number of laws dating back to the period of the British Mandate of Palestine continue to be of full force and effect in Israel. The Banking Ordinance of 1941 is one of these laws).

---

[1] Banking Ordinance (Amendment No. 9), Statute Book No. 552 of March 24, 1969, p. 58 (English translation, Israeli Ministry of Justice, Laws of the State of Israel, volume 23, p. 62).

Banking Ordinance of 1941

19-003 The Knesset amendment of 1981 (which incorporates the 1969 amendment) became section 15A(a) of the Banking Ordinance of 1941, and it reads as follows:

> "15A(a) Secrecy
>
> A person shall not disclose any information delivered to him or show any document submitted to him under this Ordinance or under the Banking (Licensing) Law of 1981: Provided that it shall be lawful to disclose information if the Governor deems it necessary so to do for the purposes of a criminal charge or if the information or document was received from a bank and that bank consents to its disclosure."

A contravention of the provisions of this section 15A(a) constitutes a criminal offense, for which imprisonment of up to one year may be imposed by the criminal courts.

The reference in the body of section 15A(a) to the Banking (Licensing) Law of 1981 means that all information relating to any transaction between a bank and its customer is protected from disclosure by the prohibition set out in section 15A(a) of the Banking Ordinance of 1941, since section 10 of the Banking (Licensing) Law of 1981 is particularly wide, embracing every conceivable field of banking activity.

The "Governor" referred to in section 15A(a) of the Banking Ordinance of 1941 is the Governor of the Bank of Israel, a person appointed by the President of Israel on the recommendation of the Government, under terms of section 8 of the Bank of Israel Law of 1954.

The same principle of secrecy is imposed by the Banking Ordinance of 1941 on the deliberations of advisory committees to the Governor of the Bank of Israel, established under terms of this Ordinance to advise the Governor of the Bank of Israel on "matters relating to banking business" (the wording of section 6(1) of the Banking Ordinance of 1941.

Thus, section 6(5) of the Banking Ordinance of 1941 (as amended in 1969) reads as follows:

> "The proceedings of the Committee and of every subcommittee thereof shall be secret, and no person shall without the approval of the Governor divulge any information regarding them."

The same criminal penalties as are applicable in the case of a contravention of section 15A(a) of the Banking Ordinance of 1941, apply to a contravention of section 6(5) set out above.

Bank of Israel Law of 1954

Section 65(a) of the Bank of Israel Law 1954[2] bears a strong resem- **19-004** blance to the above-quoted section 15A(a) of the Banking Ordinance of 1941 (as amended). It reads as follows:

> "A person shall not disclose information supplied or produce a document submitted to him under this Law; provided that he may disclose information other than information received under section 64, if the Governor deems this necessary for the purposes of a criminal action."

The reference in section 65(a) of the Bank of Israel Law of 1954 to section 64 of the same Law, is interesting. Section 64 of the Bank of Israel Law of 1954 reads as follows:

> "The Governor or any person authorized by him may inspect any individual return and any document and receive any information destined for statistics prepared for the purposes of the Statistics Ordinance, 1947 as if he were a person employed for the purposes of that Ordinance."

Evidence Ordinance (New Version) of 1971

Section 38 of the Evidence Ordinance (New Version) of 1971[3] also **19-005** relates to the survey under discussion. This section 38 reads as follows:

> "A banker or officer of a bank shall not, in any legal proceeding to which the bank is not a party, be compelled to produce any banker's book the contents of which can be proved under this article, or to appear as a witness to prove the matters, transac-

---

[2] Bank of Israel Law 1954, Statute Book Number 164 of September 3, 1971, p. 192 (English translation, Israeli Ministry of Justice, Laws of the State of Israel, volume 8, p. 163).

[3] Evidence Ordinance (New Version) 1971, Statute Book Number 18 of April 18, 1971, p. 128 (English translation, Israeli Ministry of Justice, Laws of the State of Israel, New Version, volume 2, p. 206).

tions or accounts recorded therein, unless by order of a court made for special cause."

No precedents have been found relating to the interpretation to be given to the words "special cause" in section 38.

Section 39(a) of the Evidence Ordinance (New Version) of 1971 would seem, on the face of it, possibly to erode the principle of secrecy reflected by the aforesaid section 38.

Section 39(a) reads as follows:

"On the application of any party to a legal proceeding, a court may order that such party be at liberty to inspect and take copies of any entries in a banker's book for any of the purposes of such proceedings."

However, the Supreme Court of Israel (the court of ultimate appeal in Israel) has given this section's predecessor, which is in substantially the same language as the present section 39(a), a meaning which, it is submitted, renders section 39(a) a complete deadletter for any person seeking to contend that this section erodes the principle of secrecy.

The Supreme Court held, *inter alia*, that an applicant under terms of the section which was a predecessor to section 39(a) of the Evidence Ordinance (New Version) of 1971 must satisfy the court by way of affidavit that the specific entry in the banker's book that he wishes to inspect and copy is relevant and admissible in the proceedings before the court.[4]

From this, it is logical to conclude that the applicant must, on affidavit, persuade the court that the entry in fact exists, no mean task for an applicant who is, as yet, unaware as to whether a particular entry in a banker's book in fact exists or not.

In 1988, the Supreme Court of Israel held, in a case also dealing with section 39(a), that an order under terms of section 39(a) should be granted by a court only "in the rarest of circumstances".[5]

---

[4] Civil Appeal 182/65 in the Supreme Court of Israel, Jerusalem, *Hendler* v. *Company Portion 66 Block 6126 Ltd and Others*, reported in Supreme Court Judgments 19, volume 3, p. 113.

[5] Civil Appeal 174/88 in the Supreme Court of Israel, Jerusalem, *Gozlan* v. *Company Prizion*, reported in Supreme Court Judgments 42, volume 1, p. 565.

Protection of Privacy Law of 1981

A further law re-affirming the principle of banking secrecy in Israel **19-006**
is the Protection of Privacy Law of 1981. While this law does not
deal specifically with banks or banking, its provisions can no doubt
be used to reinforce the submission that the principle of banking
secrecy is well-established in Israel.

Thus, a number of subsections of section 2 of the Protection of
Privacy Law of 1981, are applicable to this survey.

Section 2 of the Protection of Privacy Law prefaces its subsections
with the words:

"Infringement of privacy is one of the following:

Subsection 7

". . . Infringing a duty of secrecy laid down by law in respect of a **19-007**
person's private affairs".

Subsection 8

". . . Infringing a duty of secrecy laid down by express or implicit **19-008**
agreement in respect of a person's private affairs". (I will deal more
fully with the issue of "express or implicit agreement" in my
survey of the practice in Israel in relation to banking secrecy).

Subsection 9

". . . Using or passing on to another, information on a person's **19-009**
private affairs otherwise than for the purpose for which it was
given".

There can be no doubt that a breach of the duty of secrecy by a
banker or an employee of the bank, constitutes a contravention of
the provisions of subsection 7 and of subsection 9 of section 2 of the
Protection of Privacy Law of 1981, in light of the clear provisions of
section 15A(a) of the Banking Ordinance of 1941, considered above.

A contravention of subsection 7 or 9 constitutes a criminal offense, for which imprisonment of up to one year may be imposed
by the criminal courts.

A contravention of subsection 7, 8, or 9 creates a cause of action
in civil law.

Israel applies the Common Law and, therefore, the judgments of the courts also constitute precedents which become part of the law.

In the context of a survey of the law relating to banking secrecy in Israel, it would, therefore, not be out of place to refer to a 1985 Supreme Court decision in which the court accepted without question the existence of the principle of banking secrecy in Israel but pointed out that this principle would not apply to relevant and admissible information contained in civil proceedings brought by a bank against its own client.[6]

THE PRACTICE

19-010 Even before 1981 (the year of the enactment of section 15A(a) of the Banking Ordinance of 1941 in its present form), Israeli banks honored the principle of secrecy in both letter and spirit.

The principle of banking secrecy is invariably expressly provided for in documents furnished by an Israeli bank to its customer, at the time that the customer-bank relationship is created. Moreover, the obligation to observe banking secrecy is, in consequence of the well-published practice of banks in Israel, now regarded as an implicit term of the agreement between an Israeli bank and its customer.

This well-established practice is of relevance to the question of whether section 2, subsection 8, of the Protection of Privacy Law of 1981[7] has any bearing on the topic now under consideration. It is submitted that a breach of the duty of secrecy by a banker or an employee of the bank constitutes an infringement of the provisions of subsection 8 of section 2 of the Protection of Privacy Law of 1981.

Israeli banks invariably have a "confidentiality" provision in their contracts with all of their employees, including of course managers. These "confidentiality" provisions prohibit, needless to say, the disclosure of any information relating to clients of the bank.

---

[6] Civil Appeal 230/83 in the Supreme Court of Israel, Jerusalem, *Abraham Leor and Zipora Leor* v. *Bank Igud Le'Yisrael Ltd.* (unreported).

[7] Protection of Privacy Law of 1981, Statute Book Number 1011 of March 11, 1981 (English translation, Israeli Ministry of Justice, Laws of the State of Israel, volume 35, at p. 136).

Israeli banks are prepared, and are permitted by Israeli law, to maintain numbered accounts and, for the customer who requests that his numbered account be known only to the manager of the particular bank where the numbered account is maintained, this request also will be honored.

CONCLUSION

From the above survey, it is submitted that the principle of banking secrecy is fully entrenched in Israel, in both law and practice. **19-011**

Banking secrecy is but one aspect of professional secrecy. The "Trapezitica Oration", written by Isocrates between 393 and 391 BC, is the first document which refers to banking secrecy.[8]

Indeed, the principle of banking secrecy is a doctrine of very ancient legal origin. It is, therefore, not surprising that this doctrine forms an integral part of the law of the newly established State of Israel, whose very sources of law pre-date even the writings of Isocrates on the subject.

---

[8] Palmiéri, "Nuove Brecce nel Segreto Bancaro", (1981) 34 *Banca Borsa e Titoli di Credito*, at p. 77.

CHAPTER 20

ITALY

Cesare Vento and Raffaella Betti Berutto
Gianni, Origoni, Tonucci
Rome, Italy

Chapter 20

ITALY

INTRODUCTION

Historical perspective

It must be said at the outset that, in Italy, the duty of a bank to not **20-001** disclose information regarding its customers has been in existence for decades and only recently its scope of application greatly diminished.

Historically, the legal basis of banking secrecy has been much debated and uncertain, since the Italian legislation does not contain specific rules on this topic.

To identify such basis, initially most scholars pointed to the Italian Banking Act[1] and, in particular, to its article 10, according to which all the data and information regarding banks, subject to the control of the Bank of Italy, are protected by the *segreto di ufficio* vis-à-vis any person, including other public agencies.

The expression *segreto d'ufficio* stands for the duty of an individual or entity (*e.g.*, the office of the public prosecutor) to not disclose to others confidential information acquired by reason of his position.

It was then observed that article 10 of the Banking Act is intended to establish an obligation of confidentiality binding on the staff of the Bank of Italy (the controlling agency), not on the banks controlled by it; thus, the doctrine of banking secrecy based on the *segreto d'ufficio* was abandoned.

Scholars and case law then gradually reached the conclusion that, in the Italian system, there exists a banking secrecy "custom", having the force of law. Accordingly, banking secrecy is considered

---

[1] Law Number 141 of March 7, 1938.

an "integrative legal custom" of banking contracts, pursuant to article 1373 of the Civil Code.[2]

In other words, there is an unwritten, yet customarily observed (thus, legally binding) covenant included in any relationship between a bank and its customer whereby the bank undertakes to not disclose information regarding such relationship to third parties.

Recent contraction of banking secrecy

20-002 Even before recent developments, the banking secrecy, though recognized as a principle hosted in the Italian system, did not have an unlimited scope of application.

As in other countries, both in the area of criminal laws and in the area of tax law, there were statutory provisions forcing the banks, without liability to their customers, to "breach the secrecy", and to disclose information to investigating judges and tax authorities. It was believed, however, that the circumstances under which such breach could occur were too limited to permit an effective enforcement of criminal and tax laws.

Recently adopted legislative measures have substantially enlarged such circumstances, and commentators now maintain that the Italian system has come to, or very close to, a total abolition of banking secrecy.

In this paper, such new measures will be summarized and analyzed by comparison with the provisions previously in force. In particular, the most important new laws are the new Code of Criminal Procedure,[3] the 1992 Budget Law,[4] and the so-called new Anti-Mafia Law.[5]

CRIMINAL LAW AND BANKING SECRECY

20-003 According to article 340 of the former Criminal Procedure Code, only the criminal judge, personally, had the power to order seizure, at a bank's premises, of valuables (such as sums deposited in bank

---

[2] Integration of contract: A contract binds the parties not only as to what it expressly provides but also to all the consequences deriving from it by law or, in its absence, according to usage and equity.

[3] Presidential Decree Number 447 of September 12, 1988.

[4] Law Number 413 of December 30, 1991.

[5] Law Number 197 of July 5, 1991.

accounts and negotiable instruments) and/or to review and take possession of any documents or material deemed relevant for an investigation.

In order for the criminal judge to exercise such power, it was not necessary that the valuables in question be registered in the name of the individual being investigated, the only limitation being, as said, that the valuables and documents be "relevant for the investigation". Articles 248 and 255 of the new Criminal Procedure Code have confirmed the same wide powers of the criminal judge.

A relevant change, however, was introduced by simplifying the procedure to be followed in exercising such powers. The criminal judge has now the authority, in connection with any type of investigation, to delegate criminal police officers to perform inspections and to order seizures.

Under previous legislation,[6] criminal police officers could be delegated by the criminal judge to exercise such powers only in connection with investigations regarding terrorism and organized crime offenses.

Naturally, banks are required to cooperate with criminal magistrates. They cannot refuse to permit inspections and to disclose the requested documentation. In the event that a bank fails to comply with an order of a judge or of a criminal police officer, the bank officials involved are subject to imprisonment for up to three months or to a fine of up to Lire 400,000.[7]

TAX LAW AND BANKING SECRECY

The tax reform of 1972-1973

A major tax reform was enacted in Italy in 1972 and 1973. That **20-004** reform introduced for the first time the possibility that tax authorities, independently of the pending of an investigation of a criminal judge, could "pierce" the banking secrecy during the course of tax audits of administrative nature, i.e., not necessarily involving a criminal violation.

However, as seen below, the powers of the tax authorities were limited to certain circumstances and, moreover, could be exercised only by complying with a burdensome procedure.

[6] Law Number 15 of February 6, 1991.
[7] Criminal Code, article 650.

The 1972-1973 reform was brought about through the enactment, *inter alia*, of the act on personal income tax ("IRPEF Law"),[8] and of the Act on Value Added Tax ("VAT Law").[9]

Article 35 of the IRPEF Law and article 51 of the VAT Law contained the key provisions on investigations of the banking affairs of taxpayers, which remained in effect until the changes just recently introduced by the 1992 Budget Law. Such provisions were amended and enlarged in 1982, in an effort to prevent a particular form of tax evasion (so-called invoicing of fictitious transactions), and can be summarized as follows.

The IRPEF Law

20-005　Under the article 35 of the IRPEF Law, the tax authority was entitled to obtain from a bank any documents and information concerning a bank's customer and, if necessary, perform an inspection at the bank's premises only in the presence of the following circumstances:

(1) The taxpayer failed to file a return and the authority had evidence showing that during the relevant fiscal year the taxpayer earned income or purchased property in excess of Lire 100,000,000;

(2) The taxpayer filed a return, but the authority had evidence showing that during the relevant fiscal year the taxpayer earned income four times higher than the income disclosed in such return and the undisclosed income exceeded Lire 100,000,000;

(3) A so-called "synthetic" assessment (tax audit based on assumptions triggered by expenses of the taxpayer in excess of specified amounts) showed that during the relevant fiscal year the taxpayer earned income four times higher than the disclosed income, and the undisclosed income exceeded Lire 100,000,000;

(4) Improperly maintained financial statements and accounting records of the taxpayer, or omitted or false entries in such statements and records, provided that income in excess of Lire 100,000,000 was ascertained by the authority;

(5) The taxpayer took part in a scheme involving invoices for fictitious transactions (regardless of the amount involved).

8 D.P.R. Number 600 of September 19, 1973.
9 D.P.R. Number 633 of October 26, 1972.

Only in the presence of the above circumstances were the tax authority officers entitled to require documents and, if necessary, to perform inspections at the banks. In addition, to take such actions tax officers had to comply with a complex procedure involving the approval of a hierarchically higher office (Tax Department) and the authorization of the Chief of the local Tax Court.

With respect to the scope of the investigation of banking affairs of taxpayers which the Italian authorities could carry out, it must be noted that the documentation and/or the inspections could only concern the bank accounts regarding the taxpayer's fiscal years being investigated or the following fiscal years, while previous fiscal years were excluded.

In addition, the tax authorities (unlike the criminal judge) could extend their investigations only to bank accounts of the taxpayer's spouse (not legally separated) and sons and daughters, if still dependent (so-called "linked individuals").

Only in case of investigations of invoices for fictitious transactions, the linked individuals could also include the taxpayer's partners in a *de facto* partnership as well as the general partners in a limited partnership where the taxpayer had an interest, provided that the linked individuals qualified as such during the fiscal year(s) being investigated.

The VAT Law

Article 51 of the VAT Law set forth rules essentially identical to those provided for by article 35 of the IRPEF Law.   **20-006**

Thus, the power of the officers to "pierce" the banking secrecy while investigating VAT violations was subject to the same thresholds and conditions summarized in the preceding section.

Reform of 1992

Article 18 of the 1992 Budget Law abrogated articles 34 and 35 of   **20-007**
the IRPEF Law and article 51 of the VAT Law, and introduced new rules on the investigation of banking affairs of taxpayers.

Pursuant thereto, it can be said that Italian fiscal authorities have been provided with new and far-reaching tools in connection with such investigations.

Conditions and authorizations

20-008 First, as a consequence of the abrogation of the afore-mentioned provisions, tax officers, with regard to both IRPEF and VAT matters, may now obtain from banks any documents and information concerning a client, as well as perform inspections, regardless of the occurrence of the circumstances specifically required under the previous legislation.

In other words, the only circumstance now sufficient to trigger the power of tax authorities to force banks to disclose information on a taxpayer is the previous pending of an audit of such taxpayer, regardless of the nature of the suspected violation, of the amounts involved or of any other circumstance.

Moreover, in order to simplify the procedure, inspections are now subject only to an approval of an hierarchically higher officer (Superior Officer or Tax Department). The authorization of the Chief of the Tax Court is no longer required. The nature of the approval of the Superior Officer or Tax Department is still unclear.

Prevailing opinion among commentators so far maintains that such approval technically is not an authorization but, rather, a mere "receipt of notice", with the exclusion of any evaluation of the merits of the case. However, it must be noted that, unlike in the past, the investigating officer has no recourse to a higher authority if the Tax Department or Superior Officer denies the approval.

Obligations of banks for customers' protection

20-009 Information regarding a customer may be sought only through the head office of the bank, which must be contacted "directly" by the investigating authority.

This provision is intended to protect confidentiality of taxpayers' affairs since banking investigations have now become easier. It was taken into account that directing investigations to low-level, peripheral employees of banks could cause undesirable rumors around investigated customers.

The bank must give notice of the investigation to its customer in due course. The law does not expressly provide for any penalty in case of failure to comply with this requirement. Accordingly, the majority of scholars believe that such requirement is relevant only within the bank/customer relationship of private law, that is to say, its violation can constitute a reason to terminate the contract for the bank's fault and, consequently, to claim damages. In addition, damages could be claimed by a customer under article 2043 of the Civil Code (the general rule on tortious liability in the Italian system).

Additional protection of taxpayers

The new legislation furthermore provides the following. The spe- **20-010** cific tax officer (Superior Officer or officer of the Tax Department) issuing the approval of a banking investigation is responsible to give proper instructions to the investigating officers as to the correct and confidential use of the data and information collected in the course of the investigation.

An administrative penalty from Lire 1,000,000 to Lire 10,000,000 may be applied to whoever reveals, without a justifying reason, the material collected during an investigation or use said material on his or a third party's behalf, provided that such disclosure does not constitute a more serious offense, *i.e.*, a breach of the *segreto di ufficio*, in which case more severe criminal sanctions would apply under article 326 of the Criminal Code.

Scope of banking investigations

As mentioned above, under prior legislation, an investigation could **20-011** be extended to certain individuals qualifying as "linked individuals". The new legislation, instead, is silent as to the individuals or entities to which a banking investigation can be extended.

Accordingly, two interpretations have been proposed:

(1) Investigations cannot be extended to any linked individual, since the new law does not expressly contemplate such extension, or

(2) Investigations can be extended to any individual or entity having some link with the taxpayer being audited (not only to those qualifying as "linked individuals" under the previous system), provided solely that such link is relevant to the audit.

The latter interpretation seems more consistent with the spirit of the reform introduced by the 1992 Budget Law. The issue, however, is still unclear.

Bank's failure to cooperate

Penalties are imposed by the new law in the event that a bank fails **20-012** to cooperate with the tax authorities during an investigation. In particular, in case a bank fails to transmit documents which were specifically requested, or transmits untrue or incomplete documents, a fine from Lire 3,000,000 to Lire 30,000,000 is applicable.

Additionally, a fine ranging from Lire 1,000,000 to Lire 10,000,000 is personally applicable to a bank's employee who signs an untrue or incomplete reply to a tax authority's inquiry. Even in case a bank simply fails to return a tax authority's general questionnaire, a fine ranging from Lire 300,000 to Lire 3,000,000 can be applied.

Finally, in case of very serious violations, the authorization to exercise banking business can be revoked.

THE ANTI-MAFIA LAW

New regulations on money laundering

20-013   Since money laundering tied to organized crime activities is viewed as a very sensitive problem in Italy, legislation aimed at preventing this phenomenon has been in existence since several years.

Under articles 648 bis and 648 ter of the Criminal Code, a person who trades monies or profits derived from certain specified crimes (robbery, larceny by extortion, kidnapping, or drug-related offenses,) or knowledgeably invests monies or profits deriving from such crimes, commits a heavily sanctioned criminal offense. In addition, a set of rules requiring banks to identify and record personal data of customers executing transactions in excess of Lire 20,000,000 was introduced by the previous Anti-Mafia Law.[10]

Similar recording requirements were introduced in connection with foreign money transfers (to and from Italy) by the so-called tax monitoring regulations.[11]

This system of identification and registration requirements has been greatly strengthened by the new Antimafia Law, which also implemented the recent European Community (EC) Directive of June 10, 1991, concerning the prevention of the use of the financial system for money laundering purposes.

In summary, the most relevant aspects of the new Antimafia Law are:

(1) Increased restrictions on the transfer of cash, bearer instruments, and other negotiable instruments;
(2) More stringent obligations of identification and registration in connection with money tranfers, and
(3) A new duty of reporting so-called "suspect transactions".

10 Law Number 55 of March 3, 1990.
11 Law Number 227 of August 4, 1990.

Increased restrictions

Pursuant to article 1 of the Antimafia Law, transfers of cash and 20-014
bearer instruments are void, if the total amount involved exceeds
Lire 20,000,000.

The same holds true in the event of several transactions, which
separately do not exceed such threshold but for their nature, time,
and manner of execution may be considered as a single transaction
exceeding the amount of Lire 20,000,000.

Transfers in excess of the Lire 20,000,000 threshold ("registrable
transactions") can only be made through so-called "authorized intermediaries", namely, governmental agencies, banks, stock brokers, SIMs (brokerage companies), investment funds, fiduciary
companies, insurance companies, and other intermediaries specifically authorized by the Ministry of Treasury.

Note that the practical result of the new restrictions is that, at
present, in Italy it is not possible to conclude any transaction with a
cash payment or payment by a freely transferable check, when the
amount involved exceeds the Lire 20,000,000 threshold.

Identification and registration requirements

According to article 2, the authorized intermediaries must identify 20-015
the person who executes a registrable transaction and/or the person on behalf of whom the registrable transaction is executed.

Moreover, the intermediaries must record the following data in
connection with any registrable transaction: date, reason and
amount, name, address and tax identification number of the person
who executes the transaction or on behalf of whom the transaction
is made.

Within 30 days of the date of a registrable transaction, all of this
data must be filed in a computerized archive held by the intermediary and kept for 10 years.

Heavy fines (Lire 5,000,000 to Lire 25,000,000) are imposed on the
staff of the intermediary in case of violations of the aforesaid identification and registration requirements. Even heavier penalties,
including imprisonment from six to 12 months, can be applied to a
person who provides false data to an intermediary when requested
by the latter in connection with a registrable transaction.

Transactions between authorized intermediaries are exempt
from the requirements in question.

Communication of "suspect transactions"

20-016 A completely unprecedented requirement has been introduced by the new Antimafia Law.

Under it, an intermediary must communicate to a high police officer any registrable transaction with respect to which the intermediary has reasons to believe that it is connected with certain specified crimes (robbery, larceny for extortion, kidnapping, or drug-related crimes.) The violation of this duty is sanctioned with a fine of up to 50 percent of the amount transferred.

In the event a registrable transaction is communicated to persons other than the high police officer, imprisonment from six to 12 months or a fine ranging from Lire 10,000,000 to Lire 100,000,000 can be applied.

CONCLUSION

20-017 The practical impact of the recent "revolution" remains to be seen. Extensive banking searches continue to be carried out in connection with organized crime investigations. Since organized crime is a significant problem in Italy, no objections are raised. However, outside of this area and, in particular, as far as the elimination of banking secrecy as a tool to prevent tax evasion is concerned, the public debate is intense.

It should be noted that there is a link between Italy's new tax legislation and the computerized archives of registrable transactions required under the new Anti-Mafia Law. The strategy of lawmakers would seem to be to have imposed this requirement not only for anti-money laundering purposes, but also to create a centralized, easily accessible "banking database". Additional legislation in this respect is being considered. Thus, the issue is likely to continue to stir controversy in Italy.

JERSEY

David Lyons
Lyons & Caplan
St. Helier, Jersey, Channel Islands

Chapter 21

JERSEY

INTRODUCTION

In order to consider the present status of banking secrecy in Jersey,   **21-001**
it is necessary to understand the constitutional position of the
Island and its close relationship with the United Kingdom Home
Office and law enforcement agencies.

It is also necessary to appreciate the close trading and commercial relationship between the Island and the United Kingdom, particularly in the development of the banking industry in the Island.
The Bank of England has lent a friendly guiding hand in the development of banking supervision in the Island.

CONSTITUTIONAL POSITION OF JERSEY

The constitutional position of the Island of Jersey is dealt with in   **21-002**
some detail in the Home Office Report of the Royal Commission on
the Constitution.[1]

This part of the report has been published by HMSO as "Relationships between the United Kingdom and the Channel Islands and
the Isle of Man" (1973). The Island of Jersey is the largest and most
populous of the Channel Islands.

---

[1] Home Office Report of the Royal Commission on the Constitution, 1969-1973,
Part XI, volume 1.

Nature of government

21-003 The Commission was required to consider whether any changes were desirable in the constitutional and economic relationships between the United Kingdom and the Channel Islands. The report starts with some general background as to how the Islands are governed and their relationships with the United Kingdom.

The Islands are dependencies of the Crown; they are neither part of the United Kingdom nor are they colonies. They have their own legislative assemblies, systems of local administration, fiscal and legal systems, and courts of law. Legislative measures passed by the Insular assemblies depend for their validity on Orders made by the Queen in Council. Subject to these prerogative powers, the Islands have general responsibility for the regulation of their own affairs.

The Channel Islands were part of the Duchy of Normandy before the Norman Conquest, but they remained in allegiance to the King of England when continental Normandy was lost in 1204. The King of England continued to rule the Islands as though he were the Duke of Normandy, observing their laws and customs and liberties which secured for them their own judiciary and freedom from process of English courts. At no times have the Islands amalgamated with or become subject to the government of the United Kingdom.

The Lieutenant Governor is the Queen's personal representative in Jersey and the official channel of communication between the Crown and the United Kingdom Government and insular authorities. The most important of the other offices held under the Crown are those of Bailiff and Deputy Bailiff who share the duties of presiding over the legislative assembly (the States) and the Royal Court; and the Attorney-General and Solicitor-General who are the legal advisers both of the Crown and of the States.

The Attorney-General is also responsible for the conduct of the Honorary Police System in Jersey whose Centeniers undertake the prosecution of minor offences in the lower (Magistrates) courts.

The constitutional position of the Islands is unique. In some respects, they are like miniature states with wide powers of self government, while their method of functioning through committees is more akin to that of the United Kingdom Local Authorities.

The Finance and Economics Committee of the States of Jersey has charge of banking supervision in Jersey and generally of the finance industry. It has the assistance of and delegates certain functions to its Economic Adviser and to the Director of the Financial Services Department (formerly the Commercial Relations Officer and the Commercial Relations Department) which acts as a company registry and which has senior officers dealing with, *inter alia*, banking supervision.

The Crown has ultimate responsibility for the good government of the Islands. The Crown acts through the Privy Council on the recommendations of the Ministers of the United Kingdom Government in their capacity as Privy Councillors. Legislative measures are submitted to the Privy Council for ratification.

Acts of United Kingdom Parliament

The Islands are not represented in the United Kingdom Parliament. **21-004** Acts of the United Kingdom Parliament do not extend to them automatically, but only if they expressly apply to the Islands.

If an Act of the United Kingdom Parliament is intended to apply to the Islands, it is so applied by order in Council with such exceptions, modifications, and adaptations made to meet the special needs of the Islands. By convention, the United Kingdom Parliament does not legislate for the Islands without their consent in matters of taxation or other matters of purely domestic concern.

The Report concludes that the United Kingdom Parliament does possess an ultimate paramount power to legislate for the Islands on all matters and in any circumstances, despite the existence of the convention that it does not legislate for the Islands without their consent on domestic and tax matters.

The Report recommended maintaining the existing constitutional relationships, either without change or furnished with additional defenses against encroachment on the Islands autonomy.

External and internal affairs

The United Kingdom Government retains executive responsibility **21-005** for the Islands' external affairs and has a residuary power to legislate to give effect to an international agreement.

The external affairs of the Island are, therefore, controlled by the Foreign Office, but the means of communication between the Islands and the United Kingdom is through the Home Office.

Jersey, therefore, has its own legislation dealing with its internal fiscal and domestic affairs. Certain United Kingdom statutes, however, do apply to Jersey, but these are generally in matters of defense, international responsibilities, and the domestic interests of the United Kingdom.

In the fight against international fraud and drug trafficking, certain United Kingdom statutes have been specifically extended to Jersey pending the enactment of local legislation and Jersey also has passed legislation essentially similar to that of the United Kingdom. This legislation has had a profound effect upon the law of banking secrecy.

Relationship with European Community

21-006 Jersey is not a member of the European Community (EC) but, in negotiating its own terms of entry, the Government of the United Kingdom negotiated terms of entry for Jersey under article 227(4) of European Economic Community (EEC) Treaty of Rome.

This allowed for free trade arrangements with the EC in industrial and agricultural products, the application of the non-discrimination clause in respect of the movement of EC citizens, and the application of the safeguard clause.

The first term allows for the continuation of free trade between the United Kingdom and Jersey, as well as the extension of this principle to the Island's trading relationships with other Community members. The non-discrimination clause will be applied so as to allow the Island a choice between granting United Kingdom Citizens the rights of movement, work, and residence which they possess currently, and extending these to other citizens of the EC, or curtailing, to the same extent, the rights in these matters of citizens of the United Kingdom and other EC Member States.

The safeguard clause allows for ad hoc measures to be taken to meet particular problems that may arise and applies only to those parts of the Treaty concerned with free trade and non-discrimination. No other provisions of the Treaty will apply to the Island, thus allowing it to maintain its financial autonomy in respect of matters such as taxation.

It is clear, however, that, insofar as the United Kingdom and its European Community partners are *ad idem* on the fight against international organized crime, Jersey will observe and - where necessary - legislate to enforce international agreements consented to by the United Kingdom.

DEVELOPMENT OF BANKING INDUSTRY

21-007 A brief synopsis of the development of banking on the Island has been prepared by G.C. Powell, the Economic Adviser to the States of Jersey. He wrote:

"Banking developed in Jersey in the 19th century along similar lines to banking in the United Kingdom. Private banks mushroomed in the early part of the century, followed by the establishment of local joint stock banks. When harsh economic times were experienced in the 1870s there was a period of banking collapse, the financial scene then being reconstructed by British enterprise and the inclusion of local banks in the wave of mergers in the early part of the 20th century which created the London Clearing Banks as known today. The process of development is typified by the history of the English and Jersey Union Bank, which opened its doors in 1862, suspended payments in 1873, and was salvaged by the Hampshire Banking Company. The latter was consolidated into the Capital and Counties Bank, which in turn amalgamated with Lloyds Bank in 1919.

The Midland absorbed the Channel Island Bank in 1897. The Jersey Commercial Bank was absorbed by Parr's Bank in 1908, which in turn merged with the London County and Westminster Bank in 1918. Barclays entered the Island in 1921 and National Provincial in 1926. The Island thus had branches of the 'big five' well established by the 1930s. The smaller clearing banks of Martins and Williams and Glyn were relatively late in arriving, the former in 1951 and the latter in 1963".[2]

Since the Economic Survey was published, Martins has merged with Barclays, National Provincial and Westminster Banks merged to become National Westminster, and Williams and Glyn was absorbed into The Royal Bank of Scotland.

Following the repeal in 1962 of the Code of 1771 which limited the rate of interest to five percent, there was a significant increase in the number of United Kingdom merchant banks which established subsidiaries in the Island. Since that date, of course, Jersey has developed and flourished as an international finance center of some significance.

As at June 1992, there were 64 registered deposit-taking institutions on the Island, being branches or subsidiaries of banks established in 17 jurisdictions around the world. Total deposits held in Jersey by these institutions amounted to £45-billion, of which £21-billion was in Sterling and £24-billion in other currencies.

[2] G. C. Powell, the Economic Adviser to the States of Jersey, *Economic Survey of Jersey*, at p. 147, paragraphs 443 and 444.

Numerous non-United Kingdom international banks and merchant banks have established branches and subsidiaries in the Island. However, United Kingdom banks dominate the local banking scene and compete in the international arena.

All banks in the Island follow United Kingdom banking practices and adapt United Kingdom banking forms for local use where changes are needed to accommodate legal differences, *e.g.*, in real property, bankruptcy, and inheritance law. Training of bankers is undertaken by the United Kingdom Institute of Bankers which has a flourishing local branch.

BANKING SECRECY AT COMMON LAW

21-008   There is no statutory law in Jersey setting out the nature and extent of the law relating to banking secrecy. It is, therefore, necessary to consider the Common Law position.

The roots of the Common Law of Jersey are the customs of Normandy and, therefore, the underlying legal philosophy of the Common Law is civil rather than English. This leads to some philosophical conflict, particularly as statutory law in Jersey is in the English language and usually follows equivalent legislation in the United Kingdom and has to be approved by the Privy Council.

In the absence of any decision of the Royal Court on the subject, Jersey law will have regard to the customary law of Normandy and to the commentators on that law in order to determine the Jersey law on a particular topic. English law, however, is also referred to, especially where Norman customary law is silent on a particular topic, and is of strong persuasive authority.

Application of English law

21-009   In the field of banking law in general and banking secrecy in particular, it is believed that the law of Jersey follows and will follow the law of England.

As outlined above, the English banks imported the banking customs and usages in use in the United Kingdom and which were in turn incorporated as implied terms into the contract between the banks in the Island and their customers.

This does not conflict with the law of contract in Jersey where the governing maxim is *la convention fait la loi des parties*. Where legislation has been introduced in Jersey relating to banks and to bankers, it closely follows English form.[3]

There are no Jersey cases setting out the basis and extent of the bankers duty of secrecy to its customers, but the Royal Court has applied English law cases relating to the nature of the contractual relationship of bank and customer[4] and has recognized the existence of a duty of confidentiality.[5]

In English law, the duty of secrecy which a bank owes to its customer is founded on the contractual relationship which exists between them. It is uncommon for this contract to be embodied in a written agreement or for the duty of secrecy to be specifically referred to. The courts, however, have implied terms into the contractual relationship which arises when a customer opens an account with a bank.[6] With respect to secrecy, the implied term can be stated as follows:

"The banker must not disclose to third persons, without the consent of the customer express or implied, either the state of the customer's account, or any of his transactions with the banker, or any information relating to the customer acquired through the keeping of his account, unless the banker is compelled to do so under the provisions of an Act of Parliament or by order of a court, or the circumstances give rise to a public duty of disclosure, or the protection of the banker's own interests requires it".[7]

In English law, therefore, the duty of secrecy falls within the civil rather than the criminal law. Breach of the duty by a banker will not give rise to criminal sanctions but to an action for damages by a customer arising from breach of contract. In neither England nor Jersey has it been felt necessary to embody the duty in statute. This contrasts with the position in many civil law jurisdictions, for example, France.

[3] See in particular the Bankers Books Evidence (Jersey) Law 1986 and the Banking Business (Jersey) Law 1991.

[4] *Viapree v. Citibank (C.I.) Limited*, 1987 Unreported Judgments 72.

[5] *Citibank (Channel Islands) Limited and Others v. Jersey Evening Post Limited and Another*, 1990, Unreported Judgments 125.

[6] See *Foley v. Hill and Others* (1848) 2 H.L.C. 28, and *Joachimson v. Swiss Bank Corporation* [1921] 3 K.B. 110, cited in the *Tournier* Case.

[7] J. Milnes Holden, *The Law and Practice of Banking* (4th ed.), p. 37, paragraph 2-16, and see *Tournier v. National Provincial and Union Bank of England* [1924] All E.R. 550.

In France, the perception of the banker as a professional rather than a commercial man under the law has been recognized by statute and his obligation of professional secrecy set out therein.[8] Any breach of duty will give rise to criminal sanctions under article 378 of the Penal Code.

The extent of the duty and the information covered by it was the subject of some disagreement between the members of the Court of Appeal in the *Tournier* case, but the judgment of Atkin L.J. was accepted by Bankes L.J.:

> "The first question is: To what information does the obligation of secrecy extend? It clearly goes beyond the state of the account, that is, whether there is a debit or a credit balance, and the amount of the balance. It must extend at least to all the transactions that go through the account, and to the securities, if any, given in respect of the account; and in respect of such matters it must, I think, extend beyond the period when the account is closed, or ceases to be an active account. It seems to me inconceivable that either party would contemplate that once the customer had closed his account the bank was to be at liberty to divulge as it pleased the particular transactions which it had conducted for the customer while he was such. I further think that the obligation extends to information obtained from other sources than the customer's actual account, if the occasion upon which the information was obtained arose out of the banking relations of the bank and its customers - for example, with a view to assisting the bank in conducting the customer's business, or in coming to decisions as to its treatment of its customers."[9]

Bankes L.J. said:

> "The case of the banker and his customer appears to me to be one in which the confidential relationship between the parties is very marked. The credit of the customer depends very largely upon the strict observance of that confidence. I cannot think that the duty of non-disclosure is confined to information derived from the customer himself or from his account. To take a simple illustration. A Police Officer goes to a bank to

[8] Law of January 24, 1984,. article 57.
[9] *Tournier, supra* n. 7, at p. 560.

make an inquiry about a customer of the bank. The Police Officer is asked why he wants the information. He replies because the customer is charged with a series of frauds. Is the banker entitled to publish that information? Surely not. He acquired the information in his character as a banker".[10]

Disclosure within a group

Where the bank is part of a group of companies, disclosure by one **21-010** company in the group to another may constitute a breach of the duty secrecy. In *Bank of Tokyo v. Karoon*,[11] there was an argument as to whether there had been a breach of the obligation of secrecy when Bank of Tokyo Trust Co. (BTTC), a New York corporation, disclosed confidential information to its parent company Bank of Tokyo (BT), a London bank.

Ackner L.J. said:

"There is an arguable case that BTTC, a separate judicial entity, owing Mr. Karoon an obligation of secrecy, broke that obligation when, without his consent, they revealed to BT [confidential information] concerning his account in New York."[12]

The Court of Appeal in the *Tournier* case also examined the cases where disclosure was justified. Bankes L.J. said:

"At the present day I think it may be asserted with confidence that the duty [of secrecy] is a legal one arising out of contract, and that the duty is not absolute but qualified. It is not possible to frame any exhaustive definition of the duty. The most that can be done is to classify the qualification, and to indicate its limits. . . . In my opinion it is necessary in a case like the present to direct the jury what are the limits and what are the qualifications of the contractual duty of secrecy implied in the relation of banker and customer. There appears to be no authority on the point. On principle I think that the qualifications can be classified under four heads: (a) where disclosure is under compulsion by law; (b) where there is a duty to the public to disclose; (c) where the interests of the bank require disclosure;

---

[10]*Id.*, at p. 555.
[11]See *Bank of Tokyo v. Karoon* [1986] 3 All E.R. 468, at pp. 475-476.
[12]*Id.*

(d) where the disclosure is made by the express or implied consent of the customer".[13]

I shall deal with these four headings where disclosure is justified in reverse order.

Disclosure made by express or implied consent of customer

21-011　With regard to express consent, any argument usually centres on the extent of disclosure pursuant to the consent.

Whether a customer has impliedly consented to the disclosure of information concerning his accounts depends upon the facts of each particular case. Where a bank gives a reference or an opinion as to the creditworthiness of a customer without express consent, it must rely upon some implied consent.[14]

The Report of the Committee on Privacy, issued by HMSO as Cmnd. 5012 (1972), recommended that banks should inform their customers of the reference system and seek a blanket express consent or an express consent on each specific occasion.

Disclosure required by interests of the bank

21-012　The most common occasion is where the bank and its customer are in litigation, for example where the bank has demanded repayment, called in its security and the customer or a guarantor is resisting.[15]

Where there is duty to the public to disclose

21-013　In *Tournier*, the court spoke about disclosure where a higher public duty of disclosure would override the private duty of secrecy. More specifically, Atkin L.J. said that the right to disclose exists "to the extent to which it is reasonably necessary. . .for protecting the bank, or persons interested, or the public, against fraud or crime".[16]

---

13 *Tournier, supra* n. 7., at p. 554.
14 See Atkin L.J., *Tournier, supra* n. 7.
15 See generally *Sunderland* v. *Barclays Bank Limited, The Times*, November 24-25, 1938, a case decided in favor of the bank on this ground and on the basis of implied consent.
16 *Tournier, supra* n. 7, at p. 461.

In the *Law of Banking*,[17] Lord Chorley suggested that in time of war disclosure would be warranted where a customer's dealings with his bank account indicate trading with the enemy. Similarly, disclosure may be warranted where such dealings indicate breach of internationally accepted United Nations trade embargoes, whether or not local statutes are specifically breached.

In *Libyan Arab Foreign Bank* v. *Bankers Trust Company*,[18] a case involving the effect of a United States Presidential Decree blocking property and interest of the Libyan Government, its agencies, instrumentalities, and controlled entities, the Libyan bank claimed, *inter alia*, damages for breach of confidence against Bankers Trust for disclosing information concerning the account of the Libyan bank with Bankers Trust London to the Federal Reserve Bank of New York.

Bankers Trust said that it was entitled to act as it did because their own interests required them to do so, because the Libyan bank must be taken impliedly to have consented, or pursuant to a higher public duty.

In brief, the facts of the case were that at 4.10 p.m. New York time on January 8, 1986, the United States President issued an immediate blocking order on Libyan property and interests. The previous day, an order had been made preventing the grant or extension of credit or loans to Libya. On the morning of January 8, 1986, Bankers Trust told the Federal Reserve Bank of New York that "it looked like the Libyans were taking their funds out of the various accounts". Staughton J. said:

"I do not accept that disclosure was required in Bankers Trust's own interests, in the sense of the first exception relied upon; or that there was implied consent by the Libyan Bank. But I have more difficulty over the point about higher public duty. In England there is statutory power in s. 4(3) of the Bank of England Act 1946, and s. 16 of the Banking Act 1979, for the Bank of England to obtain information from banks. It was not argued that I should presume a similar legal power in the New York Fed in relation to banks in New York. But presuming (as I must) that New York law on this point is the same as English law, it seems to me that the Federal Reserve Board, as the central banking system in the United States, may have a public duty to perform in obtaining information from banks. I accept the argument that higher public duty is one of the exceptions

[17] Lord Chorley, *The Law of Banking* (6th ed., 1974), at p. 23.
[18] In *Libyan Arab Foreign Bank* v. *Bankers Trust Company* [1988] Lloyd's Rep. 259.

to a banker's duty of confidence, and I am prepared to reach a tentative conclusion that the exception applied to this case".[19]

In addition to statute, a banker may be compelled to make disclosure where he is called to give evidence in a criminal prosecution or civil proceeding, there being no legal privilege protecting the banker on such occasions.[20]

However, giving information to the police investigating the case of a customer suspected of a crime would not be justified under this head.

Disclosure under compulsion of law

21-014   This is dealt with separately in the text below.

MODIFICATION OF COMMON LAW POSITION BY COMPULSION OF LAW

21-015   The Common Law position set out above which imposes the duty of secrecy has been considerably modified by statute. Initially, these modifications were designed to assist parties to civil cases or competent prosecuting authorities in criminal cases, in or outside Jersey, to obtain information.

In recent years, however, legislation has been introduced based upon similar United Kingdom legislation to meet perceived threats to Jersey's integrity as an international financial center and to discharge Jersey's duty to the international community. Certain of this legislation allows disclosure, notwithstanding that legal action has not commenced, or may never commence.

It is convenient to consider this heading under several sub-headings according to whether or not criminal or civil proceedings have commenced inside or outside Jersey.

[19] *Id.*, p. 286.
[20] *Tournier, supra* n. 7, p. 561.

Where criminal proceedings are pending in Jersey

All criminal proceedings in Jersey are prosecuted by a Centenier or **21-016** the Attorney-General. Documents or other confidential information might be obtained from a bank, or assets of a bank arrested by the police or the Attorney-General in Jersey, pursuant to an order of the court made in criminal proceedings in Jersey

Specific legislation has now largely replaced the general duty. The Banker's Books Evidence (Jersey) Law (BBEL)[21] is described as a law to amend the law of evidence with respect to banker's books.

"Bank" and "banker" mean a person who is for the time being registered under the Depositors and Investors (Prevention of Fraud) (Jersey) Law.[22] Article 6 provides that, upon the application "of any party to a legal proceeding", the court may order the inspection and copying of entries in a bankers book. Further, "in a criminal legal proceeding an order . . . may be made either with or without summoning the bank or any other party . . . ."

It will be seen that the BBEL requires, in criminal cases, for proceedings to have commenced before an order can be made. The author is not aware of any extensive use of the BBEL as a means of the prosecuting authorities in Jersey obtaining confidential information from a bank. However, it is likely that the Investigation of Fraud (Jersey) Law 1991, which does not require proceedings to have commenced, will be used extensively if the experience of the Criminal Justice Act 1987 (Jersey) Order 1989 is followed.

The Drug Trafficking Offences (Jersey) Law 1988 applies equally to criminal proceedings within and outside Jersey. Whilst not providing specifically for disclosure of information or the provision of confidential documents by a banker, it does provide for the seizure of bank accounts. An order can be made under this Law against a "defendant" who is defined as "a person against whom proceedings have been instituted for a drug trafficking offense (whether or not he has been convicted)".

Under article 9, an application may be made *ex parte* to the bailiff in chambers by or on behalf of the Attorney-General for a *saisie judiciaire*. On the making of the *saisie*, all realizable property of the defendant in the Island (including any bank accounts) shall vest in an officer of the court.

[21] Banker's Books Evidence (Jersey) Law 1986.
[22] Depositors and Investors (Prevention of Fraud) (Jersey) Law 1967 (now replaced by the Banking Business (Jersey) Law 1991).

The power under article 9 may be exercised where the court has made a confiscation order under article 3 of the Law or where, by article 8:

> "(b) (i) proceedings have been instituted in the Island against the defendant for a drug trafficking offence;
>
> (ii) the proceedings have not been concluded; and
>
> (iii) the court is satisfied that there is reasonable cause to believe that the defendant has benefited from drug trafficking; or
>
> (c) The Court is satisfied:
>
> (i) that proceedings are to be instituted outside the Island against a person for a drug trafficking offence; and
>
> (ii) that there is reasonable cause to believe that person has benefited from drug trafficking."

Article 17 of the Law is of interest (and concern) to bankers in Jersey. This article creates an offense of assisting another to retain the benefit of drug trafficking. Although knowledge or suspicion is required for the commission of the offense, under article 17(4)(a) and (b), the burden of disproving knowledge or suspicion is on the defendant.

However, if any action is committed which would otherwise constitute an offense, it does not do so if the person (banker) concerned discloses to a police officer his suspicion or belief that the funds or investments concerned are derived from or used in connection with drug trafficking or any matter on which such suspicion or belief is based, provided the disclosure is made before the act concerned and the act is done with the consent of the police officer or after the act concerned, but on the bankers own initiative and as soon as is reasonable for him to make it. Such disclosure will not be treated as a breach of the duty of confidentiality owed to the customer or potential customer.[23]

---

[23] See the Drug Trafficking Offences (Jersey) Law 1988, article 17(3).

Where civil proceedings are pending in Jersey

Where civil proceedings are commenced in the Island, the Royal   21-017
Court has powers to order particulars to be furnished, interrogatories to be delivered, and discovery and inspection of documents to
be made.[24]

These rules relate to the obtaining of information by and from
parties to a lawsuit. Information obtained in legal proceedings by
one party from another by means of the discovery process should
not be used for any purpose other than the immediate purpose for
which it was obtained unless the court so authorizes.

In granting leave for documents obtained on discovery in Jersey
proceedings to be used in Bermuda, the Royal Court has held that
there must be a common link between the proceedings. The court
will balance confidentiality against the merits of justice.[25]

Materiality and good faith

As against a non-party, the basic rule prior to the introduction of the   21-018
BBEL was that the parties to an action have no right to compel
disclosure of relevant documents in their possession.

Article 6(3) of the BBEL provides that

"In a civil legal proceeding an application for an order. . .shall
be made by summons which shall be served on the bank and
the other party and shall be supported by an affidavit showing
the materiality of the inspection and that the application is
made in good faith".

It would appear that this requirement for "materiality" and "good
faith" override the Common Law requirement of confidentiality.

At Common Law, a subpoena duces tecum could be issued by a
party to a civil action requiring the non-party to attend at the
hearing with requested documents but they are not entitled to
inspect them before the hearing unless the non-party has "facilitated the commission of the alleged wrong".[26]

The same case established that, even though the information
sought is confidential, The Royal Court of Jersey may order disclo-

---

[24]Royal Court Rules, 1982, rules 6/14, 6/15, and 6/16.
[25]*Dalamad and Others* v. *Rhone Company Limited and Another*, 1988 Unreported
Judgments 14.
[26]*In the Matter of the Representation of Lucas* (1981) J.J. 83.

sure where the interest of justice outweighs the confidentiality of that information. It is submitted that such will be the case where the information sought is relevant to the proceedings before the court.[27]

Thus, where the bank itself is not a party to the litigation, it can still be made to produce its books under *subpoena duces tecum*. It is no answer to such an order that the document is held by the institution on terms that its delivery up requires the authority of the customer.[28]

Bankers Trust v. Shapira

21-019 In *Bankers Trust Company* v. *Shapira*,[29] the Court of Appeal held that the court's powers to order discovery of information at the earliest stages of an action to assist a plaintiff to trace and recover property of which he claimed to have been wrongfully or fraudulently deprived may be exercised to require a bank to disclose material normally subject to the banker/customer obligation of confidentiality; such disclosure is, however, to be strictly confined to the purposes of the action. The above English authorities would be applied by the Jersey courts in similar cases.[30]

Injunctions or arrests may be obtained on a person's movable estate, *i.e.*, his bank account where the plaintiff has reason to believe that the defendant may otherwise dispose of his assets or remove them from the jurisdiction pending litigation. The general principles applicable to an interim injunction pending suit are those established in England.[31]

Where the plaintiff and defendant are resident outside the jurisdiction, the court will raise an injunction placed on the defendant's Jersey assets where the parties have not submitted to the court's jurisdiction, unless the plaintiff has a proprietary interest in the

---

27 See also *IBL Limited and Another* v. *Planet Financial & Legal Services Limited and Another*, 1990 Unreported Judgments 167.

28 *R* v. *Daye* [1908] 2 K.B. 333.

29 In *Bankers Trust Company* v. *Shapira* [1980] 3 All E.R. 353.

30 See *Guinness Plc* v. *Marketing & Acquisition Consultants Limited and Others* [1987-88] JLR 104, at p. 106.

31 See *Cerqueira* v. *Bilbao International Bank (Jersey) Limited and Another* (1981) J.J. 141, where the court quoted from p. 537 of *Halsbury's Laws of England* and accepted that Jersey Law was the same.

assets or is claiming to arrest the monies as a form of *saisie conservatoire*, pending an action in the Royal Court.[32]

In recent years, there have been numerous Mareva orders made in Jersey and consequent applications to the Royal Court to have the orders raised. The Royal Court has applied the principles laid down in the English authorities.[33]

As in England, it is possible to obtain an Anton Piller order from the bailiff, requiring a defendant to allow a plaintiff to enter property and search for documents, take photographs, preserve property, and take custody of and detain property, in certain circumstances. Generally, there must be a strong *prima facie* case; damages, actual or potential, must be very serious; and the defendant must have documents or material in his possession which is essential to his case, and which would be destroyed if the application was on notice.[34]

The bailiff has a general discretion to sign such orders and, again, the principles derived from English case law are generally applied. *Ex parte* injunctions have been regularly issued on affidavit evidence where some allegation of fraud or wrongdoing is made.

The above rules should not, however, allow a plaintiff to engage in a "fishing expedition", that is, discovery will not be allowed to enable a party to "fish" for witnesses or for a new case.[35]

Where criminal proceedings are pending outside Jersey

Criminal matters arising in the Island are subject to the exclusive jurisdiction of the insular courts.[36] This is now subject to the exceptions given below. The charter also stated that, with a few exceptions, English writs and other processes could not run into the Island. **21-020**

[32] *Middle East Engineering Limited* v. *Edwards* (1980) J.J. 265; *Dailey International Sales Corporation* v. *Middle East Petroleum*, 1985 Unreported Judgments 20, where the court distrained upon the defendant's bank account in the Island pursuant to an interim injunction which was raised in the action.

[33] See, for example, *A.C. Mauger & Son (Sunwin) Limited* v. *Victor Hugo Management Limited and Others*, 1989 Unreported Judgments 212 and, on appeal, 1990 Unreported Judgments 137.

[34] *Anton Piller KG* v. *Manufacturing Processes Limited and Others* [1976] 1 All E.R. 779.

[35] *Board* v. *Thomas Hedley & Co. Ltd.* [1951] 2 All E.R. 431, CA; *Edmiston* v. *B.T.C.* [1955] 3 All E.R. 823, C.A.

[36] See the Charter of Queen Elizabeth I, June 27, 1562.

However, it has been recognized by the Royal Court that every court has an inherent right to ask a foreign court to lend it assistance by hearing evidence for use in a hearing pending before it.[37]

Under the provisions of the United Kingdom's Extradition Act 1873, which applies to Jersey, a magistrate, if required to do so by a Secretary of State, for the purposes of any criminal matter (not of a political character) pending in any court or tribunal of any foreign state, must take the evidence of every witness appearing before him for the purpose. Witnesses may be compelled to attend and give evidence, answer questions and produce documents.[38]

The Evidence (Proceedings in Other Jurisdictions) (Jersey) Order 1983, extended by Order in Council the provisions of the Evidence (Proceedings in Other Jurisdictions) Act 1975 of the United Kingdom. However, the United Kingdom Act was extended only insofar as concerns criminal proceedings. By virtue of the provisions of the 1983 Order, a foreign court or tribunal may, in relation to criminal proceedings which have been instituted before it, request the Royal Court for an order making provision for obtaining evidence in Jersey and, in particular, for the examination of witnesses, either orally or in writing, or for the production of specified documents, as provided in sections 1, 2, and 5.

Under sections 3 and 5, a person cannot be compelled to give any evidence or produce any documents which he could not be compelled to give or produce in criminal proceedings in Jersey or, with exceptions, in criminal proceedings in the country of the requesting court.

The United Kingdom Customs and Excise made use of the Order to obtain documentation relating to transactions in Krugerrands from Brown Shipley (Jersey) Limited and Standard Chartered Bank (C.I.) Limited.[39]

Prosecuting authorities in other jurisdictions also have made use of the Order to obtain information from banks in the Island.[40] Some restriction on the procedures set out in the Order is imposed by section 2 of the Protection of Trading Interests Act 1980, which provides that, if it appears to the Finance and Economics Committee that (a) a requirement has been or may be imposed on a person in Jersey to produce to any court, tribunal, or authority of an overseas country any commercial document which is not within the

---

[37] *Falle* v. *Vincent* (1908) 225 Ex. 446.
[38] See *Representation of Voisin and Others* v. *Kaminski*, 1990 Unreported Judgments 149.
[39] See J.E.P., February 17, 1984, p.11.
[40] See *In re Imacu Limited* [1989] J.L.R 17.

territorial jurisdiction of that country or to furnish any commercial information to any such court, tribunal or authority or that (b) any such authority has imposed or may impose a requirement on a person or persons in Jersey to publish any such document or information, the Finance and Economics Committee may give directions for prohibiting compliance with the requirement where:

(1) The requirement infringes the jurisdiction of the United Kingdom or Jersey or is otherwise prejudicial to the sovereignty of the United Kingdom, or

(2) If compliance with the requirement would be prejudicial to the security of the United Kingdom or Jersey or to the relations of the government of the United Kingdom with the government of any other country.

Moreover, the Committee will make an order in respect of a requirement in (a) above if it is made otherwise than for the purposes of civil or criminal proceedings which have been instituted in the overseas country or if it requires a person to state what documents relevant to any such proceedings are or have been in his possession, custody, or power or to produce for the purposes of any such proceedings any documents other than particular documents specified in the requirement.

Use of the Order to obtain information has declined following the extension of section 2 of the Criminal Justice Act 1987 of the United Kingdom to Jersey by the Criminal Justice Act 1987 (Jersey) Order 1989. This Order, which had a limited life of two years, has been replaced by the Investigation of Fraud (Jersey) Law 1991. Neither the Order nor the Law require proceedings to have commenced.[41]

Where civil proceedings are pending outside Jersey

The Charter of Queen Elizabeth I, mentioned above, equally applies to civil proceedings as it does to criminal proceedings.   **21-021**

Certain judgments emanating from civil proceedings in England and Wales, Scotland, and Northern Ireland may be registered and

---

[41] See also the provisions of the Drug Trafficking Offenses (Jersey) Law 1988, pursuant to which have been made the Drug Trafficking Offenses (Designated Countries and Territories) (Jersey) Regulations 1991. These Regulations extend the provisions of the Law (with modifications) to external confiscation orders and to proceedings which have been or are to be instituted in any of 22 designated countries.

enforced in Jersey, but as yet there is no provision for the registration or enforcement of judgments obtained in other jurisdictions.[42]

By virtue of article 1 of the Service of Process and Taking of Evidence (Jersey) Law 1960 (as amended), ("the 1960 Law") and rules 2-3 of the Service of Process (Jersey) Rules 1961, it is possible to serve a person within the Island with a process or citation in any civil or commercial matter pending before a court or tribunal of a foreign country.

Articles 3 and 4 of the 1960 Law provide that the Royal Court may, where an application is made for evidence to be obtained in the Island by a requesting court for the purpose of civil proceedings which have either been instituted before the requesting court or where institution before that court is contemplated, by order make such provision for obtaining evidence in the Island as appears appropriate including, for example, the examination of witnesses, the production of documents, and the preservation of property.

However, article 4A of the 1960 Law provides that a person cannot be compelled to give any evidence which he would not be compelled to give in civil proceedings in Jersey or, in certain circumstances, in civil proceedings in the jurisdiction of the requesting court.[43]

Furthermore, a court in Jersey will not make such an order under the 1960 Law if it is shown that the request infringes the jurisdiction of Jersey or is otherwise prejudicial to the sovereignty of the United Kingdom; and a certificate signed by or on behalf of the Finance and Economics Committee to the effect that it infringes that jurisdiction or is so prejudicial shall be conclusive evidence of the fact.[44]

Where no legal proceedings are pending in Jersey or elsewhere

21-022   For some years, the Comptroller of Income Tax in Jersey has had the power to demand information from a bank concerning a customer, and the Commissioners of Income Tax may summon and examine the servants or agents of a bank regarding such matters.[45]

---

[42] See the Judgments (Reciprocal Enforcement) (Jersey) Law 1960 and related provisions; and the Protection of Trading Interests Act 1980, section 5-7, as extended to Jersey.

[43] See *Wrigley and Others* v. *Dick*, 1989 Unreported Judgments 193c.

[44] Protection of Trading Interests Act 1980 section 4 ,.

[45] Income Tax (Jersey) Law 1961, articles 17, 18, and 35 .

In respect of information obtained by the insular authorities regarding taxation, such information is treated in the strictest confidence.[46]

However, the Jersey taxation authorities may exchange information with the United Kingdom and Guernsey taxation authorities for the purposes of carrying out the provisions of the double taxation relief agreements concluded with those jurisdictions or for the prevention of fraud or for the administration of statutory provisions against legal avoidance in relation to the taxes which are subject to such agreements.[47]

More recent developments have enabled prosecuting authorities both within and outside the Island to obtain confidential information from bankers within the Island in circumstances where proceedings have not been commenced against the bank's customer and may never commence.

Balancing individual and societal interests

The balance between the rights of the individual to confidentiality 21-023 in respect of his business with his bankers and of society is held by the Attorney-General under this legislation, and it is not possible to perceive how he achieves that balance.

It appears that any allegation of fraud or other major crime by a prosecuting authority will result in the issue of an order by the Attorney-General.

This follows from the introduction of the Criminal Justice Act 1987 (Jersey), Order 1989. By this Order in Council, section 2 of the Criminal Justice Act 1987 of the United Kingdom was extended to Jersey for an initial period of two years. Upon expiry, it was replaced by the Investigation of Fraud (Jersey) Law 1991.

It is interesting to note that the Order gave powers to the Attorney-General only in respect of offenses being investigated by the Serious Fraud Office in the United Kingdom. Section 2 conferred sweeping powers upon the Attorney-General to order the person under investigation "or any other person whom he has reason to believe has relevant information to answer questions or otherwise furnish information . . .".

[46] First Schedule to the Income Tax (Jersey) Law 1961.
[47] Double Taxation Relief (Arrangement with the United Kingdom) (Jersey) Act 1952, article 10(1); Double Taxation Relief (Arrangement with Guernsey) (Jersey) Act 1956, article 10(1).

Section 2(2) confers similar sweeping powers to order the production and copying of documents.

No requirement to commence criminal proceedings

21-024   The Act broke new ground in that no criminal proceedings need be commenced. The powers of the Attorney-General were exercisable "only on a request made by the Director of the Serious Fraud Office . . ." in any case in which it appears to him that there is "good reason to do so for the purpose of investigating the affairs, or any aspect of the affairs, of any person."

If the Attorney-General is satisfied that a person has failed to comply with a notice or that it is not practicable to serve notice or that "the service of such a notice . . . might seriously prejudice the investigation. . ." he may issue a warrant to enter and search premises and to take possession of documents.

There is power for the Attorney General to enter into agreements for the supply of information on the basis of limited disclosure and for non-disclosure on the basis of legal privilege. Section 2(10) provides:

> "A person shall not. . .be required to disclose information or produce a document in respect of which he owes an obligation of confidence by virtue of carrying on any banking business unless -
>
> (a) the person to whom the obligation of confidence is owed consents to the disclosure or production; or
>
> (b) the Attorney General has authorised the making of the requirement."

It is a criminal offense to fail to comply with a notice or to make false or misleading statements as this effectively reverses the principle of innocence until proven guilty. It is also an offense to conceal or destroy documents which a person "knows or suspects are or would be relevant" to an investigation into serious or complex fraud.

The Law contains identical provisions to the Order, save that there are no references to the Serious Fraud Office. The Attorney-General now has equivalent powers in respect of investigations into crimes both inside and outside the Island.

Company Securities (Insider Dealing) (Jersey) Law 1988

Two other statutes also give to prosecuting and supervisory **21-025** authorities in the Island wide powers to obtain information from bankers and others which may be confidential.

Article 15 of the Company Securities (Insider Dealing) (Jersey) Law 1988 provides that, if it appears to the Finance and Economics Committee that there are circumstances suggesting that there may have been "insider dealing" in contravention of the Law or that there may have been a contravention of the laws of another country or territory relating to insider trading and that a person in the Island:

> "(i) may have been concerned (directly or indirectly) in any such contravention; or

> (ii) may have information or documents which may be of assistance in the investigation of such contravention

> then the Finance and Economics Committee may appoint inspectors to investigate and report. By article 15(3) such inspectors may require a person who they consider is or may be able to give information concerning such contravention:

> (a) to produce to them any document . . .

> (b) to attend before them; and

> (c) otherwise to give . . . assistance. . .

> and it shall be the duty of that person to comply with that requirement".

There are exceptions in article 15(7) in respect of legal professional privilege, and article 15(8) refers specifically to bankers. That article states that:

> "Nothing in this article (15) shall require a person carrying on the business of banking to disclose any information or produce any document relating to the affairs of a customer unless:

> (a) The customer is a person who the inspectors have reason to believe may be able to give information concerning a suspected contravention; and

(b) the (Finance and Economics) Committee is satisfied that the disclosure or production is necessary for the purpose of the investigation".

Banking Business (Jersey) Law 1991

21-026   Finally, it should be noted that, on October 1, 1991, the Banking Business (Jersey) Law 1991 (BBL), which replaces the Depositors and Investors (Prevention of Fraud) (Jersey) Law 1967, came into force.

The BBL draws extensively upon the Banking Act 1987 of the United Kingdom to provide a "banking supervisory infrastructure". In the Report which accompanied the presentation of the proposed Law to the States of Jersey on July 3, 1990, it was stated:

> "Whilst the States of Jersey is not required to alter its laws in compliance with European Community Banking Directives, the Finance and Economics Committee recognises the need to adopt similar prudential requirements for its banks in areas like capital adequacy, consolidated supervision, financial reporting standards and so on. The Committee has also for many years through its officers played a part in the work of the Basle Committee on Banking Supervision established under the Bank for International Settlements. The Basle Committee has been successful in encouraging not only the gradual convergence of supervisory standards but also co-operation between national authorities by promoting the development of supervisory policies. One of its main achievements has been agreement on the Concordat, revised in 1983 and supplemented in 1990, which sets out the principles for determining the shared responsibilities for banks' international establishments. This Jersey seeks to follow. Another has been the securing of international convergence of capital measurement and capital standards for banks which again Jersey has implemented. The legislative framework must keep pace and be flexible enough to cope with these developments. The new Banking Business (Jersey) Law seeks to reflect this changing environment".

Although the BBL is concerned with the licensing and supervision of banks in the Island (which function is exercised by the Finance and Economics Committee), Part II of the Law gives power to the Committee to obtain from a bank "prudential information" on a regular basis to assist the Committee in carrying out its functions under the Law.

The Committee also may call for accountants reports and the urgent production of "relevant documents and information". For the first time, the Committee is able to appoint persons to carry out investigations on its behalf into the nature, conduct, or state of business of a bank. These extensive powers are contained in articles 25, 26, and 27 of the Law.

An offense of obstructing investigations is created by article 30 where a person who knows or suspects that an investigation is being or is likely to be carried out ". . . falsifies, conceals, destroys or otherwise disposes of, or causes or permits the falsification, concealment destruction or disposal of documents which he knows or suspects. . ." are relevant to the investigation. He will escape conviction if he proves lack of intent. The burden of proof is again reversed.

Inevitably, confidential information concerning the business of the bank and perhaps of its customers will be obtained by the Committee and/or its inspectors. While Part IV of the Law provides for restrictions on the disclosure of any information obtained from banks for the purpose of the Law, there are exceptions.

Disclosure may be made:

(1) To auditors and others for the purpose of enabling the Committee to discharge its functions under the law;

(2) To persons exercising any other statutory function in the Island and designated by the States in Regulations; this could apply to a situation where inspectors have been appointed under other Jersey legislation, e.g., Company Securities (Insider Dealing) (Jersey) Law 1988;

(3) To other regulatory authorities in territories outside the Island who are carrying out similar functions to those of the Committee (for example, the Bank of England) or who are supervising other financial areas (for example, the Securities and Investments Board in the United Kingdom); and

(4) In connection with the institution of criminal proceedings and in various other cases.

These provisions are contained in articles 41, 42, 43, 44, and 45 of the Law.

CONCLUSION

21-027   The duty of secrecy which is owed by a banker to his customer is alive and well. Customers not involved in crime can still enforce their contractual rights.

However, the statute law examined above which has been introduced to assist in the efforts against international crime in general and drug trafficking and money laundering in particular have imposed public duties or obligations on bankers which overrides the private (contractual) duty to their customers.

Bankers in Jersey have adopted or have been forced to adopt a much more critical approach to new customers and new business and are more observant of transactions placed through customers accounts. In common with their brethren in the outside world, they are conscious of their reputation in the eyes of their regulators.

In many ways, the new laws have been of positive benefit to bankers anxious in previous years to cooperate in criminal investigation but caught in difficult legal grey areas. The existence of clearly defined laws is of positive assistance. There may be some danger now of too many overlapping laws.

The Jack Committee on Banking Services in the United Kingdom which reported in 1989 recommended that all existing statutory exemptions from the duty of confidentiality should be consolidated into one statute.[48] This may be appropriate to Jersey which might also benefit from a clear and unequivocal statement of the principle of customer confidentiality save as set out in such a statute.

Although not a full member of The Basle Committee on Banking Regulation and Supervisory Practices ("the Committee"), Jersey is a member of the Offshore Group which is a sub-group of the Committee and which meets at the same time as the Committee. In December 1988, the Committee issued a paper on the "Prevention of Criminal Use of the Banking System for the Purpose of Money-Laundering". This paper was accompanied by a Statement of Principles which provides:

> "Banks and other financial institutions may unwittingly be used as intermediaries for the transfer or deposit of money derived from criminal activity. The intention behind such transactions is often to hide the beneficial ownership of funds. The use of the financial system in this way is of direct concern to police and other law enforcement agencies; it is also a

48 HMSO Cmnd. 622, recommended at p. 37.

matter of concern to banking supervisors and banks' manage-
ments, since public confidence in banks may be undermined
through their association with criminals.

With a view to ensuring that the financial system is not used as
a channel for criminal funds, banks should make reasonable
efforts to determine the true identity of all customers requesting the institution's services. Particular care should be taken to
identify the ownership of all accounts and those using safe-
custody facilities. All banks should institute effective procedures for obtaining identification from new customers. It
should be explicit policy that significant business transactions
will not be conducted with customers who fail to provide
evidence of their identity.

. . . As regards transactions executed on behalf of customers, it
is accepted that banks may have no means of knowing whether
the transaction stems from or forms part of criminal activity.
Similarly, in an intentional context it may be difficult to ensure
that cross-border transactions on behalf of customers are in
compliance with the regulations of another country. Nevertheless, banks should not set out to offer services or provide active
assistance in transactions which they have good reason to
suppose are associated with money-laundering activities.

Banks should co-operate fully with national law enforcement
authorities to the extent permitted by specific local regulations
relating to customer confidentiality. Care should be taken to
avoid providing support or assistance to customers seeking to
deceive law enforcement agencies through the provision of
altered, incomplete, or misleading information. Where banks
become aware of facts which lead to the reasonable presumption that money held on deposit derives from criminal activity
or that transactions entered into are themselves criminal in
purpose, appropriate measures, consistent with the law,
should be taken, for example, to deny assistance, sever relations with the customer and close or freeze accounts"

The December 1988 Statement of Principles concludes:

"All banks should formally adopt policies consistent with the
principles set out in this Statement and should ensure that all
members of their staff concerned, wherever located, are informed of the bank's policy in this regard. Attention should be
given to staff training in matters covered by the Statement. To
promote adherence to these principles, banks should imple-

ment specific procedures for customer identification and for retaining internal records of transactions. Arrangements for internal audit may need to be extended to establish an effective means of testing for general compliance with the Statement".

This Statement was circulated to Jersey Bankers by the Finance and Economics Committee and was followed, in July 1991, by the circulation of detailed guidance notes on money laundering and advice on "policies procedures and controls" to prevent bankers unwitting assistance.

There is no doubt that Jersey is and will continue to be party to international efforts to combat organized crime, but this policy should in no way cause any grief to the law-abiding banker and customer. As the Bailiff, Sir Peter Crill, said in *Citibank (Channel Islands) Limited and Others* v. *Jersey Evening Post Limited and Another*:

> "It cannot be said too often that the Island's success in financial circles depends on the strictest confidentiality being observed by all to whom confidences are given . . .".[49]

Note: The author wishes to acknowledge the advice and assistance of Advocate P. R. Cushen of Crills and, in particular as to French law, T. P. Clemens-Jones of Holman Fenwick & Willan, Paris, France.

---

[49] *Citibank (Channel Islands) Limited and Others* v. *Jersey Evening Post Limited and Another*, 1990 Unreported Judgments 125.

LIECHTENSTEIN

Andreas Batliner
Dr. Dr. Batliner & Partner
Vaduz, Liechtenstein

Chapter 22

LIECHTENSTEIN

INTRODUCTION

Historical Perspective

The Principality of Liechtenstein, with its 160 square kilometers, is one of the smallest countries in Europe. It is situated between Switzerland and Austria, consists of 11 villages, and numbers some 29,000 inhabitants. In 1699 and 1712, Prince Johann Adam Andreas purchased the Lordship of Schellenberg and the County of Vaduz and, in 1719, he united them in the Principality of Liechtenstein.   22-001

In 1806, Liechtenstein achieved full sovereignty through admission to Napoleon's Confederation of the Rhine. From 1815 to 1866, the country was a member of the German Confederation, and today it is the only State of that alliance to have remained independent.

After the collapse of the Austro-Hungarian monarchy at the close of the World War I, Liechtenstein's parliament abrogated the customs treaty with Austria-Hungary and began negotiations with Switzerland.

In 1921, a new Constitution was introduced and is still in effect today. Two years later, the Customs Treaty with Switzerland was signed. Since that time, there has been a customs union between the two countries.

In the 1920s, many new statutes were enacted, among others the Persons and Companies Act (PGR) of 1926 and the Law of Trust Enterprises of 1928.

After 1945, Liechtenstein experienced extraordinary development, making it one of the most highly industrialized and richest countries in the world.

Since 1921, the Principality of Liechtenstein has been a "constitutional hereditary monarchy on a democratic and parliamentary foundation." This means that the Prince and the people govern jointly, that neither the Prince nor the people can make laws without the consent of the other entity.

The people are represented by Liechtenstein's Parliament (*Landtag*), composed of 25 deputies. Only two parties are represented in the Parliament of Liechtenstein. Both are conservative-liberal and, since 1938, they have formed a coalition government.

Liechtenstein also has a modern system of justice. Jurisdiction in civil and penal matters is exercised on three judicial levels. Matters of public law are the province of administrative review by administrative court (*Verwaltungsbeschwerdeinstanz*) and the State Court of Justice (*Staatsgerichtshof*) as constitutional court.

Liechtenstein is a member of the International Court of Justice at The Hague, the European Free Trade Association (EFTA), a number of special United Nations organizations, the Council of Europe, and the Conference for Security and Cooperation in Europe (CSCE). Since 1990, Liechtenstein has been a full member of the United Nations.

Economically, Liechtenstein is almost totally unified with Switzerland. In addition to the Customs Treaty of 1924, Liechtenstein and Switzerland have concluded several other important treaties, such as the Postal Treaty, the Currency Treaty, the Patent Treaty and treaties in the area of social security. Liechtenstein's currency is the Swiss franc, and banking practices are similar to those of Switzerland.

Banking in the Principality of Liechtenstein

22-002   In 1861, the first Liechtenstein bank, the *Zins- und Credit-Landes-Anstalt*, now the *Liechtensteinische Landesbank* (LLB, National Bank of Liechtenstein), was founded. This bank is an independent public-law institution, chartered by a statute of its own and owned by the State of Liechtenstein.

The Bank in Liechtenstein AG (BIL) was founded by a group of investors in 1920. Later, the Prince of Liechtenstein invested money in the bank. Since then, the princely family, or the Prince of Liechtenstein Foundation, has been majority stockholder of the BIL.

In 1956, the *Verwaltungs- und Privat-Bank AG* (VPB, Private Trust Bank Corporation) was founded. Like the BIL, it is in the nature of a private bank, whose majority stockholder is likewise a Liechtenstein private-law foundation.

There is a fourth bank, the Sinit Bank AG, with a limited banking concession. But, since it is practically inactive, it will not be mentioned again here. A fifth bank, Neue Bank AG, was established in Spring 1992.

The favorable conditions for strong growth of the Liechtenstein bank lie especially in the economic and political stability of the country, liberal company and tax law and the associated multitude of Liechtenstein holding and domiciliary companies, banking legislation, banking secrecy, and specifically the Swiss franc. In January 1920, Liechtenstein unilaterally declared the Swiss franc to be the official currency of the country, and created the appropriate foundation in the Act of May 26, 1924, concerning introduction of the franc currency.

By the treaty between Switzerland and the Principality of Liechtenstein of March 29, 1923, concerning adjunction of the Principality of Liechtenstein to the customs territory of Switzerland (Customs Treaty), a customs union was created. A currency union had existed *de facto* since 1920, but it was officially created with clear rules of international law by the Currency Treaty of June 18, 1980.

The Landesbank is chartered under an express statute. Today, this is the Act of November 4, 1981, concerning the *Liechtensteinische Landesbank* (LBG). The other banks were not regulated by statute until the Banking Act (BaG) of 1960, the Act of December 21, 1960, concerning banks and savings funds), which, with certain amendments, remains in force. Liechtensteinian banking legislation is patterned after Swiss law.

Liechtenstein banks are subject to surveillance by the Liechtenstein Banking Commission and by the Government of Liechtenstein. In addition, under the Currency Treaty with Switzerland, they are bound to report to the National Bank of Switzerland and to observe its rules on capitalization and liquidation. This applies to the Landesbank, as well.

Growth of the three Liechtenstein banks has been rapid in recent decades. Thus, the balance sheet total for all three rose from SFr. 38-million in 1945 to SFr. 244-million in 1960, SFr. 1,479-million in 1970, SFr. 4,364-million in 1980, and SFr. 17,348-million in 1990. The 1990 balance sheet totals were SFr. 6,516- million for the Landesbank, SFr. 6,967-million for the Bank in Liechtenstein AG, and SFr. 3,865-million for the *Verwaltungs- und Privat-Bank AG*.

DEFINITION OF BANKING SECRECY

Neither the Landesbank Act (LBG) nor the Banking Act (BaG) **22-003** contains a definition of the term "banking secrecy". Still, the term "banking secrecy" is used in article 48 of the Landesbank Act, though not in the Banking Act.

Article 47, paragraph 1, letter b), of the Banking Act mentions "obligation of reticence" and "professional secrecy". Nevertheless, it is undisputed that banking secrecy is what is meant, for private-law banks, as well. The term "banking secrecy" may be defined step by step, as follows.[1]

"Secrecy:

By a secret is meant facts known to certain persons only and not to become known to others.

Private Secrecy:

Private secrets are facts in the private life of a private individual that relate to his personal affairs (including his affairs of property), are known only to himself or certain individuals, and are not to become known to others.

Professional Secrecy:

Professional secrets are a third party's private secrets entrusted by him (repositor) to a certain circle of persons qualified by their profession (repositees).

Banking Secrecy:

A bank's professional secrecy is called banking secrecy. It embraces all secrets entrusted to a bank by its customers. A special relationship of confidentiality exists between the bank and the customer."

The bank's own business and operating secrets are not subject to banking secrecy.

Banking secrecy - like any professional secrecy - presents itself in two legally distinguishable manifestations and, accordingly, has two different meanings.

First, banking secrecy means the obligation of a bank to give no information concerning the banking connections of a customer or other facts having come to its knowledge because of the business connection, absent exceptional provisions of statute.

---

[1] S. Sichtermann, *Bankgeheimnis und Bankauskunft* [Banking Secrecy and Banking Information] (Frankfurt-am-Main, 1984), 3rd ed., at p. 31.

Second, banking secrecy means the bank's right to withhold information concerning a customer's accounts and situation.[2]

In this connection, reference also may be made to the legal definition of banking secrecy in section 23, paragraph 1, of the Austrian Banking Act (*Kreditwesengesetz*):

> "The banks. . .may not divulge or use secrets. . . entrusted or made accessible to them exclusively by reason of their business connection with customers (banking secrecy)".

To be distinguished from banking secrecy is the official secrecy of officials and authorities in the performance of their duties.[3] The question arises whether the Landesbank, and its agents and employees, in addition to banking secrecy, are perhaps subject to official secrecy as well.

Here, sections 302 *et seq.* of the Penal Code (StGB) must be read with the legal term "officials" in section 74, number 4 thereof. According to this, "an official is anyone appointed . . . to perform legal acts in the name . . . of another public law person . . .".

According to article 1, paragraph 1, Landesbank Act, the Landesbank is an independent public law institution having its own legal personality. This at least suggests that the Landesbank is subject to official secrecy as well. Against this, however, in general, the term "official" in section 74, paragraph 4, Penal Code, does not subsume the activity of independent economic bodies (*e.g.*, carrier operations).[4]

Yet a close inquiry should be made whether official secrecy does apply to the Landesbank. For there is the consideration that the Landesbank clearly partakes of sovereign authority. Thus, for example, according to article 42, Landesbank Act, the books and statements as well as the instruments executed for public registers by the Landesbank have the evidential force of public instruments. According to articles 43-45, Landesbank Act, the Landesbank has privileged executory rights, within the scope of which even a bare application for execution made by the Landesbank constitutes a judgment in the sense of the Executory Code, so that neither court

---

[2] Heinz J. Frommelt, *Das liechtensteinische Bankgeheimnis* [Banking Secrecy in Liechtenstein] (Zurich, 1988), at pp. 15-24.

[3] Sichtermann, *supra* n. 1, at p. 39.

[4] Foregger-Serini, StGB [Penal Code], MKK (Vienna, 1988), 4th ed., Commentary IV.2 on number 4, section 74, Penal Code.

judgment nor similar verdict of an independent forum is required for compulsory execution.[5]

STATUTORY FOUNDATIONS

22-004 The statutes of Liechtenstein contain no legal definition or other explicit provision as to the content of banking secrecy (see text above). The content and scope of banking secrecy must be derived and ascertained primarily from general provisions and principles of private law (see text below).

However, the protection of banking secrecy arises not only from private law but also and especially from (public law) banking legislation and law on professions (see text below).

Banking Act (BaG)

22-005 The Banking Act contains only a penal protective provision in favor of banking secrecy. Article 47 provides:

"1) One who deliberately

a) . . .

b) As an officer, official, bank employee, auditor or auditor's assistant, Banking Commission member, official or employee of its secretariat, breaches professional secrecy and the obligation of reticence [or] who procures or seeks to procure such breach, . . . shall be punishable. . .

2) If the perpetrator has acted through negligence, he shall be punishable . . . .[6]

---

[5] Article 1, letter r), Executory Code; Principality of Liechtenstein Superior Court Decision of January 10, 1986, LES 1986, at p. 57.

[6] The nature of the punishable act and the penalty rates were amended by the Penal Law Adaptation Act of May 20, 1987, LGBl. 1988, number 38, to the effect that the offense under article 47, paragraph 1, Banking Act, and article 48, paragraph 1, Landesbank Act, constitutes a misdemeanor punishable by detention for up to six months or fine of up to 360 per diem rates, whereas that under article 47, paragraph 2, Banking Act, and article 48, paragraph 2, Landesbank Act, constitutes an infraction punishable by fine of up to SFr. 20,000 or, if not collectable, detention for up to three months.

The Banking Act thus protects banking secrecy and thereby acknowledges the existence and subsistence thereof.

Landesbank Act (LBG)

The Landesbank Act, in article 25, under the heading "Reticence", **22-006** contains a formulation of the specification of banking secrecy by content, in that it provides:

> "All offices and governing bodies of the Landesbank and all its employees are laid under a duty of strictest reticence concerning the business relations of the Landesbank with its clientele as well as concerning their situation as to earnings and assets. This obligation shall continue in effect even after quitting the service of the Landesbank."

Penal protection follows in article 48 of the Landesbank Act, which, in terms similar to those of article 47 of the Banking Act, provides:

"1) One who deliberately

a) As a member of the directorate, member of the supervisory board, employee of the Landesbank or auditor, breaches banking secrecy or the duty of reticence, or who procures or seeks to procure such breach;

b) . . .

c) . . .

. . . shall be punishable. . .

2) If the perpetrator has acted through negligence, he shall be punishable . . . .[7]

---

[7] Id.

Attorney-at-Law Act and Penal Code (StGB)

22-007 Somewhat surprisingly, the Act concerning attorneys-at-law, legal advisers, trustees, auditors and patent attorneys,[8] under the heading "Professional Obligations and Disciplinary Power", also contains provisions on the obligation of reticence and supervision thereof. Thus, article 33 of the Attorney-at-Law Act provides:

> "Trustees, auditors, patent attorneys, banks and managers of banks. . .are to perform their duties conscientiously and honestly, and safeguard the honor and dignity of the profession by their conduct. They shall be bound to reticence concerning the matters entrusted to them. Statutory provisions concerning duties of witnesses and the duty of information vis-à-vis an authority are reserved."

Article 34, paragraph 1, Attorney-at-Law Act, provides:

> "Disciplinary power over trustees, auditors, patent attorneys, banks and managers of banks . . . shall be exercised by the Superior Court."

The background of these provisions is that banks, under article 29, paragraph 4, Attorney-at-Law Act, are authorized by statute, through the banking concession, in other words, without special trusteeship grant, to engage in the business of exercising the trusteeship services designated in article 29, paragraph 2, Attorney-at-Law Act.

These fiduciary activities include the assumption of trusteeships (letter a), administration of assets (letter b), and financial counseling (letter d). Hence, if banks are by statute trustees in the sense of the Attorneys-at-Law Act, they must be subject to the same professional obligation and the same disciplinary power as trustees.[9]

Banks, therefore, as to their services in the sense of the Attorney-at-Law Act, are subject by article 33 thereof to the rules of the guild and the obligation of reticence. Supervision and protection are exercised, according to article 34, Attorney-at-Law Act, as a matter of disciplinary law, by the Principality of Liechtenstein Superior Court.

---

[8] Of November 13, 1968, LGBl. 1968, number 33, in the version of Statutes of July 5, 1979, LGBl. 1979, number 44, and April 29, 1987, LGBl. 1987, number 29.

[9] Report and Recommendation of the Parliamentary Commission to Deliberate on a Statute To Amend the Statute concerning Attorneys-at-Law, Legal Advisers, Trustees, Auditors and Patent Attorneys, Vaduz, April 10, 1987, p. 12.

However, there is also penal protection for the obligation of reticence. Section 121, paragraph 1, Penal Code provides:

> "One who divulges or uses a secret entrusted or made accessible to him
>
> 1. ...
>
> 2. As attorney-at-law, legal advisor, trustee, auditor or patent attorney,
>
> 3. ...
>
> 4. ... and the divulgation or use of which is of a nature to injure a legitimate interest of the person who engaged his services or for whom they were engaged, shall be punishable by detention for up to six months or by fine of up to 360 per diem rates."

This penal provision also must apply to banks in those areas in which they engage in activities under the Attorney-at-Law Act and so are, by statute, trustees in the sense of the Act.

However, it must be left unsettled as to the relationship which banking legislation and the Attorney-at-Law Act have to each other; in particular, whether indeed every assumption of trusteeships and every administration of assets or counseling by a bank is a fiduciary activity under the Attorney-at-Law Act and hence subject to its provisions. In practice, the banks do not always abide by the Attorney-at-Law Act, at least not by the prohibition against business denominations of importunate effect[10] or the prohibition against advertising.[11]

Law of Contract

The customer stands in a contractual relationship with the bank. **22-008** Appropriate provisions concerning the obligation of reticence on the part of the bank may figure in the contract.

But, even if no such contractual provisions are explicitly stipulated, there is a duty of reticence on the part of the bank. In this respect, a distinction is to be made between two groups of contracts.

---

[10] Ordinance of October 31, 1972, LGBl. 1972, number 57.
[11] Pursuant to general canons of professional ethics; ELG 1967-1972, at p. 54; ELG 1973-1978, at p. 127; LES 1984, at p. 13.

If there is an agency or contractual relationship in the nature of an agency, the provision of sections 1002 *et seq.* of the General Civil Code concerning the "agency contract" are applicable. From the provision of section 1009, General Civil Code, a general obligation of trust and specifically an obligation of reticence on the part of the agent arises:.

> "From the fact that the business relationship between customer and bank is one of confidence, a far-reaching obligation of reticence on the part of the bank towards the customer is derived."[12]

It is further provided:

> "The obligation of reticence embraces all that has been entrusted to his man of business by the client and/or has come to his knowledge in connection with the transaction of business, and in some particular cases otherwise, concerning which it has been stated or is apparent to him that disclosure would injure the client's interest, to wit not matter whether disclosure leads to material or merely immaterial disadvantages (cf. EvBl 1988/5)."[13]

For those contracts and legal relations with a bank which are not subject to the law of agency under sections 1002 *et seq.*, General Civil Code, the legal doctrine derives the bank's obligation of reticence from the general principle of trust in the law of obligations. The contracting parties would have known, or should have known, that it was in accordance with the custom of the trade to observe banking secrecy. Hence, the contracting parties would, at least tacitly, stipulate the obligation of reticence.[14]

---

[12] Stanzel, in Klang, *Kommentar zum Allgemeinen bürgerlichen Gesetzbuch* [Commentary on the General Civil Code] (Vienna, 1968) 2nd ed., section 1009, at p. 820.

[13] Strasser, in Rummel, *Kommentar zum Allgemeinen bürgerlichen Gesetzbuch* [Commentary on the General Civil Code] (Vienna, 1990), 2nd ed., volume 1, marg. 20, on section 1009.

[14] Maurice Aubert, Jean-Philippe Kernen, and Herbert Schönle, *Das schweizerische Bankgeheimnis* [Banking Secrecy in Switzerland] (Berne, 1978), at p. 33.

For the Principality of Liechtenstein Supreme Court, observance of banking secrecy is an incidental obligation resting upon the principle of trust, even in contracts lacking any element of the law of agent and principal.[15]

In Germany, the bank's obligation of reticence is even regarded as customary law.[16] Such a construction of banking secrecy, as a matter of customary law, is no longer required in Austria since the Banking Act of 1979 went into effect.[17]

These principles also hold for the pre-contractual relationship, even when no contract comes to be concluded.[18]

Law of Personal Rights

Banking secrecy is rooted in the law of personal rights.[19] The Liechtensteinian Persons and Companies Act (PGR) of January 20, 1926, contains provisions, in articles 38 *et seq.* thereof, on "protection of personal rights". Article 39, PGR, protects against attacks from without, and provides:

22-009

> "One who is unwarrentedly injured or threatened in his personal situation (rights of personal privacy), as for example in correspondence, business and similar relationships, and in the right to respect and dignity of the person, except insofar as rights of personal privacy. . .are regulated by special statute, and insofar as their protection is compatible with the interests of his fellow men . . .".

Thus, article 39, paragraph 1, PGR, is the fundamental and central rule concerning the subsistence and the content of banking secrecy, and moreover confers the corresponding claims at private law upon the protected person (see text below).

The provisions of articles 38 *et seq.*, PGR, expressly apply, according to article 115 thereof, to legal persons as well, who enjoy "the same protection of personal rights as natural persons. In particular, they [the legal persons] are protected in their right to . . . secrets of correspondence, business, and others meriting protection".

[15] Principality of Liechtenstein Supreme Court Decision of October 25, 1989, A 234/88.

[16] Sichtermann, *supra* n. 3, at pp. 62 *et seq.*

[17] Peter Avancini, in Avancini-Iro-Koziol, *Östrreichisches Bankvertragsrecht* [Austrian Law of Banking Agreements] (Vienna, 1987), volume I, marg. 2/4.

[18] Aubert-Kernen-Schönle, *supra* n. 14, at pp. 33 *et seq.*

[19] Principality of Liechtenstein Supreme Court Decision, *supra* n. 15.

Other Points

22-010 On June 19, 1980, the Principality of Liechtenstein and the Confederation of Switzerland signed a Currency Treaty, which went into effect on November 25, 1981.[20]

Thereafter, the National Bank of Switzerland, vis-à-vis persons in the Principality of Liechtenstein, in particular vis-à-vis banks, has exercised the same powers as vis-à-vis banks and other persons in Switzerland. Accordingly, the Currency Treaty provides that all Swiss provisions, legal and administrative, concerning monetary, credit, and currency policy shall be valid in the Principality of Liechtenstein, as well. But the National Bank of Switzerland is likewise subject to a strict obligation of secrecy, to wit firstly under the provision of international law in article 4 of the Currency Treaty (Observance of Secrecy), and secondly under the Swiss law applicable in Liechtenstein, as provided by article 16k, paragraph 4, National Bank of Switzerland Act, and article 9, Swiss Banking Act.

LEGAL CONSEQUENCES OF BREACH OF BANKING SECRECY

Civil Law consequences

Extra-contractual liability

22-011 Article 39, Persons and Companies Act (PGR), contains the central provision concerning banking secrecy. This provision of law holds in principle vis-à-vis everyone and, above all, extra-contractually.

The legal consequences of violation of rights of personal privacy by third parties are contained in articles 39-41, PGR. Article 39, paragraph 1, PGR, confers an affirmation and a claim to removal of the injury, to restoration of the status in *quo erat*, and to cessation of further injuries. All of these claims subsist even if there is no fault of the injuring party.

With fault of the injuring party, the injured party, under article 40, paragraph 1, PGR, has a claim for damages, as well. Article 40, paragraph 2, PGR, confers a further claim to payment of a sum of

---

[20] On the Currency Treaty, see LGBl. 1981, number 52; Emil-Heinz Batliner, *Der Währungsvertrag Schweiz-Liechtenstein - mit einem währungsgeschichtlichen Rückblick* [The Swiss-Liechtenstein Currency Treaty - With a Review of Monetary History] (Vaduz, 1981).

money as satisfaction (for immaterial damage) if warranted by the special severity of the injury and by deliberate fault.

In the case of malice, the court may award other forms of satisfaction in lieu of or in addition to the sum of money, as for example a court declaration of honor, publication of the judgment, or donation of a sum of money to a benevolent institution, as provided by article 40, paragraph 3, PGR.

Article 41, paragraph 1, PGR, incidentally, makes supplementary reference to "provision concerning illicit acts". These are chiefly the provisions of sections 1293 *et seq.*, General Civil Code, concerning the law of damages and satisfaction, and section 47, Final Part, PGR, concerning master's liability for servants.[21]

Article 38, Banking Act, likewise refers to sections 1273 *et seq.*, General Civil Code, and to section 47, Final Part, PGR.

Pre-contractual liability *ex culpa in contrahendo* also should be mentioned in this connection.

Contractual liability

The general provisions of the law of contract are contained in   **22-012**
sections 859 *et seq.*, General Civil Code. In connection with the breach of banking secrecy, reference should be made in particular to sections 920 *et seq.*, General Civil Code.[22]

Specifically, compensation for damages is again due, to be governed by sections 1293 *et seq.*, General Civil Code.

In a continuing-obligation relationship, breach of banking secrecy will as a rule constitute weighty cause for premature dissolution.[23] "In grave cases, breach of the reticence obligation may warrant extraordinary revocation of an irrevocable power-of-attorney (agency)."[24]

Contractual liability for servants is regulated in section 44, Final Part, PGR.

---

[21] An important provision concerning liability for servants is contained, however, in section 1315, General Civil Code, as well.
[22] Frommelt, *supra* n. 2, at pp. 52 *et seq.*
[23] Avancini, *supra* n. 17, marg. 2/148.
[24] Strasser, in Rummel, *supra* n. 13, marg. 20, on section 1009.

Provisions governing the Landesbank

22-013 Article 47, Landesbank Act, under the heading of "Responsibility", provides:

> "The liability of the Landesbank and the liability of its officers and employees shall be subject in particular to the provisions of the Official Liability Act."

The Landesbank, in other words, shall be liable under the Official Liability Act.[25] This applies at least to extra-contractual liability. Whether the Official Liability Act applies to the bank's contractual liability as well is at least to be doubted. It would seem unreasonable for the Landesbank to make private-law contracts with its customers and yet have public-law responsibility under the Official Liability Act.

However, the relationship between such public-law liability under the Official Liability Act and private-law liability (including liability for illicit acts under articles 38 *et seq.*, PGR) cannot be clarified here.

Still, it should be briefly mentioned that, under the Official Liability Act, the provisions of civil law apply "analogously", except as otherwise provided in the Official Liability Act itself.

Departing from civil law, in article 3, paragraph 4, the Official Liability Act provides that the public legal person, while likewise liable in the case of any fault, including, minor negligence has no liability in the absence of fault. On the other hand, the public legal person must prove absence of fault on the part of agents, as provided by article 3, paragraph 5 of the Act. Under article 3, paragraph 5, of the Act, damage can be compensated in money only; in other words, there is no restitution in kind. Article 5, paragraph 2, provides that aliens have indemnity claim only if so provided by treaty or if reciprocal rights are accorded.

Competence to decide complaints under the Official Liability Act does not belong, in the first instance, to the State Court, but to the Superior Court, according to article 10, paragraph 1. The procedure too is somewhat different from that of ordinary civil process.

---

[25] Act of September 22, 1966, concerning official liability, LGBl. 1966, number 24.

Penal law consequences

The penal consequences appear in article 48, Landesbank Act, and article 47, Banking Act, and have already been outlined above.

22-014

Where a bank acts as trustee in the sense of the Attorney-at-Law Act, a breach of banking secrecy is punishable also under section 121 of the Penal Code (see text above).

Disciplinary law consequences

Where a bank acts as trustee in the sense of the Attorney-at-Law Act, it is subject under article 34 thereof to the disciplinary power of the Principality of Liechtenstein Superior Court (with right to petition for review by the Principality of Liechtenstein Supreme Court). Under article 35, paragraph 1, Attorney-at-Law Act:

22-015

"Disciplinary penalties to be applied are reprimand, disciplinary fine up to SFr. 5,000, suspension from practice for a determinate period, and permanent bar from practice of profession".

Breach of convention on due diligence (see text below) may, in principle, have the disciplinary consequences under Articles 34 *et seq.* Attorney-at-Law Act.

Administrative law consequences

The private-law banks of Liechtenstein must hold a concession from the Government and Parliament. This concession, under article 5, paragraph 4, Banking Act, may be withdrawn "if facts are present whereby it appears that the management lacks the requisite reliability for its operations or if the bank offers no warrant for the security of assets entrusted to it or if it violates important general interests".

22-016

According to article 5, paragraph 5, Banking Act, however, the bank may in appropriate cases be assigned a time limit within which to remedy shortcomings.

Official liability

Not only the Landesbank (see text above) but all public legal persons are liable for damage they unlawfully inflict on third parties in

22-017

the exercise of their official duties, as provided by article 3, paragraph 1, Official Liability Act.

In the present context, this is of importance primarily concerning the Banking Commission and the Government, both of which act as supervisory and control bodies for the Liechtenstein banks.

However, the National Bank of Switzerland also is liable, not under private law, but under public law, that is to say, under the (Swiss) Federal Act of March 14, 1958, on Responsibility of the Federacy, its Agencies, Members and Officials.[26]

Swiss Bankers' Association

22-018   The three main Liechtenstein banks are members of the Swiss Bankers' Association. Under article 5 of the Charter of that organization, an affiliated bank may be expelled for violation of banking secrecy.

OVERRIDING OF BANKING SECRECY

Tax law[27]

Liechtenstein tax law

22-019   The most essential source for the tax law of Liechtenstein is the Act of January 30, 1961, concerning State and Parish Taxes (Tax Act), with numerous amendments since.

Article 7 of the Tax Act affirms tax secrecy and provides that persons who are charged with or co-opted in the application of the Tax Act must observe silence concerning the business and private situations of taxpayers as apprehended in the course of their official duties and concerning proceedings within the tax agencies. However, the tax administration, upon demand of a taxpayer showing a legitimate interest, must release information from the tax register, as provided by article 7, paragraph 2.

As for the taxes to be paid by holding companies, domiciliary companies, and annuitant taxpayers, tax secrecy is absolute under article 7, paragraph 3 of the Tax Act.

[26] Appendix II to the Liechtenstein-Switzerland Currency Treaty; Aubert-Kernen-Schönle, *supra* n. 14, at pp. 62 *et seq.*
[27] See detailed account by Frommelt, *supra* n. 2, at pp. 229 *et seq.*

Article 9, Tax Act, specifies the tax authorities' rights of control in the assessment of taxpayers, in other words, whether any repositees of secrets are bound to furnish information. In principle, the tax authorities have the right, for the determination of the facts material to tax assessment, to demand information from all persons subject to the fiscal sovereignty of the State and to examine their books and records, according to article 9, paragraph 1, Tax Act.

However, article 9, paragraph 3, Tax Act, expressly provides that the powers conferred upon the tax authorities in paragraph 1 are not theirs vis-à-vis such persons as are bound by official or professional secrecy to observe reticence concerning the affairs of third parties. This statutory provision refers expressly, by way of examples, to attorney secrecy and banking secrecy. Thus, the Liechtensteinian Tax Act respects, and therefore protects, banking secrecy expressly, and does not in principle provide for any override of banking secrecy. This applies both in the banks' own tax affairs and in those tax matters in which the bank might be involved as a third party.

This absolute protection of banking secrecy in the tax law of Liechtenstein, however, requires closer examination, and some relativization, in the cases of inheritance tax, tax evasion, tax fraud, and Swiss tax legislation applicable in Liechtenstein.

In the event of death of a taxpayer, the Board of Inventory of the parish in which decedent was a taxpayer must within eight days after death take an inventory of all assets of the deceased, as provided by article 101, paragraph 1, Tax Act. The taking of this inventory, however, cannot override banking secrecy, since the protective provision of article 9, paragraph 3, has precedence.

In the case of tax evasion, article 156, paragraph 1, Tax Act, refers to the procedural provisions of the Code of Administrative Procedure (LVG, administrative penal procedure), which in turn further refers subsidiarily to the Code of Penal Procedure (StPO), petty offense procedure). The reference of article 156, paragraph 1, Tax Act, however, holds only in the absence of other provisions in the Tax Act. Article 9, paragraph 3, Tax Act, does contain such other provision, protecting banking secrecy absolutely, as already set forth. In the case of tax evasion also, there is thus no override of banking secrecy.

It is otherwise in the case of tax fraud (tax fraud under Liechtensteinian law, in other words to the detriment of the State of Liechtenstein), for such an action, according to article 156, paragraph 2, Tax Act, is subject to the provisions of the StPO without exception. And, in penal procedures, the bank cannot invoke banking secrecy (see text below).

Under article 156, Tax Act tax fraud is committed by one who commits tax evasion through the deliberate use of false, falsified, substantively untrue books of account or other documents.

Swiss tax law

22-020   On March 29, 1923, Switzerland and Liechtenstein concluded the Treaty concerning Adjunction of the Principality of Liechtenstein to the Customs Territory of Switzerland.[28]

According to article 4 of that Treaty, owing to the customs union, both the whole of Swiss tariff legislation and other (Swiss) Federal legislation insofar as the customs union entails its application, have application in Liechtenstein in like manner as in Switzerland. This applies also to the (Swiss) Federal Act concerning Stamp Fees[29] and to turnover tax.

Execution of Swiss legislation applicable in Liechtenstein under the Customs Treaty is in principle up to the Swiss authorities. The same applies to jurisdiction in the prosecution and punishment of infractions. However, within the sphere of the Customs Treaty, Liechtenstein has the same legal standing as the Swiss cantons, according to article 6, Customs Treaty, so that the agencies and courts of Liechtenstein have original jurisdiction in some instances. Even so, Swiss law of process is applicable in every case.

Of special significance is the Swiss Federal legislation concerning stamp duties. Accordingly, on 14 May 1974 the Government of the Principality of Liechtenstein and the Federal Revenue Administration covenanted provisions to implement execution of Federal legislation concerning stamp duties.[30]

The Swiss Federal Act concerning Stamp Duties of June 27, 1973, comprises an issuance levy (such as on issuance of domestic shares of stock and investment fund certificates), a transactions levy (such as on transactions in domestic and foreign bonds, stocks, if a contracting party or an intermediary is a domestic securities dealer), and a levy on insurance premiums.

Under articles 35-37, Stamp Act, the bank, both as taxpayer and as third party, must afford information and inspection of records to

---

28 Customs Treaty, LGBl 1923, number 24.
29 Article 37, Customs Treaty; article 31, Act of March 29, 1923, to introduce the Customs Treaty with Switzerland, LGBl. 1924, Number 11; in the version of the Act of December 29, 1966, LGBl. 1967, number 2.
30 LGBl. 1974, number 33.

the tax administration. However, article 37, paragraph 5, Stamp Act, explicitly provides that banking secrecy is to be preserved.

Turnover tax and tariff legislation are not of great moment in the context of banking secrecy. It should be noted, however, that in event of tax or revenue fraud in these areas, banking secrecy is overriden.[31] In the case of tax or revenue evasion, the bank as a third party has as a rule not to supply any information.[32]

Double taxation agreements

Liechtenstein has made a double taxation agreement only with Austria.[33]   **22-021**

In addition, Liechtenstein has made compacts with certain Swiss cantons concerning certain taxes, as with the cantons of St. Gallen and Graubünden concerning taxation of earnings of cross-border commuters and the tax treatment of donations by will or gift for purposes of common weal, with the canton of Schaffhausen in the area of inheritance and gift taxes, and with the canton of Freiburg concerning tax treatment of donations by will or gift for purposes of common weal.[34]

Penal actions

Penal actions are regulated in principle by the Code of Penal Proce-   **22-022**
dure (StPO) of October 18, 1988. The code contains provisions on competence of courts, rights and duties of parties, penal investigation, acquisition of evidence, and procedure before the courts.

In penal investigation and in penal action before the courts, the object is to inquire into material truth and to serve the public's

---

[31] Aubert-Kernen-Schönle, *supra* n. 14, at pp. 146 *et seq.*

[32] *Id.*, at p. 148.

[33] Convention of November 5, 1969, between the Principality of Liechtenstein and the Republic of Austria to Avoid Double Taxation in the Fields of Income and Property Taxes, LGBl. 1970, Number 37, and Agreement of September 27 and October 12, 1971, between the Government of the Principality of Liechtenstein and the Federal Minister of Finance of the Republic of Austria concerning the Treatment of Refund of Taxes Collected by Deduction at Source, LGBl. 1971, number 43.

[34] Unpublished; enumeration in *Rechtsdienst der Regierung des Fürstentums Liechtenstein, systematische Sammlung der liechtensteinischen Rechtsvorschriften* [Legal Services of the Liechtenstein Government, Systematic Collection of Provisions of Liechtenstein Law], LR Register 1987 (Vaduz, 1988), p. 135; reprinted in Eduard Hilti and René Melliger, *Steuern in Liechtenstein* [Taxes in Liechtenstein] (Vaduz, 1989), 3rd ed., Appendix G.

interest in the detection of punishable actions. There is no weighing against private interests, in particular that of protecting secrets of third parties.[35]

Bank as a party

22-023 If the bank or an officer of the bank is suspect, culpable, or accused in a penal action, then in principle all acts of investigation are possible on the premises of the bank, including visitation, search, and seizure of papers.

There are exceptions to this only in actions for petty offences or misdemeanors insofar as the latter are punishable only by monetary fine or detention not exceeding six months, according to section 317, StPO. In these cases, specifically, search of third parties' papers and seizure or opening of correspondence are not allowed, as provided by section 322, number 4, StPO.

However, under sections 152 and 193, paragraph 2, StPO, a party cannot be compelled to speak, and untrue utterances are not punishable.[36]

Bank as witness

22-024 As a rule, under section 105, StPO, anyone called as a witness is bound to appear in court and testify; under section 122, StPO,, to take an oath, and under section 118, StPO, to tell the truth. These duties of witnesses may be compelled, according to sections 113 *et seq.*, StPO, and section 288, Penal Code.

The StPO provides certain exceptions to the obligation to speak in court. Section 106 regulates the prohibition of interrogation. According to this, the following may not be interrogated as witnesses, their testimony being otherwise null and void:

> "State officials, if by their testimony they would breach the official secrecy incumbent upon them, provided they are not released from that obligation by their superiors."

In this context, the question again arises whether the agents and employees of the Landesbank are State officials, specifically State

---

35 Frommelt, *supra* n. 2, at pp. 166 *et seq.*, with further references to precedents and doctrine.
36 Penal Code, section 288 .

officials in the sense of section 106, number 2, StPO. Certain commentators do not accord any special legal status to dependents of the Landesbank with respect to duties of witnesses.[37]

Section 107, StPO, regulates the right of refusal, under which the following are discharged from the obligation to give evidence: dependents of the inculpated, defense counsel and attorneys-at-law, legal advisers, auditors and patent attorneys, concerning that which has been entrusted to them in that capacity by their principal.

It is striking in this provision that, under section 107, number 3, StPO, most repositees of secrets in the sense of the Attorney-at-Law Act have the right of refusal, but trustees and banks do not.

Section 108, StPO, regulates the right of exemption from giving evidence:

> "If the giving of evidence or the answering of a question would entail ignominy or the risk of penal prosecution or a direct and significant disadvantagement in property rights to the witness or any of his dependents, and he therefore declines to testify, he shall be bound to give evidence only if indispensable by reason of the special importance of his evidence."

The primarily essential ground is the risk of penal prosecution, in particular if the bank and/or its dependents are implicated (section 12, Penal Code, cites direct perpetrator, instigator, or accomplice) in the penal action under investigation. The second important ground is the danger of direct and significant property disadvantagement. "Such disadvantagement is present if a lasting impairment of general economic position, effective over some length of time, is present."[38]

Such a severe impact may, for example, result from the discovery of banking secrets; it is essential, however, that the impact be severe, and not a mere encumbrance over a matter of months.[39] In other words, the bare fact that the banking secret would have to be discovered does not suffice.

If any of the grounds of exemption of section 108, StPO, is present, the court may insist on testimony if "indispensable by reason of special importance." In other words, the court must balance interests.

---

[37] Frommelt, *supra* n. 2, at pp. 170 *et seq.*

[38] Foregger-Serini, StPO (Code of Penal Procedure), MKK (Vienna, 1989), 4th ed., Commentary I on section 153.

[39] *Id.*

Bank's duty to surrender

22-025 Under section 96, paragraph 2, StPO, everyone is bound to surrender articles that may be pertinent to the investigation, in particular including documents, upon demand of the court.

Surrender may be compelled, but not if the possessor "is exempted by statute from the obligation to give evidence", as provided by section 96, paragraph 2, StPO. In other words, if the rare case should befall that the bank is not bound to give evidence, then no compulsory process may be exercised against it to enforce the surrender of documents or other articles. However, such articles may be taken from the bank by sequestration.[40]

> "By sequestration, the right to decline to give evidence may not be avoided. Thus for instance it is not licit to seize the journals of a dependent entitled to decline, in order therefrom to learn what the dependent has rightfully withheld."[41]

In the penal action itself

22-026 Under section 181, StPO, the concluding procedure before the court is public, unless the court decides, for reasons of morality or public order, to hold a closed session.

However, the risk of discovery of a banking secret does not suffice as grounds for a closed session, so that the revelation of a banking secret to the public in the concluding procedure cannot be ruled out.[42]

Another risk of loss of banking secrecy consists of the right of a private plaintiff to inspect records under section 31, paragraph 2, StPO, and that of a private party under section 32, paragraph 2, number 2, StPO. There is opinion, however, that in the case of abuse, the private party, but not the private plaintiff, may be excluded from the right to inspect records under section 32, paragraph 2, number 2, StPO.[43]

---

40 Christian Bertel, *Grundriss des österreichischen Strafprozessrechts* [Outline of the Austrian Law of Penal Process] (Vienna, 1984), 2nd ed., marg. 491.

41 Foregger-Serini, *supra* n. 38, Commentary II on section 143.

42 Frommelt, *supra* n. 2, at p. 181.

43 *Id.*, at p. 182.

Mutual assistance in criminal matters

Sources of law

Liechtenstein has no judicial assistance statute embodying the ma-   **22-027**
terial prerequisites for the allowance of judicial assistance and the
procedural regulations. There are plans, however, to enact a judicial
assistance statute. Such a government proposal was in fact presented to the public for hearings in 1990.

The granting of judicial assistance is based on international conventions. Absent such conventions, judicial assistance may be
granted voluntarily.

The most important international agreement is the European
Convention of April 20, 1959, on Mutual Assistance in Criminal
Matters. With the Republic of Austria, a treaty supplementary to the
European Convention was made on June 4, 1982. Other agreements
have been made with Germany, especially concerning direct correspondence in criminal matters between the judiciary authorities. In
practice, the pertinent international agreements in the field of narcotics offenses, especially the Unitary Convention of March 30,
1961, concerning narcotics is important. (The extradition conventions, among which the European Convention on Extradition of
1957 and the bilateral Extradition Treaty of 1936 with the United
States are the most important, need not be more fully discussed
here).

"Insofar as judicial assistance is extra-contractually rendered
voluntarily, in the first place the principles of international
customary law become applicable, which according to the
precedents in the State Court of Justice [constitutional court] of
our State requires no specific transformation into intra-State
law and is therefore a direct constituent part of the domestic
legal order. According to international customary law, States
are indeed entitled, but not bound, to voluntarily accord each
other judicial assistance. In extra-contractual judicial assistance, Liechtenstein applies those principles which are contained in the European Convention on Mutual Assistance in
Criminal Matters. The judicature of the State Court of Justice
concurs in this time-honored practice. Application of the prin-

ciples of the European Convention on Mutual Assistance to extra-contractual reciprocity of mutual assistance conforms to the postulate of equality before the law."[44]

In practice, it is moreover usual, in the granting of extra-contractual judicial assistance, invariably to demand a declaration of reciprocity from the requesting State.[45]

Principles

22-028 Since Liechtenstein adheres to the principles of the European Convention on Mutual Assistance in granting either contractual or voluntary judicial assistance, that Convention is often referred to.

Thereunder, in particular the principles of parallel punishability (required under the Liechtensteinian reservation in the employment of any compulsory measure), reciprocity,[46] commensurability,[47] and subsidiarity.[48]

In addition, Liechtenstein requires assurance that Liechtensteinian results of inquiry are not used in fiscal actions, inasmuch as Liechtenstein regularly requires a declaration to that effect from the requesting state. This declaration, binding under international law, secures an absolute prohibition of use of evidence in fiscal matters.[49]

This principle is applied rigorously. Thus, it recently has been reported that a Liechtensteinian result of inquiry was published in the foreign press, whereupon the foreign State instituted a fiscal action. Liechtenstein forthwith refused judicial assistance to that state until the fiscal action had been dropped.

In the practice of judicial assistance, the procedural provisions of Liechtenstein's Code of Penal Procedure are applied analogously. This is in accord with the provisions in article 3, paragraph 1, of the European Convention on Mutual Assistance. The consequence of this is that for example in the case of petty offense, certain compulsory measures are not available.

---

44 Benedikt Marxer, in Liechtenstein Seminar 1988 (Vaduz, 1989), at p. 106.
45 *Id.*, at p. 114.
46 *Id.*, at pp. 113 *et seq.*
47 Frommelt, *supra* n. 2, at pp. 278 *et seq.*
48 *Id.*, at pp. 280 *et seq.*
49 Benedikt Marxer, *supra* n. 44, at pp. 112 *et seq.*

"Furthermore, acquisition of evidence called for from abroad is rendered difficult when the procedural ordinance of the requesting State provides stronger restrictions than that of the requested State. The principle holds that the requesting state may not demand more abroad than its own procedure law allows. A witness may invoke grounds for declining to testify even if they are known only in the place of the trial court, and not in the place of deposition."[50]

Exceptions

No judicial assistance is allowed in the case of military, political or 22-029
fiscal offenses, nor of endangerment of sovereignty, security, public order (*ordre public*), or other essential interests of the State of Liechtenstein.

By fiscal offenses are meant fiscal offenses in the proper sense of the word (violation of tax and other revenue legislation, as well as tariff and monopoly provisions), violations of foreign exchange legislation (currency legislation), and provisions concerning stewardship of goods and foreign trade (commercial and economic policy legislation).[51]

The line between fiscal and other punishable acts often is difficult to draw, but certain criteria have been worked out in practice.[52] Thus, regarding fraud, the following rule holds:

"If by fraudulent acts, public law claims are curtailed, a fiscal offense is present; but if benefits to which one would have had no claim are fraudulently acquired, common fraud is present, as for example export defalcation or subsidy fraud."[53]

Civil actions

Civil process is regulated basically in the Act of December 10, 1912, 22-030
concerning court procedure in civil litigation (the Code of Civil Procedure).

---

[50] Wolfgang Strub, *Der Geheimnisschutz im liechtensteinischen Treuhandwesen* [Protection of Secrecy in Liechtenstein Fiduciary Affairs] (Berne, 1987), at p. 263.
[51] Benedikt Marxer, *supra* n. 44, at pp. 110 *et seq*.
[52] *Id.*, at pp. 111 *et seq*.
[53] *Id.*, at pp. 112 *et seq*.

Bank as party

22-031   Under section 380, paragraph 3, Code of Civil Procedure, a party to an action can be compelled neither to appear in court nor to testify. Refusal would have adverse effects only in the context of the free consideration of evidence by the court and in that the evidence could not be furnished.

As to the submittal of documents by a party to an action, the rule is, under section 304, Code of Civil Procedure, that submittal may not be refused:

(1) If the party itself has referred to the document for the purpose of furnishing evidence in the case;

(2) If the party is bound under civil law to surrender or present the document, or

(3) If the document by virtue of its contents is one common to both parties.

Presentation of any other documents may be refused under section 305, number 4, by the bank as a party, provided the bank has a state-recognized obligation of reticence (such as banking secrecy is) from which it has not been validly released. Failure to appear, despite an obligation to testify, would have negative trial consequences primarily insofar as the court might interpret the bank's conduct accordingly.

Bank as witness

22-032   A witness who has been summoned must appear in court, as provided by section 329, Code of Civil Procedure; testify in court, as provided by sections 320 *et seq.*, and take an oath, as provided by sections 336 *et seq.*

Under sections 325 and 333, these duties of witnesses may be compelled, and false evidence would be punishable according to section 288, Penal Code.

To this obligation to testify in court, the Code of Civil Procedure provides certain exceptions:

Section 320, number 3, Code of Civil Procedure, provides that "State officials, if by their testimony they would breach official secrecy incumbent upon them, insofar as they have not been released by their superiors from the obligation of secrecy," may not be questioned as witnesses. Here again, the question arises whether the officers and employees of the Landesbank are State officials in the sense of this provisions.

Section 321, Code of Civil Procedure, regulates the right to refuse testimony as follows:

"A witness may refuse to testify:

1. On questions to answer which would tend to bring down ignominy or jeopardy of penal prosecution upon the witness, his spouse or a [well-defined, closely associated] person;

2. On questions to answer which would occasion a direct disadvantagement of property rights for the witness or a person as referred to in number 1;

3. Respecting facts concerning which the witness could not testify without breaching a State-recognized obligation incumbent upon him, insofar as he has not been validly released therefrom;

4. Regarding that which has been entrusted to the witness in his capacity of counsel to his party;

5. On questions which the witness could not answer without divulging a business or trade secret."

The banks and/or their employees as witnesses, by contrast with the situation in penal procedure, are entitled by virtue of banking secrecy to a right of refusal to testify provided the bank has not been validly released from the duty of reticence by the repositor. Even in these cases, some one of the other grounds of refusal enumerated in section 321, Code of Civil Procedure, might apply.

Bank's duty to surrender

If the bank is not a party to the action, but a third party, under 22-033 section 308, Code of Civil Procedure, it is bound to surrender documents required in evidence only if the bank is obligated under the provisions of civil law to surrender and present the document, or because the document by virtue of its contents is one common to the party to the action and the third party (the bank).

In these cases (obligation to surrender and submit under civil law and common instrument), the bank has no right of refusal. Only a party to an action is entitled to the right of refusal provided by section 305, Code of Civil Procedure.

In the civil action itself

22-034 Under section 171, Code of Civil Procedure, proceedings before the court are public. Under section 172, Code of Civil Procedure, the public is to be excluded if it appears that morality or public order would be endangered or if their is warranted concern that the public would abuse the occasion for the purpose of interfering with the proceedings or impeding ascertainment of the facts.

In addition, the public may be excluded from discussion and deposition of facts of family life. Hence, if a party to a case must reveal essential business secrets in the action, or if the bank as a witness must override banking secrecy, the court is to exclude the public if ascertainment of the facts would otherwise be impeded.

However, even an exclusion of the public in a civil action will not hinder parties to the action in the exercise of their unrestricted right to examine records under section 219, Code of Civil Procedure.

Mutual assistance in civil matters

22-035 Concerning legal assistance in civil matters, Liechtenstein has a treaty (dated April 1, 1955) only with Austria. It may be noted that there are enforcement agreements with Austria and Switzerland, and the Hague Convention of April 15, 1958, on recognition and enforcement of decisions in the field of maintenance obligation in respect of children has been adhered to.

Otherwise, the rules of mutual assistance are governed by sections 27-29 of the Jurisdiction Ruling of December 10, 1912.[54] According to the Jurisdiction Ruling, the courts of Liechtenstein must render mutual assistance to foreign courts insofar as not otherwise expressly provided, no statutes of Liechtenstein are violated, and reciprocity is accorded. Procedure is governed by the Code of Civil Procedure, whereby in particular the provision of section 321 is again applicable, according to which the bank as a witness may decline to testify on grounds of banking secrecy.

Injunctions

22-036 Injunctions are regulated in articles 270 *et seq.* of the Act of November 24, 1971, concerning executory and security actions (Executory

[54] LGBl. 1912, number 9.

Code). Under article 270, paragraph 1, Executory Code, temporary injunctions may be issued either before litigation is introduced or during the same, and during proceedings of execution, to secure the rights of a party.

In such security actions, the Liechtenstein banks are very often involved, since claims of the defendant party upon the bank may be secured as assets. Security is given, among other methods, by a third-party injunction ordered by the court against the bank. The third-party injunction is executed by an order to the third party (the bank) not to pay what is due to the defendant upon own liability, and not to restore matters to which the defendant is entitled, nor otherwise do anything respecting them that might defeat or substantially impede execution, until further orders from the court.

By such an injunction, the complainant acquires a lien on the assets placed in security, as provided by article 275, Executory Code. This has the result that the bank, in analogous application of article 223, Executory Code, is bound to furnish a third-party debtor statement respecting the assets secured and under lien. This statement in particular must indicate whether the bank recognizes the secured claim as founded and is prepared to perform it.

If the bank declines to furnish a statement, it cannot indeed be compelled to do so, but it becomes liable for damages to the complainant, as also if it furnishes untrue or incomplete information.[55] So-called search decrees, however, are illegal, according to Liechtenstein precedent.[56]

Enforcement proceedings

Compulsory enforcement of executable claims under an award (by a court, as a rule) is termed *Exekution* in Liechtenstein. Such execution is governed by articles 1-269, Executory Code.   **22-037**

In the context of execution, claims of the constrained party upon a Liechtenstein bank for payment or restoration may be attached and realized. The bank, under article 223, Executory Code (as explained above), is bound to furnish a third-party debtor statement and, under article 229, Executory Code, to make payment or restoration to the complainant creditor. To that extent, banking secrecy is likewise overriden.

[55] Principality of Liechtenstein Supreme Court Decision of May 27, 1986, LES 1987, at p. 166, confirmed by the Principality of Liechtenstein Supreme Court in LES 1990, at pp. 29 and 32.
[56] Principality of Liechtenstein Supreme Court Decision of May 27, 1986, *supra* n. 55.

Bankruptcy and compulsory composition

22-038   Bankruptcy proceedings are regulated in the Act of July 17, 1973, concerning bankruptcy actions (Bankruptcy Ordinance). If bankruptcy proceedings are opened on the assets of a debtor, the court will appoint a trustee.

The trustee is empowered to perform all legal transactions and legal acts vis-à-vis third parties that pertain to the settlement of the bankruptcy, according to article 4, Bankruptcy Ordinance. Thus, if bankruptcy proceedings are opened on the assets of a bank, the trustee has full rights of inspection of the entire banking operation and all records. If bankruptcy proceedings are opened on the assets of a customer of a bank, the trustee is entitled to demand information from the bank and to make dispositions. The bank cannot invoke banking secrecy.

As regards foreign bankruptcy actions, essentially the principle of territoriality applies, according to which foreign bankruptcy actions have no legal effects in Liechtenstein. However, this principle has been relaxed by the Principality of Liechtenstein Supreme Court decision of April 1, 1981, to the effect that the foreign estate in bankruptcy has trial and party standing in Liechtenstein.[57]

From that decision, it must doubtless be inferred that in general foreign trustees and administrators in bankruptcy are qualified to prosecute claims in Liechtenstein.[58] Hence, foreign trustees in bankruptcy should be able to demand payment or surrender from a Liechtenstein bank, and the bank could not invoke banking secrecy.

Much the same applies to the so-called composition agreement action, under the Act of April 15, 1936, concerning composition agreements.[59] A composition agreement is the court-ordered moratorium on a debtor's obligations and the conclusion of an agreement between the debtor and the creditor concerning reduction of the obligations. The court will appoint an administrator.

Administrative actions

22-039   General administrative procedure is regulated in the Act of April 21, 1922, concerning the Code of Administrative Procedure (LVG). Article 68, LVG, makes reference, respecting the duty of informa-

---

[57] LES 1982, at p. 81.

[58] Helmut Neudorfer, "*Das liechtensteinische Insolvenzrecht* [The Liechtenstein Law of Insolvency]", *Liechtensteinische Juristen-Zeitung* 1988, at p. 136.

[59] LGBl. 1936, number 8.

tion of parties and the obligation of non-parties (*i.e.*, witnesses) to testify, subsidiarily to the Code of Civil Procedure.

Therefore, by analogy with the provisions on civil procedure, the bank can invoke banking secrecy in administrative actions as well. There is an exception, under article 67, LVG, in the action to avert public dangers to life, limb, health and property, where the Code of Penal Procedure becomes subsidiarily applicable.

Deputation

If the bank's customer appoints a deputy for himself with appropri-   22-040
ate powers, then of course the bank cannot invoke banking secrecy vis-à-vis the deputy respecting the bank's relations with the principal.

Much the same applies as a rule to statutory deputation. Thus, parents, guardians, and spouses, often have the same rights vis-à-vis the bank as does the principal. In such case, the bank cannot invoke banking secrecy.

Law of inheritance

When a bank's customer dies, other persons enter into his rights   22-041
and duties. These persons are termed heirs or legatees according as they are general or particular successors in interest.

The decedent's successors in interest enter into the rights and duties of the decedent regarding the bank. Accordingly, the bank has in principle, the same rights and duties as to the successors and the deceased customer. In detail, however, manifold problems arise, specifically who the successors are, to what rights they are entitled, whether third parties also have rights of information vis-à-vis the bank (*e.g.*, the forced heirs, the curator of the estate, the testamentary executor, the estate administrator), and whether the interests of the deceased customer have ongoing effects.

The latter, according to a widespread view concerning the confidentiality interest of the bank's deceased customer with regard to his own successors and third parties, is supposed to be the case, so that, as a rule, no information is given concerning the period prior to the decedent's death. All these questions and problems are very largely unsettled in Liechtenstein law. In clarifying them, it must first be ascertained, according to the rules of conflict of laws, what substantive law is applicable to all these issues.

Rules of private international law

22-042 From the Liechtenstein point of view, the Liechtenstein rules of private international law are to be applied. To take the Liechtenstein point of view is justified for the reason that the Liechtenstein banks have their seat in Liechtenstein.

In Liechtenstein, there is no special statute concerning private international law. The rules of conflict of laws, insofar as any exist, are scattered through various statutes. In the field of inheritance law, primarily the Act of December 4, 1911, concerning Settlement of Aliens' Estates, applies.[60]

This statute contains some peculiar rules. According to the Principality of Liechtenstein Superior Court Decision of November 23, 1977, Liechtenstein law proceeds from the principle of unity of estate.[61]

However, this principle is overriden respecting immovable property (division of estate). On this point, in any case, the *lex rei sitae* holds. According to the Act concerning Settlement of Aliens' Estates, the application of Liechtenstein law is determined by exclusively procedural considerations. Not the law of the home State, of residence, or of the location of the estate, but the jurisdiction of the Liechtenstein court, decides as to the applicable substantive law.

Therefore, if a Liechtenstein court has jurisdiction of the settlement of the estate, at all events substantive Liechtenstein law will be applied. Whether the Liechtenstein courts have jurisdiction is determined by what State the deceased belongs to and what principles that State would apply if the case were reversed. Even if the foreign State would then have jurisdiction, the Liechtenstein court sometimes may take jurisdiction on motion of the parties.

The statutes of Liechtenstein do not determine what substantive law is applicable if a foreign court has jurisdiction of the settlement of the estate. To solve this problem, an attempt may be made to find an answer in the Austrian legal position. Both in the field of inheritance law and in the field of conflict of laws, Liechtenstein has traditionally followed the same principles as Austria, or at least similar ones.

Thus, the Liechtenstein law of inheritance was taken over almost verbatim from Austria. The Act concerning Settlement of Aliens' Estates corresponds largely to the former provisions of interna-

---

60 LGBl. 1911, number 6.
61 A 80/76, ELG 1973-1978, at p. 233.

tional inheritance law in the Austrian Statute on Non-Contentious Matters. Hence, we may begin by referring to Fritz Schwind.[62]

He states that the earlier Austrian doctrine premised that the status of the thing (*lex rei sitae*) applied. The more recent doctrine, however, proceeds from the personal status of the decedent (law of that State to which the decedent belonged), at least as to the movable estate. Now the Principality of Liechtenstein Supreme Court, in decisions on the law of indebtedness, has held that by reason of a legal kinship with Austria, the guidelines and provisions of the Austrian Federal Act of June 15, 1978, concerning private international law, which went into effect on January 1, 1979, may be subsidiarily adduced in the Principality of Liechtenstein as well, at least to fill existing gaps of statute in the realm of Liechtenstein law.[63]

In analogous application of these remarks, one may arrive at the conclusion that section 28 of the Austrian Statute on Private International Law is applicable in Liechtenstein as well. Accordingly, as a rule, the principle will hold that the whole succession in interest by reason of death is subject to the decedent's personal status (law of that State to which the decedent belonged) at the time of death.

Development of banking practice

This remains an extremely complex and unsettled region of the law in Liechtenstein. Court precedents are wholly absent. The practice of the Liechtenstein banks has developed some rules concerning the treatment of rights of information after the death of a customer. They are to the following effect.   **22-043**

Anyone who can evidence to a bank by means of a public instrument that he is heir (successor in interest) to the bank's customer will receive information. Foreign authorities and courts will not, as a rule, receive information, since their competence does not extend to Liechtenstein.

For any other persons, as for example executors, the position of fact and of law will be examined on a case-by-case basis. In so doing, as a rule, the law of last domicile and the decedent's home law will be referred to.

---

[62] Fritz Schwind, *Handbuch des Österreichischen Internationalen Privatrechts* [Manual of Austrian Private International Law] (Vienna, 1975), at pp. 253 *et seq.*

[63] Principality of Liechtenstein Supreme Court Decision of March 13, 1984, LES 1986, p. 7; Principality of Liechtenstein Supreme Court Decision of June 28, 1988, 4 C 206/85-66.

Banking surveillance

22-044   As mentioned above, the Liechtenstein banks are subordinate to the National Bank of Switzerland. However, the control authority conceded to the National Bank of Switzerland is limited in such manner that the interests of bank customers are hardly affected.[64]

Both the banking legislation and the Persons and Company Act (PGR) provide that the banks must establish an audit authority (control office) having certain supervisory powers. According to article 34, Landesbank Act, the audit authority will examine the annual statements and is entitled, under article 35, paragraph 2, Landesbank Act, to inspect the books and records at any time. The same function and rights devolve upon the audit authorities of the other banks.[65]

The secrecy obligation, and with it the observance of banking secrecy by the audit authorities, is affirmed in articles 37 and 38, Landesbank Act; article 20, paragraph 5, and article 47, Banking Act. Since the audit authorities are moreover subject to the Attorney-at-Law Act, the reticence provision of article 33 thereof is applicable to them just as to trustees and banks.

In penal actions, the secrets of the auditors (audit authority), in like manner as the secrets of attorneys-at-law, *viz.* more extensive than the secrets of trustees and banks, are protected. Under section 107, paragraph 1, number 3, Code of Penal Procedure, the auditor has a right of refusal concerning that which has been entrusted to him in that capacity by his principal, *i.e.*, the bank under audit.

The Landesbank is an institution of public law. Naturally, therefore, political forums also would have certain powers respecting the Landesbank. Thus, the Liechtenstein Parliament (*Landtag*) makes decisions on capitalization and interest, elects members of the directorate and supervisory board, approves the annual statements, and resolves certain conflicts between the Government and the directorate.

However, since the Government enjoys no far-reaching competence in relation to the directorate, the parliament's right of mediation does not touch any interests of the individual bank customer.

Under article 29, Landesbank Act, the government has perquisites respecting the election of officers and approval of the order of business, regulation, annual statements, and money loans to Liechtenstein parishes. To that extent, no interests of the bank customers are affected. However, it is otherwise as to the government's com-

---

64 Wolfgang Strub, *supra* n. 50, at pp. 227 *et seq.*
65 Banking Act, articles 18 and 19, paragraph 2 .

petence under article 30, Landesbank Act, according to which the government has a comprehensive right of supervision over the business conduct of the Landesbank as a whole.

Unfortunately, an express secrecy obligation of the Government in this respect is lacking in the Landesbank Act. However, the Government and its several members are generally subject to official secrecy, and would incur punishment by detention for up to three years in the case of breach, as provided by section 310, paragraph 1, Penal Code.

The banks, under the Banking Act, are subject to surveillance by the Banking Commission and by the Government. The competence of the Banking Commission, it is true, is limited. Still, under article 21, paragraph 5, Banking Act, it may demand all information and documents if the audit authority reports violation of statutory provisions, punishable acts, improprieties, loss of half of own resources, or other facts endangering the security of creditors, to the Banking Commission.

The Banking Commission is required to report to the Government currently on its activity, according to article 23, paragraph 3, Banking Act. Hence, banking secrecy cannot be maintained vis-à-vis the Banking Commission and the Government. Article 55, Banking Act, expressly provides that the members of the Government and of the Banking Commission must observe secrecy concerning facts coming to their knowledge in the execution of the Banking Act. Incidentally, reference is made again to the official secrecy protected by section 310, Penal Code.

Convention on due diligence

On July 1, 1977, the Government of Liechtenstein concluded the 22-045 first convention on due diligence with the banks. That agreement was influenced by the agreement between the Swiss banks and the Swiss Bankers' Association, on the one hand, and the National Bank of Switzerland, on the other hand, concerning the duty of Swiss banks to exercise care in the reception of monies and the treatment of banking secrecy.

However, the Liechtenstein agreement was more weakly formulated, in particular as to identification of the economic rightsholder in the case of juridical persons. In the years 1982, 1987, and 1991, the Swiss Convention was made more strict. In Liechtenstein, the Agreement of June 1, 1977, was not replaced until October 5, 1989, by an agreement which went into effect on December 1, 1989.

The later agreement was made between the four banks domiciled in Liechtenstein and the Government of the Principality of Liechtenstein. Its purpose is to safeguard the reputation of the Liechtenstein banking industry at home and abroad. This purpose is accomplished in that the banks bound themselves to identify their customers and ascertain the true holder of economic rights, and not to render any active aid to flight of capital or tax evasion.

To be sure, the economic rightsholder need not be disclosed if a Liechtenstein attorney-at-law, legal adviser, trustee, auditor, or patent attorney furnishes a statement to the bank that he is bound to professional secrecy but at the same time affirms that the identity of the person holding economic rights to the items of value to be placed with the bank is known to him.

Such professional repositees, however, can furnish such a declaration only if they in turn personally bind themselves by an agreement with the Government of the Principality of Liechtenstein, to observe the due-diligence agreement between the banks and the Government. A violation would result in information to the Principality of Liechtenstein Superior Court, as disciplinary authority for professional repositees of secrets.

Thus far, banking secrecy has not been affected by the agreements in question. However, the audit authorities under the Banking Act must report violations of the agreement to a special arbitration commission, to the Government and to the Banking Commission.

In general, the settlement and sanction of violations of the due-diligence agreement is the province of a special arbitration commission. Its members comprise the chairman of the Liechtenstein Banking Commission and one representative each of the Liechtenstein Banking Association and the government. This arbitration commission can award a stipulated penalty against an offending bank. However, in order to ascertain a violation and sanction the bank, it is indispensable that the position of fact be first exactly ascertained.

By this process of investigation and the reports of the Banking Act audit authorities, banking secrecy is clearly overriden. Nor is this altered by the fact that the due-diligence agreement binds the members of the arbitration commission to observe strict reticence concerning the facts that have become known.

As in Switzerland, in Liechtenstein it is difficult to explain why the audit authorities, under the Banking Act, may render reports and why the banks may furnish information to the arbitration commission without having previously obtained the consent of the bank's customers.

"Insider" actions

Liechtenstein has no statutory rules respecting so-called "insider" **22-046** dealings (abusive exploitation of insider knowledge on the part of persons of trust in stock exchange transactions).

For this reason, in principle no international judicial assistance is available in penal matters, and the Liechtenstein banks may not give up any banking secrets in a foreign "insider" action. Were an insider action to be instituted abroad against a Liechtenstein bank, however, substantial disadvantages to the Liechtenstein bank might result. For this reason, the Liechtenstein banks have, in part, adopted the practice of requiring a statement on insider actions from their customers.

The bank is thereby empowered by the customer to release the name and address of the customer and the bank records in question to the proper foreign authority if the bank or the customer becomes involved in an official insider action. This statement amounts to a contractual authorization of the bank by the customer to release information.

Conclusion

In Liechtenstein, it does not seriously occur to anyone to eliminate **22-047** banking secrecy. However, in order to abate abusive use of banking secrecy, there are certain tendencies to relax it. In the following, the more important statutory amendments planned and other tendencies are discussed.

Banking Act review

The Banking Act is to be reviewed in its entirety. The Government **22-048** has submitted its Bill of February 28, 1992, for an act concerning banks and financial companies (Banking Act) to the parliament. The Landesbank is to be subject to the new statute as well, "insofar as the Act concerning the Landesbank does not otherwise determine."

Banking secrecy is to be expressly regulated, and it is to relate to the banks, financial companies, their officers, employees, other persons performing services for banks, and authorities.

The obligation to observe banking secrecy does not stand in penal actions when the customer consents in writing, to customary bank information in general terms concerning the economic position of an enterprise, or in litigation between bank and customer. Of special importance would appear to be the enlargement of the circle of persons under obligation. In other words, banking secrecy is to be retained, at least, to the past extent.

International judicial assistance

22-049   On JSeptember 17, 1991, the Government submitted to the parliament a bill regarding an act concerning international judicial assistance in penal matters (Judicial Assistance Act). That statute is to regulate details of requirements for granting legal assistance and for conduct thereof.

There is not to be any substantial change in past practice. Specifically, as heretofore, judicial assistance will not be granted if the subject of the action is an act appearing to be addressed to a curtailment of fiscal levies, or violating provisions concerning measures of monetary, commercial or economic policy. The draft contains express provisions of protection in the realm of secrecy. Reference is made to the provisions of the Code of Penal Procedure.

In addition, it is provided that disclosure of the secret domain of a person not under suspicion is licit only "if it appears indispensable for ascertaining the state of the facts, there is no other way to achieve this, and the importance of the act so warrants." However, even in such a case, secrets may not be given up if that course "would threaten any substantial disadvantage to the Liechtenstein economy, and that disadvantage would not be acceptable in view of the offense."

Money laundering and insider transactions

22-050   The Government has submitted two other bills of importance in this connection, the Bill of August 28, 1989, concerning introduction of a penal rule regarding money laundering and want of care in money laundering, and the Bill of August 17, 1990, concerning introduction of a penal rule regarding abuse of a business or trade secret for illicit stock exchange transactions ("insider" transactions).

Such statutes would not only have the result that money laundering and want of care in ascertaining the identity of the economic rightsholder on the occasion of professional acceptance of alien assets, and the exploitation of insider knowledge, would become punishable in Liechtenstein. Rather, on the basis of the then-satisfied criterion of parallel punishability, foreign States could be granted judicial assistance in such penal matters. To that extent, banking secrecy would have been limited.

Convention on due diligence

The last convention on due diligence was made only in late 1989.   **22-051**
Still, it cannot be said that no change will occur here within the
foreseeable future.

Liechtenstein is to some extent influenced by the Swiss model,
and it also is subject to a certain amount of Swiss pressure. In
Switzerland, as of July 1, 1991, agreement on due diligence was
rendered considerably more strict, *i.e.*, use of the so-called Form B,
Swiss Bankers' Association 1987, was prohibited, so that in any case
the economic rightsholder must be made known to the banks and
no professional respositee of secrets may be interposed.

This relaxation of Swiss banking secrecy, sooner or later, will
have repercussions on banking secrecy in Liechtenstein.

European integration

Finally, Liechtenstein has, for some time, attempted to become   **22-052**
involved in European integration. Liechtenstein, as a member state
of the European Free Trade Association (EFTA), is party to the
agreement with the European Community in the creation of the
European Economic Area, and it does not rule out membership in
the European Community.

In either case, Liechtenstein must adapt to the present and future
rules of law of the European Community. This applies to the realm
of banking and taxation, as well.

CHAPTER 23

LUXEMBOURG

Guy Harles
Arendt & Medernach
Luxembourg

Chapter 23

LUXEMBOURG

INTRODUCTION

Banking secrecy in Luxembourg is based on the fundamental prin-　**23-001**
ciple of the protection of the interests of the individual.

The client of the bank has a right that information regarding his
assets and his banking transactions be kept confidential.

However, banking secrecy does not mean protection of criminal
activities; there are exceptions to the principle of banking secrecy in
this context.

Some other exceptions relating to the public sector or certain
private persons exist but, generally, the principle of banking secrecy
is protected.

BASIS OF BANKING SECRECY

Banking secrecy is implied essentially from article 458 of the Penal　**23-002**
Code, which governs professional secrecy in general:

> "Doctors, surgeons, health officers, pharmacists, midwifes,
> and all other persons who, by their functions or profession,
> come into possession of secrets entrusted to them, and who,
> except where they are called upon to testify in the courts of law
> and in cases where the law requires them to make these secrets
> known, divulge such secrets shall be punished by fine of be-
> tween LUF 10,000 and LUF 50,000".

Since the World War II, Luxembourg has considered that article 458 applies to bankers. This fact has become indisputable since the adoption of the Law of April 23, 1981. Article 16 of the Law (which has become article 31 of the Law of November 27, 1984) provides a general recognition to the principle of banking secrecy.

According to this text, article 458 of the Penal Code prohibits directors, members of the managing and supervisory boards, executive staff, and other employees of credit institutions (banking establishments) from disclosing the secrets which are entrusted to them by reason of their position as bankers.

BANKING SECRECY AND THE STATE

Tax administration

23-003 Before World War II, banks were not obliged to divulge information to the tax administration.

During World War II, German fiscal legislation (*Reichsabgabenordnung*) was introduced in Luxembourg.

This legislation prohibits the keeping of professional secrets from the tax administration, under its article 175, and the *Reichsabgabenordnung* remains in force in Luxembourg.

While the tax administration has never invoked this text, there was a juridical insecurity, essentially towards third countries in the case of mutual assistance of the tax authorities.

International aspects

23-004 Although all of the double taxation treaties signed by the Grand Duchy of Luxembourg (*i.e.*, with Germany, Austria, Belgium, Brazil, Canada, the United States, the United Kingdom, Finland, France, Ireland, Italy, Morocco, Norway, The Netherlands, and Sweden) provide clauses for mutual assistance, it is admitted that the Luxembourg authorities would not divulge any information which these authorities themselves would not seek under their normal day-to-day practice; in particular, the Luxembourg authorities would not divulge information covered by Luxembourg banking secrecy.

Under article 8 of European Community (EC) Directive Number 77/799 on mutual assistance between Member States in direct and indirect matters, a Member State may refuse to seek information on behalf of another Member State's authorities if its domestic authorities would not seek the same information under their usual practice. This clause always has been fully applied in Luxembourg.

In February 1989, the EC Commission presented a draft Directive, modifying EC Directive Number 77/799, relating to the mutual assistance of the competent authorities of the EC Member States in the matter of direct taxes and value-added taxes. The main effect of the draft would have been to discontinue application of the term "usual practice".

The draft proposition to abolish article 8 has been abandoned due to the negative attitude of some Member States, among them the Grand Duchy of Luxembourg.

Decree of March 24, 1989

However, on March 24, 1989, Luxembourg adopted a Grand-Ducal **23-005** Decree to establish additional provisions regarding banking secrecy in fiscal matters and to restrain the investigation rights of fiscal administrations.

The Decree of March 24, 1989, has clarified the application of banking secrecy in tax matters. The rights of investigation of the Luxembourg tax authorities are considerably restricted by article 1 of the Decree, which provides in very simple and clear words that the domestic tax authorities are not allowed to seek information from the banks concerning their clients.

Article 1 of the Decree provides that:

> "Fiscal administrations are not authorized to require from financial institutions any individual information about their clients, except for the case foreseen by the January 28, 1949, Act to assure a just and exact perception of registration and succession duties".

The Law of January 28, 1948, now constitutes the main exception to the general system of the inviolability of banking secrecy of the fiscal administration.

The tax authorities can address questions to banks for the assessment of inheritance tax on the estate of a deceased Luxembourg tax resident. Some further exceptions exist, under certain circumstances, for the assessment of registration and mortgage duties, as well as of the value-added tax. However, the new Decree has effectively insulated banking secrecy from the domestic tax authorities.

BANKING CONTROL ADMINISTRATION

National supervision

23-006 The control of banks is the main function of the Luxembourg Monetary Institute (IML), which was created by the Law of April 20, 1983.

The Law of November 28, 1984,[1] provides that the IML may investigate credit establishments to verify the management of such establishments.

The IML can obtain access to the account books, registers, or other records or documents of credit establishments operating under the privilege of banking secrecy.[2]

The bank is obliged to make full disclosure to the IML, acting in its role as supervisory authority of the financial sector.

However, article 37 of the Law of April 20, 1983, provides expressly that the employees of the IML are required to observe professional secrecy.

In addition, the IML is bound by article 458 of the Penal Code. In order to allow full banking supervision, the bank, its independent auditors, and the IML are authorized, however, to exchange information.[3]

The IML also may inform all Luxembourg banks regarding the magnitude of loans given by Luxembourg banks to certain individual or corporate clients.[4]

In addition, the IML can communicate to a foreign country administration the information which is known to it regarding supervision of the financial sector. But the IML is obliged to refuse communication of such information when the foreign administration is not required to observe professional secrecy and if such information is not used exclusively for the purpose of supervising credit establishments.

International supervision

23-007 EC Council Directive Number 83/350 of June 13, 1983, provides for the supervision of credit institutions within the European Community.

Luxembourg has implemented the provisions of this Directive in articles 31.1 to 31.8 of the Law of November 28, 1984.

---

[1] The legislation also is known as the Banking Act of 1984.

[2] Banking Act of 1984, article 17.3.

[3] *Id.*, article 17.6.

[4] *Id.*, article 30.

Insofar as such supervision is the function of the IML, the EC Directive does not result in a new exception to Luxembourg's banking secrecy practice.

If the IML receives information from a foreign control authority in the matter of the supervision of banks, it may not utilize such information for any purpose other than supervision.

The monetary authorities

It is the Belgo-Luxembourg Exchange Institute (IBLC) which executes the provisions of the law and Grand-Ducal regulations relating to exchange control.   **23-008**

The mission of the IBLC is to search for and record any infringements of these provisions.

Banks are obliged to provide to the officers of the IBLC all evidence concerning transactions subject to its supervision and to authorize inspection by the IBLC of all the documents necessary to verify these transactions.

The representatives of the IBLC are liable to criminal proceedings if they divulge any information which has come into their possession in the exercise of their functions.

Customs

Under the provisions of article 8.1, the Belgian Law of June 1, 1967,   **23-009**
introduced into Luxembourg law by the Decree of August 1, 1967, Luxembourg banks are required to provide transactional information to the Customs Authority.

BANKING SECRECY AND THE COURTS

National courts

When the banker is confronted with civil or commercial proceedings, two cases can be distinguished.   **23-010**

If the banker is called as a witness, he can choose to testify or to refuse to testify. The Supreme Court of Luxembourg has decided several times that any person required to observe professional secrecy according to article 458 of the Penal Code may disclose confidential information when he is required to testify, but the court may not oblige the person to disclose such information.[5]

If the banker is a party to a lawsuit, he may disclose information covered by banking secrecy in the interest of his own defense.

However, this exception to banking secrecy is narrowly construed.[6] The banker also may be called to testify before a Luxembourg criminal court. In such event, the banker is obliged to appear in court, but article 458 of the Penal Code permits the witness to adopt either of two attitudes:

(1) He may answer the questions asked by the court, or
(2) He may refuse to answer questions covered by banking secrecy.

The situation is the same, in fact, as in civil or commercial matters; the court has no authority to oblige the banker to disclose his information.

Under articles 65 and 66 of the Criminal Procedure Code, the investigating judge (*Juge d'instruction*) has wide ranging powers to investigate the offices of the bank and to take possession of all documents relevant to a criminal offense under the jurisdiction of the investigating judge.

However, the banker may use article 458 of the Penal Code to justify refusal to answer questions regarding such documents.

International judicial cooperation

23-011 Luxembourg judicial authorities are frequently requested by foreign judicial authorities through letters rogatory to investigate in Luxembourg matters on behalf of foreign prosecutors.

If the Grand Duchy of Luxembourg has not signed a bilateral treaty with the foreign authority's country, or if the foreign country is not signatory to one of the multinational treaties signed by the Grand Duchy of Luxembourg, the investigating judge may execute such a letter rogatory only if he has been previously authorized to do so by the Minister of Justice.[7]

---

[5] Cour. Sup. Justice, March 21, 1957; June 6, 1961, and November 3, 1976.

[6] See Luxembourg, June 15, 1983, number 6516, *Rogalla* v. *Herstatt Bank*.

[7] The Law of 7 March 1980, article 59, concerning the organization of judicial power.

The Grand Duchy of Luxembourg is a party to the European Convention on judicial cooperation in criminal matters, signed in Strasbourg on April 20, 1959,[8] and to the Benelux Treaty on judicial cooperation in criminal matters, signed in Brussels on June 27, 1962.[9]

Letters rogatory may be executed only in cases in which the offender also may be extradited. This excludes any cooperation in matters relating to taxes, customs, exchange control, and restrictions on trade (except narcotics).

It is fair to say that the Luxembourg authorities are very cautious in allowing judicial cooperation only in cases of serious criminal offenses, in particular as to whether a letter rogatory hides an alleged tax offense behind a *prima facie* criminal offense.

In a recent case, the Court of Appeal of Luxembourg refused to a foreign *partie civile* access to criminal files in Luxembourg in circumstances in which a foreign authority would have received information which it could not otherwise have obtained through a letter rogatory.[10]

BANKING SECRECY AND PRIVATE PERSONS

Authorization from client

Although article 458 of the Penal Code is a statutory provision of **23-012** public policy and although a potential victim may generally not waive his or her protection under criminal law, whether the client may authorize the bank expressly to give information to third parties which would normally fall under banking secrecy is subject to discussion in Luxembourg.

At any rate, the bank is authorized to provide information, but it is not obliged to do so.[11] Thus, professional secrecy is not only a duty for the bank but a right, as well.

---

[8] Applied in Luxembourg through the Law of July 21, 1976.

[9] Applied in Luxembourg through the Law of February 26, 1966, and the Law of June 2, 1977.

[10] See Luxembourg, July 1, 1988, Number 71/88 ChdC, *Bco Ambrosiano S.p.A.* v. *Bco Ambrosiano Andino S.A.*

[11] See Luxembourg, June 6, 1961, Pas XVIII 351.

Majority shareholders

23-013 A bank may give to its majority shareholder information requested by the supervisory authority of the majority shareholder in cases relating to banking supervision (article 31.5, Banking Act of 1984).

However, only information relevant to banking supervision may be provided, and clients' names are not considered relevant for purposes of banking supervision.

As noted above, in 1981, a law was enacted which indirectly confirms the application of article 458 to bankers.

In fact, article 16 of the Law of April 23, 1981[12] introduced an exception to banking secrecy. It provides that, by derogation from article 458 of the Penal Code, the persons responsible for management of credit establishments may communicate to any person who holds at least half the registered capital or funds of the establishment information relating to:

(1) The amount, nature, and terms of loans granted to the debtor when total of such loans exceeds an absolute amount or is higher than a specified co-efficient applied to specific items of the balance sheet of the establishment, and

(2) The amount, nature, and term of commitments to another credit establishment where the total of such commitments exceeds an absolute amount or is higher than a specified co-efficient applied to specific items of the balance sheet of the establishment.

The banker and persons linked to his clients

23-014 The principle in Luxembourg is that banking secrecy may be invoked by third parties, even as between spouses.

However, there are some exceptions resulting from statute, case law, and commentaries.

Regarding estates

23-015 After death, legal heirs and legatees have universal title to the assets of the client of a bank and are entitled to obtain information concerning the assets and to give instructions relative to the account if they establish that they are the sole heirs of the deceased client.

12 Now, Banking Act of 1984, article 31.

In a judgment of May 5, 1989, confirmed by a judgment on appeal of October, 27, 1989, the District Court of Luxembourg decided that the heir entitled to a compulsory share of the estate must receive all information relating to the assets existing both before and after the death of the account holder.

However, there is support for the position that the deceased has a right to the protection of his private life and, consequently, his heirs should have no right to obtain information relating to the transactions made by the deceased before his death.

Regarding bankruptcy

In a bankruptcy proceedings, the judge-commissioner can obtain   **23-016**
from the bank all information relating to the bankruptcy.

Article 485 of the Commercial Code allows the judge-commissioner to hear the bankrupt or any other persons to verify balance sheets and to investigate the reasons, causes, and circumstances of the bankruptcy.

Regarding other cases

The legal commentaries consider other cases. For instance, the legal   **23-017**
representatives of the company have access to banking information. However, a distinction is made based on the form of the company.

In the case of the *société en nom collectif* (general partnership), it appears that all the partners have the right to obtain information relating to the accounts of the company.

In the *sociétés de capitaux* (financing companies), the right to access banking information is reserved to the persons who have the responsibility for management: the board of directors and the auditors in a *société anonyme* (joint stock company) and the manager in a *société à responsabilité limitée* (company with limited liability).

Banking secrecy is opposable to the shareholders or the partners of such companies.

The authorized agent may take note of the bank assets of his client. This authorization is limited to his mandate, *i.e.*, the authorized agent may not obtain information regarding the operations made outside the period of duration of the mandate or which have no links with the object of the mandate.

CONCLUSION

23-018   Banking secrecy is well protected in Luxembourg. A banker or an employee of a bank who discloses the secrets which are entrusted to him commits a punishable offense.

The Member States of the European Community sometimes criticize Luxembourg's banking secrecy. Banking secrecy is seen by some Member States of the EC as an obstacle to free movement of capital and to tax harmonization.

However, Luxembourg does not share this point of view. Luxembourg is ready to adopt certain measures relating to the maintenance of the propriety and integrity of the financial jurisdiction, as in the law against money laundering,[13] but it refuses to impose significant restrictions on banking secrecy.

---

[13] The Law of July 7, 1989.

MEXICO

Daniel del Río and José F. Salem
Basham, Ringe & Correa
Mexico City, Mexico

Chapter 24

MEXICO

INTRODUCTION

The Mexican banking system was composed until September 1982 **24-001** of the *Banco de Mexico* (Central Bank) and private and government-owned banks. Thereafter, a Presidential Decree was issued, ordering the expropriation and nationalization of banking institutions. The Decree also transformed banking and credit services into a restricted and exclusive activity of the State.

In 1990, as a result of the opening of the Mexican economy, President Carlos Salinas de Gortari initiated the re-privatization of various industries, including banking, thus authorizing private investment.

Pursuant to the above policy, in July 1990 the new Credit Institutions Law (CIL) was enacted, regulating banking and credit services and providing that such activities may be performed and rendered only through multi-service banks and development banks.

PROFESSIONAL SECRECY

Although there is no specific definition of banking secrecy in Mex- **24-002** ico, there are similar regimes, such as the concept of professional secrecy.

Acosta Romero has defined professional secrecy as:

"The silence and discretion that, for ethical reasons, certain persons must keep with respect to facts, circumstances or information disclosed, or documents delivered to them by their clients in the course of their professional activities."[1]

Professional secrecy also is defined as:

"That [information] which must be kept undisclosed, unknown or hidden [from third parties] by the wish of the party who may be negatively affected or damaged as a consequence of disclosure thereof."[2]

Pursuant to the above, professional secrecy has its basis in the ethics of those professionals who have knowledge of the facts and in the public regulations established by society to protect privacy or legal security.

Mexican legislation provides rules on secrecy in many different areas and activities. As an example, the Federal Labor Law provides for an employee's obligations to keep in secrecy all technical, industrial, commercial, and manufacturing information considered as secret. Failure by the employee to comply with such obligation shall be sufficient cause for terminating the labor relationship with the employee.

In addition, the Law Regulating Professional Activities provides for every professional to keep as secret the information of their clients. In addition, the Securities Market Law restricts inside trading information for all individuals involved in securities transactions including stock brokers, directors, examiners and officers, shareholders owing 10 percent or more of a stock brokerage house, as well as their directors, officers, and employees.

All such persons are prohibited from carrying out any transaction involving inside trading information and from revealing such information to any third party.

BANKING AND TRUSTEE SECRECY

24-003 Articles 117 and 118 of the CIL provide the basis of banking secrecy and trustee secrecy.

---

[1] Acosta Romero, *Las Instituciones Fiduciarias y el Fideicomiso en México*, Banco Mexicano Somex, S.A., México, D.F., at p. 123.

[2] *Diccionario Jurídico Mexicano* (Mexican Legal Dictionary), Editorial Porrua, S.A., Universidad Nacional Autónoma de México, Instituto de Investigaciones Jurídicas, México, D.F., 1988, at p. 2876.

Banking secrecy

In relationship to banking secrecy, article 117 provides: 24-004

"Article 117 - Banking institutions shall in no event provide information on any deposits or transactions to any person other than the depositor, obligor, the holder of title or the beneficiary thereof or to their legal representatives or persons empowered to handle the account or participate in the services, unless said information shall have been requested by a court of law pursuant to a ruling issued in a legal action where the holder of title is either plaintiff or defendant, or by the federal tax authorities through the National Banking Commission, for tax purposes. Employees and officers of banking institutions shall be liable, under applicable law, for the violation of the secrecy obligation established herein and the banking institutions shall be liable for any damages sustaineddue to the disclosure of said secret.

The above is without prejudice of the obligation banks have to provide information to the National Banking Commission (in the exercise of its activities) which information and documents may be requested in connection with the transactions carried out in the normal course of business and the services rendered by said banks".

Trustee secrecy

As regards trustee secrecy, article 118 provides: 24-005

"Article 118 - Except for information requested by the National Banking Commission, the violation of the secrecy obligation on the transactions contemplated by section XV of article 46 of the Law (trusts, commissions and agency agreements), including disclosure to government authorities and courts of law in legal actions or proceedings, other than those filed by a trustor, beneficiary or principal against the banking institutions or vice versa, shall make the banking institution incur in civil liability for damages without prejudice of any criminal liability".

Scope of banking secrecy protections

24-006 Pursuant to the above provisions, banking secrecy shall protect:

(1) Banking and credit operations (active and passive), and
(2) Confidential and private information provided by the clients to the banks, their officers, and their employees.

However, banking secrecy is not considered to encompass general information which is or becomes part of the public domain; information provided by the client not related to its private matters or the transactions carried out with the banks; and information which has been expressly authorized by the client to be disclosed to any third parties in connection with the granting of credits, or regarding the commercial or moral solvency of such client.

In addition to the above and as provided by article 117 of CIL, courts of law may request any information pursuant to a ruling issued in a legal action whereby the client is involved, either as plaintiff or defendant, or in the event the federal tax authorities so request through the National Banking Commission for tax purposes.

In addition, the National Banking Commission is entitled to request all information on transactions carried out by the banking institutions in order to review and supervise the legality of such transactions.

Nature of trustee secrecy protections

24-007 Article 118 of the CIL regulates trustee secrecy regarding activities carried out by the banks in connection with trusts, commissions, and agency activities. In this respect, banking institutions may only provide information to the courts of law pursuant to a ruling issued in connection with a legal action whereby the banks as trustors, beneficiaries, commissioners, or principals are plaintiffs or defendants.

In the event of a violation of their duties, banking institutions shall be liable for any damages that may be produced without prejudice of criminal liability.

SECURITIES SECRECY

Securities secrecy also may be considered as part of the banking **24-008**
secrecy regime in Mexico since it involves credit operations in the
securities market.

In this respect and as provided in article 25 of the Securities
Market Law, securities agencies or brokers shall in no event provide
any information to any third party regarding transactions carried
out for their clients, unless their clients or their legal representatives
have authorized them to do so.

This provision does not apply to the information provided to
courts of law regarding any legal action whereby the client is either
plaintiff or defendant; to the information provided to government
authorities through the National Securities Commission; and to the
statistical information that the securities agencies or brokers are
required to supply to the Commission on activities and transactions
carried out by them.

Any information provided to the National Securities Commission shall be submitted in general terms without mentioning the
client names or private information.

In the event of a breach of securities secrecy, the client may
submit its claim to the National Securities Commission in order to
resolve the controversy through a conciliatory or arbitration procedure, as provided in the Securities Market Law, without prejudice
to any criminal liability before the courts of law.

DISCLOSURE OF BANKING SECRETS

Depositors or beneficiaries of bank accounts have a right to lodge a **24-009**
legal action with the National Banking Commission or the courts of
law for collection of damages against banks and the officers and
employees of such institutions that, by breach of their obligations
thereunder, disclose any information considered as protected by
banking secrecy.

In addition, articles 210 and 211 of the Criminal Code for the
Federal District establish violations of professional secrecy, including banking secrecy, as a crime. Article 210 provides:

> "Article 210 - A fine of five to fifty pesos, or imprisonment from
> two months to one year shall be imposed to any individual
> who, without cause and the prior consent of the person who

may be negatively affected, discloses any secret or privileged information received because of his or her employment or position".

Article 211 provides:

"Article 211 - A penalty of imprisonment from one to five years, fine of 50 to 500 pesos and cancellation of the right to exercise the profession, in the event, from two months to one year, shall be imposed if the disclosure is made by any individuals who renders professional or technical services or by public servants, provided the secret disclosed or published is of an industrial nature".

In case of violation of the banking secrecy obligation, the depositor, obligor, holder of title, or beneficiary may initiate a criminal action through the competent courts of law or may petition the National Banking Commission or the National Securities Commission for relief.

THE NETHERLANDS

Sebastiaan A. Boele
Buruma Maris Scheer Van Solkema
The Hague, The Netherlands

Chapter 25

THE NETHERLANDS

INTRODUCTION

The Law on the Supervision of Credit Institutions (*Wet toezicht* **25-001**
kredietwezen), bringing Dutch banks under the supervision of the
Dutch Central Bank (*De Nederlandsche Bank*), distinguishes among
the following types of banks:

(1) Credit institutions (*i.e.,* general banks and cooperative
banks);
(2) Securities credit institutions;
(3) Saving banks;
(4) Near banks;
(5) Mortgage banks, and
(6) Other capital market institutions.

Since these distinctions are not relevant for the present subject, the
term "bank" will be used throughout this contribution, encompassing all the previously-mentioned types.

There are no specific laws or regulations in The Netherlands
dealing with banking secrecy. The duty of confidentiality is not
codified in statutory form. It is, therefore, necessary to rely on
general principles of law and jurisprudence in examining this topic.

Only in the field of taxation has a code of conduct been established, laying down rules with regard to the duty of banks to
disclose certain information to the tax authorities. This subject will
be dealt with below.

The concept of banking secrecy can be differentiated into two
categories:

(1) The bank's *duty* of confidentiality to its customers, and
(2) The *right* of a bank to keep information about its customers
confidential.

The first category is concerned with the question of whether a bank owes a duty toward its customers to keep their affairs and details secret and whether it is a breach of contract or a criminal offense for the bank to disclose such information.

The second category is concerned with the question of whether a bank has a right to keep secret any information concerning its customers in criminal or civil proceedings and whether it has the right to do so in fiscal matters involving the tax authorities.

BANK'S DUTY OF CONFIDENTIALITY

25-002　The bank's duty of confidentiality may be approached from two different aspects, that of criminal law and that of civil law. As has been mentioned, there are no express statutory provisions under criminal or civil law which impose a duty of confidentiality on banks.

Criminal law

25-003　Regarding criminal law, article 272 of the Penal Code[1] does provide that it is a criminal offense to purposely disclose a secret, which the disclosing party knows or should know he must keep confidential by reason of his office or his profession or by reason of any statutory provision.

The Dutch Supreme Court has held that, except in the case of explicit statutory regulations, article 272 applies only when the office or profession, by its very nature, entails a duty of confidentiality.

Whether this is the case with the banking profession is doubtful. In its judgment of December 18, 1984, the Amsterdam Court of Appeal held that article 272 does not apply to banks or their employees and that they are, therefore, not punishable by law whenever they purposely disclose a secret that is entrusted to them by one of their customers.

Although the judgment of the Court of Appeal has been criticized, the Supreme Court has not yet had an opportunity to decide on this issue. However, it should be noted that, even if it were decided that banks fall under the provision of article 272 and it would be considered a criminal offense to disclose confidential

1 Law of March 3, 1981, *Official Gazette*, number 35, as subsequently amended.

information about a bank's customers, this would not mean that the employees of a bank would fall into the category of those persons who are subject to the rules as to professional secrecy and who, for that reason, cannot be compelled to testify. Banks and/or their employees do not enjoy this privilege.

Act on Registration of Personal Data

In 1989, the Act on the Registration of Personal Data[2] came into force. This Act has as its objective the protection of the privacy of natural persons whose personal data is registered with governmental or private-sector institutions, including banks.

25-004

Among other things, the Act forbids the distribution of such records to third parties without the prior consent of the person registered, except when this is in conformity with the purpose of a registration (*e.g.*, the bank receives an application for an insurance policy and sends it to the insurance company) or as required by law (*e.g.*, in the context of a criminal investigation). The violation of this provision is a criminal offense.

The Act allows for the distribution of records consisting of name, address, and other such data for the purpose of communication. Dutch banks, however, have stated as a matter of policy that they will not make use of this possibility.

Uniform General Banking Conditions

Although no statutory provisions to this effect exist, there is no doubt that, under civil law, banks owe a duty of confidentiality to their customers. This duty is based on the law of contract.

25-005

Nearly all Dutch banks use the Uniform General Banking Conditions as a basis for their relations with their customers. Although even these General Conditions do not contain any explicit provision as to banking secrecy, the basis for the bank's duty in this respect is to be found in article 2 of the General Conditions.

Article 2 of the General Banking Conditions reads:

---

[2] Law of December 28, 1988, *Official Gazette*, number 665, as subsequently amended.

"The bank shall exercise due care in complying with the customer's instructions and the performance of other agreements
with the customer, as well as respect the interests of its customers to the best of its abilities. On all occasions, the bank
shall exercise due care in its relation with the customer. . . ."

It is generally assumed that this provision implies a duty of confidentiality on the part of the bank toward its customers. This view
has, in any case, been adopted by the Dutch Commission on Banking Disputes, which has been established to settle disputes between
banks and their private customers. The Commission has held on
several occasions that a bank acted in breach of its duty to its
customer by disclosing information to third parties.

Furthermore, under Dutch law, a contract does not have only the
juridical effects agreed to by the parties but also those that, according to the nature of the contract, result from the law, usage, or the
requirements of reasonableness and equity. It has been argued that
the bank's duty of confidentiality to its customers rests on this rule
of law since, in practice, this duty is respected and accepted as a
legal obligation.

Registration of credit transactions

25-006 Most banks and other credit institutions, such as insurance companies, credit-card organizations, and mail-order companies, are
members of the *Stichting Bureau Krediet Registratie* (BKR).

This is an agency that registers all loans or other credit arrangements granted to private persons. The BKR also maintains a record
of whether the borrower fulfills his obligations on outstanding
loans.

Members of the BKR do not only have the duty to furnish the
BKR with all such information but also to consult the BKR database
before granting any private person a loan or providing him any
other form of credit. Apparently, the banks do not believe this
constitutes a breach of confidentiality on their part since only banks
and other financial institutions can become members of the BKR
and all members are obliged to keep secret all information they
receive from the BKR database.

BANK'S DUTY TO DISCLOSE

The bank's duty of confidentiality naturally gives way before a 25-007 statutory duty to disclose information, *e.g.*, to the judicial or tax authorities. The extent of this duty to disclose is discussed below.

Duty to identify

Regarding the question of what information banks are able to 25-008 supply, it is important to know that Dutch banks are under a duty to ascertain with due diligence the identity of all customers with whom they wish to enter into a relationship for the provision of financial services.

If the bank is unable to identify the customer with a sufficient degree of certainty, it is not allowed to enter into a relationship with that customer. This rule is founded in an agreement that the Dutch Central Bank concluded in 1986 with the banks and which was given force of law in 1988.

Duty to testify

When the employees of a bank (including its managing directors) 25-009 are lawfully called upon to appear in court as witnesses, whether in civil or in criminal proceedings, they are obliged to give testimony insofar as it has any bearing on the case.

Like all witnesses, the employees of a bank may testify only as to facts that are known to them from their own observation. No obligation rests on a witness to produce documents or other records.

A bank cannot be ordered in civil proceedings to surrender documents as evidence, unless the bank itself is a party to the litigation. In civil proceedings, the court only may order the litigating parties to produce certain documents relevant and necessary for the case at hand.

The exemption from giving testimony on the basis of professional secrecy that is granted to lawyers, doctors, and members of the clergy is not conferred on banks or their employees. They are, therefore, compelled to give evidence without restriction when lawfully called upon to do so.

Nevertheless, a special rule applies to officials of the Dutch Central Bank who obtain confidential information concerning banks. In its judgment of 11 December 1985, the European Community (EC) Court of Justice in the *Hillegom* Case[3] ruled on the interpretation of article 12 of the First Council Directive of December 12, 1977,[4] requiring Member States of the EC to ensure that all persons currently or previously employed by banking authorities are bound by the obligation of professional secrecy.

The Dutch Supreme Court, on the basis of this decision, has ruled that, when an official of the Dutch Central Bank is questioned as a witness concerning confidential information that he obtained in the exercise of his duties and he refuses to give evidence on the basis of professional secrecy, the examining judge must decide for each question that the witness is asked which should prevail: the public interest that the truth comes to light or the public interest that certain confidential information is kept secret.[5]

Means to compel disclosure

25-010   A common means to compel a bank to reveal at least some information about a specific customer is to attach the customer's assets and accounts with a bank after a judgment against that customer has been obtained. The bank is then obliged to state what assets of the customer are deposited with it and what money the bank owes the customer.

In the case of criminal investigations or proceedings, the judicial authorities have extensive powers to compel third parties, such as banks, to hand over documents and other materials that can help to bring the truth to light. Generally, these powers can be exercised only by or under the authority of the examining judge, charged by the court to conduct the investigations, when there is a reasonable suspicion that a criminal offense has been committed.

The rules that govern these proceedings are no different for banks than for other private or legal persons. They will be dealt with briefly to provide some insight into the investigations to which banks may be subjected.

Often, when banks are compelled to cooperate in criminal proceedings, the offense under investigation is tax fraud or a related criminal offense. The specific rules that apply in those cases are dealt with below.

The examining judge may order a bank to surrender certain objects that he reasonably suspects that the bank has in its possession and which can help to reveal the truth. The examining judge

---

3 [1985] E.C.R. 3947.
4 First Council Directive of December 12, 1977 (77/780/EEC).
5 H.R. July 22, 1986; N.J. 1986, 823

must, however, indicate with some degree of precision which specific objects are to be surrendered.

The refusal to comply with this order is a criminal offense, except for those persons, such as doctors and lawyers, who can raise the defense of professional secrecy.

If the examining judge intends to order the handing over of objects consisting of letters or other documents, several restrictions apply; the judge may order the handing over of such letters and documents only when they:

(1) Originate from the suspect;
(2) Are destined for him;
(3) Belong to him;
(4) Are the object of the offense under investigation, or
(5) Have served to commit it.

The examining judge also may request the court to issue a search warrant, with which a search may be conducted in a bank's offices. The sole object of such a search is the seizure of objects which can help bring to light the truth.

During the search, however, letters and other documents may be seized only when they are the object of the offense under investigation or have served to commit it, unless the court explicitly has given its permission to seize other documents as well.

DISCLOSURE TO FISCAL AUTHORITIES

Article 49 of the General Law of the Kingdom's Taxes (*Algemene Wet* **25-011**
inzake Rijksbelastingen)[6] imposes a duty on certain bodies to produce information to the tax authorities. Its main provisions can be summarized as follows:

(1) Persons and bodies operating a business or practicing an independent profession within the Kingdom have the duty, when so ordered, to give the tax inspector access to their books and other documents when the examination thereof may be of importance for the levy of taxes on third parties. This includes the duty to allow the tax inspector to make copies.

[6] Law of July 2, 1959, *Official Gazette*, number 301, as subsequently amended.

(2) Such persons and bodies have the duty, when so ordered, to furnish the tax inspector with such other data and information as may be of importance for the levy of taxes from third parties.

It should be noted that this duty exists irrespective of any actual suspicion of wrongdoing, since these powers are conferred on the tax inspector for the purpose of verifying tax returns submitted to him. The decision as to whether the information is of importance for the levy of taxes against third parties is essentially left to the discretion of the tax inspector.

So-called "serial questions" are allowed under article 49. Serial questions are those that are not individualized as to persons or bodies and that may cover more than one fiscal year.

Lawyers, doctors, and members of the clergy are, by reason of their professional secrecy privilege, exempted from complying with the tax inspectors' orders. As has been mentioned, banks do not enjoy this privilege.

Article 49 makes no exception for banks in this respect, and its provisions, therefore, in principle also apply to banks. Banks, however, have always enjoyed a special status in The Netherlands as to their duty to disclose information about their customers to the tax authorities, insofar as the tax authorities have never fully exercised their powers to demand such information from banks.

Code of Conduct

25-012 In 1984, the Ministry of Finance and the banking community agreed on a Code of Conduct, which lays down certain rules concerning the use by the tax inspector of his powers under article 49.

The Code of Conduct states that article 49 applies to banks without any limitation. Nevertheless, it establishes certain rules whereby the use of the tax inspector's powers are, in fact, restricted.

The most important rules contained in the Code of Conduct are the following:

(1) An order to have access may be given in all those instances in which Dutch taxation interests are at stake. This means that the right to information also extends to non-residents, either because they may be subject to the levy of Dutch taxes or because the information obtained about non-residents may be of importance in other respects for Dutch taxation purposes (*e.g.*, for the levy of tax against a Dutch resident).

(2) Before giving an order to have access to information that is in the possession of a bank, the tax inspector shall first try to obtain the desired information from the taxpayer himself, unless the interest of the investigation requires otherwise. In addition, the taxpayer should be given the opportunity to collect the required information from the bank before the tax inspector approaches the bank.

(3) If the tax inspector requires information concerning a specific customer, the bank shall allow complete access to the financial relation that exists between the bank and that customer. Financial relations are understood as including bank and similar accounts, deposits, loans, security accounts, safe rentals, and insurance agencies.

(4) The "individualization" of the bank's customer by the tax inspector may take place either through the usual personal identification methods, or by means of an account number.

(5) The bank is only obliged to provide access and to allow copies to be made. No duty rests on the bank to provide information that goes beyond what appears from books and documents.

(6) The duty of a bank to allow access to information concerning one of its customers is not conditional upon the authorization by that customer.

(7) The submission of complete credit and client files and the allowing of access to documents therein will be required only under special circumstances, *i.e.*, when such access may be of considerable importance with respect to a certain customer. The tax authorities will decide whether such special circumstances exist.

(8) No access need be allowed to reports of meetings with the customer, reports to the bank by the bank's accountants, internal notes, correspondence between the offices of the bank, and other such information with which the client is wholly or partially unacquainted.

(9) Except when information about premium bonds, dividend-stripping, and interest is required, the tax inspector shall only be allowed to request information about specific customers who are to be individualized in the way mentioned previously (either through the usual identification methods or by means of an account number).

(10) The tax authorities may ask serial questions concerning the balance on all bank accounts, bonds, mortgage bonds, certificates of deposit, savings certificates, and all other yields generated by securities or financial relations that are to be regarded as interest for taxation purposes, as well as the payment of interest by financial institutions as intermediaries to third parties.

As will be seen, perhaps the most important aspect regarding the Code of Conduct is that no serial questions are allowed (thus precluding "fishing expeditions"), except in the case of an investigation on accrued interest.

The latter exception is due to the widespread practice of the Dutch to exclude from their tax returns the interest they have received on their savings accounts, since they are of the opinion that it is unfair to have to pay tax on interest. The Code of Conduct was amended in 1987 to allow for serial questions concerning accrued interest.

It should be noted, however, that the Code of Conduct contains a proviso allowing the tax authorities to ask serial questions on other subjects, provided that the Minister of Finance has given prior public notice of any such change in policy.

For the sake of completeness, it should be mentioned that the Amsterdam Stock Exchange also is a party to the Code of Conduct. Stockbrokers who are not also banks, therefore, profit from the rules of the Code of Conduct, as well.

The powers of the tax authorities examined in the previous paragraphs may be exercised at any time, even when no actual suspicion of tax fraud exists. When such a suspicion does arise, the same powers are conferred on the tax authorities as are mentioned above at paragraph 25-010, the most important difference being that, whereas in (common) criminal investigations and proceedings it is the examining judge who exercises these powers, in the case of tax fraud, the tax authorities directly exercise the investigatory powers.

It should be noted that similar powers are granted for the investigation of other economic offenses, such as insider trading.

Ministry of Finance directive

25-013 To avoid a loss of confidence in Dutch banks and a possible flight of capital to other countries, the Minister of Finance has issued a directive that makes all proposed measures against banks for the purpose of investigating tax fraud subject to review by a joint committee.

This committee consists of officials from the Tax Directorate and the Directorate of Domestic Financial Policy. If the committee members disagree as to the desirability of certain measures, it is the Minister himself who takes the decision.

It is clear that this directive confers no rights on banks or their customers. Nevertheless, it assures that the rather extensive powers of the tax authorities are used in a prudent way. Although searches within banks are not completely unknown, they have occurred only rarely.

CHAPTER 26

NETHERLANDS ANTILLES

Rudsel S. J. Martha
Minister Plenipotentiary, Netherlands Antilles
Netherlands Permanent Mission
to the European Communities
Brussels, Belgium

Chapter 26

NETHERLANDS ANTILLES

INTRODUCTION

This article surveys the extent of banking secrecy in the Netherlands **26-001** Antilles. The Netherlands Antilles, together with Aruba and The Netherlands, constitute the Kingdom of the Netherlands, a federation of autonomous countries governed by the Charter of the Kingdom of the Netherlands of 1954.

Under this Charter, each constituent part is autonomous with respect to matters concerning banking, civil, and criminal law. Consequently, each of the countries has its own laws and policies in these matters. By virtue of the operation of the principle of concordance enshrined in the Charter, there is a large degree of parallelism in the relevant legislation of the different countries.

Although the Netherlands Antilles is subject to the treaty establishing the European Community, article 227, paragraph 3, of that treaty limits its application to its part IV. Therefore, the Common Market legislation affecting banking secrecy does not apply to the Netherlands Antilles.

In the Netherlands Antilles, banking secrecy - or rather the confidentiality of financial information - is governed by both private and public law. As to private law, the Civil Code and the Commercial Code are relevant, while the legislation regarding foreign exchange, banking supervision, and criminal law are among the most relevant public laws.

Currently, the confidentiality of financial information in the Netherlands Antilles is under review. This review is induced by the fact that the Netherlands Antilles has expressed interest in accepting the obligations of the 1988 Vienna Convention on Illicit Drugs Trade, as well as its commitment to implement the recommendations of the Financial Action Task Force concerning measures to combat money laundering.

Mention also should be made of the fact that, since 1983, a treaty concerning mutual assistance in criminal matters is effective in the relations of the Netherlands Antilles with the United States. Under that treaty, the confidentiality of financial information can be pierced, except in connection with tax matters.

CONFIDENTIALITY OF FINANCIAL DATA UNDER CIVIL LAW

26-002   In the Netherlands Antilles, financial services are provided by many institutions. These include, in the first place, the banks and investment services companies, followed by the insurers.

These categories are found in both the onshore and the offshore sectors. This also applies to those engaged with ancillary services, such as accountants and tax consultants. Moreover, the so-called trust offices are found in the offshore sector.

Under Netherlands Antillean public law or imperative civil law, none of these institutions is subject to any secrecy obligation, whether general or specifically oriented towards the respective professional category. Therefore, to the extent that these actors are subject to a secrecy obligation, this obligation either arises from express contractual stipulations or from the good faith principle of article 1356 of the Civil Code of the Netherlands Antilles.[1]

Civil Code, article 1355

26-003   Cases in which providers of financial services expressly bind themselves to secrecy vis-à-vis the client are governed by provisions of article 1355 of the Civil Code of the Netherlands Antilles.

The first paragraph of that article provides that all legally valid agreements are deemed to be the law of the parties (the so-called *pacta sunt servanda* principle).

Consequently, the provider of financial services who agrees on such a stipulation with his client is legally bound to observe it, unless a legal obligation imposed by law or a *de facto* "*force majeure*", leaves him no alternative.[2]

---

[1] Compare P. W. Bartelings, "Banking Secrecy Stands or Falls with the Statute; A Few Remarks about Banking Secrecy in The Netherlands, Switzerland and Luxembourg", *TVVS 1991*, Number 91/3, at pp. 57-62.

[2] Civil Code of the Netherlands Antilles, article 1355, paragraph 2.

Generally, the agreement (written or not) will contain nothing about the obligation to secrecy. Therefore, the question will arise as to whether the secrecy is impliedly imposed by the agreement. This follows from the third paragraph of article 1355 of the Civil Code of the Netherlands Antilles, which prescribes that agreements must be implemented in good faith.

Because of the way this provision and the similar provision in the laws of The Netherlands are interpreted in case law and in doctrine, it has become necessary to evaluate in each specific case whether good faith implies secrecy. Generally, it can be asserted that parties are not only required to perform in good faith in the strict sense but, in addition, the parties moreover must do or, as the case may be, abstain from doing anything required by good faith in connection with the nature of the agreement and the circumstances.

The provision of paragraph 3 of article 1355 of the Civil Code of the Netherlands Antilles and the interpretation thus accepted is especially important to insurers, tax consultants, and accountants.

Civil Code, article 1356

A special obligation for banks to observe secrecy is derived from **26-004** article 1356 of the Civil Code of the Netherlands Antilles. That article provides that agreements do not only bind to that which has expressly been stipulated, but also to anything that is called for by the nature of the agreement, fairness, usage or the law.

It is generally accepted that, in banking, a practice - as contemplated within the meaning of this article - has evolved according to which banks ought to respect the confidentiality of the data of their clients.[3]

Within the Kingdom of The Netherlands, however, no court has ever dealt with this issue in relation to banks. Therefore, no case can be referred to in support of this conclusion. What is certainly non-existent as well is any case that contradicts the conclusion. Practice, however, confirms that the banks themselves also assume that they have a special relationship of confidence with their clients.

---

[3]Compare R. J. H. Smits, "Bankgeheimnis und Bankauskunft nach Niederländische Recht", *Bankgeheimnis und Bankauskunft in der BDR und in ausländische Rechtsordningen* (Berlin, 1986).

Banks as custodians

26-005   When banks lease safe deposit vaults to clients they act as custodian within the meaning of book 3, title 11, of the Civil Code of the Netherlands Antilles. By virtue of that provision, such banks incur the special confidentiality obligations inherent to custody.

First, article 1725 of the Civil Code of the Netherlands Antilles requires the bank to observe the same care it accords to the custody of its own valuables with respect to the custody of the safe deposit contents entrusted to it. If, as will frequently occur, something is entrusted to the bank for undisclosed safe-keeping, then the bank is bound pursuant to article 1732 of the Civil Code of the Netherlands Antilles to abstain from investigating the contents of the safe deposit box.

The doctrine confirms that this rule must be applied analogously to any other case in which it is obvious to the custodian (in this case the bank) that it has been the depositor's wish that the contents of objects given in safe-keeping be kept secret.[4]

When the bank acts as a custodian it is also bound to observe the general obligations of secrecy entailed by articles 1355 and 1356 of the Civil Code of the Netherlands Antilles. The latter is particularly important with respect to open safe-keeping of, for instance, securities.

Code of Commerce, article 9

26-006   Article 9 of the Code of Commerce of the Netherlands Antilles also plays a part within the framework of confidentiality regarding financial data.

Under that provision, a bank may only be compelled to open its books if required for the benefit of one who, as heir, an interested party in a community, a partner, an appointer of factors, or administrator, has a direct interest in the bank's doing so, and furthermore in the event of bankruptcy.

This provision limits the right to request opening of the books of a bank to a certain circle of persons. However, under article 6 of the Commercial Code of the Netherlands Antilles, courts have access to the obligatory accounts as prescribed by article 2 of the Commercial Code. In such cases, only the courts have access to these accounts.

Moreover, the authority of the courts does not extend beyond their obligatory accounts. Therefore, only the items mentioned in

---

[4] C.J. van Zeben and others, *Compendium van Bijzondere Overeenkomsten* (*A Compendium of Special Agreements*) (5th ed.), at p. 351.

article 2 of the Commercial Code ought to be disclosed to the courts[5] (see text below).

A violation of the obligation to observe secrecy pursuant to civil law may trigger civil penalties, to wit, compensation instead of or next to specific performance and the cancellation of the agreement, with or without indemnification.

CONFIDENTIALITY OF FINANCIAL DATA UNDER CRIMINAL LAW

In the Netherlands Antilles, the confidentiality of financial data is protected by criminal law in two ways: by ordinary criminal law and by the special penal provisions laid down in the Legislation on the Supervision of Financial Institutions.   **26-007**

Criminal Code, article 285

Article 285 of the Criminal Code of the Netherlands Antilles provides that one who intentionally discloses any secret which he is supposed to keep by virtue of his present or former office or profession is liable to an imprisonment not exceeding six months or a fine of no more than NaFl. 600.   **26-008**

If this crime is committed against a specific person, the offender will be prosecuted only on a complaint filed by that person. The concept of "office" refers to the *ex officio* obligation to observe secrecy,[6] whereas the concept of "profession" has a bearing on professional secrets prescribed by law.[7]

However, it does not appear that the obligation to observe secrecy, arising from an agreement (see text above) is also guaranteed by criminal law through this provision. On the other hand, it is article 286 of the Criminal Code of the Netherlands Antilles that will be applied within the framework of contractually created obligations to observe secrecy.

Given article 286 of the Criminal Code of the Netherlands Antilles, the bank can safeguard the obligation of secrecy which it has undertaken contractually vis-à-vis its customer, since bank employ-

---

[5] Compare the litigation resulting in the *Luxe Leder Lebo,* Judgment of the Supreme Court of The Netherlands, October 9, 1942, p. 821.

[6] See LMA = Civil Servants Act.

[7] Such as attorneys, see Adv.Lv. (The Lawyer's Act); or civil law notaries, see the Rgl. N. Ambt (Civil Law Notary's Act).

ees who, not being a party to the contract themselves, may be required unilaterally not to disclose secrets of the business.

This is because, as far as material in this context is concerned, article 286 of the Criminal Code of the Netherlands Antilles provides that one who intentionally reveals business secrets is liable to criminal prosecution.

This provision applies to the secrecy obligations created within the scope of civil law. According to a judgment of the Supreme Court of The Netherlands of January 14, 1935,[8] this secrecy obligation may be imposed unilaterally by the management of an enterprise. The absence of the employee's endorsement of the obligation is not deemed by the Supreme Court to be an obstacle to his criminal prosecution.

Special penal provisions on the confidentiality of financial data also apply to the employees of the Central Bank of the Netherlands Antilles and the external experts appointed by that bank. Violation of conditions, rules, and provisions imposed by or pursuant to the Foreign Exchange Act, if committed intentionally, are deemed to be crimes and render the offender liable to an imprisonment not exceeding two years or a fine not exceeding NaFl. 25,000 or both penalties (paragraph 3, article 28, of the Foreign Exchange Act).

A violation which is not intentional is deemed to be a misdemeanor and is punishable by an imprisonment not exceeding six months or a fine not in excess of NaFl. 10,000, or both. The Banking and Credit System Supervision Act (1972) also contains its own special penal provisions, to wit: paragraph 4 of article 3, paragraph 3 of article 9, and article 12.

Financial Sector Supervision Act

26-009   The unofficial draft of the Financial Sector Supervision Act provides, in its article 20, that one who performs a duty by or pursuant to the provisions of the Act is prohibited from making additional or different use of, or to make more or different disclosures about data or information obtained under this Act than is strictly necessary for the performance of his duties.

In article 21, exceptions are made as to prudential supervision. However, within the framework of international cooperation in the field of banking supervision, the bank may not exchange names of individual depositors. Violation of the prohibition contained in article 20 will, if committed intentionally, be regarded as a crime

---

[8] Judgment of the Supreme Court of The Netherlands, January 14, 1935, at p. 430.

and will be punished by an imprisonment not exceeding two years or a fine not in excess of NaFl. 500,000, or both.

Violation of the prohibition will, if not intentionally committed be considered a misdemeanor and punished with an imprisonment of one year at the most, or a fine not exceeding NaFl. 250,000, or both, under the provisions of article 28.

The draft of the Financial Sector Supervision Act introduces a provision in article 23 which prohibits a financial institution from submitting or otherwise disclosing the personal and financial data of their customers to tax agencies or any other fiscal agencies, whatever their names, unless this has been expressly provided by federal statute of the Netherlands Antilles or by a treaty. The same penal provision as mentioned above applies when this prohibition is disregarded.

LIMITATIONS ON CONFIDENTIALITY

The laws on civil procedure, criminal procedure, and monetary and financial supervision all contain exceptions as to the confidentiality of financial data. **26-010**

However, the purpose of such limitations is not to relieve the banker from all secrecy obligations in his dealings with others than the bodies referred to in those laws.[9]

Express obligations to disclose

The limitations arising from monetary-financial legislation take the shape of express obligations to disclose financial data to the administrative bodies appointed by or pursuant to the law. Such an obligation has been laid down in article 8 of the Foreign Exchange Act.[10] **26-011**

The first paragraph of article 8 provides that anyone is under an obligation to furnish to the Central Bank of the Netherlands Antilles (the BNA), on request, all information and data which the BNA needs for the preparation of the balance of payments.

[9]E.T. Fransisca, *Toezicht op het Antilliaanse Bank- en Kredietwezen, Rechtsgrondslagen* (*Supervision over the Antillean Banking and Credit System, Legal Foundations*) (1985), p. 68.
[10]Publication Bulletin Number 67 of 1981.

In the second paragraph, the BNA is granted powers to issue administrative rules in this area. Thereby, the possibility is created to have the desired provided information in most cases through the exchange banks who, in connection with their business, often are closely involved with the facts to be reported.[11]

Furthermore, the first paragraph of article 26 of the Foreign Exchange Act authorizes the BNA - apart from the powers derived from article 8 - to gather any and all information it may deem necessary for the proper performance of the duties imposed upon it by or pursuant to the Act. According to the explanatory memorandum, one of the purposes of that article is to give the BNA powers of auditing which it may delegate to other experts.[12]

Due to the term "anyone", the powers of the BNA cover anyone active in the financial sector, and all of such persons are under an obligation to give the information requested when they are required to, regardless of whether they are onshore or offshore enterprises.[13]

Under article 3 of the Banking and Credit System Supervision Act,[14] the BNA can gather any information deemed reasonable or necessary to evaluate whether the enterprise or institution concerned should be registered or not. When summoned, the respective enterprise or institution is under an obligation to allow the BNA to inspect books and records in order to satisfy itself as to the correctness of the information, and it shall cooperate with the BNA as far as possible in such an investigation instituted by or on orders of the BNA.

An appeal against this may be lodged with the Governor of the Netherlands Antilles. Pursuant to articles 7, 8, and 9 of the Banking and Credit System Supervision Act, the BNA has access to all information on the conduct of management of credit institutions within the meaning of the Banking and Credit System Supervision Act.

However, this does not apply to credit institutions whose business only consists of credits to borrowers outside the Netherlands Antilles from risk capital and/or borrowed capital, both obtained from abroad (article 14 of the Banking and Credit System Supervision Act).

---

[11] Explanatory Memorandum accompanying the Bill, Parliament of the Netherlands Antilles, session 1978-1979, at p. 7.

[12] *Id.*, at p. 14.

[13] R. S. J. Martha, "De Deviezenrechtelijke Positie van Buitengaatse Ondernemingen (The Position of Offshore Companies under the Foreign Exchange Act)", E.L. Joubert and others, *UNI KU UNA - Noten bij Van der Grinten*, 1991.

[14] Publication Bulletin Number 138 of 1972.

Due to the BNA'S new policy in granting foreign exchange licenses to offshore banks, it may result on occasions in such banks being subject to the obligations contemplated in articles 7, 8, and 9 of the Banking and Credit System Supervision Act.[15]

The legal obligation of the BNA and its employees to observe secrecy is a guarantee for the confidential handling by the BNA of the data it has gathered by virtue of the Foreign Exchange Act and the Banking and Credit System Supervision Act.

Obligation to give testimony

The obligation to give testimony in civil actions also imposes limitations on the confidentiality of financial data. Under civil procedural law, anyone summoned in a manner valid at law is under an obligation to give testimony, pursuant to article 1928 of the Civil Code of the Netherlands Antilles. **26-012**

Actually, this is a public law obligation or a civic duty of public order, based on the public interest within a society, which requires the truth to be revealed in a legal action, not only for the benefit of the litigating parties but also for the benefit of a good administration of justice and legal protection.[16]

The right to refuse to give testimony is an exception to the obligation to give testimony. Under article 1928 of the Civil Code of the Netherlands Antilles, all the persons who are bound to secrecy on account of their position, profession, or legal relationship are entitled to refuse to give testimony. Based on the jurisprudence,[17] it is accepted that the banker is not entitled to the right to refuse to appear as a witness as laid down in the second sentence of article 1928 of the Civil Code of the Netherlands Antilles.

The same that has been said above in relation to civil procedural law applies *mutatis mutandis* to criminal procedural law, which also imposes an obligation to give testimony and defines exceptions thereto under article 59 of the Code of Criminal Procedure in the Netherlands Antilles.

In 1974, the Court of Appeal in Amsterdam ruled that a banker's profession is not of a sufficiently confidential nature so as to be a basis to assume the existence, in connection with the public interest,

15 Martha, *supra* n. 13.

16 Hugenholts/Heemskerk, *Hoofdlijnen van Nederlands Burgerlijk Procesrecht* (*The Main Outlines of Dutch Civil Procedural Legislation*) (15th ed., 1990), p. 150; compare Judgment of the Supreme Court of The Netherlands, December 22, 1989, RvdW, 1990, at p. 13.

17 Judgment of the Utrecht District Court, May 17, 1964, N.J. 1966, p. 74; Judgment of the Court of Appeal in the Hague, June 6, 1922, N.J. 1924, at p. 939.

of an overriding duty of the banker to observe secrecy (vis-à-vis the court, as well) with respect to the data that came to his knowledge in his capacity of a banker.[18]

Ruling in *Hillegom*

26-013 The ruling of the Supreme Court in the action of *Hillegom*[19] has resulted in a lack of clarity about the right of the BNA, its employees or the external experts it appoints to refuse to give testimony.

The central question is whether a right to refuse to appear as a witness also arises from the legal obligations to observe secrecy in article 24 of the Foreign Exchange Act and in paragraph 4 of article 3, paragraph 3 of article 9, and article 12 of the Banking and Credit System Supervision Act.

In the *Hillegom* action, the Supreme Court held that neither the text nor the history of article 46 of the Banking and Credit System Supervision Act of The Netherlands, which corresponds to article 12 of the Banking and Credit System Supervision Act of the Netherlands Antilles, justify the conclusion that the obligation also implies a right to refuse to appear as a witness.

Although the structure of the new provision in the draft bill of the supervision favors the latter interpretation, it is not certain whether the courts also will follow this path.

---

[18] Judgment of the Court of Appeal in Amsterdam, December 11, 1974, N.J. 1975, Number 441, spec. Th.W.v.V.

[19] Judgment of the Supreme Court of The Netherlands, July 22, 1986, N.J. 1986, Number 23.

NEW ZEALAND

Gill Goodwin and Simon Fraser
Rudd Watts & Stone
Auckland, New Zealand

Chapter 27

NEW ZEALAND

INTRODUCTION

Legal bases of duty

The Constitution Act 1986[1] provides that the Parliament of New   **27-001**
Zealand, consisting of the Sovereign in right of New Zealand (acting either in person or through the Governor-General on behalf of
the Sovereign) and the House of Representatives, continues to have
full power to make laws.

Although Parliament has enacted many statutes that impinge
upon or amend the banker's duty of secrecy to a customer,[2] it has
not enacted legislation that creates such a duty.

New Zealand is a Common Law jurisdiction and, accordingly,
judge-made law supplements statute law. The Common Law of
England is incorporated into New Zealand law both by statute and
by the judicial rules of precedent. With regard to the former, the
Imperial Laws Application Act 1988[3] provides (in section 5) that the
Common Law of England, including the principles and rules of
equity, so far as it was part of the laws of New Zealand immediately
before the Act came into force on January 1, 1989, shall continue to
be part of the laws of New Zealand.

With regard to the latter, the appellate court in New Zealand, the
Court of Appeal, regards decisions of the House of Lords and the
English Court of Appeal as possessing strong persuasive authority.

[1] Constitution Act 1986 (1986, No. 114), sections 3, 14, and 15.
[2] See text below relating to disclosure under compulsion by law.
[3] Imperial Laws Application Act 1988 (1988, No. 112).

In 1971, the President of the New Zealand Court of Appeal, North P., commenting upon the judicial authority of decisions of the House of Lords, stated:

> "In my opinion, while judgments of the House of Lords without question, are entitled to the greatest respect, technically we are not bound by the judgments of that august body."[4]

In 1988, the President of the New Zealand Court of Appeal, Cooke P., said:

> "Since at least 1971 it has been recognized that the New Zealand Courts are not bound by House of Lords decisions (*Bognuda* v. *Upton & Shearer Ltd* [1972] N.Z.L.R. 741) but of course they are treated with great respect and have very high persuasive value."[5]

Similarly, the decisions of the English Court of Appeal are not regarded as binding upon the New Zealand Court of Appeal, although they are regarded as highly persuasive. In *Union Steam Ship Company of New Zealand Limited* v. *Ramstad*,[6] Cooke J. stated that:

> ". . . this Court [*i.e.*, New Zealand Court of Appeal] should, and always will, hesitate long before differing from a decision of the English Court of Appeal, and particularly so where such a decision relates to a matter that arises in the day-to-day practice of the common law."

Accordingly, the decision of the English Court of Appeal in *Tournier* v. *National Provincial and Union Bank of England*[7] is the basis of New Zealand law in relation to the nature and scope of a banker's duty of secrecy, and that case has been applied by New Zealand courts.[8]

Before further examining case law derived from the *Tournier* case, it is of note that the major New Zealand trading banks recently have subscribed to a voluntary Code of Banking Practice. This Code, published in January 1992 by the New Zealand Bankers' Association, sets out minimum standards to be observed by participating members when dealing with their customers. It also estab-

---

[4] *Bognuda* v. *Upton & Shearer Ltd* [1972] N.Z.L.R. 741, 757 (C.A.).

[5] *Askin* v. *Knox* [1989] 1 N.Z.L.R. 248, 254-5 (C.A.).

[6] *Union Steam Ship Company of New Zealand Limited* v. *Ramstad* [1950] N.Z.L.R. 716, at pp. 727-728.

[7] *Tournier* v. *National Provincial and Union Bank of England* [1924] 1 K.B. 461.

[8] See, for example, *The Queen* v. *William Bacon and Company Limited and Others* [1969] N.Z.L.R. 228.

lishes a banking ombudsman to deal with customer complaints. Clause 10 of the Code deals with the protection of customer information and essentially re-states the Common Law rules of confidentiality, together with the exceptions to those rules, as set out in Tournier's case.

The Code provides that banks must take reasonable steps to ensure that information on customers' files is accurate, complete, and up to date. In addition, before personal information is used for other than the purpose for which it was collected, or before any banker's reference is given, the appropriate customer's consent must be obtained. Customers have the right to request copies of information which a bank holds on them and, if necessary, to have that information corrected. The Code also provides that banks must act reasonably in the use of direct marketing and, in doing so, must follow the Code of Ethics of the New Zealand Direct Marketing Association.

Nature of duty

The *Tournier* case established that the contract between a banker   27-002
and a customer contains an implied term that the banker will not disclose information relating to the customer's affairs to a third party without the consent of that customer.

Bankes L.J. stated in *Tournier* that the banker's duty was not an absolute one but was qualified, and then classified these qualifications under four heads:[9]

> "(a) Where disclosure is under compulsion by law; (b) where there is a duty to the public to disclosure; (c) where the interests of the bank require disclosure; (d) where disclosure is made by the express or implied consent of the customer."

It is interesting to note that there is authority[10] in England and Australia for the view that a banker's duty of secrecy, in addition to its contractual base, also derives from equitable principles. The general equitable principle is that person who has received information in confidence must not use that information to the prejudice of the person who gave it, without obtaining that person's consent.

---

[9] *Tournier, supra* n. 7, at p. 473.
[10] *Attorney-General* v. *Guardian Newspapers Ltd and Others* (No. 2) [1988] 3 W.L.R. 776; *Coco* v. *A.N. Clark (Engineers) Ltd* [1969] R.P.C. 41, at p. 46; see also J. McI. Walter and N. Erlich, "Confidences - Bankers and Customers: Powers of Banks to Maintain Secrecy and Confidentiality", 63 A.L.J. [1989] 404.

Unlike their Australian and English counterparts, the New Zealand courts have not developed such an equitable doctrine specifically in the banking area. However, that doctrine has been generally recognized in relation to other fiduciary relationships. It is submitted that a New Zealand court would be likely to follow Commonwealth authorities in upholding a duty of confidentiality in the banking area, based upon equitable principles.

QUALIFICATIONS TO BANKER'S DUTY OF SECRECY

Disclosure under compulsion by law

27-003 A specific statutory provision requiring disclosure will override a banker's general duty of secrecy.

The United Kingdom's Review Committee on Banking Services Law, chaired by Professor R. B. Jack and, consequently, known as the "Jack Committee", viewed the United Kingdom legislation that required disclosure by a banker of confidential customer information as ". . . a serious inroad into the whole principle of customer confidentiality. . .".[11]

In New Zealand, as in the United Kingdom, there are several statutory provisions permitting or compelling disclosure that would otherwise be prohibited under the general ambit of a banker's duty of secrecy.[12] Essentially, specific exceptions to the usual banker's duty of secrecy have been developed to prevent crime and to protect the public interest.

While in the crime prevention and detection areas there is an increased awareness of the need to override an otherwise existing duty of secrecy, there also recently has been evidenced an increased awareness for the need to protect individual privacy. This awareness has been sharpened by publicity over the sale of trade and customer lists and developments in electronic banking.

---

11 Banking Services: Law and Practice, Report by the Review Committee (Cmnd 622, 1989).

12 See, for example, Companies Act 1955 (section 262A); Reserve Bank of New Zealand Act 1989 (section 99); Banking Act 1982 (sections 6 and 7); Customs Act 1966 (section 218); Family Proceedings Act 1980 (section 165); Inland Revenue Department Act 1974 (section 17); Insolvency Act 1967 (section 64); Securities Act 1978 (section 18(3)); Commerce Act 1986 (section 98); Fair Trading Act 1986 (section 47); Serious Fraud Office Act 1990 (sections 5 and 23) and Proceeds of Crime Act 1991 (sections 69 and 77).

Accordingly, privacy legislation in the form of the Privacy Commissioner Act[13] was recently enacted. At the core of the legislation is a code that sets out 14 "information privacy principles" which govern the gathering, holding, and handling of information. These include a prohibition upon disclosing personal information.

As originally introduced into parliament, the privacy legislation would have applied to virtually every agency, including banks, in both the public and private sectors. The exchange of information between certain government agencies to prevent fraud was, however, expressly authorized.

The legislation in that form appeared to promote a double standard. The government was permitting disclosure of information so as to prevent welfare abuse and tax fraud and yet, at the same time, was prohibiting the private sector practice of disclosing data for the preparation of credit references.

As a result of much private sector criticism, the legislation actually enacted relates only to the narrow issue of swapping information between government departments. The Privacy Commissioner Act also establishes the office of the Privacy Commissioner, whose role is to monitor data making and to investigate, conciliate, and seek a remedy for any breach of the provisions of the Act. The privacy concepts of the original bill remain before the New Zealand Justice and Law Reform Committee for further consideration.

The principal New Zealand statutory exceptions to a banker's Common Law duty of secrecy are contained in the Banking Act 1982, the Inland Revenue Department Act 1974, the Companies Act 1955, the Commerce Act 1986, the Serious Fraud Office Act 1990, and the Proceeds of Crime Act 1991. Brief consideration of each of these statutes follows.

Banking Act 1982

Under the Banking Act 1982, any party to a legal proceeding may apply to the court for an order under section 7(1), permitting that person to inspect and take copies of any entries in the business records of a bank for any of the purposes of such proceedings. **27-004**

The business records of the bank in respect of which inspection is sought need not relate to the applicant or to any other party involved in the litigation.

New Zealand courts have, however, displayed a reluctance to exercise a wide discretion in requiring the production of the banking records of a person who is not a party to the litigation. That

13 Privacy Commissioner Act (1991, No. 126).

approach is exemplified in *James* v. *Mabin (No. 3)*[14] in which the court considered a summons, issued under section 21 of the Banking Act 1908, a predecessor of section 7 of the Banking Act 1982, for an order to inspect the books of a bank relating to the account of a person who was not a party to the litigation.

Adams J. held that such power should seldom, if ever, be exercised, except where the account sought to be inspected was in form or substance really the account of a party to the litigation or was kept on his behalf, so that entries in it would be evidence against that person at the trial. In addition, Adams J. suggested that on such an application, the party whose account was to be inspected should be given the right to be heard by the court.[15]

Similarly, the operation of section 7 was considered in *Allingham* v. *Bank of New Zealand*.[16] In that case, the defendant bank was alleged to have closed out a forward-rate exchange contract undertaken on behalf of the plaintiffs at a time which was disadvantageous to the plaintiffs.

Consequential damages were claimed. In order to prove those damages, the plaintiffs sought discovery of documents that would reveal not only the identity of other clients who had purportedly suffered loss in the same way but also would reveal the extent of those losses.

These documents were required to support an allegation that the bank had pursued a deliberate policy of disadvantaging smaller clients by closing out their contracts at different times, in order to protect the interests of larger clients.

The bank maintained that it was under a duty of confidentiality to its other clients. In the High Court, Barker J. stated that:

> ". . . it is the fundamental right of an (*sic*) bank customer that his or her affairs not be made known to any third party, without very good reason."[17]

Accordingly, although the judge allowed the plaintiffs to inspect certain documents, he did not consider that the plaintiffs' interests were such as to require the defendant bank to disclose the names of other customers and the individual amount for which each of those customers may or may not have had a claim against the bank.

---

[14] *James* v. *Mabin (No.3)* [1929] N.Z.L.R. 899, at p. 900.

[15] *Id.*, at p. 900, citing *South Staffordshire Tramways Co.* v. *Ebbsmith* [1985] 2 Q.B.D. 669.

[16] *Allingham* v. *Bank of New Zealand* [1988] 2 P.R.N.Z. 616; cf *Barclays Bank PLC* v. *Taylor* [1989] 1 W.L.R. 1066, per Croom-Johnson LJ, at p. 1077.

[17] *Id.*, at p. 620.

Finally, it is of note that, in New Zealand, the record of interviews between a bank manager and a client and a bank manager's diary both fall within the definition of "business records of the bank" for the purposes of the Banking Act and that, accordingly, those papers may be the subject of an order for discovery.[18]

Inland Revenue Department Act 1974

The Inland Revenue Department Act 1974[19] gives the New Zealand **27-005** Commissioner of Inland Revenue wide information-gathering powers and rights.

The Commissioner may, by virtue of section 17(1) of this Act, require any person to furnish in writing any information and produce for inspection any books and documents which the Commissioner considers necessary or relevant for any purpose relating to the administration or enforcement of any of the Inland Revenue Acts or for any purpose relating to the administration or enforcement of any matter arising from or connected with any other function lawfully conferred on the Commissioner.

The Judicial Committee of the Privy Council was recently called upon, in the case of New Zealand Stock Exchange & The National Bank of New Zealand v. Commissioner of Inland Revenue,[20] to consider the width of the information-gathering powers afforded to the Commissioner pursuant to, inter alia, section 17(1) of the Inland Revenue Department Act.

The Commissioner, in the case of the first appellant, required members of the Stock Exchange to produce a list of their largest clients and details of those clients' purchases and sales of shares; in the case of the second appellant, the Commissioner required them to produce the names and details of bank customers who had bought and sold commercial bills.

Both appellants contended that the Commissioner could obtain confidential information regarding their clients and customers respectively only where he had a specific taxpayer in mind in respect of whom there was a serious question as to the tax liability of that taxpayer.

---

[18] The Queen v. William Bacon and Company Limited and Others, supra n. 8.
[19] Inland Revenue Department Act 1974 (1974, No. 133).
[20] New Zealand Stock Exchange and The National Bank of New Zealand v. Commissioner of Inland Revenue [1991] 15 T.R.N.Z. 824; [1991] 3 W.L.R. 221.

Although it was acknowledged by the Judicial Committee that a confidential relationship existed between a bank and its customers, it was held that such a confidential relationship was not such as to require a limitation to be placed upon the plain wording of the statute.

The Judicial Committee upheld the judgment of the Court of Appeal[21] in deciding that the information requested by the Commissioner had to be disclosed by the bank and by the members of the Stock Exchange, notwithstanding the fact that no specific taxpayer had been named in the information sought. In delivering the judgment of the Judicial Committee, Lord Templeman stated:

> "If the Commissioner, exercising his undoubted powers under s 17(1) of the Act of 1974, requires the bankers of a specified taxpayer under investigation to produce information about that taxpayer's activities, then the confidentiality that attaches to the relationship between banker and customer must be broken. The whole rationale of taxation would break down and the whole burden of taxation would fall only on diligent and honest taxpayers if the Commissioner had no power to obtain confidential information about taxpayers who may be negligent or dishonest."[22]

Companies Act 1955

27-006 Under the Companies Act 1955, both the courts and a liquidator are afforded wide powers to require the production of accounting records, deeds, instruments, or other documents or papers relating to the company from any person who has those documents in his or her control.[23]

The statutory language is wide and has been described as creating ". . .an extraordinary provision of an inquisitorial nature".[24] The statute is designed to assist a liquidator in discovering all circumstances of a company in liquidation. Hence, the requirement in the Banking Act for there to be a court order made for "special cause" before a bank officer may be compelled to appear does not extend

---

21 *New Zealand Stock Exchange & The National Bank of New Zealand* v. *Commissioner of Inland Revenue* [1990] 3 N.Z.L.R. 333.

22 *New Zealand Stock Exchange and the National Bank of New Zealand* v. *Commissioner of Inland Revenue, supra* n. 20, at p. 827.

23 Companies Act 1955, sections 262(3) and 262A(1)(c).

24 The Coachman Tavern (1985) Limited (in liq): *Currie* v. *Gooch* (1990) 5 N.Z.C.L.C. 66,321, *per* Anderson J., at p. 66,322.

to protect that bank officer from being summoned before a court under the Companies Act.[25] The absence of any "special cause" will not be an excuse.

Commerce Act 1986

The Commerce Act 1986 was enacted with the objective of promot-   **27-007** ing competition in New Zealand markets by introducing measures to control restrictive trade practices and also a complaints mechanism to resolve business grievances.

The statute establishes a Commerce Commission headed by a Commissioner. The Commissioner is charged with dealing with applications for the clearance of trade practices and merger or takeover proposals and to take enforcement proceedings in respect of contraventions of certain provisions of the Act.

To enable the Commission to fulfill its duties under the Commerce Act, the Commissioner may require any person to furnish any information or class of information to the Commission or to produce any documents or class of documents.[26] These powers may, however, only be exercised where the Commissioner considers it necessary or desirable for the purposes of carrying out the functions of the Commission and the exercise of the powers under the Act.

Judicial comment has upheld the requirement that any request for information must be relevant to a particular investigative situation:

". . .in my view the primary right to decide as to relevance [of information requested] under s 98 of the Commerce Act as in s 17 of the Inland Revenue [Department] Act, reposes in the investigative body or officer but it is incumbent upon the investigative body or officer to show a degree of relevance bearing in mind that in an investigative situation and in the context of the section, the onus must be a very easy one to discharge. Nevertheless, it will still be open to the person from whom the information is sought, to seek to establish that the

---

25 In *re Hartley and Riley Consolidated Gold Dredging Co. Ltd* [1931] N.Z.L.R. 977, *per* Smith J, at p. 981.
26 Commerce Act 1986, (1986, No. 5), section 98(1).

information or the document is not relevant and in the appropriate case the issue may have to be determined by the Court."[27]

Serious Fraud Office Act 1990

27-008 The New Zealand Serious Fraud Office was established with the aim of combating white collar crime. The director of the Serious Fraud Office is charged with making investigations where he believes that a serious or complex fraud has arisen.

In furtherance of his duties, the director is given wide powers to require the production of documents and to require persons to answer questions as to the whereabouts or existence of further documents that may be relevant.[28]

The statute expressly overrides a banker's duty of secrecy by providing that the director may require any person who claims to have a duty of confidentiality to his or her client, including any person carrying on the business of banking, first, to comply with any of the disclosure requirements imposed under the Serious Fraud Office Act and, second, to answer questions, supply information and produce documents relating to any persons whose affairs are being investigated under that Act.[29]

Although the statute seeks to limit the dissemination of confidential information by imposing "strictest secrecy" on the members of the Serious Fraud Office, the director is entitled to disclose such information to the extent that the information is available to the public under any Act[30] or to any person who the director is satisfied has a proper interest in receiving such information.[31]

Proceeds of Crime Act 1991

27-009 New Zealand has followed a worldwide trend toward legislating to provide specifically for disclosure of information that may assist with the detection of criminal offending.

In particular, Part V of the Proceeds of Crime Act sets out the information gathering powers permitted to the police. Although the

---

[27] *Telecom Corporation of NZ Limited* v. *Commerce Commission* [1991] N.Z.A.R. 155, *per* Gallen J., at p. 163.
[28] Serious Fraud Office Act 1990 (1990, No. 51), section 5(1).
[29] *Id.*, section 23(1).
[30] *Id.*, section 36(2)(b).
[31] *Id.*, section 36(2)(e).

statute generally permits the making of orders requiring the production of documents, such production orders are not permitted to be made in respect of any accounting records used in the ordinary course of banking.[32]

On the other hand, a court may make an order directing a financial institution to supply to the Commissioner of Police information obtained by the institution about transactions conducted through the account of a particular person, where there are reasonable grounds for believing that a person has committed or has benefitted from or is about to commit or will benefit from a drug-dealing offense.[33]

International aspects of duty of confidence

A bank is placed in a difficult position when a request for information or a subpoena originates from a foreign jurisdiction. The difficulty for the banker is whether to refuse the request for information or the subpoena, and thereby risk being held in contempt of the court of foreign jurisdiction or to obey the subpoena and so breach the bankers' local the duty of secrecy. **27-010**

This difficulty was well described by Hoffmann J. in *Mackinnon* v. *Donaldson Lufkin & Jenrette Securities Corp. and Others*[34] as follows:

"Banks are in a special position because their documents are concerned not only with their own business but with that of their customers. They will owe their customers a duty of confidence regulated by the law of the country where the account is kept. That duty is in some countries reinforced by criminal sanctions and sometimes by 'blocking statutes' that specifically forbid the bank to provide information for the purposes of foreign legal proceedings .... If every country where a bank happened to carry on business asserted a right to require that bank to produce documents relating to accounts kept in any other such country, banks would be in the unhappy position of being forced to submit to whichever sovereign was able to apply the greatest pressure."

There are no direct New Zealand case law authorities. In the United States, however, courts have attempted to exercise jurisdiction over

---

[32] Proceeds of Crime Act 1991,(1991, No. 120), section 69(4).

[33] *Id.*, section 77(1) and (2).

[34] *Mackinnon* v. *Donaldson Lufkin & Jenrette Securities Corp. and Others* [1986] 1 All E.R. 653, at p. 658.

the acts of foreigners committed outside the jurisdiction. This practice has been criticized in the United Kingdom as being ". . . not in accordance with international law".[35]

When requested to grant disclosure orders that are intended to take effect in foreign jurisdictions, United Kingdom courts seem to have been more reluctant than their United States counterparts to grant such orders. It appears that international regulation would be of assistance in clarifying this area.

DISCLOSURE PURSUANT TO DUTY TO PUBLIC

27-011   The second of the qualifications, cited by Bankes L.J. in *Tournier*, to the duty of secrecy and implied into the banker-customer relationship has been described by commentators in New Zealand, Australia, and the United Kingdom respectively as "very uncertain",[36] "undoubtedly

the worst defined",[37] and "the most difficult of Bankes L.J.'s instances of where a bank might be justified in disclosing".[38]

Echoing these opinions, the Jack Committee[39] stated that this qualification, with its uncertainty of application, was no longer needed, given the fact that the statutory provisions that required disclosure were so extensive.[40] The Committee recommended,[41] albeit unsuccessfully,[42] that this exception should be deleted and that the statutory codification of the *Tournier* rules which the Committee advocated should make it clear that no such general disclosure provision exists.

---

[35] *Re Westinghouse Uranium Contract* [1978] A.C. 547, at p. 631.

[36] Mark W. Russell, *Introduction to New Zealand Banking Law* (2nd ed., 1991), at p. 60.

[37] G. A. Weaver and C. R. Craigie, *The Law Relating to Banker and Customer in Australia* (2nd ed., 1990), paragraph 6.650.

[38] M. Hapgood, *Paget's Law of Banking* (10th ed., 1989), at p. 256.

[39] Banking Services: Law and Practice, Report by the Review Committee (Cm 622, 1989).

[40] *Id.*, paragraph 5.30.

[41] *Id.*, paragraph 5.41.

[42] In its response to the Review Committee's recommendations the United Kingdom Government in its White Paper *Banking Services: Law and Practice* (Cmnd. 1026, 1990) rejected the recommendation that this particular qualification should be abolished (see paragraph 2.14).

Scope of qualification

The difficulty in ascertaining the scope of this qualification to the **27-012** general rule can be explained for the following reasons. First, at its inception, the qualification was a general statement of principal rather than a summary of established practice. Although Bankes L.J. stated that there were "many instances" of the qualification that might be given, he did not, in fact, refer to any case in which such a qualification had been ruled upon by the court.[43] Bankes L.J. referred instead to obiter comments made by Viscount Finlay in the House of Lords' decision in *Weld-Blundell* v. *Stephens*[44] where he had stated that, as a general rule, an agent is not entitled to disclose confidential information relating to his principal unless a superseding or higher duty is involved:

> "Danger to the State or public duty may supersede the duty of the agent to his principal."[45]

The *Weld-Blundell* case was not cited by either counsel for the appellant or counsel for the respondent in the *Tournier* case, and neither Atkin or Scrutton LL.J. referred to it in their judgments. This leads to the conclusion that the appearance of the *Weld-Blundell* case in Bankes L.J.'s judgment is due to the fact that he sat in the Court of Appeal when it considered *Weld-Blundell*, and his comments in the earlier case[46] regarding a public duty to disclose which may override a private contractual duty foreshadowed the comment subsequently made by Viscount Finlay in the House of Lords.

Second, subsequent case law that might be referred to in order to assess the scope of the qualification is scarce. The only case directly relevant to the banker-customer relationship- as opposed to, for example, the relationship between an employer and its former employee,[47] a television company and its sources,[48] or an accountant and its client[49] - would appear to be *Libyan Arab Foreign Bank* v. *Bankers Trust Co.*[50] In that case, the plaintiff bank claimed, *inter alia*, that the defendant bank had breached its duty of confidence by revealing information to the Federal Reserve Bank of New York

---

[43] *Tournier, supra* n. 7, at p. 473.

[44] *Weld-Blundell* v. *Stephens* [1920] A.C. 956.

[45] *Id.*, at p. !95-196.

[46] [1919] 1 K.B. 520

[47] See *Initial Services Ltd* v. *Putterill* [1967] 3 All E.R. 145.

[48] See *British Steel Corp* v. *Granada Television* [1981] 1 All E.R. 417.

[49] See *Price Waterhouse* v. *BCCI Holdings (Luxembourg) SA and Others, The Times,* October 30, 1991.

[50] *Libyan Arab Foreign Bank* v. *Bankers Trust Co.* [1988] 1 Lloyd's Rep 259.

about the movement of funds between accounts immediately prior to the issue of the Presidential order "freezing" Libyan assets within the United States on January 8, 1986.

Staughton J. recognized that the public duty qualification existed and reached "a tentative conclusion that the exception applied in this case".[51] In reaching this conclusion, the judge presumed that the Federal Reserve Bank of New York possessed similar statutory powers for obtaining information from New York banks as did the Bank of England from English banks. It may, therefore, be argued that the judge, in reaching his tentative conclusion, blurred the distinction between disclosure pursuant to a duty to the public and disclosure due to compulsion of law. In any event, no final conclusion was reached by the judge who expressed himself "convinced" that any breach of confidence could not have caused the loss complained of by the plaintiff.

Third, those cases concerning the disclosure of confidential information that do not specifically relate to the banker-customer relationship (for which, see the preceding paragraph) are dependent to a certain extent upon the particular facts of each case and do not generally introduce new guidelines that are of use in the banker-customer context.

In *Price Waterhouse* v. *BCCI Holdings (Luxembourg) SA and Others*,[52] however, Millett J. suggested that one factor that might be taken into account in deciding whether or not to permit disclosure was whether the interests of the party resisting such disclosure would be contrary to the interests, as well as contrary to his wishes).

Entitlement to disclose

27-013   In determining the instances in which the banker is entitled to disclose confidential information under this head, it appears to be well-established that disclosure will be justified where that customer is trading with the enemy in times of war.[53]

It is also possible that the banker may be entitled to disclose confidential customer information when the banker believes a crime has been committed.[54]

Even this is not certain, however, as it should always be borne in mind that it is the function of the court and not the bank to decide

---

[51] *Id.*, at p. 286, column 1.
[52] *Price Waterhouse* v. *BCCI Holdings (Luxembourg) and Others, supra* n. 49.
[53] *Weld-Blundell* v. *Stephens, supra* n. 44, at p. 965.
[54] *Tournier, supra* n. 7, at p. 486, *per* Atkin L.J.

whether a crime has been committed and, therefore, whether it is in the public interest for confidential information to be disclosed.

In addition, in *Tournier*, Bankes L.J. appears to have stated that the banker would not be entitled to disclose customer information even when presented with a request for information by a police office conducting an investigation into a series of frauds[55] (presumably such investigation being conducted prior to obtaining the appropriate court orders). In all other cases, the banker will, of necessity, be involved in weighing whether the public interest is served by disclosure.

Accordingly, bankers should be most reluctant to exercise their own discretion in the matter, and the obvious way of proceeding would be for the banker to seek an order of the court.

WHERE INTERESTS OF BANK REQUIRE DISCLOSURE

In the third of Bankes L.J.'s qualifications in *Tournier*, he acknow- **27-014** ledged that a banker is entitled to disclose certain confidential information relating to a customer where the interests of the banker require disclosure. Examples include:

(1) Where a bank issues a writ claiming payment of an overdraft stating on the face of the writ the amount of the overdraft, and

(2) Where a bank brings an action against a guarantor.

However, a bank's right to disclose information to protect its own interests is not unlimited. As stated in *Tournier*, a bank has:

". . . the right to disclose such information when, and to the extent to which it is reasonably necessary for the protection of the bank's interests, either as against their customer or as against third parties in respect of transactions of the bank for or with their customer, or for protecting the bank, or persons interested, or the public, against fraud or crime."[56]

In New Zealand, it has been held that a bank has duties both to disclose to a guarantor those facts about the person whose obligations are being guaranteed that are unusual or that are different

---

[55] *Id.*, at p. 474, *per* Bankes L.J.
[56] *Id.*, at p. 486, *per* Atkin L.J.

from those which a guarantor might naturally expect and also not to conceal from a guarantor those facts as need to be mentioned in answer to a guarantor's questions put to a bank.[57]

To comply with these duties, where the person whose obligations are being guaranteed is a bank's customer, that bank will be obliged to disclose confidential information about that customer to the guarantor. A balance must be found between satisfying the bank's duty not to disclose any more information than is required to protect the bank's interests and disclosing information that in the circumstances of a particular case should be disclosed to a guarantor.

A bank would be well advised to obtain its customer's consent to such disclosures in order to avoid the need to make judgments in this difficult area.

DISCLOSURE WITH EXPRESS OR IMPLIED CONSENT OF CUSTOMER

27-015   The fourth of Bankes L.J.'s qualifications to the general duty of secrecy owed by a banker to a customer has its widest application in the giving of banker's references or opinions.

It is axiomatic that a banker will be entitled to disclose confidential customer information to a third party where such disclosure has been expressly authorized by the customer. It is, however, less clear that a banker is entitled to disclose confidential customer information where the basis for such disclosure rests upon consent that is to be implied into the banker-customer relationship.

In *Tournier*, neither Bankes L.J. nor Atkin L.J. gave clear examples of whether or not they considered a banker's reference an instance of express or implied consent. For example, Bankes L.J. referred to a bankers reference as example of disclosure "made by the express or implied consent of the customer",[58] while Atkin L.J. commented that, if the practice of giving bankers' opinions were justified (upon which he expressed no final opinion), it would be upon the basis of an implied consent.[59]

A banker who relies upon the implied consent of a customer for the disclosure of confidential information faces the fact that the exact amount of information disclosed and the party to whom it is

[57] *National Mortgage and Agency Company of New Zealand Limited* v. *Stalker* [1933] N.Z.L.R. 1182; *Goodwin* v. *National Bank of Australasia Ltd* [1968] 42 A.L.J.R. 110.
[58] *Tournier, supra* n. 7, at p. 473.
[59] *Id.*, at p. 486.

disclosed have not been expressly considered by the customer. In the former case, it has been recommended that implied consent must relate to the release of the minimum of information.[60] In the latter case, judicial opinions have been at variance between whether references can only be given to other banks or to other individuals.

The code of Banking Practice, promulgated by the New Zealand Bankers' Association, overcomes many of these difficulties in that it states that banks are not to provide bankers' references without the prior consent of the customer on whom the reference is to be based.[61]

---

[60] G. A. Penn, A. M. Shea, and A. Arora, *The Law Relating to Domestic Banking*, (1987), at p. 56.

[61] Code of Banking Practice, New Zealand Bankers' Association, January 1992, clause 10.4.2.

NORWAY

Finn Arnesen
Advokatene Haavind & Haga
Oslo, Norway

Chapter 28

NORWAY

INTRODUCTION

The principle of banking secrecy has been cemented in the present **28-001** Norwegian Act on Savings Banks,[1] Act on Merchant Banks,[2] and Act on Finance Institutions[3] (hereinafter "the Banking Acts"), but it has been a recognized principle since the first independent savings bank was established in Norway in 1824.

The first merchant bank came some years later. Until 1814, Norway was under Danish rule and had no banks of its own. Danish law prevailed in Norway.

The right of confidentiality belongs, according to the banking laws, both to the customer and to the bank.

Both civil and criminal statutory provisions contain exceptions to the basic rule of confidentiality, and may, as will be shown below, permit or compel the disclosure of confidential information or knowledge.

[1] Act Number 1 of May 24, 1961.
[2] Act Number 2 of May 24, 1961.
[3] Act Number 40 of June 10, 1988.

BANK'S DUTY OF CONFIDENCE

28-002 The Act on Savings Banks stipulates the following secrecy rules:

> "Officers, employees and auditors in a savings bank have an obligation of secrecy about matters which they in their positions become acquainted with in respect to the bank's, or a bank customer's or another bank or its customer's relations, if they, according to this or any other law are not under obligation to disclose information. The secrecy obligation does not relate to information which the Board of Directors or someone who has a power of attorney from the Board of Directors, gives on behalf of the bank to another bank. This paragraph, however, does not prevent banks from conducting credit information business in accordance with the laws regulating such business."[4]

Similar stipulations are contained in the Act on Merchant Banks and in the Act on Finance Institutions.

OFFICERS, EMPLOYEES, AND AUDITORS

28-003 Under the acts, "officers" include the members of the board of directors and members of the boards of subsidiaries of the bank, the control committee (audit committee), the board of representatives, and district governors and their deputies.

The law does not distinguish between members having been appointed by the government or elected by the employees and other members of the various bodies, and it also relates to that specific member of the control committee who according to the law must have special qualifications and be recognized by the Finance, Insurance and Securities Commission (for merchant banks, the recognition is provided by the Bank of Norway).

The officers also are under secrecy obligations towards those who have elected or appointed them. Thus, they are not permitted to disclose more information to the electing bodies than to third parties. The secrecy obligation also rests upon officers appointed by the government towards political organs and employee representative officers toward other employees in the bank.

---

[4] Act on Savings Banks, *supra* n. 1, paragraph 21.

"Employees" includes all employees, among them those working part time or for short periods or filling in for others.

"Auditors" means external auditors having been elected or employed as auditors by the board of representatives and their personnel. Internal auditors performing daily audits without being elected by the board of representatives or by the external auditors to work for them are considered to be employees.

The secrecy obligation imposed on the groups mentioned above continues to exist even after the individual in question has ended his position with the bank.

WHAT DOES THE SECRECY OBLIGATION ENCOMPASS?

Basically, the secrecy obligation relates to all matters as to which the **28-004** person concerned acquires knowledge in his position in the bank (as an officer, employee, or auditor) - whether financial or personal. It is not required that the knowledge is acquired or received in connection with the work in the bank, as long as the person has acquired the information in his capacity as officer, employee, or auditor.

The secrecy obligation does not extend to matters that are publicly known or available, or can be discovered through investigation of publicly available protocols or registers. Information involving evaluations that are based upon the bank's special knowledge regarding its customer or customers may, of course, not be disclosed.

For the members of the board of directors, it should be emphasized that the secrecy obligation also relates to discussions which take place during board meetings and to decisions by the board unless they are made publicly known. Board members who disagree with a board decision have the right to have their opinions minuted but, under no circumstances, may they disclose the fact that the board's decision is not unanimous.

The reason for this is, of course, that a board acts - insofar as external perception is concerned - as one body and that it is very difficult to disclose a disagreement without also disclosing the reason behind it and thereby also the discussion within the board.

The secrecy obligation relates not only to the bank's own customers but also to information relating to other banks and their customers, and to information regarding guarantors for the obligations of a customer.

The secrecy obligation covers all matters, both financial and personal, relating to a customer, which have been disclosed to the board of directors, and the board has a duty to ascertain that there are procedures within the bank that eliminate the risk of sensitive information going astray.

SECRECY OBLIGATION AND INFORMATION WITHIN THE BANK

28-005 The control committee can, according to the law, demand all types of information from everyone in the bank. Accordingly, every employee, officer, or auditor has a duty towards the control committee to disclose such information as the committee may demand.

Although nothing is explicitly stated in the law, it is obvious that a subordinate officer must be able to give his superiors any information they require. It is also supposed that an employee must have the right to disclose information to another employee under the condition that the latter is in need of such information in relation to his work for the bank. This is irrespective of whether there exists a superior/subordinate relationship between the two.

The auditors, of course, also must have the right to have disclosed to them all such information as is necessary to enable them to carry out a satisfactory audit.

OBLIGATION TO DISCLOSE INFORMATION TO OTHERS

28-006 The main exception to the secrecy rule in Norway is the one stated in the acts: ". . .if they, according to this or any other law, are not under obligation to disclose information".

There are many other laws which put banks, their officers, or employees under an obligation to disclose information. But it should be noted that any demand for information should be in written form, stating the reason for the demand and the law that gives the right to demand such information and the obligation to disclose it. How far the duty to disclose information goes depends on the interpretation of the various laws.

The main laws in this connection will be the Criminal Procedure Act,[5] the Civil Procedure Act,[6] the Acts relating to Tax (income tax,[7]

---

[5] Act Number 25 of May 22, 1981.
[6] Act Number 6 of August 13, 1915.
[7] Act Number 8 of August 18, 1911.

inheritance tax,[8] and value added tax),[9] acts relating to the regulation of prices, import and export restrictions, competition, trading in securities, and of course the laws governing the supervision and control of the banks and other financial institutions.

RIGHT TO GIVE INFORMATION TO OTHER BANKS

The law provides that "[t]he secrecy obligation does not relate to information which the board of directors or someone who has a power of attorney form the board of directors, gives on behalf of the bank to another bank". **28-007**

It is only the board of directors as such, and not any individual member of the board, that may give information on behalf of the bank or give a personal power of attorney to someone to give such information. Such power of attorney may follow from a person's position in the bank.

The information must be given on behalf of the bank, and not as private individuals. It is the board of directors or the attorney who decides whether information should be given or not.

The bank must assure itself that the information is given to the appropriate person or body in the other bank and not to some individual falsely claiming to represent the other bank.

The Act restricts the recipients of information to "another bank", but it is commonly presumed that it also covers other credit institutions governed by law, under the condition that they themselves have the same secrecy obligations as a bank.

In addition, banks and credit institutions in other countries are included, providing one can rely on their discretion.

SECRECY OBLIGATION AND POLICE

The secrecy obligation also is normally in force regarding the police. The police may, however, ask for a court to order the lifting of the secrecy obligation. **28-008**

How far a bank may go in assisting the police in matters regarding punishable crimes must be evaluated individually from case to case. The result, of course, also will depend on the bank's own

8 Act Number 14 of June 19, 1964.
9 Act Number 66 of June 19, 1969.

interest in the matter. If the bank is an interested party to the prosecution, it is considered that the bank should release any information which may be relevant for the prosecutor.

The same, of course, is valid in relation to the bank's external lawyers in court proceedings against the bank's own customers.

PRACTICAL EXAMPLES

28-009   A married person does not have the right to demand information from the bank concerning the spouse's affairs with the bank without his/her consent. This is true even if the spouses have a duty between themselves to inform each other about such matters.

A guardian has the power to demand information regarding his ward's financial matters, and the manager of an estate (bankruptcy or death estate) has the power to demand information concerning the financial affairs of the debtor or the deceased.

Persons having an interest in a death estate as inheritors often may have a personal interest in obtaining information regarding the financial matters of the deceased from the period prior to the death or the opening of the estate. However, such persons should, however, normally not receive such information automatically from the bank on request. The Ministry of Justice provided a written opinion on this issue, in reference to the Act on Settlement of Estates[10] in July 1975:

> "The Ministry of Justice is of the opinion that a commercial bank probably is under no obligation to give any individual part owner of an estate information with respect to the deceased or a death estate's bank accounts relating to the time prior to the time of death. No rule relating to an information obligation follows from the Act on Settlement of Estates, and the Ministry has found no other base for such a rule. The situation is different if the inheritor is actually acting on behalf of the estate itself. On the other hand, one is of the opinion that the bank normally will not be bound by any secrecy obligation in accordance with the Commercial Banking Act, paragraph 18, if an inheritor asks for information. An inheritor may have a justifiable interest in and need for information relating to the deceased's financial dispositions, and one cannot find any

[10] Act of February 21, 1930.

decisive reasons indicating a different solution, unless the request relates to information of a more personal character. Information asked for by the inheritor would in any case be
subject to release if all the inheritors or their attorney should
demand it, or if the estate becomes subject to public settlement.
If the bank has to act as a witness in a court case relating to the
estate's assets, the bank would normally not be bound by any
secrecy obligation in accordance with paragraph 18."[11]

A person who, according to law or by agreement, has the same right
to act towards the bank as the customer himself also has the right to
receive the same information as would be given to the customer.
The secrecy obligation is not in force in this case.

It has been discussed whether the secrecy obligation is in force
towards lawyers acting on behalf of the customer. The secrecy
obligation here is the same as towards other private persons: a
lawyer demanding information about his client's affairs with the
bank must produce a specific power of attorney from the client.

CREDIT INFORMATION

The Banking Acts contain an exemption from the secrecy obligation   **28-010**
related to credit information carried out by a bank in accordance
with the laws regulating such activities.

After the Law on Registration of Personal Information[12] was
enacted in June 1978, all Norwegian banks decided to discontinue
their credit information activities, and thus the exemption is no
longer relevant.

CHINESE WALLS AND INSIDER DEALING

The Law on Dealing in Securities[13] was enacted in June 1985. After   **28-011**
that date, trading or dealing in securities may be done only by
securities brokerage firms. Banks that want to act as brokers must

[11] Ministry of Justice Opinion of July 26, 1975.
[12] Act Number 48 of June 9, 1978.
[13] Act Number 61 of June 14, 1985.

establish separate securities' departments for this purpose with "Chinese walls" between such a department and the rest of the bank.

In 1989, another Act[14] was passed which further developed the principle of "Chinese walls" by laying down rules which, among other things, also stipulate that the securities department should be organized as a separate company, that officers of the bank cannot act as chairman of the board of the securities company, that employees or officers may not be a majority in the board, that the bank and the securities company must conduct their respective activities from separate buildings, and that separate data services and switchboard services are required.

A company dealing in securities is under the supervision of the Finance, Insurance and Securities Commission, and it is under obligation to give the Commission any information the Commission seeks in relation to the company's business, even if the information normally would be subject to a secrecy obligation.

14 Act Number 28 of June 9, 1989.

PAKISTAN

Aliya Yusuf
Orr, Dignam & Co.
Karachi, Pakistan

Chapter 29

PAKISTAN

INTRODUCTION

Pakistani law imposes a duty of secrecy on bankers in respect of the **29-001**
bona fide transactions of their customers.

The secrecy obligation of banks was established in the area now
constituting Pakistan during the British Raj in the then-British India. This obligation originally was based on English Common Law
which, prior to the partition of British India into India and Pakistan
and their independence from Great Britain, had authority in the
courts of the subcontinent. Such pre-independence decisions of the
courts of England have continued to have authority in the courts of
Pakistan.

The *Tournier* decision

Thus, the case of *Tournier* v. *National Provincial and Union Bank of* **29-002**
England,[1] which is considered to be the most important English
decision on the point, has authority in Pakistan and the principles
enunciated in this judgment would be followed in Pakistan.

In substance, the judgment in the *Tournier* case (which has not
been overruled in Pakistan) states that bankers are under a general
duty of confidentiality which goes beyond the state of an account
and covers all transactions which go through an account, as well as
any securities given in respect of the account. This duty was expressed to extend beyond the period when the account is closed, or
ceases to be active, and to extend to information obtained from
sources other than the customer's account if this was obtained by
reason of the relations of the bank and its customer.

---

[1] [1924] 1 K.B. 461.

However, according to the *Tournier* judgment, there are four generally accepted categories of exception to the restrictions over disclosure, each of which was discussed in that judgment. These are when the bank is required to disclose information under compulsion of law, by reason of any public duty owed by it, where its own interest requires disclosure, or where disclosure is made with the express or implied consent of the customer.

Banks (Nationalization) Act 1974

29-003 In 1974, the legislature of Pakistan for the first time recognized the general right of a customer to confidentiality in the Banks (Nationalization) Act 1974.[2] Section 12 of the Act, dealing with fidelity and secrecy, reads:

> "12. (1). . .every bank, the President, members of the Board, members of the Executive Committee and Chief Executive, by whatever name called, shall observe, except as otherwise required by law, the practices and usages customary among bankers and, in particular, shall not divulge any information relating to the affairs of its constituents except in circumstances in which it is, in accordance with law or practice and usages customary among bankers, necessary or appropriate for a bank to divulge such information.
>
> (2). . .the President, members of the Board and members of the Executive Committee of every bank, every Administrator, Auditor, Adviser, Officer or other employee of the Council or a bank shall, before entering upon his office, make a declaration of fidelity ans secrecy in such form as may be prescribed."

The Banks (Nationalization) Act 1974, however, applies only to those commercial banks which were nationalized by the Government of Pakistan. These banks included all the commercial banks formed or incorporated in Pakistan but did not include foreign banks operating in Pakistan.

Thus, the statutory duty of confidentiality imposed by the Act applies only to nationalized banks in Pakistan. Almost all major banks operating in Pakistan fall into this category. However, two major banks which were nationalized have since been privatized and it is likely that (barring a reversal of this policy) all nationalized

---

[2] Legislation whereby local banking companies were nationalized.

banks will be privatized in due course. Nevertheless, for so long as a bank remains a nationalized bank, it will be bound by the duty of secrecy imposed on it by the Bank (Nationalization) Act 1974.

This does not mean that other banks are not bound by this duty; they are bound by the Common Law duty of confidentiality discussed above and by a statutory duty imposed by the Protection of Economic Reforms Act 1992, as discussed below.

State Bank of Pakistan

Notwithstanding the Common Law and statutory duty of secrecy **29-004** imposed on banks, the State Bank of Pakistan (which is the central bank of the country) has wide powers to demand and receive information from banks (see text below). However, the confidentiality of the information so provided by a bank to the State Bank is protected by section 53 of the State Bank of Pakistan Act 1956 as follows:

> "(1) Except in the performance of his duties under this Act every officer or servant of the Bank shall preserve and aid in preserving secrecy with regard to all matters relating to the affairs of the Bank not published by it, and with regard to all matters relating to the financial or monetary affairs of any institution, person, body of persons, any Government or authority whether in Pakistan or outside that may come to his knowledge in the performance of his duties.

> "(2) Every such officer or servant who communicates any such matter, except when required by law to do so or in the discharge of his duty as such, shall be guilty of an offence and shall on conviction by a Court of competent jurisdiction be punished with imprisonment of either description for a term which may extend to six months or with fine which may extend to Rs. 500 or with both. . . ."

The wording of section 53 ensures the secrecy of any information furnished by a bank to the State Bank in regard to any of the bank's customers.

Similarly, the Establishment of the Federal Bank for Cooperatives and Regulation of Cooperative Banking Act 1977 empowers the Federal Bank for Cooperatives to call for information but, at the same time, protects under the confidentiality of such information by requiring its employees to maintain secrecy and protects "unpublished" information from the authority of the courts.[3] These sections state in part:

> "32. (1) Except in the performance of his duties under this Act or, subject to section 34, when required by law, every officer or servant of the Bank shall observe, and aid in preserving, secrecy in all matters relating to the affairs of the Bank not published by it and with regard to all matters relating to the financial and monetary affairs of any Provincial Cooperative Bank or cooperative society affiliated to it or any multi-unit cooperative society of any institution, person or body of persons or any Government or authority in or outside Pakistan that may come to his knowledge in the performance of his duties.
>
> (2) Every such officer or servant who communicates any such matter except, save as otherwise provided in section 34, when required by law to do so or in the discharge of his duties as such shall be punishable with imprisonment of either description for a term which may extend to six months, or with fine, or with both.
>
> 34. (1) No Court, Tribunal or authority shall have authority to compel the Bank or any of its officers or servants to produce or, as the case may be, give any evidence derived from any unpublished records of the Bank.
>
> (2) No Court, Tribunal or authority shall take notice of, or permit any one to produce or give any evidence derived from, unpublished records of the Bank except with the prior written permission of the Managing Director who may give or withhold such permission."

Protection of Economic Reforms Act 1992

29-005 In 1991, in furtherance of the government's policies of encouraging private investment in Pakistan and implementing policies to attract foreign exchange into Pakistan, the Protection of Economic Reforms Ordinance 1991 was promulgated by the President of Pakistan.

---

[3] Establishment of the Federal Bank for Cooperatives and Regulation of Cooperative Banking Act 1977, sections 32 and 34.

This Ordinance, which came into force in December 1991, has now been promulgated as an Act of Parliament as the Protection of Economic Reforms Act 1992. This Act, which came into force in July 1992, specifically protects the confidentiality of bona fide banking transactions in the following terms:

> "(9) Secrecy of bona fide banking transactions shall be strictly observed by all banks and financial institutions, by whosoever owned, controlled or managed."[4]

This is the most recent legislative measure to provide legal cover to the Common Law obligation of secrecy of banking transactions. This may be considered the most important concrete step taken by the government for protecting the secrecy of banking transactions in Pakistan.

The holding of foreign currency by nationals and foreigners (whether resident or non-resident) recently has been permitted, and foreign currency accounts now may be freely opened and maintained by all. Protection is given to such foreign currency accounts under the provisions of the Protection of Economic Reforms Act 1992 which enacts a specific provision in the following words:

> "The banks shall maintain complete secrecy in respect of transactions in the foreign currency accounts."[5]

It is interesting that, in relation to such foreign currency accounts, the requirement of secrecy is absolute and is not linked to the bona fides of the transaction involved, as is the case with the protection afforded to other banking transactions under section 9 of the Act; it will be observed that the term "bona fide" used in section 9, quoted above, does not appear in section 5(3).

This difference in the wording of the sections 5(3) and 9 of the Act indicates that the government is keen to ensure complete and unconditional secrecy by banks in respect of foreign currency transactions. The purpose appears to be to attract foreign currency deposits by assuring the depositors that complete secrecy will be maintained by banks in regard to their foreign currency deposits and dealings.

A further observation of equal significance is that no penalty has been prescribed under the Act for breach by banks and financial institutions and their employees of the requirement for secrecy imposed thereby.

[4] Protection of Economic Reforms Act, section 9.
[5] *Id.*, section 5(3).

It also is worth noting that, by using the term "secrecy" rather than "confidentiality" in sections 5(3) and 9 of the Act, it would appear that the government intends to cover all information which is in possession of or is received by a bank or financial institution in its capacity as a banker or financial institution.

It is submitted that this is the correct position since, if the term "confidentiality" had been used, the implication would have been that the protected information would itself have to be confidential in nature and the duty imposed for that reason rather than by reason of the nature of the relationship of banker and customer.

The Protection of Economic Reforms Act 1992 states that it shall have effect notwithstanding anything to the contrary contained in any other law. Accordingly, the benefit of any statutory exceptions to the secrecy obligation should not be available to any governmental or any other authority except to the extent discussed below.

In other words, by virtue of sections 5(3) and 9 of the Act, a bank or financial institution should not be obliged to divulge any information regarding bona fide banking transactions and transactions pertaining to the foreign currency accounts of its customers to any governmental or other competent authority which may have a right of access to such information under any other law.

The actual effect of the provisions of the Act and the statutory protection it affords to a customer's right to confidentiality or secrecy regarding his banking transactions and upon the four general exceptions to secrecy obligation mentioned above nevertheless will be open to interpretation by the courts should the matter come before them.

Each of the four categories of exceptions and the possible effect of the Protection of Economic Reforms Act 1992 upon them are discussed below.

IMPACT OF BANKING SECRECY EXCEPTIONS

Express or implied consent of customer

29-006   Of course, it will remain open for the customer to give express consent to a bank to reveal any confidential information.

Since, by the very nature of the secrecy obligation, it is intended to protect a customer from disclosures which he would prefer to avoid, the obligation will cease to have effect once instructions for or consent to disclosure have been given by a customer.

Such disclosure could be made under the authority of the contract between bank and customer or by the bank obtaining the customer's consent, or receiving the customer's instructions to disclose on each occasion upon which the question of disclosure arises.

In case of the customer going into bankruptcy or liquidation, the trustee or liquidator will stand in the shoes of the customer and will be entitled to require or authorize disclosure and the bank may properly make such disclosure. If a disclosure is made to a trustee or liquidator, it would be considered as if the bank is acting under the express instructions of its customer.

As regards implied consent, it is possible that the rationale for the Protection of Economic Reforms Act could be brought into play to support the argument that consent cannot be implied by a course of dealings between bank and customer or by reason of the customer's having refrained from objecting to disclosure on a previous occasion or occasions.

This is particularly so in cases involving information pertaining to foreign currency accounts of the customer as a distinction has been drawn in the Act by specifically requiring banks and financial institutions to observe complete secrecy in regard to transaction of such accounts and not merely bona fide transactions. This requirement goes beyond the general duty of secrecy imposed on banks and financial institution under the Act.

Bank's interest requiring disclosure

Since the obligation imposed on banks under the Protection of **29-007** Economic Reforms Act 1992 is to maintain "secrecy" in relation to bona fide banking transactions, it is unlikely that a plea that a disclosure was made to protect the interest of the bank would remain a valid defense in most circumstances.

One of the instances which could be asserted by a bank as justifying disclosure in its own interest is the exchange of information which is usual between banks and other credit giving agencies, regarding the financial position of their customers for the purposes of considering the advisability of giving a loan or financial facility to its customer.

The necessity of such exchange of information was recognized by the legislature when enacting of the Banking Companies Ordinance 1962, which specifically permits banking companies to exchange information regarding their customers and protects them when doing so in the following terms:

"93-C. (1) Banking companies may exchange on a confidential basis amongst themselves, either directly or through the Pakistan Banking Council, information about their respective clients.

(2) No suit or other legal proceedings shall lie against the Pakistan Banking Council or any banking company or any officer of the Pakistan Banking Council or banking company for anything which is in good faith done in pursuance of this section or for any damage caused or likely to be caused by anything done or intended to be done as aforesaid."[6]

The effect of the Protection of Economic Reforms Act on these provisions is not clear, as the transactions about which information is exchanged are likely to be bona fide. However, since what is usually revealed is the general state of the customer's finances and his credit worthiness and not any specific "transactions", it is probable that banks may, in view of the specific statutory provision, continue to make such general information available to other banks on the basis that those banks also maintain the confidentiality of this information.

In the circumstances discussed above, an additional argument in favor of disclosure is available in that a customer seeking an advance or financial facility impliedly consents to the giving of credit information by his bankers.

A further case where banks may continue to disclose information regarding the state of its customers' accounts would be disclosure to the court in the event of legal action to which the bank and the customer are both parties, as this would be required under the general rules of discovery and would be pursuant to a court's order.

Public duty

29-008 It is unlikely that a situation would arise in which it would be in the interest of the public to disclose information about a customer.

If, however, an incident arose in which it was in the public interest to disclose information, such as a case in which funds are received which the bank involved reasonably believes may be used in the commission of a serious offense (such as a terrorist offence), it is arguable that the bank would be entitled to disclose the information to the authorities on the basis that such disclosure was not

6 Banking Companies Ordinance 1962, section 93C.

in regard to a transaction which was, by its nature, bona fide, and thus protected and that disclosure was in the public interest.

In this connection, it is interesting to note that the State Bank of Pakistan in Regulation XII of the Prudential Regulations for Banks issued by it in January 1992 under the powers contained in the Banking Companies Ordinance 1962, has provided guidelines concerning the "criminal use of banking channels for the purpose of money laundering and other unlawful trades".

These regulations require banks to take precautions against involvement in money laundering and related activities, but they do not specifically require those banks to disclose any such suspected activity to the State Bank. It could, however, be argued that in such circumstances, disclosure to the State Bank or other authorities would be in the "public interest" and, thus, a proper disclosure.

Compulsion of law

Disclosures which are required to be made under law can be further categorized into overlapping subheads: disclosure under order of the courts, disclosure to investigating authorities, and disclosure under statute. **29-009**

Disclosure under order of court

The courts have various powers to compel the attendance of witnesses and production of relevant documents in proceedings before them in which powers have been granted under various procedural and evidentiary statutes. **29-010**

The Bankers Books Evidence Act 1891 is the main enactment pertaining to the production of bankers books in court proceedings. This Act provides:

> "4. Subject to the provisions of this Act, a certified copy of any entry in a banker's book shall in all legal proceedings be received as *prima facie* evidence of the existence of such entry, and shall be admitted as evidence of the matters, transactions and accounts therein recorded in every case where, and to the same extent as, the original entry itself is now by law admissible, but not further or otherwise.
>
> 5. No officer of a bank shall in any legal proceeding to which the bank is not a party be compellable to produce any banker's book the contents of which can be proved under this Act, or to

appear as a witness to prove the matters, transactions and accounts therein recorded, unless by order of the Court or a Judge made for special cause.

6. (1) On the application of any party to a legal proceeding the Court or a Judge may order that such party be at liberty to inspect and take copies of any entries in a banker's book for any of the purposes of such proceeding, or may order the bank to prepare and produce, within a time to be specified in the order, certified copies of all such entries, accompanied by a further certificate that no other entries are to be found in the books of the bank relevant to the matters in issue in such proceeding, and such further certificate shall be dated and subscribed in manner hereinbefore directed in reference to certified copies."

The primary purpose of the Act was to relieve officials of banks from the obligation to appear personally in Court to give evidence and in order to mitigate the difficulties of hearsay rules. In addition, the Act follows the principle that if a customer is involved in civil or criminal proceedings, he thereby subjects himself to the necessity of disclosure of facts which are relevant to such proceedings.

As regards the general principles governing disclosure in civil proceedings, these are set out in the Civil Procedure Code 1908. Under the Code, the court has power to order discovery in proceedings, either of its own motion or upon the application of any party to the proceedings.

Discovery in cases involving information in the hands of bankers would be ordered by the courts on the same basis as discovery in other cases, except that the Banker's Book Evidence Act could be asserted to allow banks to submit certified copies of their books.

In criminal law proceedings, the provisions of the Criminal Procedure Code 1898 would apply. Section 94 of the Code states:

"94. (1) Whenever any Court or, any officer in charge of a police-station considers that the production of any document or other thing is necessary or desirable for the purposes of any investigation, inquiry, trial or other proceeding under this Code by or before such Court or officer, such Court may issue a summons, or such officer a written order, to the person in whose possession or power such document or thing is believed to be, requiring him to attend and produce it, or to produce it at the time and place stated in the summons or order.

Provided that no such officer shall issue any such order requiring the production of any document or other thing which is in the custody of a bank or banker as defined in the Bankers' Books Evidence Act, 1891 (XVII of 1891), and relates, or might disclose any information which relates, to the bank account of any person except -

(a) for the purpose of investigating an offence under sections 403, 406, 408 and 409 and section 421 to 424 (both inclusive) and sections 465 to 477-A (both inclusive) of the Pakistan Penal Code, with the prior permission in writing of a Sessions Judge; and

(b) in other cases, with the prior permission in writing of the High Court."[7]

The sections referred to relate to the offenses of dishonest misappropriation of property, criminal breaches of trust, dishonest or fraudulent acts, and forgery.

It is felt that the above quoted provisions of law will have overriding effect, and a bank will be required to disclose relevant information to a court or other competent authority if such court or competent authority directs that disclosure be made to it in terms of the above quoted provisions of law.

Disclosure to investigating authorities

It will be observed from the above quoted provisions of the Criminal Procedure Code that the Powers of the Police to require disclosure are the same as those of the courts.[8] **29-011**

The investigative powers of other investigating authorities, such as the Federal Investigation Agency in relation to financial matters, are in general the same as those of the police.

Statutory provisions

There are numerous statutory provisions requiring banks to make disclosure in certain specified instances or for specific purposes. **29-012**

---

[7] Criminal Procedure Code, section 94.
[8] *Id.*

Banking laws

29-013 Various enactments pertaining to banks and financial institutions contain provisions requiring banks to make disclosure for certain specific purposes, and these are discussed in the text below.

The main enactment governing the activities of banking companies in Pakistan is the Banking Companies Ordinance 1962. Section 25A of the Ordinance obliges banks to furnish to the State Bank of Pakistan such credit information as the State Bank may require, but the State Bank is requested to maintain confidentiality as to the source of this information.

This section also provides that this credit information may be made available to banks at a fee and obliges the banks availing of this facility to use the information only for the purpose for which it was disclosed, to keep the information confidential, and to reveal it only with the prior permission of the State Bank.

Under section 25AA of the Banking Companies Ordinance, the State Bank is required to prepare a report of cases in which banks have written off or restructured loans or the usual banking practices have been departed from and submit this report to the Federal government which, if it believes that the report to be of public interest, may submit it to Parliament or one of the Standing Committees of Parliament dealing with finance.

In case of the winding up of a banking company, its books of account are specifically made admissible in evidence by the provisions of section 65 of the Banking Companies Ordinance.

Similarly, the State Bank, under the State Bank of Pakistan Act, 1956 (referred to above), has considerable powers to demand and receive information and to issue directives regarding the conduct of banks.

In respect of cooperative banks, the Federal Bank for cooperatives has power to call for information, but such information is protected by the confidentiality provisions contained in the statute under which it was set up (see text above).

Other statutory banking corporations, such as the Industrial Development Bank of Pakistan and the Agricultural Development Bank, have certain statutory guidelines regarding disclosure, fidelity, and secrecy.

Income Tax Ordinance 1979

29-014 Under the Income Tax Ordinance 1979, the income tax authorities have power to call for information regarding assessees. This section, in the relevant part, states:

"144. The Income Tax Officer, the Inspecting Assistant Commissioner, the Commissioner, or any other officer authorized in this behalf by the Commissioner or the Central Board of Revenue, may, by notice in writing, require . . .

(c) any person, including a banking company, to furnish such information or such statement or accounts as may be specified in such notice:

Provided that no such notice shall be issued to any banking company as respects any client, except with the prior approval of the Commissioner in the case of an Income Tax Officer, or the Central Board of Revenue or any other income-tax authority authorized by it in this behalf in the case of the other officer."[9]

As indicated above, the Protection of Economic Reforms Act 1992 states that it is to override the provisions of all other laws and expressly refers to the Income Tax Ordinance. In interpreting the effect of this provision on the powers of the income tax authorities referred to above, it is relevant that foreign currency accounts are expressly made exempt from income tax, and the reference to the Income Tax Ordinance could be to protect this position.

Further, as the main secrecy provisions refer to bona fide banking transactions, it could always be asserted that the authorities would require this information in order to investigate transactions which appear to be other than bona fide as being designed to evade tax liability which would otherwise accrue and thus disclosures required by tax authorities under the above which are not in regard to foreign currency accounts would continue to be permissible.

Foreign exchange control

The Foreign Exchange Regulation Act 1947 and regulations made thereunder also could have some impact on disclosure of customer information by banks in that they impose certain reporting requirements upon customers and banks in respect of the official remittance of currency into and out of Pakistan. 29-015

Such reports and information would, however, be protected by the general right of confidentiality discussed above and the terms of the Protection of Economic Reforms Act thus would not be available outside the banking community.

[9] Income Tax Ordinance, section 144.

Drugs legislation

29-016   In Pakistan, there are various enactments pertaining to medicinal and narcotic drugs. The relevant enactment for the purposes of banking secrecy is the Dangerous Drugs Act 1930, which was amended in 1987 to permit the tracing of assets acquired as a consequence of drug trafficking offenses and states:

> ". . . any officer referred to in subsection (1) may, after obtaining approval in writing from his senior officer authorized by the Head of the Department concerned, trace the assets of a person who has committed an offence punishable under Chapter III and may, for that purpose, require a bank or other financial institution to furnish such information as he may specify."[10]

In addition, under the Act, a court trying an offence of drug trafficking punishable under the Act has power to freeze the assets of the accused if it has reasonable grounds to believe the accused may have committed such offense.[11]

Upon conviction, the assets of the accused are liable to be forfeited if acquired during or as a result of the commission of the offense.

Thus, any person convicted of an offense in relation to narcotic drugs becomes liable to have his assets traced, and these assets are liable to forfeiture. It is likely that such tracing and confiscation provisions may be extended to other cases where an offense has been proved to have been committed.

Insolvency

29-017   If a person is the subject of insolvency proceedings, the Court may, under the provisions of the Insolvency Act 1909, on the application of the official assignee or any creditor who has proved his debt:

> ". . . summon before it in such manner as may be prescribed the insolvent, or any person known or suspected to have in his possession any property belonging to the insolvent, or supposed to be indebted to the insolvent or any person whom the court may deem capable of giving information respecting the

10 Dangerous Drugs Act 1930, section 23(3).
11 *Id.*, section 35A.

insolvent, his dealings or property; and the Court may require any such person to produce any documents in his custody or power relating to the insolvent, his dealings or property."[12]

Similarly, in case of winding-up under the Companies Ordinance 1984, the court has power to order discovery in cases in which the property of the company is involved.

In these cases, as well, a bank may be requested to disclose information which otherwise may be protected by secrecy obligation.

Customs Act 1969

Under the Customs Act 1969 certain customs officers have the power to require the giving of evidence or production of documents in connection with an enquiry which such officer is making in respect of the smuggling of any goods.[13]   **29-018**

The Customs Act is another enactment which is apparently over-ridden by the Protection of Economic Reforms Act 1992. However, if the account or transaction in question is not connected with a foreign currency account, it would seem that a bank would be obliged to produce any information required by a customs officer on the basis that transactions pertaining to monies earned by reason of smuggling or illegal activities would not be a bona fide transaction, even if the transaction itself is not in any way inappropriate.

REMEDIES FOR WRONGFUL DISCLOSURE

The Protection of Economic Reforms Act, while enunciating a principle regarding banking secrecy does not enact any penalties for breach of the duty of secrecy and, although there is provision for the Federal government to make rules for "carrying out the purposes of" the Act, no rules have as yet been published. Perhaps such rules will be framed now that the Ordinance has become an Act of Parliament.   **29-019**

---

12 Insolvency Act 1936, section 36.
13 Customs Act 1939, section 166.

Thus, at present, it would be appropriate only to discuss the remedies available for breach of the implied condition regarding confidentiality which would be available to the customer in case where a bank makes a disclosure which is not permitted under any of the exceptions discussed above.

Damages

29-020 The remedy for a breach of the terms of a contract would be damages, and these are calculated in accordance with the terms of the Contract Act 1872, which provides:

> "73. Compensation for loss or damage caused by breach of contract. When a contract has been broken, the party who suffers by such breach is entitled to receive, from the party who has broken the contract, compensation for any loss or damage caused to him thereby, which naturally arose in the usual course of things from such breach, or which the parties knew, when they made the contract, to be likely to result from the breach of it.
>
> Such compensation is not to be given for any remote and indirect loss or damage sustained by reason of the breach."[14]

The actual damage caused to a customer in respect of whose accounts or banking transaction details have been improperly released by the bank is likely to be nominal and thus the level of damages recoverable likely to be proportionately small.

Injunction

29-021 The other remedy open to the customer in case of breach or threatened breach by a bank of its duty of confidentiality or secrecy is that of an injunction restraining the bank from revealing details of the customer's accounts or banking transactions.

Thus, prevention of disclosure would, in normal circumstances be a suitable case for an injunction. In cases of necessity and urgency, temporary injunctions may be obtained speedily and by means of *ex parte* proceedings and thus do not require notice to the bank.

[14] Contract Act 1972, section 73.

Although in many ways the injunction is an ideal remedy for the customer, this remedy may, however, not be available due to the fact that the customer is likely to discover the breach after it has occurred or when it is already too late to prevent it, or the customer has no evidence to support the contention that disclosure is about to be made and support the consequent plea for the injunction.

Defamation

In addition, there is the possibility of a suit for defamation, which **29-022** may be their civil or criminal (defamation being a penal offence under section 499 of the Pakistan Penal Code), if the customer has in fact been defamed by the disclosure.

In either case, in general, truth may be asserted as a defense. However, truth will be accepted as a legitimate defense only if the disclosure was made in the public interest, in the interest of the disclosing party or the party about whom information was disclosed, or was a privileged communication.

CONCLUSION

In general, it would seem that the trend in Pakistan is towards more **29-023** and greater banking secrecy as it is realized that confidentiality must be preserved in banker-customer relationships for promotion of confidence in the banking system of the Country and attraction of foreign private investment in Pakistan.

The prime example of this trend is the promulgation of the Protection of Economic Reforms Ordinance 1991, which for the first time imposes a general statutory duty of secrecy upon all banks and financial institutions.

Against this, it is necessary to balance the demands of legitimate public purpose for which disclosure of information may be necessary, such as the prevention of drug trafficking, financing of terrorist and illegal activities, and for providing effective controls against insider trading and evasion of taxes.

The trend in such cases does not appear to be towards the disclosure of information to authorities by banks on suspicion of funds being used or received as a result of such activity (although some discretion is left to the banks by the use of the words "bona fide banking transactions" to reveal such suspicions to the State Bank or authorities). However, it is probable that as in the case of drug traffickers, the funds of convicted offenders in certain categories of crimes may be traced and if linked to the illegal transaction be liable to forfeiture.

Given the government's avowed desire to open the economy and privatize state owned businesses, to attract as much private investment in Pakistan and form as broad a base of investors (both foreign and local) as possible, and to attract investment of foreign exchange into Pakistan, it is unlikely that, apart from the exceptions mentioned above, any limitation on secrecy obligations will be imposed in the future.

If the present trend continues, it is hoped that the Protection of Economic Reforms Act and the right of secrecy given therein will be clarified by the issue of rules determining the scope of secrecy, the instances in which a transaction may be considered to be other than "bona fide", and the sanctions which would apply in case of breach of this duty.

It is not possible to complete this discussion without raising the other general trend in Pakistan's laws, that of the Islamization of the economy and laws of Pakistan. In addition to endeavoring to encourage private investment and liberalize laws relating to exchange control, the avowed policy of the government is the Islamization of Pakistan's economy and laws.

Enactments such as the Enforcement of Shari'ah Act 1991, while imposing provisions of Sharia (Islamic law) also protect foreign international obligations (such as those in connection with foreign loans which may provide for the payment of interest) even though these obligations may be contrary to Sharia.

However, it is unlikely that this process would have any impact upon the secrecy provisions discussed above, as this concept would be acceptable under an Islamic legal system.

PORTUGAL

Francisco Santana Guapo
Advogado
Lisbon, Portugal

Chapter 30

PORTUGAL

INTRODUCTION

"Considering that the reconstruction of the country implies the **30-001** establishment of a feeling of confidence in the banking system which enables the seizure and recovery of hoarded money, the Government has been showing its concern for the safeguarding of banking secrecy".

The above paragraph, which is a part of the brief report issued in connection with Decree Law Number 2/78,[1] shows clearly the objectives that the Portuguese Government intended to achieve through the statute.

In fact, it is necessary to understand the Portuguese situation as it was in 1978 in order to have an accurate knowledge of the number of solutions defined by the legislature.

After the revolution of 25 April 1974 and until the end of 1979, the Portuguese political situation was generally characterized by periods of great instability, as well as social problems and a preponderance of left wing political forces.

This situation stimulated a decrease in economic activity and a retraction of national and foreign investments, aggravated by the instability of 1975, with the nationalization of some sectors of the economy, among them the banking industry.

Among the various consequences caused by the political situation was the loss of confidence in the Portuguese banking industry.

The Portuguese Government attempted to remedy the situation in 1978 by enacting Decree Law Number 2/78, the main intention of which was to re-establish confidence in the banking system.

---

[1] Decree Law Number 2/78 of January 9, 1978.

The legislature's intentions do not, therefore, aim at a technical perfection of the legal concept of banking secrecy and its protection, seeking instead to create a system guaranteeing maximum privacy to the client in matters of personal and patrimonial nature.

This intention was taken to its extreme by adopting a pattern of full protection of the right to the banking secrecy, with regard to the public and to the State itself.

The level of banking secrecy which previously applied to credit institutions and members of the board and employees now takes into consideration the latter, subjecting them to the requirements of professional secrecy.[2]

The implications of this are many, since persons subject to professional secrecy may abstain from testifying or producing confidential documents.

With regard to credit institutions which are not mentioned in the Decree Law Number 2/78, the responsibility lies in civil liability for illicit actions or through contractual civil liability.

Decree Law Number 2/78 has been effective since 1978, with only a few minor amendments. However, the demands of European Community (EC) rules imply deep changes in this matter; thus, it is not likely that the Portuguese statute will be effective for much longer.

CONCEPT OF BANKING SECRECY

30-002   Decree Law Number 2/78 does not define, in abstract terms, banking secrecy.

Under article 1 of Decree Law Number 2/78, banking secrecy is regarded as an obligation that binds certain persons in accordance with their positions, such as directors, managers, and employees of the credit institution.

It is, however, difficult to include every person who should be submitted to the statute. There are those not expressly encompassed by the law but who are involved in banking and who are excluded, in fact, from the secrecy obligation.

These persons who have no position with the credit institution and are not directly linked to it, nevertheless have access to important information concerning clients and the bank due to their functions as, *i.e.*, auditors.

---

[2] Judgment of the Tribunal da Relacao of February 13, 1980; Judgment of the Supremo Tribunal de Justica of May 21, 1980; Judgment of the Supremo Tribunal de Justica of October 20, 1988.

There is a further difficulty in determining when the secrecy obligation arises.

Article 1, number 1, Decree Law 2/78, determines the obligation of secrecy in relation to the facts "which knowledge comes exclusively by virtue of the practice of their performance".

Article 1, number 2, presents a series of factors which imply the obligation of secrecy, *i.e.*, the names of the clients, deposit accounts and movement of funds, bank transactions, and information related to current procedures in the Credit Inspection of the Bank of Portugal.

Nevertheless, the legal formulation leaves several questions open.

In effect, there is the issue of knowing as to when the obligation of banking secrecy arises, or if only the factors cited in the statute, the incidence of which are susceptible of causing loss to clients, are sufficient to trigger the obligation. In addition, it is not settled whether in formation concerning clients of the bank, that come by accident within the knowledge of the person bound to banking secrecy, are subject to such secrecy.

In respect to the system adopted by Decree Law 2/78, the lack of answers to these questions has caused great difficulties.

The following definition of banking secrecy is worth noting here:

> "Banking secrecy consists in the discretion that the banks and its personnel should observe over economic data and personal information of the clients that may have come to their knowledge through the exercise of banking functions. By client, here we have to consider not only the one who makes transactions in the bank, but also everyone who through him establishes unaccomplished negotiations in result of which the bank is left with a set of information about the person, his property and business".[3]

Generally, the interpretation of the law concerning banking secrecy has been very broad attempting to involve every type of relationship between the client and the bank.

---

[3] Alberto Luis, "Banking Secrecy in Portugal", *Lawyers Magazine* (May/August 1981), at pp. 461-462.

RELEASE OF THE BANKING SECRECY OBLIGATION

By the client

30-003 According to Decree Law 2/78, both the client and the bank hold the right to the banking secrecy.

As far as the client is concerned, article 2, number 2, of the statute determines that only the client can release those subject to banking secrecy in relation to facts concerning himself:

> "The discharge of duty of banking secrecy related to facts and elements of the relations between the client and the institution of credit can only be granted through an authorization of the client conveyed to the institution".

Nevertheless, this disposition should be narrowly interpreted. Effectively, it is not the credit institution that is bound to banking secrecy but rather the members of its administration and finance departments and employees. Therefore, the authorization of the client, although conveyed to the credit institution, should be understood as being an authorization addressed to the member of the administration or to the employee of the Institution, so that he can reveal facts or elements concerning the client. Through this authorization, the person obliged is released from the duty of banking secrecy.[4]

Must the authorization be given in writing or orally? The law does not mention anything about this question; therefore, it is deemed that any form is acceptable as long as it expresses clearly the intention of releasing the obligation to secrecy.

By the credit institution

30-004 Article 2, number 1, Decree Law 2/78, declares: "The discharge of the observance of the duty of secrecy, related to facts and elements of the institution, can be granted by an authorization from the board of the credit institution".

In this case, the party entitled to the right of banking secrecy is the credit institution, that is, the members of the administration and finance departments and employees.

---

[4] *Id.;* see also José Patricio Paúl, "Banking Secrecy, Extent and Limits in Portuguese Law", *Banking Magazine* (1989), at p. 75.

In the situation relating to the client's right to secrecy, he has entrusted the institution with facts of his private life. These facts should be kept in confidentiality, as indicated by law.

In the situation relating to the credit institution's rights to secrecy, everything happens within the institution. Persons in high positions and employees are bound to the duty of secrecy regarding matters covering the activities of the institution.

This obligation results from one imposed by the General Law of Labor, which imposes the duty of loyalty, forbidding the employee to divulge information regarding the organization, methods of production, or business of the management. The violation of this duty has implications at civil and disciplinary liability level if the employer suffers loss.

Decree Law 2/78, while imposing in article 2, number 1, the obligation of secrecy about facts or elements of the credit institution itself, reinforces the duty already imposed by General Law of Labor, conceding to it the character of professional secrecy. The main consequence of this fact resides in the circumstance of its violation implying disciplinary, civil and criminal liability under article 184, Penal Code.[5]

As mentioned earlier, the holder of the right of banking secrecy is the bank institution. Therefore, only the institution can release the person obliged to secrecy, through a competent authorization. Although the law does not refer it, the authorization must be in writing, since the board of the institution must deliberate about the release, and the decision must be mentioned in the board's minutes.

DUTY TO PROVIDE INFORMATION

Article 5, Decree Law 2/78, declares that "the contents of the actual **30-005** statute does not in any manner prejudice the duties to provide information, statistics, or otherwise which, in terms of the present legislation, are impending over the institution of credit."

Effectively, in face of the statute and bearing in mind the nature of banking secrecy (professional secrecy), there is the following question: should any duty of information, mentioned in the above statute, be sufficient to release an entity bound to the duty of secrecy?

[5] M. Maia Goncalves, The Portuguese Penal Code (1986), at p. 132.

The Attorney General has issued an opinion according to which

".. .apart from the cases where the release of secrecy is permitted, board members, managers and employees of the credit institution cannot reveal facts that came to their knowledge exclusively through the exercise of their duty, since such duty of information is part of the law. There is no legal disposition that foresees the duty of information of the entities referred to above.. .concerning facts subject to professional secrecy."[6]

The Attorney General, therefore, considered that the existence of a legal duty of information of generic nature was not enough to discharge compliance with the banking secrecy, but that another disposition was necessary to expressly enable such dispensation.

Due to absence of such disposition, neither the judicial authorities nor the police have access to information and documents in the possession of the credit institutions, regarding their clients (except for proceedings, regarding checks without sufficient funds, where the law foresees the obligation of banks provide the authorities with information about the clients).[7]

This position was often confirmed by the Portuguese courts. However, the situation changed significantly with the publication of the Penal Code (1982) and the Code of Criminal Procedure (1987).

The Code of Criminal Procedure, article 135, foresees the possibility of persons subject to professional secrecy (among which are representatives of credit institutions) of refusing to testify.

However, article 135, number 2, of the statute enables the judicial authorities to proceed with the necessary investigations and, if the claim of secrecy is proved to be insufficient to compel testimony.

Article 135, number 3, provides that the Iimmediate Superior Court, after hearing the representative of the profession, can order testimony with "loss of professional secrecy".[8]

Article 185 of the Penal Code determines that violation of professional secrecy is not punishable if such violation occurs during the performance of a superior legal duty, public interest, or private interest.[9]

Finally, under article 181 of the Code of Criminal Proceedings, the confiscation of property, titles, values and other objects deposited in the banks is possible "whenever there are good reasons to believe that they are related to a crime and prove be of great utility

[6] Opinion of the Attorney General of November 30, 1978.
[7] Judgment of the Supremo de Justica of October 20, 1988.
[8] M. Maia Goncalves, The Code of Criminal Procedure (1991), at p. 229.
[9] M. Maia Goncalves, *supra* n. 5, at pp. 322-323.

to discover the truth or its proof". The article also enables the judge to examine or order to be examined by experts correspondence and bank documentation to facilitate the discovery and apprehension of such property.

As to information of fiscal nature, the situation is quite different. There are no rules which expressly grant fiscal authorities the power to demand information or access to the property and documents from the entities obliged to banking secrecy.

In fact, the law grants the Direction General of Contributions and Taxes ample powers for inspection purposes, requests for information, and access to premises. However, the Attorney General and the Portuguese courts consider that the duty of professional secrecy can be excluded only by rules which expressly provide for its derogation.

Since such rules do not exist, only the holder of the legally protected interest, in this case the client, can release the employees of the credit institution from the obligation of secrecy. In other words, tax authorities will only have access to the client's information if he gives permission.[10]

In case authorization is refused, the law allows the tax authorities resort to the possibility of recurring to judicial process to obtain the required authorization. Nevertheless, not even through the judicial proceedings can tax authorities have access to information in possession of the credit institution against the client's will.

In conclusion, the tax authorities can obtain information only from the employees of the credit institution if the client allows it.

Mention also should be made of article 618, number 1(e), of the Code of Civil Proceedings, that

> ". . .those who, due to their condition of profession being bound to professional secrecy, concerning facts covered by such obligation, are unable by motive of moral reason to testify".[11]

Article 519, number 3 of the same statute provides that persons obliged to professional secrecy can legally refuse to cooperate with the court, if such cooperation implies the violation of such obligation.

---

[10] José Patricio Paúl, "Banking Secrecy, Extent and Limits in Portuguese Law", *Banking Magazine* (1989), at p. 78.
[11] Abilio Neto, *The Code of Civil Proceedings* (1985), at pp. 423, 464.

CONCLUSION

30-006   The development of banking secrecy in Portugal has encompassed two phases.

The first phase was one during which a full protection of facts connected to banking secrecy was guaranteed, under a policy which stresses the recovery of credibility and confidence in the Portuguese banking system.

The second phase, connected with the promulgation of the Code of Criminal Proceedings (1989), where it was recognized that, under certain circumstances, it was necessary, specifically as to criminal proceedings, to consider a derogation of legal principles with reference to banking secrecy, taking into consideration the protection of values and interests preserved by the Penal Law.

Decree Law 2/78 has been in force for fourteen years. Essentially, its rules have not been significantly amended but the duty of secrecy was extended to persons involved peripherally in the financial activities of the credit institution.

However, there is a likelihood that banking secrecy in Portugal will undergo changes in the near future, re-defining its concept as well as to assure that it will not conflict public or private interests.

It is also important to stress that certainly EC regulations will be taken into consideration.

CHAPTER 31

SINGAPORE

Angeline Yap
Allen & Gledhill
Singapore

Chapter 31

SINGAPORE

INTRODUCTION

In Singapore, the duty of banking confidentiality or secrecy in **31-001** respect of his client's affairs stems from two sources:

(1) The duty of confidentiality implied by the Common Law by virtue of the banker-customer relationship, and
(2) A statutory duty imposed by section 47 of the Banking Act (referred to herein as the "section 47 duty" or "the statutory duty").[1]

The Common Law principle is imported as part of the commercial law of England and the Banking Act is part of the legislation enacted by Singapore's Parliament.

This article will first present an overview of Singapore's economy and legal system and briefly explain why the commercial law of England is applicable in Singapore. This will be followed by a description of the Common Law duty as articulated by the courts in England and the statutory duty outlined by section 47 of the Banking Act.

The article will then examine how much of the English Common Law duty is applicable in Singapore in view of the existence of the statutory duty. Thereafter, changes and possible modifications to

---

[1] Chapter 19 of the 1985 Revised Edition of the Singapore Statutes.

the duty of confidentiality will be considered in the context of past and future regulatory trends.

Singapore's strategic location

31-002 Singapore is one of the newly-industrialized countries of Asia. Located four miles north of the Equator at the tip of the Malayan peninsula, Singapore is surrounded by Malaysia, Indonesia, and Thailand.

This strategic geographical location on traditional international trade routes has resulted, over the years, in her present importance to international trade, transportation and finance.

Singapore is now the world's busiest port in terms of tonnage handled[2] and the focal point of about 700 shipping lines, through which she is linked to more than 600 major world ports. Her airport handles in excess of 10-million passengers a year[3] and is amongst the busiest in the world.[4]

In addition, she has a well-developed infrastructure, efficient telecommunications, and a capable, pragmatic, and productive workforce, rated the among most productive in the world.

All these factors together have made Singapore the choice of many business or multinational corporations seeking to establish a presence in Asia. For example, the Hong Kong-based Political & Economic Risk Consultancy Ltd. (P. & E.) has ranked Singapore second only to Japan as a low-risk business site in its projections for 1991 and 1992.[5] This importance as a commercial center has in turn fuelled the growth and importance of her financial sector.

Financial center

31-003 Singapore's financial sector, which is supervised by the Monetary Authority of Singapore (MAS), has sustained double digit growth for the latter half of the 1980s.

---

[2] The port handled 483.7-million gross registered tons from 44,606 vessels in 1990 alone.

[3] In 1988, 12,569,788 passengers; in 1989, 14,136,4767, in 1990, 15.6-million.

[4] See "Business Environment Risk Intelligence (BERI) Survey", *The Business Times*, May 3, 1991.

[5] *The Business Times*, November 12, 1990.

Singapore is a center for Asian dollar dealings and, in all, 198 institutions participate in the Asian dollar market based in Singapore.[6] Singapore is the world's fifth largest foreign exchange center, after London, New York, Tokyo, and Zurich, in terms of trading activity.[7] In addition to the Asian dollar market, the 71 merchant banks operating from her shores have been active in interbank lending and have been increasingly busy in underwriting flotations and fund management.[8]

As at March 1991, a total of 137 (13 local and 124 foreign) commercial banks operated in Singapore, and her 13 home-grown commercial banks operated a network of 239 banking offices in Singapore.

THE LEGAL FRAMEWORK

Legislation enacted by the Parliament of Singapore

Singapore, which is a republic, was a colony of the United Kingdom   **31-004** and briefly part of the Federation of Malaya. She has a unicameral parliament and a government patterned after the Westminster model, in which Parliament enacts laws and confers executive powers thereunder upon ministers,[9] who form a cabinet headed by the Prime Minister.

The President is the constitutional Head of State. Although the President does not have executive powers, his assent is required before any legislation can have the force of law.[10] Local legislation comprises acts passed by Parliament and assented to by the Presi-

---

[6] As at March 1991, see *The MAS Annual Report* 1990/91, at p. 32. The Asian Dollar Market (ADM) was created in the early 1970s and has grown steadily since. For example, total assets in the ADM grew by 16 percent to US $390-billion in 1990, according to *The Business Times*, February 27, 1991.

[7] Trading activity averaged a daily forex turnover of US $79-billion in 1990, an increase of almost 30 percent over the previous year and 84 percent higher than in 1988 (*MAS Annual Report* 1990/91, at pp. 50-51). This daily average has apparently leveled off at US $80-billion per day for the first seven months of 1991; see *The Business Times*, November 15, 1991.

[8] See *MAS Annual Report* 1990/91, at p. 41. Singapore's budding fund management industry has also witnessed almost a doubling in total funds under management in the last three years; *MAS Annual Report* 1990/91, at p. 29.

[9] The Ministers usually are empowered under their respective Acts to promulgate such subsidiary legislation as in necessary for the implementation of the Acts.

[10] Article 58 of the Singapore Constitution provides that "the power of Legislature to make laws shall be exercised by Bills passed by Parliament and assented to by the President."

dent,[11] and subsidiary legislation promulgated thereunder by ministers exercising their delegated authority.

Judiciary

31-005   Singapore's judicial system comprises three tiers of courts:

(1) The Subordinate Courts, consisting of the Coroners' Courts, the Juvenile Courts, the Magistrates' Courts, and the Small Claims Tribunal;

(2) The Supreme Court, which comprises the High Court, the Court of Appeal, and the Criminal Court of Appeal, and

(3) The Judicial Committee of the Privy Council, which traditionally has been the highest court of appeal for Britain's former colonies.

Appeals to the Privy Council on civil matters must involve matters amounting to, or to the value of at least S$5,000, or the case must by its nature be a fit one for appeal, and the parties must, prior to the hearing in the Singapore Court of Appeal, have consented in writing to be bound by an appeal made to the Privy Council.[12]

ENGLISH COMMON LAW AND STATUTES

Second Charter of Justice

31-006   The reception of English law in Singapore was effected by the Letters Patent issued on November 27, 1826, more commonly referred to as the Second Charter of Justice, which established the Court of Judicature of Prince of Wales Island, Singapore, and Malacca and required the court "to give and pass Judgement and Sentence according to Justice and Right".

---

11 All Acts passed are compiled in the 12 volumes of the Singapore Statutes, of which the latest edition is the 1985 Revised Edition. Periodically, important Acts which have undergone substantial amendment are reprinted embodying all amendments up to the date of reprint, e.g., the Companies Act which has send a number of amendment exercises.

12 See the Judicial Committee Act, CAP 148, 1985 Revised Edition.

This phrase traditionally has been interpreted to mean that the English law and equity, as it stood in England in 1826, was part of the law of the Straits Settlements.[13]

Common Law

As a result of the foregoing, matters which have not been legislated   **31-007** upon by the Singapore Parliament are governed by English Common Law, embodied in decided cases of the English courts, with such adaptations as are required by local circumstances.[14]

The Common Law enjoys continuous reception in Singapore as "the Common Law was traditionally conceived of as having existed from time immemorial and was merely declared by the judges from time to time. . .".[15]

According to this interpretation of the Common Law, the courts in England deciding a case today simply would be declaring the law as it has always been (and, hence, as it was at the date of the Second Charter of Justice), and applying it to the facts before them.

Consequently, current decisions of the courts of England are still referred to and cited for guidance on principles where local statutes are silent, although at least one commentator takes the view that post-1826 Common Law developments made by the English courts may not *ipso facto* be applicable in Singapore.[16]

---

[13] *Regina* v. *Williams* (1858) 3 Kyshe 16; *Fatimah* v. *Logan* (1871) Kyshe 255.

[14] See *The Singapore Legal System*, edited by W. Woon, at p. 119, where he states "Again in its application to Singapore, the Common Law is subject to modification to suit the customs, manners, usages and religions of the native inhabitants." As an example, he cites the relaxation, in colonial days, of the common law concept of monogamous marriage in the case of the Chinese.

[15] See G. W. Bartholomew, Dean, Faculty of Law, New South Wales Institute of Technology, *English Law in Partibus Orientalium; The Common Law in Singapore and Malaysia*, at p. 15.

[16] Woon, *supra* n. 14, at p. 123. The view that the courts do make law is gaining acceptability, and it is increasingly recognized that the Common Law is not static but changes. However, the Privy Council, which is Singapore's final appellate court on civil matters, is composed of the same judges as the English House of Lords with the result that even Woon concludes, "Unless legal circumstances dictate otherwise, it may well be that Singapore courts are constrained to follow decisions of the English courts expounding well settled principles of the common law. Where the decision is that of the House of Lords, the Privy Council is unlikely to diverge from it unless some local circumstance justifies divergence."; see Woon, at p. 121.

Legislation in force on November 27, 1826

31-008   As a result of the Second Charter of Justice, all statutes that were in
force in England on November 27, 1826, are applicable in Singa-
pore,
provided they are of general application and suited to the conditions of Singapore,[17] and are not inconsistent with or precluded by
local legislation.[18]

Any English legislation enacted after that date is not applicable,
unless it is imported as part of the commercial law as discussed
below.

English commercial law

31-009   In instances where no local provision has been made on an issue or
question relating to certain enumerated categories of law, including
the law of banks and banking[19] and insurance, or with respect to
mercantile law generally, section 5 of the Civil Law Act[20] provides
for the matter to be governed by English law with such modifications as are necessitated by local circumstances.[21]

---

[17] This was made clear in *Yeap Cheah Neo* v. *Ong Cheng Neo* (1975) L.R. 6 P.C. 281,
an appeal from the Straits settlements, where the Privy Council stated,
"statutes relating to matters and exigencies peculiar to the local condition of
England, and which are not adapted to the circumstances of a particular
colony, do not become part of its law, although the general law of England may
be introduced to it."

[18] The Imperial Parliament at Westminster also passed legislation governing
Singapore as a colony of the British Empire from 1824 to 1963. Such of these
statutes as have not been repealed continue to from part of the law of
independent Singapore.

[19] Other categories enumerated are the law of partnerships, corporations,
principals and agents, carries by air, land and sea, marine insurance, average,
and life and fire insurance.

[20] CAP 43 of the Singapore Statutes.

[21] The exceptions to this reception are set out in section 5(2) of the Civil Law Act.
No part of English land law, statutes regulating or controlling any business or
activity through fines or registration, or statutes enacted to give effect to any
international agreement to which Singapore is not a party, or any United
Kingdom provision of which there is a corresponding written law in force in
Singapore, are applicable by virtue of section 5 of the Civil Law Act. Singapore
legislation is regarded as corresponding to United Kingdom legislation "if
(notwithstanding that it differs, whether to a small extent or substantially) the
purpose or purposes of the written law are the same or similar" to that or those
of the United Kingdom Act; section 5(3)(b) of the Civil Law Act.

CONTRACTUAL DUTY OF SECRECY

Contractual duty imported from Common Law

The banker's duty to his customer to keep confidential information **31-010** regarding the affairs of his customer (such information being referred to hereafter as "confidential information") arises out of the banker and customer relationship and is a term of their contract, implied by the Common Law.[22]

It is referred to herein as "the contractual duty of confidentiality" or "the contractual duty". The customer enforces this contractual right by suing the banker for damages in the event of a breach of this duty.

When he does so, the contractual duty of confidentiality, and its scope and application would, in the words of section 5 of the Civil Law Act, be "questions or issues which arise or which have to be decided in Singapore with respect to the law. . .of banks and banking."[23]

Since there is no other provision made by any law having force in Singapore imposing a contractual duty of secrecy, and since the exceptions enumerated in section 5 of the Civil Law Act do not apply, in the words of section 5, "the law with respect to those matters to be administered shall be the same as would be administered in England in the like case, at the corresponding period, if such question or issue had arisen or had to be decided in England . . ." subject to modifications required to adapt the Common Law to local circumstances.

As a common factor to both the Common Law and statutory duties is the fact that they are owed by the banker to his customer, the meanings of "customer" and "bank" will need to be set out first.

Meaning of "customer"

The authoritative *Halsbury's Laws of England* succinctly states: **31-011**

"A customer is someone who has an account with a bank or who is in such relationship with the bank that the relationship of banker and customer exists, even though at this stage he has

---

[22] See *Tournier v. National Provincial & Union Bank of England* [1924] 1 K.B. 461.
[23] Cap. 43 1988 Ed.

no account. An occasional or even regular encashment of a check is not sufficient to establish the relationship of banker and customer. At the same time the duration of the relationship is not of the essence".[24]

Similarly, Lord Dunedin observed in *Commissioners of Taxation* v. *English, Scottish and Australian Bank Ltd.*:

". . . the word 'customer' signifies a relationship in which duration is not of the essence. A person whose money has been accepted by a bank on the footing that they undertake to honor checks up to the amount standing to his credit is. . .a customer of the bank . . . irrespective of whether his connection is of short or long standing. The contrast is not between a habitue and a newcomer, but between a person for whom the bank performs a casual service, for instance cashing a check for a person introduced by one of their customers, and a person who has an account of his own at the bank."[25]

Hence, it is now clear that opening an account with a bank will suffice to constitute a person the bank's customer, whether the account is a savings, current, deposit or overdraft account. Professor E. P. Ellinger notes that it is also possible to be a customer without an account, such as where a clearing bank, "as a matter of regular business dealings, collects checks remitted to it by a non-clearing bank on behalf of that bank's customers."[26]

Furthermore, the relationship of banker and customer comes into existence when the bank agrees to open an account in the customer's name, thus signifying its consent to enter into a regular business relationship with him. By entering into this relationship of banker and customer, the bank agrees, *inter alia*, to accept the duty of keeping his affairs confidential.

Meaning of "bank"

31-012   A bank is defined in the Banking Act as "any company which carries on banking business" and holds a valid license granted by the MAS under the Banking Act.[27]

---

[24] See Fourth Edition Reissue, volume 3(1), paragraph 148.

[25] [1920] A.C. 683, at p. 687.

[26] See *Modern Banking Law* (Clarendon Press, 1987), at p. 78.

[27] For a fuller discussion, see Myint Soe, "Banks and Banking Business in Singapore and Malaysia", [1974] 2 M.L.J. ii.

"Banking business" is defined as "the business of receiving money on current or deposit account, paying and collecting checks drawn by or paid in by customers, the making of advances to customers", and includes "such other business" as the MAS may prescribe for the purposes of the Banking Act.[28]

DUTY OF SECRECY UNDER COMMON LAW

Implied contractual term

Under the Common Law, it is an implied term of the contract **31-013** between a bank and its customer that the bank will not divulge information to third persons, without the express or implied consent of the customer, either:

(1) The state of the customer's account;
(2) Any of his transactions with the bank, or
(3) Any information relating to the customer acquired through the keeping of his account.

These conditions apply unless the bank is compelled to release information:

(1) By order of court;
(2) Where circumstances give rise to a public duty of disclosure, or
(3) Where protection of the bank's own interests requires it.[29]

Tournier v. National Provincial and Union Bank of England

The *locus classicus* in which this duty was established by the English **31-014** Court of Appeal is *Tournier v. National Provincial and Union Bank of England.*[30]

This duty has been described by the United Kingdom Review Committee on Banking Services Law in its Report (hereafter referred to as the "Jack Report") as a legal principle which has stood the test of time.[31]

---

[28] See the Banking Act, section 2.
[29] See *Halsbury's Laws of England*, Fourth Ed., Reissue Volume 3(1), paragraph 240.
[30] [1924] 1 K.B. 461.
[31] See "Banking Services: Law and Practice Report by the Review Committee", Her Majesty's Stationary Office (1989), paragraph 5.05.

The plaintiff was the defendant bank's customer. His bank account was in debit and they agreed that the plaintiff would reduce the debt by paying one pound weekly to the defendant. The plaintiff broke the agreement after making three payments. The defendant bank's branch manager noticed that another customer of theirs had issued a check in favor of the plaintiff for 45 Pounds which the plaintiff did not put into his account.

Instead, the check was presented for collection through another bank and, on making inquiries with that bank, the branch manager discovered that the check had been collected for the account of a bookmaker. He then rang up the plaintiff's employer to find out the plaintiff's private address and in the course of the conversation told him about the plaintiff's debt to the defendant and about the plaintiff's check being diverted into the bookmaker's account.

Owing to this disclosure, the plaintiff's contract of employment was not renewed when it expired, and the plaintiff successfully sued the bank for slander and for breach of the banker's duty of confidentiality. The Court of Appeal took the view that a bank customer has a legal right to confidentiality regarding his bank account and that the bank's duty is not an absolute, but a qualified duty. Bankes L.J. said:

> "The duty is a legal one arising out of contract, and that the duty is not absolute but qualified."[32]

Exceptions at Common Law

31-015   Bankes L.J. identified four general exceptions to the duty which have been accepted as an accurate statement of the law:[33]

(1) Where disclosure is under compulsion by law (*e.g.*, where the bank is compelled to obey an order under the Bankers' Books Evidence Act);

(2) Where there is a duty to the public to disclose (*e.g.*, where danger to the state or public duty supersede the duty of the agent to his principal);

(3) Where the interests of the bank require disclosure (*e.g.*, where a bank issues a writ claiming payment of an overdraft stating on the face of the writ the amount of the overdraft), and

[32] *Tournier, supra* n. 22, at pp. 471-472.
[33] See the Jack Committee Report, paragraph 5.04.

(4) Where the disclosure is made by the express or implied consent of the customer (the familiar instance is where the customer authorizes a reference to his banker).[34]

Scope of duty not confined to information derived from account

Both Bankes and Atkin L.J.J. thought that the duty is not confined **31-016** to information derived from the customer's account. In their opinion, the duty extended to information derived from sources other than the customer's account.

The information in the *Tournier* Case, for example, was derived from another customer's account rather than from the plaintiff's own account. Nevertheless, the Court of Appeal held that the banker's duty did extend to it.[35] Furthermore, Atkin L.J. said:[36]

"I further think that the obligation extends to information obtained from other sources than the customer's actual account, if the occasion upon which the information was obtained arose out of the banking relations of the bank and its customers - for example, with a view to assisting the bank in conducting the customer's business, or in coming to decisions as to its treatment of its customers."[37]

The *Encyclopaedia of Banking Law* also states:

"The duty of secrecy goes beyond the state of the account. It extends at least to all the transactions that go through the account, and to the securities, if any, given in respect of the account."[38]

---

34 *Tournier, supra* n. 22, at p. 473.
35 ". . . the confidence is not confined to the actual state of the customer's account. It extends to information derived from the account itself . . . .", *per* Bankes L.J., *Tournier, supra* n. 22,at pp. 473, 475.
36 *Tournier, supra* n. 22, at p. 485.
37 Scrutton L.J., however, felt that the duty did not extend to information derived from the account of another customer. His Lordship said (at p. 482), "It appears to me, therefore, that we cannot imply an obligation to keep secret information about a customer derived not from that customer or his account, but from the account of another customer."
38 See *Encyclopaedia of Banking Law*, Cresswell, Blair, Hill & Wood, Volume 1, C142.

Therefore, it can be concluded that the scope of the duty extends to:

(1) Information derived from the account itself, and
(2) Information derived as a result of the banker-customer relationship from sources other than the account.[39]

Duration of duty

31-017 Information gained during the currency of the account remains confidential unless released under one of the four exceptions.

Their Lordships in the *Tournier* Case were of the view that the duty to keep information confidential continues even after the customer ceases to be a customer of the bank. That is, the bank is under a duty to keep the customer's affairs confidential:

(1) During the currency of the banker-customer relationship, and
(2) After the banker-customer relationship has been terminated.

Disclosure in the public interest

31-018 In the *Tournier* case, Bankes L.J. took the view that danger to the state may supersede the duty of confidentiality,[40] and a more recent example discussed below examines the inter-relation of the Common Law duty and section 47 of the Banking Act.

Disclosure in the bank's interest

31-019 A simple example of this exception is where a bank issues a writ claiming payment of an overdraft and stating on the face of the writ the amount of the overdraft.[41]

Sunderland v. *Barclays Bank Ltd.*, discussed below, is also a good example. Du Parq L.J.'s first ground of decision there was that the interests of the bank would permit disclosure, to the customer's husband, of the wife's dealings with bookmakers.

---

[39] In relation to information of this nature, the *Encyclopaedia of Banking Law* takes the view that the duty relating to information as to the customer which is obtained after he has ceased to be one. *Id.*, C144.

[40] *Tournier, supra* n. 22, at p. 473.

[41] See *Encyclopaedia of Banking Law, supra* n. 38, C121.

Consent Under English law

As Bankes L.J. stated in *Tournier*, the duty of confidentiality may be   **31-020**
waived by the customer either expressly or impliedly.[42] How the
English court would imply consent from circumstances surrounding a case is demonstrated in *Sunderland v. Barclays Bank Ltd.*[43]

The plaintiff in this case had an overdraft account with the
defendant bank. She had called the manager of the bank on the
telephone to lodge a complaint over the bank's decision to dishonor
one of her checks, drawn in favor of her dressmaker, for lack of
funds. However, the real reason was that the bank manager thought
it was unwise to grant her overdraft facilities because of her involvement with bookmakers.

During the conversation, the plaintiff relinquished the telephone
to her husband, who was told that most of the checks that had
passed through his wife's account were made in favor of bookmakers. The English Court of Appeal decided that the interests of the
bank in this case warranted disclosure and that, in the circumstances, the plaintiff had impliedly consented to the disclosure
made by the bank manager to her husband. Lord Justice du Parq
said:

> "The husband having taken over the conduct of the matter, the
> manager was justified in thinking that the wife did not object
> to his offering to the husband the explanation which might
> satisfy the husband that the complaint made was unjustified."

It also it sometimes argued that the practice of giving credit references without the express consent of the customer is permitted by
the customer's implied consent. It is widely known that it is accepted banking practice for banks to forward such information on
request and it has been submitted that by opening the account, the
customer impliedly consents to such references being given by his
bank.[44]

In giving such references, banks would obviously be required to
ensure that they exercise due care and are not negligent, as it is
accepted that a duty of care is owed in giving references to a third
party if the bank knows or ought to know that third party will rely
on such information.[45]

---

[42] *Tournier, supra* n. 22, at p. 473.
[43] (1986) V L.D.A.B. 163; *The Times*, November 25, 1938.
[44] See *Encyclopaedia of Banking Law supra* n. 38, 1, C131, and Poh Chu Chai, *Law of Banking* (2nd ed., 1992) at p. 170.
[45] See *Hedley Byrne & Co Ltd.* v. *Heller & Partners Ltd.* [1964] A.C. 465.

SECTION 47 OF THE BANKING ACT

Disclosure of information is an offense

31-021 In Singapore, in addition to the contractual duty, the bank's employees have a statutory duty, imposed by section 47 of the Banking Act, to keep the affairs of a bank customer confidential. Section 47(3) provides for a general prohibition against disclosure. Section 47(3) reads:

> "Subject to subsection (4), no official of any bank and no person who by reason of his capacity or office has by any means access to the records of the bank, registers or any correspondence or material with regard to the account of any individual customer of that bank shall, while his employment in or professional relationship with the bank, as the case may be, continues or after the termination thereof, give divulge or reveal any information whatsoever regarding the money or other relevant particulars of the account of that customer."

This is followed by a number of exceptions in section 47(4), which provides that section 47(3) shall not apply:

(1) Where there is consent (which, since the 1984 amendment to section 47, must be written);

(2) Where the customer is declared a bankrupt (or is being wound up, in the case of a company);

(3) In civil proceedings -
   (a) between the bank and the customer or, since the 1984 amendments, between the bank and its customer's guarantor relating to the customer's banking transaction, or
   (b) in which the bank is one of a few parties making adverse claims to money in the client's account where the bank seeks relief by way of interpleader;

(4) Where the officials of the bank are compelled under any written law in force in Singapore to cooperate with authorities investigating or prosecuting a crime;

(5) Where the client's monies are attached under a garnishee order (introduced in the 1984 amendments);

(6) Where the branch of a foreign bank forwards information required by its head office relating solely to credit facilities which it has granted the customer (introduced in the 1984 amendments), or

(7) Where information which, since the 1984 amendments may only be of "a general nature", is required to assess the customer's creditworthiness in connection with a bona fide commercial transaction or a prospective transaction.

The full text of section 47(3) and (4) is set out at Appendix B to this chapter.

Consent under section 47

It will be noticed that, whereas in England consent can be implied from the surrounding circumstances of the case, since the 1984 amendments to the Banking Act, permission must be granted in writing under section 47.[46]

31-022

However, the position on banker's references is provided in section 47(4)(g), which permits the disclosure of information required

> ". . . to assess the creditworthiness of a customer in connection with or relating to a bona fide commercial transaction or a prospective commercial transaction, so long as the information required is of a general nature and in no way related to the details of a customer's account."

Hence, the statutory exception in relation to the whole area of consent and banker's references may be restated as follows:

> Except for information relating to a customer's creditworthiness, it is an offence to divulge information relating to the money or relevant particulars of a customer's account without his written consent. In relation to requests for credit references, the information required must be:
>
> (1) Required to assess the customer's creditworthiness;
> (2) Required in connection with or relating to a bona fide commercial transaction which may be a prospective transaction, and
> (3) Of a general nature, unrelated to the details of the customer's account.

---

[46] This would appear, at least on one view, to still leave open the possibility of "implied written permission". See Soh Kee Bun, *Current Developments in International Banking and Corporate Financial Operations*, at p. 298.

Of course, banks must bear in mind that in giving such references, they have a duty towards the recipients not to be negligent in addition to their duty to the customer to exercise due care in doing so.[47]

Compulsion by law

31-023 It has been said that banking secrecy takes second place to criminal investigations in Singapore.[48] Wide powers to obtain information about bank accounts are conferred by legislation.

The list of such legislation is set out in section 47(8) of the Banking Act, which defines "written law" to mean Part IV of the Evidence Act, the Criminal Procedure Code, the Internal Security Act, the Income Tax Act, the Prevention of Corruption Act, the Kidnapping Act, and the Companies Act. Failure to cooperate renders the party concerned liable to legal penalties under the relevant legislation.

However, it is interesting to note that this list of legislation appears scanty compared to the position in the United Kingdom, where the Jack Committee has identified at least 19 Acts requiring disclosure to the authorities.[49] Such investigations are also the exception rather than the norm, and the vast majority of banking transactions are protected by the general rules of secrecy at Common Law and under section 47, outlined above.

Furthermore, wide as these powers may apparently be, it must be remembered that the officers conducting such investigations would arguably fall within the scope of persons "who by reason of . . . capacity or office has by any means" access to the bank's records, registers, correspondence, or material regarding an account.

Accordingly, they would appear to be under a duty to maintain the confidentiality of information relating to the account. The discussion relating to persons prohibited from divulging confidential information below deals with the question of whether section 47 applies to government officers.

---

[47] See Poh Chu Chai, *supra* n. 44, at p. 170.

[48] *Id.*

[49] See the Jack Committee Report, paragraph 5.07. The legislation requiring disclosure is listed at Appendix Q to the Report.

Civil proceedings

Where civil proceedings such as those outlined take place, banking   31-024
secrecy is enhanced by giving the courts the power to hold them *in
camera* with the consequence that neither the name, address or
photograph of any of the parties, or any information likely to lead
to their identification may be published, either during the proceedings or after they have ended. This is provided for in section 47 (5)
& (6) of the Banking Act.

Persons prohibited from divulging confidential information

The statutory duty under section 47 covers officials of any bank,   31-025
defined in subsection (8) to include directors and employees. The
definition is not exhaustive.

The statutory duty also applies to any "person who by reason of
his capacity or office has by any means access to the records of the
bank, registers or any correspondence or material with regard to the
account of any individual customer of the bank". That is, apart from
accountants, it apparently also applies to officials of government
bodies who are authorized to look into bank accounts, as well as all
others who have access to the bank's records by virtue of their
capacity or office.

One argument against the extension of section 47 to government
officials is that the provision that the duty is to last "while his
employment in or professional relationship with the bank, as the
case may be, continues or after the termination thereof" would seem
to imply that only employees or those subject to some form of
contractual relationship with the bank are subject to the section 47
duty.

Against that, it could be countered that section 47 utilizes the
term "employment in" the bank as opposed to "employment by" the
bank and also that the term "professional relationship" is defined by
section 47 to include, *i.e.*, it is not confined to, the bank's relationship
with a computer bureau. Furthermore, there is no restriction in
section 47 that the persons who would thereby gain access to the
bank's records need do so as a result of their office or capacity
within the bank.

This would have been easy enough to provide for had it been the
legislative intention. It would therefore appear that section 47 could
be wide enough to cover government officials. The matter has not
been deliberated upon by the courts in Singapore.

By its Notice to Banks, MAS 614, issued pursuant to the 1984
amendments to the banking secrecy provisions, the MAS has laid
down requirements aimed at ensuring that auditors of the head

offices of foreign banks comply with the statutory duty of secrecy. MAS 614 spells out clearly that the prohibition under section 47 of the Banking Act "covers all persons regardless of whether they are residents or non-residents".

It also provides that internal auditors or inspectors from the head offices of foreign banks are required to comply with section 47 should they gain access to the records of the accounts of individual customers in the course of the audit or inspection. Prior to such audit or inspection, they are also required to submit to the MAS statutory declarations that they are aware of the requirements of section 47 of the Banking Act and will strictly observe them. A copy of the inspection or audit report to the head office must also be submitted to the MAS.

Duration of statutory duty

31-026   A banking officer or other person who acquires information relating to an account is required, in the words of section 47(3), not to "give, divulge or reveal" it "while his employment in or professional relationship with the bank, as the case may be, continues or after the termination thereof". Since no mention is made of the duty lapsing after a reasonable period, it would appear to impose a perpetual vow of silence!

Subject matter of statutory duty

31-027   Section 47 prohibits those concerned from giving, divulging, or revealing "any information whatsoever regarding the money or other relevant particulars of the account of [the bank's] customer". It will be noticed that a moratorium is imposed on "any information whatsoever", that relates to:

(1) The money in the customer's account, or
(2) Relevant particulars of the account.

It would appear that an omission has been made in respect of the affairs of the customer other than the money in, or relevant particulars, of the account. The situation in *Tournier*, for example, would apparently fall outside the wording of section 47 as the information divulged in that case was that the banks' customer had diverted the proceeds of a check to his bookmaker. This neither relates to the money in his account, nor is it a particular of his account.

Penalty

The penalty for a failure to observe this statutory duty is a fine not **31-028** exceeding S$50,000 and/or a term of imprisonment not exceeding three years.[50]

In addition, section 66 of the Banking Act provides that "any person[51] being a director, managing director or manager of a bank" who, willfully,[52] (*inter alia*) "fails to take all reasonable steps to secure compliance" with the provisions of the Banking Act (*i.e.*, including section 47) shall be liable, on conviction of the offence so created, to a fine of up to $50,000 or imprisonment for a term of up to three years, or to both such fine and imprisonment".[53]

Enhanced protection

The statutory framework for banking secrecy is further enhanced **31-029** by the fact that despite having a wide supervisory jurisdiction over banks, which empowers it to conduct investigations of banks' books, the MAS is required by sections 44 and 45 of the Banking Act to do so under conditions of secrecy.

Furthermore, section 47(1) of the Banking Act specifically states that the MAS is not authorized to inquire into the affairs of any individual customer of any bank. Finally, section 47(2) provides that any incidental information relating to the affairs of an individual customer obtained by the MAS shall be secret between the MAS and the bank. Doubtless, any MAS official who comes into possession of such information in the course of investigations also would be under a section 47 duty of secrecy.

The position regarding merchant banks is broadly similar. It is to be found in Directives 11 and 12 of the MAS Directives to Merchant Banks. Directive 6 of the MAS Directives to Merchant Banks also provides that any information which a merchant bank is required to furnish to the MAS to enable the latter to supervise the merchant bank "shall be secret as between that merchant bank and the Authority".

---

[50] Section 47(9) of the Banking Act, Cap. 19, Singapore Statutes, 1985 Ed.

[51] The word "person" is defined to include a "corporation" for the purposes of the Banking Act.

[52] See section 66(3) of the Banking Act.

[53] *Id.*, section 66(1)(6).

RELATIONSHIP BETWEEN COMMON LAW AND STATUTE

Comparison of Common Law and statutory duties

31-030   A comparison between the Common Law duty and the statutory duty shows that:

(1) The banking secrecy laws of Singapore provide for contractual liability for the bank with criminal liability for the bank's directors, employees, accountants, and other persons whose office or capacity would give them access to the bank's records, who would not be contractually liable;

(2) Until the 1984 amendments, the section 47 exceptions were almost identical to the Common Law exceptions;

(3) The exceptions provided under section 47 are (since the 1984 amendments) more numerous than those available in England under the Common Law;

(4) The consent exception in section 47 now requires the customer's authorization to be written while, under the Common Law position, consent can either be express or implied, and

(5) The public interest exception is not included in section 47, with the result that academic opinion on its applicability in Singapore is divided.

That a contractual duty of confidentiality is implied into the banker-customer contract by the Common Law applied *vide* section 5 of the Civil Law Act is clear as section 47 does not deal with implying a contractual duty. That a statutory duty exists on the part of its employees, directors, and others with access to confidential information and the extent of that duty is clear from section 47 of the Banking Act.

However, in the light of the existence of section 47 of the Banking Act, what is not so clear is the exact extent of the contractual duty. In particular, would it be possible for the bank to be excused from its contractual duty due to consent implied from circumstances, or because the disclosure would be in the public interest, even though the actual employee who makes the disclosure in each case would thus be criminally liable under section 47 of the Banking Act? Academic views differ.

Whether the public interest exception applies in Singapore

One author, for example, takes the view that "it is arguable that the   **31-031**
Common Law exception of disclosure in the public interest can be
applied."[54]

It also has been argued that section 47 is not exhaustive as "such
an interpretation is too restrictive" as section 47 "does not cover
certain situations where banking secrecy will be justifiably en-
croached upon" such as the situation in *Sunderland,* where it was in
the bank's interest to make a disclosure in circumstances other than
those provided in section 47.[55]

The same author also argues against interpreting section 47 as
being exhaustive as the provision "does not deal with situations
where banking secrecy can be violated if the bank has a public duty
to disclose other than under compulsion of law." He cites the example of legislation amended or enacted to enable the accounts of
suspected drug smugglers to be disclosed, which he says "may not
be written law as defined".[56]

One line of reasoning supporting such views would be as follows. Applying section 5 of the Civil Law Act, the issue or question
of whether a banker is permitted to make disclosure in the public
interest would be decided in the affirmative under English Common Law. The application of Common Law would not be ousted by
the existence of section 47, as section 5 of the Civil Law Act only
provides that English law will not apply where there is a corresponding piece of legislation enacted by the Singapore parliament.
Since section 47 imposes a statutory duty, it is not such a piece of
legislation.

Furthermore, besides being a Common Law duty, the banker's
duty of confidentiality is a contractual one, giving rise to civil
liability, while section 47 serves a different purpose, namely that of
making the persons responsible for divulging the information, who
would not be contractually liable, subject to criminal liability.

The opposing view is that the issue should be characterized as
what exceptions to the contractual duty operate in Singapore. Characterized in that way, the Common Law exceptions would have to
be modified by section 47 because section 5(3)(a) of the Civil Law

[54]See Soh Kee Bun, "Banking Secrecy and Taking Evidence Abroad", *Current
Developments in International Banking and Corporate Financial Operations,*
(Butterworths, 1989), at p. 298, n 13.

[55]See Myint Soe, "Changes in the Law Relating to Banking Secrecy, The Banking
(Amendment) Act 1983", [1983] 25 Mal. L.R. 387, at p. 391.

[56]*Id.,* at p. 390.

Act requires the Common Law to be applied "subject to such modifications and adaptations as the circumstances of Singapore may require."

Hence, the position would be that criminal liability for disclosure is imposed by section 47 of the Banking Act while the Common Law operates concurrently to impose contractual liability, but the Common Law exceptions are modified in that they are restricted by the exceptions listed in section 47. It also may be argued that, in respect of a customer's affairs, apart from the money in or other relevant particulars of an account, the Common Law contractual duty applies without modification.

For example, one author argues that, since one of the cardinal principles observed by the courts in implying terms into a contract is that an implied term must not be contrary to law, the Common Law exception of public interest cannot apply in Singapore.[57]

This school of thought would point out that there is yet another weakness in the view that the Common Law exceptions can apply if they are excluded from section 47. That is, it relies on an unnatural distinction between the bank and its employee, excusing on the part of the institution acts which it could only do through its employees and which are crimes under the written law.

It is submitted that the contractual duty is separate and distinct from the statutory duty imposed by section 47 and that the legislature never intended section 47 to replace it. This is supported by the fact that the purposes or functions and the subject matter of the two duties differ.

The Common Law imposes a contractual duty on the bank because of the intimate knowledge that a bank acquires into its customer's affairs, whereas section 47 imposes criminal liability on persons described therein who would not be contractually liable to the customer since they are not party to the contract between the customer and his bank.

Considering the width of investigative powers given to the authorities in Singapore, the public interest exception might not be very useful even if it were applicable in Singapore. First, most investigations would be conducted under the respective pieces of legislation mentioned above. Second, the disclosure of information under the Common Law public duty exception would be subject to restrictions very similar to those outlined in the statutory provisions.

As outlined above, when the MAS conducts investigations, it does so under conditions of secrecy, only general information may be sought, it may not inquire into the affairs of any specific cus-

---

[57] Poh Chu Chai *supra* n. 44, at p. 167.

tomer, and any incidental information acquired is to be kept secret. That this is very similar to the factors applicable to the public interest exception will be apparent from the discussion below.

Public interest exception at Common Law

An interesting Common Law decision on the public duty exception **31-032** is the recent case of *Price Waterhouse* v. *BCCI Holdings (Luxembourg) S.A. & Others,* reported in *The Times* on October 30, 1991.

In this case, the High Court of England decided that the public interest in maintaining the confidentiality owed by a bank to its customers might be outweighed by some countervailing public interest in disclosure, and the latter was not limited to the public interest in detecting or preventing wrongdoing.

Hence, it ruled that Price Waterhouse (PW) could be permitted under the exception to make disclosures of certain confidential information to an enquiry set up to review BCCI's past performance of its statutory functions. PW was seeking to give evidence voluntarily without BCCI's consent as the enquiry, not having been convened under the Tribunals of Enquiry and Evidence Act 1921, could not compel the disclosure of confidential information.

At issue was the question whether voluntary disclosure could be made without the consent of BCCI, to whom PW owed a duty of confidentiality. The court decided that, as the United Kingdom legislature had conferred a general power of supervision upon the Bank of England, there was an important public interest in the effective regulation and supervision of authorized banking institutions and the protection of depositors. It held that this public interest ought to prevail over the interest in confidentiality. A few points from Millet J.'s decision are worth noting:

(1) The scope of disclosure was limited - The interest in disclosure to the enquiry was at least as wide as the interest in disclosure to the Bank of England, "provided that dissemination of such information was no wider in the latter case than would be authorized in the former case" (the powers of the MAS and the Bank of England are similar).

(2) Infrequent and less serious invasions - The enquiry would be dealing with matters more abstract and remote from the details of the underlying banking transactions than the Bank of England in its routine supervision; it was less likely that details of particular accounts would require to be identified, and the occasions when banking confidentiality was invaded were likely to be fewer and less serious.

(3) The enquiry had undertaken to respect confidentiality - It would do this where it could properly do so. The extent to which confidentiality would be invaded would depend upon the judgment of responsible persons at several different levels.

Public interest and compulsion by law

31-033 In the BCCI case discussed above, the court inferred the existence of a public interest in the proper supervision of financial institutions from the fact that section 1 of the United Kingdom Banking Act 1987 imposes a duty on the Bank of England "generally to supervise the institutions authorized by it in the exercise of" its powers.

In Singapore, the MAS has a similar duty. Section 28 of the Monetary Authority of Singapore Act, Cap 186 (MAS Act), empowers the MAS to approve financial institutions and control their operations and section 27 of the Act provides that the MAS may, if it thinks necessary in the public interest, request information from and make recommendations to such financial institutions as the Authority may from time to time determine.

The MAS also may issue directions under section 27 for the purpose of securing that effect is given to such requests or recommendations.

The similarity between the approach of the Common Law "public interest exception", as outlined above, and the "compulsion by law" provisions of which the MAS provisions provide an example, does not need to be belabored. So great is the similarity between the two that the Jack Committee has described the compulsion of law exception as a codification of the public duty exception and the purpose of the latter as being "to catch those items which have not yet been codified".[58]

In the United Kingdom, there were 19 Acts requiring disclosure to the authorities at the date of the Jack Committee's Report, and the Committee therefore recommended an exhaustive codification of all relevant legislation, requiring disclosure, with the further recommendation that all subsequent disclosure requirements should only be added by way of amending that provision.

At the same time, it advocated the abolition of the public duty exception as being vague, as well as unnecessary, in the light of the long list of legislation.[59] If these proposals are accepted, they would

[58] See the Jack Committee Report, paragraph 5.06.
[59] See the Jack Committee Report, paragraph 5.30.

have the effect of making the English position on the compulsion of law/public interest exception the same as that in Singapore.

Bankers books

A detailed examination of every piece of legislation permitting **31-034** disclosure of confidential information under compulsion of law would be outside the scope of this paper.

However, one important piece of general applicability should be discussed, *i.e.*, discovery under the Evidence Act.

The Evidence Act

The civil litigant cannot invoke the legislative provisions enumer- **31-035** ated in section 47. He has to rely on the Common Law exceptions and Part IV of the Evidence Act when he wants a bank to make disclosure.

In England, section 7 of the Bankers' Books Evidence Act 1879 is the general provision that can be invoked during discovery in civil litigation. Part IV of the Evidence Act, Cap. 97, Statutes of the Republic of Singapore, Rev. Ed. 1985,[60] is similar in effect to the English Act.

The main object of the provisions of the Act is to enable evidence to be procured and given and to relieve bankers from the necessity of attending and producing their books in court but not to give the litigant a new right of discovery. They are not intended to give a litigant a right to go on a fishing mission.[61] A bank cannot be compelled to give evidence unless a judge makes an order "for special cause".

TRENDS AND DEVELOPMENTS

An understanding of the role and approach of the MAS in oversee- **31-036** ing the development and integrity of Singapore's financial sector is crucial to a proper understanding of past and future trends in the financial sector.

---

[60] See sections 168 - 174.
[61] *Per* Arulanandom J. in *Goh Hooi Yin* v. *Lim Teong Chee & Others*, [1977] 2 M.L.J. 26. See also Poh Chu Chai, *supra* n. 44, at pp. 270 *et seq.*

These trends have in turn affected past developments in banking secrecy and they also may give some indication of future changes.

Supervisory policy - prudence and caution

31-037   The overall approach of the MAS may well be described as one of prudence and caution. Examples abound, and a few illustrations will be discussed below.

The strong growth of Singapore's finance sector has been patiently husbanded by conservative policies aimed at ensuring sound development. This conservatism is perhaps best explained by Dr. Richard Hu, Chairman of the MAS, in his opening statement in the MAS Annual Report 1990/1991 where he said:

> "Against the background of increased fragility in the international financial environment, the need to enhance prudential standards and ensure a stable financial system remains of paramount importance."[62]

Indeed, the specter of expensive bailouts, such as those in the United States savings and loans industry, seem to be ever present in the minds of Singapore's regulators, and Dr. Hu has attributed the successful development of Singapore as a financial center to the maintenance of sound, prudent standards linked to strict enforcement of these standards.

Giving a talk on The Regulation and Development of Financial Markets in June 1991, Dr. Hu explained the MAS approach to managing the growth of the financial sector:

> "A balance ha[s] to be struck between the opposing needs of giving markets freedom to grow, and the fiduciary responsibility for protecting the interests of depositors and investors. . . . Given that the long term viability of a financial center hinges upon investor confidence, regulators must uphold stringent prudential standards and exercise vigorous supervision in order to maintain the stability and soundness of the financial system."[63]

[62] See MAS Annual Report 1990/91, at p. 2.
[63] See *The Business Times* and *The Straits Times* for June 19, 1991.

Dr. Hu pointed out that:

(1) There has not been a single bank failure in Singapore since its independence in 1965;

(2) The financial sector has withstood severe volatility in international financial markets, such as the October 1987 stock market crash, and

(3) The sector has expanded at an average rate of 19 percent annually, or twice the overall rate for the economy, in the past decade.

He, therefore, concluded that "the MAS insistence on strict prudential standards . . . is a small price to pay to protect the financial system."

Examples of prudence and caution

The foregoing remarks encapsulate the conservative approach of the Singapore authorities demonstrated by a handful of examples: **31-038**

(1) The MAS has consistently rebuffed the persistent overtures of Luxembourg-based Bank of Credit and Commerce International (BCCI) since 1973. This policy of only approving institutions with proven track records has been vindicated in 1991 when the Singapore financial sector was spared the runs and suspensions which attended the BCCI scandal worldwide, from Hong Kong and Japan to the United Kingdom;

(2) MAS issued a Directive in 1983, requiring banks to consult the MAS before considering the extension of credit facilities exceeding S. $5 million to non-residents or to residents who intend to use them outside Singapore. Dr. Hu reiterated in June 1991 that the MAS has ruled out the internationalization of the Singapore dollar.[64] In July, the MAS clarified that the 1983 Directive is aimed particularly at discouraging "external speculative activities in the local financial or property markets";[65]

(3) In June 1991, the Minister for Finance announced an increase in the capital adequacy ratio requirement for banks to 12 percent; a hike from the previous eight percent, and four percent more than the ratio recommended by the Bank

[64]See *The Business Times*, June 19, 1991.
[65]See *The Business Times*, July 1, 1991.

for International Settlements (BIS). The MAS has explained that the higher ratio takes into account banks' exposure to market risks in their trading and investment portfolios, *e.g.*, in relation to share and money markets, foreign exchange rates, interest rates, and other investment price risks which the BIS recommendation does not cover. MAS has warned that defaulting banks may be directed to scale down their Asian Currency Unit activities and dividend payments.[66]

Supervisory policy - an overview

31-039   A few conclusions may be drawn from the foregoing:

(1) The overall approach of regulators is one of caution and prudence;

(2) The MAS tries to safeguard investor confidence and protect the interests of depositors (Hence, its insistence on strict prudential standards and vigilant enforcement. This, in turn, gives rise to two considerations: the need to insure the confidentiality of investor's and customer's accounts, and the need for efficient investigation mechanisms such as those built into the compulsion by law exception under section 47 - The two are apparently at odds but in reality serve the same purpose of protecting investor confidence.), and

(3) It counter-balances against this protective need the desire to give markets maximum freedom to grow.

Impact of policy on banking secrecy

31-040   The impact of these policies on past developments can be seen from a consideration of the 1984 amendments to the statutory duty of secrecy. An examination of section 47 in Appendix B, in which the 1984 amendments have been highlighted, will demonstrate that the original provision was almost identical to the position at Common Law.

The amendments introduced by Act Number 2 of 1984 to the then section 42 of the Banking Act were passed:

---

[66] *Id.*

(1) To extend the operation of section 42(2), which is now section 47(2), so as to permit the MAS to acquire incidental information of a customer's account in the discharge of its duty to supervise the financial condition of banks;

(2) To extend the existing exception relating to civil proceedings between the bank and its customer to a guarantor of a customer;

(3) To insert two new exceptions to banking secrecy that would have the effect of allowing a bank to make disclosure when the bank has been served with a garnishee order and enabling a head office of a bank incorporated outside Singapore to obtain information from its branch in relation to credit facilities granted by the branch, and

(4) To limit, to information of a general character unrelated to details of the customer's account, the existing exception on providing information about the credit worthiness of a customer.[67]

These amendments exemplify all three points mentioned above.

The first amendment strengthened the supervisory role of the MAS by specifically providing that it could acquire incidental information in the course of exercising its general supervisory role as well as in the course of its investigations under the Banking Act. Simultaneously, it made such information subject to the same duty of secrecy between the bank and the MAS.

The next two amendments could be viewed as facilitating the easier operation of banks in Singapore by widening one exception and introducing two new ones.

Finally, the fourth amendment exemplifies a refinement and strengthening of an existing exception to ensure that no specific information relating to an account is disclosed. By limiting the credit reference to general information, the amendment sought to enhance the customer's existing right of secrecy.

Hence, section 47 in its present state reflects the policy of ensuring banking secrecy in the bulk of bona fide accounts and transactions while ensuring that investigative authorities have enough teeth to see that banking secrecy cannot be taken advantage of by wrongdoers. All the while, the needs of the banking community for a sufficiently free environment in which to function are seen to in the provisions expanding on their right to make disclosures in their own interests.

---

[67] See the Explanatory Statement to the Banking (Amendment) Bill Number 15 of 1983, dated December 27, 1983.

Money laundering guidelines

31-041   Recent developments have illustrated even more of this delicate balancing operation between competing considerations.

January 1990 saw the introduction, by the self-regulating Association of Banks in Singapore (ABS), of a set of Guidelines pursuant to the Association's adoption, in January 1989, of the Basle Committee's "Statement of Principles" pertaining to the prevention of the misuse of the banking system for money laundering.[68]

The Guidelines are not legislation. They are examples of what may be called the "know your customer" approach to fighting money laundering, which have been described as essential to ensure the effectiveness of any laws which may be employed. They are:

> ". . .discretionary steps a bank may take to minimize the likelihood that it does business with money launderers, and thereby minimizing the likelihood that it incurs legal liability for wrongdoing . . . the banker responsible for managing [a] customer's account takes steps to ensure that the customer is who he purports to be . . . not a front for laundering ill gotten gains."[69]

The Guidelines enjoin bankers to require references and proper identification before opening new accounts and to scrutinize large deposits, withdrawals, and transfers, particularly if they are inconsistent with the nature of the customer's alleged line of business. While accepting that they in no way modify the banks' obligation of confidentiality, the Guidelines encourage the banks to cooperate with law enforcement authorities.

Code of Conduct for banks

31-042   The ABS is drawing up a Code of Conduct for the banking industry. The draft Code is being studied by the Association's 133 members, and it has been reported that the section on general guidelines for all areas of banking practice stresses confidentiality of accounts, dealings, and relations between banks and their customers.[70]

---

[68] See Guidelines on "Prevention of the Misuse of the Singapore Banking System for Drug Trafficking and Money Laundering Purposes", issued by the Association of Banks in Singapore.

[69] See Raj Bhala A. B., Dora S. S. Neo, and Choong Yeow Choy, "Legal Aspects of Money Laundering" [1991] 3 MLJ xxxiii at pxlix.

[70] See *The Straits Times*, July 20, 1991.

In relation to crime detection, the Code says that, if an officer suspects a customer's activities to be illegal, senior management must immediately be alerted, and the possibility of making a police report should not be ruled out.[71]

Electronic banking and credit information

Like money laundering by drug traffickers, electronic banking, and the pressures on banks to share credit information are features of modern banking which could not have been contemplated at the time of *Tournier*, and these also may have an impact on banking secrecy.

31-043

Electronic banking

The MAS supports the development of electronic banking services. For example, it has permitted full licensed banks to offer home banking services to individuals, through telephone and personal computer facilities, in addition to the increasingly widespread use of automated teller machines and the more recently introduced electronic funds transfers at points of sale, known in Singapore as NETS.[72]

31-044

This has necessitated the development of safety procedures by banks seeking to safeguard confidentiality. These precautions usually take the form of secret access codes, more commonly known as Personal Identification Numbers (PIN), in conjunction with passcards. Most banks take the precaution of warning their customers that the PIN must be kept secret, and not written on or stored together with the passcard.

Although electronic banking is a recent development, the maintenance of confidentiality may necessitate the passing of legislation or the promulgation of banking guidelines by the banks themselves in time to come.

---

[71] While this may seem alarmingly wide, it should be remembered that police officers investigating a crime probably also would be under a statutory duty of secrecy as persons acquiring information about an account by reason of their capacity or office as provided by section 47 of the Banking Act.
[72] See MAS Annual Report, at pp. 37-38.

Credit information

31-045   The burgeoning of credit and the attendant rise of defaults on payment are a phenomena of modern society. To protect themselves against default and to improve the services that they offer, banks in Singapore may increasingly be tempted to participate in computer network schemes involving the mutual sharing of electronic data with other banks.

The ease with which individuals can obtain access to credit through multiple credit, charge or even store discount cards has also prompted the MAS to tighten credit card regulations in 1991, even though the default rate in Singapore is relatively low. A large proportion of credit cards are offered by banks in Singapore.

If the rate of default increases, banks may be pressured to supply credit information to networks established to provide information on creditworthiness in the interests of protecting themselves from affording additional credit to defaulters, as well as in the general interest of other institutions in a similar position. If this development occurs, it may require some enabling legislation in the form of an amendment to section 47 of the Banking Act.

A trend towards pressuring banks to participate in such networks has already been reported by the Jack Committee in the United Kingdom.[73] However, the early action of the MAS in tightening credit card requirements so as to make them less easily accessible may dispense with, or at least delay, the need for such creditworthiness networks altogether.

CONCLUSION

31-046   The recent reiterations by the authorities that the Singapore financial sector is not over-regulated would indicate that they intend to stay their present course of delicately balancing competing needs for secrecy and supervision.

At a recent seminar on "Trends in the 1990s: Implications for Stock Market Investments", a keynote speaker noted the recent trend of deregulation of financial institutions in developed countries is now being reversed. If this is, indeed, an accurate forecast of international trends, as an international finance center, the Singapore authorities would, given their present inclinations, in all probability follow suit.

---

73 See the Jack Committee Report, paragraph 5.18.

Future regulation of the financial sector, including the banking industry, is likely to reflect the present concerns for soundness and stability, investor confidence, and an environment favoring growth.

Note -   The writer wishes to thank E.P. Ellinger, Professor of Law, National University of Singapore, for his comments on an earlier draft of this paper. For a brief overview of the contractual duty, see the writer's discussion, "To Disclose or not to Disclose?" in *Singapore Law Gazette* July/August 1992, at p. 19. A discussion of the interplay of the Section 47 duty and the Common Law duty can be found in the writer's paper, "Banking Secrecy Obligations in Singapore" to be published in the first volume of the *Nanyang Business Law Review*, a forthcoming publication of the Nanyang Technical University, Singapore.

APPENDIX I

Civil Law Act (Cap 43), section 5

5(1)   Subject to the provisions of this section, in all questions   **31-047**
or issues which arise or which have to be decided in
Singapore with respect to the law of partnerships, corporations, banks and banking, principals and agents, carri-
ers by air, land and sea, marine insurance, average, life
and fire insurance, and with respect to mercantile law
generally, the law with respect to those matters to be
administered shall be the same as would be administered
in England in the like case, at the corresponding period,
if such question or issue had arisen or had to be decided
in England, unless in any case other provision is or shall
be made by any law having force in Singapore.

(2)   Nothing in this section shall be taken to introduce into
Singapore -
    (a) any part of the law of England relating to the tenure
        or conveyance or assurance of, or succession to, any
        immovable property, or any estate, right or interest
        therein;
    (b) any law enacted or made in the United Kingdom,
        whether before or after the commencement of the
        Civil Law (Amendment Number 2) Act 1979 (*i.e.*,
        October 5, 1979) -
        (i) giving effect to a treaty or international agree-
            ment to which Singapore is not a party; or
        (ii) regulating the exercise of any business or activ-
            ity by providing for registration, licensing or any
            other method of control or by the imposition of
            penalties; and
    (c) any provision contained in any Act of Parliament of
        the United Kingdom where there is a written law in
        force in Singapore corresponding to that Act.

(3)   For the purposes of this section -
    (a) the law of England which is to be administered by
        virtue of sub-section (1) shall be subject to such
        modifications and adaptations as the circumstances
        of Singapore may require; and
    (b) a written law in force in Singapore shall be regarded
        as corresponding to an Act of Parliament of the
        United Kingdom under paragraph (c) of sub-section

(2) if notwithstanding that it differs, whether to a small extent or substantially, from that Act) the purpose or purposes of the written law are the same or similar to those of that Act.

APPENDIX II

Section 47(3) and (4), Banking Act, Cap 19, Singapore Statutes　　　**31-048**

Italicized words are those added by the amending of the Act of 1984.

Section 47(3) of the Banking Act provides:

> "Subject to subsection (4), no official of any bank and no person who by reason of his capacity or office has by any means access to the records of the bank, registers or any correspondence or material with regard to the account of any individual customer of that bank shall, while his employment in or professional relationship with the bank, as the case may be, continues or after the termination thereof, give, divulge or reveal any information whatsoever regarding the money or other relevant particulars of the account of that customer."

The exceptions to the general prohibition are contained in section 47(4) (the 1984 amendments which have been bracketed), which reads:

> "Subsection (3) shall not apply in any case where -
>
> (a) the customer or his personal representatives gives his or their *written* permission so to do;
> (b) the customer is declared bankrupt in Singapore or Malaysia or if the customer is a company, the company is being wound up;
> (c) 　civil proceedings arise -
> 　(i) between the bank and the customer [*or his guarantor relating to the customer's banking transaction*]; or
> 　(ii) between the bank and two or more parties making adverse claims to money in a customer's account where the bank seeks relief by way of interpleader;
> (d) the officials of any bank by compulsion of any written law in force in Singapore are required to give information to the police or a public officer who is duly authorized under that law to obtain that information or to a court in the investigation or prosecution of a criminal offence under any such law;
>
> [(e) *the bank has been served with a garnishee order attaching moneys in the account of the customer;*]

[(f) *the information relates solely to credit facilities granted by a branch of a bank incorporated outside Singapore and the information is required by its head office; or*]

(g) the information is required to assess the creditworthiness of a customer in connection with or relating to a bona fide commercial transaction or a prospective commercial transaction [*so long as the information required is of a general nature and in no way related to the details of a customer's account*].

APPENDIX III

Notes on the history of banking secrecy in Singapore   31-049

Colonial period

While Singapore was a British colony, banking secrecy would pre-   31-050
sumably have been governed by the Common Law. The Common
Law was applicable by virtue of the general reception of English
law via the Second Charter of Justice.

More specifically, British banking secrecy law would have been
made applicable by section 5 of the Civil Law Ordinance 1878, the
predecessor to the present day section 5 of the Civil Law Act, Cap
43, Singapore Statutes, 1988 Ed., which provided for the application
of British commercial law.

Malaysian law

Thereafter, Singapore joined the Federation of Malaya, Sabah, and   31-051
Sarawak to form Malaysia in 1963. This brought her banks under
the Banking Ordinance 1958 of Malaysia, section 22 of which prohibited the Malaysian Central Bank from enquiring specifically into
the affairs of any individual customer of a licensed bank, but otherwise did not make provision for a general duty of secrecy.

Singapore became a fully independent and sovereign state on
August 9, 1965, when it separated from Malaysia. The Malaysian
Banking Ordinance continued to be used by Singapore even after
that date, until the passing of the Singapore Banking Act in 1970.

The Banking Act 1970

Section 47 of the Banking Act, Cap 19, the present day banking   31-052
secrecy provision, can be traced to section 42 of the Banking Act of
1970 ("the 1970 Act").

The 1970 Act can generally be described as a piece of supervisory
legislation governing the banking industry. Section 42 of the 1970
Act did not lay down a general duty of secrecy but preserved the
provision in the Malaysian Ordinance protecting the account of the
individual customer from specific inquiry by the supervising
authorities. It further provided that such incidental information as
was obtained in the course of investigations was to be kept secret.

The beginning of section 42(2) is similar to the present day
section 47(3) in some respects. It provided:

"(2) No official of any bank and no person who by reason of his capacity or office has by any means access to the records of the bank registers or any correspondence or material with regard to the account of any individual customer of that bank shall give, divulge or reveal any information whatsoever regarding the moneys or other relevant particulars of the account of such customer to -

(a) any person who, or any bank, corporation or body of persons which, is not resident in Singapore; or

(b) any foreign government or organization, unless -
(i) the customer or his personal representatives gives or give his or their permission so to do;
(ii) the customer is declared bankrupt; or
(iii) the information is required to assess the credit worthiness of the customer in connection with or relating to a bona fide commercial transaction or a prospective commercial transaction."

Section 42(2) of the 1970 Act prohibited disclosure of information relating to the moneys or other relevant particulars of an account by a banking official or any other person who, by means of his office or capacity, would have access to bank records, to two classes of persons, namely:

(1)   Any non-residents without exception, and

(2)   Any foreign government or organization, except under any of three conditions -
(a) where the consent (presumably either written or oral) of the customer or his personal representatives was obtained;
(b) the customer was declared bankrupt (referred to below as "the bankruptcy exception"), or
(c) where the information was required to assess the credit worthiness of the customer (referred to below as "the credit worthiness exception").

What was not completely clear was whether the word "foreign" qualified both "governments" and "organizations", or only "governments" in category (2). On the latter reading, a bank would have been justified under section 42(2)(b)(iii) in giving a credit reference to another organization, without the customer's consent. This issue had not been judicially considered when the Banking Act was amended by the Banking (Amendment) Act 1983 ("the 1983 Amendment").

The Banking (Amendment) Act 1983

The 1983 Amendment repealed section 42 of the Banking Act 1970   **31-053** and substituted it with a new section. The new section 42(1) was divided into two provisions, the first providing for the immunity of a specific customer's account against inquiry, and the second providing that incidental information acquired in the course of supervision by the banking authorities would be kept secret.

Section 42(2) also was divided into two provisions, now numbered section 42(3) and section 42(4), respectively. The new section 42(3) contained the opening paragraph of the old section 42(2) and was amended in three respects:

(1)   To delete the references to the classes of persons to whom information was not to be divulged (*i.e.,* non-residents and foreign governments and organizations);

(2)   To make it clear that the persons having access to the bank's records who were prohibited from making disclosure would include not only those employed by the bank, but also those having a "professional relationship with the bank", and

(3)   To make it clear that the obligation not to disclose was to exist even after the employment or professional relationship ended.

The effect of the amendment was that section 42(3) provided for a general prohibition against disclosure, which was made an offence by section 42(9).

The new section 42(4) contained the exceptions to the prohibition against disclosure. The three existing exceptions were retained, and the bankruptcy exception was extended to Malaysian bankruptcies and to companies being wound up.

Some new exceptions were added, namely:

(1)   Section 42(4)(c) in civil proceedings between the bank and the customer and between the bank and two or more parties making adverse claims to money in a customer's account where the bank sought relief by way of interpleader, and

(2)   Section 42(4)(d) where the officials of any bank were compelled by any written law in force in Singapore to give information to the police or a duly authorized public officer or to a court in the investigation or prosecution of a criminal offence under any such law.

The 1983 Amendment also provided for civil proceedings to be held in camera where information relating to a customer's bank account was likely to be disclosed and prohibited the publication of information likely to lead to the disclosure of the parties thereto. In addition, the court's power to obtain evidence under the Evidence Act was preserved. Lastly, section 42(9) provided that any contravention of section 42 was an offence.

The Banking (Amendment) Act 1984

31-054   The Banking Act was further amended in 1984 by the Banking (Amendment) Act, 1984 ("the 1984 Amendment"), which produced the banking secrecy provisions in force today, the relevant portions of which are reproduced at Appendix B.

Section 42 was amended to permit the MAS to acquire incidental information not only in the course of conducting inspections and investigations, but also in the course of discharging its duty to supervise the financial condition of a bank.

Section 42(4) was amended to require that consent be in writing and to extend disclosure in civil proceedings between the bank and the customer's guarantor. Two new exceptions also were introduced: where the bank had been served with a garnishee order attaching the money in a customer's account and where a foreign bank operating in Singapore needed to furnish its head office with information relating solely to credit facilities.

A qualification was also introduced in respect of the creditworthiness exception. The qualification required that answers to credit enquiries be limited to information of a general nature which was in no way related to the details of the customer's account.

SOUTH KOREA

Young Moo Kim and Soo Man Park
Kim & Chang
Seoul, South Korea

Chapter 32

SOUTH KOREA

INTRODUCTION

Korean law clearly provides for legal protection of confidential 32-001 information relating to financial transactions. However, the exceptions to such protection are also specifically enumerated under Korean law, and they permit government ministries, agencies, and courts relatively unhindered access to such confidential information when deemed necessary.

Furthermore, to some limited extent, financial institutions are permitted to share otherwise privileged information with each other. For these reasons, the protection of confidential information is far from absolute. This chapter recognizes these limitations and focuses on what information is protected and how it is protected by law.

LEGAL FOUNDATIONS FOR SECRECY OF FINANCIAL INSTITUTIONS

Laws protecting confidentiality of transactions with financial insti- 32-002 tutions ("confidentiality" or "secrecy") are based on the Constitution of Korea. The Korean Constitution specifically enumerates that "the privacy of citizens shall not be infringed",[1] and that "the privacy of communication by citizens shall not be infringed".[2]

Although constitutional protection of privacy as applied to secrecy has not been directly addressed by the Supreme Court of Korea or the Constitutional Court of Korea, legal scholars widely view the relevant provisions in the Constitution as extending to commercial and financial transactions.

Legislation specifically prescribing protection of secrecy are found in, *inter alia*, the Real Name Financial Transaction Law, as well as in the Securities and Exchange Law, the Bank Act, and the Credit Card Business Law. Further, the Foreign Exchange Control Regulations promulgated by the Ministry of Finance provide for protection of secrecy as it applies to foreign exchange transactions.

SCOPE OF PROTECTED CONFIDENTIAL INFORMATION

32-003 Generally, all information relating to transactions with and between financial institutions is protected as confidential and privileged information. The basis for such protection arises from the principle of good faith, under which a financial institution has the implicit fiduciary duty to its clients. This duty obligates the financial institution to protect the confidentiality of its clients. This duty continues to exist even after the transaction is completed.

Further, special statutes provide specific protection for secrecy regarding "financial transactions", "foreign exchange transactions", "credit card transactions" and "securities related transactions".

Financial transactions

32-004 The Real Name Financial Transaction Law,[3] in general, provides for the protection of secrecy with respect to information and materials concerning "financial transactions" handled by financial institutions. This law provides that an employee of a "financial institution"

---

[1] Constitution, article 17.

[2] *Id.*, article 18.

[3] The Real Name Financial Transaction Law was passed on December 31, 1982. The purpose of this law was to induce the general public to transact with financial institutions on a real name basis. Some used, and to some extent still use, nominees' names, for example, in order to avoid taxation. Under the Real Name Financial Transaction Law, if financial transactions are carried out on a real name basis, then tax benefits are given and the information relating thereto is treated confidentially.

shall not disclose or divulge to others any material or information concerning a "financial transaction" without the written request from or consent of only the person who is party to such financial transaction; no other person shall request an employee of a financial institution to disclose or divulge such material or financial information.[4]

A "financial institution", for the purposes of the Real Name Financial Transaction Law includes,[5] among others, banks, short-term finance companies, merchant banks, trust companies, mutual savings and finance companies, securities companies, securities finance companies, and post offices.

Further, for the purpose of this law, a "financial transaction" is a transaction involving receipt, sale, purchase, intermediation, discount, issuance, redemption and refund of "financial assets", or payment of interest on these financial assets.[6]

"Financial assets" include, *inter alia*, deposits, installment deposits, trust assets, shares, debentures, beneficial certificates, participation certificates, bills of exchange, or promissory notes handled by financial institutions, as well as other assets which produce interest payment, discount or dividend, or are paid in excess of principal amount.[7]

In sum, the definition of a "financial transaction" includes deposits and other transactions similar to the making of deposits. However, extension of credit or loan transactions involving a financial institution are not included in the definition of "financial transactions" under the Real Name Financial Transaction Law. Although credit and loan transactions are not accorded protection under the Real Name Financial Transaction Law, as mentioned earlier, a fiduciary duty, nevertheless, requires financial institutions to protect the confidentiality of information regarding credit or loan transactions.

Foreign exchange transactions

Analogous to the Real Name Financial Transaction Law, the Foreign   32-005
Exchange Management Regulations provide, as a general rule, that foreign exchange banks may not disclose content or information or "any other matters regarding a foreign exchange transaction which are obtained in the course of their business".[8]

---

[4] *Id.*, article 5(1).
[5] *Id.* article 2, item 1.
[6] *Id.*, article 2, item 3.
[7] *Id.*, article 2, item 2.
[8] Foreign Exchange Management Regulations, article 2-9.

However, the interpretation of "any other matters which are obtained in the course of business" is problematic. One view is that this clause refers to any matter which relates to foreign exchange transactions which are conducted by foreign exchange banks. A more expansive view is that it refers to any matter which is obtained in the course of banking business irrespective of whether or not it relates to a foreign exchange transaction.

Credit card transactions

32-006   The Credit Card Business Law provides, as a general rule, that credit card companies shall not disclose or divulge confidential information relating to their clients, such as card holders and member stores, without their consent.[9]

Securities transactions

32-007   Under the Securities and Exchange Law, information regarding purchase, sale, or other transactions of securities, or the money or securities deposited are protected as confidential information.[10] Accordingly, no person shall request the disclosure of, and no officer or employee of securities companies shall disclose, such information.

Likewise, information regarding transactions with investment advisory companies and the Korean Securities Settlement Corporation also is protected as confidential.[11]

Accounting books and materials of banks

32-008   Under the Commercial Code, a shareholder having five percent or more of total issued and outstanding shares of a corporation can examine and copy the accounting books of the corporation in which he or she holds shares.[12]

However, as such right in the case of banks may require the disclosure of confidentiality of financial transactions of bank clients, the bank may refuse the request by a shareholder to examine or copy accounting books and materials in the event such request risks

9 Credit Card Business Law, article 14.
10 Securities and Exchange Law, articles 59(1) and 60.
11 *Id.*, articles 70-7 and 278.
12 Commercial Code, article 466(1).

disclosing or divulging confidential information of a bank client protected under the principle of fiduciary duty.[13]

This right to refuse disclosure is applicable only to banks and such other institutions deemed as banks under the Bank Act and is unavailable to other financial institutions. Furthermore, in case the bank fails to properly refuse the request for aforesaid access, no sanctions against the bank are specified in the Bank Act.

CIRCUMSTANCES REQUIRING OR PERMITTING DISCLOSURE

Plainly, the scope of coverage of confidentiality as it relates to **32-009** financial or securities transactions is very expansive. More importantly, however, although disclosure of Confidentiality is generally prohibited, broad exceptions requiring or permitting disclosure do exist as set forth below.

However, all confidentiality obtained pursuant to the exceptions below are prohibited from being further disseminated or divulged to others; the use of confidential information so obtained is limited to the purposes for which the disclosure was required or permitted.[14]

The Real Name Financial Transactions Law, Foreign Exchange Management Regulations, Credit Card Business Law, and Securities and Exchange Law use different wording to describe the exceptions when disclosure is required or permitted; however, such exceptions are applied substantially in the same manner.

Written request or written consent by client

The confidential information can be disclosed at the client's written **32-010** request or written consent. Oral consent does not constitute legitimate consent, except for under the Credit Card Business Law. The purposes of requiring written consent or request are to prevent confusion or misunderstanding; to evidence consent; and to prevent unintended disclosure.

---

[13] Bank Act, article 26-2.
[14] Real Name Financial Transaction Law, article 5(2); Foreign Exchange Management Regulations, article 2-9; Credit Card Business Law, article 14(2); and Securities and Exchange Law, article 59(2).

Such requirement is designed to avoid dispute between the financial institution and the client as to whether or not the consent or request was granted or made.

Disclosure among financial institutions

32-011   The confidential information can be disclosed to employees within the financial institution or to other "financial institutions" under the Real Name Financial Transaction Law.[15] The intent of such permitted disclosure is to allow the financial institutions to share information regarding creditworthiness of their clients.

Such disclosure to employees of credit card companies and credit guarantee funds is permitted under the Credit Card Business Law for the purpose of confirmation of creditworthiness of card holders and member stores.[16]

The Foreign Exchange Management Regulations provide that a foreign exchange bank may disclose information regarding foreign exchange transactions to other banking institutions.[17] It is not entirely clear whether a "banking institution" under the said regulations includes "financial institutions" under the Real Name Financial Transaction Law.

Audit or supervisory review

32-012   The confidential information is not privileged against audit or inspection by the Ministry of Finance, the Office of Bank Supervision of the Bank of Korea, the Korean Stock Exchange, or the Securities Supervisory Board.[18] Such exceptions do not include inspection or audit by supervisory authorities of foreign countries.

Similar exceptions requiring disclosure also apply to audit of corporations pursuant to the Law Concerning Independent Audit of Corporations. Pursuant to this law, certain types of corporations

---

[15] Real Name Financial Transaction Law, article 2, item 1; Foreign Exchange Management Regulations, article 2-9, item 1.

[16] Credit Card Business Law, article 11.

[17] Foreign Exchange Management Regulations, article 2-9, item 2.

[18] Real Name Financial Transaction Law, article 5(2); Foreign Exchange Management Regulations, article 2-9, item 2; Credit Card Business Law, article 14(1), item 1; Presidential Decree to the Securities and Exchange Law, article 38, items 4 and 5.

are required to be audited by independent auditors (*e.g.*, corporations having assets exceeding 4-billion won). In performing the audit, the independent auditors are permitted access to the confidential information as deemed necessary for the audit.

Tax

Not surprisingly, the confidential information may be disclosed to tax authorities when so requested in writing for purposes of investigating taxable transactions and assets under tax laws.[19] However, such request for disclosure must be in writing and made separately to each business office of the financial institution from which the tax authorities desire to obtain information.

For example, a tax office can request such office which is suspected to have transacted with a delinquent tax payer to provide information regarding the balance of the delinquent taxpayer's funds maintained with such office.

32-013

Court order

Under the Criminal Procedure Code, courts may order or issue warrants with or without the motion of a prosecutor to require production of confidentiality which is necessary for evidentiary purposes in a criminal proceeding.[20] Similarly, under the Civil Procedure Code, courts may require disclosure of confidentiality for evidentiary purposes.[21]

Orders for disclosure issued by courts of foreign jurisdictions do not constitute the court order in this context.

32-014

Other circumstances

The Real Name Financial Transaction Law,[22] states in broad terms that confidential information may be disclosed to the general public if such disclosure is specifically required by law.

32-015

[19] Income Tax Law, article 201; Corporation Tax Law, article 68; Inheritance Tax Law, articles 24 and 34-7; National Tax Collection Law, article 27; Tax Crime Punishment Procedure Law, article 2.
[20] Criminal Procedure Code, article 272.
[21] Civil Procedure Code, article 318.
[22] Real Name Financial Transaction Law, article 5, paragraph 1, item 5.

Finally, the Presidential Decree to the Securities and Exchange Law permits a securities company to disclose to a public prosecutor Confidentiality regarding securities transactions when requested by the prosecutor in writing even without a court warrant.[23]

Although the court has not ruled on this issue, the authors note that this provision may be in conflict with the Criminal Procedure Code, which requires that a court warrant be obtained for the prosecutor to require the disclosure of confidentiality in connection with his criminal investigation.[24]

LIABILITIES ARISING FROM WRONGFUL DISCLOSURE

Civil actions

32-016   In general, when a confidentiality is disclosed in breach of fiduciary duty owed to the client, and in particular when the disclosure is made which does not fall under the exceptions enumerated above, damages may be claimed on grounds of wrongful disclosure. It is possible that, under the general fiduciary duty, even a confidentiality which is not specifically protected by law, if wrongfully disclosed, can incur civil liability.

If a client is aware that his privacy will be violated by wrongful disclosure, he may seek court injunction to prevent such disclosure.

Criminal sanctions

32-017   Under the Real Name Financial Transaction Law, the penalty for wrongful disclosure is three years maximum imprisonment and/or a fine of 3-million won,[25] and under the Securities and Exchange Law, three years maximum imprisonment and/or 20-million won;[26] under the Foreign Exchange Control Regulations, no criminal sanctions are provided.

[23] Presidential Decree to the Securities and Exchange Law, article 38, item 7.
[24] Criminal Procedure Code, article 199(1), Proviso.
[25] Real Name Financial Transaction Law, article 6.
[26] Securities and Exchange Law, article 208.

CONCLUSION

It appears that the actual practice of protecting secrecy under Ko- **32-018** rean law is adequate for purposes of protection against third parties. However, it is unclear whether such protection has been equally adequate against government intrusion in light of the strong regulatory power of the Korean government over the financial institutions.

Further, because as a practical matter confidentiality may be disclosed without the knowledge of the client, the means to prevent such disclosure or to recover damages for such disclosure seem to be rather limited.

The trend, however, is to strengthen the protection accorded to confidentiality. Recent steps taken by the Korean government to liberalize the financial markets, such as the securities industry and market, have heightened competition among the financial institutions to provide better services to their clients and have enhanced awareness of the importance of protecting confidentiality as a means to liberalizing and internationalizing the Korean financial industries.

Finally, the authors anticipate that the relevant Korean laws and regulations protecting secrecy in the context of transnational financial transactions will continue to develop commensurate with the internationalization of Korean financial industries, in particular the securities industry and market.[27]

---

[27] J. Park, "Internationalization of the Korean Securities Market", 7:1 *International Tax & Business Lawyer* (1989), at pp. 3-56.

Appendix

Summary of relevant legislation

Constitution

Article 17 - The privacy of citizens shall not be infringed.   **32-019**

Article 18 - The privacy of communication by citizens shall not be infringed.

Real Name Financial Transaction Law

Article 5 - (Guarantee of confidentiality of financial transactions)   **32-020**

(1) An employee of a financial institution shall not provide or disclose to others any material or information concerning financial transactions ("confidential information") without the written request from or consent of the nominal party (trustor or beneficiary in case of a trust) and no person shall request an employee of a financial institution to disclose or divulge such confidential information; provided that this provision shall not apply to a case that falls under one of the items specified below:

1. In case that the confidential information is provided within the same financial institution or between the financial institutions enumerated in items 1 through 12 of article 2, item 1.

2. In case that the confidential information is provided as a necessity with respect to the audit or inspection by the Ministry of Finance, the Office of Bank Supervision of the Bank of Korea, the Securities Supervisory Board (including audits by independent auditors pursuant to the Law Concerning Independent Audit of Corporations).

3. In case that the confidential information is provided pursuant to the court order or warrant.

4. In case that the chief officer of the relevant tax office requests the involved business office of the financial institution in writing the provision of confidential information for the purpose of inquiry or investigation pursuant to the tax laws,

and the provision of materials for taxation which are required to be provided pursuant to the tax laws.

5. In case that the disclosure of confidential information to the general public is permitted under other laws.

(2) If a person acquires confidential information pursuant to provisions of items 1 through 4 above, he shall not provide or disclose nor make use of such confidential information to any person or any other purpose. No person shall request a person who acquires such confidential information to provide it for any other purpose.

Securities and Exchange Law

32-021 Article 59 - (Prohibition of offer or disclosure of information)

1. Unless an officer or employee of a securities company receives a written request or a written consent from a customer who purchases or sells or intends to purchase or sell securities through the securities company (including those who make securities savings referred to in article 50; the same shall apply hereinafter), the officer or the employee of such securities company shall not provide or disclose the information with respect to the customer's buying, selling or other transactions of securities and the money or securities deposited by such customers; provided, however, that this provision shall not apply to cases when the securities company is inspected by a supervisory institution, or when it receives a request pursuant to article 60 hereof.

2. If a person acquires information in the course of performing the duty of a supervisory institution, he shall not provide or disclose such information to any other person, nor make use of the information for any other purpose.

Article 60 - (Prohibition of request for information)

1. No person shall request an officer or an employee of a securities company to provide the information referred to in article 59, paragraph 1, except when a court issues an injunction to submit such information, or a court issues a warrant, or other cases as may be prescribed by the Presidential Decree.

2. Even if the provision of the relevant information may be requested in accordance with paragraph 1 above, the inquiry or

investigation thereon shall be limited to the necessary scope of purpose.

Article 61 - (Refusal of illegal investigation)

An officer or employee of a securities company shall refuse any request, inquiry or investigation made in violation of article 60 hereof, stating the reason therefor.

(The above provisions shall apply *mutatis mutandis* to investment advisory companies and the Korean Securities Settlement Corporation (articles 70-7 and 278).)

SPAIN

Felix López Antón
Abogado
Madrid, Spain

Chapter 33

SPAIN

INTRODUCTION

Banking secrecy is an institution which has been traditionally ac-   **33-001**
cepted in Spain and which has been questioned only in recent years,
due to the fact that investigation of the bank accounts has been
largely used by the Spanish fiscal authorities as a device to discover
and control tax evasion.

As a result, the controversial issue now in Spain in connection
with banking secrecy is to determine its scope as a right of private
citizens *vis-à-vis* the right of inspection and the capacities to obtain
information granted to the government and, in particular, to the tax
authorities.

BANKING SECRECY IN SPANISH LAW

Notwithstanding the traditional and general acceptance of banking   **33-002**
secrecy in Spain, there is no express or general provision in Spanish
law which establishes banking secrecy for financial institutions.

This has produced a number of attempts by Spanish legal commentators to discern the legal basis for banking secrecy in the
Spanish norms.

Banking law

There is an express provision for banking secrecy in article 23 of the   **33-003**
by-laws of the Bank of Spain of 1947, which sets forth the prohibition for the Bank of Spain to give any information with respect to

the funds held in checking accounts, in deposit, or for any other reason and which belong to a certain person, except for the information given to such person or his representative, or by virtue of a court order.[1]

It should be noted, however, that the above provision is included in the by-laws of the Bank of Spain; therefore, it is mandatory for the Bank of Spain, but it is not binding with respect to any other bank.

Article 16 of the Decree-Law of Nationalization and Reorganization of the Bank of Spain of 1962 also refers to banking secrecy, in connection with a centralized service of information concerning banking transactions created at the Bank of Spain and for the use of Spanish banks. According to this provision, the data and information obtained by the banks from such service shall be kept secret.

Other banking norms, concerning the relations between the Bank of Spain and the financial institutions also refer to banking secrecy, but always within the context of the entities belonging to the banking system.

There is no norm, however, establishing banking secrecy for the relationship between banks and customers.

Commercial law

33-004   Such absence of legal provisions sustaining banking secrecy in the banking laws has caused the development of an artificial construction in order to support the legal basis for banking secrecy in Spain.

According to such construction, banking secrecy results from the norms of the Commercial Code which establish the general rule that the accounting of business and merchants (and, therefore, of the banks) are secret (subject always to exceptions to the general rule, as provided by the law).[2]

Therefore it could be maintained that the accounting of the banks is secret and, consequently, the information included in such accounting is also secret, so that the customers of the banks enjoy such secrecy.

This position has been criticized by arguing that accounting secrecy intends to protect the information related to the business (in

---

[1] In favor of this theory as the legal basis for banking secrecy in Spain are Jiminez de Parga, R., *"El secreto bancario en el Derecho Español"*, *Revista e Derecho Mercantil* (1969), number 113, and L. M. Cazorla, *El secreto bancario* (1978).
[2] See articles 32 and 33 of the Commercial Code.

this case, the banking business), while banking secrecy has as its main objective the privacy of the customers of the banks. More important, from a practical point of view, is that accounting secrecy is a right granted by the law to merchants and it may be renounced, while banking secrecy is more of an obligation of the banks to their customers; therefore, it can be waived only by the customers and not by the banks.[3]

Criminal law

Another possible source of support for banking secrecy is found in the criminal law. **33-005**

Some authors have maintained that banking secrecy is merely an extension or a branch of professional secrecy, which is protected in the Criminal Code.[4]

The problem under Spanish law is that there are only a few and very specific norms in the Criminal Code related to professional secrecy. Those norms refer to the breach of secrecy by civil servants (which would not be applicable, in principle, to banking secrecy), by lawyers and barristers with respect to the information obtained from their clients (not applicable either to banking secrecy), by employees and officers with respect to the information related to their employer, and by anyone who takes possession, without title, of documents belonging to a third party in order to reveal the information contained in such documents (which is not applicable to banking secrecy, given that the offense criminally sanctioned is to take possession without title of the documentation, regardless of whether or not the information obtained is revealed).

Consequently, since there is no legal norm in the Criminal Code referring specifically to professional secrecy, the possibility to seek legal protection of banking secrecy within the norms of the Criminal Code is extremely doubtful.[5]

---

[3] G. Battle, "*El secreto de los libros de contabilidad y el secret bancario: Dos manifestaciones del derecho a la intimidad privada*", Revista General de Legislación y Jurisprudencia (1975).

[4] J. M. Otero Novas, "*El secreto bancario: vigencia y alcance*", Revista de Derecho Bancario y Bursátil (1985), number 20.

[5] G. Fajardo, "*Fundamentación y protección del secreto bancario*", Revista de Derecho Bancario y Bursátil (1990), number 39.

Tax law

33-006   The more solid legal basis for banking secrecy existed in the fiscal norms, which expressly recognized banking secrecy.[6]

However, the fiscal norms have represented, at the same time, the legal basis for the crisis of banking secrecy in Spain. This is so because the provisions referred to above have been rendered without effect by other fiscal norms enacted subsequently.

In this respect, article 111 of the Law of December 28, 1963, established the obligation to cooperate with the tax authorities of any individual or legal entity. In addition, article 41 of the Law of November 14, 1977, expressly declared that such obligation to co-operate with the tax authorities was fully applicable to banks and other financial institutions.

The direct implication of such provisions is that banking secrecy does not exist when the requirement of information comes from the tax authorities.[7]

This issue has focused the main debate with respect to banking secrecy in Spain in recent years; therefore, it will be analyzed in more detail below.

Commercial uses and customs

33-007   Given that the laws do not contain any direct reference generally applicable to banking secrecy, while banks and financial institutions have the obligation to keep confidential information concerning their customers (except where a legal norm establishes an obligation of disclosure), an alternative is to ground banking secrecy in commercial uses and customs.[8]

This position maintains that, throughout the years, there has been an implicit understanding between the banks and their customers to the effect that any information obtained by the bank from the customer would be treated as confidential and would not be disclosed by the bank to any third party, except in case such disclosure is legally required.

---

6 Article 62 of the Law of December 16, 1940, and article 7.4 of the Decree-Law of April 7, 1975.

7 See J. M. Perulles, "*El secreto bancario en el ámbit tributario*", *Impuestos*, number 9, and F. Cervera, "*El secreto bancario desde la perspectiva del derecho tributario*", *Crónica Tributaria,* number 15. Such implication has been confirmed by the provisions of various tax laws enacted in Spain in recent years.

8 J. Garrigues, *Contratos Bancarios* (1975).

Such understanding produces, in turn, for the customer a belief in good faith that the information which is provided to the bank shall not be revealed to any third party.[9]

Such confidentiality, inherent to banking secrecy, remains even if finally the bank and the customer do not enter into any transaction or formalize any contract between them (*i.e.*, the information which the customer delivers to the bank as a requirement or prior step when the customer requests a credit from the bank shall remain confidential, even if the credit requested is not granted and therefore no legal relationship exists between the bank and the customer).

Court decisions

In the absence of legal provisions, it becomes important to examine the court decisions in order to determine the extension and scope attributed to banking secrecy.   **33-008**

Unfortunately, however, there are no court decisions (apart from those related to the confrontation between banking secrecy and the obligation of the banks to provide information to the tax authorities, which shall be analyzed below) dealing with banking secrecy.

This may well be due to the fact that banks in Spain have traditionally maintained banking secrecy and, therefore, customers have not initiated actions against banks before the courts in connection with breaches of confidentiality.

Only the decision of the Supreme Court of January 3, 1975, deserves to be mentioned, and mainly because it states that banks must keep confidential the information obtained from their customers, at the same time stressing that this obligation of confidentiality is recognized world-wide.

The judgment also mentions that banking secrecy is an essential element of banking and, as such, it is implicit and accepted in the context of the relations between a bank and its customers.

CONSEQUENCES OF BREACH OF BANKING SECRECY

From the foregoing, it could be concluded that banking secrecy is considered in Spain as an obligation assumed by the bank as a direct   **33-009**

---

[9]J. San Roman and R. Sebastian, "*El secreto bancario*", *Cuadernos de Derecho y Comercio* (December, 1988).

consequence of its relationship with the customer, and that the confidentiality involved in such obligation must be maintained except in cases where the bank is legally obliged to disclose information concerning its client.

The immediate question, then, refers to the consequences or implications derived out of an eventual breach by the bank of its obligations of confidentiality.

It is quite clear that the beneficiary of banking secrecy is the customer of the bank and, consequently, the customer is entitled to request from the bank the maintenance of such confidentiality.

If the bank fails to comply with its obligation of confidentiality, the customer will be entitled to sue the bank before the courts in order to obtain compensation for the damages caused by such breach.

It is necessary to distinguish two situations with respect to the basis for the customer to request compensation from the bank.

If the bank and the customer have entered into a contract (such as for deposit, checking account, or loan), the customer may claim compensation on the basis of the failure by the bank to comply with its contractual obligations.

Such liability by the bank may be exacted on the basis of article 57 of the Commercial Code and article 1258 of the Civil Code and pursuant to article 1101 of the Civil Code, even if - as it normally happens in Spain -banking contracts do not contain a specific clause establishing the obligation of the bank to maintain confidentiality related to information obtained from the customer or regarding the development of the contractual relationship.

If the bank and the customer have not executed any contract (which is the normal situation in the preliminary negotiations when the customer applies for credit from the bank), the customer might claim responsibility by the bank according to articles 1902 and 1968,[10] of the Civil Code in the event that disclosure by the bank of information provided by the customer produces damages to the customer.

It is important to bear in mind that, in the absence of an express legal provision establishing the obligation of the bank to maintain confidentiality, the claim against the bank may be initiated only if two requirements are met:

(1) That the disclosure of information has caused damages to the customer, and
(2) That those damages can be proven.

10 See also articles 32 and 33 of the Commercial Code.

If both requirements exist, in the event of breach of its confidentiality duties by the bank, the customer may seek compensation for the damages caused by such breach.

If it is not possible to prove that the breach of confidentiality has produced damages to the customer, and given that the failure by the bank to maintain secrecy does not violate any legal provision, the customer would not have any legal basis to initiate a court action against the bank.

SCOPE OF BANKING SECRECY AND THE TAX AUTHORITIES

The Law of November 14, 1977, which implied that banking secrecy   **33-010** should be subordinated to the requests of information from the tax authorities, has been challenged on the basis of the Spanish Constitution and of the Law of May 5, 1982.[11]

Article 18.1 of the Spanish Constitution of 1978 declares the right of Spanish citizens to personal and familiar privacy. Such article was developed by the Law of May 5, 1982, which regulates the right to privacy. These norms also have been considered as the basis in Spanish law for banking secrecy.[12]

Access to checking account information

The conflict between the right of the tax authorities to obtain infor-   **33-011** mation from the banks and the right of the individuals to personal privacy was brought before the courts in a situation where the tax authorities required the documents evidencing the credits and debits of a checking account of an individual.

The customer opposed the request on the basis that the information reflected in such documents affected his right to privacy and, therefore, the knowledge by the tax authorities of such information implied a violation of such right.

The National Court issued its decision on such matter on June 18, 1983, establishing that the right of individuals to privacy did also include financial aspects, that such right was constitutionally pro-

---

11 J. Aguilar, "*El secreto bancario*", *Estudios de Derecho Público Bancario* (1987).

12 A. Vergara, "*Sobre el fundamento del secreto bancario*", *Revista de Derecho Financiero y Tributario* (March-April, 1988).

tected, and consequently that the tax authorities were not entitled to obtain information from the bank concerning the checking account of the individual.

The decision of the National Court, however, was rejected by the decision of the Supreme Court of July 29, 1983.

The Spanish Supreme Court upheld the view that the information related to bank accounts does not belong to the context of the personal and familiar privacy, that the right to privacy could not be conceived in absolute terms, and that the inspection of the fiscal duties of the individuals by the tax authorities, through the possibility of obtaining information with respect to the bank accounts, could not be deemed as a violation of the right to privacy set forth in the Constitution.

The Supreme Court decision was appealed to the Spanish Constitutional Court. The Constitutional Court, in its decision of November 26, 1984, confirmed the judgment of the Supreme Court, establishing that the tax authorities are entitled to request and obtain information related to the financial situations of citizens and that such information does not form part of the privacy which is legally protected.[13]

In a similar case, the Territorial Court of Burgos, in its decision of October 25, 1984, determined the right of the tax authorities to investigate the banking transactions of a citizen, and such judgment was confirmed by the Supreme Court in its decision of July 25, 1985.

Opposition by banks

33-012 Banking secrecy in respect of the request of information from the tax authorities has been argued not only by individuals, as in the cases mentioned above, but also by banking institutions (in a position which is consistent with the statement that banking secrecy, although ultimately protecting the privacy of the customers of the banks, is also an essential element of the banking system).

A resolution issued by the General Directorate of Taxes, requesting banks to provide information about the checking accounts and deposits of their customers, was appealed by a number of banks, on the basis that the delivery of such information would infringe the right to privacy of the customers.

[13] For a detailed study of the decisions of the Constitutional Court on this matter, see N. Nogueroles, "*La intimidad económica en la doctrina del Tribunal Constitucional*", *Revista de Derecho Administrativo*, number 52; E. Pinel, "*El Tribunal Constitucional y el Secreto Bancario*", *Revista de Derecho Bancario y Bursátil*, number 17, and J. J. Arunaga, "*La sentencia del Tribunal Constitucional sobre la investigación de las cuentas corrientes*", *Gaceta Fiscal*, number 19.

The issue was brought again to the Constitutional Court, which in this case admitted in its decision of July 23, 1986, that the economic information concerning the citizens also is included within the scope of the right to privacy.

However, the Constitutional Court said that, notwithstanding this, banking secrecy should be subordinated to the requirements from the tax authorities in the exercise of the capacities which are established in legal norms (such as in the case of the investigation of bank accounts under the Law of November 14, 1977) since the possibility to grant such authority by virtue of a legal norm to the public administration is also recognized in the Constitution.[14]

LIMITATIONS TO BANKING SECRECY

There are two exceptions to the obligation of the banks to maintain **33-013** confidentiality with respect to the information received from their customers (taking into account that the authorization given by the customer to the bank to reveal the information provided can not be considered as an exception or limitation to banking secrecy, but rather as the exercise by the customer of the right to waive banking secrecy).

The first exception, which has been discussed in detail above, is the obligation of the banks to provide the information required by the authorities in the exercise of capacities legally granted for the request of such information. Such capacities have been legally attributed to the tax authorities, as indicated above.[15]

The second exception relates to the requirement of information addressed to the banks by judges and courts. Such exception is based on reasons of public policy, and it is reflected in norms such as article 17 of the Law of July 1, 1985, and article 603 of the Civil Procedural Law.

According to article 603 of the Civil Procedural Law, the judge has the capacity to require documents from someone who is not a party to the court proceeding, provided that this is requested by one of the parties to the court proceeding and that the judge decides that

---

[14]On this decision of the Constitutional Court, see J. Aguilar, "E segundo pronunciamiento constitucional sobre el secreto bancario: El Auto del Tribunal Constitucional de 23 de julio de 1986. Un comentario de urgencia" Revista de Derecho Bancario y Bursátil, number 24.

[15]R. Falcon,"El levantamiento del secreto bancario frente a la Administración Tributaria", La Ley, number 824, and J. M. Cabra de Luna, "Derecho a la intimidad y funciones investigadoras de la Inspección Financiera y Tributaria" in Impuestos (June, 1985).

the knowledge of such documents is relevant in order to issue the court decision on the proceeding.

Some authors[16] also consider as an exception to banking secrecy the possibility for the Bank of Spain to request information from private banks in the exercise of its capacity of supervision and inspection of the banking system.

It is possible, however, to maintain that the exercise of such capacity does not represent an exception or limitation to banking secrecy, as long as the Bank of Spain has the obligation, according to article 23 of its by-laws, to maintain confidentiality with respect to the information obtained from the financial institutions. Therefore, the Bank of Spain may be considered, in this respect and for these purposes, as a branch of the banking system.

CONCLUSION

33-014   As a general rule, banking secrecy is recognized in Spain, in spite of the absence of legal provisions specifically establishing the obligation of the banks to maintain confidentiality with respect to the information obtained from their customers.

From the point of view of customers, they may require the confidential treatment by the banks of the information received from the customers, on the basis that this is privileged information delivered exclusively to the bank, but which must be excluded from the general knowledge since it belongs to the sphere of privacy which is legally protected.

Consequently, in case of a violation of banking secrecy, the customer would be entitled to initiate legal actions against the bank claiming compensation for the proven damages caused by the violation by the bank of his right to privacy.

Banking secrecy is subordinated to the requirements of information which the banks may receive from the authorities with respect to the banking transactions of their customers (which occurs relatively often in connection with tax matters) or when the information is requested by a court order.

---

[16] San Roman and Sebastian, *supra* n. 9.

CHAPTER 34

SWEDEN

Olof Wærn and Monica Petersson
Advokatfirman Vinge
Stockholm, Sweden

Chapter 34

SWEDEN

INTRODUCTION

The interest in having one's businesses with banks kept confidential 34-001
has long been recognized in Sweden. The first provision in law in
this regard, applying to the Swedish Central Bank, was given in the
late seventeenth century. As regards private banks, one must wait
until the late nineteenth century to find any law mandating banking
secrecy; however, prior to that, similar rules could be found in the
banks' articles of association.

Today, Swedish banks are obliged to adhere to a provision which
requires that "the relations of individuals to a bank may not be
disclosed without legal cause". As can be guessed, "without legal
cause" signals an important restriction in the degree of confidentiality accorded to a customer. Thus, a bank is obliged to provide
certain information to various authorities, such as the tax authorities, the police, prosecutors, the Enforcement Service Authority and,
of course, the Financial Supervisory Authority (formerly the Bank
Inspection Board and the Insurance Inspection Board).[1]

A bank's auditors will learn about the individual customers
during the audit. The auditors are subject to the provision on
secrecy restated above and in addition to some rules limiting, *inter
alia*, the information to be given to an individual shareholder.

The purpose of this article is to provide a general idea of banking
secrecy in Sweden, its scope, and its limits.

---

[1] The Enforcement Service Authority (*Kronofogdemyndigheten*) is the Swedish
execution authority which, *inter alia*, assists in attaching liens, collecting
judgments, levying on property, administering garnishments, and with official
(forced) sales. The Financial Supervisory Authority (*Finansinspektionen*) is
responsible for the supervision of financial institutions, such as banks.

WHAT IS SECRET?

The customer criterion

34-002   Banks are obliged to keep their relations with customers confidential. Therefore, the relation to be kept confidential must be with a customer. Naturally, contracts with employees, suppliers, and even the bank's legal advisers are not entitled to secrecy based upon the rules about banking secrecy.

It is considered that the mere fact that a certain person is a customer of a certain bank is subject to secrecy. In many cases, companies and natural persons are only too keen to let it be known that they are customers of a certain bank and a generally known fact is, of course, not subject to secrecy.

Technically, only the bank that indeed has business relations with a certain entity is obliged to keep the relationship secret, and other banks are free to disclose that a certain company is not a customer in the bank. However, it is also the practice that banks which do not do business with a certain company or person will refuse to answer inquiries.

The confidentiality criterion

34-003   It is generally true that only matters which are exclusively known to a company and its bank, and perhaps to a few other persons, are subject to banking secrecy. On the other hand, it is clear that publicly known facts are not subject to confidentiality. The "gray area" in between is the most difficult to deal with, and banks are restrictive in what they communicate to outsiders.

The business criterion

34-004   Should someone have entered into negotiations with a bank, *e.g.*, with a view to obtaining credit but without the negotiations having led to any business relations, banking secrecy applies both to the fact that negotiations have occurred and to what the bank may have learned about the company's business during such negotiations.

Information relating to a customer learned by an officer of a bank while on vacation or otherwise on his free time also is normally subject to banking secrecy.

Banks engaged in the securities business are not subject to the provision on banking secrecy in that part of the business. A similar provision in the Act on Securities Business[2] states that a member of the board or an employee with such a company may not, without legal cause, disclose what he may have learned about the client's business or personal relations, nor use such knowledge to the detriment of the client.

SECRET FOR WHOM?

Consent

A bank is entitled to divulge a customer's secrets when the cus- **34-005** tomer has given his permission thereto. Such permission shall be given for a specific case. It is considered that such permission can be tacit.

Within the bank

A bank also is entitled to disseminate information internally on a **34-006** "need to know" basis.

The tax authorities

The tax authorities have wide powers to obtain information from **34-007** banks without the hindrance of banking secrecy; indeed, these powers are so wide that it has been discussed whether banking secrecy exists vis-à-vis the tax authorities.

Banks must send information annually to the tax authorities regarding the interest they have paid to natural persons and regarding the balance on each such customer's accounts.

Banks which have rendered assistance to natural persons with their foreign businesses must report each transaction, to or from Sweden, amounting to at least SEK 50,000 and the aggregate amount of such payments.

Furthermore, banks are, upon request, required to furnish the following information regardingt a named individual or company to the tax authorities:

[2] Act on Securities Business (1991:981).

(1) Interest accrued on the person's (legal or natural) accounts;

(2) Interest paid by the person, and

(3) Balance - positive or negative - on such accounts by a certain date and transactions on the accounts in a certain period.

Such control shall be made only when it is suspected that a person has not been entirely truthful on his tax return. It is within the discretion of the tax authorities to decide when this is the case. The bank is required only to deliver the requested information as long as it is required for named persons or companies. The legislative history shows that the legislator expected the tax authorities to use these powers with restraint and judgment.

Unfortunately, this has not always been the case, and one request was struck down by an appellate administrative court.[3] In that case, a diligent, though misguided, tax official had requested information about an impressive number of named persons from local branches of a bank. However, the requests were made after the tax returns for one year had been processed by the tax authority but before the tax returns for the next year had been filed. Consequently, there could be no suspicion of wrongful information by the taxpayers.

When a demand for information is served upon the bank, the bank may petition the administrative courts for an order of injunction. An injunction will be granted only in very special circumstances, *e.g.*, if a trade secret is at risk. In exceptional circumstances, when great loss could result for the customer, it might be argued that a bank should have an obligation towards its customers to move for an injunction.

A bank also may be subjected to a tax audit. Such audit may be made to gather information about third parties. In recent years, such audit need not be limited to named persons or certain transactions but may have a general scope. As was true for the demand for information, a bank may petition the administrative courts for an injunction if there are special reasons why documents should not be disclosed to the auditor. Again, there could be situations in which a bank should move for an injunction.

Information obtained by the tax authorities in the aforementioned ways is subject to secrecy also after it has been delivered to the tax authorities. However, should a trial by a tax court follow the audit, the confidentiality may be threatened.

---

[3] Docket Number 2080-1985, the *Appellate Administrative Court of Jönköping*.

On the witness stand

Should a bank official or employee be called to testify in court, **34-008** banking secrecy will not prevent him from doing so. It should be noted that a bank's in-house counsel must testify, while the same information, had it been entrusted to an attorney or a member of a law firm, would have been subject to the attorney-client privilege. Should the lawyer have obtained the information while representing the client-customer in court, the information will be privileged.

A bank official, as any other witness, is allowed, and is indeed expected, to confine his testimony to what is relevant in the case and should not indulge in any extensive discussion regarding the customer's relations with the bank. Further, there are certain possibilities under Swedish law to restrain the witness from disclosing trade secrets, including those of a third party, at the witness stand.[4]

Should a bank be ordered to produce documents in discovery, the same principles will apply. It should be noted that pre-trial discovery is not known to Swedish law.

Criminal investigations

When someone is suspected of a crime, the police and the prosecu- **34-009** tor in charge of the investigation may seize documents which may be thought to be of importance for the investigation if they are available. Should the law enforcement officials wish to search a safe deposit box in a bank, they must obtain a search warrant. Such a warrant may be issued by a commanding police officer, a prosecutor, or the district court. A search warrant will be issued only for crimes punishable by imprisonment.

The bank's auditors are required to provide information to the prosecutor in charge of a criminal investigation about the bank's business relations.

Generally, information given at a trial or in a criminal investigation will not be kept confidential.

---

[4] The Swedish Code of Judicial Procedure of 1948, as amended, chapter 36, section 6, states: ". . . Further, witness may refrain from giving testimony that would involve disclosure of a trade secret, unless there is extraordinary cause for examining the witness on the matter".

Information sought by the Enforcement Service Authority

34-010   A bank is required to give information to the Enforcement Service Authority in order to enable the Authority to ascertain whether a certain debtor has assets which can be levied upon. The Authority should inform the bank about how much money is sought.

Should the debtor's assets with the bank exceed that amount it is considered suitable that the bank only informs the Authority that assets covering the debt are deposited with the bank. The exact amount of the assets should not be disclosed.

The shareholders

34-011   The owners of a bank, the shareholders, have a legitimate interest to be kept informed of the bank's business. On the other hand, such information may give away confidential business relations. Under Swedish law, any shareholder may ask questions at the shareholders' meeting, but the board of directors is not obliged to answer in certain cases, *inter alia*, if the answer could cause a customer any inconvenience.

It is sufficient that the answer would reveal a business relation that the customer may wish to keep confidential for the board not having to reply. Should the board exercise such right the information shall, if the shareholders so request, instead be given to the bank's auditors.

The employees and their unions

34-012   The labor unions organizing employees at a bank may be entitled to information about the bank's business. Should the unions obtain any information regarding individual customers in connection therewith, such information will be subject to the same secrecy requirement with the unions.

Spousal interests

34-013   Under Swedish law, a married couple is considered to consist of two separate individuals and, consequently, the spouses are regarded as two separate economic entities. That notwithstanding, it has been authoritatively suggested that a bank should be entitled, though perhaps not obliged, to inform one spouse of the other's relations with the bank upon request.

The rationale for such an entitlement should be that, under the Swedish Marriage Act,[5] the spouses are obliged to keep each other fully informed of their economic conditions and there would consequently not be any reason to keep a spouse's relations with banks confidential towards the other spouse.

This holds true also in divorce proceedings, while an ex-spouse has no such rights, although he may be entitled to alimony or child support. In this context, an ex-spouse is looked upon as any other creditor. A partner in a couple merely living together - a form of quasi-matrimonial cohabitation which is very common in Sweden and in some respects is awarded the same protection as a marriage by the legislator - has no right to learn anything about the other partner's relations with banks.

A customer's auditor

Normally, a company's auditors have no reason to approach a bank **34-014** directly to obtain information about the company's business. Should the management, however, be uncooperative, a bank may give the auditor the desired information, but care should be taken to ask the auditor to be precise about the information he wishes to obtain, to communicate only that which the auditor has asked for and, some suggest, to give the management an opportunity to consider the auditor's request before submitting any information.

Protecting the bank's interests

A bank may make an otherwise confidential relationship public in **34-015** a trial to which the bank is a party in order to protect its own interests.

Credit check

In Sweden, it is possible to make a so-called credit check, on both **34-016** natural and legal persons, through a simple inquiry to a company which is jointly owned by the banks.

The company can provide information about where somebody lives, if and to whom the person is married, when he was married, information as to whether the couple has a prenuptial agreement, if

5 The Swedish Marriage Act of 1987.

the person has not fulfilled his financial respectabilities within the last three years (but only if such non-performance has been determined by a court or other authority if the party questioned is a natural person), and if the person has applied for other loans.

Information regarding a natural person should be given only to someone who may be supposed to have a genuine need thereof because he has, or is considering, lending money to the person. It should be noted that a bank may give even more information to another bank as regards a certain person's management, or mismanagement, of his accounts. Inter-bank information about a natural person not handling his accounts in a desired manner could well be given, although no court has ruled on the matter.

The receiving bank is obliged to keep the information confidential as though it pertained to a customer of its own. Notwithstanding the aforesaid, banking secrecy does apply between banks, and it is not suggested that banks freely share information about their customers.

Bank subsidiaries and foreign branches

34-017   A bank is considered to be able to obtain information about customers of its wholly-owned subsidiaries. Information from the bank to the subsidiary should be given restrictively and on a need to know-basis. The bank will be held responsible if the subsidiary, or somebody employed thereby, breaches the confidentiality to which the information is subject.

A prudent bank would see to it that the subsidiary itself, as well as its board of directors, the managing director, and other officials promise to adhere to the same rules on banking secrecy as those to which the bank is subject.

Should, however, the subsidiary, or its employees, not make good on their promise, the bank will be liable for damages towards its customers.

Foreign subsidiaries of Swedish banks engaging in banking business abroad are subject to the rules in their place of incorporation, and one must look to each foreign jurisdiction to see whether - and to what extent - the subsidiary may keep the Swedish bank informed about its customers.

The Swedish bank would have the same possibilities to communicate information to its foreign as to its domestic subsidiaries. The Swedish bank ought to be extremely careful, however, if it has a subsidiary in a country with rules on banking secrecy less stringent than those of Sweden.

A branch abroad is subject to Swedish banking secrecy rules but also can be subject to the rules at its place of business. In practice, it would, thus, have to adhere to the more stringent rule.

Foreign banks in Sweden

Foreign-owned banks in Sweden are incorporated under Swedish **34-018** law and subject to Swedish rules on banking secrecy.

Financial Supervisory Authority

The Financial Supervisory Authority is entitled to obtain the infor- **34-019** mation about a bank's customers which it needs to fulfil its duty to control the bank. Such information shall be kept confidential by the Authority.

Subpoenas is ued by a foreign sovereign

A different problem is at hand relative to a foreign subpoena to **34-020** produce documents. A Swedish bank is required to adhere to Swedish law on banking secrecy. By doing so, it may however subject itself to various problems in the other jurisdiction, such as stiff fines.

It should be noted that, whatever problems a bank may encounter in foreign jurisdictions, it is, first and foremost, required to obey the Swedish law on banking secrecy.[6]

Evidence in foreign trials

Swedish courts may take evidence in foreign proceedings. A bank **34-021** official then will have to testify as to confidential matters in accordance with what has been said about testimony in Swedish proceedings.

Foreign tax authorities

Should foreign tax authorities request information from Swedish **34-022** banks, such requests should be made to the Swedish tax authorities.

---

[6] Richard Ziegler, "What To Do When the American Subpoena Arrives", *Financial Law* (May 1991), at p. 27.

The Swedish authorities should then - assuming the request comes from a country with which Sweden has entered into an agreement regarding assistance in tax matters - assist in the investigation using the least intrusive of the possibilities given by Swedish and the requesting state's laws.[7] Trade secrets should not be disclosed by such information.

Extradition

34-023   A bank may be obliged to provide information when a foreign state has requested the extradition of a suspected criminal. The Swedish police authorities may make an investigation before such surrender, and banks may then be required to provide information, by analogy to what was stated above, regarding crimes to be tried in Sweden.

SANCTIONS WHEN SECRECY IS BREACHED

34-024   A customer who has been damaged by a bank not respecting confidentiality is entitled to damages. However, the offending employee cannot, except in extreme circumstances, be subjected to criminal proceedings. However, he could be subjected to disciplinary actions as permitted under Swedish labor laws.

The bank is responsible towards its customers for breaches of confidentiality by its directors and employees. It seems likely that the bank also should be liable for breaches occurring after a certain employee has left the bank. A bank is not considered to be responsible for what its shareholders or auditors may do. Under general Swedish contract law, negligence is a prerequisite for damages.

It has been authoritatively discussed whether damages for breach of banking secrecy could be awarded on the basis of strict liability and suggested that perhaps the bank has to show that it, or someone for whom it is responsible, has not been negligent. Naturally, sheer ignorance on the part of the offender is not an excuse.

Members of the board, the managing director, and the auditors are responsible towards third parties for damages which they may have caused. A shareholder also can be held responsible for damages which he has caused, but only if he has caused them through gross negligence or willful misconduct. Should the management of

---

[7] Such agreements include those with Austria, Canada, Japan, Switzerland, the United States and, except for Portugal, the Member States of the European Community.

the bank have permitted, or perhaps even ordered, some information to be given to an outsider, the bank must reimburse the person who has been held liable for damages towards the customer.

In the cases mentioned above, the bank and the offender(s) are jointly and severally liable towards third parties, except when a shareholder is at fault.

As to "ordinary" employees, these do not have a contractual relationship with the customer and cannot be responsible for damages towards him but may well, at least in theory, be obliged to reimburse the bank for whatever damages the bank may have had to pay because of the employee's ignorance or carelessness.

A consequence of the aforesaid is that a breach of confidentiality will go unsanctioned, except possibly for disciplinary actions, if no damages can be proved.

Conclusion

Swedish law on banking secrecy has remained virtually unchanged **34-025** for decades. One important exception is that tax authorities have gained increased possibilities to obtain information regarding a bank's customers through tax audits. For many years, however, tax audits were carried out in the manner permitted by law until the highest administrative court declared it unlawful.[8] The law was subsequently changed.

Banking secrecy often has to give way to inquiries made by various, particularly tax, authorities. The information revealed will, in most cases, be kept secret by the receiving authority. The most "dangerous" way to breach banking secrecy for a superior interest would be in a court proceeding or a criminal investigation.

Sweden, like many other countries, is keen to do something about white-collar crime, and it may be suspected that a court would be more ready to order an obstructing witness to disclose otherwise confidential information in such proceedings. As noted above, the information would most likely thereafter become a part of the public record.

On balance, we do not foresee any major changes in Swedish banking secrecy rules. Sweden will have to adapt to the requirements of the Common Market, at such time as it becomes a member.

[8] The Swedish Supreme Administrative Court 1986, Case Number 69.

SWITZERLAND

Hans Bollmann
Pestalozzi Gmuer & Patry
Zürich, Switzerland

Chapter 35

SWITZERLAND

INTRODUCTION

Switzerland fulfills, according to a widespread belief, the highest **35-001** standards of a banking haven. This opinion still prevails, despite the tendency of foreign newspapers to take a more balanced position and point out that other countries also have banking secrecy.

In fact, all countries have a certain amount of banking confidentiality, the differences being only incremental.

Although Swiss bank secrecy has some unique features, it is far from being absolute. The critical task is, therefore, to define its content and to lay down its limitations.

In the following, we shall begin by outlining the factual and legal aspects and describing the concept of Swiss bank secrecy. Thereafter, the limitations resulting from domestic procedural law and international legal assistance shall be discussed. Finally, two special subjects shall be presented: Switzerland's new Insider Trading Code and the Due Diligence Agreement of 1977.

Background

Basically there are two reasons for the actual status of Swiss bank **35-002** secrecy. The first must be seen historically in connection with Switzerland's tradition of neutrality, which extends back for centuries.

In the 17th century, thousands of Huguenots from France fled to Switzerland because of religious persecution. Some of them became bankers and, for obvious reasons, had to maintain secrecy regarding the affairs of customers in their homeland. Similar situations developed in connection with the political changes at the end of the 19th century and the beginning of the 20th century.

The second important reason is the persecution of Jews and other persons by the Nazi regime in Germany in the 1930s and the 1940s. The dictatorship led to a direct connection between Swiss neutrality and bank secrecy. When a banking act was proposed in the early 1930s, the relevant bill did not contain any provision regarding bank secrecy, and bankers did not press to have it included.

After Hitler's rise to power in 1933, increasing pressure was exerted on Swiss banks to disclose information concerning German customers, particularly Jews. The Swiss Parliament then considered it necessary to include a secrecy provision in the banking regulations.

However, neutrality has not been the only factor leading to Switzerland's current position within the spectrum of financial markets; another factor is that its domestic political, social, and economic stability, and particularly its monetary stability, have inspired worldwide confidence in Swiss banking facilities.

Legal aspects

35-003 The primary source of the Swiss legal system is the law and, failing that, legal custom. Within the general term "law", the Constitution is the main source, followed by statutes enacted by Parliament. Governmental legislation also falls within the ambit of "law" as a primary source.

Therefore, one must examine at which of these levels bank secrecy has its legal basis, *i.e.*, which are the concrete legal provisions protecting and reinforcing it.

Constitutional level

35-004 The right to privacy is usually one of those fundamental rights included in and protected by the constitutions of democratic countries. The Swiss Constitution, perhaps surprisingly, does not include the right to privacy as a specially protected fundamental right. In fact, individual rights are hardly dealt with expressly by the Constitution.

The lack of such a provision should not, however, be regarded as a lack of protection of fundamental rights by the Swiss Constitution. The Federal Supreme Court continues to uphold the existence of individual rights and considers those not specifically enumerated in the Constitution to be unwritten fundamental rights with constitutional validity and protection.

Civil Code

Independent of any contractual relationship, the right to privacy **35-005** refers to a person's right to the protection of his or her person in the sense referred to by article 28(1) of the Swiss Civil Code, which declares:

> "Whosoever suffers an illegal offense against his person is entitled to ask the judge for help against anyone joining in the offense". (unofficial translation)

This provision refers to both natural and legal persons. Furthermore, it refers to all aspects of the personal sphere, including the right to privacy. Therefore, in its widest sense, professional secrecy has its basis in a person's right to have his or her person as a whole protected, as promised, in the Civil Code.

As a consequence, priests, doctors, lawyers, notaries, and bank personnel have a particularly strict duty of secrecy, since they are the ones whose professional activity leads them to learn about the personal lives of their clients, patients or customers.

Violation of the right to privacy is also tantamount to a tort under articles 41 *et seq.* of the Code of Obligations. Thus, a bank can not only be held liable on contractual grounds but also towards third parties.

Code of Obligations

The contractual relationship between the bank and its client is **35-006** another legal basis for the bank employees' duty of secrecy. Nevertheless, under Swiss law, the legal nature of this contractual relationship is unclear since it includes a wide spectrum of banking activities which do not have a common legal nature.

For most relationships, however, the laws concerning mandates are (at least by analogy) applicable. The duty of secrecy thus derives generally from the duty of loyalty to be observed by the bank as an agent.[1]

Certain kinds of agreements between the bank and its customers (*e.g.*, credit agreements and safekeeping agreements) cannot be included within the category of agency contracts. In those cases, the question arises whether the bank still has a duty of secrecy. The Federal Supreme Court has stated on several occasions that the

---

[1] Code of Obligations, article 398(2).

bank's obligation to observe secrecy becomes part of the contractual relationship through the principle of "good faith" inherent in customary law.[2]

Regardless of the relationship between a bank and its client, a duty of secrecy is, therefore, a further obligation in all contractual and extra-contractual relationships linked to bank activities.

Breach of contract entitles the customer to remedies. The bank is, in this case, also strictly liable for faults of its employees and other persons acting in fulfillment of the contractual duties. (In tort claims, by contrast, the bank is liable only for the acts of employees and may, under certain circumstances, even exculpate itself from any liability for their faults).

Criminal law

35-007   Criminal law deals with bank secrecy to the extent that it has already been breached.

Breach of bank secrecy is mentioned in two different sources of the law, namely, specific banking regulations and the Swiss Penal Code. Whereas the former deals with breach of bank secrecy within the framework of the banking business, the latter deals with it as a disclosure of domestic information that might damage important Swiss economic interests.

35-008   **Specific regulation of breach of bank secrecy** The specific consequences under the criminal law of infringing the duty of bank secrecy are described in article 47 of the Bank and Savings Bank Federal Act of June 8, 1934, as amended in 1971 (hereinafter referred to as the "Banking Act").

This is the primary administrative statute governing the business operations, financial security, statement of accounts, control, and supervision of banks and related institutions.

Article 47 provides that:

(1) Every person working at a bank has a duty to keep secrets;
(2) Third parties who lead others to infringe the secrecy duty are also to be punished, even if the offense never takes place;
(3) Infringement due to pure negligence, as well as intentional infringement, is to be punished;

---

[2] See, *e.g.*, BGE 63 (1937) II 240, 242.

(4) The infringement of bank secrecy may be prosecuted by the court on its own initiative;

(5) The penalties are a prison term not to exceed six months or a fine not to exceed SFr. 50,000; either penalty may be cumulated;

(6) Breach of professional secrecy remains punishable even after termination of a public or private employment relationship or the practice of a profession, and

(7) Bank secrecy is not absolute; in specific legal circumstances, Swiss authorities are to be granted the right of access to private banking records.

Article 47 of the Banking Act applies only to individuals and not to banks as legal entities, since the principle *societas delinquere non potest* is accepted by the Swiss legal system.

Notwithstanding the above, all managers and employees of a bank or any entity falling within the ambit of the applicable banking regulations are under the obligation to observe bank secrecy. The Banking Act was amended in 1971 to make bank mandatories, of whatever kind, subject to the obligation of discretion. Mandatories include independent contractors to whom a bank- related task (*e.g.*, data processing) is entrusted.

The duty of secrecy is not territorially limited; thus, its breach abroad also is punishable under Swiss criminal law.

Swiss Penal Code Article 273 of the Swiss Penal Code contains the following provision: 35-009

"Whosoever obtains a manufacturing or business secret in order to make it available to a foreign public authority or foreign organization or to a private organization or to its agents,

whosoever makes available a manufacturing or business secret to a foreign public authority or foreign organization or to a private organization or to its agents,

shall be punished with imprisonment or, in severe cases, with penal servitude. In conjunction with detention a fine may be imposed."

This article is primarily intended to protect Swiss public interests. It seeks to secure Swiss economic sovereignty by guarding matters from undesirable intrusion on behalf of foreign countries. Private individuals and legal entities, in the context of their economic activity in Switzerland, are considered part of the Swiss public economy and, therefore, are protected by this provision.

It is immaterial whether there is a specific legal or contractual obligation to observe secrecy with regard to information that qualifies as secret. As stated above, bank secrecy obliges the banks to observe secrecy with regard to the affairs of their customers *vis-à-vis* all persons in Switzerland and abroad, while article 273 of the Swiss Penal Code prohibits any person from transmitting manufacturing or business secrets abroad.

Inasmuch as this provision is intended to protect the Swiss public (economic) interest, it may be violated, even if the person or legal entity legitimately in possession of secret information consents to the disclosure of such information.

Notwithstanding the above, not every communication of information of an economic character to foreign authorities is prohibited. Such disclosure is punishable only if it involves manufacturing or business secrets. Such secrets include not only trade secrets of economic enterprises but also any kind of information concerning economic conditions which is neither obvious nor generally accessible, and for the secrecy of which there is an interest deserving protection.

However, it is difficult to determine the "sphere of secrecy"; the Swiss Penal Code does not provide conclusive guidelines on the matter, so the courts must examine the circumstances of each case in order to determine whether particular information is subject to secrecy.

CONCEPT OF BANK SECRECY

Objective scope

Characteristics of bank secrecy

35-010   Swiss law does not provide a statutory definition of bank secrecy. The term may be defined, nevertheless, by summarizing the characteristics suggested by the different legal materials dealing directly or indirectly with the matter and by court decisions.

Bank secrecy is factual bank discretion, which can be defined as a banker's professional obligation to keep, in strictest confidence, all business and affairs related to the financial and personal circumstances of clients and some third parties to the extent that knowledge of such matters is acquired in the course of business.

A special feature of bank secrecy in Switzerland is, as mentioned above, that a violation of trust is subject to criminal prosecution. As with a violation of official secrecy, a breach of bank secrecy is prosecuted by the court on its own initiative, whereas violations of professional secrecy (such as with doctors and attorneys) are prosecuted only upon the express request of the injured party.

In order to establish the real meaning of bank secrecy, it is necessary to specify the activities to which it refers. Bank secrecy - or, more precisely, banking discretion - is generally considered to refer to all types of activities performed within the framework of bank business. However, in order to avoid doubt, the following examples can be mentioned:

(1) The relationships between the clients and the bank;
(2) Information given by the clients to the bank concerning economic issues, even the information related to the client's relationships with other banks, and
(3) Information concerning financial operations performed by third parties.

Concept of a bank

Swiss banks in general Since the concept of a bank is the main feature to be taken into account when defining the scope of Swiss bank secrecy, it is necessary to describe the different institutions which can be included within the widest meaning of the term "bank". **35-011**

The Banking Act, which is the starting point for defining a "bank", adopts a functional definition of the entities subject to it. Article 1 declares that the Banking Act applies to all banks, private bankers (individual bankers, partnerships, limited partnerships), and savings banks (hereafter referred to by the Banking Act as "banks").

Furthermore, the Banking Act establishes in article 1(2) that all kinds of entities with financial functions are to be considered, for the purposes therein referred to, as banks to the extent that they publicly solicit customer deposits.

To the extent that they do not engage in banking activities, stockbrokers, notaries, investment managers, and the like are expressly excluded from the concept of a bank and, therefore, from the ambit of the Banking Act and the regulations concerning bank secrecy.

35-012 **Savings banks** Savings banks also are governed by the Banking Act. Since the Banking Act does not specially distinguish savings banks, exactly the same rules that apply to banks in the strict sense of the term also apply to savings banks.

For practical reasons, the Banking Act uses the general term "bank" for banks and savings banks without distinction.

35-013 **Foreign banks with establishments in Switzerland** Article 2(1) declares that the Banking Act also applies to subsidiaries, branch offices, or agencies of foreign banks established in Switzerland.

These entities are subject to the Swiss secrecy rules to the same extent as Swiss banks; their employees are subject to the same secrecy duty as the employees of a Swiss bank and are, therefore, not allowed to reveal any information regarding customers of the Swiss entity to their parent company, head office, foreign auditors, or foreign authorities.

Notwithstanding the above, the exercise of control by a foreign bank over its Swiss banking operation is not excluded. In the case of a subsidiary, for example, control may be effectively achieved by the foreign parent company's designation of one or several senior officers to the board of directors of the Swiss subsidiary.

In their capacity as directors, those officers will have the right to obtain comprehensive information regarding the operation of the Swiss subsidiary and, therefore, will be entitled to control and inspect whatever transaction takes place within the subsidiary. Of course, members of the board of directors of a bank also are subject to article 47 of the Banking Act, so they, too, may not disclose information to the parent bank or to foreign authorities, regardless of whether such members are Swiss citizens or foreigners.

The management report of a bank in Switzerland, regardless of its purpose, may not disclose information about the identity of the clients. This should present no problem since the individual identity of the clients is usually a mere portfolio question of the Swiss entity with no significance for general reporting to the controlling company.

In cases where the identity of a customer may be an important piece of information for the parent company or for third banks (for instance, in connection with granting credit facilities), special care should be taken by the Swiss entity, before the identity of the customer is disclosed for whatever purpose, about the fact that certain information regarding the customer needs to be disclosed in order to have the transaction executed. In particular, the customer should be asked to consent to the disclosure and the consent should be received and evidenced.

Concerning auditors, if the foreign auditors of the parent company or head office exercise their functions directly in Switzerland, the management of the Swiss bank must furnish only information of a general nature which would not entail a breach of bank secrecy. If, in exceptional cases, the foreign bank intends to make a direct and unrestricted audit of the Swiss entity, the auditors should be cautioned that they are deemed mandatories of the Swiss subsidiary or branch and that, as such, they are subject to Swiss law, particularly to article 47 of the Banking Act.

No official agent or representative of a foreign government may undertake any investigation of a bank in Swiss territory, even if foreign-controlled, without the permission of the competent Swiss governmental authority. Provisions of foreign law mandating such an investigation do not exclude the application of this rule; the managers and employees of a foreign-controlled bank are therefore fully subject to article 47 of Swiss Banking Act when providing such persons with information directly related to the Swiss entity.

As a counterpart to the requirements that it imposes upon foreign banks operating in its territory, Switzerland recognizes that foreign legislation is applicable to foreign branches of Swiss banks and assumes that those foreign entities are not subject to Swiss legislation. Information relating to customers of such branches is, therefore, not protected by Swiss bank secrecy rules but is governed by the bank legislation of the country in which those entities are located.

Subjective scope of bank secrecy

The subjective scope of bank secrecy is defined by the persons **35-014** involved. The persons affected may be divided into two groups, namely, the persons obligated by bank secrecy and the persons benefiting from it.

For clarity's sake, we will call the first group "secrecy debtors" and the second group "secrecy creditors".

Secrecy debtors

Article 47 of the Banking Act applies to persons who are subject to **35-015** the confidentiality obligation arising from bank secrecy rules.

This article declares that the following persons will be punished if they violate the obligation of secrecy: "managers, employees, mandatories, liquidators, or commissioners of a bank, representatives of the Banking Commission, managers or employees of a recognized auditing firm, anyone who attempts to induce another person to violate professional secrecy." To be more precise:

(1) The term "managers" means directors, officers, principals, partners, and any other persons with managerial functions.

(2) "Mandatory" means any person to whom the bank has given a bank-related task, regardless of its extent. By analogy, in cases where the mandatory (or agent) is a legal person, all persons who have any kind of relationship with the mandatory legal person (once again, managers, employees, officers) are subjected to the duty of confidentiality owed by the legal person; as stated above, *societas delinquere non potest* applies so that the breaches of secrecy are directly imputable to the individuals responsible for them.

(3) Inducing another person to infringe the law is also an offense; as a result, the scope of article 47 of the Banking Act becomes universal.

Secrecy and creditors

35-016   As a general principle, and without prejudice to the exemptions dealt with below, bank secrecy is a personal right of the banks' clients.

They are the persons within whose disposal bank secrecy falls, so they may waive such a right at any time and by any means, even by an action which merely implies such a waiver. The bank has no right to raise the objection that the maintenance of secrecy is in the public interest.[3]

This means that, if so required by the customer, the bank is not only authorized but obligated to provide all information concerning the client's banking transactions, even to courts, tax authorities and other third parties. However, if third parties are involved in the client's banking transactions, the bank may refuse to disclose information to the extent that it would breach the bank secrecy obligation towards those third parties.

In addition to waiver, the client's extra-contractual and contractual relationships may also lead the bank to release information. For example, if the client grants a power of attorney in favor of a third person concerning his or her bank accounts, the bank will no longer be obligated - more precisely, it will not be allowed - to raise objections referring to bank secrecy against that empowered person.

[3] BGE 74 (1948) I 485, 492/493.

The same applies to contractual relationships between the client and third parties which confer on the latter the right to obtain information. If the contractual relationship expires or if the power of attorney is revoked, the third party's right to obtain information will disappear.

All the holders of a joint bank account are entitled to comprehensive information on the status of the account as a whole.

Peculiarities of Swiss bank secrecy

Some circumstantial factors have led public opinion to the false idea   **35-017** that bank secrecy as such is peculiar to Swiss law. It is unnecessary here to clarify how far this statement is from reality, but it should once again be stressed that Swiss law does have one peculiarity concerning bank secrecy, namely the fact that it is protected by criminal law.

Moreover, such prosecution takes place by the court on its own initiative whereas the prosecution of breaches of secrecy in most other jurisdictions takes place only upon the request of the injured party.

Numbered accounts are another part of public opinion's false notions about Swiss bank secrecy. Contrary to popular belief, anonymous numbered accounts - a term which is misused and which does not correspond to reality - do not exist. The bank always knows the name of the last beneficiary party holding each account, even if the account is designated by a number or a password.

The public's misconception originated when Swiss banks - like banks in some other countries - offered the clients the possibility of having accounts listed under a number or a code word. This practice offers the owners of such accounts the advantage of being personally known only to a restricted number of bank officers or employees instead of to all the officers of the bank dealing with the account.

However, the owner of a numbered account is always known to at least one person at the bank, all the more because the client may become the bank's debtor at some future date. No bank would ever take the risk of accepting an anonymous client; in fact, holders of such accounts are usually depositors who were already customers of the bank before opening the account or, if new customers, depositors whose circumstances have been examined by the bank through references and interviews so that the bank has had the possibility of evaluating whether the customers have legitimate reasons for wishing such protection.

RESTRICTIONS UNDER DOMESTIC PROCEDURAL LAW

35-018 Bank secrecy is restricted mainly by domestic procedural law and by international judicial assistance. These two topics shall thus be discussed at some length in the next two sections.

The limitation of the bank secrecy by procedural law is grounded on article 47(4) of the Banking Act. This provision contains a reservation concerning federal and cantonal regulations which might create an obligation for the banks to testify and to furnish information to a governmental authority. This provision, together with the client's consent referred to above, forms the legal basis for all exceptions to bank secrecy.

Civil proceedings

35-019 Since the Swiss political and administrative system allows the existence of different cantonal regulations on certain matters, three kinds of solutions have been found by the different cantons in order to regulate the extent of application of article 47(4) of the Banking Act in connection with the duty to testify.

The cantons of Aargau, Berne, Geneva, Jura, Neuchâtel, St. Gallen, and Vaud have exempted all persons bound by a professional secret from the duty to testify. Bank secrecy is usually understood to fall within this exemption. The canton of Valais is deemed to be included in this group, even if some authors dispute it.

The solution chosen by Appenzell, Basel, Glarus, Grisons, Obwalden, Schaffhausen, Solothurn, and Thurgau is the express mention of all categories of professionals who are exempted from the duty to testify. Banking people are not mentioned; thus, they are obliged to testify.

The final means of regulating the application of article 47(4) is to allow the judge to decide, in each case, whether it is necessary for the bank officer to testify. This applies to Fribourg, Nidwalden, Schwyz, Ticino, Uri, Zug, and Zürich. The canton of Lucerne seems to be moving from laws like that of the second group towards a system similar to that of the last group.

In proceedings governed by the Federal Code of Civil Procedure, a system analogous to that of the third group applies.

Independent of the underlying legal basis, in all those cases where the court is authorized to require the testimony of the bank, special protective measures are adopted in order to infringe bank secrecy only to the strictest necessary extent.

Arbitrators are not entitled to compel testimony, but article 184 of the Swiss Statute on Private International Law provides that, if the assistance of state judiciary authorities is necessary for the taking of evidence, the arbitral tribunal may request the assistance of the state judge and thereby gain access to privileged information, including bank information; that would otherwise be protected.

Inheritance law

According to the Swiss principle of direct and immediate succession, the heirs acquire the rights and obligations of the deceased immediately upon his or her death, except for highly personal rights. The right of secrecy, including the correlative rights to release the bank from its secrecy obligation and to obtain information, is a right of the property owner. **35-020**

It is not considered a highly personal right; it, therefore, is one of those rights which pass to the heirs. Secrecy concerning such information must be preserved vis-à-vis the heirs only if some of the information related to the decedent's affairs is of a highly personal character.

Whether the nature of the information has a sufficiently highly personal character to justify the non-disclosure of information must be judged by objective criteria; the customer may not simply label it "highly personal." If the information turns out to be of a highly personal character, the bank will not disclose it to the heirs and the executor.

Some authors and, to a certain extent, the Swiss Bankers' Association, hold that the bank must disclose information only with regard to the status of the assets at the time of the decedent's death, but not with regard to any transactions performed prior to his or her death. Other authors, supported to a large extent by court decisions, are of the opinion that the bank must furnish all information contained in its files.

The obligation of the bank to disclose information is effectively limited in time by the provisions referring to the obligation to preserve records, which is governed by the general Swiss statute of limitation, *i.e.*, 10 years. The heirs, moreover, are entitled to obtain any information which had already been furnished to the decedent.

As a general rule of Swiss inheritance law, heirs can dispose of the inheritance only when acting jointly and, therefore, must instruct the bank jointly, but they may severally require the bank to provide them with information.

Legatees are not entitled to obtain information from the bank since they do not succeed the decedent.

Marriage law

35-021 The extent of bank secrecy in connection with married couples is determined by the economic regime of the married couple involved, as laid down in their marriage covenant. If they have agreed on a joint property regime, the bank is not bound by the bank secrecy obligation when dealing with the bank matters of one spouse vis-à-vis the other.

Each spouse is entitled to be provided with bank information relating to the other spouse. Otherwise (*i.e.*, if they agreed to any other common economic regime), the bank does have to observe bank secrecy rules in matters referring to the other spouse.

Bankruptcy and collection of debts

35-022 The Federal Statute on Debt and Bankruptcy of April 11, 1889 (hereinafter the "Bankruptcy Act") applies to bank secrecy in connection with bankruptcy or the collection of debts.

35-023 **Bankruptcy and collection of the client's debts** Under the terms of the Bankruptcy Act, banks must disclose information at an early stage of the bankruptcy proceedings but, in practice, no coercive measures can be taken by the authorities before the seizure becomes definitive.

Thus, until the execution officer has seized a bank account and such seizure has become definitive, the bank can refuse information by invoking bank secrecy.

In bankruptcy proceedings, the trustee in bankruptcy is entitled to full disclosure of account information pertaining to a client's account.

35-024 **Bank's bankruptcy** The bankruptcy of banks may create conflicts of interest since, on one side, creditors must be allowed to satisfy their rights, and on the other, clients must continue to be protected by bank secrecy.

In practice, the Federal Supreme Court has decided that bank secrecy may not be invoked by the bank vis-à-vis the bank's creditors. The trustee in bankruptcy or the officially appointed liquidator, therefore, will have full access to all information concerning the bank's business.

In spite of some special provisions of the Banking Act related to bankruptcy proceedings, creditors of a bankrupt bank or a bank in forced liquidation due to a settlement under the Bankruptcy Act are granted wide access to client-related information in order to protect their interests in the liquidation proceedings.

Criminal proceedings

Proceedings related to criminal matters clearly delimit the scope of   35-025
application of bank secrecy.

In principle, as long as the police are still investigating, bank
secrecy remains fully protected. Notwithstanding the above, banks
might be required to testify before official prosecutors and criminal
courts by virtue of the Federal Code of Criminal Procedure and all
cantonal statutes on criminal procedure.[4]

The fact that bank secrecy concerning uninvolved third parties
might be infringed by answering certain questions must be brought
to the judge's attention so that the judge or prosecuting officer can
decide whether the information must nevertheless be disclosed. In
criminal proceedings against a bank or any officer thereof, secret
information relating to clients remains protected and may not be
used against them.

In order to avoid the problems that could be caused by the
disclosure of information related to third parties, the Federal and
Cantonal Codes of Criminal Procedure provide for protective measures, such as sealing documents seized at the bank until a judge or
a judicially-appointed expert has examined them and has decided
whether their disclosure is necessary.

However, in Switzerland, it is not possible to make documents
available only to the public prosecutor and not to the other parties
since such activity would imply the acceptance of secret files, which
infringes Swiss criminal procedure rules.

Administrative proceedings

In principle, banks do not have to testify in administrative proceed-   35-026
ings since article 16(2) of the Administrative Procedure Act of December 20, 1968, exempts all persons bound by professional secrecy
from the obligation to testify.

However, this applies only as far as not otherwise expressly
provided for by statute; thus, a bank must testify, for example, in
connection with the acquisition of interests in Swiss real estate by
foreigners.

If administrative matters are brought before any administrative
or civil court, civil rules concerning bank secrecy will apply. On the
other hand, the Federal Act for Criminal Administrative Procedure
declares that, if involved in such proceedings, banks will not be
entitled to invoke bank secrecy when required to testify.

[4] See, e.g., Banking Act, article 47(4).

Taxation

35-027 As a preliminary matter, it is necessary to distinguish between tax evasion and tax fraud. The former refers to cases where payment of taxes has been insufficient on the basis of negligently or wilfully provided incorrect information in the tax returns or the non-compliance with procedural obligations by the taxpayer.

Tax fraud, on the other hand, means the deception of the tax authorities by fraudulent means, especially by false or falsified documents which results in an underpayment of tax. The sanction for tax evasion usually consists of penalty taxes, whereas the sanction for tax fraud includes higher penalty taxes and occasionally fines or even imprisonment.

As a general principle, when dealing with tax evasion, the tax authorities are to address themselves directly to the taxpayer and not to third parties. This means that, in general, banks will not be involved, and bank secrecy, therefore, will remain protected. However, this statement is not absolute. Bank secrecy will be observed in the following cases:

(1) Evasion of federal taxes (administrative prosecution in this respect rests exclusively with the tax authorities), and

(2) Cantonal and municipal taxes insofar as prosecution rests with the tax authorities, which is the case in practically all cantons with regard to tax evasion (and, in some cantons, even with regard to tax fraud).

On the other hand, bank secrecy does not operate in proceedings relating to:

(1) Direct federal taxes insofar as tax fraud is concerned, and in proceedings relating to all other federal taxes insofar as tax evasion and tax fraud are concerned; in such proceedings bank officials must testify and furnish information and have no right to invoke bank secrecy, and

(2) Cantonal taxes, insofar as the provisions of the cantonal codes of criminal procedure apply, which is the case in some of the cantons with regard to tax fraud.

All Swiss banks and Swiss branches of foreign banks have to account for stamp duties on certain transactions and withholding taxes on dividends and interest. Within these limited areas, Swiss federal tax authorities are entitled to inspect the relevant files; this means they have access to information on customers.

However, information on clients that is obtained in this way must not be used for any other purpose, not even for the enforcement of any other federal taxes. The bank must testify in criminal proceedings regarding evasion of stamp duties, withholding taxes, turnover tax, and customs duties by its customer.

With regard to its own taxes, the bank must furnish all the necessary information to the tax authorities. This seems quite obvious since otherwise bank secrecy could become a way for the bank to avoid its own tax obligations. However, the information obtained may be used only against the bank and for no other purposes and particularly not against the bank's customer.

Other disclosures

Apart from the exceptions referred to above, some special situations 35-028 require disclosure of information.

Legal disputes with a customer

The existence of bank secrecy in such disputes depends on the kind 35-029 of situation, *i.e.*, on the position of the bank and the customer within the lawsuit.

If the customer institutes legal proceedings against the bank, the latter is no longer bound by bank secrecy. By bringing suit, the customer tacitly releases the bank from its secrecy obligation with regard to any facts directly related to the lawsuit.

Although the Banking Act does not contain any specific provisions on this matter, most authors are of the opinion that a customer who sues a bank and then insists that the bank abstain from disclosing facts covered by bank secrecy in defending its position would be acting against the general principle of good faith as set forth in article 2 of the Swiss Civil Code.

This means that a bank may disclose information that is necessary or useful for its defense without breaching its duty of confidentiality. Information unrelated to the dispute remains confidential.

In the opposite case, *i.e.*, if a bank institutes legal proceedings against a client, the legal situation is more complicated. The bank may disclose otherwise protected information only if specially justified in some manner, *e.g.*, in order to protect its legitimate interest. Therefore, in each individual case, the interests at stake must be taken into account.

As a rule, the bank must inform the customer in advance of its intention to bring an action against him or her. Once again, the disclosure of information is justified only if it is directly related to the dispute. As a general rule, in criminal proceedings, the bank may disclose the necessary facts since, in such cases, its legitimate interests are undoubtedly at stake.

In the most common case, the bank is involved as a third party claimant. The bank is involved in litigation between a client and a third party because it holds the assets which are the object of the dispute. In these cases, banks are supposed to protect their own interests and usually must be able to enforce preferential rights such as pledges, rights of set-off, or any other right arising from securities.

Swiss courts have stated that banks must disclose their interests in a timely manner if they wish to avoid forfeiture; hence, such disclosure is not a breach of bank secrecy. Notwithstanding the above, in cases of attachments granted in summary proceedings, such disclosure may be contrary to the interests of the client if made prematurely because, *inter alia*, it could furnish important information to the other party before it is even certain whether its claim is at all justified.

Disclosure to supervisory authorities

35-030   Swiss banks and Swiss branches of foreign banks must provide all information concerning their Swiss business to Swiss regulatory authorities. Those authorities are mainly the Swiss National Bank and the Banking Commission.

Both authorities may use the information disclosed to them only within the scope of their statutory functions, and their officers and employees are strictly bound by their own secrecy obligation.

Some cantonal regulations provide for further authorities with a similar controlling function, such as the Zürich Stock Exchange Commission. Officers and employees of those authorities also are bound by the bank secrecy provisions.

Furthermore, pursuant to article 18(1) of the Banking Act, banks must have their annual accounts audited by an independent, recognized bank-auditing company. Since the auditing company must verify the bank's compliance with a large number of provisions of banking law and related legislation, disclosure of information becomes unavoidable. Bank secrecy, however, extends to the auditing companies.

Since foreign branches of Swiss banks are not subject to the Swiss Banking Act, disclosure of relevant information to foreign authorities or auditing firms does not fall within the application scope of article 47 of the Banking Act but, rather, within the scope of the applicable foreign law.

RESTRICTIONS UNDER INTERNATIONAL JUDICIAL ASSISTANCE

International judicial assistance has become the most important limitation of the bank secrecy, besides the procedural provisions concerning the duty to testify, to furnish information, and to edit documents. 35-031

If, according to the provisions regarding judicial assistance, coercive actions in order to obtain information and documents are allowed, the bank secrecy is rescinded. Because of the direct nexus between these provisions and bank secrecy, a more detailed treatment of the requirements and modalities of such coercive actions grounded on judicial assistance is necessary.

Concept of mutual assistance

The obtaining of information is a way of exercising authority; thus, it cannot extend beyond the boundaries of the state which has vested the officials with their authority. 35-032

Everything that goes beyond those limits must be included in the general category of mutual assistance, which is any kind of activity by the authorities of one country to help the authorities of another in legal proceedings.

Like most countries, Switzerland grants mutual assistance to foreign courts or authorities on the basis of multinational conventions, bilateral treaties, declarations of reciprocity, or international customary law. As a general rule of procedure, the Federal Justice and Police Department first summarily examines the relevant requests and subsequently refers them to the competent cantonal judicial or administrative authority. Those authorities consider the applicable cantonal procedural rules and decide on the grant and scope of the mutual assistance.

Mutual assistance in civil matters

35-033   Like most European countries, Switzerland is a signatory to the Hague Convention of July 19, 1905 (as amended in 1954), concerning mutual assistance in civil matters.

Furthermore, Switzerland has entered into agreements with countries which are not parties to the Hague Convention. Moreover, Switzerland renders mutual assistance on the basis of reciprocity even if it is not obligated to do so by bilateral or multilateral treaties, provided no compulsory measures need be employed.

The Hague Convention

35-034   The Hague Convention, like other treaties addressing this form of cooperation, is restricted to regulation of the general prerequisites for mutual assistance.

The material extent of the cooperation is subject to the rules of the applicable national law. The precedence of national law over the provisions of the Convention is expressly provided in article 11(1). In the case of Switzerland, this means that the success of a mutual assistance application may depend on the terms of the applicable cantonal law, which could lead to a negative reply to having a banker testify in Geneva, whereas the same banker could have been compelled to testify in Basel.

In other words, no bank may be compelled to disclose information subject to bank secrecy which it would not be compelled to disclose under the applicable cantonal rules of civil procedure.

Mutual assistance in bankruptcy proceedings

35-035   Insofar as there are no international treaties, bankruptcy proceedings abroad have no effect in Switzerland. The foreign receiver in bankruptcy, thus, may not obtain information from Swiss banks without the consent of the bank customer.

As a consequence, the bankrupt client of a Swiss bank can (assuming the bankruptcy proceedings take place abroad) continue to control his or her bank accounts in Switzerland.

This situation caused very critical reactions from international forums since it chilled international economic cooperation. The Swiss Private International Law Statute departs, therefore, from the principle of territoriality and recognizes, in principle, foreign bankruptcy proceedings.

According to article 166 of the Private International Law Statute, a foreign bankruptcy decree that was issued in the country of the debtor's domicile may be recognized (under certain specified conditions) in Switzerland upon a motion by the foreign receiver in bankruptcy or by one of the creditors.

The recognition of a foreign bankruptcy decree leads to the debtor's assets in Switzerland becoming subject to the consequences of Swiss law - that is, a follow up bankruptcy proceeding is executed.[5]

However, only the Swiss authority executing the bankruptcy has the right to obtain information from the banks.

Difficult problems arise if there are neither international treaties nor follow-up bankruptcy proceedings and the bankrupt client is a corporation. If the corporate organ's power to act ceases to exist in case of bankruptcy, the view that the receiver in bankruptcy has no rights in Switzerland would lead to the result that neither the receiver in bankruptcy nor the organs may act for the company.

However, the latest position of Swiss authors tends to be that article 47 of the Banking Act could never apply to a Swiss bank that discloses information to the receiver in bankruptcy of a corporate customer since such a receiver should legally not be considered a third party, but the universal successor of the bankrupt customer's rights and obligations, including the right to information on and disposal over bank accounts.

Bankruptcy proceedings in France

As a result of the bilateral treaty between France and Switzerland of June 15, 1869, bankruptcy proceedings instituted in France put Swiss banks in the same position as if the proceedings had been instituted in Switzerland. **35-036**

The Federal Court has stated that banks holding assets of a client who has been declared bankrupt by French authorities are to furnish information to the trustee in bankruptcy and to French authorities if required to do so in order to complete the inventory of the bankruptcy.

Mutual assistance in criminal matters

The increase of criminal offenses related to drug trafficking and terrorism has led the authorities of most countries to try to prevent legal institutions such as bank secrecy from becoming an easy way **35-037** to cover up such illicit activities.

---

[5] See Swiss Private International Law Statute, article 170.

Until 1983, it was unpredictable whether compulsory measures could be taken because it was a domain of cantonal law. Even though such drastic procedures as house searches, seizures, and compulsory process were concerned, the legal status of the person involved and his right of appeal were unclear.

All of these matters were settled by the Swiss Legal Assistance Act of March 20, 1981, which - along with the ordinance of February 24, 1982, on Legal Assistance in Criminal Matters - entered into force on January 1, 1983.

Swiss Legal Assistance Act

35-038   The Legal Assistance Act governs not only extradition, as the prior law did, but also all kinds of international legal assistance in criminal matters.

It specifies the circumstances under which Switzerland can guarantee such assistance. Furthermore, it lays down general statutory guidelines for compulsory measures of mutual assistance.

35-039   **General provisions** In spite of the existence of the Legal Assistance Act, whether or not judicial assistance must be granted by Switzerland is still determined primarily by the provisions of applicable treaties.

The Legal Assistance Act does not oblige Switzerland to grant assistance to the requesting country beyond the assistance resulting from treaties. On the other hand, if no treaty applies or if a request is beyond Switzerland's treaty obligations, legal assistance still remains possible and may be granted under the provisions of the Legal Assistance Act.

The determination of whether or not Switzerland will grant legal assistance leading to the lifting of bank secrecy is subject to a special procedure in which the persons concerned, including the banks who are asked to provide information, are granted several possibilities of appeal to cantonal courts and to the Federal Supreme Court.

35-040   **Scope of application** Since the Legal Assistance Act refers to "criminal matters," it is necessary to clarify what is meant by that term. Article 1(3) of the Legal Assistance Act specifies that criminal matters are those proceedings in which, according to the laws of the country requesting legal assistance, a criminal court may intervene.

Therefore, proceedings in which the determination of whether the law was violated and the pronouncement of the decision are pure administrative matters and are excluded. However, if administrative proceedings can be challenged and can, therefore, become a criminal matter, legal assistance can be applied for.

In order to avoid double jeopardy, Switzerland normally will refuse judicial assistance if the incriminated person is staying in Switzerland and a Swiss proceeding concerning the same offense is pending.

General conditions of applicability As set forth in article 1(2) of the   35-041
Legal Assistance Act, protection of sovereignty, security, public order, or any other essential Swiss interests must be taken into account when applying the Act.

Banking secrecy belongs to these essential interests only if the requested information undermines the principle of secrecy or damages the whole Swiss economy.

Article 4 of the Legal Assistance Act allows the rejection of an application for legal assistance "if the gravity of the offense charged does not justify proceedings thereon."

As a general rule, article 8(1) of the Legal Assistance Act provides that a request for legal assistance will "generally be granted only when the requesting State guarantees reciprocity." However, this is not an absolute requirement. Article 8(2) details several exceptions which are not to be deemed an exhaustive list.

For example, reciprocity is not necessary for the service of court notifications, summonses or subpoenas or even for any other action if such granting "aids in the investigation of a crime committed against a Swiss citizen." The necessity of combating certain crimes through international cooperation is another situation where reciprocity may not be required.

The same protection granted by domestic procedural rules to witnesses bound by the professional secrecy obligation is granted within the scope of international legal assistance. Thus, as a result of the right of refusal to testify established in cantonal law, persons entitled to such rights cannot be obliged to furnish evidence to foreign authorities.

There is extensive protection of secrecy concerning persons "who according to the request (for legal assistance) are not a party to the criminal proceedings undertaken abroad. . . ".[6] Therefore, it can be said that protection of third parties is particularly strict.

In all these cases, witnesses may be compelled to disclose information only if it appears to be indispensable in order to clarify the facts of the case and if the gravity of the offense justifies it.

---

[6] Legal Assistance Act, article 10(1).

Judicial assistance will operate as an exception to bank secrecy only if coercive measures can be applied by the Swiss authorities because otherwise the bank is obliged to refuse to cooperate. However, under the Legal Assistance Act coercive measures are (as a rule) permissible only if the offense being prosecuted contains elements, other than intent or negligence, of an offense punishable under Swiss law (*i.e.*, it must be a criminal offense in both countries) unless the assistance is demanded only to exonerate an incriminated person.

The Legal Assistance Act excludes the prosecution of certain kinds of criminal offenses from legal assistance and gives priority to the applicability of Swiss law over legal assistance to the offense under prosecution.

35-042   *Excluded offenses* As a general rule, political, fiscal, and military offenses are excluded from legal assistance.

According to long-standing Federal Supreme Court case law, an offense is political if it is aimed directly against the power of the state, such as an attempt to overthrow a government by force through high treason or creation of a forbidden intelligence network. Bank connections often turn out to be necessary for the preparation of such crimes and for the storage or safekeeping of the resulting profits.

A political offense also may be an ordinary criminal act which serves political ends (political motivation is predominant), and which proves to be an appropriate means to attain those ends. However, reflecting current efforts to restrict the scope of political offenses and to refuse the protection of legal assistance for the use of violence, article 3(2) of the Legal Assistance Act states that crimes against humanity, genocide, or particularly repugnant crimes cannot be considered political offenses.

Non-fulfillment of military obligations and opposition to military discipline are considered military offenses, *i.e.*, crimes directed against a state's national defense or military power. In principle, they are excluded from legal assistance.

Fiscal offenses, in the broad sense of the term, are excluded from legal assistance by virtue of article 3(3) of the Legal Assistance Act. Switzerland rejects legal assistance if the offense "seems to be aimed at a reduction of taxes or if it violates provisions concerning currency, trade or economic policy measures".

Nevertheless, the Legal Assistance Act contains an important exception whereby a request for accessory legal assistance may be granted if the target of the proceeding is fiscal fraud.

According to article 24(1) of the Act, fiscal fraud shall be understood in the sense given to it by article 14(2) of the federal law on administrative criminal law, which states that fiscal fraud is an act of willful deceit on the part of the offender whereby "a substantial tax, contribution or other service is illegally withheld from the community or harms the latter in some other material way. . .".

Long-standing Federal Supreme Court case law shows that the concept of willful deceit in the provision on fraud means more than making use of a lie. Willful deceit consists of a series of lies, especially deceitful actions or artifices. The term particularly applies to those cases in which false or falsified documents are used for the purpose of tax evasion.

Article 24(2) of the Act provides that a request for legal assistance may not be rejected merely "because Swiss law does not provide for the same kind of tax or tax regulations". Article 24(3) requires the Federal Office for Police Matters or the cantonal executive tax authorities to obtain the opinion of the Federal Tax Administration "when there are doubts as to the features of the tax mentioned in the request. . .".

A fiscal offense, in the broad sense of the term, may lead indirectly to legal assistance if committing it involves an ordinary criminal offense such as falsification or bribery. For a common offense connected with a fiscal offense, known as the connected fiscal offense, Switzerland has always granted legal assistance on the condition that the information disclosed by Switzerland be used exclusively for the criminal proceedings which led to the assistance and under no circumstances for the prosecution of a political, military, or fiscal offense excluded from legal assistance. This is known in Swiss law as the principle of specialty of legal assistance.

Excluded proceedings Switzerland does not grant legal assistance if **35-043** the foreign legal proceedings requiring legal assistance do not meet certain constitutional standards or if they have any other noteworthy defects.

Article 2(a) of the Legal Assistance Act rules out legal assistance if the foreign proceedings "do not follow the procedural guidelines of the European Convention of November 4, 1950, for the protection of Human Rights and Fundamental Freedoms. . .".

The Convention requires, in particular, that the defendant be given sufficient opportunity to defend himself and that the final decision be handed down after public proceedings before an impartial court. This means, *inter alia*, that legal assistance is impossible if the proceedings are conducted and the decision rendered by ad hoc courts, which do not include special courts, *e.g.*, courts such as military courts or traffic courts that are established by the Constitution or general statutes to judge specific criminal offenses or special groups of people.

Switzerland does not grant legal assistance if the foreign proceedings violate the principle of equality before the law and "are undertaken in order to prosecute or punish a person because of his political views, membership of a certain social group, race, religion, or ethnic origin. . ." as set forth in article 2(b) of the Legal Assistance Act, or if the proceedings "could lead to a deterioration in the accused person's situation for one of the reasons mentioned under letter b. . ." as article 2(c) foresees. These provisions are obviously inspired by article 3(2) of the European Convention on Extradition of 1957.

35-044   *Priority of sub judice or terminated proceedings* Article 5(1) of the Legal Assistance Act excludes legal assistance if the offense charged in the state requesting assistance has already been tried or if proceedings have already begun in Switzerland or in the country where the offense was committed.

The Swiss authorities also are entitled to refuse legal assistance if the penal sanctions imposed by any state have already been executed.

35-045   *Statute of limitations* If providing legal assistance means that the Swiss authorities will be forced to take compulsory measures, the granting of legal assistance is excluded under the terms of article 5(1) of the Legal Assistance Act if the offense could not be prosecuted in Switzerland due to the Swiss statute of limitations or if a sentence handed down for the offense could not be executed in Switzerland.

International conventions on legal assistance in criminal matters

35-046   Two international conventions are important when referring to the international scope of legal assistance in Switzerland, namely the European Convention on Legal Assistance signed in Strasbourg in 1959 (hereinafter the "ECLA") and the Swiss-American treaty which has been in force since 1977 (hereinafter the "Treaty").

Both documents start from a common basis and have several provisions in common. Most of the contents of both conventions are quite similar to the material provisions of the Swiss Legal Assistance Act, so there are few compatibility problems when simultaneously applying national and international legislation.

35-047   **Common principles in the ECLA and the Treaty** Both legal instruments foresee in their respective article 1 that a judge will be entitled to discharge a witness from his or her confidentiality duty if an application for legal assistance from a signatory party has been presented within the framework of the prosecution of a common crime. However, this is a general principle with some exceptions and limits.

Like the Swiss Legal Assistance Act, both conventions refuse to grant legal assistance if the proceedings are related to political, fiscal, or military matters.

As a consequence of the exception of legal assistance in connection with political, fiscal, or military matters, and linked with the general principles set forth by the Swiss Legal Assistance Act, Switzerland made a reservation in both conventions concerning the specialty principle, by virtue of which Switzerland requires the authorities benefiting from the letter rogatory to abstain from using the acquired information for any purpose other than the one for which legal assistance was granted, and particularly for no political, fiscal, or military matter.

When it became a signatory of the ECLA, Switzerland abandoned the double incrimination principle, according to which legal assistance is to be granted only when the offense for which assistance is requested is punishable both in the requesting and in the granting country. Because it abandoned this principle, Switzerland may grant legal assistance in relation to prosecution of crimes which are not punished in Switzerland. However, in such cases, coercive measures will not be executed by Swiss authorities.[7]

Special provisions of the Treaty The treaty, which has been in force **35-048** since 1977, is much more detailed than the ECLA, but it contains the same principles.

The efforts to conclude a bilateral treaty on legal assistance in criminal matters between the United States and Switzerland date to the period prior to World War II. At that time, the differences between the two legal systems rendered the achievement of an agreement impossible. After Switzerland became a party to the ECLA in 1966, the idea of a bilateral Swiss-American treaty was relaunched, although there were still problems deriving from the huge differences between the two countries' legal systems.

It took the negotiating parties more than five years to reach a compromise combining the Anglo-Saxon and Civil Law systems, particularly because of the problems in delimiting the scope of the treaty, i.e., in defining "criminal matter".

As in every treaty, each party had to concede certain points. However, the Swiss delegation was able to achieve some concessions, partly because the negotiations had as their starting point the

[7] See ECLA, article 5(1), and Swiss Reservation, the Treaty, article 4, respectively.

draft prepared by Swiss experts (which had already been used as background for the ECLA).

The main features of the treaty are that it includes all aspects of accessory legal aid, is based upon the ECLA, and generally corresponds to well-established Swiss legal practice in these matters.

According to its article 1(1), the Treaty applies to investigation or court proceedings concerning offenses which fall within the jurisdiction of the requesting country or its member states. Jurisdiction of the member states had to be mentioned because criminal procedure in the United States is still mainly a matter of state rather than federal law.

The most important differences between the Treaty and the ECLA are the following:

35-049   *General procedure for common crimes* Special protection for third parties - In connection with bank confidentiality, secrecy affecting uninvolved third parties will be lifted only if all of the following requirements are fulfilled:

(1) The crime for which legal assistance is requested is a grave one;
(2) The disclosure of secret bank information is important for the articles of evidence, and
(3) Appropriate efforts have been made in the United States to obtain the information by other means but no results have been achieved.

This provision is, therefore, a balance between the interest of the United States in having information available when prosecuting a grave crime and the interest of Switzerland in keeping its bank secrecy untouched, with the sole exception of obligations deriving from its duty to collaborate against international crime.

The protection of the private sphere - The Sixth Amendment of the American Constitution was an obstacle to the requirements of Swiss representatives since that amendment entitles the accused to a public trial, whereas Switzerland required American authorities to keep the disclosed information secret.

Only an informal solution could be found. Through the correspondence sent by the American ambassador to Swiss authorities within the framework of the treaty, American authorities undertake to reduce the publicity of the acquired information as far as possible.

Presence of American representative - Swiss authorities will allow the presence of such a representative only if it is essential; otherwise, the interrogation will be carried out exclusively by Swiss authorities.

General safeguard clause - If legal assistance threatens national security, sovereignty, or any other essential interest of the requested state, legal assistance may be refused. In principle, bank secrecy does not fall within this clause.

Appearance of witnesses - The requesting state may, under certain circumstances, ask a witness to appear before its own jurisdiction; however, this appearance is not compulsory. Furthermore, the treaty expressly states that the person appearing before the authorities of the requesting state may not be compelled to testify about facts protected by bank secrecy within the framework referred to by article 25 of the treaty.

This kind of provision, which is unique among the international treaties to which the United States is a party, represents a tacit recognition by American authorities of Swiss bank secrecy.

Special procedure in prosecution of organized crime In chapter II of **35-050** the treaty, special provisions are made in order to allow somewhat more far-reaching legal assistance for the prosecution of members of organized crime.

Organized crime is defined as

> ". . . an association or group of persons combined together for a substantial or indefinite period for the purposes of obtaining monetary or commercial gains or profits for itself or for others, wholly or in part by illegal means, and of protecting its illegal activities against criminal prosecution."

The special features of legal assistance in such cases are, according to article 2(2)(a) of the treaty, that in exceptional cases political offenses and violations of antitrust laws may be prosecuted if these acts were committed in support of the purposes of an organized criminal group. (Political offenses must be mentioned because interference with election and voting rights, political bribery, and manipulation of elections are some of the means by which organized crime seeks to gain political influence). Furthermore, if the special provisions of article 7 (mentioned below) are satisfied, legal assistance for tax offenses also is permitted.

Article 5(2)(c) allows the use of information and materials which were obtained through legal assistance in proceedings against persons who are members of organized crime.

According to article 7(1), compulsory measures may be employed for this special legal assistance even if the offense in question is not punishable in Switzerland; however, this applies only if "the securing of the information or evidence is not possible without the cooperation of the authorities in the requested State, or . . . it would place unreasonable burdens on the requesting State . . .".[8]

Procedurally, in all cases related to organized crime, article 8(1) stipulates that the requesting state shall furnish to the requested state "information in its possession on the basis of which such suspicion, conclusion, or opinion has been arrived at." The identity of the persons providing the information can be kept secret.

The effects of special provisions for organized crime upon bank secrecy are not especially significant, with two exceptions. First, if a bank is not willing to provide requested information, compulsory measures can be employed against it even if the offense concerned is not punishable in Switzerland.[9]

According to article 7(2), a bank is obligated to provide information in legal assistance proceedings against leading members of organized crime, even when the act committed is only tax evasion - which, however, is punishable by imprisonment under United States law.

Apart from these two exceptions, a bank's position in special legal assistance proceedings is the same as in any other proceeding requested in accordance with the Treaty.

Information exchange in tax matters

Without treaty

35-051   Besides the fact that legal assistance constitutes an administrative procedure under Swiss law (even in criminal matters), no legal assistance involving fiscal information is to be granted if no treaty applies.

General provisions in double taxation treaties

35-052   The issue of personal privacy protection in tax matters is especially significant in those bilateral treaties intended to avoid double taxation.

8 Treaty, article 7(3).
9 *Id.*, article 7(1).

Most of those treaties provide for the protection of commercial, professional, and industrial secrets. The conventions with France, Germany, and Denmark provide expressly for the protection of bank secrecy, whereas the ones concluded with Great Britain and the United States do not. However, this omission does not matter since the protection of commercial secrets in the treaties with Great Britain and the United States includes protection of bank secrecy.

Switzerland has a long standing policy of granting the exchange of information only for the purposes of applying the double taxation treaty, but not for the assessment of taxes covered by the treaty as long as the taxpayer has not claimed any treaty benefits. The exchange of information being an administrative procedure, the same restrictions apply as for domestic purposes; bank secrecy is, therefore, preserved.

The Swiss-American Treaty for avoidance of double taxation

In article 16, Swiss and American authorities agreed to exchange the information necessary to avoid tax frauds. This provision did not have much effect until the Swiss Federal Supreme Court held, on December 23, 1970, that this obligation would be enforced even if the lifting of bank secrecy was necessary. **35-053**

However, the provision has no practical importance anymore because the whole subject is covered by the Legal Assistance Act.

INSIDER TRADING

Even though insider trading has been a criminal offense since July 1, 1988, and therefore receives the same treatment as criminal matters in general, its particular legal nature justifies this separate section. **35-054**

Under article 161 of the Swiss Penal Code, any director, manager, auditor, attorney, or agent of a company or a cooperative or an entity controlling it or controlled by it, and any member of the government or an agency or a public servant or any auxiliary person thereof may be considered an insider.

Persons directly or indirectly informed by an insider are considered tippees if they knew or should have known that the information was illegally disclosed by the insider.

Disclosure and use of inside information is punishable only if it refers to shares, stock certificates, bonds, debentures, or any other negotiable instruments or rights issued by Swiss or foreign companies listed on an official stock exchange or an official second market in Switzerland or even if it concerns options for the purchase or sale of such securities. Information is considered to be inside information if the following requirements are fulfilled:

(1) It is confidential;
(2) It refers to a planned issue of securities, a merger, or any other transaction of comparable significance, and
(3) It can be foreseen that its disclosure to the public will directly affect the price or the transaction itself.

There are three types of insider trading crime:

(1) Disclosure to third persons for a profit;
(2) Own use of information for purpose of obtaining own profit, and
(3) Own use of information for purpose of causing third parties to obtain a profit.

The penalties are stiff and range from a fine to imprisonment of up to three years.

Banks have been affected by the introduction of insider trading in the Swiss Penal Code to the extent that bank secrecy can be lifted in domestic insider trading cases of a criminal nature as well as in judicial assistance proceedings concerning such crimes.

Legal assistance in insider trading cases related to the United States receive somewhat special treatment by virtue of the memorandum of understanding dated November 10, 1987, and signed by both parties within the framework of the treaty. In this memorandum, Switzerland agreed to grant assistance in so-called "civil proceedings" concerning insider trading conducted by the United States Securities and Exchange Commission.

DUE DILIGENCE AGREEMENT

35-055 In 1977, the Swiss banks and their professional organization, the Swiss Bankers' Association, responding to discrete pressure from Swiss authorities, in 1977 entered into the Agreement on the Observance of Care by the Banks in Accepting Funds and on the Practice of Banking Service (hereafter the "Agreement") which has been amended and renewed several times.

The Agreement is a convention containing the standards of behavior expected from Swiss banks. It is no more than a transcription of the rules which had governed bankers' behavior prior to that date.

The preamble of the Agreement establishes that the goal of the convention is the preservation of the well-known reputation of Swiss banks as well as the financial status of Switzerland itself. Banks are free to refuse to join the Agreement, but all of them have joined.

Obligations of the banks

The obligations imposed on the banks signatory to the Agreement 35-056 are mainly as follows:

(1) Knowledge of the identity of their clients - The Agreement requires the banks to ascertain the identity of their clients on a systematic basis. Even lawyers opening accounts on behalf of clients have to disclose the name of the beneficial owner unless the account is closely connected to legal work. As a result, if a lawyer is used only for the purpose of protecting the identity of the beneficial owner by the attorney-client privilege as an additional screen, the banker must refuse to open the account or lease a safe-deposit box if no disclosure of the identity of the last beneficiary follows.

(2) Refusal of funds with criminal origin - If they suspect that funds which are about to be deposited into an account have a criminal origin, bankers are obliged by the Agreement to refuse to open an account or to keep such funds.

(3) Assistance in capital flight and tax fraud - The agreement, even stronger since a revision in 1982, prohibits the banks from maintaining accounts for persons and companies known by the bank to use their accounts professionally to assist capital flight or tax evasion. The prohibition extends to the renting of safe-deposit boxes; the Agreement requires the banks to rent such facilities only to persons whose trustworthiness gives no cause for doubt.

Verification of compliance with the Agreement is the responsibility of the bank controlling authority, which may impose a fine not to exceed SFr. 10-million for non-compliance.

Effect on bank secrecy

35-057   The existence of the agreement does not modify the scope and extent of bank secrecy. The obligations imposed on the banks refer to disclosure of information, if any, only vis-à-vis Swiss bank controlling authorities, which have the right to be provided with such information anyway and which, moreover, are subject to their own bank secrecy obligation.

The real goal of the Agreement is to assure that banks know the underlying reality of their business; the goal is not the easier disclosure of information to Swiss or foreign authorities, especially tax authorities.

CONCLUSION

35-058   As can be seen from the preceding sections, Swiss bank secrecy is not as absolute as people outside Switzerland tend to believe.

Like every democratic state, Switzerland must constantly try to strike a balance between individual rights and the interest of the community so that stability can be maintained. Due to Switzerland's historical development and the political system, the traditionally high importance of individual rights is still embodied in the public mind and can thus be preserved in the legal system to a larger degree than in most other countries.

However, Switzerland's interest in keeping its long-cherished bank secrecy does not prevent it from complying with the requirements that the ever-changing worldwide community expects it to respect in connection with international cooperation and joint development. There is definitely a tendency to lift bank secrecy more easily than in the past, particularly in view of the growing need for transnational cooperation in combating international and organized crime.

The description of the actual content of Switzerland's bank secrecy shows that it cannot simply be condemned as an institution that protects criminal persons. Rather, Switzerland is willing not to sacrifice a worthy principle, but to regulate its use in order to avoid isolated cases in which bank secrecy could be used for illegitimate purposes.

APPENDIX

Unofficial translations of relevant parts of certain Swiss statutes and regulations:

35-059

Swiss Banking Secrecy

(Article 47 of the Federal Law on Banks and Saving Banks of November 8, 1934, as amended)

35-060

1. Whosoever discloses a secret that has been entrusted to him or of which he has received knowledge in his capacity as officer, employee, agent, liquidator or commissioner of a bank, as representative of the Federal Banking Commission or as officer or employee of a recognized auditing firm, or whosoever attempts to induce somebody else to commit such a violation of professional secrecy, shall be punished with imprisonment up to six months or with a fine amounting up to 50,000 francs.
2. If the act has been committed by negligence, the penalty shall consist of a fine up to 30,000 francs.
3. The violation of professional secrecy remains punishable beyond the termination of the official or professional relationship, or the exercise of the profession.
4. Remaining reserved are federal and cantonal provisions concerning the duty to testify in court to give information to a government authority.

Insider Transactions

(Article 161 of the Swiss Penal Code of 1937, as amended)

35-061

Taking advantage of knowledge of confidential facts

1. Whosoever as a member of the board of directors, of the management, of the auditing entity or as delegate of a joint stock company or of a controlling or of a controlled company thereof, as a member of a public authority or as an official, or as an aide of any of the aforementioned persons, takes for himself or provides for others a material benefit by taking advantage of knowledge of confidential facts or passes such facts on to a third party and such facts, by virtue of having become public knowledge anticipate a

considerable influence on the price of shares, other forms of securities or respective book securities or of related options of a given company traded in Switzerland on or outside exchanges will be subject to punishment by imprisonment or a fine.

2. Whosoever receives knowledge of such facts from anyone mentioned under paragraph 1 above, either directly or indirectly and provides himself or others with a material benefit by taking advantage of such communication will be subject to imprisonment of up to one year or a fine.

3. As fact in the sense of paragraphs 1 and 2 above apply the imminent issue of new equity rights, a merger or acquisition or similar facts of comparable consequence.

4. In the event of a merger or acquisition between two joint stock companies, paragraphs 1-3 apply to both companies.

5. Paragraphs 1-4 find similar application if taking advantage of confidential facts refers to share certificates, other securities, book claims, or respective options of a cooperative or of a foreign company.

Economic Espionage

35-062   (Article 273 of the Swiss Penal Code)

Whosoever obtains a manufacturing or business secret in order to make it available to a foreign public authority or foreign organization or to a private organization or to its agents, whosoever makes available a manufacturing or business secret to a foreign public authority or foreign organization or to a private organization or to its agents, shall be punished with imprisonment or, in severe cases, with penal servitude. In conjunction with detention a fine may be imposed.

Money Laundering

35-063   (Articles 305 bis of the Swiss Penal Code)

1. Whosoever undertakes actions which lend themselves to defeat the ascertainment of origin, the discovery or collection of assets which, as he knows or must assume, emanate from crime, will be subject to punishment by imprisonment or a fine.

2. In severe cases punishment is penal servitude up to five years or imprisonment. Added to this penalty of detention is a fine of up to 1-million francs. A severe case is if the perpetrator:

   a) acts as a member of a criminal organization;
   b) acts as a member of a criminal organization whose purpose is the continued practice of money laundering;
   c) realizes a large turnover or considerable profit from professional money laundering activities.

3. The perpetrator will also be subject to sentencing if he commits the principal act of violation abroad and such act is also punishable in the place of perpetration.

Lack of Due Diligence in Financial Transactions

Whosoever professionally accepts, keeps in safe custody, assists in the investment or transfer of assets which are the property of others and fails to apply the relative due diligence called for in establishing the identity of the economic beneficiary, is subject to punishment by imprisonment of up to one year or a fine. **35-064**

Note - The draft of this report is based on the following publications: Aubert/Kernen/Schönle, *Das Schweizerische Bankgeheimnis* (Bern, 1978); Aubert, *Le secret bancaire en droit suisse* (Basle, 1979); Steiner, *Switzerland: Bank Confidentiality*, Neate/McCormick ed.,.(London/Boston, 1990); Schultz, *Banking Secrecy and Mutual Assistance in Criminal Matters* (Switzerland, 1983); Schultz, *Banking Secrecy and the Swiss-American Treaty on Legal Assistance in Criminal Matters* (Switzerland, 1977); Swiss Bankers' Association, *Secrecy in Swiss Banking* (Basle, 1984).

UNITED STATES

Melanie Rovner Cohen
James E. Carroll
Terry Robin Horwitz Kass
Altheimer & Gray
Chicago, Illinois

Chapter 36

UNITED STATES

INTRODUCTION

This chapter examines the bank secrecy laws of the United States as **36-001** they apply to individuals, entities, and financial institutions. The chapter begins with brief descriptions of various statutes governing bank secrecy, money laundering and the right to financial privacy.

The United States imposes fines and other penalties for violating various currency reporting and recordkeeping requirements. Such requirements are described in some detail.

Many different acts fall into the category of money laundering. The crime of money laundering and its elements are examined quite extensively. In addition, the role of financial institutions in the crime of money laundering is also examined. This chapter addresses enforcement of United States bank secrecy laws by both the United States Department of the Treasury and the United States Justice Department. The impact of enforcement of bank secrecy laws on United States financial institutions also is considered.

Finally, the chapter probes the current view of the effectiveness of the United States bank secrecy laws, which are commended while the supporting statistics are criticized.

History and purpose of United States banking laws

The Bank Secrecy Act

36-002   On October 26, 1970, the United States Congress enacted the Bank Secrecy Act and the Currency and Foreign Transactions Reporting Act[1] (the "Records Act").

The Records Act requires financial institutions to make reports and keep records. Such requirements are designed to identify the sources, volumes and movements of United States currency being transported into and out of the United States through financial institutions. These records and reports result in an audit trail for law enforcement agencies to use in the detection and investigation of criminal activities.

Title I of the Records Act (Financial Recordkeeping) requires financial institutions to make and retain certain records.[2] Title II of the Records Act, The Currency and Foreign Transactions Reporting Act, commonly known as the Bank Secrecy Act, requires financial institutions and individuals to report certain domestic and foreign financial transactions to the federal government.[3]

Criminal and civil penalties, as well as civil forfeiture, may result from the failure to comply. Congress enacted the original Bank Secrecy Act in part to reduce white-collar crime by improving the detection and investigation of regulatory, tax and criminal violations. Prior to the Bank Secrecy Act, some Americans used foreign bank accounts to avoid United States taxes on money earned in the United States and to hide money obtained from illegal transactions.

However, the Bank Secrecy Act, as it originally was created, was not completely successful in curbing the use of foreign bank accounts to avoid compliance with United States laws. In 1986, organized crime in America netted income in excess of US $67-billion.[4]

---

[1] Pub. L. No. 91-508, 84 Stat. 1114, 1118 (1970), as amended (codified in scattered sections of 12 U.S.C. and 31 U.S.C.).

[2] Title I appears as 12 U.S.C. 1730d, 1829b and 1951-1959. The requirements under Title I are not covered in this chapter.

[3] Title II formerly appeared as 31 U.S.C.S. 1051 *et seq.*, prior to the enactment of Title 31 into positive law by Act September 13, 1982, Pub. Law 97-258, 1, 96 Stat. 995; similar provisions now appear as amended 31 U.S.C. 5311-5326. The requirements under Title II are covered *supra*.

[4] Wharton Econometric Forecasting Associates, Inc., *The Income of Organized Crime* (1986), reprinted in President's Commission on Organized Crime, Report to the President and the Attorney General, *The Impact: Organized Crime Today* 413 (1986).

Each year, between US $5-billion and US $15-billion in illegal drug money earned in the United States moves into international financial channels.[5]

Due to the purchases of United States equities by Latin American and Caribbean investors increasing 250 per cent from 1984 to 1985, it was feared that narcotics traffickers controlled enormous amounts of United States government securities. Such equities reached a total of US $1.7-billion in 1985.

Similarly, investments in government bonds reached US $4.3-billion, representing a three-fold increase during that time. Flight capital and drug trafficking are equally plausible explanations for this surge; however, the proportionate share due to each is unknown.

Money Laundering Control Act

The ability to move and hide its enormous profits is crucial to the current success of organized crime. The concealing of a paper trail connecting funds to the illegal source from which they were obtained is known as money laundering.[6]

36-003

On October 27, 1986, President Reagan signed the Money Laundering Control Act of 1986[7] (MLCA) into law as part of the Anti-Drug Abuse Act of 1986.[8] The MLCA was enacted to prevent the Bank Secrecy Act from being circumvented by money launderers.

The MLCA codified the following primary recommendations of the President's Commission on Organized Crime:

(1) That money laundering be made a substantial criminal offense, and

(2) That the Right to Financial Privacy Act be amended to facilitate the flow of information from financial institutions to enforcement authorities, and

(3) That new money-laundering offenses be given extra territorial effect.[9]

---

[5] President's Commission on Organized Crime, Interim Report to the President and the Attorney General, *The Cash Connection: Organized Crime, Financial Institutions and Money Laundering* 13 (1984).

[6] The crime of money laundering is discussed in the text at paragraph 36-009.

[7] Subtitle H of Title 1 of the Anti-Drug Abuse Act of 1986, Pub. L No. 99-570, 100 Stat. 3207 (introduced September 8, 1986 as H.R. 5484) (codified as amended in scattered sections of 18 U.S.C. and 31 U.S.C.).

[8] Pub. L. No. 99-570.

[9] President's Commission on Organized Crime Interim Report to the President and the Attorney General, the Cash Connection: *Organized Crime, Financial Institutions, and Money Laundering* 13 (1984).

The MLCA performs four basic functions. First, it makes criminal any financial transactions involving the proceeds of crime. Second, it also raises the seriousness of asset tracing and forfeiture of those convicted. Third, the MLCA addresses the same issues on an international level. Fourth, the MLCA strengthens the importance attached to the currency reports and the requirements of the Internal Revenue Code and the Bank Secrecy Act.

While addressing the international drug problem, the MLCA recognizes other nations' sovereign interest in the financial affairs of their citizens. The MLCA adopts the criminal laws of other nations prohibiting the manufacture, importation, sale, or distribution of controlled substances.

First, the various money-laundering offenses prohibit the laundering of proceeds from narcotics trafficking committed in violation of the laws of another nation.

Second, the civil forfeiture of assets found in the United States, representing the proceeds of drug trafficking conducted in violation of foreign laws, are available to foreign nations through American courts.

Right to Financial Privacy Act

36-004 The Right to Financial Privacy Act of 1978[10] ("Privacy Act") was enacted to restore the balance between the commonly asserted right to privacy of an individual and the need for enforcement of banking laws.

The name of the Privacy Act is misleading in light of the fact that Congress opted for enumerated procedural safeguards in lieu of creating a substantive and legally enforceable right of financial privacy.

While the Privacy Act originally was intended to provide banking customers with a reasonable amount of protection from government intrusion into their financial records, it enumerates the process available for federal agencies to legally access a customer's account information.

Access is conditioned upon obtaining only one of the following: customer authorization, administrative subpoena or summons, search warrant, judicial subpoena, grand jury subpoena, or formal written agency request. Absent one of the aforementioned, disclosure is prohibited.

---

[10] 12 U.S.C. 3400-3422.

Therefore, if the government or its agents fail to fulfill any Privacy Act requirement, the financial institution is forbidden from complying with the disclosure request. The requesting agency also is required to certify that it is in compliance with certain notification requirements in providing customers with notification prior to disclosure. A description of the records and a general statement of the inquirer's response is included in proper notification.

Information on how a customer may judicially challenge the requested disclosure also must be provided. However, challenges are limited to objections based on the relevancy of the requested records or whether the agency did not substantially comply with the Privacy Act's notification requirements.

Amendments to the Privacy Act clarify circumstances under which customer notification is not required or may be delayed. The Financial Institutions Reform, Recovery, and Enforcement Act of 1989 amended the Privacy Act such that the notification requirements of the Privacy Act are inapplicable when a grand jury is investigating a suspected violation against a bank or its supervisory agency.

In such a circumstance, disclosure by a financial institution that it was served a grand jury subpoena is strictly prohibited. Such disclosure could result in both criminal and civil penalties.

The Privacy Act was previously amended in 1986 to specify exactly what information a bank could reveal to the government about a suspected violation. A bank may furnish the requesting agency with only specific limited information such as: identifying information about the suspected perpetrator by a name; the type of suspected infraction; and information regarding the affected accounts. Moreover, a bank must act in good faith when making disclosures to a government agency.

There are many exceptions to the application of the Privacy Act. The Privacy Act is inapplicable with regard to records not identified with particular customers. Nor does the Privacy Act apply to records required pursuant to the exercise of supervisory or regulatory authority. Various other classes of records, such as those requested by subpoena or court order issued in conjunction with a grand jury proceeding, also are outside the scope of the Privacy Act. Since corporations do not to have privacy rights, the Privacy Act does not protect the records of corporations.

The Privacy Act does not authorize withholding financial information that is required to be reported under any federal statute or rule promulgated thereunder. The MLCA identifies three specific pieces of information that may be disclosed without fear of private suits:

(1) The name or other identifying information relating to any individual involved in the conduct of a suspect transaction;

(2) Any account number or other identifying information concerning the account involved, and

(3) The nature of any suspected illegal activity.

Any disclosure on the part of the disclosing bank is entirely voluntary. Financial institutions providing voluntary disclosure are granted a limited "good faith defense." The principal shortcoming of the Privacy Act is its failure to provide substantial financial privacy. Protection is afforded only to individuals of partnerships of less than six members.

Another limitation is that the application is limited to federal agencies. State and local agencies, organizations, and private individuals are not required to comply. Recognition of financial privacy at the state level flows from three sources: state constitutions, state financial privacy legislation, and a Common Law duty of financial confidentiality.

A Common Law duty of financial confidentiality has been recognized by a number of state courts. The principle theory behind this duty is based on an implied contract between a customer and his chosen financial institution. None of the states whose courts recognize the right to financial privacy have substantively fashioned the right by statute.

SCOPE AND REQUIREMENTS OF UNITED STATES BANKING LAWS

36-005   The Bank Secrecy Act authorizes the Secretary of the Treasury to require financial institutions to keep specific records of certain foreign and domestic transactions.

The subject transactions are those the Secretary deems as useful in criminal, tax, or regulatory investigations or proceedings. Among other transactions, all domestic and foreign currency transactions of more than US $10,000 must be reported within 15 days. The scope of the reporting requirements was broadened in order to allow earlier apprehension of offenders before they leave the United States. Congress modified the requirements to compel a report when one is about to transport a monetary instrument, rather than when one actually attempts transportation.

The Bank Secrecy Act does not compel financial institutions to report suspicious transactions that do not exceed US $10,000 when aggregated. However, the Privacy Act, as amended, provides clear authority for financial institutions to report information regarding such transactions without fear of civil liability under the Right to Financial Privacy Act that requires prior notice to the customer before disclosure of a customer's financial records.

As amended, the Privacy Act provides that it shall not preclude any financial institution, or any officer, employee, or agent of a financial institution, from notifying a government authority that such institution, or officer, employee, or agent has information that may be relevant to a possible violation of any statute or regulation. Such information may include only the name or other identifying information concerning any individual or account in and the nature of any suspected illegal activity.[11]

In addition, the Privacy Act clearly exempts institutions from liability to the customer under federal, state, or local law, either for disclosure or the failure to notify the customer of disclosure. Banks have several substantial reasons for making such disclosures voluntarily. There is the need for prompt disclosure to assist in discovering and apprehending money launderers.

Furthermore, an officer's or employee's failure to make further inquiry regarding suspicious transactions or to call such transactions to the attention of law enforcement authorities may later constitute evidence of the institution's intent to violate the Bank Secrecy Act.

In contrast, efforts by an institution to bring the suspicious transaction promptly to the attention of the authorities indicates the institution's lack of intent to violate the Bank Secrecy Act. Another consideration in making a voluntary disclosure of suspicious transactions to law enforcement agencies is the prevention of federal supervisory agencies from requiring reports of possible Bank Secrecy Act violations.

Bank Secrecy Act reports

The Bank Secrecy Act requires reports to be made on transactions **36-006** involving the transfer of currency from one person or entity to another. Currently, four primary types of reports must be filed under the Bank Secrecy Act and the implementing regulations promulgated thereunder.

The first is the Currency Transaction Report (CTR). Financial institutions, other than casinos, must file a CTR (also known as Internal Revenue Service (IRS) Form 4789) for "each deposit, with-

---

[11] 12 U.S.C. 3403(c).

drawal, exchange of currency, or other payment of transfer, by, through, or to such financial institution which involves a transaction in currency of more than $10,000."[12]

The Bank Secrecy Act was amended to clarify that a CTR must contain the identity of the person on whose behalf the transaction was conducted.[13] Certain transactions by specific categories of customers (generally retailers, restaurants, and similar enterprises) are exempt from the CTR filing requirements.

The Currency Transaction Report by Casinos (CTRC) is the second type of required report. A CTRC (also known as IRS Form 8362) is a casino's equivalent to other financial institution's CTR.

The third type of report is the Report of International Transportation of Currency or Monetary Instruments (CMIR). Every person or entity must file a CMIR (also known as Customs Form 4790) who "physically transports, mails, or ships, or causes to be physically transported, mailed, or shipped, currency or other monetary instruments in an aggregate amount exceeding $10,000 on any one occasion,"[14] regardless of whether that transportation is into or out of the United States.

A CMIR also is required by a person who receives in excess of US $10,000 in the aggregate, in United States currency or other monetary instruments from outside the United States, on which no CMIR was filed.

The fourth type of required report is the Report of Foreign Bank and Financial Accounts (FBAR). A FBAR (also known as a Treasury Form TDF 90-22.1), applies to persons subject to the jurisdiction of the United States, including a United States citizen residing abroad. A FBAR must be filed by a person who, at any time during a given year, has a financial interest in, or signature or other authority over one or more bank accounts, security accounts, or any other financial accounts in foreign countries, if the aggregate value of those accounts exceeds US $10,000.

In addition, the Treasury imposes special reporting requirements on domestic financial institutions. This occurs when it is deemed appropriate in order to obtain information on certain transactions between those institutions and foreign financial agencies. Moreover, financial institutions are required by the Bank Secrecy Act to maintain, for a five-year period, a variety of records, such as copies of signature cards, bank statements, and checks drawn for more than US $100.

---

[12] 31 C.F.R. 103.22(a)(1) (1987).
[13] 31 C.F.R. 103.27 (1987).
[14] 31 C.F.R. 103.23(a) (1987).

Additional requirements

In addition to the four types of reports mentioned above, agencies **36-007** are required to establish regulations requiring the financial institutions they regulate to create and maintain procedures designed to assure and monitor compliance with the Bank Secrecy Act.

The Bank Secrecy Act also authorizes agencies to issue monetary penalties and cease and desist orders for financial institutions that fail to comply with regulations or fail to correct problems with regard to its procedures after being notified of the problems.

The MLCA amended provisions relating to supervisory compliance requirements under two other federal acts, the Change in Bank Control Act[15] and the Change in Savings and Loan Control Act.[16] Banking agencies are authorized under the MLCA to disapprove changes of control of financial institutions within their jurisdictions.

One reason Congress enacted the MLCA was to prevent dishonest persons, such as those with a history of insider abuse or those who have a criminal background, from controlling financial institutions.

Furthermore, the MLCA requires the Secretary of the Treasury, working with the Federal Reserve Board, to initiate discussions with central banks as well as appropriate government officials of other countries to create an information exchange system to assist cooperating countries in their efforts to eliminate the international flow of money derived from criminal activities such as illicit drug operations.

The Secretary of the Treasury, in consultation with the Board of Governors of the Federal Reserve System, also is required by the Act to conduct a study of money laundering through foreign branches of domestic institutions.

MONEY LAUNDERING

The MLCA was drafted to combat the increase in money launder- **36-008** ing. In the late 1980s, it was estimated that in excess of US $300-bil-

---

15 Pub. L. No. 95-630, 92 Stat. 3641 (1978) (codified in scattered sections of 12 U.S.C.).
16 *Id.*

lion was annually generated from the sale of illegal drugs world-wide. More than US $110-billion supposedly came from the United States.[17]

The enactment of the MLCA in 1986 created new federal money-laundering crimes. There are three categories of laundering offenses; they are conducting or attempting to conduct:

(1) Financial transactions involving the proceeds of specific unlawful activity;
(2) The international transportation of proceeds of specific unlawful activity, and
(3) Monetary transactions involving property constituting, or derived from, the proceeds obtained from a criminal offense.

The first two categories often are grouped together under the heading of "Money Laundering Crimes", while the last is considered a "Monetary Transaction Crime". Avoiding transaction reporting requirements under state or federal law is also a crime under the MLCA.

The money laundering crime

36-009 The money laundering crime involves promoting "specific unlawful activity," a term of art used to describe crimes commonly associated with narcotics trafficking, financial misconduct and organized crime.

Although the MLCA does not provide a definition for the term "proceeds", such proceeds must be generated by specific unlawful activity. The MLCA seizes for the proceeds of more than 30 criminal offenses, ranging from espionage to trading with the enemy to narcotics trafficking. To curtail money laundering activities, the MLCA prohibits such activities as designing transactions or transporting monetary instruments for the purpose of concealing or disguising the nature, location, source, ownership, or control of the proceeds of specific unlawful activities.

These activities are divided into two categories of certain specific financial transactions (the "Transaction Offense") and certain transportation activities (the "Transportation Offense").

[17] "Drug Money Laundering, Banks and Foreign Policy," a report on anti-money-laundering law enforcement and policy based on oversight hearings before the United States Senate Foreign Relations Committee on September 27 and October 4, 1989.

The Transaction Offense prohibits conducting financial transactions in property that represents the proceeds of a "specified unlawful activity." While the commission of a "specified unlawful activity" is fundamental to the Transaction Offense, the definition of a "specific unlawful activity" is perhaps the most significant limitation to the application of the MLCA.

"Specified unlawful activity" defines the particular crimes that generate the proceeds that are subsequently involved in the transaction constituting a Transaction Offense. To commit a Transaction Offense, the defendant must either intend to promote the "specified unlawful activity" or know that the transaction is designed either to conceal or disguise proceeds of a "specified unlawful activity" or avoid a reporting requirement.

"Specified unlawful activity" is defined by reference to several federal statutes. Bank Secrecy Act offenses are not "specified unlawful activities," based on the theory that there are no identifiable "proceeds" of Bank Secrecy Act violations.

The Transportation Offense prohibits money laundering by transferring a monetary instrument or fund into or out of the United States. The term "transportation" is undefined. Therefore, the most significant limitation to the application of the statute involves the definitions of "monetary instrument" and "funds."

To be guilty of either of the MLCA's two component offenses, *i.e.,* the Transaction Offense and the Transportation Offense, a defendant must have conducted the prohibited acts with the requisite *scienter*. A defendant is deemed to have the necessary level of *scienter* in one of two ways. A defendant has the requisite scienter if he:

(1) Acted with the intent of promoting a specific unlawful activity, or

(2) Acted knowing that the transaction or transportation was designed in whole or in part to either conceal or disguise the nature, the location, the source, the ownership, or the control of the proceeds of specific unlawful activity or to avoid a transaction reporting requirement under state or federal law.

The *scienter* standards of both the Transaction Offense and the Transportation Offense may be summarized as "intent to promote" or "knowing." The current interpretation of "knowing" is a high scienter standard. Mere negligent involvement in a money laundering scheme is not punishable. However, "willful blindness," such as intentional and knowing disregard of the nature of the funds involved, is punishable.

While the defendant need not know that the crime generating the funds was a "specified unlawful activity", or even what crime was involved in the transaction, the defendant must know that the monetary instrument or funds involved in the transportation represent the proceeds of some form of felonious activity under federal or state law.

The Monetary Transaction Crime

36-010   The Monetary Transaction Crime, a creation of the House Judiciary Committee, potentially has the broadest application of the new transaction crimes.

The Monetary Transaction Crime prohibits monetary transactions involving criminally derived property. The Monetary Transaction Crime requires that the defendant "knowingly" engages or attempts to engage in a prohibited monetary transaction.

The Monetary Transaction Crime also has the potential for extraterritorial application. Punishment for a violation of the Monetary Transaction Crime is a fine under Title 18 or imprisonment for not more than ten years, or both.

If either a Money Laundering Crime or a Monetary Transaction Crime is committed, all gross receipts and property traceable to such crimes are subject to civil forfeiture. To deter the laundering of foreign crime proceeds in the United States, the proceeds of an offense against a foreign nation also are subject to forfeit.

Role of financial institution

36-011   For banking and financial institutions, there exists an uncertain connection between the concept of avoidance of knowledge and their increased ability to communicate with enforcement authorities.

Permissible disclosure under the Privacy Act was broadened, yet made more specific under the MLCA. Information identifying a customer and account and the nature of any suspected illegal activity may be released to law enforcement authorities without a subpoena, court order or liability for such disclosure.

This liberalization trumps any state disclosure law that is more restrictive. As long as the disclosure is authorized by law and is made in good faith, the disclosing institution is protected from liability.

However, disclosure is voluntary rather than mandatory. One dilemma for financial institutions is how to avoid crossing the line between passive complicity and unreported suspicion. Professional money launderers have developed various means to evade the Bank Secrecy Act's reporting requirements to prevent disclosure of their association with large cash transactions.

The most common evasion technique, known as "structuring" transactions, consists of multiple cash transactions, such as deposits or purchases of money orders or cashier's checks, in amounts that individually do not exceed US $10,000 but aggregate more than US $10,000.

Thus, each transaction remains below the threshold for CTR reports. Such behavior also is known as "smurfing", and the perpetrators are referred to as "smurfs." Thus, persons desiring to evade the CTR requirements are able to transfer amounts for greater than US $10,000 without having to file.

Financial institutions and individuals have been federally prosecuted for structuring transactions to evade the Bank Secrecy Act reporting requirements. While some of these prosecutorial efforts have been successful, appellate courts have reversed convictions on various grounds, holding that structuring transactions was not a federal crime.

The MLCA augmented the Bank Secrecy Act by prohibiting the structuring of transactions under the Anti-Structuring Statute[18] in the MLCA. The Anti-Structuring Statute is controversial, as it prohibits the structuring of transactions to evade reporting requirements, while the act of "structuring" is not defined.

Under this new statute, it is both a civil and a criminal violation of the Bank Secrecy Act to attempt to evade the CTR reporting requirements by causing or attempting to cause a domestic financial institution to:

(1) Fail to file a required CTR, or
(2) File a required CTR that contains a material omission or misstatement of fact.

It is also both a civil and a criminal violation to structure or assist in structuring, or to attempt to structure or assist an attempt to structure any transaction with one or more domestic financial institutions. Some banking and financial institutions are concerned that they may be liable for assisting in structuring if they handle multiple transactions for a particular customer who later proves to have been structuring his transactions, even though they were unaware that the transactions, once aggregated, exceeded US $10,000.

[18] 31 U.S.C. 5324 (Sup. IV. 1986).

The institutions' fears are largely unfounded, however, because the MLCA requires more than inadvertent conduct. Liability attaches only to conduct entailing willfulness or negligence.

Furthermore, an institution handling multiple currency transactions of US $10,000 or less is not "assisting in structuring," for purposes of the MLCA, because the conduct of those transactions is not for the purpose of avoiding the CTR reporting requirement. However, mere knowledge of the source of the illegally obtained funds establishes a violation of the MLCA.

Despite the MLCA's requirement that a financial institution act with at least willfulness or negligence, a bank's mere failure to notice certain transactions conducted by its customers may meet the MLCA's negligence requirement. Bank compliance experts and law enforcement authorities have observed that the following acts are characteristic of persons conducting large cash transactions or seeking either to structure transactions to avoid the CTR reporting requirement or to engage in money laundering:

(1) The person seeks to exchange large amounts of small-denomination bills (i.e., US $1, $5, $10, and $20 bills) for large-denomination bills (i.e., US $50 and $100);

(2) The person presents a transaction that involves large numbers of US $50 and $100 bills;

(3) The person presents a transaction without having counted the cash;

(4) The person expresses concern about the financial institution's intention to file a CTR on the transaction;

(5) The person, after being informed that the institution intends to file a CTR on the transaction, seeks to take back part of the cash in order to reduce the amount of the transaction to US $10,000 or less;

(6) The person, after being informed that the institution intends to file a CTR on the transaction, asks the officer or employee handling the transaction whether he should deposit less than US $10,000;

(7) The person initiates a transaction involving more than US $10,000 in cash but appears reluctant to provide identification for the CTR, even though he has no account relationship with that institution;

(8) The person conducts multiple transactions, each involving less than US $10,000 but totalling more than US $10,000 over the course of several consecutive or near-consecutive days (e.g., Monday, Wednesday, and Friday), whether at the same financial institution, different branches of the same institution, or different institutions;

(9) The person deposits multiple cashier's checks or money orders (each for US $10,000 or less) into an account from which funds are subsequently wire transferred to a foreign bank account or otherwise withdrawn;

(10) Two or more persons enter a financial institution together and separately make cash purchases of monetary instruments (such as cashier's checks) that individually do not exceed US $10,000, but total more than US $10,000 from different tellers in the same institution.[19]

If a financial institution encounters evidence of a suspicious cash transaction, four actions should be taken immediately by an officer of the financial institution encountering such a transaction.

First, this information should be brought to the attention of the institution's compliance coordinator or other supervisor responsible for assuring the institution's compliance with the Bank Secrecy Act.

Second, the institution's internal procedure should be implemented to determine whether the person or persons who conducted the suspicious transaction also conducted other currency transactions at that institution, including its branches, during the same business day or over the course of several consecutive or near-consecutive days.

Third, the institution must complete a CTR and should submit that CTR to the IRS as soon as possible.

Fourth, the institution should immediately contact the local IRS office to report the matter to a Special Agent of the IRS Criminal Investigation Division, whether or not a CTR is required.

Structuring is the primary loophole used to elude authorities. To combat structuring, banks are instructed to view multiple transactions as a single transaction under certain circumstances. If a financial institution has knowledge that multiple currency transactions are by or on behalf of any single person or entity and result in either cash in or cash out totalling more than US $10,000 during any one business day, those transactions shall be treated as a single transaction.

However, three conditions must exist before multiple transactions are treated as one. First, the transaction must be "by or on behalf of any person." Second, the transaction must amount to more than US $10,000 cash in or cash out in a single day. Third, the bank must have knowledge of both of these conditions.

[19] Rusch, "Hue and Cry in the Counting-House: Some Observations on the Bank Secrecy Act", 37 *Cath. U.L.Rev.* 465 (1988).

In these situations, the existence of a single person or single account requires that any and all transactions involving that person or account must be combined and treated as a single transaction. Whether multiple transactions must be treated as one if all three conditions are met, although the cash in or cash out is transferred at more than one bank, is an unanswered question.

Clearly, if a financial institution is without knowledge of the various transactions, they will remain separate. Ambitious launderers have some interesting options as a result of the amended regulations.

Congress broadened the scope of the MLCA in 1988 by increasing the record keeping and currency reporting responsibilities of financial institutions. For example, in an attempt to curtail smurfing, the 1988 amendments created a recordkeeping requirement for the sale of monetary instruments that exceed US $3,000. In addition, civil penalties for non-compliance were increased.

ENFORCEMENT OF UNITED STATES BANKING LAWS

36-012 Recently, both legislation and judicial decisions have provided mechanisms for stronger enforcement of United States banking laws. Congress has given various branches of the government new weapons of enforcement and efforts to increase compliance with the new regulations are intense. The courts also have forced a sleepy financial community to come to terms with its responsibility.

Enforcement by Department of Treasury

36-013 The Bank Secrecy Act empowers the Secretary of Treasury to demand that financial institutions keep records and file reports that the Secretary of the Treasury deems to be useful in criminal, tax or regulatory matters.[20]

The Treasury has the authority to make disclosures of information reported under and consistent with the Bank Secrecy Act. The Treasury is authorized to impose civil penalties for violations of the Bank Secrecy Act.

[20] Pub. L. No. 91-508, as amended.

The compliance function of the Treasury Department was strengthened after an amendment to the MLCA granted the treasury an enforceable summons authority.[21] Notwithstanding the many amendments clarifying regulations and increasing enforcement authority, the government's enforcement of the Bank Secrecy Act is criticized heavily.

For example, the CTR regulations in the Code of Federal Regulations are confusing,[22] and the requirements for filing CTRs and CMIRs are inconsistent. The Treasury also does not encourage the banking industry to voluntarily disclose CTR violations.

Furthermore, the Treasury permits financial institutions to exempt from the CTR reporting requirements those businesses that customarily deal in large amounts of cash, regardless of the potential for abuse. This leaves much room for discretion. Banks are permitted to unilaterally exempt certain limited types of currency transactions (such as deposits or withdrawals), by specific categories of customers such as retail sellers of certain goods and services. Moreover, a bank may apply to the IRS for authority to exempt other types of transactions and businesses.

The Treasury also is criticized for devoting an exorbitant portion of its available resources to extracting civil penalties from institutions who voluntarily come forward and disclose past Bank Secrecy Act violations. The Treasury justifies its actions in several ways. Most significantly, there are few Treasury personnel relative to the number of voluntary disclosure cases. Thus, effective enforcement is a struggle.

Moreover, the Treasury has no resources to pursue the non-volunteers. However, considering the difficult circumstances of insufficient staff, poorly drafted statutes (prior to the MLCA), and lack of enlightened congressional insight, many feel the Treasury has performed quite well in this sector.

Enforcement by Justice Department

The Justice Department was given a significant new weapon **36-014** against financial institutions in the mid to late 1980s in the form of a new standard of compliance.

Bank compliance officers were jolted to life in 1985 after vast numbers of financial institutions were prosecuted for lack of Bank

[21] Section 1356, Subtitle H of Title I of the Anti-Drug Abuse Act 1986, Pub. L. 99-570.
[22] 31 C.F.R. 103.

Secrecy Act compliance under the "flagrant organizational indifference" standard.

Moreover, the "collective knowledge" concept was applied in 1987 when a jury was instructed that to determine the knowledge of the bank as an institution, it should "sum" up the knowledge of the bank's various employees.[23]

Thus, if the "sum" of that collective knowledge amounted to knowledge of the applicable facts in law, the bank could be deemed to have knowledge of its duties. The court's instructions were upheld on appeal. The basis for the court's decision was that knowledge, obtained by employees of a corporation acting within the scope of their employment, is imputed to the corporation.

The traditional principles of corporate criminal liability were significantly expanded as the equating of "willfulness" with "flagrant organizational indifference" fundamentally eroded the level of scienter prescribed by the Bank Secrecy Act.

Impact on United States financial institutions

36-015 The Bank Secrecy Act, like the more recent laundering statutes, reflects a Congressional belief that law enforcement goals can be more effectively achieved by severely punishing federally regulated banking institutions than by developing enforcement programs in cooperation with the financial industry.

The enactment of the MLCA severely impacted financial institutions. For example, the MLCA amended the Bank Control Act and the Savings and Loan Control Act, making the acquiring parties' past record of Bank Secrecy Act violations relevant to approval of bank acquisitions. Federally-insured banks are required to adopt Bank Secrecy Act compliance procedures.

The procedures for monitoring Bank Secrecy Act compliance require each bank to develop and provide for the continued administration of a program designed to reasonably assure and monitor compliance with record keeping and reporting requirements.[24] The compliance program will be reduced to a writing, approved by the board of directors and noted in the corporate minutes. The compliance program shall minimally provide for the following:

(1) A system of internal controls to assure ongoing compliance;
(2) Independent testing for compliance to be conducted by bank personnel or by a third party;

[23] *Bank of New England,* 821 F.2d 844 cert. denied, 484 U.S. 943 (1987).
[24] See 12 C.F.R. Ch. 111, 326.8(b); 31 U.S.C. 53; 31 C.F.R. 10

(3) Designation of an individual or individuals responsible for coordinating and monitoring day-to-day compliance, and

(4) Personnel training.

Financial institutions must wrestle with many ambiguities in both the MLCA and the Bank Secrecy Act. Conducting transactions that involve "criminally derived property" is strictly prohibited. However, terms such as "proceeds" and "conduct" are undefined and as a result, financial institutions have little chance of applying them accurately. A financial institution risks incorrectly deciding to terminate business activities with a suspected customer, which could result in a major civil law suit.

Such apprehension is matched by the fear of violating the law through passivity. Many American financial institutions function under what might prove to be damaging misconceptions regarding the MLCA. Some financial institutions believe corporate liability for Bank Secrecy Act offenses is minimized if the financial institution employs only foreign citizens in their overseas branches.

In reality, the drug money-laundering process often includes conduct beginning in the United States. Consequently, the laundering conduct of a foreign bank employee could render an overseas bank criminally responsible because the bank's liability under such circumstances depends solely on *respondeat superior* principles.

Albeit limited, the MLCA gives the Bank Secrecy Act an international dimension. Extraterritorial jurisdiction is asserted over those who know that a transaction or transportation intends to evade a reporting requirement under federal or state law.

PUNISHMENT FOR VIOLATION OF UNITED STATES BANKING LAWS

Penalties under the Bank Secrecy Act and the MLCA escalated in **36-016** both the criminal and civil arenas. The Treasury Department is authorized to impose civil monetary penalties for failing to comply with the reporting requirements.

Both criminal penalties and civil sanctions are imposed on laundering offenses created by the MLCA. Civil penalties and criminal penalties assessed due to the same violations are now cumulative. The criminal penalties include fines, forfeiture, and imprisonment, while the civil sanctions are limited to forfeiture and severe monetary penalties.

Criminal penalties

36-017   The criminal penalties for structuring transactions to avoid the reporting requirements of the Bank Secrecy Act were intensified by the MLCA. Jail terms of up to 10 years and fines from US $1,000 to US $500,000 are some of the criminal penalties for violating the Bank Secrecy Act. Furthermore, criminal enforcement authorities are now provided with additional tools for their trade.

The combination of new money laundering offenses, legislation directed against organized crime, and electronic surveillance probably will produce more serious high-tech intrusion into potential criminal conduct, even in non-organized crime cases.

One goal of this new strategy is to enable American courts to reach laundered monies anywhere in the world. As a result, banks often are pitted against their own customers and depositors who seek the protection of foreign laws and foreign courts to hide transfers. Certainly, customers might issue instructions contrary to a bank's corporate resolutions.

American banks with foreign branches undoubtedly will be forced to choose whether to obey the directions of American courts, foreign courts or their own customers.

The historical concepts of criminal behavior were discarded with the enactment of the MLCA. Currently, a person is unable to do business with or for another simply because unlawful conduct created the funds for the transaction. Those who are merely suspected of crimes may be unable to engage in everyday commerce. The threat of criminal liability will prevent anyone from dealing with them.

Civil penalties

36-018   In an attempt to curtail money laundering, the MLCA also expands the civil penalties available for violations of the Bank Secrecy Act. Negligent violations of the recordkeeping and reporting requirements, willful violations of the foreign financial agency transaction prohibitions, and willful reporting violations have newer, steeper penalties.

The statute of limitations for assessment of penalties under the Bank Secrecy Act was extended from five years to six years. Attempts to avoid Bank Secrecy Act reporting requirements now result in the imposition of civil penalties.

Furthermore, maximum civil penalties were increased and now range from US $25,000 to US $100,000 for each willful violation of the Bank Secrecy Act. Significant long-term results probably will be more the result of an increase in cross-border enforcement of civil forfeiture provisions than in the prosecution of individual money launderers. Since many laundering offenses, as well as Bank Secrecy Act violations, are organized crime predicate offenses, private civil consequences certainly will increase.

THE BANK SECRECY ACT'S EFFECTIVENESS

The Bank Secrecy Act reporting requirements have proved highly successful in aiding civil and criminal law enforcement. Using the Bank Secrecy Act, the government has prosecuted several leading money launderers, both in the United States and abroad.

36-019

A single CTR (Currency Transaction Report) can furnish substantial leads for criminal investigators. The reports provide investigative leads, information corroborating other sources of information regarding criminal activities, as well as probative evidence for federal criminal cases.

The Bank Secrecy Act reports are also highly useful in identifying or proving various other types of financial crimes. For example, one federally-insured financial institution filed reports that, when analyzed, provided leads regarding the disposition of millions of dollars that had been embezzled from the financial institution through devices such as illegal loans.

Due to the reporting requirements, data regarding large domestic and international movements of cash is constantly provided to enforcement authorities. This data furnishes the grounds for either initiating or expanding an investigation.

The voluntary process for filing these reports provides law enforcement agents with valuable information on suspicious movements of cash in a less cumbersome and more timely fashion than a compulsory process. The Internal Revenue Service Criminal Investigation Division has steadily increased the number of investigations pursued and prosecutions recommended for criminal violations of the Bank Secrecy Act.

Furthermore, the numbers of indictments and convictions for these violations also increased. The Treasury also has increased the number of civil money penalties against financial institutions for civil violations of the Bank Secrecy Act.

However, it should be borne in mind that the number of statistical units of money-laundering prosecutions are misleading. Every time a bank files a bad report or fails to file a required report, it counts as one unit of prosecution. Similarly, every time a customer attempts to cause such a result, it equals one unit of prosecution. The number of units of prosecution should relate to the total amount of the money laundered rather than during an arbitrarily selected time period. Using money as a base would provide more uniform and accurate data ensuring that liability is commensurate with culpability and harm.

EUROPEAN COMMUNITY

Fergus Randolph
Brick Court Chambers
Brussels, Belgium

Chapter 37

EUROPEAN COMMUNITY

INTRODUCTION

The aim of this chapter is to examine the issue of banking secrecy **37-001** from the perspective of the European Community (EC). Some of what is said here will be echoed in other parts of the work, which is unavoidable given the fact that the laws relating to banking secrecy originated in individual states.

Banking secrecy is not an original Community principle; rather it has become part of the fabric of the EC through a process akin to osmosis. However, in recent years, the EC has shown itself willing to take the initiative in areas relating to banking secrecy and indeed roll back some of the protection engendered by it.

This chapter will first briefly examine the background to banking secrecy, its *raison d'etre* and its modern-day transformation. There will then follow sections dealing with two issues which have recently had a great impact on the principle of banking secrecy: money laundering and 1992.

Within these sections, the various EC instruments and European Court of Justice decisions covering aspects of banking secrecy, of course, will be examined. In the final concluding section, the question of whether there is a continued need for banking secrecy will be raised, with special regard paid to the BCCI affair.

BACKGROUND TO BANKING SECRECY

The right of bank clients to privacy with regard to their financial **37-002** transactions is one which is recognized throughout the world. The differences which arise in different jurisdictions relating to this right are of degree rather than substance. Thus, the obligations relating to disclosure of "confidential" information are more strict in the United States than they are in Panama, for example.

It is generally understood that individuals and companies have the right to regulate their own financial affairs with banks with the understanding that such regulation will be confidential. However, the freedom of the individual and the rights of states and statutory authorities may come into conflict here, as in other areas, and this will generally lead to the erosion of the right to privacy in favor of greater knowledge by the state or its authorities.

Having said this, there are still many countries which specialize in not restricting the right to privacy, which become known as tax havens.[1] Two issues have arisen recently which have had important consequences for the principle of banking secrecy.

The first is the growing perception that banking secrecy rules were being abused to a greater and greater extent, especially by those involved in the drug trade.

Second, and specifically with regard to the EC, the concept of the internal market, set for completion on January 1, 1993, is inimical to different jurisdictions within that internal market having differing degrees of secrecy permitted for financial transactions within their territories.

The very idea of only one authorization being needed to trade in any of the Member States - the single "passport" concept - must in itself lead to a harmonization of the rules relating to, *inter alia*, banking secrecy. Tied to this is the harmonization of the exchange of information between the Member States of the EC in matters relating to taxation. These issues have come to dominate the whole issue of banking secrecy as can be seen from the following sections.

MONEY LAUNDERING

International action

37-003 One of the main financial issues which has gripped the global headlines for some time is that of money laundering. Money laundering has been defined as follows:

---

[1] Switzerland, the Bahamas, the Cayman Islands, the Isle of Man, Liechtenstein, Gibraltar, Panama, and the Dutch Antilles are examples.

".. . the conversion or transfer of property, knowing that such property is derived from criminal activity or from an act of participation in such activity, for the purpose of concealing or disguising the illicit origin of the property or of assisting any person who is involved in the commission of such activity to evade the legal consequences of his action;

the concealment or disguise of the true nature, source, location, disposition, movement, rights with respect to, or ownership of property knowing that such property is derived from criminal activity or from an act of participation in such activity;

the acquisition, possession or use of property, knowing, at the time of receipt, that such property was derived from criminal activity or from an act of participation in such activity;

participation in, association to commit, attempts to commit and aiding, abetting, facilitating and counselling the commission of any of the actions mentioned in the foregoing paragraphs."[2]

It has been estimated[3] by the Financial Action Task Force on Money Laundering (GAFI) that the value of sales of drugs to final consumers in 1990 was in the region of US \$500-billion. It also was estimated that, of the US \$122-billion representing cocaine, heroin, and cannabis sales in the United States and Europe, up to US \$85-billion could be available for laundering/ investments. These figures are huge and capable of seriously affecting the international financial system.

The fact that the largest bank scandal ever seen - that of BCCI - arose out of allegations of money laundering on a hitherto unimaginable scale is yet more proof of the widespread use of money laundering. The issue is clearly a global one and, thus, it would seem fitting that the first attempts to bolster up the financial markets against this type of manipulation were of an international nature.

International action has been active in two ways. The first approach has been to tighten international cooperation among judicial and law enforcement agencies and to view money laundering as a

2 EC Council Directive 91/308, article 1.

3 See the Economic and Social Committee Opinion on the proposal for a Council Directive on prevention of the use of the financial system for the purpose of money laundering; *Official Journal* 1990 No. C 322/86, December 31, 1990.

crime to be combated mainly by penal means. Two agreements have followed this approach:

(1) The Recommendation of the Council of Europe of June 27, 1980, and
(2) The United Nations Convention against Illicit Traffic in Narcotic Drugs and Psychotropic Substances, adopted December 19, 1988, in Vienna, Austria ("the Vienna Convention").

It should be noted that the Vienna Convention specifically deals with the question of banking secrecy, stating that the principle of banking secrecy should not impede criminal investigations taking place in the context of international cooperation.

The second approach has been to use the financial markets themselves as a means of tackling money laundering, the aim being to prevent the markets being used for money laundering. Two agreements have followed this approach:

(1) The Declaration of Principles adopted on December 12, 1988, in Basle, Switzerland, by the banking supervisory authorities of the Group of Ten ("the Basle Declaration"), and
(2) The Council of Europe Convention on laundering, tracing, seizure, and confiscation of proceeds of crime, opened for signature on November 8, 1990, in Strasbourg, France.

The Basle Declaration sets out three basic ways in which money laundering can be tackled, two of which directly impinge on the principle of banking secrecy:

(1) Client identification;
(2) Refusal to deal with operations apparently tied to money laundering operations, and
(3) Cooperation with the relevant authorities, taking into account existing rules and the obligations relating to confidentiality.

These three principles neatly sum up the problem facing international action in this area: the desire for transparency in financial operations tied to the need to ensure the continuation of confidentiality in banking transactions.

International action has also lead to the creation, in 1989, of the Financial Action Task Force on Money Laundering, which published its first report on February 7, 1990, and which has conducted useful work in the area. The group consists of participants from the following countries: The United States, Japan, Canada, the United Kingdom, Germany, France, Italy, The Netherlands, Belgium, Luxembourg, Spain, Sweden, Switzerland, Austria, and Australia.

The group's report noted that one of the main problems was that many countries had banking secrecy rules which made it impossible for banks to communicate confidential client information to the competent authorities. This was causing the banks in these countries not to report doubtful financial transactions to the authorities as there were no safeguards established to protect the banks from allegations of breach of confidentiality.

This was to be contrasted with the position in the United States, where the banks were compelled by law to disclose doubtful financial transactions to the relevant authorities.

The above approaches have been incorporated in the recent EC Council Directive on money laundering, which will now be examined in detail.

EC Council Directive 91/308

The EC Council adopted Directive 91/308[4] on the prevention of the **37-004** use of the financial system for the purpose of money laundering on June 10, 1991.

The importance and potential effect of money laundering on the international financial system can be seen in the first recital to the Directive:

> "Whereas when credit and financial institutions are used to launder proceeds from criminal activities. . ., the soundness and stability of the institution concerned and confidence in the financial system as a whole could be seriously jeopardized, thereby losing the trust of the public."

This raises one of the anomalies surrounding banking secrecy. One of the reasons cited for the continued existence of banking secrecy rules is that they preserve the clients' trust in the banking system as a whole; the move towards "piercing" the secrecy surrounding banking transactions in certain circumstances in order to stop abuses may in fact cause there to be a certain loss of confidence in the banking system as more details of these abuses become known.[5]

---

[4] *Official Journal* 1991 No. L 166/77, June 28, 1991.
[5] See Jack Guttentag and Richard Herring, "Disclosure Policy and International Banking", *Journal of Banking and Finance* 10 (1986), at pp. 75-97.

The extent to which client identification is seen to be significant in the fight against money laundering can also be noted from the 11th recital to the Directive:

> "Whereas ensuring that credit and financial institutions require identification of their customers when entering into business relations or conducting transactions, exceeding certain thresholds, are necessary to avoid launderers' taking advantage of anonymity to carry out their criminal activities; whereas such provisions must also be extended, as far as possible, to any beneficial owners."

Finally, insofar as the recitals are concerned, the impact of banking secrecy on effective action against money laundering can be seen from the Directive's 15th recital:

> "Whereas preventing the financial system from being used for money laundering is a task which cannot be carried out by the authorities responsible for combating this phenomenon without the cooperation of credit and financial institutions and their supervisory authorities; whereas banking secrecy must be lifted in such cases; whereas a mandatory system of reporting suspicious transactions which ensures that information is transmitted to the above-mentioned authorities without alerting the customers concerned, is the most effective way to accomplish such cooperation; whereas a special protection clause is necessary to exempt credit and financial institutions, their employees and their directors from responsibility for breaching restrictions on disclosure of information."

In the text of the Directive itself, the following articles fall to be considered as impacting on the principle of banking secrecy:

Article 3(1)

37-005
> "Member States shall ensure that credit and financial institutions require identification of their customers by means of supporting evidence when entering into business relations, particularly when opening an account or savings account, or when offering safe custody facilities."

Article 3(2)

"The identification requirement shall also apply for any trans-   **37-006**
action with customers other than those referred to in paragraph 1, involving a sum of amounting to ECU 15,000 or more,
whether the transaction is carried out in a single operation or
in several operations which seem to be linked. When the sum
is not known at the time when the transaction is undertaken,
the institution concerned shall proceed with identification as
soon as it is apprised of the sum and establishes that the
threshold has been reached."

Article 3(5)

"In the event of doubt as to whether the customers referred to   **37-007**
in the above paragraphs are acting on their own behalf, or
where it is certain that they are not acting on their own behalf,
the credit and financial institutions shall take reasonable measures to obtain information as to the real identity of the person
on whose behalf those customers are acting."

Article 6

"Member States shall ensure that credit and financial institu-   **37-008**
tions and their directors and employees co-operate fully with
the authorities responsible for combating money laundering:

   - by informing those authorities, on their own initiative, of
   any fact which might be an indication of money laundering

   - by furnishing those authorities, at their request, with all
   the necessary information, in accordance with the procedures established by the applicable legislation.

The information referred to in the first paragraph shall be
forwarded to the authorities responsible for combating money
laundering of the Member State in whose territory the institution forwarding the information is situated. . .

Information supplied to the authorities in accordance with the
first paragraph may be used only in connection with the combating of money laundering. However, Member States may
provide that such information may also be used for other
purposes."

Article 8

37-009   "Credit and financial institutions and their directors and employees shall not disclose to the customer concerned nor to
other third persons that information has been transmitted to
the authorities in accordance with Articles 6 and 7 or that a
money laundering investigation is being carried on."

Article 9

37-010   "The disclosure in good faith to the authorities responsible for
combating money laundering by an employee or director of a
credit or a financial institution of the information referred to
in Articles 6 and 7 shall not constitute a breach of any restriction on disclosure of information imposed by contract or by
any legislative, regulatory or administrative provision, and
shall not involve the credit or financial institution, its directors
or employees in liability of any kind."

Article 15

37-011   "The Member States may adopt or retain in force stricter
provisions in the field covered by this Directive to prevent
money laundering."

The above articles divide neatly into two sections, the first relating
to the identification of clients by the banks and the second relating
to the communication of "confidential" information by the banks to
the relevant authorities. Although it is true to say that the issue of
client identification does not impact directly on banking secrecy, it
does have some effect.

Take, for example, article 3(5). This not only provides that the
identity of the client should be ascertained but also provides that
the banks should take reasonable measures to obtain the real identity of the client. To the extent that this involves communication
between the bank and a third party, there will be an effect on the
confidential relationship between the bank and its client. This is on
the basis that banking secrecy not only covers the financial affairs
of the client as are known/dealt with by the bank but also the
knowledge that a particular bank has relating to a particular client.

The communication of confidential client information by banks
to third parties, on the other hand, clearly impacts on the principle
of banking secrecy. This is made clear in article 9, which provides
that the transmitting of confidential information to the competent

authorities for the purposes of combating money laundering will not be in breach of what is described as "restriction(s) on disclosure of information imposed by contract or by any legislative, regulatory or administrative provision, and shall not involve the credit or financial institution, its directors or employees in liability of any kind." In other words, the relevant persons will not be in breach of the rules relating to banking secrecy.

This is not to say that the rules per se will not have been breached; it simply means that the disclosure (which clearly is a *prima facie* breach of the rights of the client) will not lead to liability. Thus, the provisions are somewhat loosely worded when they describe the communication of confidential information as not being in breach of the relevant restrictions.

One point which should be born in mind is that one general principle in the provisions is that the transmitted information can only be used for the purposes of combating money laundering. However, article 6(3) provides that Member States "may provide that such information may also be used for other purposes." Not only is this clause rather vague and unclear, but it also will hardly comfort bank clients who may find that their confidential information is being disseminated for reasons other than helping to combat money laundering.

Thus, in the fight to control illegal activities, *in situ* money laundering, the principle of banking secrecy has had to be curtailed. This is neither surprising, nor to be criticized. However, with the possibility open to Member States to exploit this further, by having the possibility of using the once-confidential information for uses other than those relating to the combating of money laundering, the principle of banking secrecy per se is at risk.

It is maybe interesting to note that the possibility to use the information for purposes other than for combating money laundering did not appear in the earlier drafts of the text and only appeared for the first time in a late Council draft at the end of May 1991; it did not appear in earlier Commission drafts.

1992 AND CONFIDENTIALITY

General concept

The EC Commission's task in completing the internal market by **37-012** 1992 was spelt out in its 1985 program:

"Unifying this market presupposes that Member States will agree on the abolition of barriers of all kinds, harmonization of rules, approximation of legislation and tax structures, strengthening of monetary cooperation and the necessary flanking measures to encourage European firms to work together."

The Commission's aim was and is to create a market in which goods, services, capital and people all move freely within the EC.

One major consequence of this which impacts on the principle of banking secrecy is that harmonization must, by its nature, restrict the opportunities for some jurisdictions to have more stringent rules relating to the communication of client information than other jurisdictions, affecting their positions as tax havens.

In addition, with the closer coordination and cooperation between authorities in the Member States, there will be greater opportunities for creating exceptions to the principle of banking secrecy in the name of approximation. Thus, it is not surprising that over the years, there has been a significant weakening of the principle of banking secrecy in the EC. One clear example of this has been in the field of taxation.

Taxation

37-013 EC Council Directive 77/799[6] concerns mutual assistance by the competent authorities of the Member States in the field of direct taxation. The directive was conceived as a means of combating tax evasion and avoidance, as can be seen from its recitals.

From these, a clear message is communicated; given the multinational character of tax evasion and avoidance, it is necessary to increase collaboration between different tax administrations in different Member States and one form of collaboration is the communication of information between the Member States concerning particular cases.

To this general approach of increased communication and thus coordination is added a rider; in all cases, it will be necessary to protect the basic rights of persons and companies. Thus, once again, it is possible to see the permanent conflict between the powers of the state in upholding the law and the rights of its citizens to confidentiality with regard to their financial transactions.

6 *Official Journal* No. L 336/15, December 27, 1977.

The competent authorities can exchange information between themselves "that may enable them to effect a correct assessment of taxes on income and on capital", according to article 1 of the Directive.

Articles 7 and 8 of the Directive deal specifically with the question of communication of confidential information and the rights of individuals and are given in full.

Article 7

"Provisions relating to secrecy   **37-014**

(1) All information made known to a Member State under this Directive shall be kept secret in the State in the same manner as information received under its domestic legislation.

In any case, such information:

- may be made available only to the persons directly involved in the assessment of the tax or in the administrative control of this assessment

- may in addition be made known only in connection with judicial proceedings or administrative proceedings involving sanctions undertaken with a view to, or relating to, the making or reviewing the tax assessment and only to persons who are directly involved in such proceedings; such information may, however, be disclosed during public hearings or in judgments if the competent authority of the Member State supplying the information raises no objection

- shall in no circumstances be used other than for taxation purposes or in connection with judicial proceedings or administrative proceedings involving sanctions undertaken with a view to, or in relation to, the making or reviewing the tax assessment.

(2) Paragraph 1 shall not oblige a Member State whose legislation or administrative practice lays down, for domestic purposes, narrower limits than those contained in the provisions of that paragraph, to provide information if the State concerned does not undertake to respect those narrower limits.

(3) Notwithstanding paragraph 1, the competent authorities of the Member State providing the information may permit it to be used for other purposes in the requesting state, if, under the legislation of the informing State, the information could, in similar circumstances, be used in the informing State for similar purposes.

(4) Where a competent authority of a Member State considers that information which it has received from the competent authority of another Member State is likely to be useful to the competent authority of a third Member State, it may transmit it to the latter competent authority with the agreement of the competent authority which supplied the information."

Article 8

37-015   "Limits to exchange of information

(1) This directive shall impose no obligation to have enquiries carried out or to provide information if the Member State, which should furnish the information, would be prevented by its laws or administrative practices from carrying out these enquiries or from collecting or using this information for its own purposes.

(2) The provision of information may be refused where it would lead to the disclosure of a commercial, industrial or professional secret or of a commercial process, or of information whose disclosure would be contrary to public policy.

(3) The competent authority of a Member State may refuse to provide information where the State concerned is unable, for practical or legal reasons, to provide similar information."

The following points can be noted from the above. First, the general principle that the information disclosed should only be used for matters relating to tax assessment is clearly made. However, important exceptions to this general principle also appear. The second indent to article 7, paragraph 1, for example, allows for information communicated to a competent authority, pursuant to this Directive, to be disclosed during public hearings relating to tax assessment as long as the competent authority communicating the information raises no objection.

Article 7, paragraph 3, goes further and provides that information disclosed may in certain circumstances be used for purposes other than the assessment of tax by the competent authorities. Although restricted, the possibility exists and that in itself may be somewhat worrying.

It is interesting to note that, in the Opinion[7] given by the Economic and Social Committee on the proposal to amend Council Regulation 77/799 so as to include indirect tax matters in its scope, two points relevant to the discussion were made. First, the Committee stated that taxpayers and third parties should be given an assurance that their private affairs and their business and trade secrets would be adequately protected by not being pried into any more than was necessary to assess the tax in question. Second, the Committee stated that information passed from one authority to another should be used for no other purpose than that for which it was disclosed. Noble sentiments all. But, when the proposal came into being, in the form of Council Directive 1070/79,[8] no amendment was made to article 7 and thus the possibility exists now, both in the fields of direct and indirect taxation, for previously confidential information to be used by Member States for purposes other than tax assessment.

Finally, it should be noted that there are plans to restrict the possibilities for Member States to refuse to provide information for tax assessment purposes. It will be remembered that article 8(1) of EC Council Directive 77/799, as amended, provides that a Member State is not obliged to provide information following a request from another Member State if its laws or administrative practices prevent it from collecting the information for its purposes.

A proposal to amend article 8(1) was put forward by the Commission[9] in mid 1989 which was to add to the existing article 8(1) the following subparagraph:

"However, where the appropriate authority of the Member State making the request shows specific grounds for supposing that one of its residents has transferred, either directly or through another country, significant funds to the Member State to which the request is made without declaring the corresponding income, the appropriate authority of the Member State to which the request is addressed may not rely on the fact

---

[7] *Official Journal* No. C 283/28, November 27, 1978.

[8] *Official Journal* No. L 331/8, December 27, 1979.

[9] Proposal for a Council Directive amending Council Directive 77/799/EEC concerning mutual assistance by the competent authorities of the Member States in the field of direct taxation and value added tax; *Official Journal* No. C 141/7, June 7, 1989.

that its administrative practices do not permit it to carry out these enquiries or to collect or use this information for the purpose of correctly establishing the taxes due by its own residents."

This proposal has yet to be adopted.

Disclosure

37-016   While it is clear from the above that the specific EC provisions relating to the communication of confidential information for the assessment of tax impact on the principle of banking secrecy, it is not so clear whether banking secrecy per se is affected by disclosure rules. The term "disclosure rules" is here used to mean those rules required of institutions in the financial sector which have to disclose certain facts about themselves to competent authorities in order to be given a license to trade.

These rules have become more prevalent in the EC in recent years, as more effort has been put into establishing a common financial market. One of the main foundations upon which the single financial market is based is the principle that a financial institution only needs authorization from one Member State in order to trade throughout the EC. This is the so-called single passport system. The system clearly relies on common rules as to the disclosure of certain relevant data relating to the soundness of the institution in question.

This disclosure of relevant data may impact on banking secrecy, but only in a secondary fashion, as the essence of that which is secret under the banking secrecy principle are the communications between the bank and its client and activities undertaken by the bank on behalf of its client.

Secondary and primary impact

37-017   Disclosure rules, as described above, only relate in general terms to financial institutions' activities and do not necessarily seek to have access to individual clients' records. The secondary impact will turn into primary impact if individual client information is disclosed together with the general information relating to the bank.

However, it is to be noted that in the Community legislation at least, only those persons employed by the competent authorities are bound by the obligation of professional secrecy. The competent authorities are not the financial institutions such as banks, insurance companies or stock exchanges and thus the obligation on the banks, for example, to keep confidential its dealings with individual customers is not specifically affected.

The banking directives can be taken as an example. EC Council Directive 77/780[10] and EC Council Directive 89/646[11] (the so-called First and Second Banking Directives, respectively) deal with the establishment and harmonization of rules relating to the trading of banks in the EC. In order to trade, the banks must show to the relevant competent authorities that their solvency and liquidity ratios are such that they should be allowed to trade.

The Second Banking Directive also provides, in article 5, that the "competent authorities shall not grant authorization for the taking-up of the business of credit institutions before they have been informed of the identities of the shareholders or members, whether direct or indirect, natural or legal persons, that have qualifying holdings, and of the amount of those holdings."

"Qualifying holdings" are defined as being a direct or indirect holding in an undertaking which represents 10 percent or more of the capital or of the voting rights or which makes it possible to exercise a significant influence over the management of the undertaking in which a holding subsists.

Despite the fact that, pursuant to this provision, the identities of the relevant persons with qualifying holdings have to be made known to the competent authorities, the principle of banking secrecy is only impacted indirectly as the information given only relates to a shareholder, not necessarily a client, and to the amount of the holding, not any activities carried on for the holder by the bank.

In any event, both banking directives specifically deal with the issue of professional secrecy from the point of view of the competent authorities and what persons employed therein may or may not disclose. It should be noted that the term "competent authority", although not defined in the two directives themselves, is defined at article 1 of EC Council Directive 83/350[12] as follows:

---

[10] First Council Directive of December 12, 1977, on the coordination of the laws, regulations, and administrative provisions relating to the taking up and pursuit of the business of credit institutions; *Official Journal* No. L 322/30, December 17, 1977.

[11] Second Council Directive of December 15, 1989, on the coordination of laws, regulations, and administrative provisions relating to the taking up and pursuit of business of credit institutions and amending Directive 77/780; *Official Journal* No. L 386/1, December 30, 1989.

[12] Council Directive of June 13, 1983, on the supervision of credit institutions on a consolidated basis; *Official Journal* No. L 193/18, July 18, 1983.

> "[C]ompetent authorities means the national authorities which are empowered by law or regulation to supervise credit institutions."

All information given to the competent authorities pursuant to the two directives is covered by professional secrecy. The Second Banking Directive, in amending the provisions of the First Banking Directive on professional secrecy, provides as follows at article 16:

> "(1) The Member States shall provide that all persons working or who have worked for the competent authorities, as well as auditors or experts acting on behalf of the competent authorities, shall be bound by the obligation of professional secrecy. This means that no confidential information which they may receive in the course of their duties may be divulged to any person or authority whatsoever, except in summary or collective form, such that individual institutions cannot be identified, without prejudice to cases covered by criminal law. Nevertheless, where a credit institution has been declared bankrupt or is being compulsorily wound up, confidential information which does not concern third parties involved in attempts to rescue that credit institution may be divulged in civil or commercial proceedings."

It is interesting to note that in its explanation of the meaning of professional secrecy, article 16(1) provides that only information in summary or collective form can be disclosed, so that individual institutions cannot be identified.

This would seem to add weight to the argument that disclosure relates to information about the financial institutions themselves rather than the individual clients thereof. In any event, where confidential information is received by the competent authorities, it may only be used in the course of their duties:

(1) To check that the conditions governing the taking-up of the business of credit institutions are met and to facilitate monitoring of the conduct of such business, or
(2) To impose sanctions, or
(3) In an administrative appeal against a decision of the competent authority, or
(4) In court proceedings.

Article 16(7) of EC Council Directive 89/646 also allows for the information to be transmitted from the competent authorities in that it provides that:

"... the Member States may, by virtue of provisions laid down by law, authorize the disclosure of certain information to other departments of their central government administrations responsible for legislation on the supervision of credit institutions, financial institutions, investment services and insurance companies and to inspectors acting on behalf of those departments."

Insider dealing and stock exchanges

Similar provisions relating to competent authorities and the obligation of professional secrecy exist in EC legislation affecting insider dealing[13] and stock exchanges.[14]   **37-018**

The precursor to article 16 of EC Council Directive 89/646 - article 12 of EC Council Directive 77/780 - has been interpreted by the European Court of Justice in Case 110/84: *Municipality of Hillegom v. Hillenius.*[15]

The case concerned the right of an individual employed by a competent authority - *in situ*, the Dutch central bank - to rely on article 12(1) of the first banking Directive as a basis for refusing to answer certain questions put to him in the course of bankruptcy proceedings. The individual had been subpoenaed to give evidence about matters relating to a bankruptcy of a particular bank.

The Court of Justice found that article 12(1) laid down a general obligation on the Member States to maintain professional secrecy but left the specific substance and scope to be determined by the Member States themselves. The judgment concerns itself with the principle of "professional secrecy" rather than "banking secrecy".

As the German government stated in its intervention "(p)rofessional secrecy is an important precondition for proper bank supervision". This should be distinguished from banking secrecy per se which has as its main *raison d'etre* the protection of the banks' clients; it has no direct impact on bank supervision.

[13] Council Directive 89/592 of November 13, 1989, coordinating regulations on insider dealing; *Official Journal* No L 334/30, November 18, 1989.

[14] Council Directive 80/390 of March 17, 1980, coordinating the requirements for the drawing up, scrutiny, and distribution of the listing particulars to be published for the admission of securities to official stock exchange listing; *Official Journal* No. L 100/1, April 17, 1980.

[15] Text of Footnote

CONCLUSION

37-019 As was said at the start of this chapter, banking secrecy is a national rather than an EC concept. In recent years, specific measures have
been taken by the EC institutions which have had a direct impact on the principle of banking secrecy - initiatives against money laundering and legislation relating to mutual assistance across the EC in the field of taxation, as noted above.

With the move towards an integrated internal market, the present national discrepancies on banking secrecy laws will narrow. This has already been seen in those areas mentioned above where the Community has acted, where EC-wide norms have been established. However harmonized the system becomes, it is not likely that the principle of banking secrecy will disappear. This is because, despite the fact that the principle can be abused, its advantages outweigh its disadvantages.

This can be seen in the wake of the BCCI affair. The closure of BCCI, and the subsequent scandal which arose, have tainted Luxembourg to the extent that the liberal banking regime there allowed the situation to develop so that the only action available to the authorities was to close it down. However, at stake is really the supervisory rules for banks in Luxembourg, not the secrecy rules. For, although Luxembourg has extremely strict banking secrecy laws, making it a suitable tax haven for example, these only played an indirect part in the downfall of BCCI.

Far more important in the whole saga were the lax supervisory rules. This is something which the EC will have to address if its system of home country control and a single "passport" authorising a bank to trade throughout the EC is to survive. In contrast to a general harmonized system for banking supervisory rules and disclosure thereunder, the rules on banking secrecy per se will only need to be affected in particular key areas in which abuse has been prevalent.

Note: The author would like to thank Mlle. Laurence Gourdou for her preparatory work on this article.

INDEX